Philological and Historical Commentary
on Ammianus Marcellinus XVII

Philological and Historical Commentary on Ammianus Marcellinus XVII

by

Dr. P. de Jonge

Groningen
Bouma's Boekhuis b.v. Publishers
1977

ISBN 90 6088 052 8

© Copyright 1976 by Bouma's Boekhuis b.v. Groningen, Netherlands.

All rights reserved. No part of this book may be reproduced or translated
in any form, by print, photoprint, microfilm or any other means
without written permission from the publisher.

This book was translated and printed with financial support from the
Netherlands Organisation for the Advancement of Pure Research (Z.W.O.).

Translated into English by Mrs. P. de Waard-Dekking.
Printed in the Netherlands.

S. D. M. Gothofredi

Preface

In this text we offer you the annotations on book XVII in the series of commentaries on Ammianus Marcellinus published by the author, which began with book XIV.

More emphasis has been laid on text criticism, summary of interpretation and on reference to sources.

The excursus in caput 4 on the hieroglyphs and obelisks and that in caput 7 on earthquakes have been extensively explained.

These digressions should not be considered as appendices, but rather as an organic part of the entire work of A.M., which makes them of interest with respect to the technique of composition of the "res gestae", as well as to an appreciation of the style of the work and insight into the sources used by A.M.

In spite of the many new studies on A.M. and the late imperial era, much remains unexplained in the text handed down to us and its background.

It is gratifying that lately more attention is being paid to Roman economy, as witnessed by the works published in 1974 by A. H. M. Jones, The Roman Economy, ed. by P. A. Brunt, and R. Duncan-Jones, The Economy of the Roman Empire.

Another work which will be important for our further investigations is that by Dietrich Hoffmann, Das Spätrömische Bewegungsheer, published in 1970.

We should be very careful when determining the standpoint that A.M. is believed to have taken in his time. We should also abstain as much as possible from schematizing persons and situations, as well as from too schematic a periodisation of A.M.'s work, unless this is absolutely essential for the sake of clarity.

Thanks are due to Z.W.O. (= Netherlands Organization for the Advancement of Pure Research), who subsidized the translation and publication, to the publisher, Mr. Egb. Forsten of Bouma's, who in spite of the unfavourable times is willing to publish this work, as well as to the staff and co-workers of the Buma Library at Leeuwarden and those of the University Library at Groningen.

Hengelo, 1974.

Bibliography

Please refer also to the bibliographies of my Commentaries on Books XIV, XV, XVI.

A.

A. Alföldi, A conflict of Ideas in the Late Roman Empire. The Clash between the Senate and Valentinian I, Oxford, 1952.

Ammien Marcellin, Histoire II (XVII-XIX), texte établi, traduit et annoté par G. Sabbah, Paris, 1970.

R. Asmus, "Kaiser Julians Misopogon und seine Quelle", Philologus, LXXVI, 1920, p. 266-292 and LXXVII, 1921, p. 109-141.

B.

G. J. M. Bartelink: Nu de wereld oud wordt (Dutch), Hermeneus 42.2.1970. p. 91-98; ibid. 44.2.1972 p. 85-87 (Mundus senescens).

G. Böhlig, Untersuchungen zum rhetorischen Sprachgebrauch, Berlin, 1956.

M. B. O'Brien, Titles of Address in Christian Latin Epistolography, Washington, D.C., 1930.

F. Buffière, Les mythes d'Homère et la pensée grecque, Paris, 1956.

F. Buffière, Héraclite, Allégories d'Homère, Paris, 1962.

C.

P. M. Camus, Ammien Marcellin, 1967.

M. Cary, The geographical Background of Greek and Roman History, 1949.

W. R. Chalmers, Rhein. Mus. N. F. 102, 1959, p.183 sq.: An alleged Doublet in Amm. Marc.

M. P. Charlesworth, "The virtues of a Roman Emperor: Propaganda and the Creation of belief". Proc. of the Brit. Acad., XXIII.

R. Chevallier, Les voies Romaines, Paris, 1972.

D. Conduché, Latomus 24, 1965, p.359 sq. Ammien Marcellin et la mort de Julien.

D.

L. Dautremer, Une anecdote tirée d'Ammien Marcellin, Mél. Boissier, Paris 1903, p.157 sq.

O. A. W. Dilke, The roman land surveyors. An introduction to the Agrimensores. Newton Abbot. 1971.

L. Dillemann, La Haute Mésopotamie orientale et les pays adjacents (= Tome LXXII de la Bibliothèque historique et archéologique de l'Institut français de Beyrouth = H.M.P.A.), 1962.

G. Downey, Ancient Antioch, 1963, Princeton Univ. Press.

G. Downey, The Olympic games of Antioch in the 4th Century A.D. T.A.P.A., LXX, 1939, p.428-438.

G. Downey, Julian the Apostate at Antioch, Church History, VIII, 1939, p.303-315.

G. Downey, "Personifications of Abstract Ideas in the Antioch Mosaics", Transactions of the Am. Phil. Assoc., LXIX, 1938, p.349-363.

F.

L. F. Field, The Epilogues of Amm. Marc. Diss. Baltimore, 1968.

J. A. de Foucault, Recherches sur la langue et le style de Polybe, Paris, 1972. (Collect. d'Etud. Anc.).

A. J. Fridh, Terminologie et formules dans les Variae de Cassiodore, Stockholm, 1956.

G.

J. L. Le Gall, Le Tibre, fleuve de Rome, dans l'antiquité, Paris, 1953.

J. A. Mac Geachy Jr., Quintus Aurelius Symmachus and the Senatorial Aristocracy of the West, Diss. Chicago, 1942.

M. Grant, Roman History from coins, Cambridge, 1958.

H.

G. Haddad, Aspects of social life in Antioch in the Hellenistic-roman period, 1949.

J. Hagen[2], Römerstrassen der Rheinprovinz, Bonn, 1931.

L. Harmand, Discours sur les patronages, texte traduit, annoté et commenté, Paris, 1955.

H. Hinz, Xanthen zur Römerzeit[2], Xanthen. 1963.

C. Hopkins, The siege of Dura, Class, Journal, 42, 1947, p.251 sq.

K. Hopkins, Eunuchs in Politics in the Later Roman Empire, Proc. Cambridge Philol. Soc., N.S.9, 1963, p.62 sq.

I.

E. Iversen, Obelisks in Exile. I The Obelisks of Rome, 1968.

J.

A. H. M. Jones, Constantine and the Conversion of Europe, London, 1948.

P. de Jonge, Review of E. Galletier - J. Fontaine, Ammien Marcellin, Histoire, Tome I, 1968, in Mnemos., s.v., vol. XXIII[4], 1971.

K.

J. Karayannopulos, Das Finanzwesen, München, 1958.

M. Kaser[2], Das Römische Privatrecht. Abschnitt I. 1971. Handb. der Alt. Wiss.

G. Kolias, Ämter und Würdenkauf, Athens, 1939.

B. Kötting, Peregrinatio religiosa, Wallfahrten in der Antike und das Pilgerwesen in der alten Kirche, 1950.

K. Kraft, Die Taten der Kaiser Constans und Constantius II. Jahrb. für Numism. u. Geldgesch., 9, 1958, 141-186.

W. Krebs, Elefanten in den Heeren der Antike, Wiss. Ztschr. der Univ. Rostock 13, 1964, Gesellsch.- und Sprachwiss. Reihe, Heft 2-3, p.205-220.

F. Kretzschmer, Bilddokumente Römischer Technik (Beiträge zur Technikgesch.), Düsseldorf, 1967³.

L.

S. Lauffer, Diokletian, Preisedikt, 1970.

J. H. W. G. Liebeschuetz, Antioch. City and imperial administration in the later roman Empire. Oxford 1972.

A. Lippold, Theodosius der Grosse und seine Zeit. Stuttgart 1968.

M.

S. Mazzarino, La fine del mondo antico, Milaan, 1959.

P.

R. T. van der Paardt, L.Apul.Mad., The Metamorph. A Commentary on book III with text and introduction. Diss., Amsterdam, 1971.

Christian Parma, Pronoia und Providentia. Der Vorsehungsbegriff Plotins und Augustins, 1971.

F. Paschoud, Roma aeterna. Études sur le patriotisme romain dans l'Occident latin a l'époque des grandes invasions, Bibl.Helv.Rom.7, 1967.

D. A. Pauw, Karaktertekening bij Amm.Marc., Diss. Leiden, 1972.

J. Pépin, Mythe et allégorie, Paris, 1958.

H. von Petrikovits, Das römische Reinland, Archäologische Forschungen seit 1945, Köln, 1960.

H. Pinkster, On latin Adverbs. Amsterdam, 1972. North-Holland Ling.Ser.6.

Ernst Posner, Archives in the ancient world, Harv.Univ.Press, 1972.

Q.

Quintilianus, Ausbildung des Redners. Zwölf Bücher. Hrsg.u.übers. von H. Rahn. Teil I, Darmstadt, 1972.

R.

K. Rosen, Stud. zur Darstellungskunst und Glaubwürdigkeit des Amm.Marc. Diss. Heidelberg, 1968.

A. Roullet, The Egyptian and Egyptianizing Monuments of Imperial Rome, 1972, Leiden.

S. Runciman, Byzantine Civilisation, London, 1933.

S.

C. Samberger, Die "Kaiserbiographie" in den Res Gestae des Amm.Marc. Eine Untersuchung zur Komposition der ammianeischen Geschichtsschreibung, Klio 51, 1969, p.349-482.

A. E. Samuel, Greek and Roman chronology. Calendars and years in classical antiquity. München 1972. Hanb.d.Alt.Wiss.

J. A. Sawhill, The use of Athletic Metaphors in the Biblical Homilies of St.John Chrysostom.Diss., Princ.Univ.Press, 1928 (with index of athl. terms).

A. Selem, Annali della Scuola norm. sup. di Pisa, Serie 2, vol. 33, 1964, p.147 sq.

K. M. Setton, Christian Attitudes towards the Emperor in the Fourth Century, New York, 1941.

Stauffenberg, Die röm. Kaisergeschichte bei Malalas, Stuttgart, 1931.

J. Steinhausen, Arch. Siedlungskunde des Trierer Landes, Trier, 1936.

J. Szilágyi, Prices and Wages in the Western Provinces of the Roman Empire, Acta Antiqua 11, 1963, 3-4, 325-389.

T.

Tschudin, Isis in Rom, Diss. Basel, 1962.

V.

J. Vannerus, Le limes et les fortifications gallo-romaines de Belgique, 1943. (Mém. de l'Acad. Royale de Belgique, 2e série, tome 11, fasc.2).

W.

M. Waas, Germanen im römischen Dienst, Diss. Bonn, 1965.

D. A. White, Litus Saxonum, New York, 1971.

E. M. Wightman, Roman Trier and the Treveri, London, 1970.

K. A. Wittfogel, Oriental Despotism, Yale, 1957.

Z.

O. J. Zimmermann, The late latin Vocabulary of the Variae of Cassiodorus. Cath. Univ. of Am., Stud. in Mediev. and Renaissance Lang. and Lit. 15. Washington, 1944.

Zosimus, Histoire Nouvelle, Texte ét. et trad. par F. Paschoud, Tome I, Paris, 1971. (Budé).

I, 1

Hac rerum varietate ... ita conclusa. = his variis rebus... ita conclusis. p. 104. 1
Cf. ad 15.4.4 (= III p.58); ad 14.6.23 (= I p.99); ad 14.8.13 (= II p.80);
Hagendahl Stud. Amm. p.117 sq.

1. varietas. Cf. ad 16.12.56, p.100.20-21; Hassenstein (op.cit.I) p.18; p. 104. 1
Liesenberg (op.cit.I) 1888 p.18 sq. (subst. on -as).

1. conclusa = finita, perfecta. Cf.Cic.Verr. 2.33(82): invenietis enim id p. 104. 1
facinus natum a cupiditate, auctum per stuprum, crudelitate **perfectum atque conclusum** (Quoted by Georges). The last two underlined words are almost synonymous. Meaning: brought to an end, concluded. It should be pointed out, however, that in Latin **concludere** has a wider meaning. Cf. Souter, p.68; Krebs Antib.I p.318. The subst. **conclusio** term. techn. mil. and as t.t. rhet. and philos., which is frequently used by Cic., does **not** occur in Amm. Cf. et Oder Mul.Chir. p.165.18-19; Amm.23.5.24; **Conclusa** oratione ad hunc gratissimum finem.

a **1. digessimus** = narrated, told. Cf.14.7.21: p. 104. 1
per orientales provincias; quas recensere nunc puto oportuna, absque Mesopotamia, iam **digesta** cum bella Parthica dicerentur; 22.2.6; cuius super adventu ... in actibus Commodi principis **digessimus** per excessum (= digression); 28.1.4: hoc argumentum paulo postea **digestum** tumore tragico Frynichus in theatrum induxerat Athenarum; Vopisc.Aurel.1.6: et tamen, si bene novi, ephemeridas illius viri scriptas habemus, etiam bella charactere historico **digesta** ...; Cod.Theod.11.22.4; 12.6.14.
b A different meaning 14.6.14: et si **digesto** plene consilio, id placuerit fieri (= secum considerare, animo revolvere; cf.Thes. s.v.). Cf. et Stat. Theb.2.316 sq.:
> tunc quos excedens hilaris, quis cultus iniqui/praecipuus ducis, et profugo quos ipse notarat/ingemuisse sibi, per noctem ac luce sub omni/ **digerit**; ...

In Stat. here = secum computat, enumerat, Cf. Mulder Comm.Theb.II p.216; Cod.Just.10.48.12.2; Claud.28.590 sq. (De VI cons. Honor.).
c to expound orally, to discuss: cf.17.8.3: hos legatos **negotio plene digesto** oppositaque condicionum perplexitate... muneratos absolvit; 21.11.2: reque digesta per secreta colloquia et alto roborata silentio.
d 24.2.7 hanc peditatus omnis **pontibus caute digestis** transivit (= con fectis, constructis, iunctis). As this probably refers to a ship's bridge, the use of **digerere** can be easily explained.

p. 104.2 **Martius iuvenis** Sabbah annotates: "**Martius iuvenis** n'est pas un cliché rhétorique mais garde une valeur religieuse, à une époque où la théologie politique venait de s'efforcer d'associer Dioclétien (284-305) à Iupiter et Maximien à Hercule (286-305). Dans la pensée d'Ammien, la victoire de Strasbourg est un signe qui révèle en Julien le protégé de Mars".
Although possible, it here seems better to me to be wary of a religious interpretation. **Mars** and **Martius** are part of the most hackneyed metaphorical language. Cf.23.6.83: et gentes plurimas praeter eas ... sub iugum haec natio miserat ita audax et **ad pulveres Martios erudita** (= rebus bellicis exercita); Claud.22.347 sq. (Laud.Stilich.II):

... iam creverat infans,
Ore ferens patrem; sed avus maturior aevi
Martia recturo tradit **praecepta** nepoti.
(= praecepta belli).

Claud. has more examples like this one, in which he alternates **Martius** with **Mavortius**. It is wholly superfluous to quote more examples from the classical and post-classical litterature. Cf.et. Krebs Antib.II p.59 (Mars). It therefore seems to me far-fetched in connection with 17.1.11 (et dum nullus obsisteret, munimentum quod in Alamannorum solo conditum Traianus suo nomine voluit appellari), as well as 14.8.13: hanc (Arabiam) ... obtemperare legibus nostris Traianus compulit imperator ... cum **glorioso Marte** (= glorioso bello) Mediam urgeret et Parthos (cf. ad 14.8.13 = II p.81) and finally with Martialis 12.8:

Terrarum dea gentiumque Roma
cui par est nihil et nihil secundum
Traiani modo laeta cum futuros
tot per saecula conputaret annos
**et fortem iuvenemque Martiumque
in tanto duce militem videret** etc.,

to see in the epitheton **Martius** an allusion to **Traianus**, as Sabbah wants to do.

p. 104.2 *a* **Rheno ... fluente** Cf.16.12.57: spumans denique cruore barbarico, decolor alveus insueta stupebat augmenta. (with the annot.ad. p.101.2-3).
b **Rheno.** Cf. ad 14.10.6 (p.29.3); ad 16.11.8 (p.89,17-18)c.
c **post Argentoratensem pugnam:** (cf.16.12) Augustus 357.
d Cf.14.6.6: et olim licet **otiosae** sint tribus, pacataeque centuriae et nulla suffragiorum certamina, set Pompiliani redierit **securitas** temporis..., Krebs Antib.II p.233 sq.
Note. Apart from the usual meaning, we find in later and late Latin also

the meaning: unnecessary, superfluous and: **free from burden** (= ± immunis). This last judicial term **not** in A.M.

securus sollicitusque = without cares, **but also** worried, concerned. Note p. 104. 3
the alliteration in line 3.

dirae volucres. Dirus t.t. of the religious language. Cf.Plin.N.H. 18.1: **dirarum alitum** modo; ibid.10.16: Bubo **funebris,** et maxime abominatus publicis praecipue auspiciis, deserta incolit; nec tantum desolata, sed **dira** etiam et inaccessa; Suet.Claud.22: utque **dira avi** in urbe aut in Capitolio visa, obsecratio haberetur; Ovid.Met.5.550: Ignavus bubo, **dirum** mortalibus **omen;** Cic.leg.2.8(21): Quaeque augur iniusta, nefasta, vitiosa, **dira** defixerit, irrita infectaque sunto; Cic.divin.2.15: Quum enim **tristissima exta** sine capite fuerunt, quibus nihil videtur esse **dirius;** Horat. Od. 1.2.1:

> Iam satis terris nivis atque **dirae**
> Grandinis misit Pater et rubente
> Dextera sacras iaculatus arces
> Terruit urbem etc.

Stat.Theb.2.263 sq.:

> ... Cunctos tamen **omina** rerum
> **dira** movent, variisque metum sermonibus augent

(with the excellent annot. edit. Mulder p.103, p.192, p.193, p. 201); Claud. 28.326 sq. (VI cons.Honor.):

> Circum membra rotat doctus purganda sacerdos,
> Rore pio spargens, et **dira** fugantibus herbis
> **Numina,** purificumque Iovem Triviamque precatus etc.

It seems to me that with **dirae volucres** Amm. has vultures (vultures) in mind, who, however, to my knowledge did not (and do not) occur in these regions, although they were to be found in his native country. Iulianus' fear is not only based on violation of the body by vultures, but also on the religious contamination, which could be caused by these animals. The **soldier** A.M. does not go too deeply into this macabre mass funeral: à la guerre, comme à la guerre!

Sine discretione. Cf.23.6.67: nentesque subtemina conficiunt sericum ad p. 104. 4
usus antehac nobilium, nunc etiam infimorum sine ulla discretione proficiens; 26.6.7: qui ad nudandos sine discretione cunctos immaniter flagrans nocentes pariter et insontes. The expression, as well as the word, are late-Latin. Cf. Krebs Antib.I p.455 (with lit. quoted); Georges I 2201; Souter p.107. Meaning: separation (sometimes separation of

3

meanings = ± definition; cf. e.g. Veget.Mulomed.16.1 = Lommatzsch p.32). distinction, **difference**. The last meaning only in Amm., not with others. Without difference here means: without difference between Germans and Romans.

Cunctos. Cf. ad 14.1.6 (= I p.61); Krebs Antib. I p.383; Hofm.-Leum. (op.cit.I) p.391 E (cuncti c. genit).

Cunctos humari mandavit. For **mandare c.acc.c.inf.** (not-class.) cf.Krebs Antib. II p.53; Hofm.-Leum. p.585. The construction of **mandare** here is that of **iubere** in class. Latin, when the person to whom the command is given, is not mentioned. With conjunct. without ut 26.6.2: **mandaratque** (sc. Procopio) ... pro cognitorum **ageret** textu et, si subsidia rei Romanae languisse sensisset, imperatorem ipse se **provideret** ocius nuncupari.

Humari. Here Amm. uses correctly (also on purpose?) this verb, which is found with the subst. **humatio** in judicial texts, besides **sepelire** and **sepultura.**

a **absolutisque legatis** = to release. Cf.25.3.23: (Iulianus) vita facilius est absolutus; 27.11.1: Per haec tempora Vulcacio Rufino absoluto vita. Cf. Hagendahl St.Amm.p.101 (annot.1): "Quoniam haec locutio (sc. **vita absolvi**) in litteris latinis alibi non reperitur (Thes.I 173,44), haud scio an Amm., homo natione Graecus, usum quendam suae linguae proprium imitando expresserit... es scheint hier ein in späterer Prosa häufiger Sprachgebrauch zuerst aufzutauchen, nach dem ἀπολύεσθαι den Sinn von **discedere** hat".

For **absolutus** (= planus atque perspicuus) cf. ad. 14.10.13 (= II p.110). Cf. et Krebs Antib. I p.55 sq. (absolvere and absolutus), with litt.

b **legatis.** Cf. ad 16.12.3, p.91.16-17.

p. 104. 4-5   *a* **quos ... praediximus.** Allusion to: 16.12.3: satis pro imperio Caesari mandaverunt, **ut terris abscederet virtute sibi quaesitis et ferro,** viz. that part of Gallia which was conquered by the Alamanni after the death of Magnentius (353).

b **praediximus** = supra diximus, memoravimus.

Especially post-class. and late Latin. Cf. Krebs Antib. II p.351 (with lit.); Heum.-Seckel p.446. Cf.et. ad 14.3.4 (= I. p.81); 16.7.10, p.80.14-17f; ad 15.5.4, p.47.11.

c **Superba quaedam portasse.** Cf.Verg.Aen. 2.114:

Suspensi Eurypylum scitantem oracula Phoebi/mittimus; isque adytis haec tristia dicta **reportat;**

Liv.45.1.10: ludis relictis, domus magna pars hominum ad coniuges liberosque laetum nuntium **portabant.** In both cases **refert** and **(re)fere-**

bant would have been more "correct". Krebs Antib.II p.326. who gives both these examples, says that in the vernacular **portare** is preferred to **ferre** and that for this reason the verb **portare** is also connected with non-concrete objects. As shown above and here in Amm. However, the combination is still remarkable. In this meaning **not** in judicial lit. Perhaps here a Grecism? Cf. Bauer, Wörterb.N.T.² (1928) 1365 ß
d   **quaedam.** Cf. ad 16.12.53. p.100.7.

Tres tabernas. Cf. ad 16.2.12, p.73.27; cf.et. Sabbah A.M. II p.161 sq.   p. 104. 5-6
(with lit.).

I, 2
Mediomatricos Cf. ad 15.11.9 (= IV p.63).   p. 104. 6

a   **Servandam - praecepit.** For this late Latin construction cf.Hofm.-   p. 104. 6-7
Leum.p.595 B. Praecipior c.infin.act.15.3.9; c.infin.pass.15.7.2; 20.4.6; 29.3.5. For the former construction compare Oros.hist.4.3.5; hoc facinus in tam sceleratos defectores puniendum Genucio consuli **iussum est;** Eutr.1.16.1: **promittentes** senatui et populo per se omne certamen implendum; etc. (although not quite comparable).
b   **ad... usque.** Cf. ad 14.7.17 (= II p.42) and 14.8.5 (= II p.64)

a   **et petiturus ... ut ... transgressus ... requireret ... vetabatur.**   p. 104. 7-9
vetabatur Imperfectum pro perfecto. Cf. ad 14.2.14 (= I p.75). Clausula II. Cf.17.1.5: Quo ita disposito, solis primo exortu, visis per montium vertices barbaris, ad celsiora **ducebatur** alacrior miles; 17.10.9: ad colloquium tandem accitus a Caesare, trementibus oculis adorato, victorisque superatus aspectu, condicione difficili **premebatur;** 17.13.8: Iamque vergente in vesperum die, cum moras rumpere lux moneret excedens, erectis vexillis, in eos igneo miles impetu **ferebatur;** 17.13.12: Vixdum populis hostilibus stratis, gregatim peremptorum necessitudines **ducebantur,** humilibus extractae tuguriis. ... et fastu vitae prioris abolito, ad infimitatem obsequiorum venere servilium et exiguo temporis intervallo decurso, caesorum aggeres et captivorum agmina **cernebantur;** etc.
b   **petiturus.** Cf. ad 16.12.33, p.96.14-15*a*
c   **ponte compacto.** By this is meant a **ship's bridge** still to be constructed. Therefore p.c. is an ablativus absolutus. Cf.Dig.45.1.83.5: nam et si navem, quam spopondit, dominus dissolvit et isdem **tabulis compegerit.** Does Amm. have in mind Verg.Aen12.672 sq.:
  ecce autem flammis inter tabulata volutus/ad caelum undabat vortex

turrimque tenebat,/turrim, **compactis trabibus** quam eduxerat ipse/ subdideratque rotas **pontisque instraverat** altos?

These ship's bridges have been frequently pictured, among others on Traianus' column. I agree with Sabbah that one should not imagine a bridge as in Caes.d.b.Gall.4.17 (cf.comm. Meusel [17]I p.315 sq., with drawing). Cf. et Kretzschmer (op.cit.) p.132 sq.

d **in suis**, sc. terris. × **in nostris** (p.104.9). This use is late Latin: nostra × peregrina.

e **refragante ... exercitu** = (a) refraganti ... exercitu. But **part.praes. in ablat.absol.** with causal meaning are fashionable in late Latin.Cf. Hofm.-Leum.57γ p.443; 60ζ p.448 **refragari** (× suffragari): t.t. originally of public law, and then used in a wider and also metaphorical sense. Cf.et. ad 16.12.5, p.91.22.

p. 104. 9-10 *a* **verum (exercitum sc.) ... allectum ... traduxerat** = verum ... allexit et traduxit. The main idea, as so often, is expressed by the participium. For **plusq. perf. pro perfecto** cf. ad 14.7.12 (= I p.37). Traduxerat suam: Clausula I.

b Cf.Cic. pro Cluent.52 (144): **traduxit** me as suam sententiam; Liv.44. 40: Post hanc orationem silentium fuit, partim **traductis** in sententiam eius, partim verentibus etc.

c **facundia**. Never with Cic.Caes. and rare with Liv. (like **facundus** and **facunde**). Cf. Krebs Antib. I p.575; Claud.28.491 sq. (De VI cons.Honor.):

Exsere (= produce) nunc doctos tantae certamina laudis
Roma choros, et quanta tuis **facundia** pollet
Ingeniis, nostrum digno sonet ore parentem (= Stilichonem).

Cf. ad 15.3.1 (= IV p.79).

d **iucunditate**. In contrast with **facundia**, iucunditas occurs quite often in Cic.Cf. De orat.3.38 (55): Tertius ille modus transferendi verbi late patet, quem necessitas genuit, inopia coacta et angustiis; post autem delectatio **iucunditasque** celebravit (sc. audiendi); ad Quint.fr.2.10.2: Nunc mihi **iucunditatis** plena epistola hoc adspersit molestiae, quod videris, ne mihi molestus esses, veritus esse atque etiam nunc vereri; etc.

e For **military discipline**, a matter of life and death for the Roman Empire, cf. Müller Milit. (op.cit.I) p.617 sq. Even a popular commander like Julianus sometimes finds these "spoilt" and often rebellious soldiers hard to handle.

p. 104. 10-
p. 105. 3 *a* **amor ... adsuetum.** Though true, these words testify to the exalted

admiration of Amm. for Julianus. **Amor etc.** For the **personificatio** cf. Blomgren op.cit.II p.87.

b **Documenta.** Cf.Cic. pro C.Rab.Post.10(27): Ergo ille P.Rutilius, qui **documentum** fuit hominibus nostris **virtutis,** antiquitatis, prudentiae...; Liv.32.10: Iam aedilitatem praeturamque fastidiri: nec per honorum gradus, **documentum sui dantes,** nobiles homines tendere ad consulatum, etc. p. 105. 1

c **flagrantior.** Cf.Tac.Hist.4.39: ... vires abolet dimissa in hiberna legione septima, cuius **flagrantissimus** in Antonium **amor;** Plin.ep.6.8.2 likewise: **flagrantissimus amor;** Krebs Antib.I p.597; Claud.3 (In Rufin. I) 220 sq.:

Crescebat scelerata sitis, praedaeque recentis/Incestus **flagrabat amor,** nullusque petendi/Cogendive pudor.

d **Sequi ... hortatus est.** For the verbs constructed with acc.c.inf. (or with inf. connected with an object accus.), against the rules of "classical" grammar, cf.Kallenberg (op.cit.I) p.21 sq.; Hassenstein (op.cit.I) p.49 sq. Cf.et. ad 14.1.3 (= I p.58); 14.5.7 (= I p.87); ad 14.9.7 (= II p.94); ad 14.9.6 (= II p.91); ad 14.11.4 (= II p.118); 14.11.6: **sororem** suam... Constantius ad se tandem desideratam **venire** multis fictisque blanditiis **hortabatur;** 14.11.15: comperit Thebaeas legiones in vicinis oppidis hiemantes consortes suos mississe quosdam eum **ut remaneret** promissis fidis **hortaturos** et firmis...

e **conturmalem.** Cf. ad 16.12.45, p.98.21-22. p. 105. 2
f **indicere.** In the same meaning Claud.29.126 sq. (Laus Serenae):

Non ludit Galatea procax, non improbus audet/Tangere Cymothoën Triton, totoque **severos/**

Indicit mores pelago pudor ... But otherwise ibid.15.16 (b.Gildon.): Quem veniens **indixit** hiems, ver perculit hostem. Cf.et.Heum.-Seckel p.260. In judicial lit. in the same meaning as here with Claud. (viz. to announce and to impose); Eutrop.8.13: Ad huius belli usum aerario exhausto, cum largitiones nullas haberet, neque **indicere** provincialibus aut senatui aliquid vellet; Arnob.adv.nat.1.3 (Reiffersch. 6.19): difficiles pluviae sata faciunt emori et sterilitatem **indicunt** terris (here probably: to announce); Iust,12.3.1; 24.3.4. Cf. et 23.5.24: sub imperatore plus sibi laboris quam gregariis indicente; 28.3.1: nihilque gregariis imperans, cuius non ipse primitias, alacri capesseret mente; Cic. pro Mur.18 (38)): nunquam iste plus militi laboris imposuit quam sibi sumpsit ipse; Michael (op.cit.I) p.26.

p. 105. 3 **g Sicut perspicue contigit.** For **perspicue** cf.Cic.Verr.Act.I 7(20): aperte iam ac **perspicue;** and more often with the same author. Sabbah: comme l'événement le montra clairement. **Contigit sc. videre** (poet., post-class., late Latin). Remarkable is the absolute use of the verbum. Cf.Hofm.-Leum.p.582,168*a* (with lit.) and ibid. p.588,171*a* (with lit.). It might be important to point out that **contingens** and **contingentia,** t.t. of logic, mean: possible and possibility (late Latin),
moxque. For **-que** cf. ad 16.12.37, p.97.6*a*. For **mox = mox ut = simulatque** cf. ad 14.10.16 (= II p.111).

p. 105. 3-4 **praedictum** Cf. ad 17.1.1, p.104.4-5*b*.

p. 105. 4 **flumine pontibus constratis transmisso.** Cf. ad 17.1.2, p.104.7-9*c*. Cf.d.b. Gall. (Hirtius) 8.14.4: **pontibus palude constrata** legiones traducit; 8.9.3: turris excitari crebras in altitudinem trium tabulatorum, **pontibus** traiectis **constratisque** coniungi... (beams covered with boards; for **traiectis** cf.Liv.30.10.5). Cf.et. ad 16.12.63, p.102.4; Liv.30.10.14: Speculatoriae naves ac levia ipsa navigia, quae **sub constratis pontium** per intervalla excurrebant ... Cf.et. ad 16.8.10, p.83.2 *f* and *h* (**compaginare**).
occupavere. Cf. ad 16.12.19, p.94.11-12.

I, 3

p. 105. 5 *a* **perstricti negotii magnitudine.** Cf.Liv.1.25.4: Ut primo statim concursu increpuere arma, micantesque fulsere gladii, **horror** ingens spectantes **perstringit:** et, neutro inclinata spe, torpebat vox spiritusque, Val.Fl.7.80 sq:

Contremuitque metu, ne nescius audeat hospes,

Seque miser ne posse putet. **perstrinxerat horror**

Ipsum etiam et maesta stabat defixus in ira;

ibid.7.194:

Virginis ecce novus mentem **perstringere** languor

Incipit: ingeminant commotis quaestibus aestus.

Cf.et. ad 14.7.10: **praestrictis** (= II p.33).

b For **negotii** cf. ad 16.12.22, p.94.26; Krebs Antib. II p.140. Here: military undertaking. In this sense more often with Amm.Cf. Eutr. Praef.: Res Romanas, ex voluntate mansuetudinis tuae, ab urbe condita ad nostram memoriam, quae in **negotiis** vel **bellicis** vel civilibus eminebant.

p. 105. 5-6. *a* **qui ... sperabant** = Qui (**putantes**) se in transquillo positos otio = who, **because** they believed etc., hoped. **Positos** = part. + ὡσ in Greek. Cf.et. ad 14.11.6, p.32.8-9.

b **(se) parum inquietari posse sperabant.**
Construction "correct". Cf. ad 14.5.7 (= I p.87); ad 14.7.5 (= II p.20).
c **inquietari.** Cf.14.3.2; 22.9.8; 30.9.5. Post-classical and late Latin. Not used in legal texts until after 200 A.D. Cf. Krebs Antib. I p.751 (with lit.); Heum.-Seckel p.271. The substant. **inquietator** Cod.Iust.12.7.1.1. Cf.et. ad 16.12.30, p.96.2c.

aliorum exitio. Aliorum = ceterorum, viz. those who were killed in the battle of Strassbourg. Cf. Krebs Antib. I p.144; Riemann (op.cit.I) p. 186 (both with lit.). p. 105. 6-7

fortunis suis. Here: fate, lot, as often. Cf.Plaut.Miles 125: Conqueritur mecum mulier fortunas suas; Caes.b.g.5.3.7; 6.7.6 (with annot. Meusel II^{17} p.142). The latter meaning of **plur.fortunae** has not always been understood. p. 105. 7

a **ut primae vertiginis impetum declinarent.** p. 105. 8
Cf.31.10.22: remotusque in ipsa **vertigine** pereuntium rerum dux cautus et diligens...; Lucan.Phars.8.14 sq.:
  Multi, Pharsalica castra/cum peterent nondum fama prodente ruinas,/ occursu stupuere ducis, **vertigine** rerum/attoniti; ... (quoted by Seyfarth).
Of an acrobate, in a different meaning, Claud.20.359 (In Eutrop, II):
  Quis melius vibrata puer **vertigine** molli
  Membra rotet? verrat quis marmora crine supino?
"In manumissione per vindictam apud praetorem" Persius used in 5.7.6: **vertigo** and replaces that in 5.78 by the synonym **turbo.**
b For **declinare** with object cf. Heum.-Seckel p.124; Curt.Ruf.4.13.37: monet ut regionem monstratam **declinent** (= vitent); Iust. Phil.: 12.2.4: ad **declinanda** fatorum pericula; ibid.3.7.9: ad invidiae **impetum declinandum;** ibidem.26.2.7: victorem hostium exercitum **declinantes;** ad 15.1.3, p.39.6.
c It seems to me that here is meant: **primum** vertiginis impetum. For this **enallage adiectivi** cf.Blomgren (op.cit. II) p.146 sq. Differently: Seyfarth, Sabbah, Rolfe. Cf.et. Blomgren ibid. p.91 sq.

cum verbis compositis. Cf.Iust. 4.1.17: Neque hoc ab antiquis in dulcedinem fabulae **compositum,** sed metu et admiratione transeuntium. In this meaning (= fictitious, faked, false) **not** used in legal texts. cf.et. Krebs Antib.I p.314. Thus also in Tac. Quint.Gell.Eutrop. p. 105. 9-10

p. 105. 9 **quae denuntiarent concordem foederum firmitatem.** Note the alliteration. Cf.14.8.13: Bostram et Gerasam atque Filadelfiam, murorum **firmitate** cautissimas. = quae denuntiarent (se) **concordium** (cf. ad p.105.8c) **foederum** firmitatem (servaturos esse). In my view the concordia refers to the foedera, not particularly to the subject of denuntiarent, as Sabbah wants: "pour proclamer leur fidélité unanime aux engagements souscrits".

p. 105. 10 **incertumque quo consilio statim instituto:** Sabbah Mommsem. aut instituto G.Stat institutos V. According to Seyfarth Phil. Probleme (op, cit. XVI), Gelenius' version is probably based on conjecture and not on M. Seyfarth: stat. ... institutos. In any case the version of Gelenius seems to me to be preferred to that of Mommsen: consilium instituere seems to me, as far as the Latin is concerned, not acceptable. Pighi St.Amm. (op.cit.I p.50 sq.): **statim ⟨in⟩stitutor(um) mutata voluntate** etc. Palaeographically quite justifiable.

p. 105. 10-11 *a* **cursu celeri venire compulsos.** Alliteration! For **cursu** cf.14.6.17: velut vim inectans naturae, eandemque ab **instituto cursu** retorquens (= literally: to turn back (trans!) away from the development already started = away from a normal development); 16.1.4: bellorum **gloriosis cursibus** Traiani simillimus (Galletier-Font.: et ses glorieuses expéditions guerrières le faisaient comparer en tous points à Trajan; in my view an incorrect translation; Seyfarth: durch ruhmreiche Kriegszüge, also inaccurate. Translation: because of the **glorious course** of his wars); 16.12.36: et properantes concito quam **considerato cursu** Germani (cf. ad 16.12.36, p.96.26-97.1). Meaning: run, course. For the poet. pluralis Hagendahl St.Amm. p.95 sq. (with some other examples).

b For **compellere c, infinit.** cf. Thes.s.v.; Hofm.-Leum. p.580, 167 **B.,** ad 15.5.14 (= III p.91).

p. 105. 10 **per alios.** Cf.17.5.12: cum duce tuo **per quosdam** ignobiles, me inconsulto, sermones conseruit super pace; Reinhardt (op.cit.I) p.33: per instrumentale; ad 14.11.1 (= II p.113).

p. 105. 11-12 **eorum regionibus** = suis r. Cf. ad 14.7.7 (= Ip.25 sq.). For **excedere** cf. ad 17.13.8, p.129.14-15.

I, 4

p. 105. 13 **Quibus clara fide compertis.** = from clear and reliable information = claris nuntiis fidelibus. Abstractum pro concreto. Cf. ad 15.4.4 (= III p.58); ad 14.8.13 (= II p.80).

noctis prima quiete = noctis prima vigilia. Amm. does not use the usual military term. Other versions: Seyfarth, Sabbah. **Quies** in my opinion not = **somnus,** as more often.

navigiis modicis et velocibus octingentos imposuit milites, Meant here are p. 105. 13-14
the lusoriae (naves). In Amm. on the Rhine: 17.1.4; 18.2.12. On the Meuse: 17.2.3. Cf. Müller Milit. (op.cit.I) p.590 sq. Cf.et. Cod.Theod. 7.17: de lusoriis Danuvii (a⁰ 412), with the extensive commentary by Gothofredus. Mentioned in Amm. 17.2.3. Furthermore S. H. A. Bonosus 15.1; ((pleasure) yacht) Sen. de ben.7.20.3: Cui triremes et aeratas (= rostratas, bellicas) non mitterem, **lusorias** et cubiculatas (= large ships, built like houses = θαλαμηγοί) et alia ludibria regum in mari lascivientium mittam. Cf.et. ad 14.10.6 (= II p.103).

a †**eorum XX sursum versum decurso egressi.** Clark. Thus Seyfarth (inst. p. 105. 14-15
of XX: viginti). Sabbah: ea re ut M P XX sursum versum decurso egressi; ea re ut vi ingenti: Valesius; eo ut amni: Mommsen. **Vmilitis eorum XX. EBG** milites.
b "**Eorum** donné par V et par G peut être la corruption de l'expression **ea re ut** combiné avec **m(p): milia (passuum)**: l'unité ne peur être le stade, car une distance de 3600 mètres seulement est incompatible avec l'importance des manoeuvres décrites" (Sabbah). Here we see an intelligent palaeographical foundation for the **conjecture** of Valesius.
c Novák: milites ⟨**ut spatio stad**⟩ **iorum XX sursum versum decurso** egressi. A principal objection against this conjecture is that in this way the distance is too small. Cf. *b* above. (Wiener Stud.33.1911. p.306 sq.).
d "**Decurso** étant juxtaposé à **sursum versum,** le verbe n'a pas son sens propre de "dévaler, descendre" (qu'on trouve en 18.2.12; 18.6.5; 20.11.22; 22.8.17; 23.6.59; 25.2.6) mais le sens neutre et élargi de "parcourir" (qu'on trouve en 22.15.9; 24.3.10; 31.12.11), appliqué à la navigation (comme en 24.6.2)". But in my view the latter meaning is not expected here, but rather that of: to sail to and fro, to patrol (cf. ad 16.2.10, p.73.21). This is a terminus technicus mil., expressed by: **discurso,** not **decurso.** I agree partly with Langen Phil.29, 1870, p.469 sq., who wants to read **discurso;** but not with his translation: to cover a distance. (viz. here). Palaeographically this small change does not give any trouble. For the ablativus absolutus **discurso** (neutrum impersonale) cf. Hofm.-Leum. p.448, 60*b*. Especially old Latin, post-classical and late Latin. Cf. et Riemann (op.cit.I) p.306 sq. (with many examples). And if one has

objections against the "hard" use of this abl.abs. here, compare Terent. Hec. 736 sq.:

Si vera dicis, nil tibi est a me pericli, mulier:
Nam iam aetate ea sum, ut non siet **peccato** mi ignosci aequom.

sursum versum. Only the vulgair Mulomedicina Chironis uses several times su(r)sum versus. The expression is **not** found in Claud.Veget.r.m. Arnob. adv.nat. Optatus Milev. Whether Amm. prefers an older, more archaic form or whether **sursum versus** and **sursum versum** existed side by side in late Latin, is not known to me. I suspect the former.
Cf. Hofm.-Leum. p.519.112 Zus. *a.*

p. 105. 15 **egressi.** The usual t.t.naut. = to land, to go on land. For the constructions with Amm. cf. Naumann (op.cit.I) p.12 sq.; and in general Krebs Antib. I p.495 sq.

p. 105. 15 **Quicquid invenire potuerint:** Coniunctivus perf. iterativus. Cf.23.4.5: Nam muro saxeo huius modi moles imposita disiectat **quidquid invenerit** subter concussione violenta...; 23.4.12: Conseruntur autem eius frontalibus... cuspides praeacutae, ponderibus ferreis graves ... ut **quidquid petierit** aculeis exsertis abrumpat; 23.6.17: In his pagis hiatus quoque conspicitur terrae, unde halitus letalis exsurgens, **quodcumque animal** proxime **steterit** odore gravi consumit; Ehrism. p.57 (op.cit.I); ad 16.7.2, p.78.27*b;* ad 14.1.5 (= I p.60); ad 14.4.1 (= I p.82).

a **ferro violarent et flammis.** Note the alliteration and the placing of the verb. Claus.I. Cf.27.4.6: urbibus multis et **castris contiguus et castellis. ferro... flammis** instead if the usual: ferro ignique. Cf. Sil.Pun.6.701 sq.:

... captam, Karthago, Saguntum
Da spectare, simul **ferro flammaque** ruentem...; ibid.16.154:
... in Libyam **flammis ferroque** trahendus;

ibid.2.315 sq.:

Sed campos fac, vane, dari. num gentibus istis
Mortales animi? aut **ferro, flammave** fatiscunt?

b One should not be misled by the flowery rhythmic words. Time and again we see in A.M. and others that the Romans commit murder and arson, when it suits their purpose; which the soldier A.M. finds quite normal. The barbarians are no better, except that in their foolishness they destroy what might in future be a source of prosperity to them. Cf.Claud.3.360:

Adspice **barbaricis** iaceant quot moenia **flammis.**

I, 5

quo ita disposito. Cf. ad 16.12.23, p.94.27; ad 16.10.1, p.84.9-10; ad 16.10.1, p.84.10; ad 16.12.27, p.95.18. p. 105. 16

a **solis primo exortu.** Cf.31.1.2: et squalidi **solis exortus** hebetabant matutinos diei candores (plur.poet.); 17.7.2: primo lucis exortu. Rare compositum, extremely rare in class. Latin. Archaism? (occurs in Gellius and Symmachus). Cf. Krebs Antib.I p.549. For the verb **exorior** cf. ad 16.12.27, p.95.18*b*. p. 105. 16

b For the many expressions for **sunrise** cf. ad 15.5.31 (= III p.117). Cf.et. ad 14.8.1 (= II p.54). p. 105. 16

I, 5-14

Unfortunately, A.M.'s report of this campaign is very obscure. The expedition takes place in the Northern region of the **agri decumates** (cf. Woordenboek der Oudheid, I, 1965, p.85, with Lit.). where the **Alamanni** had settled since ± 260, after driving away the Romans. The influence of the romanisation was quite considerable (cf. ad p.105,26 sq.). The events may have occurred as follows: p. 105. 16-
p. 107. 3

After patrolling, the 800 man sail up the river Main, and invade the **Northern** region of the **Alamanni**. In this region horse-riders are also present. Where these come from, is a mystery. Simultaneously, in order to separate the Al. North of the Moenus from those to the South, **other** soldiers (alacrior miles, 5), occupy the **Southern bank** of the Moenus, where the enemy had been sighted (5). These withdraw immediately. But when, after seeing their compatriots in the North being harassed (5, eminus ingentia fumi volumina visebantur), they want to rush to their rescue and leave the ambushes (desertis insidiis, 6), they are caught in a vice of on the one side **riders** and on the other side the **800 men**. The **alacrior miles** stay more or less in the same spot, probably to prevent a crossing, in which they fail (6). Therefore the crossing of the Alam. has to take place **East** of these, towards the North. The **Southern Al.**, realising there is nothing they can do, flee to the East (or later across the Moenus to the South), while the **Northern Al.**, already defeated on the West Side. (nostros perruptas populari terras hostiles, 5) also flee to the East. The Romans now have their hands free and ransack everything North of the Moenus, to a distance of 10 miles, until they reach the mountain forests of the **Taunus.** Here the general comes to a standstill, because according to a defector, there are ambushes there. Nevertheless they venture a little further into the forest. (ausi tamen omnes accedere, 9). Because the roads are barred by felled trees (9) which might mean lengthy detours (non nisi per anfractus longos et asperos ultra progredi posse, 9), while furthermore the ground is frozen and covered with snow (aeris urente saevitia ... nives opplevere montes simul et campos, 10). the attempt to march further is abandoned. Finally a munimentum, quod Traianus suo nomine voluit appellari, is taken without any resistance (in my view a capital negligence of the Al.: castra supra quam optari potuit occupata sine obstaculo, 12). Julianus brings in an occupational force, as well as foodstuffs (11). He realises that the fort has to be provided with certain defenses (12). After the fort had been taken, the Alam. have asked for peace, which is granted to them for a period of 10 months (12). When they see that the reconstruction of the fort is seriously taken to hand, 3 kings who have helped the vanquished at Strassbourg, offer their subjection, at which they promise to respect the foedera (= foedus) up to a previously fixed date (probably the same term as mentioned above), while they will even supply the fort with victuals, if the occupying forces run short (si defuisse sibi docuerint defensores, 13) and will never attack the fort (13).

In spite of the lyrical passage of A.M. (14), this whole expedition seems to me to be fairly limited in character and intended to let the Alam. feel, after the battle of Strassbourg, the Roman supremacy **in their own country** and thus strengthen the Rhine border against the barbarians. I doubt whether many Al. were killed in battle, as their knowledge of the terrain was to their advantage (7, subsisidium velox locorum invenere prudentes). Some women and children may have been taken prisoner, but probably only a few of the able-bodied men. The **captivi** (p.105.27) are in my view **Alam.: captivis** is used proleptically (cf. Sabbah II p.163). The terrain on which all this takes place, is relatively small (8), but the damage caused to this prosperous country (p.105,26-27) is considerable. A.M. who is very anti-German, here also pictures the enemy as unsympathetic and unreliable people. (Cf. Enzlin, Zur Geschichtsschr. etc., op.cit. I, p.30 sq.).

Although in general the **Franci** were to be found **North** of the Moenus, and the **Alam. South** of this river, we **have to** assume here that there are Alam. living North of the Moenus. Otherwise, why should they cross the river, if there were **only** Alam. living South of the Moenus? (6). The **silva** etc. (8) also points to the Taunus mountains. Thirdly the expedition against the **Franci** is described in cap. II (cf.et. ad 14.10.6 = II p.103). All this happens before Dec. 357 (cf.17.2.2). For the **Alamanni** in general cf. ad 14.10.1 (= II p.96 sq.). Still the question remains why A.M. here (and sometimes elsewhere) is so obscure in his descriptions of wars and

expeditions, although he is a professional soldier and has at least a rough knowledge of Gallia and Germania West of the Rhine. There may be the following reasons for this:
1⁰. inaccuracy of his sources (Julianus' memories). 2⁰. not very clear topography, as this area East of the Rhine, is not or hardly found on itineraria, because it did not belong to the Roman empire (Amm. will certainly have used itineraria). 3⁰. faulty 1st or 2nd revision of the text by Amm. of this description. 1 and 2 seem to me the most probable. Cf. et Seyfarth p.303 (notes 7 and 10); Sabbah II p.162 sq. (both with lit.).
As regards the **munimentum Traiani**, this ought to be situated, in connection with the above, close to Mogontiacum and not too far from the Moenus. I do not know of any archeological data which could lead to a localisation. Perhaps **Nida?** Cf. et. Seyfarth I p.304, note 12; Sabbah II p.163, note 13.

I, 5

a **per montium vertices.** For the peculiar metaphorical meaning of **vertex** cf. ad 14.7.2 (= I p.17); ad 15.5.16 (= III p.95). In the sense of top, crown, head, often in Claud.   p. 105. 16-17

b For **per locale** cf. Reinhardt (op.cit.I) p.21 sq.; 17.1.6; 17.1.10; etc.; ad 14.3.1 (= I p.78); ad 14.11.1 (= II p.113): **per modale.**

a **celsiora:** comparativus pro positivo = vertices.   p. 105. 17
alacrior: „   „   „   = alacer.
Cf.ad 14.6.12 (= I p.96).

b Cf. Claud.17 (de Fl.M.Theod.cons.) 206 sq.:
.... sed ut altus Olympi
Vertex, qui spatio (= altitudine) ventos hiemesque relinquit,
Perpetuum nulla temeratus nube serenum,
Celsior exsurgit pluviis, ... ; ibid.26.77 sq. (de bello Getico):
Adspice, Roma tuum iam **vertice celsior** hostem:
Adspice, quam rarum referens inglorius agmen/Italia detrusus eat...
Veget.r.m.4.21.

a **nulloque invento:** sed nullum invenerunt. The main point is given in the participium. Cf. ad 16.12.59, p.101.13-17. The idea is as follows: At dawn the soldiers are led to the tops of the mountains, but they do not find anybody there; (when they turn around and go back (from South to North, **but they stay on the Southern side of the Moenus**)), they see the smoke columns **North** of the river, which are also observed by the retreating Alam.

b For the usual (but not always noticed) **adversative** use of **et** and **-que** cf. Hofm.-Leum. p.660.231*d*.

p. 105. 18 *a* **hoc si quidem opinati discessere confestim. si quidem.** Cf.Hofm.-Leum. p.782: "Die spätere Latinität zeigt eine ausgesprochene Vorliebe für **si quidem;** so ist es überaus häufig bei Eccl.... (sowohl mit Indik. wie mit Konj.), wird im Anschlusz an **enim** öfters nachgestellt und erscheint wie dieses manchmal geradezu als koordinierende Partikel, namentlich in Verbindung mit dem Indik. z.B. Oros.hist.3.5.1: repente si quidem medio urbis terra dissiluit...".
What is also remarkable here is that in my view **siquidem,** placed between hoc and opinati, belongs to the last particip. (translation: because they had believed, realised this (beforehand), they had left immediately).

b **opinati.** This partic. in **passive** meaning among others in Arnob.adv. nat.1.24 (= Reiffersch.16.1): vestra sunt haec, vestra sunt inreligiose opi**nata** et inreligiosius credita; Amm. 21.6.3: postridie ludis Circensibus ... cum certamen **opinatum** emitteretur (= highly regarded, famous). The latter meaning late Latin. Cf. Krebs Antib.II p.217; Georges II 1363.

c **confestim.** Cf. ad 14.1.5 (= I p.61); Hofm.Lat. Umgangsspr. (op.cit.I) p.83. For the place of the adv. cf. ad 17.11.1, p.123.24.

d **discessere.** For the **perf.** cf. ad 14.2.9 (= I p.72) ad 14.3.4 (= I p.81).

p. 105. 18-19 *a* **fumi volumina.** Alliteratio! Cf.14.7.9, p.20.14; Domitiano ex comite largitionum praefecto provecto; Blomgren (op.cit.II) p.131.

b here = pillars of smoke, smoke columns. But 23.4.2, in the description of a **ballista:** a round, smooth surface. Cf.Ovid.Met.13.600 sq.:
... cum Memnonis arduus alto
Corruit igne rogus, nigrique **volumina fumi**
Infecere diem... ; likewise Luc.3.505.
For the meaning curve; curving, round surface, bend, etc. cf.Verg.Aen. 5.85; 2.208; 11.753; 5.408 (caestus); Georg.3.192 (of the bending horses' legs); Luc.5.565 (of waves); Claud.5.538. Furthermore in Amm. in the usual sense of: book (roll), act, written document, protocol.

p. 105. 19 *a* **indicantia nostros perruptas populari terras hostiles.** Note the use of the participia and the alliteration. Vulgar Latin and especially Latin translations of Greek texts show an abundant use of **participia praesentia.** in places where it is not allowed in archaic or classical Latin. Cf. Hoogterp, Et.sur le Latin du Cod.Bob.des Evang. p.210 sq. (with lit.) Hofm.-Leum.p.606 (182); Koziol (op.cit.I) p.106 sq.; Optat.Milev.1.18

(= Ziwsa p.19): Iubente deo indulgentiam mittente Maxentio christianis libertas est restituta; ibid.index p.300; etc.

b terras hostiles. Cf. ad 14.1.1 (= I p.55); ad 14.5.3 (= I p.85); ad 15.4.9 (= III p.62); ad 16.4.1, p.74.21.

perruptas. Thus also, without preposition: Liv.8.10.6: tantaque caede **perrupere cuneos**, ut ...; Caes.b.g. 7.19 ... si eam **paludem** Romani **perrumpere** conarentur; Horat.Carm.1.3.36:

perrupit Acheronta Herculeus labor.

Amm.31.7.4: Rheno perrupto; Claud.28.460; Veget.r.m.

I, 6

a **per arta loca et latebrosa struxerant nostris.** For the hyperbaton cf. ad p. 105. 21
15.2.9. (= III p.25); Hagendahl abund, (op.cit.I) p.187 sq.; Blomgren (op.cit.II) p.25 sq.

b Cf.Caes.b.g. 7.18.3: carros impedimentaque sua in **artiores silvas** abdiderunt. × latus. Normal adjective; but the combination **arta et latebrosa** is not known to me from other sources.

c **latebrosa.** Cf. ad 14.2.2 (= I p.67); 15.10.4: per diruptas utrimque angustias et lacunas, pruinarum congerie **latebrosas** (cf.17.12.4: flumen Histrum exundantem pruinarum iam resoluta congerie).

d **struxerant.** For simplex pro composito cf. ad 14.2.5 (= III p.18). Cf. et. Pighi St.Amm. (op.cit.I) p.172.4; Hofm.-Leum. p.548, 141d; ibid. p.793; Hagendahl, La prose métrique d'Arnobe (op.cit.II) p.157 sq.

a **trans Menum nomine fluvium.** Claus.I with synizesis, or Claus.II; cf. p. 105. 21-22
Pighi St.Amm.p.61.8 sq.

b **Menus** = Moenus. I see no grounds for correcting this version, as Heraeus wants to. **Nomine fluvium** will have been added because the **Moenus** will have been more or less unknown to the Romans. With **Rhenus**, for example, often mentioned in Amm., this addition is never found. Cf.16.3.1; ubi **amnis** Mosella confunditur Rheno; 27.6.12: gelu pervios Histrum et Rhenum; 14.8.5: ab Eufratis **fluminis** ripis; 18.8.9: ad ripas pellimur Tigridis; 19.8.9: ferebamur ad **flumen** Eufraten; 23.6.25: et Eufrates, cunctis excellens.

a **ad opitulandum suis necessitudĭnibus avolārunt.** for **opitulari** cf. ad 16. p. 105. 22
12.45, p.98.21a.

b Cf.21.16.20; 24.5.3; 31.5.5: Relatives, family. Plur. thus in Tac.Suet. Plin.min.Eutr. Cf. Krebs Antib.II p.137. Cf.et.Arnob.adv.nat.3.27

17

(= Reiffersch. p.130): in incestas libidines **necessitudo sanguinis** inardescit (with the same meaning).

c **avolarunt.** Cf.ad 16.12.19, p.94.11-12. Claus III.

I, 7

p. 105. 22-23 *a* **ut enim rebus amat fieri dubiis et turbatis.** for the hyperbaton cf.ad 17.1.6, p.105.21*a*.

b for the expression cf. ad 15.5.31 (= III p.117).

c Cf. turbata castra: Verg.Aen.6.668 sq.; folia turbata ibid.6.74 sq.; freta turbata Georg.III 259; Ovid.Met.8.859: capilli turbati; Iust.Phil. 18.2: pax turbata; Claus.7.63 sq.: (De III cons.Honor):

Interea turbata fides, civilia rursus

Bella tonant, dubiumque quatit discordia mundum;

ibid.31 (epithal.)28:

Utque fuit, turbata comas, intecta papillas,

Mollibus exsurgit stratis...

ibid.36.136: I tamen, et nullo turbata revertere casu.

d Novák (Wiener Stud.33,1911, p.307) wants to read **in** before **rebus** and refers to 16.12.40; 14.4.3; 15.5.31; 18.8.8; 21.10.1; 25.1.1; 26.9.9; 30.1.5. Palaeographically this "omission" would be easy to explain after **enim**: but in spite of numerous examples **with in** I do not see why it should be necessary.

p. 105. 23-24 **hinc... inde** = hinc ... illinc. Cf. Krebs Antib.I p.652 (with lit.). In general post-classical and late Latin.

p. 105. 23 **adcursu.** Cf.14.2.9: inopino (cf.I p.72) adcursu; 26.9.6: (Gomoarius) velut adcursu multitudinis visae subito circumsaeptus; insidiatricis manus locatae per abdita subito oppetisset accursu, ni... (27.10.11). Postclassical. Cf.et. ad 16.2.6, p.73.6-7. Not in Veget.r.m.

p. 105. 24 **vectorum militum** = **advectorum militum.** Simplex pro composito, cf.ad 17.1.6, p.105.21 *c*.; ad 14.8.8 (**advecticius**) = II p.69.

p. 105. 24 *a* **impetu repentino perterrefacti.** Note the alliterating **p** and **t**.

b Cf.28.1.48: Simplicii adventu perterrefacti; 30.1.7: ut cum tribuno milites universi perterrefacti vividius quam venerant remearent ad muros; Terent.Andr. 169; also late Latin.

c Cf.Cic. de orat.2.55 (225): vis... repentina; Caes.b.g.5.39: repentino equitum adventu; ibid.3.3: cum tantum repentini periculi... accidisset; Ovid.Met.5.5 sq.

Inque repentinos convivia versa tumultus/Assimilare freto possis...
Claud.1.211: ...unde repentinus coeli fragor; ad 15.2.4 (= III p.17);
Blomgren (op.cit.II) p.118, note 2.

d cf. **adsultu subito** ad 15.2.4 (= III p.16).

a **evadendi subsidium velox locorum invenere prudentes.** Cf.26.8.9: p. 105. 24-25
undique **facultate evadendi** exempta; 30.7.11: postquam eum (Macrianum) **evasisse Burgundios**... maerens didicisset et tristis; 25.8.18: Iovianus... quem in obsidione civitatis Maozamalchae **per cuniculum** docuimus **evasisse** cum aliis; 19.8.5: obscurae praesidio noctis **postica,** per quam nihil servabatur, **evado.**

b **subsidium** here: refuge, haven. Cf.Tac.Ann.3.60: complebantur templa pessimis servitiorum; **eodem subsidio** obaerati adversum creditores suspectique capitalium criminum receptabantur; ibid.4.67: quoniam inportuosum circa mare et vix modicis navigiis pauca **subsidia** (= refuges = resting-, anchoring places); ibid.2.63: Maroboduo undique deserto **non aliud subsidium quam** misericordia Caesaris fuit. Cf.16.12.54: ad subsidia (poet.plur.) fluminis petivere.

c Here we do have a kind of **abundantia.** Cf.26.9.8: hoc praeter spem omnium viso, Procopius **salutis intercluso suffugio,** versus in pedes, circumiectorum nemorum secreta (petebat) et montium (V.Lind.Vales; suffragio: E.B.G., Clark, Seyfarth. suffragio wrong in my opinion: cf. 26.8.9, above); 31.13.5: circumspectantes ademptum esse **omne evadendi suffugium;** Oros.adv.pag.2.19.13: ... et Gothi relicta intentione praedandi ad **confugia salutis,** hoc est sanctorum locorum. agmina ignara cogentes; Hagendahl abund. (op.cit.I) p.200 sq.; ad 15.10.4 (= IV p.55); ad 15.8.7 (= IV p.33).

d In "normal" Latin the sentence would read: **velociter** subsidium invenerunt, quo evaderent, prudentes locorum (the last 2 words: causal). For this **enallage** cf. Blomgren (op.cit. II p.146 sq.).

e Cf.Terent.Eun.135 sq.:
hic meus amicus: emit eam dono mihi
inprudens harum rerum **ignarusque** omnium.

The first underlined adj. used since Terent., the 2nd since Plautus with the genit. (Other adj. c.genit. Hofm.-Leum. p.403 sq.). Cf.et.b.Afr. 7: reliquae (naves), ut est ei nuntiatum, **incertae locorum** Uticam versus petere visae sunt; Riemann (op.cit.I) p.270. Cf.et. ad 16.2.10. p.73.21 **(locorum gnaritate).**

a **quorum digressu miles libere gradiens.** Cf.27.3.10: unde accensorum p. 105. 25,26 iracundiam pauperum, damna deflentium crebra, aegre potuit **celeri** vitare **digressu;** 25.3.19 hunc merui clarum ex mundo **digressum** (= dead). Cf. **discessus** ad 16.10.16, p.87.9.

b **gradiens** = progrediens. Cf. ad 17.1.6, p.105.21*c*. In the clausula (II). Perhaps a literary reminiscence: Cic.Verg? Cf.Claud.99.17; ibid.21.47 sq:

Quacumque alte **gradereris** in urbe,
Cedentes spatiis assurgentesque videbas,
Quamvis miles adhuc (Stilicho).

Cf.et. ad 15.5.2 (= III p.68): **grassari.** Not in Veget r.m. (gradi).

p. 105. 26 *a* **opulentas pecore villas et frugibus rapiebat.** For the hyperbaton cf.ad 17.1.6, p.105.21*a*.

b Cf.Liv.22.3.3: Etrusci campi... **frumenti ac pecoris** et omnium copia rerum **opulenti.** The adj. often connected with **praeda:** ibid.4.34.4; 9.36. 12-13; 35.1.11.

c **rapiebat** = diripiebat (as seen more often). Claus.III. Cf. ad 17.1.6, p.105,21 *c*.

p. 105. 26 **villa.** The word already indicates that here one should think of fairly large, non-primitive houses and barns, which is further adstructed by: domicilia, curatius ritu Romano constructa. The class. word **domicilium** is also used of larger houses.

p. 105. 26 **nulli sc. villae.**

p. 105. 27 *a* **extractisque captivis.** Captivis: "proleptically" used, as said before. Sabbah quotes 19.8.4, where **praedatoribus** was to have been used in this way. For the more normal form of the **prolepsis** (cf.18.2.12: ... perculsi reges eorumque populi, qui **pontem** ne strueretur studio servabant intento...) cf. Blomgren (op.cit.II) p.99.

b Cf.15.4.8: plerique ... periculoque praesidio tenebrosae noctis extracti; 15.5.31: Silvanum extractum aedicula, quo exanimatus confugerat; 17.13.12: gregatim peremptorum necessitudines ducebantur, humilibus extractae tuguriis; 17.13.13: nec quemquam casa, vel trabibus conpacta firmissimis, periculo mortis extraxit (note the close repetition in 17.13.12 and 17.13.13); 18.6.16: hoc extracti periculo; 24.5.4: hic et Nabdates vivus exustus est, quem extractum cum octoginta e latebris expugnatae docui civitatis; 25.1.2: Maurus frater ... infirmatus et ipse umerum telo... Macameum extrahere pugna viribus valuit magnis; 25.8.3: tandemque universi (praeter mersos) ad ulteriores venimus margines favore superi numinis discrimine per difficiles casus extracti; 27.6.4: imperator... vixque se mortis periculo contemplans extractum; 29.6.14: geminatibus ictibus omnem paene delessent, ni periculo mortis aliquos citum extraxisset effugium (in all the preceding places probably **ablat.**) 26.9.9: ad veteris Pepernae exemplum... e frutectis, ubi latebat **extractus** oblatusque Pompeio eius iussu est interfectus; 16.6.2: nam etiam alia munimenta isdem diebus rapta sunt et incensa **unde** hominum milia **extracta** complura Cf. Krebs Antib.I p.565; Heum-Seckel p.201. Not in Claud.

a **domicilia.** Cf.Caes.b.g.6.30.3: Sed hoc factum est, quod **aedificio**   p. 105. 27
circumdato silva, ut sunt fere **domicilia Gallorum,** qui vitandi aestus causa plerumque silvarum ac fluminum petunt propinquitates... Also used by judicial authors, often in a technical meaning: fixed abode. Metaph. Arn.adv.nat. 7.11 (= Reiffersch.p.245): nonne alios inquiunt, videmus ex illis **domicilia** esse **morborum** (= dwelling places of diseases) ...?
b For the **dwelling habits** of the Germans in conquered territory cf. ad 16.2.12, p.74.1.2. **cuncta.** Cf. ad 14.1.6 (= I p.61); Krebs Antib.I p.383; Hofm.-Leum. p.391, 22 E. Also used by judicial authors and Claud.

a **curatius ritu Romano constructa.** Cf.19.1.10: circaque eum lectuli   p. 105. 27
decem sternuntur figmenta vehentes hominum mortuorum ita **curate** pollincta...; 23.2.7: ut fama de se nulla praeversa-id enim **curatius** observarat – improvisus Assyrios occuparet. **Curatus** = **accuratus:** post-classical and late Latin. Similarly the comparativus **curatius** (Cf.Tac.ann. 2.27; 14.21; 16.22). Cf.et. Krebs Antib. I p.386; ad 17.1.6, p.105.21 *c.*
b Note the alliterating **c** and **r.**
c **ritu.** Cf.14.2.7: pecudum ritu (Cic.Lael.9.(32)); ad 15.5.31 (= III p.118); Liesenberg (1888) p.18; Krebs Antib.II p.519 sq. (with lit.) For Amm. cf. et. ad 16.12.43, p.98.15-16. Generally post-class. and late Latin. Frequently in Claud. Cf.28.151 sq.

... an iura perosus
Ad priscos **pecudum** damnaret saecula **ritus;**
ibid.20.499 sq.:
Hi **pecudum ritu** non impendentia vitant
nec res antevident...; 26. 173 sq.:
Ex illo, quocumque vagos (barbaros) impegit Erinys,
Grandinis aut morbi **ritu** per devia rerum
Praecipites per clausa ruunt (gr.r. also in Amm.). Not in Veget r.m.

a **flammis subditis exurebat.** Cf.b.Afr. 26: animadvertebat enim **villas**   p. 106. 1
exuri, agros vastari, **pecus diripi,** trucidari, oppida castellaque dirui deserique etc. (the normal military exploit); Caes.d.b.G.1.5.4: **oppidis** suis vicisqie **exustis;** Verg.Aen.1.39 sq.: ...Pallasne **exurere classem** Argi-

vum atque ipsos potuit submergere ponto...; Claud.50.46: Nec gemat **exustas** igne furente **domos.**

b Cato agric.38.4: Cum **ignem subdideris,** siqua flamma exibit nisi per orbem summum, luto oblinito (of the fornax calcaria); ibid.105.1: **ignem subdito;** Cic.nat.deor 2.10 (27): Quam similitudinem cernere possumus in iis aquis, quae effervescunt **subditis ignibus;** Verg.Georg.3.271: ... avidis ubi **subdita flamma** medullis... In **this** combination not in Claud. and Veget.r.m. (For the adj. **subditivus** cf.14.9.1).

I, 8

p. 106, 1 *a* **emensaque aestimatione decimi lapidis.**

lapis = miliarium. Cf. Nepos T.Pomp.Att.22: Sepultus est iuxta viam Appiam, ad quintum **lapidem,** in monumento Q.Caecilii avunculi sui; Liv.5.4.12: Nos intra vicesimum **lapidem,** in conspectu prope urbis nostrae, annuam obpugnationem perferre piget; Varro r.r.3.2.14: Axio admiranti, Certe nosti, inquam, materterae meae fundum, in Sabinis qui est ad quartum vicesimum **lapidem** via salaria a Roma; etc. (Tac.Hist. 2.24; 3.15 omits **lapis**) The expression here is, of course, quite unusual = emensoque aestimatione (abl. limit.) decimo lapide = emensoque aestimatione spatio decimi lapidis.

What is covered is not the estimate of the distance, but the distance itself. Abstractum pro concreto. Cf. ad 17.1.1, p.104.1.

b Cf.Claud.31 (Epith.Pall. et Cel.) 66 sq.:

Per cunctos iit ille gradus, aulaeque labores
Emensus, tenuit summae fastigia sedis.

p. 106. 2 **silvam:** Taunus.

squalore tenebrarum horrendam. Cf.19.1.9: per acervos caesorum et scaturrigines sanguinis, aegre defensum **caligine tenebrarum** extrahitur corpus; 31.13.12: primaque **caligine tenebrarum;** Firm.err.19.1: illic sordes, **squalor, caligo** et perpetuae noctis dominatur **horror;** Hagendahl abund. (op.cit.I) p.200; ad 17.1.7, p.105.24-25 *c.* Cf.et.Claud.35 (rapt.Proserp.) 329 sq.:

Rumpunt insoliti **tenebrosa** silentia cantus./Sedantur gemitus. Erebi se sponte relaxat/**Squalor** et aeternam patitur rarescere noctem.

(cf.Tac.ann.2.82: passim **silentia et gemitus).** Not in Veget.r.m.

p. 106. 2-3 *a* **stetit ⟨dux⟩ diu cunctando.** dux: Clark, Seyfarth. stetit diu: Sabbah. Grammatically **miles** should be the subject of **stetit;** but this does not fit in with: indicio perfugae doctus. The subject has therefore been shifted from **miles** to **dux (Caesar)**, but this is not expressed because of an understandable carelessness.

b **cunctando.** Cf. ad 14.1.6 (= I p.61 sq.).

a **per subterranea ... latere plurimos.** Between latere and plurimos Clark assumes a gap, Novák inserts **hostium.** I agree with Seyfarth and Sabbah that this is unnecessary. **plurimos** = pl. hostes. This is quite obvious without adding anything. However the difficulty lies in the metrics: lătĕrĕ plūrĭmōs.

Although in this commentary "unusual" clausulae have been pointed out before, the above clausula seems to me somewhat strange. Neither do I endorse the view of Pighi (Aevum 11,1937,396). It is not quite impossible that we are dealing here with a vulgar Latin phenomenon: **lătĕre.** For many verbs of the 2nd conjugation shift in vulgar Latin to the 3rd. Cf. **respondere** (Georges 2353); Bourciez (op.cit.II) 83 *d*, p.81 (with inst.); Ernout (op.cit.I) 215, p.109; Grandgent (op.cit.I) 399,p.167.

b **per subterranea quaedam occulta.** For the neutr.plur. of the adject. cf.ad 14.1.1 (= I p.55); ad 14.1.3 (= I p.57); ad 14.10.16 (= II p.111); ad 14.7.21 (= II p.50); ad 14.2.6 (= I p.69).

c Cf.Cic. 15.26.4: paucos **specus** in extremo fundo et eos quidem **subterraneos;** Florus 1.12.10: sed cuniculo et **subterraneis** dolis peractum urbis excidium; Tac.Germ.16: solent et **subterraneos specus** aperire; more over among others Colum., Seneca Nat.Quaest., Plin.H.N., Iuven., Pallad.Veget r.m.; not in Claud.

occulta is here a substantive. Cf.Caes.b.c. 3.105.4; Tac.ann.1.61.

d An unusual meaning of latere 15.11.1 (= to be unknown): Temporibus priscis, cum **laterent** hae partes ut barbarae, tripertitate fuisse creduntur, in Celtas eosdemque Gallos divisae et Aquitanos et Belgas...

e **quaedam** cf. ad 16.12.53, p.100.7 *a*.

a **ubi habile visum fuerit erupturos.** = fuisset, with the well-known repraesentatio. Conjunct. orat.obliq. = orat.rectae indic.perf. or **ind. fut. exacti.** "Correctly" used. For **ubi** cf. ad 14.2.7 (= I p.70); 14.2.20 (= I p.78). Cf.et.14.6.2 (= I p.89: **part.fut.**); ad 16.10.18, p.87,22 (**conjunct.iterat.**); ad 16.11.9, p.89.24. *a* and *c* (**part.fut.** and **si iuvisset fors**); ad 17.1.4, p.105.15 (**conj.iterat.**); ad 16.11.13, p.90.19-21 (**part.fut.**); ad 16.7.2, p.78.27 (**fut.exact.**).

b Cf.25.3.20: Super imperatore vero creando caute reticeo, ne per imprudentiam dignum praeteream aut nominatum, **quem habilem reor,** anteposito forsitan alio ad discrimen ultimum trudam. Also class. adj. Claud. 26.338.

19.5.2: duae legiones Magnentiacae... virorum fortium et pernicium, ad planarios conflictus **aptorum,** ad eas vero belli artes, quibus stringebamur, non modo **inhabiles**...; among others in Liv.Curt.Colum.Seneca ep. legal authors. Not in Claud. Cf.et. ad 16.2.6, p.73-6. Veget.r.m.2.14.

a **fossasque multifidas.-que** here probably explicative. Cf.Stat.Theb. 2.265 sq.: infaustos ... ornatus... dirum**que** monile.

b Cf.23.4.14: Malleoli autem, teli genus, figurantur hac specie: sagitta est cannea, inter spiculum et harundinem **multifido ferro** coagmentata...; 24.3.14: prope locum venit, ubi pars maior Euphratis in **rivos** dividitur **multifidos;** Claud.1.56; 35.15; 49.59. Poetic word. Cf.Hagendahl St. Amm.p.60 (with more examples). Not in Vegetr.m.

I, 9

p. 106. 5-6 *a* **ausi - constratas.** The order of words is here very artificial, as **ilicibus - magno** are 3 ablativi instrumentales.

b **ilicibus.** Here the inhabitant of the Mediterranean region is mistaken. **Quercus ilex** does not (and did not) occur in these regions, With the olive tree it is the characteristic tree of the territory around the Mediterranean and still grows in some places in the Lombardic sub-alpine lake district and in South-West France.

c **ilicibus incīsis et frāxinis.** Hyperbaton. Cf. ad 15.2.9 (= III p.25). Claus.II.

d **incisas.** Incidere means: to cut into, to cut off, to cut through. (cf. Krebs Antib. I p.708 sq.), not: to fell (of trees), to cut down; which one expects here. For that the simplex **caedere** or **succidere** (from below-) or **excidere** are used.

e **robore abietum** = robustis truncis abietum. It is generally known that **robur** is used especially of **oakwood,** and then of any firm, strong wood or heart-wood. Cf.Stat.Theb.2.619 sq.:

tunc audax iaculis et capti pelle leonis

pinea nodosam quassabat **robora** clavam.

(**pinea robor:** is object, **nodosam clavam** apposition).

(Cf.et. Mulder Comm.Stat.Theb.2 p.319.351).

f **constratas.** Cf.ad 17.1.2, p.105.4.

p. 106. 6 **ideoque.** Cf. ad 16.12.37, p.97.6.

p. 106. 6 **gradientes.** For the simplex cf. ad 17.1.6, p.105.21 *c*.

cautius. Cf. ad 14.6.12 (= I p.96). Claus.I (cautius retro). Cf.et ad 16.11.14, p.90.23. p. 106. 7

anfractus. Cf.15.4.2: inter montium celsorum amfractus; 24.4.10: nam p. 106. 7 accessus undique rupibus **amfractu celsiore** discissis flexuosisque **excessibus** ob periculum anceps adeundi copiam denegabat (excessus = protuding, offshoot). = curve, bend. In Claud.5.379; 35.156; 1.105; 28.517 sq.:

    Non procul amnis abest, urbi (Narniae sc.) qui nominis auctor,
    Ilice sub densa silvis arctatus opacis,
    Inter utrumque iugum **tortis anfractibus** albet.

Also class.substantive. Veget.r.m. 4.2.

a **vix indignationem capientibus animis, advertebant.** The punctuation is p. 106. 8 that of **Clark**, who divides his sentences metrically. Not so **Seyfarth**, who does not give any punctuation marks here. **Sabbah** like Clark. But in my opinion the punctuation here is not without significances. Because meaning and metric division are connected and cannot be viewed separately, I believe **Clark's** view to be as follows: **capientibus animis**: abl.abs.; **advertebant**: observed, realised (as often seen); cf. Krebs Antib.I p.107). No objection can be made against this. But one can also punctuate as follows: non... ultra progredi posse, vix indignationem capientibus, ănimis advertēbant (claus.III). **Vix indign.cap.** is an abl.abs., which **here** therefore stands for the partic.coniunctum. Cf.Hofm.-Leum. p.448, 60*a* ε; Tac. Nipperdey-Andresen[11] p.88 (ad I 29); ibid.p.390 (ad V 10). In vulgar or late Latin the construction which I believe possible here occur more often. But perhaps the Greek syntax also is of some influence here. Cf.Thucyd.4.32: οἱ δὲ ᾽Αθηναῖοι τοὺσ μὲν πρώτουσ φύλακασ, οἷσ ἐπέ δραμον, εὐθὺσ διαφθείρουσιν... οἰομένων αὐτῶν τὰσ ναῦσ κατὰ τὸ εἰωθὸσ ἐσ ἔφορμον τῆσ νυκτὸσ πλεῖν; etc.

b Cf.24.3.3: cum eos parvitate promissi percitos (alliteration: p) tumultuare sensisset, ad **indignationem** plenam gravitatis erectus. Cf. et Krebs Antib.1 p.725. Not in Claud. For the subst. **indignitas** cf. ad 16.4.3, p.75. 1-2*b*. The adverbium **indignanter** 15.1.3; 27.3.5; Arnob.adv.nat.3.7, not in Claud.

I, 10

a **aeris urente saevitia.** Sabbah: Alors, comme la rigueur **cuisante** du p. 106. 9 climat fait que etc.; good translation. Cf.Sall.Jug. 37.3-4: magnisque itineribus **hieme aspera** pervenit ad oppidum Suthul... quod quamquam et **saevitia temporis** et opportunitate loci neque capi neque obsideri poterat;

Curt.Ruf.8.4.13: Excepere... alios castra, quae, in humido quidem, sed iam caeli mitescente **saevitia,** locaverunt; Tac.ann.2.87: **Saevitiam annonae** incusante plebe statuit frumento pretium (= high corn-, food price).

b **aer** = caelum = climate. This meaning quite rare, although class. and post-classical. Cf.Horat.Epist.2.1.241 sq.:

quodsi iudicium subtile videndis artibus illud

ad libros et ad haec Musarum dona vocares/Boeotum **in crasso** iurares **aere** natum; Plin.min.ep. 5.19.7: Qua ex causa destinavi eum mittere in praedia tua, quae Foro Iuli possides. audivi enim te saepe referentem esse ibi et **aera salubrem** et lac eiusmodi curationibus accommodatissimum. Cf. Krebs Antib.1.p.116; Thes.s.v. The transition of meaning: (thick lower)air→sky→climate, is sometimes hard to determine and is not always determined correctly, in my opinion. Among the many examples of **aer** in Claud. I could not with certainty establish the meaning: **climate.**

c **urente.** Urere is also used with frost damage, freezing, etc. Cf.Cic. Tusc.2.17 (40): Pernoctant venatores in nive: in montibus **uri** se patiuntur; Ovid.Fasti 1.679 sq.:

Vos date perpetuos teneris sementibus auctus,

Nec nova per gelidas herba sit **usta** nives; Iust.2.2.9: Lanae iis usus ac vestium ignotus, quamquam continuis frigoribus **urantur;** Verg.Georg. 1.92 sq.: ne tenues pluviae rapidive potentia solis/acrior aut Boreae penetrabile frigus **adurat;** etc.

a **Cum discriminibus ultimis laboratur in cassum.** discrimen = danger, also class.; **very frequent in Amm.** Cf. ad 16.2.1, p.72.14-15.

b For the use of **cum** with this **ablat. of the attendant circumstances** cf. Hofm.-Leum.p.430,51 *b* Zusatz. The "classical" rule for the above **cum** does not apply to many late Latin authors, among whom Amm.

c **in cassum.** Cf. ad 14.2.9 (= I p.72). For this adverbial expression, which does not occur in Cic.Caes.Quint. and only once in Tac.(ann.1.4), cf. Krebs Antib.1.p.264 (with lit.); Riemann p.98 (op.cit.I) (who mentions 2 places in Liv. and calls it an "expression archaique": 2.49.8 and 10.29.2); Sall.Orat.Macri tr.pl.11; Claud.5.302; 26.614.

p. 106. 10 *a* **aequinoctio quippe autumnali exacto.** Cf.Liv.31.47: Jam **autumnale aequinoctium** instabat... **Aequinoctium** among others in Cic.Caes.Mela, but not very frequent. **Autumnalis** non-class.adj.: arch., post-class., poet. Both words not in Claud. The adjective **aequinoctialis** 22.15.31: apud Meroen, Aethiopiae partem **aequinoctiali circulo** (= aequator) proximam.

b **exacto.** Cf. ad 16.12.62, p.101.26-27.

c **quippe,** with the abl.abs. (since Livius). Cf.Hofm.-Leum.p.448, 60γ.

Cf.et.Kalb, Röm.Rechtsspr. (1912) §96; Grandgent (op.cit.I) p.8.11; Lindsay, Lat.Gramm.², p.96,160. Probably in late Latin no longer part of the spoken language. Also rare in late Latin lit.; except with historians, therefore an archaism. In Amm.17.1.10; 19.6.1; 19.11.7; 23.6.41; 26.6.4; 29.1.9; 30.6.2; 31.10.14; 31.12.1. (Fesser, op.cit.I, p.48).

per eos tractus. Cf. ad 16.3.1, p.74.8-9. Cf.et.Claud. (very often, with this and other meanings) in Index edit.Gesner s.v. Not in Veget r.m.

superfusae nives. nives = nix: Plur.poet. The part. may be derived from **superfundere** or **superfundi** = to pour out (oneself). Not in Claud. Infrequent in class. Latin. Also used by legal authors. Cf.et. **infundere** ad 16.5.4, p.76.1-2. In Veget. once as t.t.milit. and once in the normal literal meaning.

opplevere. Of rare occurrence in class. Latin. Not in Claud. Archaism? Also in judicial lit.

opus arreptum est. Thus one says **occasionem arripere**: Liv.35.12.17. Cf. et. Cic. ad fam.5.12.2: ... ac statim **causam** illam totam **et tempus arripere** Claud.20.406 sq. (In Eutrop.2):

Protinus excitis **iter** irremeabile signis
Arripit, infaustoque iubet bubone moveri
Agmina ...

ibid 28.210 (De VI cons.Honor.):

Oblatum Stilicho violato foedere **Martem**/Omnibus **arripuit** votis, ubi Roma periclo/Iam procul...; ibid. 44.34 sq. (Phoenix); Pars (sc.pinus) cadit assiduo flatu; pars imbre peresa
Rumpitur; **arripuit partem** vitiosa vetustas.

Veget.r.m.3.6 (= Lang p.77): primi ergo equites iter arripiant, deinde pedites. The verb does not occur in Arn.adv.nat. and Opt.Milev.

memorabile. This class.adj. we see again a little further on (14): hoc memorabili bello. Comparable with this place 16.11.9: **facinus memorabile** si iuvisset fors patraturos. Also 22.8.41; etc.

I, 11

et dum nullus obsisteret. For **dum** with the coniunct. cf. ad 14.10.1 (= II p.95). Cf.et. ad 14.11.5 (**dum** = usque ad id tempus quo) (= II p.118).

munimentum quod in Alamannorum solo conditum Traianus suo nomine voluit appellari.

a For **munimentum** cf. ad 16.12.58, p.101.6-7 *d*.
b For **Alamanni** cf. ad 14.10.1 (= II p.96).
c **solo.** Cf.16.12.59, p.101.8-9: et quia non nisi Rheno transito ad

territoria sua poterat pervenire (sc. rex Chnodomarius) and comment, ad h.1.

d **conditum.** The appropriate word for the construction of a complex of buildings, such as urbs, colonia etc. Cf. Krebs Antib. 1.p.320.

e **Traianus** (98-117 A.D.), the famous example. Cf.16.1.4: bellorum gloriosis cursibus Traiani simillimus (sc. Julianus). As regards the **fort itself** cf. ad 17.1.5-14, p.105.16-p.107.3, in fine.

p. 106. 13-14 *a* **dudum violentius oppugnatum.**

dudum. here: just now, recently; probably during the events narrated in 16.12, or just before or after.

b **violentius.** Cf. ad 14.6.12 (= I p.96). Claus.III.

p. 106. 14 **tumultuario studio**: with a zeal which was hasty and irregular (precipitate) (due to the circumstances). For they were not prepared to repair part of the **limes** (or a frontline just behind it). That was not the intention of this expedition. Cf. ad 17.1.5-14, p.105.16-p.107.3. The adject. also: 25.6.4; 26.8.7; 31.5.9. For the meaning of the word cf. Krebs Antib.2.682 (very good).

a **locatisque.** For - que cf. ad 16.12.35, p.96.22; 16.12.35, p.96.23; 16.12.37, p.97.6; 16.5.7, p.76.14-16 *c*.

b Cf.Cic. pro Cael. 28(67): fortis viros, ab imperatrice **in insidiis** atque **in praesidio** balnearum **locatos** (collocatos T, locatos Pπ Sbψ) v. Wageningen ad h.l. in comment.p.102: "**collocatos.** huic lectioni et usus favet et clausulae lex". I doubt whether this is right.

Iust.2.8: dux Atheniensium Pisistratus iuventutem **in insidiis locat.** But **locare defensores** will have been an invention of Amm.Cf.et.16.11.11: et victum **defensoribus ibi locandis...** condidit; 16.12.49. Term.techn. milit? Veget r.m.1.20; 2.16; 2.15; 4.32.

p. 106. 15 **defensoribus.** Cf. ad 16.11.11, p.90.9.

p. 106. 14 **pro tempore**: according to the circumstances of time. Cf. ad p.106.14: **tumultuario.** For the use of **pro modale** cf. ad 14.11.4 (= II p.118); Liesenberg (1890), op.cit.I, p.16; Krebs Antib.2 p.384; Caes.d.b.G.5.8.1: ... consiliumque **pro tempore** et **pro re** caperet (c.annot. in edit. Meusel[17] p.17).

p. 106. 15 *a* **ex barbarorum visceribus alimenta congesta sunt.** V barbarum. E B G barbarorum. Similarly Seyfarth, Clark; Sabbah like V.Cf.annot.14 p.163, Amm.2: "Le génitif en - um est un archaïsme mais il s'est maintenu dans des expressions spéciales de la langue technique et pour éviter l'accumulation des **r**: on trouve le génitif pluriel **barbarum** chez Nepos (Milt.2.1; Alc.7.4) Sénèque (clem.1.26.5), Tacite (ann.14.39; 15.25);

Florus (epit.2.30.31 et 36) et Ammien (31.16.5). Le choix de cette forme donne un relief épique à une image (**viscera**) familière à Cicéron et à Tite-Live". I agree with this. In the edit. Halm-Andresen (1918) of Tac. this genit. in **barbarorum** has been changed. Clark, Seyfarth read 31.6.5: **barbarorum**. Rolfe also reads in both places of Amm. **barbarorum**. For this genitive on -**um** cf. et Hofm.-Leum.p.279, 195 *d.* However, one should remember that to the Greek-speaking Amm. βάρβαροσ is an ordinary word, which, because it sounds almost exactly the same, can easily lead him to this gen. on -**um**.

b **visceribus**. Cf.Verg.Aen.3.575:
Interdum scopulos avulsaque **viscera montis**/Erigit eructans; Cic.Cat.1.13: periculum autem residebit et erit inclusum penitus **in venis** atque in **visceribus rei publicae**; Cic.Tusc.4.11: permanat **in venas**, et inhaeret **in visceribus** illud malum; Cic.Phil.1.15 (36): O beatos illos, qui... aderant tamen et in medullis **populi Romani** ac **visceribus** haerebant!; Aen.6.834; etc. But in my view Amm. has in mind Ovid.Met.1.137 sq.:
  Nec tantum segetes **alimentaque** debita dives
  Poscebatur humus, sed itum est in **viscera terrae.**
Cf.et.Claud.28.503:
Admittitque viam **sectae** per viscera **rupis;** ibid.33.175 sq.:
  Seu mare sulphurei ductum per **viscera montis**
  Oppressis ignescit aquis...; ibid.48.5 sq.:
  Unde fluant venti, trepidae quis **viscera terrae**
  Concutiat motus...; not at all in Veget.

c **alimenta**. Cf.14.6.19; 14.7.5. Also in Claud. The adj.20.8.20: **res alimentaria** (= provisions, supplies) Veget. does not have **alimenta**, though he does have **alimonia (f)**, viz. IV 7, vulgar and late Latin. Cf. Thes.sub v.; Krebs Antib.1.p.138 (with litt.); ad 16.11.12, p.90.12.

I, 12

illi. Cf. ad 16.12.38, p.97.17-21 *i*. p. 106. 16
perniciem. This ordinary class.subst. also in Veget.r.m. Not in Claud. The equally ordinary and class.adj. **perniciosus**: 14.10.14: tum autem ut incruenti mitigemus ferociae flatus **perniciosos** saepe provinciis (for **flatus** cf. ad 14.6.22 = I.p.99. Note the alliteration: **f.** and **p.**) Also in Veget r.m., not in Claud.

a **contemplantes ... congregati**. Because in my opinion **contemplari** p. 106. 16-17
should precede **congregari**, the first **part. (praes).** has been used perfecti-

vely, which we often find in late Latin. Cf.Hofm.-Leum. p.604 sq., 182 *a*.
Congregati precedes **petiere**.
b **contemplari** not in Veget.r.m. (though **contemplatio** is) and Claud.
congregare (-ri) not in Veget.r.m., nor in Claud.

p. 106. 16   **metuque rei peractae** = out of fear for the ending (with success) of the undertaking.

p. 106. 17   **volucriter.** Cf.21.9.6; 28.6.21; 29.1.18; 14.6.20 (?) 20.4.21. Not in Claud. Veget.r.m. Only in Amm.?

p. 106. 17   **humilitate.** Literally used: 15.10.4; 21.10.4.

p. 106. 17   **petiere.** Cf. ad 16.12.19, p.94.11-12.

p. 106. 17-18   **oratoribus.** Cf. ad 14.10.13 (= II p.110); ad 15.8.4 (= IV p.31).

p. 106. 18-19   **quam ... intervallum.** At first sight this passage is definitely obscure. Büchele: "nachdem er jedoch allen Ränken den Zugang abgeschnitten und eine Menge wahrscheinlicher Gründe seines Verfahrens vorgebracht hatte." The underlined is a free translation or rather an explanation of: quam... firmatam. Sabbah: "César s'assura de toute sorte de **précautions**". Seyfarth: "nachdem er ihn durch Beratungen über alles Für und Wider gesichert". The last translation is in my view the most accurate. But mentally one should add: against the mala fides of the barbarians. None of the 3 authors give a satisfactory explanation of the 2nd part of the passage: **causatus ... plurima. Causari** means: to give as (professed) reason, to excuse oneself (with pretenses). That does not fit in here. (Cf. Krebs Antib.1.p.268). However, the late Latin meaning is: to complain, to raise objections. One could paraphrase as follows: and **although** he raised many objections (1. to them? 2. to himself? 3. to the army? viz. to make peace), which had some truth in them (and therefore could refute rising criticism (3); so that they could defend the short period (1)), he nevertheless assigned it etc. For **consiliorum via** cf. ad 14.10.10 (= II p.107); ad 16.5.16, p.78.1*b*.
The subst. **causatio**: 18.6.5.

p. 106. 19   **mensuum** V Seyfarth Sabbah. mensium HBG Rolfe. For this form cf. Amm.M.Sabbah 2. p.163 sq. note 15; Thes.s.v.; Amm.26.1.13; Veget.r.m.

4.39 (mensum E. **mensuum** α. mensium ΠVPλ); ibid.4.40 (mensum E. **mensuum** Aμ. mensium ΠGP vulgo). In both cases Lang gives E.'s version.

per decem mensuum tribuit intervallum (sc.pacem). A contaminatio of: intervallum (belli) tribuit per decem menses and: pacem decem mensuum tribuit. This **pax** is a cease-fire **(indutiae)** of 10 months, which Julianus believes is the time he needs to reinforce the fort (id-communiri). For the time being his plans for "peace" go no further. And the enemies asking for peace have to be satisfied with this term.
Intervallum refers in Claud. and Veget.r.m. only to places, **not** to time. **Indutiae** not in Claud. In Veget.1 time (4.36): siquidem et adhuc solidae arbores et iam divisae per tabulas duplices ad maiorem siccitatem mereantur **indutias**. (Cf. et.Souter p.201). It suggests that to Amm. **indutiae** (= **cease-fire**) is no longer a living word. Cf.et. ad 16.12.19, p.94.8 *b*.

colligens. Cf.ad 16.5.7, p.76.13 **b**. p. 106. 20

quod ... deberent. Cf. ad 14.7.5; 14.7.14; 14.10.14; 14.11.7. (= II p.22; p. 106. 20-21
II p.41; II p.111; II p.120).

a **quod castra supra quam optari potuit occupata.** Cf.Sall.5.3: corpus p. 106. 20
patiens inediae algoris vigiliae **supra quam** cuiquam credibile est; Cic. Orat.40 (139): saepe **supra** feret sc. rem **quam** fieri possit...; Aur.Vict. Epit.14.3: memor **supra quam** cuiquam credibile est; ibid.1.21: porro autem dominandi, **supra quam** aestimari potest, avidissimus; Hofm.-Leum. p.732, 295 II, Cf.et. ad 15.6.1 (= IV p.6); verum contra quam speratum est contigit.
b **castra ... occupata**: as above: **rei peractae**.

obstaculo. Cf.17.13.4: Parthiscus ... accolas... a barbaricis vero excursi- p. 106. 21
bus suo tutos praestat **obstaculo**; 21.10.4: inferior (planities) ita resupina et panda, ut nullis habitetur **obstaculis** adusque fretum... Subst.non-class., once in Seneca nat.quaest.2.52.1, for the rest late Latin. Cf.et. Krebs Antib.2 p.190; Georges II 1272-1273; not in Claud. or Veget.r.m., though it does occur among others in Arnob.adv.nat.

a **tormentis muralibus.** Cf.19.6.6: **tormentis** ad emittenda undique **saxa** p. 106. 21
telaque dispositis; 19.6.10: tormentorumque machinae stridebant sine iaculatione ulla **telorum**; 19.7.4: Persae pedites **sagittas tormentis** excussas e muris aegrius evitantes; 18.9.1: locatoque ibi conditorio (= store-

room) **muralium tormentorum** fecit hostibus formidatam (civitatem); 31.15.6: et ad emittenda undique **tela vel saxa tormenta** per locos aptata sunt habiles; Müller Mil. (op.cit.I) p.607 sq.; Kretzschmer (op.cit.) p.93 sq. It is obvious from the above mentioned projectiles that the **tormenta** include several different sorts of machines. **Tormentum** is therefore not a specific term (That **tormentum** also means: torture, e.g. 14.5.9; 15.6.1 etc., need hardly be mentioned). Cf.et.Verg.Aen.12.921 sq.:...
  Murali concita numquam
  Tormento sic saxa fremunt...

b Cf.23.4.15: hactenus de **instrumentis muralibus,** e quibus pauca sunt dicta (= siege works).

c **apparatus** has here almost the same meaning as above (b): military equipment. With the usual meaning e.g.14.5.1: theatrales ludos atque circenses **ambitioso** editos **apparatu.** Cf.et. ad 16.5.9., p.76.23-25 *b*.

I, 13

p. 106. 22 **hac fiducia.** Seyfarth: Im Vertrauen auf diese Lage. Sabbah: Usant de cette garantie. Büchele: **Auf dieses gegebene Wort hin.** In my view only the last translation is correct. (hac fiducia = huius rei fiducia; as so often). The confidence of the 3 reges should refer to the peace allowed by Julianus to the Alamanni, at least to those of them that had sent **oratores.** For the rest the men, on both sides, will have had very little faith in each other's intentions.

p. 106. 22 **immanissimi.** Cf.Cic.Verr.2.51: Mithridates... Hostis, et hostis in ceteris rebus nimis ferus et **immanis.** When one reads how Sulla etc. acted against non-Romans and Romans, one views the term **immanissimi** with some suspicion. To Amm. and many of his contemporaries the Germans are, after all, very disreputable people. Cf. ad 16.12.61, p.101.20-21 *a*. The adj. also in Claud. Not in Veget.r.m. The subst. **immanitas** (= monstrous size) 19.7.6: quorum stridore **immanitateque** corporum (sc. elephantorum).

a **tandem aliquando iam.** For this abundant use of adverbia cf.26.5.13 **(tandem denique);** 17.12.10; **(denique tandem);** 17.4.14 **(tandem sero);** 17.9.3 **(nondum etiam);** 27.10.3 **(inde post);** etc.; Hagendahl abund. (op. cit.I) p.213; Hofm.Lat.Umg.spr. (op.cit.I) p.69 sq.; Hofm.-Leum. p.827 sq. (with lit.).

b However, it is possible to connect **iam** with **trepidi** (= finally).

p. 106. 23 *a* **apud Argentoratum.** For **apud** cf. ad 14.11.21 (= II p.137); Liesenberg (op.cit.I) 1890 p.9; Reinhardt (op.cit.I) p.51.

b For **Argentoratus** cf. ad 15.11.8 (= IV p.63).

auxilia. Seyfarth: Hilfstruppen. Sabbah: des secours. Rolfe: **aid.** The last translation is correct, in my opinion. **Auxilia** is pluralis poet. as the **plural** is a typical t.t.mil., which is not used for non-"Roman" troops, which are sent to help invading Germans, for instance, as here. Cf.31.7.3: Frigeridum ducem cum Pannonicis et transalpinis **auxiliis** adventantem; 16.11.9: **auxiliares** velites; 20.1.3: moto igitur **velitari auxilio** (note the variatio with 16.11.9 and the singular), Aerulis scilicet et Batavis; 20.4.2: **auxiliares** milites. For the **auxilia** cf. Müller Mil. (op.cit.I) p.581 sq. (in Amm.); Grosse Mil. (op.cit.I) p.38 sq. (general); ad 15.5.30 (= III p.115); ad 17.2.1, p.107.10; ad 16.2.4, p.72.25.

a **iurantes conceptis ritu patrio verbis nihil inquietum acturos.** Thus Clark Seyfarth Sabbah. G verbis nihil inquietum. V vero (lac.10 litt.) linquietum. One of the many examples of Gelenius, in which the original version of the manuscript is rendered correctly, or almost correctly.
b **(se) acturos(esse).** Cf.21.5.10: **verbis** iuravere **conceptis** omnes pro eo casus ... perlaturos; 25.4.12: (Iulianus) **discessurum** ad vitam minaretur privatam, ni tumultuare desistent (but 15.4.7: minabatur **se discessurum**; 28.6.19: **relaturum se** cuncta ... minabatur ad principem). As Kuehner says: "Ziemlich oft wird das Pronomen bei dem Particip des **aktiven Futurs** und **pass.Perf.** weggelassen, wo alsdann gewöhnlich auch esse weggelassen wird". Cf.et. ad 14.5.7 (= I p.87): acc.c.inf.fut.; ad 15.7.4 (= IV p.13): **se** "omitted" in the acc.c.inf. (with lit.); ad 14.2.17 (= I p.76).
c **conceptis verbis.** Cf.Tac.Hist.4.41: Senatus inchoantibus primoribus **ius iurandum concepit**; ibid.4.31: et cum cetera **iuris iurandi verba** conciperent; Cic.Cluent. 48 (134) dixit se scire illum **verbis conceptis peierasse**; Petron.113(13): **Iurat verbis** Eumolpus **conceptissimis**; Epist.Cornel.: **Verbis conceptis deierare** ausim; Seneca Apoc.1.3: **verbis conceptis** affirmavit; Heum.-Seckel p.86. This expression not in Claud. and Veget r.m.
d **ritu.** Cf. ad 17.1.7, p.105.27 *c*. Amm. does not tell us how this ancestral way is.

a **ad praestitutum usque diem.**
   ad ... usque. Cf.ad 17.1.2, p.104.6-7 **b**.
b Cf.Terent. Phormio 3.2.38-39:
   Certe hercle, ego si satis commemini, tibi quidem est olim **dies**,
   Quam ad dares huic, **praestituta**; Plaut.Pseud.2.2.30 sq.:
   ... nam olim cum abiit, argento haec **dies**
   Praestitutast, quoad referret nobis, neque dum rettulit;
Nepos Chabr.3.1: Athenienses **diem** certam Chabriae **praestituerunt,** quam

33

ante domum nisi redisset, capitis se illum damnaturos denuntiarunt; Curt.Ruf.3.1.8: ... ad **praestitutam diem** permisere se regi; Cic.Liv. judicial authors. Not in Claud., Veget.r.m. In my view he means: the same 10-months' term as above (17.1.12). Cf.et. ad 14.11.19 (= II p.130).

p. 106. 25 *a* **quia id nostris placuerat.** Cf.20.4.4: nec dissimulare potuit nec silere... verendum esse affirmans, ne voluntarii barbari militares, saepe sub eius modi legibus assueti transire ad **nostra,** hoc cognito deinceps arcerentur; 24.4.29: Exin profecto imperatori index nuntiaverat certus... subsidisse manum insidiatricem latenter, ut ... agminis **nostri** terga feriret extrema; 24.8.6: Quidam arbitrabantur... nonnulli Persas **nobis** viantibus incubuisse firmabant; 18.6.16: docetque ... speculatorem se missum ad **nostra** saepe veros nuntios reportasse; 30.6.2: (Quadorum legati) firmabant, nihil ex communi mente procerum gentis delictum asseverantes in **nostros**...; Reiter (op.cit.I) p.13 sq.: "Persona eius, qui res narrat, cum significari soleat pronomine **ego** et possessivis huic affinibus, haec in Amm.libris nusquam inveniuntur, nisi quod interdum confundens suam scribentis personam cum eius persona, qui dicit vel de quo agitur, pronomina **nos** et **noster** inducit ita, ut sint loco vocis "Romani" et "Romanus"; ad 17.1.2, p.104.7-9 *d*. Besides the above examples in the **oratio obliqua** the frequent use of **nos** and **noster** is remarkable. This e.g. in 17.1.5: **nostros** 17.1.6 **nostris,** etc.

b **placuerat.** The plusquamperf. has been "correctly" used. As regards the indicativus, cf. ad 16.12.14, p.93.9; ad 16.10.3, p.84.19-20*b*; ad 15.6.1 (= IV p.7); ad 15.12.4 (= IV p.76). As so often, one is struck with Amm. by the **obvious use** of the indicat. in the orat.obl., of which Reiter gives many examples.

p. 106. 25 **Munimento** cf. ad 16.12.58, p.101.6-7 *d*.

servaturos. Servare (= to respect, to observe) with **foedera** is quite normal, but the connection with **munimentum** seems to me unusual. What is meant here is, they swear that they will respect the treaties and **will not attack the fort.** As Sabbah translates: "en s'interdisant toute attaque contre le fort" and Seyfarth: "ohne das Kastell anzutasten". It therefore seems to me to be a kind of **zeugma.** Cf. Blomgren p.53 sq. (op.cit.II).

p. 107. 1 **portatŭros hŭmeris(suis). Suis** Clark Her. Rolfe. V Sabbah Seyfarth: **(h)umeris** only. A different version of Clark, Novák: **humeris portaturos,** apparently metri causa (claus.III). But this is not palaeographically justified. Although V's version does not give a normal clausula, yet the lack of this is no reason for arbitrary changes in the text. In this commentary **irregular clausulae** have already several times been pointed out.

si defuisse sibi docuerint defensores. Note the alliteration. Docuerint = docuissent. Repraesentatio cf. ad 14.7.9 (= II p.31), as more often. **Docuerint**: conj.perf. = **conj.fut.ex.orat.rectae.** Cf. ad 16.7.2, p.78,27 *b* and ad 17.1.4, p.105.15. (Unless one wants to consider docuerint (= docuissent) as a **conj.perf.iterat.**). For **defensores** cf. ad 16.11.11, p.90.9.

I, 14

memorabili. Cf. ad 17.1.10, p.106.11. This adj. does not occur in Veget. r.m. or Claud.

Conparando Punicis et Teutonicis. This, of course, is a gross rhetoric exaggeration, of which I believe. Amm. was very well aware. Both series of wars were, after all, a serious peril to the Roman empire. However, when one views the **continuing wars with the Germans** from a distance, one is in a position to grant that together these were comparable to the **Punica et Teutonica bella** and even were far more dangerous. Such objective insight can hardly be expected from a contemporary. But he who lives in a certain established social order and feels himself a part of this order, may on rare occasions percieve the approaching catastrophe, but for the sake of mental self-preservation, if nothing else, he will turn away his imagination towards the past and hope for a future however unlikely, which is better than the present. Thus also Amm. **Teutonicis**: the wars with the **Cimbres** and the **Teutons** (113-101 B.C.). Cf.31.5.12: Inundarunt Italiam ex abditis oceani partibus **Teutones** repente cum **Cimbris,** sed post inflictas rei Romanae clades immensas, ultimis proeliis per duces amplissimos superati, quid potestas Martia adhibita prudentia valet, radicitus exstirpati, discriminibus didicere supremis. This is written by Amm. when the **Thervingi**, under the leadership of Alavivus and Fritigernus, secede from Valens (376) and drive away Lupicinus and his soldiers, hoping, of course, that in **ultima proelia**, under the guidance of **duces amplissimi the potestas Martia of the Romans,** will once and for all remove the German danger from the Roman state, Which proved an idle hope.

dispendiis. Cf. ad 16.12.41, p.98.9*a*.

a **ut faustus Caesar exultabat et felix.** Cf. ad 16.12.13, p.93.2-3*c*; ad 16.12.18, p.94.3-4; ad 16.12.18, p.94.5*a*.
b For the **hyperbaton** cf. ad 15.2.9 (= III p.25); ad 17.1.6, p.105.21*a*.

35

p. 107. 5 **obtrectatoribus.** Cic.Suet.Just. Not in Claud.Veget. r.m. Optatus Milev. Arnob.adv.nat. Probably a flower of speech from Cic.
potuit. The **indicative** according to the "correct" classical usage.
ideo. For **ideo(que)** cf. ad 16.12.25, p.95.9.

p. 107. 5-6 **fortiter eum ubique fecisse fingentibus.** Note the alliteration. For **fortiter facere** cf. ad 16.12.29, p.95.27; ad 15.5.33 (= III p.120).

p. 107. 6-7 *a* **quod oppetere... optabat, quam... occidi.** Note the alliteration. For **optare** c.infin., in general post-class., cf. Krebs Antib.2 p.219 sq.; Hofm.-Leum. p.581. (with acc.c.infin.ibid. p.585).
b "**oppetere** für sich allein in der Bedeutung **sterben** ist poet.-lat. und kommt nachklass. in Prosa nur beim ältern Plinius, Tacitus und ähnlichen vor; klass. und bei allen bessern steht es nur mit dem Zusatze **mortem**, poet.lat. und daher auch in der poetisierenden Prosa... mit **letum**, spätlat. z.B.Amm.20.4.8 mit **morte**" (Krebs Antib.2 p.218).
c A remarkable parallel: 20.4.8: **gloriosum** esse existimans iussa morte **oppetere**, quam ei provinciarum interitum adsignari. Cf.Veget. r.m.2.24: **gloriosa** victoria; ibid.4.praef.: ut **gloriosius** ... possideret; ad 16.12.70, p.103.9-10 *a;* ad 16. 10.3, p.84.24.
d **optabat... sperabat.** For the **indic. in the orat. obl.** cf. ad 17.1.13, p. 106.25*b*.

p. 107. 6-7 *a* **quam damnatorum sorte (sicut sperabat) ...occidi** = like a man condemned (to death) (as he expected = feared) ... to be executed.
b **damnatorum:** t.t. jurid., used especially of the condemnation for a capital crime, a grave offense.
Damnatorum sorte: far-fetched expression instead of the usual **damnatus.**
c **sperabat.** Cf. ad 14.7.5 (= II p.20); ad 15.5.9 (= III p.84 sq.).
d **occidi:** to execute. In the same way Dig.48.5.25 uses: Marito quoque adulterum uxoris suae **occidere** permittitur, sed non quem libet, ut patri...; ibid.21: **ius occidendi** adulterum; ibid.23; etc.

p. 107. 7 **frater Gallus.** Cf.Comm.I p.40; 43; 46; 47.

p. 107. 7 **pari proposito** = pari proposito **peragendo** (Nep.Att.22), p.p. **tenendo** (Caes.b.c.1.83), in pari proposito **manendo** (Suet. de gramm.24). Translation: by sticking to the same pattern of life.

excessum = **to die,** death: here: 25.3.23; 26.4.6. **The protrusion; bend:** 18.6.15; 24.4.10; **offshoots:** 18.8.9. Digression (in the story): 22.9.6: 27.4.1.

actibus. This subst. very often in Amm. Cf.14.11.26: multiplices **actus** permutando convolvit; 28.1.39: quod in variis et confragosis **actibus** vitae plerumque contingit. Often = **actio** (class.). Cf. Krebs Antib.1.77 sq. (with lit.); Heum.-Seckel p.10. Often in Claud. Not in Veget.r.m. **inclaruisset** = had become famous. Similarly: 29.5.4: quorum prior sub Nerone, alter Traiano rem regente Romanam pluribus **inclaruere** fortibus factis (cf. ad 17.1.14, p.107.5-6); day-break: 25.1.1: ubi vero primum dies **inclaruit.** Besides this **clarescere:** 17.2.1: ut postea **claruit** (became clear, appeared); 30.4.13: Tertius eorum est ordo (viz. of sollicitors, lawyers, etc.), qui, ut in professione turbulenta **clarescant** (stand out, excel)... Both verbs post-class. and not very frequent. **Both** not in Veget.r.m.; a few times we find in Claud. the **simplex,** but not the compositum, which, as so often, will have been less "chic". Cf.et. ad 14.1.9 (= I p.64).

II, 1

a **Quibus ut in tali re conpositis firmiter.** Sabbah: "Ces **conventions établies** aussi solidement que le permettaient les circonstances"; Seyfarth: "Nachdem der Cäsar **die Verhältnisse** den Umständen entsprechend sicher **geordnet hatte**"; Rolfe: "**Matters** thus **being** firmly **settled**". In my view the last two translations are correct. **Componere** has here its normal general meaning of: to arrange, to regulate; **not** that of: to agree, to settle, to make a deal. This fits better into the context, in my view. For **componere** (= to write falsehoods, to make up) cf. ad 16.11.15, p.91.12.

b **ut.** For this restricting **ut** (insofar as) cf.Hofm.-Leum. p.757,317. Cf. et.21.10.5: His **ut in re tali** tamque urgenti **compositis;** Sall.Cat.57.5: optumum factu ratus **in tali re** fortunam belli temptare; Liv.33.9.9: ceterum ad communem omnium **in tali re** trepidationem accessit; Amm. 22.9.10: exemplumque patientiae eius **in tali negotio,** licet sint alia plurima, id unum sufficiet poni...; 31.10.15: multis (**ut in tali negotio**) variatis sententiis; Sall.Jug. 107.6: ea res **uti in tali negotio** probata; Fesser (op. cit.I) p.18.

c **firmiter** = firme, both class. adv. Cf. Krebs Antib.1. p.596. Both adverbia not in Claud. Veget.r.m., though they are found in judic.lit.

ad sedes revertens hibernas: far-fetched for: ad hiberna revertens.

p. 107. 10 *a* **sudorum reliquias repperit tales.** Cf.Verg.Aen.9.457 sq.:
Adgnoscunt spolia inter se galeamque nitentem
Messapi et **multo** phaleras **sudore** receptas.
Also in this metaphorical sense several times in Cic. Almost certainly a literary reminiscence of Amm.Cf.et.Stat.Theb.4.151:
Monstrat Cyclopum ductas **sudoribus** arces;
Claud.53.4:
... Herculeus **sudor** uterque fuit
(sc. aper and leo); ibid.15.334 sq:
... Libyam nostro **sudore** receptam.
Rursus habent? ausus Latio contendere Gildo?
(and thus more often in Claud.); Veget.r.m.2.3 (= Lang p.37): Quod vitantes plerique in **auxiliis** festinant militiae sacramenta percipere, ubi et minor **sudor** et maturiora sunt praemia (An interesting place for the **auxilia!**); Cod.Theod.13.1.7: Qui in **sudore bellandi** stipendiorum gradus usque ad protectores meruerunt; H.A.Cap.Max.duo 2.7: tunc Maximinus sedecim lixas **uno sudore** devicit... Gothofr. remarks: "**Sudoris** vox militiae propria". But when one knows that **sudor** occurs already in Ennius as well as Horat. Seneca.Tac. (everywhere in the same metaph. meaning), this seems somewhat improbable to me. The **plural** also in Cod.Theod. 6.22.8: Praeterquam si de aliquibus professionum et militiae meritis **scriniorumque sacrorum emensis sudoribus** lege specialiter est statutum... (= "if specfic provisions are made by law with reference to any merits of those persons in the professions or of those in the imperial service and in the sacred imperial bureaus **who have performed toilsome service for years**": Pharr).

b Note the alliteration.

c **reliquias.** 1) In the meaning of ruins: 17.10.7: rex cum multiplices regionum vicorumque **reliquias** cerneret exustorum; 24.8.2: vicorumque **reliquiis** exustorum inopia squalentibus ultima (note the almost homonymous words). In this meaning post-class., poet., late Latin.

2) In the same way the subst. is used in Cic. de senect. 6.19: Quam palmam utinam di immortales, Scipio, tibi reservent, ut **avi** (P.Corn.Scipio maior) **reliquias** (sc. the war with the Carthaginians) persequare!; Verg.Aen. 1.29 sq.:
His accensa super, iactatos aequore toto
Troas, **reliquias** Danaum atque immitis Achilli...
(Forbiger: "Troianos, qui a Danais et ab Achille **vivi** relicti erant, qui Achivorum manus effugerant"). Ibid.3.87 (with the same words). Cf.et. Krebs Antib.2 p.496 (with lit.).

Remos. Cf. ad 15.11.10 (= IV p.64). p. 107. 10

a **Severus magister equitum.** For S. cf. ad 16.10.21, p.88.7*b*; ad 16.2.8, p.73.16 (**Marcellus**)*b*. p. 107. 10
b **magister equitum.** Cf. ad 14.9.1 (= II p.88).

a **Per Agrippinam petens et Iuliacum.** For **per** cf. Reinhardt (op.cit.1) p. 107. 11
p.8 sq. (exhausting); ad 14.3.1 (= I p.78); ad 14.11.1 (= II p.113); ad 16.11.9, p.90.1; ad 16.12.21, p.94.18-19*b*; ad 17.1.5, p.105.16-17*b*; Krebs Antib. 2 p.274 (with lit.).
b For the hyperbaton cf. ad 17.1.6, p.105,21*a*; ad 15.11.8 (= IV p.62).
c **Agrippinam** cf. ad 15.5.15 (= III p.92). Cf. et Peter La Baume, Colonia Agrippinensis[3], 1964; O. Doppelfeld, **The Dionysian Mosaic** at Cologne Cathedral 1964; F.Fremersdorf, Das römische Haus mit dem Dionysos-Mosaik vor dem Südportal des Kölner Domes, 1956; O.Doppelfeld, **Das Pratorium unter dem Kölner Rathaus**, neue Ausgrabungen in Deutschland, 1958; Woordenb. der Oudheid, 4, 1969, p.695 (with lit.); H.Clemens, Die römische Grabkammer in Weiden bei Köln, 1964. The town possessed a waterwork, which got its water from the Hocheifel, which was 77.6 kilometers long, constructed in several places as aquaductus, and considered one of the most important technical achievements of the Romans in Germany. Constantine the Great (306-337) built the abutment **Divitia** (Deutz), which was linked to Cologne with a bridge. It is not mentioned in Amm. (Cf. Kretzchmer, op.cit, p.80). The devastations of the war of 1940-1945 have made it possible to lay bare a considerable part of the old Roman city and partly preserve this, so that Cologne is one of the best-known Northern cities from Antiquity and a beautiful example of Roman urbanisation.
d **Iuliacum** (= Jülich). On the Tab.Peut.II 5-III 1 the road from **Agrippina** via **Juliacum** to **Coriovallum** (= Heerlen) is indicated. At the last place the road from Cologne to **Atuatica** (= Tongeren) (α) crosses the road from **Colonia Traiana** (= Xanten) to **Aquae** (Aachen) (β). The road to Tongeren ran via Maastricht (= **Traiectum**). The troops must have marched along the Rhine road via **Confluentes** (= Koblenz) and **Bonna** (= Bonn) to Cologne. In the Itiner.Ant.Aug. (Wesseling) p.375 we find: Iter a Colonia Traiana Coloniam Agrippinam via **Coriovallum** and **Juliacum**, therefore the part from β to Coriovallum and the part from α from Coriovallum to Agrippina. From Tongeren the road leads to Reims ((**Durocortorum (Remorum)** = **Remis** (late empire)) via **Bagacum** (= Bavay), capital of the civitas Nerviorum, also an important junction,

on the main road from **Gesoriacum** (= Boulogne) to Cologne (cf.Itin. Anton.Aug.376 sq. Wesseling). Reims is the last main station on the road which continues to **Lutetia** (= civitas Parisiorum).

Juliacum lies in Germania II (inferior), provincia of the diocesis Galliarum (Praefectura Praetorio Galliarum). From the above description of roads can be concluded where we should place the military operations mentioned in cap. II. **Severus,** leading the way with cavalry and light-armed scouts, suddenly comes upon ransacking Franks, South of the present province of South-Limburg, in the vicinity of Heerlen or Maastricht. Although far behind the Rhine front, the Franks seem to be able to plunder there unhindered. There are no Roman occupational forces there. They make use of the circumstance that **Julianus** is occupied elsewhere: in Alamannorum secessibus. There was enough loot for the taking, for this was a prosperous Romanised territory. As so often happens, the Franks are blinded by their rapacity and are more of less surprised by the returning Romans (Severus): metu iam reversi exercitus. They hastily occupy 2 forts which have long been abandoned. This certainly characterises the circumstances of that time!

We **have to** assume that **Julianus** with the main force later comes marching along **the same road.** He joins forces with Severus (?) and considers that to press on, without attacking the Franks in their forts is: 1° politically dangerous; 2° militarily unwise. Against all tradition the enemies are besieged, in the middle of winter, December and January, as is told by Amm. himself. There is a severe frost. As **the Meuse (Mosa)** washes against the walls of the munimentum, this is probably situated close to Maastricht. This is also the opinion of Sabbah. The siege lasts for 54 days. That is very long for a siege of 2 forts with 600 **light**-armed men. Apart from their pertinacia incredibilis these Franks will have developed some other talents. Probably the forts themselves, though abandoned, were in good condition. Finally the Franks are forced to surrender due to lack of food and general exhaustion. From **retento milite** it appears that **all** troops (or nearly all) remain in the neighbourhood of the forts, both for the siege and everything attendant to it (circumvallare), as to keep Frankish relief forces at bay (2.4). The sojourne of the Roman army in these inclement times will not have been very agreeable. The soldier Amm. does not waste any words on it (neither do his sources, probably). Cf.et. ad 16.8.8, p.82.9-10.

p. 107, 11-12 *a* **Francorum validissimos cuneos.** For **Franci** cf. ad 15.5.11 (= III p.86); 15.5.16 (= III p.94); ad 17.8.3: **Salios.**

b **cuneos.** Cf. ad 16.11.5, p.88.29. Here used of barbarian troops, which do **not** belong to the Roman army.

c Cf. **valida manus** ad 15.4.1 (= III p.55). If this is not a case of rhetoric exaggeration, **validissimus,** said of cunei which contain **600** men, is nevertheless somewhat exaggerated. Bearing in mind the military reality of that time, it seems sensible to me not to imagine the separate groups of invading barbarians too large (as was the case later on with the great migrations of nations); so that from Ammianus' point of view cunei, of a total of 600 men, are indeed **validissimi.**

a **in sexcentis velitibus. In** = to the number of. Cf.31.12.3: procursato-   p. 107. 12
ribus omnem illam multitudinis partem, quam viderant, **in numero** decem milium esse firmantibus; 31.7.16.: constat tamen **in numero longe minore** Romanos, cum copiosa multitudine conluctatos, funerea multa perpessos etc.; Blomgren (op.cit.II) p.107; Hofm.-Leum. p.537.131*b* Zus. β (with lit.). Cf.et.Oros.4.14.5: fuisse tunc exercitum eius **in** centum milibus peditum et viginti milibus equitum definiunt.

b Cf.Veget.r.m.3.16 (= Lang p.101): Quod si equites inpares fuerint, more veterum **velocissimi cum scutis levibus pedites** ad hoc ipsum exercitati isdem miscendi sunt, **quos velites nominabant** (note the imperfectum!); ibid.3.24 (= Lang p.117): Praecipue tamen **velites antiqui** adversum elefantos **ordinaverunt. Velites** autem **erant** iuvenes **levi armatura** et corpore alacri, qui ex equis optime missibilia dirigebant (note the perfectum and imperfectum!); Amm.19.3.1: Sabinianum crebro monebat, ut compositis **velitaribus** cunctis ... properarent, quo **levium armorum** auxilio ... aggrederentur ... (wholly synonymous). Here again used of troops **not** belonging to the Roman army (for **armorum** cf. ad 16.12.7, p.92.3-4*b*).

claruit. Cf. ad 17.1.14, p.107.8.   p. 107. 12

a **Vacua praesidiis loca vastantes.** Alliterating **va!** For the constructions   p. 107. 12-13
of **vacuus** cf. Krebs Antib.2. p.711 (with lit.). **Vacuus** is also a typically legal term for: not in someone's possession, free (cf.Heum.-Seckel p.612). Not in Veget.r.m., though found in Claud.

b Cf.Claud.26.426 sq. (De bello Getico): (Germania)
    Tam sese placidam praestat Stilichonis habenis
    Ut nec **praesidiis nudato limite** tentet
    Expositum calcare solum, nec transeat amnem
    Incustoditam, metuens attingere **ripam.**

Although the above lines are an eulogy to Stilicho, we are nevertheless informed that the border is robbed of its forts and the bank unguarded.

c Cf.Veget.r.m.3.7 (= Lang p.81): Festinanter adveisarii ad transitus fluminum insidias vel superventus facere consueverunt. Ob quam necessitatem **in utraque ripa** conlocantur **armata praesidia**, ne alveo interveniente divisi obprimantur ab hostibus. Bearing this in mind, the two forts **could** lie on both sides of the river Meuse. That the word **praesidium** should not be interpreted too narrowly, is apparent from the following passage (Veget.3.8 = Lang p.85): ... nisi per loca idonea, qua nostrorum ambulat commeatus, **praesidia** disponantur, **sive illae civitates sint sive castella murata** (civitates = towns).

d Besides vastare **vastitare**; cf. ad 16.4.4, p.75.9.

p. 107. 13 **offendit.** c.accus.class. For other meanings and constructions with this verb cf. Krebs Antib.2 p.206; Hofm.-Leum. p.407, 32c.

p. 107. 13-15 **hac oportunitate ... erigente, quod ... sunt arbitrati.** Comparable 31.3.8: **Fama tamen late serpente** per Gothorum reliquas gentes, **quod** invisitatum antehac hominum genus ... ex abdito sinu coortum apposita quaeque **convellit** modo ruinae **corrumpit** and the subordinate clauses beginning with **quod,** which refer back to a previous demonstrativum (Cf. Reiter op. cit. I p.42). For **quod** cf. et. 14.7.5; 14.7.14; 14.10.14; 14.11.11; 14.11.7.

p. 107. 13 **erigente.** For **erigere** cf. ad 16.12.37, p.97.8. Cf.et.ad 16.12.4, p.91.19-20*a*: **subrigere.** For further meanings and constructions cf. Krebs Antib.1. p.511. Like here: to incite (against) also Florus 2.17.15.

p. 107. 13 **hac oportunitate ... erigente ...** For the **personificatieo** cf. ad 14.8.13 β (= II p.80); ad 15.4.3 (= III p.58); ad 15.4.4 (= III p.58); ad 16.5.5, p.76.4-6, *d2;* ad 14.6.23 (= I p.99); ad 15.9.3 (= IV p.50); ad 15.5.14 (= III p.91); ad 15.12.5 (= IV p.77); ad 15.5.26 (= III p.111); ad 16. 12.57. p. 101.2-3*a*.

p. 107. 14 **secessibus.** Cf. ad 16.1.5, p.72.6-7*c*. Cf.Verg.Aen.1.159; 3.229. Generally poet. and post-class. Not in Veget.r.m. and Claud.

p. 107. 14-15 *a* **expleri se posse praedarum opimitate sunt arbitrati.** Note the alliterating **p.** For the construction cf. Sall.Iug.20.1: quos paulo ante muneribus **expleverat;** Cic.Phil.2.20 (50): Ibi te cum et illius largitionibus et tuis rapinis **explevisses** (si hoc est **explere,** quod statim effundas) advolasti egens ad tribunatum ...; Krebs Ant.1 p.554. Occurs in Claud., but not in Veget r.m.

b For the **poet.pluralis** (for praedarum = praedae) cf. ad 16.12.56, p. 100.20; ad 16.12.57, p.101.2; ad 14.8.5 (= II p.66); ad 14.8.14 (= II p.83); ad 14.2.1 (= I p.66 sq.); ad 16.12.2, p.91. 12*a*; ad 16.12.37, p.97.6; ad 15.6.2 (= IV p.7); ad 15.5.29 (= III p.113); ad 14.8.1 (= II p.54); ad 14.9.3 (= II p.89); ad 15.7.4 (= IV p.14); Hagend.St.Amm. p.73 sq.

c **opimitate**. Cf.16.11.9: **opimitate praedarum** onusti; annot. ad h.l. (16.11.9, p.90.2). Plaut.Tertull. Not in Claud. and Veget.r.m. Archaism? Cf. Fesser p.53.

reversi. For this part.cf. Krebs Antib.2 p.516: **revertere** etc. (in fine), with lit.   p. 107. 15

munimentis. Cf. ad 16.12.58, p.101.6-7*d*.   p. 107. 16

exinanita = deserta (a Romanis sc.). But with **this** meaning I know of no other places. The verb is found, among others, several times in Cic. and Plin.N.H. and in the judic.lit. (cf.Heum.-Seckel p.192); as well as in the Christian language, where **se exinanire** means: "se dépouiller de sa personnalité" (cf. Souter p.137; Benoist-Goelzer Dict.[10], with some examples). Not in Claud. Veget r.m.Arnob.adv.nat. As a t.t.mil.Curt. Ruf.4.13.34: Qui cornibus praeerant extendere ea iussi, ita ut nec circumvenirentur, si artius starent, nec tamen ultra modum aciem **exinanirent**. Whether Amm. uses here **also** a military term or whether he deliberately uses an "unusual" term, is hard to determine.   p. 107. 16

quoad. Cf. ad 14.4.5 (= I p.82); ad 16.11.14, p.90.27; Ehrism. p.49 sq. In the meaning: as long as c.indic., as with **donec**. Cf.et.Hofm.-Leum. p.754 (**donec**) and p.768 (**quoad**).   p. 107. 16

tuebantur: conative.   p. 107. 17

II, 2

hac Iulianus rei novitate perculsus. Note the artificial order of words. For the **hyperbaton** cf. ad 17.1.6, p.105.21*a*.   p. 107. 17

b cf.Caes.b.g.7.58.4: et **rei novitate** perterritis oppidanis; Hirt.8 praef.: quae **rerum novitate** aut admiratione nos capiunt; Ovid.Met.2.31 sq.:
    Inde loco medius **rerum novitate** paventem
    Sol oculis iuvenem, quibus aspicit omnia, vidit;
etc.

43

Krebs Antib.2 p.169.

p. 107. 18 *a* **quorsum erumperet.** Cf.20.8.2: summa coeptorum **quorsum evaderet** pertimescens; 21.13.9: summa itaque coeptorum **quorsum evaderet** ambigens; 27.3.1: idque **quorsum evaderet** ... ignorarunt; Tac.Hist.1.14: anxius **quonam** exercituum vis **erumperet;** Cic.Verr.2.74: summa expectatio **quonam** esset eius cupiditas **eruptura;** Amm.21.7.6: incertum **quonam erumpere** cogitantes; ibid.21.13.3: et speculaturos **quonam** rex **erumperet** violentus; Fesser p.25: "Die Verbindung **quorsum (quorsus) erumpere** lässt sich nur bei Cic.Att.2.21.1, Val. Max.7.4.5 und Amm. (17.2.2) belegen". Cf.Cic. ad Att.2.21.1: ut, **quorsus eruptura** sit, horreamus (note the **conj.fut.** in Cic.!); ibid.2.20.5: Haec quo sint **eruptura,** timeo; Michael p.41.

b **Quorsum.** Not in Claud.Veget.r.m. Cf.et. Krebs Antib.2. p.469 sq. (with lit.)

p. 107. 18 *a* **si isdem transisset intactis.** Coniunct.orat.obliq. = indic.fut.exact. orat.rect. Used regularly. For **si** cf. ad 14.1.7 (= I p.62); ad 14.3.2 (= I p.79); ad 14.4.6 (= I p.83).

b **intactis.** Cf.16.12.53: intactis ferro corporibus; Liv.1.25.11: **intactum** ferro corpus; 2.12.14: nunc iure belli liberum te **intactum** inviolatumque hinc dimitto; 10.27.9; hinc victor Martius lupus, integer et **intactus,** gentis nos Martiae et conditoris nostri admonuit; 10.36.3: diversique integri atque **intacti** abissent, ni cedenti instaturum alterum timuissent; 42.66.3: cum sciret nihil roboris secum esse dum liceret **intacto,** abire; Sil.Ital.10.63 sq.: ... integer, oro,

Intactusque abeas, atque intres moenia Romae;
ibid.7.399:

Plena tibi castra atque **intactus** vulnere miles
Creditur...; Liv. Drakenborch IV.1, p.99 (1822).

p. 107. 18 *c* **isdem:** refers back to **Franci,** subject of: tuebantur. For this use cf. III p.103.

p. 107. 18-19 *a* **retento milite circumvallare disposuit... (lac.16 litt.) osa fluvius praeterlambit:** V. circumvallare disposuit castellum oppidum quod Mosa BG. Pighi: disposuit (munimenta quae M)osa: "ipsum **munimentorum** vocabulum desideratur: quod si post **disposuit** addideris clausulam velocis cursus habebis". Rolfe: disposuit (castella munita quae M)osa fluvius. Sabbah: disposuit (quae ad Traiectum M) osa fluvius (cf.annot.16, p.164, II, with lit.) I agree with Sabbah that in all probability the copyist has not understood a geographical name. These mistakes occur more often. **Castella**

munita of Rolfe I consider an unlikely combination. Pighi's conjecture is too "smooth", too beautiful for me. **Castellam oppidum,** a conjecture, will have got into the text ex margine (BG) and is probably an explanation of a name (Traiectum (ad Mosam)?); i.e. **one** of the two words form the explanation. More is not clear to me at this stage.

b **circumvallare** a t.t.mil., also in Caes.b.g.7.11.1 and 7.17.1, where both times **oppidum** (see above) has to be filled in from the context as object. Cic.Liv.Colum. (and metaphor.Terent.) etc. Not in Eutrop.Veget.r.m. Very characteristically used in Claud.8.11. sq.:

Ipsa Palatino **circumvallata** Senatu
Iam trabeam Bellona gerit...

c **praeterlambit.** Cf.25.10.5: (Iuliani) cuius suprema et cineres... deberet... **praeterlambere** Tiberis. Only in Amm.Cf. **praeterlabi:** 15.11.16; 17.13.4; 21.12.8; 22.8.4; 28.2.2 (Blomgren p.93).

d **disposuit.** Cf. ad 16.10.6, p.87.10-11; 16.12.23, p.94,27.

adusque. Cf. ad 14.7.17 (= II p.42); ad 14.8.5 (= II p.64); Krebs Antib.1. p.103; Hofm.-Leum.p.498 (with lit.). Not in Veget.r.m.Claud. But the two parts of the words divided: 18.6.21: **ad** quinquagesimum **usque** lapidem; 18.7.9; 19.2.10; 22.13.2. Cf. et **abusque** Hagend.St.Amm.p.68 sq. p. 107. 20

quartum et quinquagḗsimum dĭem. This sequence of the numerals metri causa: claus.I. p. 107. 20

a **obsidionales tractae sunt morae.** Correct Sabbah: "mais les délais du siège traînèrent en longueur pendant etc.". Literally: the delay, caused by the siege, was stretched out until etc. For **obsidionalis** cf.14.2.13: nec procedebat ullum **obsidionale** commentum; 16.4.3: malis obsidionalibus Front.Gell.Aur.Vict. (Liv.7.37: gramineam coronam **obsidialem** cf. Drakenborch ad 1.IV.1, p.307, who reeds **obsidionalem**; Plin.N.H.22.4: eadem (sc. corona graminea) vocatur **obsidionalis**; Festus also speaks of an **obsidionalis** corona). Not in Claud.Veget.r.m. Arn.Adv.nat. p. 107. 21

b **morae.** Plur.poet.Cf. ad 17.2.1, p.107.14-15*b*.

a **destinatis barbarorum animis incredibili pertinacia reluctantibus.** reluctantis V. reluctantibus E Wm[2] Momms. reluctatis B G Sabbah. **reluctantibus** also: Clark, Rolfe, Seyfarth. It seems to me that all these conjectures are on the wrong track. **Reluctantis** (V) = reluctantibus. Cf.S.Bened.Reg. 30 (Linderb. p.44): hiitales, dum delinquunt, aut ieiuniis nimiis affligantur aut **acris** (= acribus) verberibus coerceantur, ut sanentur; Mulomed. p. 107. 21-22

Chir.390 (= Oder p.119): cataplasmam inpones in **omnibus cruris** ante acopo perunctis...; ibid.959 (= Oder p.286): iam de **omnibus quadrupedis** medicinam demonstrasse sufficit; and for the reverse phenomenon: dat.-abl. ending in -bus in nomina of the **2nd** declinatiom Hofm.-Leum. p.261, 181 *e*; Lucret.2.88: **tergibus** O Q; Vossius **tergo ibus**, and thus Bailey and others).

b **destinatus** = obstinate, determined. Cf.Liv.7.33.13: adeo morte sola vinci **destinaverant animis;** ibid.28.24.3: quia regnum sibi Hispaniae, pulsis inde Karthaginiensibus, **destinarant animis;** Cat.8.19: At tu, Catulle, **destinatus obdura;** adverbium **destinate** (with the same meaning): 18.2.7; 20.4.14; 27.10.5; 28.6.21; 25.5.3; 26.2.3; 23.1.3; 27.3.1 (20.4.14: comparativus, similarly 27.10.5; 28.6.21; 25.5.3; 23.1.3; 27.3.1). Only in Amm.; subst. **destinatio:** 15.10.10: **pertinaci destinatione,** with the same meaning as above, also only in Amm.Cf.et.Dig.50.17.76 (Papinianus): In totum omnia, quae **animi destinatione** agenda sunt, non nisi vera et certa scientia perfici possunt.

c Cf.25.5.3: advertens **destinatius reluctantem.**

II,3

p. 107. 22 **per(ti)miscens,** E B G. c.accus.: 22.1.3; 26.2.4; 26.8.14; 28.1.33; 28.1.47; 31.12.14; connected with **ne** (as here): 31.5.2. For the numerous **inchoativa** cf. Liesenberg (1889) p.5 sq.

sollertissimus. Cf.Amm.30.9.4: Ad inferenda propulsanda ⟨que⟩ bella **sollertissime** cautus (Thus Clark Seyfarth; I am not sure that that is the right version) The superlat. of the adverbium also in Cic.Verr.4.44 (98); Apul. de mag.2.

p. 107. 23 **nocte inluni.** The adj. extremely rare. Sil.Ital.15.619; Plin.ep.6.20.14. Not in Claud.Veget.r.m. (= νὺξ ἀσέληνος). About the moon and its role in Amm.cf.Pighi N.St.Amm. p.114 sq.

p. 107. 23 *a* **gelu vinctum amnem pervaderent.**
more usual would be: gelu, frigore concretum. Cf.Florus 4.12.18: quoties concretus gelu Danuvius iunxerat ripas; Iust.24.8.14: assidui imbres et gelu nix concreta; ibid.31.5.7: ac si quis amnes non ab ipsis fontium primordiis derivare, sed concretis iam aquarum molibus avertere vel exsiccare velit; Curt.Ruf.5.6,14: pedesque per nives et concretam glaciem ingredi coepit; ibid.8.4.6: quamquam imbrem vis frigoris concreto gelu adstrinxerat; (ibid.5.6.13: nivibus, quas frigoris vis gelu

adstrinxerat); etc. "The fettered winter streams" is also a figure of speech in the poetry of many modern languages. Cf.et.Ovid.Trist.3.10.25: Quid loquar, ut **vincti concrescant frigore** rivi...?; ibid.31 sq.: et undas p. 107. 23
frigore concretas ungula pulsat equi.
b **pervaderent** = transgrederentur, transirent, transmitterent, transveherentur (the normal verbs for the **crossing** of a river).Cf.et. Krebs Antib. 2 p.293. Not in Claud. Twice in Veget.r.m. To be compared with tha passage in Amm.Veget.3.6 (= Lang p.78): continuo enim hostes **interpellata** (n.plur.sc. aciei) pervadunt (= transeunt).

a **a sole in vesperam flexo ad usque lucis principium. ad usque.** Cf. ad p. 107. 24
17.2.2., p.107.20.
b **vesperam.** For this acc.femin. cf. Krebs Antib.II p.730 sq. Veget.r.m. 4.27 has: ad **vesperum.** Mulomed.Chir. (Oder 80.19; 296.10) has **vesperum** (= vespere = in the evening) twice; Iust.Phil.18.4.12: prima **vespera** (abl.temp.) besides **vesperi** (3.1.2) and **vespere** (appropinquante 31.2.3). In the same way Mulom.Chir. varies 3 times with **vespere** (abl. temp.) and once with **sub vespere.** But Amm. also varies; cf.26.8.13: et ignorans quod quivis beatus versa rota Fortunae **ante vesperum** potest esse miserrimus; 22.15.2: **a vespera** (= in the West) Issiaco disiungitur mari.
c Cf. Hagendahl St.Amm.p.102 sq., who points out the numerous expressions indicating the beginning of the day "quarum magna pars ampullas poetarum mirum quantum redolet".
d **flexo** = deflexo. Simplex pro composito. Cf. ad 16.5.6, p.76.12.

a **lusoriis navibus discurrere flumen ultro citroque milites ordinavit.** p. 107. 24-25
For **lusoriae naves** cf. ad 17.1.3, p.105.13-14; ad 14.10.6 (= II p.103).
b **discurrere.** Cf. ad 16.2.10, p.73.21; ad 17.1.4, p.105.14-15*d*.
c **ordinavit** = iussit. In this meaning t.t.mil. and mainly late Latin. With this meaning also in Veget.r.m., **not** in Claud. Cf. et Krebs Antib.II (with lit.); Souter p.279; Amm.27.12.7.
d **ultro citroque.** This word-combination, which is also classical, seems to occur quite often in late Latin. Cf. Krebs Antib.I p.285 (with lit.). Once in Veget.r.m.4.42 (= Lang p.161). Not in Claud.

a **crustis pruinarum diffractis.** Cf.15.10.4: per diruptas utrimque an- p. 107. 25-26
gustias et lacunas **pruinarum** congerie latebrosas; 17.12.4: flumen Histrum exundantem **pruinarum** iam resoluta congerie. Cf.Verg.Georg.3.360: Concrescunt subitae currenti in flumine **crustae**; ibid.368 sq.:

Intereunt pecudes, stant circumfusa **pruinis**
Corpora magna boum.
Cf. et Lucret.3.20; Val.Flacc.8.210. In the plural the meaning is mainly that of **winter** or **snow**.
The 2nd. meaning is required here, in my opinion. (Unless **pruinarum** here = glaciei). The (poetical) plural fairly often in Claud., once in Veget. r.m.: 3.2 (= Lang p.68): ne saeva hieme iter per nives ac **pruinas** noctibus faciant.

b **diffractis.** This verb quite rare. Among others Plaut.Vitr.Suet. **Not** in Claud.Veget.r.m.Mulom. Chir.Opt.Milev.Arn.adv.nat. Cf.20.7.13: ... turrim laxatam evertit. Qua sonitu lapsa ingenti, superstantes quoque repentina ruina deiecti, **diffractique** vel obruti, mortibus interiere diversis etc.; ibid.costā diffractā.

p. 107. 26 *a* **nullus ad erumpendi copiam facile perveniret,** This affected turn of phrase is justified by 20.4.14: **ne ad evadendi copiam quisquam perveniret** (where the "incorrect" ut ... nullus ... perveniret is replaced by: ne ... quisquam perveniret and **erumpendi** is varied with **evadendi**), as Fletcher rightly observes with reference to the conjecture by Eyss.: ad erumpendum quopiam. (Am.J. of Phil., op.cit.XVI, p.394).

b For **nullus** cf. ad. 14.7.5 (= II p.22) = **nemo.** Cf. **ullus** = **quisquam** (ad 14.2.2 = I p.68). Cf.et.Hofm.-Leum. p.483 sq. 82*b*; Bened.Reg. Linderb.3.13; 35.2; 38.11; Krebs Antib.II p.172 **(nullus)** with lit.; ibid. p.459 **(quisquam),** with lit.; Riemann (op.cit.I) p.169 sq. **(quisquam).**

c **erumpere.** With **ab:** 18.9.3; 30.4.14; 31.16.5; with **per:** 21.12.13; with **abl.:** 20.11.22; 24.5.8; 27.12.7; 22.8.44; with **adverb.loci:** 15.10.11.

p. 108. 1 **hocque.** Cf. ad 16.12.37, p.97.6*a*.

commentum = ruse, trick, also in an unfavourable sense. Cf.24.2.13: nec procedebat ullum obsidionale **commentum;** Cf. Florus 1.11.2: Apud Regilli lacum dimicatur, diu Marte vario, donec Postumius ipse dictator signum in hostes iaculatus est (novum et insigne **commentum**) uti peteretur cursu; Heum.-Seckel p.80; Iust.21.4.2: nefanda commenta. **Not** in Claud. Veget. r.m. Opt.Milev.Arnob.adv.nat. In **this** meaning not seen very often.

p. 108. 1 **inedia.** Cf. ad 14.7.5 (= II p.20).To the places mentioned there should be added: 14.2.19.

vigiliis. Unless meant in a general sense, (night-watch, lack of sleep),

48

Amm. uses here a t.t.mil. of the **Romans** (as more often) for **Franci** Cf. ad 14.3.2 (= I p.120).

desperatione postrema. Cf.19.2.4: salutis rata (= certa) **desperatione** gloriosos vitae exitus deinde curabamus. d.postrema = d.**ultima** (Tac. hist.2.48) or **extrema** (Tac.hist.2.44). This use of **postremus** by Amm. rare and mainly late Latin. Cf. Krebs Antib. 2p.336 **(postr.)** and p.689 **(ult.),** with lit. In Veget.r.m. we find **postremo** (= finally, 3 times) and **ad postremum** (= postremo). **Postr. not** found in Claud.

lassati = (de)fatigati. Mainly poet. In prose among others Cels. Curt.Ruf. **Sen.rh.Sen.phil.** Plin.nat.Ennod. Not in Veget.r.m. (who uses **lassus**, a non-class.adj., and varies this with **fatigatus**: 3.11 (= Lang p.94) without any difference in meaning), though it is used in Claud. Cf. Krebs Antib.II p.7, with lit.

a **sponte se propria de(di)derunt.** VEAG dederunt. Similarly Sabbah. dediderunt: Btl. Clark Seyf.I have to reject this conjecture. **dederunt**: simplex pro composito. (Cf. ad 16.5.6, p.76.12).
b **sponte propria.** Cf.14.6.2: summatim causas perstringam nusquam a veritate **sponte propria** digressurus; 28.4.16; 30.5.8. The expression is late Latin. Cf.et. Krebs Antib.II p.600 sq., with lit. In late Latin **proprius** often serves as a substitute of the pron.poss. tuus, suus etc. Cf. Benedicti Reg.Linderb.58.41: mox ergo in oratorio exuatur rebus **propriis** quibus vestitus est et induatur rebus monasterii; 60.16 ibid. The expression **sponte propria** not in Claud.Veget.r.m.Arnob.adv.nat. Cf.et. ad 14.5.8 (= I p.88).

ad comitatum Augusti sunt missi. From Iulianus' letter to the Athenians 280 C D it appears that he is sending to Constantius some thousand prospective recruits from the men which he has taken prisoners of war. This can be seen as one method to fill up the gaps in the army with good "material", a method which was frequently applied. For **comitatus** cf. ad 14.5.8 (= I p.129).

II, 4

eximendos periculo. For eximere cf. ad 14.2.20 (= I p.78). The exposition by Fresser p.25 sq. is important for the text criticism.

multitudo. Also used of barbarians in 17.12.10. Here Seyfarth gives the wrong translation, in my view: Gefolgschaft, Sabbah: la foule. In this place (17.2.4) the meaning is not crowd, but troup, group. Probably a t.t.mil., indicating an (irregular) army of barbarians. Cf.Veget.r.m.3.1 (= Lang p.67): Quod si infinita **multitudo** ex **gentibus ferocissimis** rebellasset; ibid.3.19 (= Lang p.105): Cuneus dicitur **multitudo** peditum etc. (the **cunei** consist of barbarians; cf. ad 16.11.5, p.88.29); ibid 4.6 (= Lang p.131): Formidatur ne **multitudo** sagittariorum de propugnaculis exterritis defensoribus adpositisque scalis occupet murum (the **sagittarii** are probably Orientals; cf. ad 16.12.7, p.92.3). **egressa**. Cf. ad 17.1.4, p.105.15. Here used absolutely = egressa ex patria sua = marching from their native country.

p. 108. 3-4 *a* **cum captos conperisset et asportatos.** Claus.III.Hyperbaton. The "omission" here of **eos** and **esse** is striking, probably metri causa. Cf. Hofm.-Leum. p.592.175*b;* Hagendahl (op.cit.II) p.53, with lit. (both dealing with the omission of the **subjects acc.** of the pronomen in the **acc.c.inf.**). Cf.et. ad 17.1.13, p.106.23-24*b*.
b **conperisset.** This verb **not** in Claud. Arn.adv.nat. Once in Opt.Milev. (conpertis rebus c.19; 21.7 Z) and in Veget.r.m. (conpertum est 4.40; 159.5 L.).

p. 108. 4 **repedavit.** Cf.17.2.4; 19.6.9; 24.4.30; 25.1.3; 29.5.37. Old Latin and late Latin = recedere, redire. Cf. Krebs Antib.II p.501, with lit. **Not** in Claud. Veget.r.m.Opt.Milev.Arn.adv.nat. Fairly rare verb. Cf.et. Fesser p.41.

p. 108. 4 **ad sua.** Cf.17.1.2, p.104.7-9*d*.

p. 108. 5 **acturus hiemen** = peracturus hiemen. Simplex pro composito. Cf. ad 16.5.6, p.76.12.
revertit. For the active form cf. Krebs Antib.II p.516 (with lit.). In Claud. and Veget.r.m. only **revertor**.

p. 108. 5 **Parisios.** Cf. ad 15.11.3 (= IV p.60).

III, 1

p. 108. 6-7 *a* **conlaturae capita sperabantur.** For **sperari** cf. ad 14.7.5 (= II p.20); ad 15.5.9 (= III p.84). Note also the alliteration.
b **capita conferre** here means: to gather one's forces, to unite, Cf.Cic. Verr.3.12 (31): **conferrent** viri boni **capita** (= to deliberate, at a secret

consultation); Liv.2.45.7: consules velut deliberabundi **capita conferunt,** diu conlocuntur. Because it is unlikely that Amm.: 1⁰ does **not** know these places; 2⁰ did **not** know their exact meaning; one has to assume that he deliberately gives this reminiscence his own nuance (not derived from others, therefore).

a   **dubia bellorum coniectans.** Cf. ad 14.2.6 (= I p.69).   p. 108. 7
b   **coniectans.** Cf.21.1.3; 27.3.1 (= to surmise, to conclude); 17.3.1; 23.5.23 (= to consider, to ponder). Not in Claud.Veget.r.m.Arnob.adv. nat.

a   **sobrius rector** = dux = ductor (cf.14.2.17 = I p.76). Cf.et.14.10.8:   p. 108. 7
rector prov. (= II p.106); 16.12.22, p.94.25-26*b* (iumenti r.). With this meaning found in Claud., not in Veget.r.m., who does not have the word at all.
b   **sobrius.** Here with the meaning also found in class. Latin: sensible, levelheaded. Cf.Veget.r.m.2.9 (= Lang p.44): Ipse (sc. praefectus legionis) autem iustus diligens **sobrius** legionem sibi creditam adsiduis operibus ad omnem devotionem (= obedience, loyalty) ad omnem formabat industriam; ibid.2.14 (= Lang p.47): centurio ... vigilans **sobrius** agilis; ibid. 3.9 (= Lang 89): dux itaque vigilans **sobrius** prudens. **Eutropius** (praepositus cubiculi of Arcadius) does not have this quality. Cf.Claud.18.229:
   Iamque oblita sui, **nec sobria** divitiis mens,
   In miseras leges, hominumque negotia ludit.

a   **magnis curarum molibus stringebatur. Stringere** used as in Ovid.Fasti   p. 108. 7-8
324:
   Stringebant magnos vincula parva pedes (= pressed);
Claud.14.19 sq. (Fesc.):
   Tam iunctis manibus nectite vincula
   Quam frondens hedera **stringitur** aesculus;
but then in a metaphorical sense.
b   Cf.Tac.Ann.12.66: In tanta **mole curarum** valetudine adversa corripitur.

dumque. Cf. ad 16.12.37, p.97.6*a*.   p. 108. 8

industias. Here also it is not exactly an **armistice.** For **no** armistice is agreed   p. 108. 8
upon with the **Franci.** Better: A cease-fire, a kind of truce. Cf. ad 16.12.19, p.94.8 *b*.

51

p. 108.8 *a* **licet negotiosas et breves.** For the constructions of **licet** cf. ad 14.1.5 (= I p.59).
b **negotiosas.** Refers here to all those activities which Julianus has to and wants to take part in and which do **not** have anything to do with the war. Only here in Amm. Not in Claud.Veget.r.m.Arn.adv.nat.Opt. Milev.

p. 108.9 **aerumnosis.** Cf.27.1.1: Alamanni post **aerumnosas** iacturas et vulnera. Not in Claud.Veget.r.m.Arn.adv.nat.Opt.Milev. Cf.ad 15.4.10 (**aerumnae**: III p.62); ad 16.12.51, p.99.22.

p. 108.9 *a* **possessorum.** Also class. = landowner. Cf. Willems (op.cit.I) p.585 (l'administration communale): "En dessous de l'ordre des **decuriones** ou **curiales** (the ruling class of the city, the "haute bourgeoisie"), il y a encore, au début de cette époque, l'ordre des **Augustales**; mais cet ordre disparaît à la suite de la reconnaissance légale du Christianisme. Il n'y a plus dès lors, en dessous des décurions, que **l'ordo plebeius**, se composant **des propriétaires (possessores) qui ne sont pas décurions,** des **negotiatores,** des **collegiati, corporati** et **artifices** de la ville, et des agriculteurs libres et des **coloni** de la campagne".
Apart from the **capitatio terrena** (= **iugatio**), including the **annona**, the **possessores** also, on the basis of possessions returned to the revenue service, and in accordance with a **formula censualis,** (cf. Willems p.468), have to pay special direct taxes on houses, slaves and cattle **(capitatio animalium)** (cf. Willems p.600). From a fiscal point of view we have here **possessores** versus the **negotiatores** (in the widest meaning of the word). The latter form a guild (corpus) and pay the so-called **lustralis collatio** (= **chrysargyrum** or **auraria functio),** which is collected every five years on the basis of a special matricula (cf. Willems p.600). The **plebei** pay the **capitatio plebeia** (= **humana).** Later however the **plebs urbana** was exempted from this, though not the **plebs rusticana extra muros (coloni),** at least the majority of these. (Cf. Karlowa, op.cit.I p.910 sq.). It is already obvious from the above rough survey that the **possessores** were extremely heavily taxed. The collecting of the taxes was done ruthlessly. (Cf. Mazzarino, op.cit.IV, cap.III, IV). Tax exemption was practically impossible (Cod.Theod.11.1.1). Pharr: "It may be said that the elaborate system of oppressive taxation was one of the most important, perhaps the most important of the factors that resulted in the complete collapse of the later Roman Empire in the West and in the fall of Rome".

p. 108.9 *a* I cannot entirely agree with this conclusion. The taxation policy was the **result** of a deteriorating economical, military and political situation. Undoubtedly the **application** of the fiscal measures has had a very bad effect, the more so for want of any checking on the part of the subiecti. Furthermore there was also considerable corruption in the tax services. In the provinces already harassed by invasions by barbarians one may well speak of a terrorism by the tax-collector. Cf.et. **(curator rei publicae)** 14.7.17 (= II p.42); 16.5.14, p.77.17-19c **(capitulum)**; Madvig, Verf.u. Verw.d.Röm.St.II p.437 sq.

b For **possessor** in the judicial lit.cf.Heum.-Seckel p.441 sq. Cf.et.: Madvig op.cit.II p.370; Stein (op.cit.I) p.70 sq. (with lit.); ibid p.174 sq.; A.M.II Sabbah note 19 (with lit.).

a **tributi ratiocinia dispensavit. Tributum** here used as in 16.5.14: quod primitus partes eas ingressus pro capitulis singulis **tributi nomine** vicenos quinos aureos repperit flagitari. It is the **general** term for **land-tax: tributum (agri),** later mostly called **iugatio** or **capitatio,** after the units on which the tax duty lay (iugum = caput) (cf.ad. 16.5.14, p.77.17-19*a*).   p. 108. 9-10

b **dispensare.** In the judic.lit. **dispensare** has 2 meanings: 1. to distribute, 2. to govern; to keep the books **(rationes dispensare** e.g. Dig.50.16.166: potest enim aliquis **dispensator** non esse servorum urbanorum numero: veluti is, qui rusticarum rerum **rationes dispenset** ibique habitet), to keep the financial records, In my view the 3 words together mean: he checked the assessments for the land-tax, he took upon himself the financial inspection of the land-tax (Differently and incorrectly: Seyf. Sabbah).

c In judic.lit. **ratiocinium** means: 1. financial administration, bookkeeping. 2. account (= ratio). The first meaning is required here.

III, 2
cumque. Cf. ad 16.12.37, p.97.6 *a*.   p. 108. 10

a **Florentius praefectus praetorio.** For **praefectus praet.** cf. ad. 14.7.9 (= II p.30). For **Florentius** cf. ad. 16.12.14, p.93.6*a*. In order to understand the contents of the following paragraphs, the following exposition is necessary (§ 2 to § 5). Every praef.praet. has control over separate funds **(arca praefecturae praetorianae),** supplied by the **annona** (cf. ad 16.5.14, p.77.17-19 *c*) and intended for the maintenance and paying of wages of the army and all the functionaries and **officiales** (subaltern civil servants) of the court and the state. But the ever-increasing expenses of the government made it necessary to support the **arcae pr.pr.** by depositing part of   p. 108. 10

the **capitatio terrena,** both of the **portoria** (cf. ad 14.7.9 = II p.29) and of the **caduca** (cf. ad 15.5.4 = III p.74, 4⁰). When the **annona,** delivered in natura, was insufficient, one requisitioned at market value **(publica comparatio)** or deducted the (previously) delivered quantity from the **next** payment. It is clear that these **arcae** took care of a considerable part of the public expenses. (The **cura viarum** and the **alimentatio** no longer exist at this time. The costs of the **cursus publicus** (national postservice) are borne mainly by the provincials). About the collection of taxes cf.16.5.14, p.77.17-19c and d. For taxes etc.cf.et.: 15.5.4 = III p.73 (comes rerum privatarum); 14.7.9 = II p.29 (comes sacrarum largitionum); 15.5.36 = III p.127 (Gallicani thesauri); 14.7.9 = II p.30 (praefectus praetorio); 15.3.4 = III p.35 (rationalis); 15.5.36 = III p.124 (rationarius); Willems p.604 (with lit.); Madvig II p.418; A.M. II Sabbah, note 19 and 21, p.164 sq. (with lit.). The **indictiones** are prescribed by the emperor (cf. ad 16.5.14, p.77, 17-19b). The duration of an indictio is at this time 15 years. The praef.praet. has no authority at all to change the **canon,** either upwards or downwards. **The emperor has to give permission for this.** From Cod. Theod.12.12.2, addressed to **Musonianus** (cf. ad 15.3.1 = IV p.78), praef. praet., can be seen that in this year (357) we have the 15th indictio. Cf. Seeck Regesten p.203. The preceding indictio therefore was in the year 342. "Florentius, en vertu des attributions financières dévolues au préfet, a sans doute **maintenu le taux de l'indiction precedente, celle de 342** (on which this reasoning is founded is not clear to me, though of course, it is possible); cette dernière correspondait à la période de prospérité que connut la Gaule sous **Constant** (337-350). Les contribuables, ruinés par les exigences de **Magnence** (cf.I p.40-42; during the years 350-353) et surtout par les invasions barbares, ne pouvant acquitter le montant prévu pour la capitation, Florentius veut combler ce déficit par une superindiction, désignée par les termes **conquisita, provisiones, indictionale augmentum, incrementum:** il s'agit d'un impôt complémentaire des **solemnia,** payable sans doute en nature (why **not** also: **adaerata?**) et destiné à assurer la couverture des besoins militaires **(commeatuum necessarios apparatus)** ... F. doit demander la signature de Julien César (as the emperor's deputy). Ce dernier la refuse, par équité et, semble-t-il, pour ne pas endosser certaines malhonnêtetés de Florentius. L'acte prend aussi une signification politique et marque une nouvelle émancipation de Iulien qui s'est libéré en 357 de ses "tuteurs militaires ..." (Sabbah).
b   The conflict with F. is also described in Ep.Iul.14(17) Bidez p.20 sq. (viz.384 d-385) and in Lib.orat.18.84 sq. (edit. Foerster 2. p.272). It is remarkable that in this letter F. is **not** mentioned by name. Bidez suspects

that this is done by way of precaution, i.e. that those who published the first collection of letters bu Iulianus, have changed the text. The entire letter, addressed to **Oribasius**, is exceedingly frank. It also clearly shows that he is conscious of the dangers of this conflict to himself. And indeed it is very audacious of the prince! (Cf.et. Wright, op.cit.I, III p.10, note 2). But in the Ep.ad Ath.282 C, F. is expressly mentioned by name (written in **361**, after his breach with **Constantius**). Cf.et.Geffcken Jul. (op.cit.I) p.42 sq.; p.135 (adnot.).

a **cuncta permensus.** For **cuncta** cf. ad 14.2.1 (= I p.66); 16.12.38 (p.97. 17-21); ad 15.5.9 (= III p.85). p. 108. 10

b **permetior.** In the literal meaning: to measure (out), also Cic.Acad. 2.51 (126): vos ergo huius (sc. solis) magnitudinem, quasi decempeda **permensi** refertis. But here the verb means: **to calculate**. Not in Veget.r.m. Twice in Claud, but only in the meaning: **to lay down.** To this metaphorical meaning: to calculate, Oros.adv.pag.6.10.19, comes very close: (Caesar) **permetiens** rem suis maximi periculi fore, si per ... silvas... dividerentur (= to consider).

a **ut contendebat.** Thus in the parenthesis also used in Cels.Med.1.praef. p.3, 28 D. Cf. Georges I, 1598; Krebs Antib.1. p.351 (= as he emphatically said, stated). p. 108. 11

b In late Latin the comparative meaning of **ut** is replaced by **quomodo**. But in set phrases **ut** was kept up for a long time (ut supra scriptum est, ut datur intelligi, ut puta, etc.) Cf. Grevander Pallad. p.509 sq. (with examples and lit.); III p.71 **(ut quasi).**

a **quicquid in capitatione deesset.** Because **quisquis** etc. occurred so often in the general language, A.M. forgot that the pronomen really refers back to the plural **cuncta**. This carelessness is very typical of the spoken language. p. 108. 11

b The **conjunct.iterat.** in later and late Latin quite normal with **quisquis**. Cf.Hofm.-Leum. p.709 (with lit.); Ehrismann (op.cit.I) p.57; ad 14.1.5 (= I p.60); ad 14.4.1 (= I p.82); ad 16.12.21, p.94.18-19*a;* ad 14.4.6 (= Ip.83).

c **capitatio**. Cf. ad 16.5.14, p.77.17-19 *a*.

ex conquisitis. Conquirere is a t.t.mil. for the recruiting, pressing of soldiers (1) and for the requisitioning of victuals, etc. (2). The meaning (2) is required here. Cf.Caes.b.g.8.10.3. Here **conquirere** can have the p. 108. 11

meaning: to make additional assessments, to claim the shortage (cf. § 4 and ad p.108.10*a* **Flor.** etc.). Whether strictly speaking there is a shortage, can **not** be disputed with the words in § 4. It seems very likely. A.M. is not interested in placing the loyal pr.pr. Florentius in a better light than he probably was in Iulianus' eyes. His mistake was that he wanted to draw blood from a stone and that his standpoint was a purely fiscal one. Apparently the **capitatio** yielded more than enough "ad commeatuum necessarios apparatus". But that does not mean to say that there was also sufficient for **other** necessary expenses, which had to be paid for from this. I believe that A.M. wrongly wants to put the blame on Flor. for a **super-indictio** (cf. ad 16.5.14, p.77.17-19*b*), while the latter has perhaps accused Iulianus of the proclamation of a **relevatio** or of an **indulgentia reliquorum** (cf. ad 16.5.14*b* and *d*). Furthermore one should bear in mind that the pr.pr. has the **highest** responsibility for the collection of taxes. The older, more formal and stiff pr.pr. feels threatened in his position by the young, emotional and determined Caesar. Hence the **relatio** to the emperor. The latter is afraid to intervene and wants to run with the hare and hunt with the hounds. By doing this he makes a political blunder of the first order, because he now (perhaps) still had the opportunity to put Iulianus in his place. The result is that Fl. feels abandoned and at Iulianus' request entrusts him **(inusitato exemplo)** with the government over Belgica II. Indeed a highly irregular affair, which must have set Constantius thinking.

p. 108. 11 **supplere.** This verb fits in with the exposé at the beginning of the previous note.

p. 108. 12 *a* **talium gnarus.** Cf. ad 14.7.21 (= II p.50); ad 14.1.1 (= I p.55); ad 14.2.6 (= I p.69).
b Cf.28.1.7: eliciendi animulas noxias et praesagia sollicitare larvarum perquam **gnarum.** (One has to pay attention to the constructions of the sentence) **Gnarus** not in Claud. Opt.Milev.Arn.adv.nat.; once in Veget. r.m. (locorum gnaris). Cf.et. ad 16.2.10, p.73.21 **(gnaritas).**

p. 108. 12-13 *a* **animam prius amittere quam hoc sinere fieri memorabat** = (se) prius (velle) amittere vitam quam hoc fieri (se) sinere. (For the "omission" of **se** cf. ad 17.2.4, p.108.3-4*a*).
For **animam amittere** cf.Sall.Cat.58.21: Quod si virtuti vostrae fortuna inviderit, cavete inulti **animam amittatis. Amittere** has here a conative (= voluntative) meaning. (Cf. ad 14.10.2 = II p.99: amendabat and ad 14.11.19 = II p.130: qua praestitutum erat etc.; ad 14.5.7 = I p.87). The

expression is found again in A.M.20.11.3: qui crebro adiurans **animam prius posse amittere** quam sententiam etc. (it should be noted that the use of **posse here** is a good illustration of the remark on **amittere** in 17.3.2)

b **memorabat.** Cf. ad 14.6.8 (= I p.93).

III, 3

norat. For this contracted form cf. Hagendahl (op.cit.II) p.186, 192; ad 16.12.69, p.102.23-24*c.;* Hofm.-Leum.244.1, p.335 sq. **Here** this form is not used metri causa.

a **huiusmodi provisionum, immo eversionum.** For the **play upon words,** frequently found in A.M., cf. ad 15.4.2 (= III p.56). This play with words is of interest not only from a stylistic point of view and important for the interpretation, but sometimes also for the text criticism: cf.19.12.9, p. 181.9 and Blomgren (op.cit.II) p.130.

b **provisio** here means: concrete measures to ensure the victualling. Sabbah, in his excellent annotation (A.M.II 21 p.165 sq.) quotes for **this** meaning S.H.A., Tyr.Trig.18.4: in **provisione annonaria** singularis (said of **Ballista**) (and in a more general sense ibid.18.7: nec est ulla alia **provisio** melior quam ut in locis suis erogentur quae nascuntur) and C.I.L. VI 1741 (= I.L.S.1243) of the susceptores Ostienses et Portuenses for the **praefectus urbi** (cf. ad 14.6.1 = I p.131) **Memmius Vitrasius Orfitus** (pr.u. roughly from 353-359 A.D.): ob eius temporibus difficillimis egregias ac salutares **provisiones.**

In the Cod.Theod.6.4.21.6 and 14.1.1 **provisio** means: rule, decision. In the meaning: measures Veget.r.m.2.3 (= Lang p.37): si **provisione** maiestatis tuae, imperator Auguste, et fortissima dispositio reparetur armorum et emendetur dissimulatio praecedentum; almost "providence": ibid.2.18 (= Lang p.52): sed huius felicitatis ac **provisionis** est perennitas tua, ut pro salute rei publicae et nova excogitet et antiqua restituat. Not in Claud.Opt.Milev.Arn.adv.nat.

eversio. On the basis of Florus 3.13.5: Reduci plebs in agros unde poterat sine **possidentium eversione?** Qui ipsi pars populi erant et tamen relictas sibi a maioribus sedes aetate (= longo tempore), quasi iure hereditario, **possidebant;** Sabbah concludes that **eversio** here = expulsio, eiectio and that "pour Amm. **provisio**, vocable noble et officiel, égale **eversio**, c'est à dire dépossession violente et illégale". I do not believe this is true. In my view **eversio** has here the same meaning as in Florus 1.12.7 and 2.16.1 = destruction, wrecking; as is found with other authors. In the judic.lit.

57

the meaning suggested by Sabbah does **not** occur either. Nor is it known to me from other sources. For a late Latin meaning of **eversio** cf. Souter p.130. Not in Claud., Veget.r.m.Arn.adv.nat.

immo. For the use of **immo** cf. Krebs Antib.1.p.688 (with lit.); Hofm.-Leum.242 p.669.

p. 108. 14 **ut verius dixerim.** Cf.28.1.57: is urbanarum rerum status (**ut ita dixerim**) fuit; 20.8.9 = 22.11.3: **ut ita dixerim.** Cf.et.20.11.30: ut diximus; 20.6.8: ut dixi; 14.8.7: ut dictum est. The writings of A.M. are full of this kind of platitudes, which form part of the verbosity of the sermo cotidianus. For the **conjunct.perf. potentialis** cf. ad 14.8.8 (= II p.69).

p. 108. 14 **insanabilia.** Cf.28.4.5: tanta plerosque labes **insanabilium** flagitiorum oppressit. Cf.et.Curt.Ruf.9.5.26: An times ne reus sis, cum **insanabile vulnus** acceperim?; 9.8.20: barbari veneno tinxerant gladios... nec causa tam strenuae mortis excogitari poterat a medicis, cum etiam leves **plagae insanabiles** essent; 10.2.21: Verum ego, tam furiosae consternationis oblitus, remedia **insanabilibus** conor adhibere (subst.). As Colum. 7.5. also connects **insanabilis** with **vulnus,** it seems almost certain that we have here a literary reminiscence. Perhaps Ammianus also had in mind Cic.Tusc.5.1.(3). The adj. not in Claud.Veget.r.m.Opt.Milev.Arn.adv. nat., nor in judic.lit.

p. 108. 14 **ad ultimam egestatem.** Cf. ad 14.2.6 (= I p.69): ex necessitate ultima. For the **variatio** cf.Hagend.St.A. (op.cit.I) p.100 sq.; Kroll, Stud.etc. (op.cit. I) p.362 sq.; Blomgren (op.cit.II) passim. **Egestas,** does not occur in Veget.r.m.Opt.Mil.Arn.adv.nat., but several times in Claud., with the heavily-laden meaning which this subst. has. Cf.Claud.3 (In Ruf.) 35 sq.:
   Et Luxus populator opum, quem semper adhaerens
   Infelix humuli gresso comitatur **Egestas;** ibid. 39 (Epist.1) 23 sq.:
   Gratia diffluxit; sequitur **feralis egestas;**
   Desolata domus; caris spoliamur amicis.

p. 108. 15 *a* **contrusisse.** Cf. ad 17.3.3., p.108.13 (norat); ad 16.12.19, p.94.11-12. In clausula (III). Cf.et. ad 15.8.1 (= IV p.26).
   b = to push in, to throw in. Cf.Cic.Verr.27 (69): quod eodem (sc.in lautumias) ceteros piratas **contrudi** imperarat; ibid.Cael.26 (63): ut in balneas **contruderentur** (= paterentur, sinerent se contrudi.). Cf.v.Wageningen comment.ad.h.l.p.100; Varro r.r.1.54.2: (uva) unde in ollulas addatur et in dolia plena vinaciorum **contrudatur;** Lucr.4.422 sq.:

stantis equi corpus transversum ferre videtur/vis et in adversum flumen
contrudere raptim; ibid.6.211 sq.:
> hasce (sc.nubes) cum ventus agens **contrusit** in unum
> compressitque locum cogens.

Not in Claud.Veget.r.m.Opt.Milev.Arn.adv.nat. Literary reminiscence?
Archaism? Cf.et. ad 15.8.1 (= IV p.26).

ut docebitur postea. Cf. ad 17.3.3, p.108.14. **docebitur** = dicetur, narrabi-   p. 108. 15
tur; cf.Veget.r.m.1.17 (= Lang p.20): ut Diocletianus et Maximianus,
cum ad imperium pervenissent ... hos ... cunctis legionibus praetulisse
doceantur.

a **penitus evertit Illyricum.** Here an adverbium. As **adj.** (only superl.   p. 108. 15-16
penitissimus): 22.8.31; 23.6.73; 29.1.24. As **adj.** also in Plaut. Varro Apul.
Gell.Jul.Val. Cf. Fesser p.58; Hofm.-Leum. p.468,76*e*.
b **evertit.** cf. ad 17.3.3, p.108.13 **(eversio)**.
c **Illyricum.** Cf. ad 16.10.20, p.88,6-7*a*.

III, 4
ob quae. Cf.15.11.4: ea **propter** quod; 18.2.15: ea **propter** ut; 23.6.87:   p. 108. 16
propter piscantium insidias; 22.8.8: qua **propter**.
Ob with **pronomina**: 14.5.5; 14.7.10; 15.3.5; 15.4.9; 15.10.5; 16.5.14;
17.3.4; 19.6.13; 28.6.16 etc.; with **subst.+participium**: 28.1.47; 29.4.7;
30.4.5; 28.1.44; 27.7.6; 28.1.19; 14.11.31 (in the last 2 examples **subst. +
gerundivum**).
Propter is used very little by A.M. In the use of **ob** A.M. conforms to
Tac. I think it is going too far to conclude from this, as Fesser wants,
an imitation of Tacitus. The matter is much more complex. The books
that A.M. read must have had some influence, in my view, but I would
certainly hesitate to point out one author in particular. Cf. Wölfflin Arch.
L.L.G. (op.cit.I) 1 p.161-169 (with lit.); Krebs Antib.2. p.182; Liesenberg
(1890) p.10; Fesser p.60 (insufficient); Hofm.-Leum.100 p.505 sq.; p.599
(with lit.); Svennung Pallad. (op.cit.II) p.36, p.372 sq.

praefecto praetorio. Cf. ad 14.7.9 (= II p.30).   p. 108. 16

a **ferri non posse clamante, se repente factum (esse) infidum.** For the   p. 108. 16-17
construction of **ferre** (= to tolerate) cf.Cic. de or.84 (344): **Ferunt** enim
aures hominum, cum **illa**, quae iucunda et grata, tum etiam illa, quae
mirabilia sunt in virtute, **laudari**; Horat.Epod.15.12 sq.:

59

Nam siquid in Flacco viri est,
non feret adsiduas potiori **te dare noctes**
et quaeret iratus parem...;
Ovid.Met.12.554 sq.: Bis sex Herculeis ceciderunt, me minus uno,
Viribus, atque **alios vinci potuisse ferendum est.** Cf.et.Hofm.-Leum.170, p.585; Thes.s.v.

b **infidum.** The explanation is given by the following words: cui - rerum, viz. untrustworthy in the eyes of the emperor.

p. 108. 17 *a* **cui Augustus summam commiserit rerum. Summa rerum.** It is doubtful whether these 2 words mean, as one would expect: the highest command, the highest government (viz. in his praefectura). When one bears in mind that under Diocletianus and Constantinus I the **aerarium sacrum** is ruled by a vir perfectissimus rationalis **summae rei** (= summae rei rationum = summarum rationum), who is later called v. inlustris comes sacrarum largitionum, that the most important **advocatus fisci** is called: advocatus (= patronus) fisci **summae rei,** that in the civil trials, in which the **aerarium privatum** or the **aerarium sacrum** is involved, **rationales summarum** or rationales rerum privatarum act as judges, then I believe that in spite of Dig.50.1.14 (... quibus **summa rei publicae** commissa est) and Cod. Iust.10.32.40: de decurionibus (quibus propter loci dignitatem **rerum summa** commissa est), **here** the highest responsibility for the finances of the praefectura is meant, particularly the highest supervision on the collection of taxes, i.e. that **summa rerum** does not have here a general, but rather a technical meaning.

b **Augustus.** Here not used accidentally, as opposed to Iulianus the **Caesar.** The official title, though, is rather **dominus.** (cf.Aur.Vict. de Caes. 39.4: Namque se primus omnium post Caligulam Domitianumque **dominum** palam dici passus et adorari se, appellarique uti deum). Cf.et.Lact. de mort.pers.18: respondit debere ipsius (sc. Diocletiani) dispositionem (cf.ad 16.12.12, p.92.24) in perpetuum conservari, ut duo sint in republica maiores, qui **summam rerum** teneant (sc. de Augusti), item duo minores, **qui sint adiumento** (sc. de Caesares). Cf.et. ad 16.10.9, p.85,23; ad 16.12.64, p.102,6-7.

c **commiserit.** Conjunct. perfecti of the oratio obliqua **per repraesentationem.** Cf. ad 14.7.9 (= II p.31).

p. 108. 18 *a* **eum sedatius leniens.** Cf.25.1.5: Postridie exercitu **sedatius** procedente. The positivus of the adverbium: Cic.Tusc.2.24 (58): Ad ferendum igitur dolorem placide atque **sedate** plurimum proficit; ibid.Orat.27(92): cuius oratio cum **sedate** placideque loquitur, tum illustrant eam etc.; Plaut. Men.5.6.15 sq.: propterea eri imperium exsequor, bene et **sedate** servo id; atque id mihi prodest. Not only the adverb is rare (neither in Claud.Veget. r.m.Arn.adv.nat.Opt.Milev.), but its comparativus is not known to me from other places. A Cic. reminiscence is very likely here.

b **leniens:** conative.

a **scrupulose conputando et vere. Scrupulose** very rare adv.Quint.Colum. August. Not in Claud.Veget.r.m.Opt.Milev.Arn.adv.nat. For the **adject.** cf. ad 16.12.10, p.92,18*b*.   p. 108. 18

b **computare** is the verb (also class.) for: to settle accounts, to calculate, to compute, to deduct etc. cf.Claud.52 (de sene Veronensi):
  Frugibus alternis, non consule, **computat** annum;
Veget.r.m.2.19: sed in quibusdam (sc.tironibus) notarum peritia, calculandi **computandique** usus eligitur. In the meaning: to take... for, to consider as, late Latin, among others in Arnob, Lact.Opt.Milev.

a **docuit - apparatus.** Cf. ad 17.3.2, p.108.11 (ex conquisitis); ad 17.3.2, p.108.10*a* (Florentius etc.). **Docuit** (eum): taught him.   p. 108. 18-20

b **exuberare.** Cf.15.4.2; 18.4.4; 22.15.14; 23.6.50; 23.6.65. Everywhere with the Ablat.copiae.

c **capitationis calculum:** illogical and short for: capit. **summae** calc.: the calculation of the **sum total** of the capit. For this **total** shows a surplus: ad comm.nec.app. Unless calculus = summa here, which is possible. The word does not occur in Claud.Veget.r.m. Arnob.adv.nat.Opt.Milev. (in Veget. we do find **calculare:** see previous note). For a special judic. meaning cf.Heum.-Seckel p.52.

d **commeatuum apparatus.** Commeatus: the plural also in 14.2.13. Similarly in Veget. twice accus.plur. and once abl.plur. For **apparatus** cf.14.5.1; ad 16.5.9 (p.76,23-25*a*). In both places singularis. Although the plural of **both** substantiva can be explained, the singular of **both** would not make for any great change in meaning, in my view. However, the style decides the usage (and the metrum? claus.III $\_\cup : \_ \cup \_ \cup$).

Apparatus has here an active meaning: acquisition, procuring. Cf.et. **alimenta** ad 16.3.3, p.74.19 and ad 16.11.12, p.90.12. For the **plur. poeticus** cf. ad 107.14-15*b*.

III, 5

a **nihilo minus tamen.** These words belong with **oblatum:** nevertheless he was offered an augmentum indictionale, but he could not bring him-   p. 108. 20

self to etc. ... and threw it down on the ground (or: so that he threw it down on the ground). The main point is contained in the participia, particularly in the first one. For this use cf.ad.15.2.8 (= III p.23); ad 15.7.5 (= IV p.14); ad 16.12.27, p.95, 18*a;* ad 16.12.37, p.97.15-17*a*.
b The combination of the 3 words is abundant.
Nihilo minus alone is sufficient, or **tamen** alone. Cf. Hagendahl abund. (op.cit.I) p.213 sq. (with lit.). One should, however, remember, that in late Latin the meaning of **nihilo minus** has faded (= aeque, pariter; = tamen; cf.Svennung Pallad.p.404 sq). A fine example of this in Linderb. S.Bened.Reg.p.38.19 and Dig.18.1.40.6: Rota quoque, per quam aqua traheretur, **nihilo minus** aedificii est quam situla.

p. 108. 20 **diu postea** = multo post, late Latin. Cf.21.12.3: hisque dispositis, ipse haud **diu postea** cognita morte Constanti... introiit. Cf. Krebs Antib.1 p.464.

p. 108. 20-21 *a* **indictionale augmentum.** Cf. ad 17.3.2, p.108.10*a* (Flor.etc.). The adject. seems to occur only in Amm. and then in this place.
b **augmentum:** post-class. and late Latin.Plin.H.N.Apul.Pallad.Firm. Fulg.August.Judic.lit. (As t.t.sacr.Varro L.L.5.112 = p.35 Goetz-Schoell and Arnob.adv.nat.7.25 = Reiffersch.p.259; and as t.t.rei coq. in Apic.). Not in Claud.Veget.r.m.Opt.Milev. The word also occurs in the **Laudes Herculis,** formerly wrongly acsribed to Claud.(101), viz. in verse 27. This "ordinary"-looking subst. is far from usual. Perhaps taken from the judic. language by A.M.?

p. 108. 21 **oblatum.** An official term. Cf.Cod.Iust.7.62.19 (de appellationibus): Quod si victus **oblatam** nec **receptam** ab iudice appellationem adfirmet, praefectos adeat, ut apud eos de integro litiget tamquam appellatione suscepta (a⁰ 331). Thus more often.
recitare. The following law in the Cod.Iust.1.14.8 is enlightening: Impp. Theodosius et Valentinianus AA ad senatum. Humanum esse probamus, si quid de cetero in publica vel in privata causa emerserit necessarium, quod formam generalem et antiquis legibus non insertam exposcat, id ab omnibus antea **tam proceribus nostri palatii** quam gloriosissimo coetu vestro, patres conscripti, tractari et, si universis tam iudicibus quam vobis placuerit, **tunc ⟨al⟩legata dictari et sic ea denuo collectis omnibus recenseri, et cum omnes consenserint, tunc demum in sacro nostri numinis consistorio recitari**, ut universorum consensus nostrae serenitatis auctoritate firmetur... (a⁰ 446). For **iudex** cf. ad 15.5.18 (= III p.101); ad 16.8.13, p.83.8.

For **consistorium** ad 14.7.11 (= II p.34). We are not told who reads out the proposal of the pr.pr. regarding a taxraise. Perhaps the **primicerius notariorum** (cf. ad 14.5.6 = I p.128; Willems p.555), perhaps a high civil servant, appointed by the **quaestor sacri palatii** (cf. ad.14.7.12 = II p.38), perhaps even the latter himself. The action will have taken place in the **consistorium** of the Caesar.

subnotare: to (under) sign. Cf.Cod.Iust.10.2.2. Post-class.verb, official   p. 108. 21
term. Cf. et **subnotatio:** Cod.Theod.8.5.22; Cod.Iust.1.23.6: Sacri adfatus (= imperial rulings, -rescripta), quoscumque nostrae mansuetudinis in quacumque parte paginarum scripserit auctoritas, non alio vultu penitus aut colore (= omnino non), **nisi purpurea tantum modo scriptione illustrentur,** scilicet ut cocti muricis et triti conchylii ardore signentur: eaque tantummodo fas sit proferri et dici rescripta in quibuscumque iudiciis, **quae in chartis sive membranis subnotatio nostrae subscriptionis** (genit.identitatis!) **impresserit** (Note the very bombastic style. Succinct and terse is no longer the fashion of the times; the law is dated 470 A.D.). The verb does not occur in Veget.r.m.Claud.Arnob.adv.nat.Opt.Milev. Cf.et. ad 16.12.69a, p.102.22; Willems p.552 **(manu divina).**

perpessus. As the person, who is not permitted to read aloud, is **not**   p. 108. 21
mentioned by name, the infinit. passivi would have been more "correct", so: recitari, subnotari. The **acc.c.inf.** construction with the verb since old Latin. Cf.et. ad 15.7.4 (= IV p.13), p.57.3; ad.14.1.3, p.2.7. The verb not in Veget.r.m.Opt.Mil., though it is found in Arn.adv.nat.Claud.1.258 sq.:
    Et Phaetonteae **perpessus** damna ruinae
    Eridanus...

humi proiecit. For **humi** cf.Hofm.-Leum.p.419 (45), p.450(61), p.453(63).   p. 108. 21-22
Probably no longer part of the spoken language. Not in Claud.Veget.r.m. Opt.Milev..Arnob.adv.nat.

Augusti. Cf. ad 17.3.4, p.108.17*b*.   p. 108. 22

monitus ... non agere. For **monere c.inf.** cf. Krebs Antib.2 p.98 sq.   p. 108. 22
(with lit.); Draeger über Synt.Tac. (op.cit.I) p.59 sq.; ad 14.1.3 (= I p. 58); ad 15.7.4 (= IV p.13).

relatione. Cf. ad 14.7.10 (= II p.34); ad 15.5.13 (= III p.90); ad 16.11.7,   p. 108. 22
p.89.11.

p. 108. 23 *a* **perplexe** = in guarded terms; an insinuation which is made even stronger by the infin.pass. **credi** (impers.), which Seyfarth rightly translates with: "damit es nicht den Anschein habe, **man schenke dem Florentius zu wenig Vertrauen**", but wrongly Sabbah: "à renoncer à une attitude tâtillonne qui faisait croire **qu'il se défiait de Florentius**".
b Cf.15.6.4; 21.16.18; 22.6.1; 23.5.20; 25.3.23; 25.7.6 (adj. and adv.). Cf. ad 15.1.1 (= III p.5). Subst. **perplexitas** 17.8.3; 18.6.19; 31.2.12. Adj. and adv. and subst. not in Veget.r.m.Claud.Arn.adv.nat.Opt.Milev.

p. 108. 23 **rescripsit:** he wrote in reply. As it is unlikely that the emperor and the Caesar, though related, would write informal letters to each other, one should bear in mind that **rescribere** is a t.t. of the legal language and of the chancellery. Cf.Heum.-Seckel p.513; Willems p.415, 553, 558.

p. 108. 23 **gratandum esse:** impersonal: that one might congratulate oneself.

p. 108. 23 **provincialis.** It is very clear that provincialis here means: the inhabitant of the country and the small towns in Gallia (and elsewhere), not as opposed to the inhabitants of Italy, but rather to the residents of the urbanised nuclear regions of the Imperium Romanum. **Constitutionally** there is no difference between these regions and the inhabitants of the peripheral "provinces", but in actual fact there is. For the **entire** empire is divided in praefecturae, doiceses and provinciae. But Rome and Constantinople, for instance, already have a separate position, and likewise other cities and regions. The word does not have the meaning "provincial" (×citified, sophisticated, cultivated); cf.Dig.50.16.190 (Ulpianus): "**Provinciales**" eos accipere debemus, qui in provincia domicilium habent, **non eos, qui ex provincia oriundi sunt.** Cf.et.Heum.-Seckel p.474; Souter p.331. It clearly means: residents of the land in the next place: Veget.r.m. 3.3 (= Lang p.70): (cattle, wine, victuals) ad castella idonea et armatorum firmata praesidiis vel ad tutissimas conferendum est civitates urguendique **provinciales**, ut ante inruptionem (sc. hostis) seque et sua moenibus condant. Just as ibid. (Lang p.70): Praecipueque vitetur ne adversariorum dolo atque periuriis decipiatur **provincialium** incauta simplicitas; and the phrase very characteristic of this period ibid. (Lang p.69): ut pabula frumentum ceteraeque annonariae species (goods, wares etc.) **quas a provincialibus consuetudo deposcit.** Cf.et. ad 16.10.9, p.85.24 - 86.1.
hinc inde vastatus. For **hinc inde** cf. ad 17.1.7 (= p.105.23-24). This expression means: robbed, cleaned out completely. This **personal** use of

vastare among others in Tac.ann.14.23; hist.2.87; Iust.29.4.1; Claud.26. 541. The verb does not occur **at all** in Veget.r.m.Arn.adv.nat.Opt.Milev.

saltem sollemnia praebeat. Note the alliteration. **Sollemnia** = **sollemnes** p. 108. 24 **et canonicae pensitationes** ((= the regular payment of taxes, in the revealing passage Cod.Iust.12.61.2: Praeter sollemnes et canonicas pensitationes multa a **provincialibus** indignissime postulantur ab officialibus (subaltern civil servants) et scholasticis (lawyers) etc. a⁰ 344)). Cf.et.Cod.Iust. 7.65.4: Abstinendum prorsus appellatione sancimus, quotiens **fiscalis calculi** (cf. ad 17.3.4, p.108.18-20c) satisfactio (= payment) postulatur aut **tributariae functionis** (= payment of taxes) **sollemne munus** exposcitur etc. (a⁰ 368). Cf.et.Heum.-Seckel p.545 sq.; Souter p.381; ad 17.3.2, p. 108.10a.

nedum. For **nedum** without the verb cf.Hofm.-Leum.306a, p.746. Not in p. 108. 24 Claud.Veget.r.m.Opt.Milev.Arn.adv.nat.

incrementa. Cf. ad 16.1.4, p.71.12; Heum.-Seckel p.258; ad 17.3.2, p.108. p. 108. 25 10a.

egenis. Cf. ad 17.3.3, p.108.14 (**egestas**). Not in Claud.Veget.r.m.Arn.adv. p. 108. 25 nat.Opt.Milev. Often in Oros.Ennod. Generally post-classical.

egenis-extorquere: hyperbaton. p. 108, 25
extorquere. Cf.16.12.14, p.93.9. Cf.et.Cic. de prov.cons.3.5: quo ille, posteaquam nihil exprimere ab **egentibus,** nihil ulla vi a miseris **extorquere** potuit, cohortes in hiberna misit; Michael (op.cit.I) p.28.

a **factumque est tunc et deinde.** For the frequent use of -que cf.p.108.22 p. 108. 26 (litterisque); ad 16.12.35, p.96.22; ad 16.12.37, p.97.6a.
b **deinde** = in posterum. Cf.24.1.12; 20.8.12; 26.1.1. Already in Cic. too. Cf. Krebs Antib.1.p.409 sq. (with lit.); Blomgren (op.cit.II) p.155.

unius animi firmitate = by the determination of one person. Somewhat p. 108. 26 comparable Cic.pro Arch.p.11(29): Certe si nihil **animus** praesentiret in posterum et si, quibus regionibus vitae spatium circumscriptum est, isdem omnes cogitationes terminaret suas nec tantis se laboribus frangeret neque tot curis vigiliisque angeretur nec totiens de ipsa vita dimicaret; where in my opinion during the greater part of the period **animus** = **homo,** es-

65

pecially in: **nec... dimicaret.** In judic.lit. the word **caput** is used to indicate a person, not: animus.

p. 108. 26 **solita** = **sollemnia** (variatio). Cf. ad 17.3.5, p.108.24.

III, 6

p. 108. 27 **conaretur** (lac.21 lit.) **inique** V conaretur. Denique Vales. Clark.Seyf. Rolfe. Sabbah can not spirit away the gap, but joins **inique** to the preceding text, referring to Blomgren (op.cit.II) p.108 sq., with numerous examples of **adverbia** placed at the end of the sentence. Cf. ad 15.13.2, p.69.14 (= IV p.80); Sabbah A.M.II note 22, p.166. This seems a good solution to me.

p. 108. 27-28 **inusitato exemplo.** Cf. ad 17.3.2, p.108.11 (ex conquisitis, in fine). For the abl.modi cf. ad 14.1.6 (= I p.62); Liesenberg (1890) p.2 sq. (op.cit.I).

p. 108. 28 **id petendo Caesar impetraverat a praefecto.** Note the alliterating consonants p.t.r. **praefecto:** Florentio (pr.praet.cf.II p.30).

p. 108. 28 **secundae Belgicae.** Cf. ad 15.11.1-18 (= IV p.57 sq.). Ruled by a **consularis** (Correction: read p.58: N.D.Occ.XXII); ad 15.11.10 **(Remi)** (= IV p.64).

p. 108. 29 **multiformibus malis.** Although the adj. also occurs in Cic. and Colum., it generally is post-classical and definitely not generally used. Here in Amm. far-fetched = **variis.** Not in Veget.r.m.Claud.Arnob.adv.nat.Opt.Milev. Cf.16.5.7: historiam **multiformem.**

p. 108. 29 **dispositio.** Cf. ad. 16.12.12, p.92.24*a;* ad 16.10.16, p.87.10-11*a* **(disponere).** = to have at one's disposal.

p. 108. 29-
p. 109. 1 *a* **ea videlicet lege** = ea v. condicione. Thus e.g. Ovid.Met.2.556; ibid. 10.50; Phaedr.3.13.5; etc.

b here: namely. In late Latin **videlicet** is used more than **scilicet.** Cf. Krebs Antib.1.p.738 (with lit.); Heum.-Seckel p.623: "während die Klassiker **scilicet** bevorzugen und z.B. Gaius immer **scilicet,** niemals **videlicet** gebraucht, hat bei Iustinian **videlicet** das Uebergewicht; in den Digesten ist **videlicet** nicht selten interpoliert...". In Opt.Milev.; not in Claud.Veget.r.m.Arnob.adv.nat.

a **nec praefectianus nec praesidalis apparitor.** For **apparitor** cf. ad 15.7.3 (= IV p.12); ad 15.5.36 (= III p.125); ad 14.11.9 (= II p.122).
b **praefectianus** = belonging to the apparitores of the pr.praet. (viz. Florentius). In Amm. only here. Furthermore in the Cod.Iust.12.52.2.3; ibid.1.40.8; C.I.L.6.33712 (quoted by Souter).
c **praesidalis.** Subst. = former praeses 22.14.4; 28.1.5: officium **praesidiale**; 29.1.6: subst. = former praeses: **praesidialis;** Heum.-Seckel p.452 (= **praesidarius:** Spart.Sept.Sev.1.7, where Hohl and Magie read: **praesidiarius).**
d not to be confused with: **praesidiarius** (cf. *c* above), which is derived from **praesidium:** Liv.Ascon. (Cic.Verr.1.34). Colum. and Amm.25.9.12; 28.2.4; 28.3.7.
e As has already been mentioned, **Belgica II** is ruled by a **consularis** (p.108.28). Amm.probably uses here **praesidalis** in a general sense, viz. of the governor of the province.

a **ad solvendum quendam urgeret.** As a comment on these words (and as an illustration of the corruption), may serve Cod.Iust.12.52,2: Praefectianos **ad perniciem provincialium** exactionibus in provinciis vel potius lucris et quaestibus suis sese immiscere vetamus: praeterea vel horreorum gerere custodiam vel curarum ius atque arbitrium sibi praesumere his denegamus (a⁰ 373). (= Cod.Theod.12.10.1 c.comm.Gothofr.). Thus in this law the civil servants just mentioned are expressly forbidden to assume the functions of exactor, of custos horreorum and of curiosus, which, of course, offered many advantages (**the Curiosi or Curagendarii** belong to the **agentes in rebus** and supervise the police, State postal service, etc, in the provinces).
b **quendam.** One would expect: **quemquam:** anybody, whoever. Cf. ad 16.8.2, p.81.1-4.*c*. 3; ad 16.4.4, p.75. 8-9*b;* ad 16.12.11, p.92.20*a*.
c **urgeret.** Cf.Dig.42.4.7.11: Plane interdum bona eius causa cognita vendenda erunt, si **urgueat aes alienum** et dilatio damnum sit allatura creditoribus; ibid.27.9.5.14: praetori enim non liberum arbitrium datum est distrahendi (= vendendi) res pupillares, sed ita demum, si **aes alienum immineat ... si urgueat aes alienum.**
a **quo levati solacio.** These words bring to mind Verg.Aen.2.452; 4.538.
b I am not sure whether the version of V.: **solatio** is "wrong". It **may** be a phonetic slip of the pen of the copyist.

cuncti. Cf.ad 14.1.6 (= I p.61); ad 14.2.1 (= I p.66); ad 15.5.9 (= III p.85); ad 16.12.38, p.97. 17-21 *h*.

p. 109.2 *a* **quos in curam ... susceperat.** Curam susceperat suam Wm². Val. curam aes alienum separat suam BG. **in cura (lac.11 lit.) separat suam V.** propriam Seyf. The version of Wm². Val. (and Sabbah) seems the best one to me; but none of the conjectures really satisfy me.

b ⟨sus⟩**ceperat.** Can be defended, among others, by 17.10.3 (of the king of the Alamanni Suomarius): et quia vultus incessusque **supplicem** indicabat, **susceptus** bonoque animo esse iussus et placido... and (of an inferior sort of lawyers) 30.4.15: et ad defendendam causam admissi, quod raro contingit, **suscepti** (= client versus **patronus**) nomen et vim negotii sub ore disceptatoris (= judge) ... instruuntur ...

c **cura** and **curare** termini technici of the official language. Often in judic. language. (Cf.Heum.-Seckel p.114 sq.). Here = government.

p. 109.3 **nec interpellati**: and not pressed (for payment). For this meaning cf. Heum.-Seckel p.282 (with examples). For **neque** cf. ad 16.12.35, p.96.23.

p. 109.3 *a* **ante praestitutum tempus debita contulerunt. praestitutum.** Thus also used in Cic.Quint. 9 (33): ut nobis **tempus,** quam diu diceremus, **praestitueres.** The rather infrequently used verb not in Claud.Veget.r.m.Arnob. adv.nat. It is found in Opt.Milev. Often used by jurists, among others in connection with **tempus, dies, annus etc.**

b **debita.** Tax debts, but then those fixed or corrected by Iulianus.

IV, 1

p. 109.4 *a* **Inter haec recreandarum exordia Galliarum.** Remarkable is with Amm. the temporal use of **inter** with substantivised adjectiva neutra; cf.17.6.1: inter quae ita ambigua; 20.7.15: inter quae tam funesta; 22.2.1: inter quae tam suspensa; 22.14.1: inter praccipua tamen et seria; 26.10.4: inter quae tam trepida; 19.11.1: inter haec ita ambigua. Comparable (but not quite equivalent) Sall.Cat.43.3: inter haec parata atque decreta Cethegus semper querebatur de ignavia sociorum. This is frequently used in late Latin. Cf. et Fesser p.5; Liesenberg (1890) p.15; Hofm.-Leum.p. 511; ad 14.6.1. (= I p.89). Compare the use of **post** with temporal meaning. Cf.Hofm.-Leum. p.501; Liesenberg (1890) p.11; ad 14.1.1 (= I p.53). For substantivised adjectiva neutra in the accus. linked with a preposition cf. ad 14.1.3 (= I p.57).

b For the **plur.poet.** cf.Hagend.St.Amm.p.72 sq. Cf.Verg.Aen.7.40: ... et primae revocabo **exordia** pugnae; Vollmer ad Stat.Silv.IV 4.87 (= p. 466 comm.); ad p.107.14-15*b*.

c V creandarum. BG recreandarum. It is the question whether V's version should be rejected. Quite probably we are dealing here with an example of **simplex pro composito** (cf. ad 16.5.6, p.76.12). I also think the simplex fits better into the rhythmics of the sentence. I do not know of any examples where creare = recreare.

d **Galliarum.** This word used in its **original** meaning! Cf. ad. 15.11.1-18 (= IV p.57 sq).

a **administrante secundam adhuc Orfito praefecturam.**   p. 109. 5
Orfito. Cf. ad 14.6.1 (= I p.130); Sabbah A.M.II p.166 (with lit.).
b **praefecturam sc. urbi.** Cf. ad 14.6.1 (= I p.130); Madvig, 2.313 sq.
c **secundam:** 357-359 p.Chr.n.
d Note the **hyperbaton.** Cf. ad 17.1.6, p.105.21*a*.

a **obeliscus Romae in circo erectus est maximo. obeliscus.** Cf. ad 17.4.12.   p. 109. 5-6
b **Romae.** For the locativus Cf. ad 14.11.21 (= II p.137); ad 15.5.34 (Romae) (= III p.122).
c. **circo maximo.** Cf.28.4.29; ad 15.5.34 (= III p.122); Woord.d. Oud-heid (no.3) p.663 (with lit.).
d For the **hyperbaton** cf. ad 17.1.6, p.105.21*a*.

a **super quo ... discurram.** Super = de. Cf. ad 14.7.12 (= II p.40 sq.);   p. 109. 6
= πρὸς τούτοις cf. ad 14.1.6 (= I p.61).
C.accusat. 25.7.3: quae **super omnia** hebetarunt ... mentem; 14.11.16: inde aliis **super alias** urgentibus litteris; 29.2.1: clades alias **super alias** cumulando; 31.10.12: hocque urgentibus aliis **super alios** nuntiis cognito; Liesenberg (1890) p.17.
b **quia tempestivum est.** Cf.28.1.43: Et quamlibet **tempestivum** est ad ordinem redire coeptorum; 25.3.15: advenit ... nunc abeundi **tempus** e vita, impendio **tempestivum** (figura etymologica).
1. For the **formula-like expressions** with which the **excursus** is introduced, cf. ad 15.11.16 (= IV p.70). Cf.et. ad 14.6.26 (= I p.101); ad 15.12.6 (= IV p.78).
2. Remarkable usage: 30.9.1: oppidorum et limitum conditor **tempestivus** (= at the right time).
c For **discurrere** cf. ad 16.2.10. p.73.21; ad 17.1.4, p.105.14-15*d*.

IV, 2-5

In this historical introduction one should pay attention to the theme of   p. 109 7-23
the obeliscus (-ci) itself, in which Amm. shows off his historical erudition.
The Thebe-with-the-100 arches, which is so solemnly introduced here, is

69

mentioned in the Iliad 9.380 sq., but it is doubtful whether the **Egyptian Thebe** is meant by this. (cf. Leaf, The Iliad, 1 p.398, note 381). Compare Od.4.126 sq. But undoubtedly A.M. knows these place(s). Sabbah rightly points out that it were not the **institutores** who gave the place that name, but the Greeks. I do not believe that the adj. "with the 100 arches" was occasioned by the numerous pylons in front of the temples, as Sabbah wants. Even a small town possessed a fair number of arches. And Thebe was quite large. The town is also mentioned in 22.16.2. **Thebais** is one of the provinciae of the **diocesis Aegyptus** (cf. ad 14.7.21 = II p.51), also mentioned in 19.12.3 and 22.16.2. That Amm. is mistaken when he tells us that the **Carthagenians** conquered Thebae, is obvious. Apparently his auditorium (and his readers) swallowed this considerable gaffe. Amm. here confuses Th. hecatonpylae with a **Lybian town Hecatonpylos** conquered by Hanno in 247 B.C. Hanno was commander of the Carthagenian troops in Libya. (He is the well-known Hanno of the last years of the first Punic war (264-241 B.C.) and the not very succesful supreme commander in the mercenaries' war of 241-238 B.C.; cf.Th. Lenschau, R.E.7, 2355-2357, with lit.). As regards **Cambyses,** the son of Cyrus maior and Cassandane, king of Persia from 530-522 B.C.: Amm. here uses as his sources **Herodotus** (3.1-28; 3.61-66; 3.89), perhaps also **Strabo** (17.27; 17.46) and quite probably **Iust.Phil.**1.9.8. (For **Herod.** cf. How and Wells, A Comm. on Herod., I, p.411 sq. Appendix IX, X; For **Cambyses**: Bury, Hist. of Greece (1924) p.232 sq.; W.Schulze, Ber.Berl.Akad.1912, p. 685 sq.; J.V.Prašek, Der Alte Orient 14.2.1913; C.F. Lehmann-Haupt, R.E. 10.1810-1823, with lit.). As regards **Gallus, praefectus** Aeqypti (cf.annot. ad 17.4.5: **procurator)** from 30 to 27 B.C., (the first one): he suppressed a tax-rising in the Thebais and does not seem to have been too gentle in this. Fallen from grace and recalled, he was banished and committed suicide. He is the same man as the poet Gallus. (Cf. Stein, R.E.4.1342 sq., with lit.; M.J.P. Boucher C.Corn.Gallus, Paris, 1966). Possible sources for Amm. concerning **Gallus** may have been: Dio Cass.53.23.5-24.1; 51.17; 51.9 sq.; Suet.Oct.66; Eutr.7.7; **Verg. Buc.**10; **Servius; Donatus;** (the last two wrote in the 4th century after Christ). Whether A.M. has still seen or read the **poems of Gallus** (4 books) which are now completely lost, can not be ascertained. When these were lost, is not known. **Oros. adv.pag.** (written ± 417 A.D.) 6.19.15 still mentions Gallus, but only as a general, which shows how his memory lived on. And his beloved **Lycoris** is to the poets a τόπος (but no longer to Claud.).

p. 109. 7-23 *a* **Note.** It is possible that the term "with the 100 arches" is **not** derived directly from the Greek lit., but from the Latin, e.g. **Pomp. Mela** 1.9.60.

b Sub dispositione viri spectabilis **ducis Thebaidos** (N.D.Or.31) is mentioned a Legio tertia Diocletiana. **Thebas.** (But the same one (?) L.III Diocl. is mentioned ibid.28: sub.disp.v.spect. **comitis rei militaris per Aegyptum,** with the addition: **Andro;** and again ibid.31 the same one (?) L.III Diocl. with the additions **Ombos** and **Praesentia.** The first information is real. The explanation of the last 3 communications seems to me rather more complicated).
c In Comm.II p.53 N.D.Or.25-28 should be corrected into: **28-31** (= Seeck N.D.p.58 sq.).
d In the Not. urbis Constant.VI (Regio V) is mentioned: Strategium, in quo est forum Theodosiacum et **obeliscus Thebaeus** quadrus. (where the obelisks were not moved to!).
e One should think of the "city" of Thebe at this time as a collection of villages, on the vast area of the former town. After the introduction of Christianity many buildings were torn down (insofar as they were still standing there), or they were reconstructed into monasteries and churches. The lime-kilns did the rest. Nevertheless **Thebae (Diospolis magna)** was a bishop's seat. But in Thebais I **Antinopolis-Antinoë** was the metropolis, and in Thebais II **Ptolemais Hermiu** (Cf. Pieper, op.cit.II, tab.8). Which clearly demonstrates the decline of the city. In the Cosmogr.Rav. (Schnetz p.33 sq.) II 2 the name of **Alexandria famosissima,** but the name **Thebae** is no longer used, not even after the words (Schnetz p.35): Item ad aliam partem, **ex regione Thebaide,** sunt civitates, id est: (there follow 5 names). In **Claud.Thebae** is not mentioned (but neither is **Alexandria,** although C. was born there).

a **ambitiosa moenium strue.** For **ambitiosus** cf. ad 14.7.6 (= II p.22); ad 14.6.9 (= I p.93). p. 109. 7
b **strues.** Comparable with Cic. ad Att.5.12.3: de **strue** laterum. In Amm. probably a literary reminiscence or archaism. Not in Veget.r.m.Claud. Arnob.adv.nat.Opt.Mil. For the verb **(prae)struere** cf. Blomgren p.141.

et portarum centum quondam aditibus celebrem. Cf.14.2.18: obseratis undique **portarum aditibus** (just as abundant as our passage). Cf. et. 18.10.2: confestim claves optulere **portarum,** patefactisque **aditibus...**; 31.15.10: barbari... in urbis obseratos **aditus** multiplicatis ordinibus inundarunt (in the last 2 examples aditus = porta: abstractum pro concreto); Liv.38. 22.7: intra vallum momento temporis compelluntur stationibus tantum firmis ad ipsos **aditus portarum** relictis (but here the word combination is p. 109. 7-8 the same, though not the meaning: "totus locus, qui ante portam erat, significatur", as Hagendahl abund. says (op.cit.I) p.199).

p. 109. 8 **institutores.** Cf.14.8.6: primigenia tamen nomina non amittunt, quae eis Assyria lingua **institutores** veteres indiderunt. Sen.Lact.Tert., with this meaning. With the meaning: instructor, teacher **not** in Amm.Souter p.211. Not in Claud.Veget.r.m.Arn.adv.nat.Opt.Mil.

p. 109. 9 *a* **ex facto cognominarunt.** Often = nominare. Cf.18.9.4; 21.1.8; 22.8.23; 22.9.7; 23.6.23; 23.6.72; 27.3.7; 27.4.8; 29.6.19; 30.7.2; 31.2.13; 31.11.2. Plin.mai.Gell.Iust.et.al. Rare verb. Post-class. late Latin. Also in Liv. Epit.55. Interesting is Macrob.Sat.1.25 sq., where one finds the following: (25) cognomentum ... (26) cognomentum- ... cognominem (adj.) ... **cognominatus...** cognomine ... cognomento ... **cognominatus** ... (27) cognominibus ... cognomina ... (28) cognomina ... cognomenta ... (29) cognomentum (from which it is apparent that Macrob. uses both **cognomentum** and **cognomen**, without any difference in meaning).
b Very simular to the words of Amm.Claud.Quadrig. in Gell.9.13.19: **Quo ex facto** ipse posterique eius Torquati sunt **cognominati.**
c For **cognomentum** cf. ad 15.12.5 (= IV p.77); Thes.sub v.; Fesser p.50 sq.
Vocabulo = nomine. Thus often in Amm.Cf. Krebs Antib.2 p.750. Similarly in the judic.lit.: expression, name.

p. 109. 9 *a* **provincia nunc usque Thebais.** For pr.Theb. cf. ad 4.2-5. p.109.7-23.
b **nunc usque** = usque adhuc (Cic.rep.2.20.36), usque ad hunc diem (Cic.Verr.4.58.130), quoted by Krebs 2.p.699, who goes on to say: "Spätlat., namentlich bei Orosius finden wir usque ad nunc; **das Kirchenlatein** schuf die Ausdrücke usque modo, usque impraesentiarum, usque nunc, usque hodie, **nunc usque.** Spätlat. und selten ist usque huc." The above communication is at least incomplete for **nunc usque.** Cf.et. **abusque** Hagend.St.Amm.p.68 (with lit.); ad 14.7.17 (= II p.42); ad 14.8.5 (= II p.64); ad 17.2.2, p.107.20.

IV, 3

p. 109. 10 *a* **inter exordia pandentis se late Carthaginis.** For the contents of § 3 cf. ad 4.2-5, p.109.7-23.
b For **inter exordia** cf. ad 17.4.1, p.109.4. The repetition after so short a time is remarkable.
c **Carthaginis.** Also mentioned in 14.11.32; 23.5.20; 24.2.16; 28.6.16

(in the last place the **new** Carthago is meant. The other passages and this one refer to the "antique" town). Cf.et. ad 14.11.32 (= II p.143).

improviso excursu. Cf.27.8.9: improvisos excursus. Meaning: attack, invasion, raid. Also 14.8.13; 17.4.3; 17.5.1; 17.13.4; 30.7.5. This typical t.t.mil. not in Veget.r.m., though we do find there the verb **excurrere**, though only once with this meaning. Cf. ad 14.2.9: **inopino adcursu.** p. 109. 10-11

Poenorum. Also mentioned 22.9.3; **adj. Poeninus:** 15.10.9. Adj. **Punicus:** 22.9.5; 22.15.8; 17.1.14; 14.8.3. p. 109. 11
posteaque reparatam. Cf. ad 16.12.37, p.97.6*a;* ad 16.12.17, p.93.23-24*b*.

Persarum rex ille Cambyses. For **Cambyses** cf. ad 17.4.2-5, p.109.7-23. For **Persarum** cf. ad 15.1.2 (= III p.7); ad 14.3.1 (= I p.119); ad 14.7.11 (= II p.66); ad 14.8.13 (= II p.81). p. 109. 11-12

quoad vixerat. Plq.perf. = Imperf.Cf. ad 14.11.8 (= II p.121). For **quoad** cf. ad 14.4.5 (= I p.82); ad 16.10.18, p.87.21; ad 16.11.14, p.90.27; 21.16.7: quod autem ... nec spuisse ... nec pomorum **quoad vixerat** gustaverit (ut dicta saepius) praetermitto; 16.10.18: Helenae ... regina tunc insidiabatur Eusebia, ipsa **quoad vixerat** sterilis; 30.1.2: inter quos erat Terentius dux demisse ambulans semperque submaestus, sed **quoad vixerat,** acer dissensionum instinctor; 14.6.1: Interhaec Orfitus praefecti potestate regebat urbem aeternam, vir ... splendore liberalium doctrinarum minus quam nobilem **decuerat** institutus; 30.3.2: quibus ille ut cunctatorem **decuerat** ducem examinatius lectis; Hassenstein p.51 (op.cit. I); Ehrism. (op.cit.I) p.49 sq. (with more examples). p. 109. 12
Note: In I p.83 Anm.21.16.17 should be corrected into 21.16.7.

a **alieni cupidus et inmanis.** Cf.Sall.Cat.5.4: **alieni** adpetens sui profusus, ardens in **cupiditatibus;** Cic. ad fam.3.8.8: non debent mirari homines, cum et natura semper ad largiendum **ex alieno** fuerim restrictior. p. 109. 12
b For the **genit. with adj.** cf. ad 14.5.6 (= I p.86); ad 14.10.3 (= II p.100); ad 14.1.4 (= I p.59); ad 14.9.3 (= IV p.50); ad 16.12.29, p.95.25-26*b;* ad 16.12.57, p.100.24; ad 17.1.7, p.105.24-25*e;* 16.7.5: bene faciendi **avidus** plenusque iusti consilii (with chiasm (cf.Blomgren 20,22,41)).
c **inmanis.** With the same highly unfavourable meaning Claud.Ruf.I 89 sq.: p. 109. 12

    Est mihi prodigium (= monster) cunctis **immanius** hydris,
    Tigride mobilius feta, violentius Austris

acribus, Euripi refluis incertius undis, Rufinus.
(Also in Claud. the very frequent meaning: "great", extraordinary). Cf. Veget.r.m.3.24 (= Lang p.118): (machinamenta) quae sint tam **inmanibus** beluis (= elefantis) opponenda (For the rest the word does not occur in Veget.) Not in Arnob.adv.nat. And again with the very unfavourable meaning: Opt.Milev.2.19: facinus **immane** commissum est; 6.2: hoc tamen **inmane** facinus a vobis geminatum est; 2.17: venistis rabidi ... in caedibus **inmanes** ... Cf.et. ad 15.4.2 (= III p.55); ad 15.8.15 (= IV p.39).

p. 109. 12 **perrupta.** Cf. ad 17.1.5, p.105.19.

p. 109. 13 *a* **ut opes exinde raperet invidendas.**
exinde here has the meaning of: **from there, out of there.** Exinde in late Latin often = **inde.** Cf.S.Bened.Reg.35 (Linderb.p.47): ... et nullus excusetur a coquinae officio nisi aut aegritudo -aut in causa gravis utilitatis quis occupatus fuerit, quia **exinde** maior merces et caritas adquiritur; Mulomed.Chir.314 (= Oder p.94): ... et ex aqua mulsa decoctam facies et **exinde** totam gregem potionabis etc. (from that = **with that, by that);** Hofm.-Leum.p.492,87*b;* Souter p.137; Krebs Antib.2 p.547 (not quite accurate); Hedfors (op.cit.I) δ 22-26. p.62.
b **invidendas.** Cf. ad 15.5.8 (= III p.84); ad 17.12.11, p.92.18-19; ad 16.12.22, p.94.26*b*.

p. 109. 13-14 **deorum ... donariis.** Wagner: "ἀναθήμασι in quibus erant et ipsi **obelisci**". This meaning: votive offering also: Aurel.Vict. de Caes.35.7: fanum Romae soli magnificum constituit, **donariis** ornans opulentis (sc. Aurelianus, 270-275 A.D.); Arnob.7.9 (138): numquid sacrilegis furtis tua **rapui** spoliavique **donaria?** This rare and probably only late Latin word (at least with this meaning) not in Claud.Veget.r.m.Opt.Milev.

IV, 4
p. 109. 14 **dum ... concursat.** Cf. ad 14.10.1 (= II p.95); ad 14.11.5 (= II p.118); ad 15.3.1 (= III p.27); Kalb Röm.Rechtsspr. (1912) § 95, p.107 sq.; p.123 ibid.; S.Bened.Reg.Linderb. (Index) p.80.

p. 109. 14 **praedatores.** Also class.
praedatrix (adj.) 14.2.1; 26.6.10. **praedatorius** (adj.) cf. ad 15.3.4 (= IV p.82).

concursat = runs to and fro. class.; 22.8.14: repeatedly clap together; 31.5.8: t.t.mil.class.
concursatorius (adj.): ad 16.9.1, p.83.15.

turbulente. class. The adv. not in Claud.Veget.r.m.Arnob.adv.nat.Opt. Milev. The adj. once in Veget.r.m.3.4 (= Lang p.72): si qui **turbulenti** vel seditiosi sunt milites... **Turbulente concursare** is no recommendation for a private soldier, let alone a general. Cf.et. ad 16.11.1, p.88.14.

a **laxitate praepeditus indumentorum.** Cf.23.6.80: (Persae) adeo autem dissoluti sunt et artuum **laxitate** vagoque incessu se iactitantes. Here **laxitas ind.** = roomy garments, too loose-fitting, uncomfortable clothes. This meaning: space, looseness, is found more often, e.g. Cic. de off.1.39 (139): sic in domo clari hominis, in quam et hospites multi recipiendi et admittenda hominum cuiusque modi multitudo, adhibenda cura est **laxitatis**.
b **praepeditus.** Cf. ad 16.2.6, p.73.9. Not in Claud.Arnob.adv.nat.Opt. Milev. Once in Veget.r.m. (2.7).

indumentorum. Cf. ad 14.7.20 (= II p.49). Not in Claud.Arnob.adv.nat. Opt.Milev. Once in Veget.r.m. Wagner: "Qualia ad nostram usque aetatem in illis regionibus solent gestari".

concidit pronus ... pugione ... subita vi ruinae nudato. Cf.Caes.b.c.2.11.4: repentina **ruina** pars eius turris **concidit**...

Suomet. Cf. ad 16.12.20, p.94.14c. Cf.et. ad 14.11.3 (= II p.117): **suopte**.

aptatum. Cf. ad 16.7.2, p.79.1-2.

a **gestabat** = ferebat, portabat. Also class., but rare with **this** meaning. Cf. Krebs Antib.1, p.624; ad 16.5.4, p.76.2 **(gestamen).** Cf.et.Heum.-Seckel p.229 (for other meanings in the judic.lit.). Of the carrying of weapons 3 times in Veget.r.m. (once = displays, demonstrates). Also in Claud. Not in Arn.adv.nat. (who does have **gestitare**) and Opt.Milev.
b Cf.Val.Flacc.Argon, 6.699 sq.:
 At viridem gemmis et Eoae stamine silvae
 subligat extrema patrium cervice tiaram
Insignis manicis, **insignis acinace dextro.**

75

p. 109. 17-18 **vulneratus paene letaliter interisset.** An incomplete, unreal and hypothetical period of the past. Complete: nisi cura medicorum eum sanavisset. Here Amm. does not follow the more general tradition, viz. that Cambyses found his death by an involuntary wound, caused by his own weapon. Another version, viz. that the Magicians should have killed Cambyses, is found among others in Strabo and in Oros.adv. p.2.8.3: post hunc (sc. Cambysen) etiam **magi sub nomine quem occiderant regis** regno obrepere ausi; qui quidem mox deprehensi et oppressi sunt. According to the official Persian version in the **inscription of Behistun** Cambyses died a natural death.

IV, 5

p. 109. 17 **longe autem postea.** Cf.14.7.17: qui haut longe postea ideo vivus exustus est.

p. 109. 17-18 **Cornelius Gallus.** Cf. ad 17.4.2-5, p.109.7-23. **Aegypti procurator.** Here Amm. is mistaken, as G. was **praefectus** Aegypti. **Procuratores,** as governors of countries (regions), subjected since the installation of the principate (where therefore the emperor has taken over the direct control), do not exist any longer in these days. The rulers of the dioceses are called **vicarii (praefectorum),** except those of the diocesis Orientis, who is called **comes Orientis** and those of the diocesis Aegypti, who is called **praefectus Augustalis.** For the denominations of the provincial governors cf. ad 14. 10.8 (= II p.106). But in Ammianus' time the name **procurator** is still used for all kinds of officials, often in the financial field, just as in previous times. It is possible that A. here consciously does not use the correct technical term (as he has done often before), but it may also be that he was misled by the abovementioned **previous** use of the term **procurator.** There was a procurator under the principate in Egypt, viz. the **procurator Alexandriae ad rationes patrimonii,** for the financial administration, placed **under** the praefectus Augusti. But I do not think that A.M. knew this (any more), so that **this** term cannot have been the reason for his mistake. Cf.Heum.-Seckel s.v.p.464.

p. 109. 18 **Octaviano res tenente Romanas.** Tenere = to control, to rule. Cf.Horat. Carm.3.14 sq.:

... ego nec tumultum
nec mori per vim metuam **tenente** Caesare terras.

Cic. ad Att.7.12.3: an cuncter et tergiverser et iis me dem, qui **tenent,** qui potiuntur? etc. However, I would like to point out that in late Latin **teneo** often is equal in meaning to **habeo**. (cf.Souter p.415).

exhausit: to exhaust = to impoverish. As in Liv.37.19.4: Restat ergo ut ... copiae ... **exhauriant** commeatibus praebendis socios; Nepos Hann.6: **exhaustis** iam patriae facultatibus (sc. bello diuturno); Cic. ad Q.fr.1.1.2 (9): non itineribus tuis perterreri homines, non sumptu **exhauriri**, non adventu commoveri? etc. class. p. 109. 18

plurimis (n.pl.) interceptis. Cf.Tac.Ann.4.45: Sed Piso Termestinorum dolo caesus habetur, quia pecunias e publico **interceptas** (sc.Termestinorum) acrius, quam ut tolerarent barbari, cogebat. = to embezzle; to rob, ransack, class. Here definitely the **first** meaning. p. 109. 19

a **cum furtorum arcesseretur:** t.t.iurid. Elsewhere Amm. has aliquem in crimen laesae maiestatis arcessere. Cf.et. ad 15.3.1 (= III p.29). p. 109. 19-20
b **furtorum** = repetundarum (see previous note).
c **populatae provinciae.** The **part.** with **pass.** meaning, as for instance, in Cic.Verr.3.52 (122): eiectos aratores esse dico ... **populatam**, vexatamque provinciam. The verb does **not** occur in Veget.r.m.; Arn.adv.nat.Opt. Milev.; it is found in Claud. For the **partic.** instead of **substantiva verbalia** cf.Hofm.-Leum.185, p.608 sq. Also quite frequent in late Latin. Cf.et. Riemann (op.cit.I) p.104 sq. For **deponentia, pass.** used, cf. Koziol (op.cit.I) p.306 sq. (in Apuleius); Hofm.-Leum.138, p.545 sq.

metu nobilitatis acriter indignatae. A.M. follows his sources. But when one reads Dio Cassius 53.23.5 sq., this indignation has a dubious flavour. p. 109. 20

a **cui negotium spectandum dederat imperator.** By **nobilitas** the **senatus** is meant, as is already apparent from the above-mentioned passage in Dio C., from which one gets the impression that the Senate left the trial to the still existing **quaestio (perpetua) de repetundis**, in whatever formation. For the changes in the jurisdiction of the **quaestiones** during the principate, cf.Mommsen Abriss des r.Staatsr.² p.234 sq. and p.254 sq. p. 109. 20-21
b **negotium** = causam, as is also often found in legal texts. **Spectandum** = investigate. Cf.Cic. de off.2.11 (38): Maximeque admirantur eum, qui pecunia non movetur: quod in quo viro perspectum sit, hunc igni **spectatum** arbitrantur; ibid Phil.2.10 (26): Quid ego de L.Cinna loquar? cuius **spectata** multis magnisque rebus singularis integritas etc. With this meaning no t.t. judic.

p. 109. 21 **stricto incubuit ferro:** drew his sword and plunged into it.

p. 109. 21-23 **is ... decantat.** Note the poetic tone of the words and the way in which A.M. pays tribute to Vergil.

p. 109. 21 **si recte existimo:** false modesty, so as not to appear conceited.

p. 109. 22 **flens quodam modo.** See previous note. The author knows exactly where the passage is to be found! **flens:** lamenting, in this context poetism, although the verb occurs with this meaning in prose (cf. Krebs Antib.1 p.598) among others in Iust.Phil.28.4.4; Opt.Milev.3.2 (Ziwsa p.69).

p. 109. 22 **postrema,** viz. in the 10th of the bucolica. The term **bucolica** (n.plur.subst.) is post-class. Gell.9.9.4. Gramm.

p. 109. 23 **decantat** = canit decantans = glorifies, chants at the end of his poem (cf.Cic.Tusc.3.22 (53)). The meaning **to chant** fits here, of course, but **decantare** does not mean: to chant. The author probably alludes to the verses 70-74. And involuntarily Propertius comes to mind (2.34.91 sq.):
    et modo **formosa** quam multa **Lycoride** Gallus
    mortuus inferna vulnera lavit aqua!

IV, 6

p. 109. 24 **delubra.** labra VEAG. Sabbah. The conjecture by Corn. is taken over by Clark, Rolfe, Seyfarth. It is a marked example of a superfluous and senseless conjecture. Instead of trying to find out which meaning **labra** could have, the text as it has come down to us, is changed. **lābrum** means basin, pond. Cf.Verg.Aen.8.22; Plin.ep.5.6.20; Liv.37.3.7; Stat. Silvae 1.5.49; Souter p.224; and in particular Sabbah A.M.II p.167, note 25, who further refers, for everything that Amm. has been able to see **in Thebe** to M. Barguet, Le temple d'Amon-Rê à Karnak, Le Caire, 1962. Thus here in Amm. the basins near the temples are meant, which served for ritual cleansing. That **labrum** is no unusual word, can be seen from a text by Ulpianus in the Dig.29.1.15: lines (lenes? = a kind of basin) et **labra,** salientes (= fountains), fistulae quoque, quamvis longe excurrant extra aedificium, aediunt sunt ... Cf.et.ad 16.10.14, p.86.24*a* **(lavacrum).**

p. 109. 24-25 *a* **diversasque moles figmenta Aegyptiorum numinum exprimentes.**
diversas = complures, varias. This meaning generally late Latin. Cf. Krebs Antib.1 p.465 (with lit.).

b   The **diversae moles**: colossal statues, will have been not only of Aeg. gods, but also of Pharao's.
c   For **figmentum** cf.14.6.8; 16.10.10; 22.16.12; 19.1.3; 19.1.10; 22.6.7; ad 15.5.5 (= III p.79). Post-class., late Latin. Not in Veget.r.m., Claud., Arn.adv.nat., Opt.Milev.

a   **obeliscos vidimus plures.** Plures = complures, multos, as more often,   p. 109. 25
also class. Cf. Krebs Antib.2.p.311 (with lit.).
vidimus. Plur. maiestatis or real plural: I together with others? In which function? Or as a tourist? This journey, as so many of Am.' travels, takes place after 360 A.D. (dismissal of Ursicinus). But the exact date is difficult to determine, as the Ammianic chronology becomes very obscure after this year.
b   The latinised diminutivum (ὀβελίσκος) does not seem to occur prior to Plin.maior.

plures ⟨alios stantes et integros⟩ aliosque. Corn.'s insertion is a good ex-   p. 109. 25
planation. But for the rest wholly superfluous.

conminutos. Thus Cic. in Pis. 38(93) uses **comminuere** of the destruction   p. 109. 26
of a **statua**. Cf.et.Opt.Milev.7.1 (= Ziwsa p.161): denique Moyses post tabulas sparsas legis et **comminutas** non damnari meruit; Arn.adv.nat.1.3 (Reiffersch.p.6): in litteris enim priscis comprehensum et compositum non videmus, etiam imbres saxeos totas saepe **comminuisse** regiones? Not in Claud.Veget.r.m. Nor in judic.lit.

a   **prosperitatibus summarum rerum elati.** Cf.24.6.17: Abunde ratus post   p. 110. 1
haec **prosperitates** similis adventare, conplures hostias Marti parabat Ultori; 20.8.6: currentium ex voto **prosperitatum;** ad 17.2.1, p.107.14-15*b*.
Cf. et Cic.nat.deor.3.36 (88): Improborum igitur **prosperitates** secundaeque res redarguunt, ut Diogenes dicebat, vim omnem deorum ac potestatem; Aug.conf.10.28: Vae **prosperitatibus** saeculi semel et iterum a timore adversitatis et a corruptione laetitiae! Vae **adversitatibus** saeculi semel et iterum et tertio a desiderio prosperitatis ... both passages quoted by Georges).
b   **summarum rerum.** In my opinion the following are placed opposite each other: **bello** domitis gentibus ... and prosp. **summarum rerum** elati (even when the version **domitis** Vm 3 EAG would not be the original one (V dotis), the antithesis remains because of the word **bello**). Seyf.: oder

aus Stolz über glückliches Vollbringen **ihrer gröszten Taten;** Sabbah: ou s'enorgueillissaient des prosperités **de leur souveraine puissance;** Büchele: auf das glöckliche Gelingen **von Staatsplanen.** It seems to me that the 3rd translation is the right one, because here **summae res** has its usual meaning of: supreme command, supreme government. Cf. et. ad 17.3.4, p.108.17*a*.

p. 110.2 *a* **apud extremos orbis incolas.** For **apud** cf.ad 14.11.21 (= II p.137); Liesenberg (1890) p.9 (with many examples).
 b **orbis incolas.** Cf. Krebs 2.p.225: "Orbis in der Bedeutung Erdkreis, Erde ohne den Zusatz **terrae** oder **terrarum** ist fast nur **poet.-lat.** und kommt erst nachklass. bei Vell.Pat., Tac., Curt., Florus und Iustinus vor". (with lit.).
 c the unusual linking of the above words is reminiscent of Cic.Tusc.37 (108): Socrates ... totius enim **mundi se incolam** et civem arbitrabatur; Claud.3 (De raptu Pros.) 430 sq.: ferus ipse quis est? **Terraene** marisne // **incola?**

p. 110.2 **perscrutatis.** Cf.Claud.17 (de Fl.Mall.Theod.cons.) 40 sq.:
 Quidquid luce procul **venas rimata** sequaces
 Abdita pallentis fodit sollertia Bessi.
The verb (also class.) does not occur in Claud.Veget.r.m.Opt.Milev.Arn. adv.nat. For the part. used **pass.** cf. Georges 2.1635 (with examples); ad 17.4.5, p.109.19.20*c*.

p. 110.2 *a* **excisos ⟨et⟩ erectos.** Without **et**: VE. erectosque: BG. **et** inserted by Clark, Seyfarth. Sabbah follows BG's version. It seems better to me to maintain the **asyndeton.** Cf. ad 15.13.2 (= IV p.80); ad 16.12.22, p.94.25*a;* Blomgren (op.cit.II) p.3 sq. When one reads out the sentence aloud, there is a pause after perscrutatis (claus.III), followed as a metric unit by **excisos erectos (Claus.I),** a further adjunct to quos (obeliscos).
 b Hewn out of the pink granite of Assuan, according to G. Jéquier, Manuel d'archéologie égyptienne, I, p.20 sq., quoted by Sabbah.

p. 110.2 **excisos.** Cf.Cic. de off.2.3 (13): Eademque ratione nec lapides e terra **exciderentur** ad usum nostrum necessarii; Verg.Aen.1.427 sq.:
 ... hinc lata theatris
 fundamenta petunt alii immanisque columnas/rupibus **excidunt.**
ibid.6.42: **Excisum** Euboicae latus ingens rupis in antrum; Suet.Claud.20: Per tria autem passuum milia, partim effosso monte, partim **exciso,**

canalem absolvit aegre. The t.t. for the carving, -cutting out of the rocks, marble, etc. X **effodere.**

erectos. Cf. ad 16.12.37, p.97.8; 16.12.65, p.102.11. For the meaning: excitare, expergefacere, stimulare cf. Blomgren p.149.   p. 110. 2

diis superis in religione dicarunt. Originally the obeliscus is a sacral stone   p. 110. 2-3 (cf. the menhir). Later, but already at an early stage, it was included in the cultus of **Râ,** sun-god of Heliopolis. Hence probably also viewed as a symbol of the rays of the sun. But the obeliscus also has a very definite decorative function (which it still has, in a somewhat altered form, in our time). The obelisci are mostly monoliths. On top they carry a **pyramidion.** These were to be found not only in or before temples, but also in front of graves and houses. The explanation of the origin and the use of ob., the study of the connection with other temple-columns in the Near East, still leaves many questions unanswered. Nor do we possess any positive information regarding "manufacture" and transport.

IV, 7

The use of the participia makes § 7 less clear. **Gracilescens — artifici** is an   p. 110. 3-6 explanation of: utque radium imitetur. = **consurgit ... et gracilescit paulatim...** productus ... levigatus ... ut radium imitetur. Cf. ad 17.3.5, p.108.20*a*.

a **asperrimus lapis.** Wagner: **durissimus** lapis, with the further explana-   p. 110. 3 tion: granites, Syenites lapis, Plinio pyrrhopoecilus, Italis granito russo. Likewise, probably in imitation of W., Büchele, Rolfe, Seyf., Sabbah. But **asper** is not: **durus**! I believe that asperrimus here means: tapering (into a fine point). Cf.Lucan.6.186:
    Iamque **hebes** et crasso **non asper** sanguine mucro;
    Perdidit ensis opus, frangit **sine vulnere** membra;
ibid.7.139:
    Nec gladiis habuere fidem, nisi cautibus **asper**
    Exarsit mucro ...

b The other meaning of **asper,** which could qualify here, viz.: uneven, bumpy, rough to the touch (because of the hewn-in hieroglyphs), as in Verg.Aen.5.267:
    Cymbiaque argento perfecta atque **aspera signis,**
    (Forbiger: figuris eminentibus caelata)
seems less suitable here.

p. 110. 3-4 **in figuram metae cuiusdam.** Wagner: "conicam, quales erant in spina circi extrema utrinque erectae" Cf.Curt.Ruf.8.11.6: Petra non, ut pleraeque, modicis ac mollibus clivis in sublime fastigium crescit, sed **in metae** maxime **modum** erecta est; cuius ima spatiosiora sunt, altiora in artius coeunt, summa in acutum cacumen exsurgunt; a place very similar to ours.

p. 110. 4 **proceritatem ... utque radium imitetur.** Cf.Plin.N.H.36.14: Trabes ex eo fecere reges ... obeliscos vocantes, **solis numini sacratos. Radiorum** eius argumentum in effigie est, et ita significatur nomine Aegyptio. With the meaning **height, length,** (as here), several times in Veget.r.m.: 1.1: Germanorum proceritatem; 1.5: proceritatem tironum; 1.6 (also of tirones); 4.17 (of turres ambulatoriae). But the word does not occur in Claud. Arn.adv.nat.Opt.Milev. and appears to me like a "literary" word for: **altitudinem.** For Veget. often fancies a figure of speech and words of a higher "order".

p. 110. 4-5 **sensim ... paulatim.** For the numerous adverbia ending in -im in Amm., usual (as these 2), as well as unusual ones, cf. Liesenberg (1889) p.14 sq. (op. cit.I).

p. 110. 5 **gracilescens.** Cf.22.8.4: (The Aegean Sea) Hinc **gracilescens** paulatim et velut naturali quodam commercio ruens in Pontum (to narrow); 22.15.29: quarum (sc. pyramidum) magnitudo, quoniam in **celsitudinem** nimiam scandens **graciliscit paulatim,** ... consumit; 20.3.10: exortus vero eius adhuc **gracilescens** (the moon crescent) primitus mortalitati videtur etc. The verb seems to occur only in Amm.

p. 110 5 *a* **specie quadrata.** Species, used **pass.** is that which is seen, outward appearance, form; **image, statue** (cf.Cic.Divin.1.12.20; 1.36.79). Cf.et. Krebs Antib.2.592 sq. (especially for the declination); Souter p.383 (for late Latin meanings); Heum.-Seckel p.549. I therefore consider the translations by Sabbah: "passant **d'une base carrée** à un sommet étroit" and Seyf.: "bei **quadratischem Grundrisz**" not quite accurate. Translation: beginning with a square (or better: four-sided) form, led upwards to etc. (as reproduced more or less by Büchele and Rolfe). I know of no place where **species** = base.

b For **specie, sub specie** etc. cf. ad 16.11.7, p.89.12-13 (abl.modi); Liesenberg (1890), p.2; Reinhardt (op.cit.I) p.42. **Variatio:** 22.8.37; 22.15.7; 23.6.28; 24.2.12; 27.4.5; Fesser p.21.

in verticem productus angustum = tapering to a narrow top, sc. the pyra- p. 110. 5
midion, or into a narrow, but blunt top. **Productus** lit.: elongated, stretch-
ed-out (also class.). For **vertex** cf.et. ad 14.7.2 (= II p.17); ad 15.5.16
(= III p.95); ad 16.12.22, p.94.24.

a **manu levigatus artifici.** Cf. Varro r.r.3.11.3: omnes parietes tectorio p. 110. 6
(a covering of plaster) **levigantur.** Further Plin.Colum.Gell.Pallad.Diom.
Arnob. Not in Veget.r.m.Claud.Opt.Milev. Archaism? Cf. et Krebs An-
tib.2 p.16.
b **artifex.** Cf. ad 15.3.4 (= III p.40).

IV, 8-11
formarum - plurima. A myth is often stronger than the scientific truth, p. 110. 6-20
to which can be added that symbolic explanations were part of the
fashion of this late epoch. There are ridiculous examples of this by many
church-fathers. Anything Egyptian was strange and mysterious, then as
well as now. This was also true of the hieroglyphs. That it was nothing
more than a system of writing, different from Latin and Greek, but
nonetheless useful and explicable, does not really enter Amm.'s head.
This is evidenced by the 2 examples given by him. Very obvious is this
in § 11, where the **bee** is indicated allegorically as the king. because of his
sting, while in reality this sign was used to indicate the king of Lower
Egypt.Amm., of course, here follows the generally held views of his time,
which he will have heard himself during his stay in Egypt, while he also
knew them from the literature. Very revealing is Plotin 5.8.6: ὡς ἄρα τις
καὶ ἐπιστήμη καὶ σοφία ἕκαστόν ἐστιν ἄγαλμα καὶ ὑποκείμενον καὶ
ἀθρόον καὶ οὐ διανόησις οὐδὲ βούλευσις', words, which he also links to
his following profound expositions, Diodorus 3.4.1-3 gives examples
like Amm. and the following explanation relating to Plotin: οὐ γὰρ ἐκ
τῆς τῶν συλλαβῶν συνθέσεως ἡ γραμματικὴ παρ' αὐτοῖς τὸν ὑποκείμενον
λόγον ἀποδίδωσιν, ἀλλ' ἐξ ἐμφάσεως τῶν μεταγραφομένων καὶ μεταφορᾶς
μνήμῃ συνηθλημένης.
Cf. et Plut. Isis et Osiris 354 E-F. Amm. will have made us of the **Hiero-
glyphica by Horapollon** (4th or 5th century A.D.), a work translated into
Greek (?) and/or other similar works. On hieroglyphs and **Horapollon** cf.
Woordenboek der Oudheid 6, 1971, 1406, **with lit.** (Vergote); Sabbah
A.M.II p.167 (note 27); Guide to the Egyptian collections in the British
Museum (1964) p.68 sq.; **J. M. A. Janssen,** Hierogliefen, Over lezen en
schrijven in Oud-Egypte (On reading and writing in Ancient Egypt)
Leiden, 1952 (in Dutch); **Erik Iversen,** The Myth of Egypt and Its Hiero-

glyphs in European Tradition (Copenhagen 1961); and further the more general works such as: **S. Morenz,** Die Begegnung Europas mit Ägypten[2], Basel, 1969; **J. R. Harris,** The legacy of Egypt[2], Oxford, 1971 (a collective work); **W. Wolf,** Funde im Ägypten, Göttingen, 1968 (deals among other things with the Rosette stone and its deciphering). Very instructive, finally, is 22.16.19-22, a lyrical glorification of the Egyptian wisdom and religion, with the words: et initia prima sacrorum caute tuentur **condita scriptis arcanis** (§ 30).

The modern edition of Horapollon is that of **F. Sbordone,** 1940, Napoli, (textcrit.edit. + comm.). **B. van de Walle** and **J. Vergote** gave a translation (in French) of Hor.'s text, in which they made use of **J. Janssen's study;** they have added a brief commentary: "Celui-ci concerne essentiellement les données égyptologiques contenues dans le texte d'Horapollon **et se propose notamment comme but d'identifier les signes hiéroglyphiques auxquels notre auteur fait allusion**". (Chronique d'Egypte, 35, 1943, p.39-89; ibid.p.199-239). Besides hieroglyphic commentary **Sbordone** also gives the correspondence with other Hellenistic sources. (Abbreviations in this comm. Sb. and v.d.W.-V.).

For the image of the **bee** (King of Lower-Egypt) cf. Guide etc. (op.cit.) p.246 sq.; for the **vulture** ibid.

Remark. Amm., who took the trouble to offer his readers the text of the hieroglyphs of the obeliscus mentioned by him, in a translation by **Hermapion,** could have concluded, from **this** translation, if he had not been misled by the fairytales about the Egyptians' script, that the contents of his obeliscus text were different from the **sapientia initialis** (§ 8), which were expressed, according to him, by the symbols of the bee, vulture, etc. His own words in § 9 do not fit in either with the above-mentioned opinion. The inscriptions are praises to the gods, devoted to them, and to kings. That with this the Egyptians **monstrabant promissa vel soluta regum vota,** ut ad aevi quoque sequentis aetates impetratorum (sc.regum) vulgatius perveniret memoria, as Amm. says, does not have to be in conflict with this. One should not be too surprised about Amm. being "blinded" by the material. Although since **Gelenius'** edition of 1533 the Greek obeliscus text was known, **no one** has ever thought to use it as a starting point for the deciphering of the hieroglyphs; if this had happened, the mystery of the Egyptian script would have been solved before Champollion and the Rosette stone.

p. 110. 6 *a* **formarum autem innumeras notas.** Cf.22.14.7: est enim Apis bos diversis genitalium **notarum figuris** expressus; 18.6.17: in vaginae internis

notarum figuris membranam repperimus scriptam. Hagendahl abund. (op.cit.I) p.196: "Hac ex origine factum est, ut genitivus ibi quoque apponeretur, ubi ad vim alterius vocis illustrandam nihil novi afferret". I do not think this statement is quite accurate for this passage and 18.6.17. In 17.4.8 I would translate: numerous signs (in the shape) of images. In 18.6.17: we found a parchment on which were written images (= signs) with (certain) meanings (code) (But it can also be translated as follows: with the signs of the **code,** as **notae** = code, cryptography). The stylistic similarity notwithstanding, every sentence should still be considered separately. Cf. ad 15.10.4 (= IV p.55); ad 17.4.2, p.109.7-8; ad 15.7.1 (= IV p.9); Hagendahl abund (op.cit.) p.192 sq. (**genit.identitatis**). Cf. et.Lucr.4.69: **formai** servare **figuram;** Cic.nat.deor.1.32 (90): sed hoc dico, non ab hominibus **formae figuram** venisse ad deos (quoted by E.Kraetsch, de abundanti dicendi genere Lucretiano, Berl.1881, p.53).

b **innumeras.** Cf. ad 14.11.29 (= II p.141). Not in Arn.adv.nat. (which does have **innumerabilitas);** Opt.Milev. (which does have **innumerabiles);** Veget.r.m. (has **innumerabilis).** The adj. does occur in Claud.

hieroglyphicas. Late Latin. Also used still by Macr.Sat.1.19.13; 1.21.12: p. 110. 6 Hunc Osirin Aegyptii ut solem esse asserant, quotiens **hieroglyphicis litteris** suis **exprimere** volunt, **insculpunt** sceptrum inque eo **speciem** oculi **exprimunt** et hoc signo Osirin **monstrant, significantes** hunc deum solem esse regalique potestate sublimen cuncta despicere, quia solem Jovis oculum appellat antiquitas. The underlined words also occur in Amm. §§ 7-10, purely by accident in my view, i.e. without being mutually influenced. Both authors, A. and M., draw on the same linguistic arsenal in these expositions. This quotation is also a fine example of the allegorical explanation of the hieroglyphs.

a **initialis sapientiae vetus insignivit auctoritas.** The adj. **initialis** late La- p. 110. 7-8 tin. The **adj.neutr.subst.** in the Scr.H.Aug.Capit.Aur.27.1: Orientalibus rebus ordinatis Athenis fuit et **initialia Cereris** addiit (viz. the Eleusinian mysteries). Cf.et. Koziol (op.cit.1) p.274; Georges 2.p.279. Not in Veget. r.m.Claud.Opt.Milev.Arn.adv.nat.

b **insignivit.** Also classical. Still a word of a higher linguistic level for: ornare, notare, distinguere etc. Cf. Krebs Antib.1 p.754 (not entirely correct); Georges 2. p.310. Found in Claud.Opt.Milev. Not in Veget.r.m. Arn.adv.nat.

c Cf.Cic. de Leg.2.7.(18): Sunt certa legum verba, Quinte, neque ita prisca, ut in **veteribus** XII sacratisque legibus; et tamen, quo plus **auctori-**

tatis habeant, paulo antiquiora, quam hic sermo est; de divin.1.18 (34): etsi ipsa sors contemnenda non est, si et **auctoritatem habet vetustatis.**

d Cf.Act.Apost.7.22: Et eruditus est Moyses **omni sapientia Aegyptiorum** et erat potens in verbis et in operibus suis.

IV, 9

p. 110. 8 *a* **volucrum.** "Literary" word for: **avium.** Also class. in prose, among others in Cic. But perhaps it means here: winged creature instead of: bird. **ferarumque etiam alieni mundi genera multa sculpentes. etiam alieni mundi** belongs to volucrum and ferarum. It is not quite clear what these last two words mean. As the text describes Egyptian hieroglyphs, they could be explained with: from a world different **from the Egyptian.** This does not quite satisfy me. The author or his source probably alludes to images like those of Anubis, Seth, Thoth, Horus, Phoenix, numerous demons, etc. The translation would then read: from a world different **from ours** (e.g. the underworld). I therefore do not agree with Ernestus (1773): "De partibus mundi universi minus cognitis, imperio Romano oppositis, qui **mundus** κατ' ἐξοχὴν dicitur".

b Cf.et.22.15.30: et **excisis** parietibus, **volucrum ferarumque genera multa sculpserunt** et animalium species **innumeras** multas, quas **hierograficas** litteras **appelarunt.** The repetition is striking. **animalium — multas** could be supplementary to the explanation given above (17.4.9, p.110.8*a*) viz. the wholly or partly theriomorphous gods and demons. Besides these, there are of course, many images of animals. These **animalia** (and a similar kind of allegorical explanation) also in Tac.Ann.11.14: Primi **per figuras animalium** Aegyptii sensus mentis effingebant - ea antiquissima monimenta memoriae humanae inpressa saxis cernuntur (= "these age-old proofs of the spiritual awareness of Man can be seen, engraved in stone", Meyer).

Cf.et.Cass.Var.3.51 (in a description of the **stadium**) Obeliscorum quoque prolixitates ad coeli altitudinem sublevantur; sed potior soli, inferior lunae dicatus est: **ubi sacra priscorum Chaldaicis signis, quasi litteris indicantur.** Evidently the limited knowledge has been obscured still more.

p. 110. 9 *a* ⟨**ut**⟩ **ad aevi quoque sequentis aetates.** Cf.30.4.6: et postea per varias **aevi sequentis** aetates (V sequentes -tis m 3) In our place: V sequentes WBG sequentis. Seyf. reads **-tis** in 30.4.6, **-tes** here, Sabbah **-tis** here. **aevum** = tempus is poet. and post-class. Although **both** versions can be defended, I see no reason to reject V's version. Cf.et.Hagend.abund. (op.cit.I) p.198; Ovid.metam.15.834 sq.:

Exemploque suo mores reget, inque **futuri**
Temporis aetatem venturorumque nepotum;
Min.Fel.38.7: Quid ingrati sumus, quid nobis invidemus, si veritas divinitatis **nostri temporis aetate** maturuit?; Prop.I.4.7: et quascumque tulit **formosi temporis aetas;** Cic.leg.1.4(13): Nam et a **primo tempore aetatis** iuri studere te nemini; Tac.: qui praesenti potentia credunt exstingui posse etiam **sequentis aevi** memoriam.

b ⟨**ut**⟩ ... **perveniret memoria.** Pervenire VEA Sabbah perveniente G perveniret Val.Clark Seyf.Rolfe. Vales. inserts **ut** after **aetates,** Clark, Rolfe, Seyf. before **ad.** Without **ut: pervenire memoriam** Sabbah. The insertion of **ut** does not seem necessary to me. But when one then reads **pervenire memoriam ... monstrabant,** as Sabbah does, the construction of the sentence is not only changed, but also the meaning. The translation of the text of Val., Clark, Rolfe, Seyf. should be: For by engraving many kinds of winged and wild animals, also those of another (strange) world, they wanted to demonstrate (or they demonstrated) the promises made, or already fulfilled by the **kings,** in order that (so that?) the memory of that which had been accomplished (by them) would be brought home also in a more general way to the generations to come. (thus **monstrabant** and **sculpentes** have the same subject). Translated Sabbah's version reads: By ... world, they wanted to demonstrate **(must** be translated conatively here) that the promises ... of the kings **also (even) reached more generally the memory of the age following the generations (periods) of their success (of that which they had achieved).** Apart from the fact that **memoria** is given by V G (not **memoriam**), I find both the construction of the period in Sabbah's translation as its meaning very strange. For it can not have been the **intention** of the founders of the obelisks to **demonstrate** that the promises (vows) ... reached the memory in a more general way, etc. That the inscriptions did reach the memory is a stated fact. It is so. The makers of the inscriptions demonstrate **by these** to the viewers the promises made by the kings. That is their real aim; **in order that (so that?) the memory (subject) ... would penetrate (reach) etc.** (according to Vales's version). In my opinion **perveniente** as given by G has almost the same meaning, while it makes intervention in the text by the insertion of **ut** unnecessary. As so often in Latin, the **part.praes.** has here a final of futural meaning. Cf.Hofm.-Leum.p.605; N.T.Marc.13.10 sq: Et in omnes gentes primum oportet praedicari Evangelium. Et cum duxerint vos **tradentes,** nolite praecogitare quid loquamini (καὶ ὅταν ἄγωσιν ὑμᾶς παραδιδόντες); Liv.30.11.6: Et, castris in propinquo positis, primo pauci equites ex tuto **speculantes** ab stationibus progredi; Hoogterp, Et. sur le latin du Cod.Bob. p.211 (414).

c It should be noted here that in this later period the **part.fut.** (and the **gerundivum**) are being used less and less and therefore have to be replaced. (cf. Svennung Pallad., op.cit.II, p.429 sq., with lit.).

p. 110.9 **aetates.** Cf. ad 15.8.21 (= IV p.44); 30.5.14: progressus ergo coacto gradu, in quantum res tulit, iugulataque **aetate promiscua;** Thes.s.v.; Krebs Antib.1 p.120.

p. 110.9 **impetratorum.** This version by V, has to be maintained. The version by BG is based on an error in writing or on a correction (**imperatorum**). **Impetratorum** is **n.plur.** of the part.perf.pass. of **impetrare** in the sense of: to get done, to achieve etc. (also class.), probably used **here** substantively (cf. Souter p.187: (late Latin)). I do not believe it is a genit. of **impetrator** (late Latin; cf. Georges 2 p.97; Heum.-Seckel p.250), although theoretically it is possible. Cf.et. ad 17.3.2, p.108.12*a*; ad 17.4.1, p.109.4*a*.

p. 110.10 **vulgatius.** Cf.15.3.6: haec augente **vulgatius** fama; 31.3.2: inpendentium tamen diritatem augente **vulgatius** fama (note the repetition, so frequent in Amm.). The adv. only in Amm.

p. 110.10-11 **monstrabant.** Simplex pro composito (cf. ad 16.5.6, p.76.12) Claus.I, similarly in 16.12.13: ardoremque pugnandi hastis inlidendo **scuta monstrantes.**

IV, 10

p. 110.11-14 The contents of this § are really contrary to the current symbolic explanations, because they show very clearly that the hieroglyphic script is a **system of writing** and nothing more (it is irrelevant here whether the contents of § 10 exactly agree with the facts).

p. 110.11 *a* **litterarum numerus praestitutus et facilis.** By this is meant the Latin or Greek alphabet, with a pre-determined number of letters, which can be easily handled.

b **praestitutus.** Certainly not a generally used word: among others: Terent.Cic.Nep.Liv.Curt.Amm. Quite often in the Digests. **Not** in Veget.r.m.Claud.Arn.adv.nat. Though found in Opt.Milev. In Amm. e.g.22.12.7.

exprimit. c.dat.: 14.1.6; 17.3.5; 28.1.56. Here: to express, in the general sense, which is late Latin, according to Krebs Antib.1 p.558; although I believe that this is hard to determine. Cf.Oros.1.5.3: et cum hoc loco nihil de incensis proper peccata hominum civitatibus quasi ignarus **expresserit.** (quoted by Krebs)

quidquid ... potest. "Correct" use of the indicativus, according to the classical grammar. Cf. ad 16.12.21. p.94.18-19a.

a **ita prisci quoque scriptitarunt Aegyptii.** Apparently Amm. is not aware of the fact that even in his time hieroglyphs were being used. The last hieroglyphic inscription comes from the island of Philae and dates from 394 A.D., under the rule of Theodosius I (379-395 A.D.). Already at that time the hieroglyphs had become a sort of cryptography, used by and readable to priests only. The **hieratic** and **demotic** script, which found its origin in the hieroglyphs, is not known to Amm. Thus his stay in the country has not contributed to better information on this facet of the Egyptian culture.
b **scriptitarunt.** Cf.Cic. de orat.2.12(51): Atqui, ne nostros contemnas, inquit Antonius, Graeci quoque ipsi sic **initio scriptitarunt,** ut noster Cato, ut Pictor, ut Piso. Cf.et. ad 14.6.8 (= I p.93): Intensiva.

a **set singulae ... verbis:** But each separate sign stood for separate substantiva and verba, Inaccurate and incomplete. Though the hierogl. script numbered many signs, ($\pm$ 700), **most of them occur in more than one function.** The signs may occur as ideograms (e.g. a book roll), have the value of 1,2 or 3 consonants, or be determinativa written behind the sound symbols, to indicate to which sort the word in question belongs.
b **nominibus.** t.t.gramm. = substantivum. Quint.Gramm. Cf. Varro 1. lat.8.4: de his Aristoteles orationis duas partes esse dicit: **vocabula** et verba, ut homo et equus, et legit et currit (vocabula bij Varro = nomina); Cic. de orat.3.49 (191): Consuetudo modo illa sit scribendi atque dicendi, ut sententiae **verbis** finiantur etc.

nonnunquam ... sensus. Cf. p.110.13-14a. Sensus t.t.gramm. Quint.Gramm. = sentence, period. Sometimes the meaning of **sentence** and **thought** merge or can not be separated, as in Stat.Silv.2.1.117 sq:
Maeonium sive ille senem Troiaeque labores
diceret aut casus tarde remeantis Ulixis:
ipse pater **sensus,** ipsi stupuere magistri.

IV, 11

p. 110. 14-15 *a* **cuius rei ... exemplis.** V scientia in his interim exemplum (sine lac.). Sabbah: cuius rei **scientia** in his interim duobus **exemplis.** Seyf.: cuius rei **scientiam** his interim duobus **exemplis.** Clark: like Seyf. Schneider (op. cit.I): cuius rei scientiam his interim duobus exemplis **expediam.** Eyssenh.: cuius rei **scientiam** his **expediam** duobus **exemplis.** Schneider: "Sed scite idem Eyssenh. verbum expediendi protulisse nobis videtur, nisi quod nos Ammiano tribuimus **exempl]is expedi[am,** quam lectionem illud **exemplum** occultare autumamus". Novák: cuius rei scientiam his interim duobus exemplis **monstrari sufficiet** (cf.25.2.5; 22.15.21; 31.14.3; 18.1.3; 22.9.10; 22.10.5; etc. Novák, Wiener Stud., 33,1911, p.307). Likewise: Rolfe.

There need not to be any objections against **interim.** cf.22.15.21: quorum sollertiae duo **interim** ostendi documenta sufficiet. In both places the meaning seems to me to be: **provisionally, for the time being,** rather than **meanwhile.** Cf. Krebs Antib.1 p.771; Dig.9.2.51.2: Multa autem iure civili contra rationem disputandi pro utilitate communi recepta esse innumerabilibus rebus probari potest: unum **interim** posuisse contentus ero. For **expedire** cf.14.4.2; 15.9.1; Krebs Antib.1 p.550 (withlit.); Vollmer ad Stat.Silv.1.4.68 p.289; Mulder ad Stat.Theb.2.240, p.180. Many editores are puzzled by **in,** as given by V. But **in** = by. Cf.Hofm.-Leum. p.438 (54α,η) and p.537 (131 b, αβ), both §§ with lit.; Souter p.190; Bauer, Wörterb.z.N.T.², p.404. Cf.et.ad 17.2.1, p.107.12*a* (**in** = to the number of) and 27.4.4: humanumque sanguinem **in** ossibus capitum cavis bibentes avidius (not quite comparable. Grecism? cf.ἐν κέρατι, ἐν λαγύνῳ πίνειν). Finally Grandgent (op.cit.I) 92.p.46.

b Of all conjectures I believe that of Sabbah to be the best, because it keeps closest to the text as given by V. A verb should not be supplemented. The omission of forms of **esse** is seen more often, and especially in Amm. Cf. Blomgren p.68 sq.; ad 17.1.13, p.106.23-24 *b*. **Exemplum** instead of **exemplis** (after his duobus) may have been caused by an abbreviation written in the manuscript of which V is a copy. Sabbah refers to Lindsay, Notae latinae p.426. When the omission of a form of **esse** is found to be too incredible, the insertion of **expediam** seems to me preferable.

p. 110. 15-16 *a* **per vulturem naturae vocabulum pandunt.** For **pandere** cf. ad 15.8.16 (= IV p.40). Places not mentioned there: 18.6.16; 19.12.3; 22.12.7; 28.6.28; 31.1.4. For **vocabulum** ad 16.12.25, p.95.11*a*. Here, however, it means: **concept.** (notio, ἰδέα).

b We find here once more the same symbolic explanation as discussed above (17.4.8-11, p.110.6-20). The image of the vulture reveals the idea of Nature, i.e. Nature in its true being, according to the neo-platonic point of view. Cf.Horap.1.11, 12; Sb.p.26; v.d.W.-V.p.50; ad 16.5.5, p.76.6-7.

IV, 11

a **quia mares nullos posse inter has ălites invenĭri, rationes memorant physicae.** The **hyperbaton** (cf. ad 17.1.6, p.105.21*a*) posse ... inveniri, metri causa: claus.III.   p. 110. 16-17

b The peculiar biological theory uttered here has its origin in the belief that the female vultures are impregnated by the wind. G. Zoëga (De origine et usu obeliscorum, p.446 sq., a⁰ 1797; quoted by Wagner) compares the scarabeus with the vulture (the scarabei have no females: Ael.hist.anim. 10.15): "Hos enim rotundam figuram effingere statuebant e stercore bubulo et semine huic immisso foetum sine femina procreare. Hoc igitur voluerunt mystae Aegyptii: uti scarabaeus **activum** rerum principium denotet, sic vulturem **passivum,** e quorum coniunctione omnia, procreentur". Cf.et.Plut.Aetia Rom.93; Aelian. de nat.anim.2.46; Horap.1.11 (quoted by Wagner).

c **alites:** sacral word; also poet. and post-class. As **adj.** 31.7.7: **aliti** velocitate regressae (vastatoriae manus sc.) Cf.Hagend.St.A.p.42; Thes. s.v.; Krebs Antib.1. p.136.

d **rationes physicae:** natural history (Rolfe); sciences physiques (Sabbah). **ratio** has here the meaning we often find in Cic.: principle, theory, system, science, scientific knowledge. The plural can be normal, although in my view the **plur.poet.** would also suitable here (cf. ad p.107.14-15*b*). Probably here a Cicero reminiscence: nat.deor.2.21 (54): ut plerique dicunt **physicae rationis** ignari.

perque speciem... regem... ostendentes. Cf. ad 17.4.8-11, p.110.6-20. I do not believe that the passage quoted by Seyf. (Seneca, de clem.1.19.2-3), a moralising dissertation on the **rex** apium, refers to this passage, as it says, among other things, rex ipse **sine** aculeo est; while here a bee (and a king) **with** sting is discussed. Cf.et.Horap 1.62; Sb. p.125; v.d.W.-V. p.86.   p. 110. 17-19

speciem. Cf. ad 17.4.7, p.110.5*a* and *b*.   p. 110. 17

mella. Plur.poet. Used not only by poets. but also by prose writers, usually metri causa. Cf.Hagend.St.A.p.78. with many examples. mēllā cõn-fĭcfĕntĭs: claus.III.   p. 110. 17

p. 110. 18 **moderatori.** Cf.26.1.3: potestatum civilium militiaeque rectores... **moderatorem** quaeritabant diu exploratum et gravem. In Claud. Not in Veget.r.m.Opt.Milev.Arn.adv.nat.

p. 110. 18 **iucunditate** = friendly, pleasant disposition.

p. 110. 18-19 **his signis ostendentes.** V signibus. V m 3 signis. E G signis. Her.signi⟨s sollemni⟩bus. Novák his ⟨rerum in⟩signibus ostendentes. N. refers to 15.6.3: fortunae superioris **insignia;** 17.11.4; 17.12.20; 18.6.22; 18.8.5; 21.9.8; 31.12.10; 14.11.3. N's objections against **signis** are partly of a metric nature: **signis ostendentes** gives the following clausala: $\overset{\text{x}}{\smile} \sim \sim \sim$ $\overset{\text{x}}{\smile} \sim$. But this objection is not valid. (cf. ad 16.12.27, p.95.19a; ad 16. 12.28, p.95.22).
But I am not sure if one should read **signis** (Sabbah) or **insignibus** (Seyf.). It is quite well possible that **signibus** is the right form. Mixing up declinations has become such an ordinary phenomenon at this time, that we may very well assume that Amm. would make "mistakes" like that. Also in our case the form **insignibus** may have been of influence. Cf. Oder Mulom.Chir.p.301 sq.; Hedfors (op.cit.I) p.90, 184, 199; Hofm.-Leum. 181 C 3e, p.261; Ernout (op.cit.I) p.27 Anm.

IV, 12-17

p. 110. 20- p. 112. 3 *a* To convenience the reader we give here a list of the obelisci, mentioned in the §§ 12-17 of 17.4.
1. In 10 B.C. taken from Heliopolis by Augustus. Erected by Psammetichus II (595-589 B.C.). Placed on the Campus Martius. Dug out in 1748 and erected in 1789 by Pope Pius VI on the Piazza di Monte Citorio. Provided with hieroglyphs. (Campus Martius: regio IX).
2. Taken by Augustus in 10 B.C. from Heliopolis. Hierogl. inscriptions from the time of Sethos I and Ramses II (1318-1237 B.C.). Placed in the Circus Maximus. In 1589 erected by Sixtus V on the Piazza del Popolo. Provided with hieroglyphs. Liv.39.7.8. (Circus Maximus: regio XI).
3. Taken away from Thebe in ± 330 A.D. by Constantinus I (307-337). Brought to Rome by Constantius II (337-361) and erected in the Circus Maximus. Found in 1587 and placed in 1588 by Sixtus V on the Piazza di S.Giovanni in Laterano. From the temple of Ammon, founded by Tuthmos III (1504-1450 B.C.). Provided with hieroglyphs.
4. Brought by Cornelius Gallus from Heliopolis to Alexandria. Taken to Rome by Caligula (37-41 A.D.). Placed in the Circus Gai et Neronis. In 1586 erected by Sixtus V on the Piazza di S.Pietro. Name: Obeliscus

Vaticanus. No hieroglyphs. Cf.Plin. N.H. 16.76.2; C.I.L.VI.882. (Circus Gai et Neronis regio XIV). Cf. et Sabbah II p.170 (38).
5. From the Horti Sallustiani. Antique Roman copy (200 A.D.) of 2, with hieroglyphs (copy). Now in the Piazza della Trinita dei Monti, where it was erected in 1789 by Pius VI. (Horti Sallustiani: regio VI).
6. Erected in 79 A.D. by Vespasianus (69-79 A.D.) in front of the Mausoleum of Augustus. Erected in 1587 by Sixtus V on the Piazza dell' Esquilino before the choir of the S.Maria Maggiore. Without hieroglyphs. (Mausoleum of Augustus: regio IX).
7. Erected by the emperor Vespasianus in 79 A.D. in front of the Mausoleum of Augustus. Erected in 1787 by Pius VI on the Piazza del Quirinale. Without hieroglyphs.

b Amm. contents himself with a rough enumeration. Among those not mentioned are the 4 obelisci erected by Domitianus (81-96 A.D.) and the obelisci of the Iseum and Serapeum (regio IX), several of which still exist to this day. Cf. **O.Marucchi,** Gli obelischi egiziani di Roma (Bulletino della Commissione Archeologica Communale di Roma, 1896, p.83-115; 129-173; 250-288; 1897, p.196-227); **J.J.Gloton,** Les obelisques romains de la Renaissance au néoclassicisme (Mélanges d'archéologie et d'histoire de l'École française de Rome, t.73, 1961, p.437-469; **Richter** Top. (op.cit.I) p.243 sq. (with lit.); p.377 sq.; R.E.17.2.1937, c.1712 **(van Buren); Sabbah** A.M.II p.167 sq.; Seyf.A.M.I p.305 sq.; Plin.N.H. 36.14 sq.

The Iseum and Serapeum is mentioned in the socalled Notitia (the description of the regiones of Rome), as well as in the Curiosum (urbis Romae regionum XIV cum breviariis suis). The Notitia dates from 354 A.D., the Curiosum from $\pm$ 357 A.D. Although Amm. must have known Rome well, I think it highly probable that, besides the knowledge he acquired while walking (?) through Rome, (and it is continuously evident that he kept his eyes wide open), he also made use of maps and/or descriptions as those in the Notitia and the Curiosum. This is not surprising: for at that time Rome was abundantly as full of places of interest as it is today, truly a **templum mundi totius.**

c That the Romans seem to have had no qualms about carting-off the obelisci (the only religious scruples reported have been Augustus'), and that Amm. does not express any objections either, may be saddening, but unfortunately a fact.

Finally we would like to draw attention to 1° an extremely comprehensive and beautifully illustrated work, viz. **A.Roullet.** The Egyptian and Egyptianizing monuments of Imperial Rome, Leiden, 1972, where the **obelisks** are discussed on p.43 sq. and p.67 sq. and secondly the **Isea** p.23 sq., p.347 (map), p.352 (map). The aforesaid maps refer to the **Iseum and Serapeum,** just next to the S.Maria sopra Minerva. 2⁰ to **E.Iversen,** Obelisks in Exile I. The Obelisks of Rome, 1968.

IV, 12

p. 110. 20 *a* **Sufflantes adulatores. Sufflare:** to inflate, to make conceited. (wrongly translated by Seyf.). No "ordinary" verb. Plaut.Cato.Varro.Persius.Plin. N.H.Petr.Mart.Gell. Marc.Emp. In Gell.7.14 (de tribus dicendi generibus) **sufflatus** is almost synonymous with **tumidus** (also mentioned there). Not in Claud.Veget.r.m.Opt.Milev.Arn.adv.nat. Cf.et.16.12.68 sq.: **inflabant** ex usu imperatorem... quocirca magniloquentia elatus **adulatorum;** 15.5.37: Constantius ... magniloquentia **sufflabatur adulatorum.**
b **adulatores.** Cf. ad 16.12.69, p.102.22.

p. 110. 20 **ex more.** Cf. ad 15.1.2 (= III p.8); ad 14.10.3 (ex usu) (= II p.100).

p. 110. 21-22 *a* **ab Heliupolitana civitate.** ab Heliopolitana EBG (Heliu-G). Like G: Clark.Rolfe.Seyf. V Heliupolitam. Likewise Sabbah: "**Heliupolita,** donné par V (Clark n'a pas remarqué le point annulant le **m** final) peut être maintenu comme l'ablativ de forme grecque de l'adjectif **Heliupolites** (employé par Pl.N.H.5.9: Heliopoliten nomum)". I agree with Sabbah, as it can reasonably be assumed that to Amm. a "Greek", this form flowed easily from his pen.
b **Heliopolis.** 12 kilometers North East of Cairo, place of worship for the sun-god Re. Frequently visited by the Greeks. Now a pitiful small village with only one obelisk left of Sesostris I (1971-1928 B.C.) This village Matarîjeh is all that remains from what has been carted off to all parts of the world, as far as the art treasures are concerned, and to other Arab villages, where the building materials were taken. The fame of the city and its priests was considerable. **Heliopolis** was situated in Augustamnica II, one of the provinciae of the diocesis Aegyptus (for the division cf. ad 14.7.21 = II p.51). A bishop's seat. But the metropolis is **Leontopolis.** From this the decline of the city is already apparent. The fragments of a stone slab, originally from H. and now in the Egyptian Museum at Turin, make it possible to reconstruct the groundplan of a temple, in the third court of which there is a chapel or altar with the name "house of **Atum** of the **sycomore**" (In H.Atum is linked with Re). This sycomore has eternal life. At Matarîjeh the tree of Maria is standing, a **sycomore,** and according to tradition a far descendant of the tree, under which the Holy

Family is said to have rested during the flight from Egypt. During the Middle Ages and later this tree was visited by many pilgrims. Cf.et. Petrus Diac. (a⁰ 1137) Geyer p.115; Woordenboek der Oudheid (1970) 5.p.1343 (with lit. Vergote).

c **civitate** = town. Cf. ad 16.2.8, p.73.14; ad 16.2.12, p.73.27-p.74.1 **(territorium)**; Krebs Antib.1p.286 (with lit.); Pighi Stud.Amm.p.139 sq.; Souter p.53; ad 16.12.59, p.101.9 **(territorium)**; Heum.-Seckel p.71 (often in judic.lit: 1. **municipality,** as a legal concept and 2. **town,** as a local concept).

Circo maximo ob.2. For the **C.max.** cf. ad 15.5.34, p.54.15 (= III p.122); Woordenboek der Oudheid 3 (1967) p.663 (with lit., Nuchelmans). In Amm.'s time still in all its glory.

alter in Campo locatus est Martio ob.1. For the hyperbaton cf. ad 17.1.6, p.105.21*a*. For the **C. Martius** cf. Richter Top. (op.cit.I) p.222 sq. (with lit.); Veg.r.m.1.10 (= Lang p.14): Ideoque Romani veteres, quos tot bella et continuata pericula ad omnem rei militaris erudierant artem, **campum Martium** vicinum Tiberi delegerunt, in quo iuventus post exercitium armorum sudorem pulveremque dilueret ac lassitudinem cursus natandi labore deponeret; Claud.18.435 sq.: p. 110. 22-23

Per te, perque tuos obtestor, Roma, triumphos
Nesciat hoc Tibris, numquam poscentibus (sc. consulatum) olim
Qui dare Dentatis annos (sc. consulatus) Fabiisque solebat.
Martius eunuchi (sc. Eutropii) repetet suffragria **campus?**

(Gesner: "Et iam ille Martius, non vano nomine, campus repetet, recitari audiet, suffragia Eunucho data?")

recens. Cf. Fesser p.48 (op.cit.I): "**recens** als Adverbium in Verbindung mit einem **part.perf.pass.** findet sich im Altlat., Sall. übernahm diesen Gebrauch, ferner Liv.u.Tac., der den Gebrauch auf Adjectiva ausdehnte, die den Sinn von Partizipien haben. Amm. gebraucht sehr oft **recens** in Verbindung mit einem part.perf.pass.; wenn er aber an einer Stelle (14.11.28) recens zu einem **part.praes.** setzt, so zeigt sich auch hier, dasz er sein Latein sich nur äuszerlich angelernt hat". (with lit.). This last conclusion is 1⁰ premature, as it seems very likely to me that the last-mentioned usage is found in more later authors, and 2⁰ incorrect, because a deviating use of a word can have other causes than a poor knowledge of Latin, such as the author's desire to be original, different etc. p. 110. 23

Note: νεωστί is also connected in Greek with a **part.praes.** This may have "tempted" Amm. unconsciously to the use as noted above.
Cf. et Souter p.342; J. H. H. Schmidt, Handb.d.lat.u.gr. Synonymik (1889) p.489 (on the meaning of **recens**); Hofm.-Leum. p.197.200; Krebs Antib. 2 p.478 (with lit.).

p. 110. 24 **territus:** to be linked with Octavianus Augustus, as is obvious from the text a little further on.

p. 110. 24 **conctrectare.** Cf.23.6.35: hostiam; 24.4.27: virginem; 17.9.5: non aurum neque argentum; 22.16.22: putealem limum contrectans. Often with an unfavourable meaning, as in the first 2 examples. Not in Claud.Veget. r.m.Opt.Milev. It is found in Arn.adv.nat. In judic.lit. especially: to appropriate, to embezzle, to steal.
movere = to remove from its stand.

p. 110. 24 **dĭscant qui ignŏrant.** For this clausula cf. ad 16.10.16, p.87.8*b*; ad 16.11.1, p.88.18-19*a*. For the **homoioteleuton** cf. ad 15.10.4 (= IV p.56) and ad 15.13.4 (= IV p.81).

p. 110. 25 *a* **veterem principem translatis aliquibus hunc intactum ideo praeterisse.** The main point is found in the partic.: **intactum:** he left this obelisk untouched and passed it by. Cf. ad 17.3.5, p.108.20*a*.
b **principem.** Cf. ad 16.12.67, p.102.16.
c **aliquibus.** The plural forms of **aliquis** are rare in class.lit. (= nonnullis). For the use of **aliquis** cf. Grandgent (op.cit.I) 13,71; Hoogterp, Cod.Bob. 314, p.164; Riemann (op.cit.I) p.167 sq; Svennung Pall. (op.cit.II) p.319 (for the plural); ad 16.11.8, p.89.19-20.

p. 110. 26 *a* **Deo Soli speciali munere dedicatus.** For the dedicatio of the obelisci cf. ad 17.4.6, p.110.2-3.
b = by way of a special gift dedicated to. For the **abl.modi** cf. ad 14.1.6 (= I p.62); ad 17.12.22, p.94.26*a;* ad 17.12.43, p.98.15-16*b;* Hoogterp Cod.Bob.117, p.95; idem Les vies des pères du Jura 63, p.52 (with lit.). For the **genit.qualitatis** ad 16.12.9, p.92.10-11*a;* Hoogterp, Les vies des pères du Jura 46, p.46 (with lit.); idem Cod.Bob.110*b*, p.88.
c **speciali.** The adj. is post-class. and late Latin X **generalis** (14.11.25: generali potentia). Not in Claud.Veget.r.m.Arn.adv.nat., though it is found in Opt.Milev. Cf. Krebs Antib.2 p.592 (with Lit.); Souter p.383; ad 16.6.2, p.78.14 **(specialiter).**

d **dedicatus.** This part., as well as the following part. **fixus,** contain the essential part of the sentence, while tamquam ... eminebat tells of a less relevant characteristic of this obelisk. For the reason why Augustus did not take this away, was not: quod ... tamquam apex omnium eminebat, but the very circumstance that it was devoted to Sol and stood within the temple domain, which could not be desecrated. Cf.ad 17.3.5, p.108, 20*a*.

a **fixusque intra ambitiosi templi delubra.** Probably **delubra** is a plur. poet. and **templi delubra** a fine example of the genit. identitatis (cf. ad 17.2.1, p.107.14-15*b* and ad 17.4.8, p.110.6*a* respectively). Cf.et. ad 14.8.14 (= II p.83); ad 16.10.14, p.86.23*a;* Hagend.St.Amm. p.90 sq. (c.annot.); Amm.22.8.25: stabilem **domiciliis sedem** (NBG) nusquam repperientes (comparable place); Claud.48.24:

p. 110. 26-
p. 111. 1

Mavors, sanguinea qui cuspide verberat urbes,
Et Venus, humanas quae laxat in otia curas,
Aurati **delubra** tenent communia **templi.**

Delubrum occurs fairly often in Claud.; not in Veget.r.m.Arnob.adv.nat. Opt.Milev.

b **ambitiosus.** For the use of this adj. in Amm.cf. ad 14.7.6 (= II p.22) = spatiosus. Cf.Claud.8. 593 sq.:

Quae tantum potuit digitis mollire rigorem
Ambitiosa colus?

Does not occur in Veget.r.m.Arn.adv.nat.Opt.Milev. Cf.et. ad 15.5.24 (= III p.109); ad 14.6.9 (= I p.93).

c **fixus.** Although **figere** is a t.t. for the hanging up of votive offerings, tropaea, etc. **this** meaning does not seem to me to fit here (Cf. Drakenborch ad Liv.38.43.11 = XI p.230). It is used here in the same sense as in Cic.Verr.5.6 (12): crucem fixeras and in Verg.Georg.4.115: figat humo plantas, i.e. to drive in, implant and erect, or: to erect while implanting somewhat pregnantly, therefore). Cf.et. ad p.111.22: **infigitur.**

contingi. Here with the well-known meaning of: to desecrate, to violate. Cf.et.15.4.4; 23.6.24; 30.9.2 **(contagium);** Hagend.St.Amm. p.28.

p. 111. 1

a **tamquam apex omnium eminebat.** Sabbah: "où il se dressait comme le **sommet de l'ensemble".** This is the correct translation, in my view. Not: "Dort ragte er empor, gleichsam als die Spitze der Welt" (Seyf). For this obeliscus (3), 32.50 meters high, rises high above all other columns, statues etc. in the sacred temple room. Also the colour (red granite) will have contributed to this. Thus **omnium** is a neutr.plur. (but omnium (obeliscorum sc.)) can be justified.

p. 111. 1

97

b **apex** has a literal, as well as a figurative meaning. Cf.Cic. Cato M.17 (61): **Apex** est autem senectutis auctoritas; Claud.5 (In Ruf.II) 4 sq.:
Iamque tuis Stilicho, Romana potentia curis
Et **rerum** commissus **apex.**
Ibid.10 (De nupt.Hon. et Mar.) 213 sq.:
Ast alii thalamum docto componite textu
Stamine gemmato, picturatisque columnis
Aedificetur **apex.** (of the canopy of the marriagebed, borne by columns). The subst. occurs fairly often in Claud., while it is also found in Arn. adv.nat. and Opt.Milev. Not in Veget.r.m. In judic.lit. it is used in its usual meaning; and particularly in the Cod.Iust. with the meaning: **letter writing from the emporor:** apices augusti, sacri etc. (cf. Heum-Seckel p.35). Cf.et. ad 15.5.12 (= III p.89).

c For **eminere**, very frequent in Amm., Cf. Naumann (op.cit.I) p.15 sq. (where this place is not mentioned).

IV. 13

p. 111, 1-
p. 111, 5 When Constantinus I has this obeliscus taken away from Thebe, he has already been a Christian for a long time, at least in name. Bur Amm. is not a Christian. **Religio** should mean, therefore, at least to Amm.'s way of thinking: the religious feelings of the Egyptians. According to A. he was not offending these: **recte** existimans. But, though Const. and Amm. may have believed this, it is very clear to us that such temple robbery (carried out on a large scale) did indeed hurt the Egyptians' feelings, that is of the large numbers who were not yet Christians. For that matter, what interest could the latter have in Rome, which to them lay so infinitely far away? A.M.'s reasoning here is more Roman than the Romans and he makes no effort to understand the mentality of this completely different and old civilisation. Cf.et. ad 17.4.12-17*c*.

p. 111, 2 **parvi ducens.** Cf.Cic. de fin.2.8 (24): sed quia parvi id duceret. Cf.et. for the **genit.pretii** Hofm.-Leum.p.400,28; Svennung (op.cit.II) p.207; p.212 sq.; Kalb, Röm.Rechtsspr. § 32, p.39; eiusd. Das Jur.lat.p.48, note 2.

p. 111, 2-3 *a* **avulsam hanc molem sedibus suis.** Cf.23.6.24: (23) post hanc Seleucia, **ambitiosum** opus Nicatoris Seleuci (24). qua per duces Veri Caesaris (ut ante rettulimus) expugnata, **avulsum sedibus** simulacrum Comaei Apollinis, perlatumque Romam, in aede Apollinus Palatini ... **collocarunt.**
sedibus is a clear example of the plur.poet.
Locare (§ 12) and **collocare** are used without any difference in meaning.

(For the pl.poet.cf. ad 17.2.1, p.107.14-15*b*). Cf.et. ad 17.1.11, p.106. 14*b*.

b **avulsam.** Cf.14.9.6: qui ... **avulsam sedibus** linguam suam ... inpegit; 29.5.42: caput tamen eius **avulsum** residuo integro corpore ... urbi inlatum est ante dictae.

committere in religionem. Cf.Cic.Verr.1.2 (6): Multa enim et **in** deos et in homines impie nefarieque **commisit;** Dig.18.3.8: Respondit secundum ea quae proponerentur non **commisisse in legem** venditionis emptorem (more examples in Heum.-Seckel p.80). **Comm.in** not in Claud.Veget.r.m. Opt.Milev.Arn.adv.nat. In Amm.15.5.28 (cf.III p.112). p. 111. 3

ablatum uno templo. Thus with the abl. only 17.13.30: plus aestimantes creare quam **auferre barbaris** regem. With **ex**: 26.10.5: quod **abstulit** Serenianum **e medio** (set phrase). p. 111. 3-4

miraculum. Here used in a peculiar way = ± object of interest. Cf.et. ad 16.10.13, p.86.14-15; Krebs Antib.2 p.87; Souter p.253; Claud.24 (De cons.Stil.III) 223 sq.: p. 111. 4

Magnarum nec parcus opum geminare profundas
Distulit impensas: sed post **miracula** castris
Edita vel genero, Romae maiora reservat.

(gener = Honorius; castris = comitatus; cf. ad 16.8.1, p.80.24. This is an allusion to events of a special nature, costly games, which Stilicho had given, while consul). Comparable also Arn.adv.nat.5.25 (= Reiffersch. p.196): vertit Baubo artes et quam (sc.Cererem) serio non quibat allicere **ludibriorum** statuit exhilarare **miraculis** (= by an extraordinary undressing-act).

Romae. Not a dat.! Locativus. Cf. ad 15.5.34 (= III p.122); ad 14.11.21 (= II p.137). p. 114. 4

sacraret sc.deis. A.M. does not seem to have been impressed, and rightly so, by Constantine's Christianity. p. 111.4
sacraret = dedicaret, without difference in meaning (§ 12).

id est in templo mundi totius. Typical polytheïstic thinking. But it is true, that when Amm. was writing this, Rome was still shining in all its unbelievable beauty. What Rome means, with its aurea templa (Claud.28.1), not only to the Romans, but also to the barbarians, can be read in the p. 111. 4

fictitious speech, or rather monologue given by **Alaric** in the panegyric on the 6th cons. of Honorius (404 B.C.), 28.291 sq.:

Haec ego continuum si per iuga tendere cursum
(Ut prior iratae fuerat sententia mentis)
Iam desperata valuissem luce; quid ultra?
Omnibus oppeterem fama maiore perustis:
Et certe moriens propius te, Roma, viderem.

(Gesner: Si **desperata iam luce** vitae huius, felicitatis certe, potuissem Italiam. quam longa est, per Apennini iuga percurrere, quid profecissem? Hoc certe ut gloriosius et propius Romam perirem).

To Amm., Claud.Veget.etc. **Rome** is the centre, not **Roma nova** = Constantinopolis, which is more of a Christian city, and moreover really a Greek one. Cf.et. ad 14.6.1 (= I p.131: **urbs aeterna**); ad 16.10.13, p.86. 13*a*.

p. 111. 5 **perpessus est.** Constructed with the acc.c.inf., as, among others, in Plaut. Terent.Ovid.Cat.Vopisc.Verg.Aen.12.643 sq:

Excindine domos (id rebus defuit unum)
Perpetiar, dextra nec Drancis dicta refellam?

The partic. also in Claud.1.258 sq.:

Et Phaetonteae **perpessus** damna ruinae
Eridanus ...

The verb also occurs in Arn.adv.nat. Not in Veget.r.m.Opt.Milev. For the **acc.c.inf.** cf.Hofm.-Leum.p.585,170. For the **acc.c.inf. (in general)** cf. 14.5.3 (= I p.85); 14.5.7 (= I p.87); 14.7.14 (= II p.41); 14.10.14 = (II p.110); 14.10.14 (= II p.111); 14.11.4 (= II p.118); 14.11.19 (= II p.130); 14.11.34 (= II p.145); 15.5.14 (= III p.91); 15.5.26 (= III p.111); 15.6.1 (= IV p.6); 16.12.35, p.96.24; 17.1.1, p.104.4; 17.1.2, p.104.6-7*a*; 17.1.2, p.105.1*d*; ad 15.7.2 (= IV p.10).

a **dum translationi pararentur utilia.** The construction with **dum** here according to the classical rule. Cf. ad 17.4.4, p.109.14; Hoogterp Cod. Bob.380, p.193; eiusd.V.d.P. du Jura p.78, § 163.4 (with lit).

b **translationi** = transport. Cf.14.10.2: dumque ibi diu moratur, commeatus opperiens, quorum **translationem** ex Aquitania... prohibebant... In spite of Cic.off.1.14(43): Quare L.Sullae et C.Caesaris **pecuniarum translatio** a iustis dominis ad alienos non debet liberalis videri, **translatio** is not the usual word for transport, in the older and class. Latin, but **vectura** (or sometimes **portatio**) or **commeatus**. Translatio (= transport) is used in the Cod.Iust. and the Cod.Theod. (cf.Heum.-Seckel p.592).

Cf.Cod.Theod.16.2.15: ut praeter ea iuga et professionem quae ad Ecclesiam pertinet ad universa munia sustinenda **translationesque faciendas** omnes Clerici debent adtineri (sc. of tax payments, a compulsory public service = **parangaria)**. This law dates from the year 360 A.D. But concerning the same subject in Cod.Theod.16.2.40 (a⁰ 412 A.D.): Nulla pontium instauratio, nulla **translationum sollicitudo** gignatur (= no obligation whatever, responsibility for forced transport; see above). From these two last passages one has to conclude that in this period **translatio** is a t.t. For other meanings in late Latin cf. Souter p.426. The word does not occur in Veget.r.m.Claud.Arn.adv.nat.Opt.Milev.

utilia. Cf. ad 17.3.2, p.108.12*a;* 17.4.1, p.109.4*a*. p. 111. 5

convecto. From reading 14.10.1-5 it appears that **(commeatus** sc.) **trans-** p. 111. 5 **latio** and (annonae) **convectio** are used synonymously. The soldiers are discontented about the lack of victuals: alimentis nondum ex usu **translatis** (§ 3). Finally the foodstuffs arrive: deinde cibo abunde **perlato** (§ 5).
For **translatio** cf. previous note. Thus **convectio** also means transport and **convehere**: to transport; for nothing is brought to it or brought together. There is only the one obeliscus. **Transferre** and **perferre**, too, are practically synonymous, unless in **perferre** one wants to see the nuance of: to bring, carry to a certain fixed destination.

alveum. Alvus does not seem to occur in Amm., contrary to alveus = p. 111. 6 alvus (22.15.18). Cf. Blomgren (op.cit.II) p.150 sq.; Thes.I 1791.

Nili. Cf. ad 14.4.3 (= I p.123); ad 14.8.5 (= II p.64). p. 111. 6

proiectoque = unloaded, brought on land. The idea of: to throw, has p. 111. 6 been completely lost here. And indeed, it does not fit in with such a giant obelisk. T.t. or vulgarism? The meaning to throw in, to push in, is contained in **proiectare.** (cf. ad 14.5.7 = I p.87).

a **Alexandriae.** For the **locat.** cf. ad 17.4.13, p.111.4. But 15.7.7: apud p. 111. 6 Alexandriam, with the same meaning.
b A. lies in the provincia Aegyptus I of the diocesis Aegyptus (for the division cf. ad 14.7.21 = II p.51). Seat of a patriarch (cf. Pieper tab.4 and 8; lit. p.32, column 3). Mentioned in Not.Urb.Const.X: Horrea Alexandrina (in the regio IX); Lat.Pol.Silv.X: Aegyptus ipsa, in qua est Alexandria; Tab.Peut.IX.3 (with illustration of the Pharus); S.Silv.

Peregr. Geyer p.41.50; Anton.Plac.Geyer p.189: Inde (viz. from the residence of "sanctus Mennas") ascendentes in navicula per stagnum (Mareotis lacus?) venimus Alexandriam. In ipso stagno vidimus multitudinem corcodrillorum. A. civitas splendida, populus levissimus, sed amatores peregrinorum; haereses multae. Ibi enim requiescit sanctus Athanasius (cf.A.M.15.7.7 = IV p.19) (Ant.Plac. writing $\pm$ 570 A.D.); Adamnanus ($\pm$ 670 A.D.) Geyer p.278-283: De Alexandriae situ et Nilo flumine; Baeda (beginning of the 8th century A.D.) Geyer p.321: De situ A. et Nilo; Ant.Plac. Geyer p.167 (**Alexandrini** come to the Jordan for the feast of the theophania); Anton.Aug.Itin.Wess.p.57,70; 124,154; Hierocl.Synecd.Wess.p.723; **Strabo** 17.1.8-10; **Dio Chrys.** orat.32 (on the population); **Amm.Marc.** 22.16.7 sq.: Alexandria enim vertex omnium est civitatum, quam multa nobilitant et magnifica; 26.10.19; 22.11 (**Alexandrini**); Pomp. Mela 1.9.60; Ravenn.2.21.2 (= Schnetz p.33); Guid.geogr.92 (= Schnetz p.133); **Expos.totius mundi et gent.** 35,62; 34,37 (with comm. by Rougé in his edit., 1966, p.262 sq.; p.267 sq.; p.257 sq.). These chapters by an author of 359 (?) A.D. are certainly worth reading, as well as those of the 3 aforementioned underlined authors. Also in late Antiquity a very large, lively and noisy city, with large heathen and Jewish minorities. In 495 part of the Eastern Roman Empire. In 642 A.D. conquered by the Arabs. Cf.et.W.d.Oudh.1 (1965), p.115 sq. (with lit. Vergote, Bartelink).

p. 111. 6 *a* **navis amplitudinis antehac inusitatae aedificata est sub trecentis remigibus agitanda.**
Cf.15.11.13: provincia Aquitanica **amplitudine civitatum** admodum culta (= amplis civitatibus); 25.2.6: (lumen) **amplitudine** vero **spatiorum** (= amplis spatiis) exinanitum in aerium solvitur corpus; 29.5.7: recepto itaque tardius milite, quem **amplitudo maris** (morabatur?); 23.6.87: capturas autem difficiles (sc. margaritarum) et periculosas et **amplitudines pretiorum** (= high prices) illa efficit ratio quod...; 30.4.3: definit **amplitudo Platonis** (= the exalted Plato; cf.Cic.Orat.1(5): nec vero Aristotelem in philosophia deterruit a scribendo **amplitudo Platonis** ∼ Plin.ep.1.10.5: frequenter etiam **Platonicam** illam sublimitatem et **latitudinem** effingit); 23.6.35: (magi) verum aucti paulatim in **amplitudinem gentis** solidae concesserunt et nomen (= but gradually they have become larger (increased) and grown to a numerous and dense population with its own name). In late Latin also titled (of emperors and high state officials cf.Heum.-Seckel p.31, Souter p.14.
b **sub.** Here the preposition is completely equal to ὑπό = through.

I suspect here the influence of Ammianus' mother tongue. For the post-class. and late Latin use of **sub** cf. ad 15.3.11 (= III p.52).
(**Correction**: Hassenstein p.62 should be changed into **Reinhardt** p.62); Liesenberg (1890) p.17 (op.cit.I); Svennung Pall. p.327 sq.; Hofm.-Leum.132*a* p.539 (with lit.); Krebs Antib.2 p.611; Heum.-Seckel p.559; Kalb, Röm.Rechtsspr.37, p.45 sq.

c Gron. is surprised at **inusitatae amplitudinis** and says that there have been more ships with larger crews. Wagner rightly objects, "Argutatur V.D., nam de inusitata tantum longitudine navis Amm. loqui voluit, ad quam, **cum nihil nisi obeliscum navis veheret, trecenti sufficiebant**".
One should bear in mind that this ship is a specially constructed **cargo vessel,** and in that case 300 men seems to me rather much; especially when one remembers that a trireme, a warship, has ± 170 rowers. For the shipping trade in Antiquity cf.L.Casson, The Ancient Mariners, New York, 1959 (particularly the lit.quoted there in the capita 15.16.17).

d **agitanda** = ± remigare. Cf.Nepos Dion 9.2: navem triremem armatis ornat Philostratoque, fratri suo, tradit eamque in portu **agitari** (= to sail to and fro) iubet, ut si (= quasi) exercere remiges vellet, cogitans, si forte consiliis obstitisset fortuna, ut haberet, qua fugeret ad salutem.The verb occurs once in Opt.Milev. Not in Claud.Veget.r.m.Arnob.adv.nat. Cf.et. ad 14.2.1 (= I p.66); 14.3.4 (= I p.81); Fesser p.10, 13; Liesenberg (1889) p.3 sq. Very frequent in Amm.

e for the **gerundivum** cf. ad 16.12.22, p.94.26*b*.

IV, 14

quibus ita provisis. For the **neutr.plur. of the pronomina substantivically used,** cf.Riemann (op.cit.I) p.185, 187, 184. Cf.17.2.1: Quibus ut in tali re compositis firmiter; 17.1.4: Quibus clara fide compertis; 16.12.67: his tot ac talibus prospero peractis eventu; 16.12.62: quibus ita favore superni numinis terminatis; 14.7.13: his cognitis; 14.1.10: quibus mox Caesar acrius efferatus; etc. Cf.et. ad 17.3.4, p.108.16; ad 14.1.4, p.2.11 (= I p.59); ad 14.5.9 (= I p.88, p.12.1). p. 111. 7-8

a **digressoque vita principe memorato.** Digredi = to **die.** For the very numerous expressions for dying, passing away cf.Hagend.St.A. p.100 sq. Cf.et 25.3.19: quod non clandestinis insidiis nec longa morborum asperitate vel damnatorum fine **decedo,** sed in medio cursu florentium gloriarum hunc merui clarum ex mundo **digressum;** but 27.3.10: iracundiam ... celeri vitare **digressu** (= flight). The subst. does not occur in p. 111. 8

Claud.Veget.r.m.Opt.Milev.Arn.adv.nat., though the latter does have **digredi** =(to die) (1.40 = Reiffersch.p.26).

b **memorato.** Cf. ad 14.6.8 (= I p.93); ad 14.3.4, p.8.25 (= I p.81).

p. 111. 8 *a* **urgens effectus intepuit.** Sabbah: et la réalisation naguère pressante se ralentit; Seyf.: und die Dringlichkeit des Unternehmens verblaszte. I believe that S. gives the best interpretation. **Urgens** = urguentia (late Latin). **Effectus** = ± work, undertaking. Souter quotes 2 late Latin meanings (p.117): 1. (human) activity. 2. (final) end (of human action); both places from Ps.Apul.Ascl. (4th cent.A.D.). Thus in judic.lit. **effectu** means: re vera and **effectus** sometimes has almost the same meaning as **factum** (cf.Heum.-Seckel p.165).

Possibly in Amm. also the influence of the Greek: ἐνέργεια = activity, practise, to take action. (cf. Bauer Wörterbuch N.T.², 1928, p.411 sq.). In Amm.14.3.4: absque ullo effectu (cf.I p.81); 17.8.4: iamque ... in oportunam clementiae partem effectu victoriae flexo; 18.2.7: Quae dum diligenti maturantur effectu (= cum diligentia et effectu ~ urgens effectus); 19.11.2: quod... exercitus ... similium spe fidenter in effectus animabitur prosperos; 27.2.4: Hoc prospero rerum effectu; 20.8.5: ut effectu multiplici claruit evidenter (cf.Pighi N.St.Amm. p.56).

b For **urgens** cf. ad 14.11.1 (= I p.114). For the syntactic use mentioned under *a*, cf.Hofm.Leum.70*a* (although not quite comparable), p.461; Riemann (op.cit.I) 22 p.105; ibid.27 p.126.

c **intepuit.** Cf.14.5.5; 17.13.17; 20.10.1; 30.4.9; 30.5.3; 31.15.3. Ovid. Colum.Sen.Petr. Not in Veget.r.m.Claud.Arn.adv.nat.Opt.Milev. **tepescere:** 28.1.9; 28.4.21. Cf.et. ad 14.7.18 (= II p.45).

p. 111. 9 **tandemque sero.** Cf. ad 17.1.13, p.106.22*a*.

p. 111. 9 *a* **per maria fluentaque Thybridis.** Twice plur.poet. Cf.22.8.4: et Abydon, unde iunctis pontibus Xerxes **maria** pedibus peragravit; Hagend.St.Amm. p.84 sq. (with lit.).

Fluenta poetism, probably first used in Lucr.Verg. In Amm.15.10.2: fluentis ... Rheni; 18.5.3; 22.8.23; 22.8.46; 22.15.27; 23.6.57; 24.1.6; 24.1.11; 24.2.12; 25.6.13; 27.5.5; 31.3.8. Cf. et Hagendahl St.A.p.28 sq. (c. annot).

"Plurale est tantum, nisi quod inde ab Apul.sing. aliquotiens invenitur" (Hag.ibid). For the **plur.poet.** cf. ad 17.2.1, p.107,14-15*b*. Vergilius imitation is highly probable. Cf.Aen.12.35 sq:

... **recalent** nostro **Thybrina fluenta**
sanguine adhuc campique ingentes ossibus albent.
(**recalere** metaph.28.1.7; Auson.5.7.15, I do not know of any other places where **recalere** is used.)
b The spelling **Thybris** in Verg.Aen.8.86; 10.421 and often in Claud.; just as the adj. **Thybrinus**. I do not think that this "Greek" way of writing is due to the Greek origin of Claud. and Amm. It is a literary affectation, sanctioned by tradition, and seemingly learned, as they occur so often in the Latin literature. **Thybris** is the river of the glorious Roman history and legends, while **Tiberis** is more a geographical concept. But, of course, the different way of spelling has become a mannerism.

velut ... inferret. Fine example of the **personificatio.** (cf. ad 17.2.1, p.107. 13). Compare also Horat.Carm.1.2.13-20. Sabbah connects our passage with C I L VI 1163 = Dessau I.L.S. 736, an inscription on the base of the obelisk, which Amm. could have read. It is possible; but personifications are so ordinary, that I do not believe that this explanation is necessary (it should be noted, however, that the inscription also reads **Thybris).** Also the difficulties attending the erection (§ 15) are mentioned in the inscr.: ... quod non crediderit ullus // tantae molis opus superas consurgere in auras (quoted by S.). The superficial similarities in Amm. and the inscription are probably more the result of **the same stylistic and literary traditions,** which put their mark on the author of the inscription as well as on Amm., when describing the **same** obeliscus. Just like the Tiber, the Nile is personified in Claud. Cf.Epist.1.(39) (Deprecatio ad Hadrianum praef.praet. Like Claud., he also comes from Alexandria) 56 sq.:

p. 111. 9-11

Audiat hoc commune solum, longeque carinis
Nota Pharos, flentemque attollens gurgite vultum
Nostra gemat Nilus numerosis funera ripis.
(For **ripae** cf. ad 16.12.57, p.101.2). And Epist.5 (43) 1 sq. (ad Gennadium ex proconsule):

Italiae commune decus, Rubiconis amoeni
Incola, Romani fama secunda fori;
Graiorum populis et **nostro cognite Nilo.**
Cf. et 16.12.57; 25.10.5; 26.10.17; Blomgren (op.cit.II) p.94.

quod paene ignotus miserat Nilus. Cf.Eid.4(47) (Nilus) 10 sq.:
Fluctibus **ignotis** nostrum procurrit in orbem
Secreto de fonte cadens, qui semper inani

p. 111. 10

105

>Quaerendus ratione latet; nec contigit ulli
>Hoc vidisse caput.

(Note **nostrum** = Romanum and **nostro** in Ep.5 = native, i.e. Egyptian).
Note. It is remarkable that the Nile is mentioned in Claud. so often and with so much praise, while the **Orontes**, though a less impressive stream, is hardly mentioned by **Amm.**, although it flows by his home town.

p. 111. 10-11 *a* **ipse parum sub emeatus sui discrimine moenibus alumnis inferret.**
Büchele: "... der eine Art von Bangigkeit fühlte das Geschenk des fast gänzlich unbekannten Nils unter den Gefahren seiner Windungen **nicht unversehrt** in die Mauern, **nunmehr seine Bewahrerinnen,** zu bringen..."
Wagner: "**Ipse** Deus Tiberis haud aeque feliciter **sub meatus sui discrimine** flexibus suis periculosis **moenibus alumnis** Romae, cuius quasi incola futurus esset. Pro **alumnis** Reinesius malebat **almis** ... Sed pertinet **alumnis** ad obeliscum" Langen Philol.29 (1870) p.471: "**Moenia alumna** bedeutet gerade das Gegenteil von dem, was Wagner den Worten unterschiebt, es sind, um es wörtlich auszudrücken, Mauern, die von irgend einer Sache genährt werden, aber nicht Mauern, die irgend etwas anderes nähren oder beherbergen. Die **passive** Bedeutung von **alumnis** ist bekanntlich die einzig richtige". This last quotation is another good example of a too classical exegesis of a late Latin text. For **alumnis** can very well have an active meaning. But this meaning seems to be restricted only to late Latin. Cf. Georges I p.350 (with examples); Krebs Antib.I p.152. Which causes no objections with Amm. So, although both the active as the passive meaning make for a satisfactory sentence, I prefer (for reasons other than Langen's) the passive. Cf.Claud.Epigr.1(51) 1 sq. (De mulabus Gallicis):
>Adspice morigeras **Rhodani** torrentis **alumnas**
>Imperio nexas, imperioque vagas.

Ibid.21 (De Laud.Stil.1) 159 sq.:
>Hic Rhodani procera cohors (sc.Galli), hic miles **alumnus**
>**Oceani** (Gesner: insulani, ut Britanni, litorum certe accolae).

Alumnus often in Claud. Not in Veget.r.m.Arn.adv.nat.Opt.Milev.
b **parum** = not proper = not as safe (viz. as the Nile). The translations given by Seyf.Sabbah Rolfe are obscure, to my view.
c for **sub** cf. ad 17.4.13, p.111.6*b*.
d **emeatus.** emeatu V emeatus G meatus EA. Probably only in Amm. Cf.29.5.5: Proinde ab Arelate secundis egressus auspiciis (sc.Theodosius) **emeatoque** mari cum classe (= to sail across, to cross). Thus here the verb does not have the meaning of: **to pour out, to flow out,** as in August.

de genes. ad litt.2.2.5 (quoted by Georges). For **meatus** cf. ad 16.1.5, p.72.8*b,c;* Veget.r.n.4.42 (= Lang p.161): Haec reciprocantis **meatus** ambiguitas cursum navium secunda adiuvat, retardat adversa (ebb and flow). Often in Claud. Not in Arn.adv.nat.Opt.Milev.

e **discrimine.** Cf. ad 17.1.10, p.106.9*a*.

defertur. It **may** means here: was carried downstream to, was brought p. 111. 11 to. Bur in connection with the preceding words also (t.t.naut.): drifted towards, found itself (for **deferri** = to be shipwrecked).

vicum Alexandri. Downstream from Rome, on the left bank of the Tiber. p. 111. 11 Here were the harbour installations of which some remains have been found. The origin of the name is unknown. Sabbah II p.169 (note 33) refers to **J. Le Gall,** Le Tibre fleuve de Rome dans l'Antiquité (1952). p.202 (with lit.). About the meagre remains of the quays of the Tiber in Rome, cf.ibid.p.194. sq. (II).

tertio lapide. lapis = "mile-post". The distance indicated is 1500 passus p. 111. 12 = ± 1½ kilometer. A.M. obviously know from, what point the distance is calculated. The starting-point may have been the **miliarium aureum** on the Forum Romanum (close to the Rostra). When one does not count this as **lapis,** the distance is about 4½ kilometers, which agrees more or less with the position of the **vicus Alexandri** (For further information: Procop.b.Goth.1.26 calculated the distance from Rome to **Portus,** the actual harbour at this time, to be 126 stadia; for this Itin.Anton.August. Wess.p.300 gives M.P.XVIIII (Iter a Roma per **Portum** Centumcellis. **In Portum** M.P.XVIIII).

seiunctum. Cf.Iust.Phil.4.1.18: Quo cum accesseris discedere ac **seiungi** promontoria, quae antea iuncta fuerant, arbitrere; Lucr.1.451 sq.:
 coniunctum est id quod nusquam sine permitiali
 discidio potis est **seiungi** seque gregari;
Claud.28.407 sq (De VI cons.Honor.).
 Quem precor ad finem Laribus **seiuncta** potestas
 Exsulat, imperiumque suis a sedibus errat?
Cic. (frequently). Nep.Lucr.Stat.Iust.Judic.lit. Not in Veget.r.m.Opt. Milev.Arn.adv.nat.

chamulcis. (χαμουλκός). Occurs only here in Amm. It must have been a enormous dray-cart, very long, to be able to transport this obeliscus. Usually cargoes were reloaded in **Portus** into a kind of Tiber barges, which were pulled by oxen (cf.Proc.b.Goth.1.26). But these barges were not big enough for this very large cargo. It must have been a fine example of river navigation to get the very large and long ship safely to the quay of **vicus Alex**. Perhaps the fact that it did land safely was due more to luck than anything else. **(defertur)**. The reloading into the **chamulcis** will have been done by a **row of cranes,** as the lifting power of even the heaviest crane still was rather limited (cf.F.Kretzchmer, Bilddokumente Röm. Techn.³, 1967, p.24 sq.). **Note.:** Proc. calls these barges βᾶρις, probably an Egyptian word. Cf. et Le Gall (op.cit.p.111.11) p.216 sq.: Les bateaux du fleuve.

p. 111. 12-13 *a* **tractusque lenius per Ostiensem portam.** Of course the cargo could only be transported slowly and carefully. The comparativus is here practically similar to **leniter.** Cf. ad 14.6.12 (= I p.96).
b Thus the transport takes place from the **vicus Alexandri** along the **via Ostiensis** to the **porta Ostiensis**, in the wall of Aurelianus. This road runs inside the wall straight on towards the **Circus maximus,** as **vicus piscinae publicae**. The aforesaid gate is the present **Porta S.Páolo**. east of the Pyramid of Cestius (i.e. the P.Ost. reconstructed by Belisarius († 565 A.D.). After going for ± 5 minutes along the vicus p.p. the **wall of Servius Tullius** is reached, which, however, had already in the late republican period been completely absorbed by the surrounding buildings. Near the **Aventinus** there were 3 gates. Through one of these, the **porta Raudusculana,** ran the v.p.p., at least if this gate was still standing (especially at this time) (there are still some remains of the Servian wall, namely at the point where the Via di Porta S.Páolo meets the Viale Aventino). At the time of A.M. the road from the Porta Ostiensis already led to the **S.Páolo fuori le mura,** a church which was founded in 368 A.D. by Valentinianus II and Theodosius. (cf. et. Richter (op.cit.I) p.40 sq., p.71; E. Nash, Bildlexicon zur Topogr. des ant.Rom. (1961-1962) 2 p.218 sq.

p. 111. 13 **piscinamque publicam.** Cf. Richter (op.cit.I) p.343 sq.: "Auf der anderen, westlichen Seite der Via Appia lag zwischen der Servianischen Mauer (cf.p.111.12-13*b*) und der Stelle, die später die Thermen des Caracalla einnahmen (= Thermae Antoninianae), die **Piscina Publica,** ein Teich, wie man ihn vor den Thoren fast aller italischen Städte findet, zum Waschen und anderen Verrichtungen (nach Festus p.213 auch: ad quam et natatum et exercitationis alioqui causa veniebat populus) dienend." The p.p. had already disappeared in the first century before Christ, but gave its name to **Regio XII** and the **vicus piscinae publicae** called for short: **piscina publica** by Amm. Cf.et. Liv.23.32.4; Festus ibid.; C.I.L. VI 167: lanii **piscinenses;** Varro GoetzSchoell p.239. **Piscina** = fish-pond, also in judic.lit. With the meaning of **baptismal font** in Opt.Milev.Ziwsa p.69.72.

obelisci.
cap. 4, 12-17. Lib. XVII A.M.

Aug. 10 B.C. obel. 1 and 2
1) **Campus Martius - Piazza di Montecitorio**
   reg.IX   1789
   Psammetich II

2) **Circus maximus - Piazza del Popolo**
   reg.XI   Liv.39.7.8
   Sethos I and Ramses II
   1 and **2** with hieroglyphs

3) **Ammon temple Thebe - Circus maximus** reg.XI found in 1587
   Thutmos III   under Sixtus V Laterane
   3 with hieroglyphs.

4) **Obeliscus Vaticanus** from **Heliopolis** (Gallus)
   Caligula in **Circus Gai et Neronis** (regio 14) brought in 1586 by Sixtus V to **Piazza di S. Pietro.**
   4 without hieroglyphs.

Sixtus V 1585-1590
Pius VI 1775-1799

5) **Horti Sallustiani - Piazza della Trinita dei Monti**
   regio VI
   With a copy of the hieroglyphs of the obeliscus of Ramses II, erected by Augustus in the circus maximus (2), constructed around 200.

6) and 7) **in front of the mausoleum of the emperor Augustus** (regio IX) (Vespas. 79 A.D.)
6) excavated in 1527. 1587 near **S.Maria Maggiore**
7) excavated in 1550. Brought in 1792 by Pius VI to the **Piazza del Quirinale.**
6) and 7) without hieroglyphs.

p. 111. 13-14 **Circo inlātus est māximo.** Hyperbaton. Claus.II For the C.M. cf. ad 17.4.12, p.110.21-22*c;* 28.4.29.

IV, 15

p. 111. 14 **erectio.** In general late Latin. Vitr.Hier.Vulg.August.Ennod.

p. 111. 15 **sperabatur posse compleri.** Cf. ad 14.7.5 (= II p.20); ad 15.5.9 (= III p.84); ad 17.3.1, p.108.6-7*a*.

p. 111. 14-15 **quae vix aut ne vix quidem.** Cf.Cic. De fin.2.34(111): nobis autem aut vix aut ne vix quidem suppetunt multo labore quaerentibus; ibid.4.13(32): quae propter exiguitatem vix aut ne vix quidem appareant; ad fam.9.8.2: mihi vero cum his ipsis vix: his autem detractis ne vix quidem; Michael (op.cit.I) p.32.

p. 111. 15-17 † **idestisque ... subtexentes.** G erectisque usque periculum B **id est** usque periculum. Clark Seyf.: † idestisque periculum. Sabbah: compleri: **usque periculum.** The conjecture by Novák, though well-founded, as always, is in my opinion, quite unacceptable (Wiener Stud.1911, 33, p.308). Haupt: **ad per(pen)diculum** I also find highly arbitrary. (cf. ad 14.8.11 = II p.76). For the other versions and speculations cf. Clark p.111 appar. crit. and **Meurig Davies,** Latomus, 1948, p.214; eiusd.Class.Quart.42, 3-4, 1948 (M.D.'s remarks are always worthy of consideration). Probably the explanatory **id est** was written in the margin, according to Sabbah per abbreviationem. From there it somewhow got into the text, written in full.

Thus there is a choice between G. and B. **erectisque** seems a conjecture by Gelenius, **erectisque usque** a duplication. Therefore the version by B. should be accepted, without **id est.**

usque periculum: lit. until danger = usque ad pericula subeunda, does not sound to me like a normal word-combination, but **usque c.acc.,** used as a preposition, is found fairly often in post-class. and late Latin; also in vulgar and old Latin. (cf.Hofm.-Leum.91, p.498 sq. (with lit.); Krebs Antib.2 p.698 sq. (with lit.)). Cf.et. **(adusque, usque ad)** ad 17.2.2, p.107.20. In Claud. only: **usque adeone?** In Veget.r.m. only: **usque ad, usque adeo, usque eo, usque in;** Stat.Theb.11.88 sq.:

... modo nempe horrendus ab astris
descendit **vos usque** fragor: ...; ibid.2.153 sq.:
... quibus ipse per imbres
fulminibus mixtos intempestumque Tonantem
has meus **usque domos** vestigia fecit Apollo; ibid.2.206.

ut machinarum cerneres nemus = ut **putares** cernere nemus machinarum. Coniunct.potent. of the past, according to the class.grammar. Just as we would say: (of ships in a port) a forest of masts; (of houses in a town) a forest of chimneys. But the combination: **machinarum nemus** is not known to me somewhere else. We find the same development of this concept in Statius Silv., where in 5.1.49 **nemus** means: (roof of) Foliage, just as **silva** in 3.1.185 and 5.5.30 (= ± closely packed mass). One finds this meaning already more or less in Verg.Georg.2.323:
Ver adeo frondi **nemorum,** ver utile silvis (there nemora = ± arbusta). Nemus and silva fairly often in Claud, but **silva** more often.

trabibus ... innectuntur. The same construction as in Horat.Epod.17.71: frustraque vincla **gutturi innectes** tuo and Sil.Ital.11.240 sq.:
... **huic** agedum, (nam cur indigna feramus?)
Magnanime o miles, meritas **innecte catenas.**
The verb appears to be a poetism. Also post-class. in prose. Fairly often in Claud. Not in Veget.r.m.Arn.adv.nat.Opt.Milev.

vasti fūnes et lŏngi. Hyperbaton.Claus.I

ad speciem. Cf. ad 17.4.7, p.110.5*b*

multiplicium liciorum. Licia (1) are really the loops which were attached to a **liciatorium** (= lath) for the purpose of separating the threads of the warp for the passage of the woof. Cf.Wunderl. ad Tib.1.6.79 (Firmaque conductis **adnectit licia telis**): "**Licia** sunt vincula, quibus textores induunt atque implicant stamina et iugo annectunt; **telae** aetem stamina, quae radius textorius percurrit. Utrum vero licia telis, an telae liciis annecti dicantur, nihil interest".
Hence (2) = woof. From there more general (3) = thread, string, ribbon, etc. Here we have the last meaning, although Amm. must have had a **fabric, weave** in mind. Cf.et.Verg.Georg.1.285: **licia** telae addere (= annectere); Aus.epigr.55 (with the meaning weaving (threads)):
   Licia qui texunt et carmina, carmina Musis,
   licia contribuunt, casta Minerva, tibi.
Amm.14.6.9: Alii ... sudant sub ponderibus lacernarum (a kind of jacket, with hood), quas ... iugulis ... **adnectunt,** nimia **subtegminum** tenuitate perflabilis ... ut longiores fimbriae (fringe) tunicaeque perspicue luceant, varietate **liciorum** effigiatae in species animalium multiformes (**subtegmen** = woof; thread, fabric. Here the 3rd meaning; **licia** = here ± embroidery. Therefore meaning (3) see above).

p. 111. 17 *a* **caelum densitate nimia subtexentes.**
    densitate. Cf.24.2.5: (Romani) ira tamen acuente virtutem clipeorum **densitate** contecti; (on the rainbow) 20.11.28: quarta ideo purpurat, quod intermicante asperginum **densitate** (density of the raindrops), per quas oritur, radiorum splendorem concipiens ostendit aspectum flammeo propiorem; etc. Cf.et. ad 14.2.10 (= I p.73): **denseta;** ad 16.10.13, p.86. 14-15*c* **(densitas).**

   b **subtexentes,** Cf.Verg.Aen.3.581 sq.:
     et fessum quotiens mutet latus, intremere omnem
     murmure Trinacriam et caelum **subtexere** fumo.
With this meaning a poetism, at any rate a very "literary" word. A fine example of imitatio. Arn.adv.nat.7.15 (= Reiffersch.p.249): Quod est honoris genus, lignorum structibus incensis **caelum fumo subtexere** et effigies numinum nigrore offuscare ferali? The verb does not occur in Claud.Veget.r.m.Opt.Milev.

Note. For **subtegmen** see previous note and 23.6.67: a quibus arborum
a fetus aquarum **asperginibus** (see for this *a*) crebris velut quaedam vellera molientes ex lanugine et liquore mixtam subtilitatem tenerrimam pectunt **nentesque subtemina** conficiunt sericum etc. (**subtilitas** = ± fine fabric; **subtemina** = ± weave, threads, as in the previous note.).

   b For **stamen** cf.23.4.14: quae in muliebris coli formam, quo nentur lintea **stamina** (= ± threads, weave, fabric).

p. 111. 18 *a* **mons ipse effigiatus scriptilibus elementis.** Cf.Min.Felix 3.1: ut tam luculento die in lapides eum patiaris inpingere, **effigiatos** sane et unctos et coronatos ("admittedly in the form of statues, but still stones". v. Wageningen);
Tert. de anima 9: omne enim **effigiatum** compositum et structile affirmat; Amm.26.7.11: aureos scilicet nummos **effigiatos** in vultum novi principis; (of the Huns) 31.2.2: ut bipedes existimes bestias vel quales in commarginandis pontibus **effigiati** stipites dolantur incompte. Late Latin. Not in Claud.Veget.r.m.Arn.adv.nat.Opt.Milev. Neither in judic.lit. (though we do find **effingere** there). Cf.et. Souter p.117; ad 14.6.9 (= I p.94). Here the part. means: ornately decorated, ornamented.

   b **scriptilibus.** Cf.29.1.30: cuius in ambitu rotunditatis extremo **elementorum viginti quattuor scriptiles formae** incisae perite diiungebantur spatiis examinate dimensis. (= the 24 characters of the alphabet). The adj. is not known to me from other places, unless from grammarians, just as **inscriptilis.**

c **elementis. Elementa** = στοιχεῖα (litterae = γράμματα). Cf.Lucr.5. 1444 sq.:

carminibus cum res gestas coepere poetae
tradere; nec multo priu' sunt **elementa** reperta;

Suet.Caes.56.6: in quibus (sc.epistolis) si qua occultius perferenda erant, per **notas** (code) scripsit id est, sic structo litterarum ordine, ut nullum verbum effici posset: quae si quis investigare et persequi vellet, quartam **elementorum** litteram, id est, *d* pro *a*, et perinde reliquas commutet; Tert.Marc.5.4: **elementa** apud Romanos quoque etiam primae litterae solent dici (quoted by Krebs): thus here the **first** letters of the alphabet (our a b c). Furthermore in gramm. In the above meaning, therefore as t.t. gramm., postclass. Cf.et. Krebs Antib.1.p.499 sq.; Souter p.119. With other meanings (our word: element, raw material etc.) ad 15.4.4 (= III p.59). Cf. et J.H.H. Schmidt Synon. (1889) p.398 sq.

a **paulatimque in arduum per inane protentus diu pensilis** † V id per arduum inane. Clark thinks that the text has been spoiled, Seyf. gives the same text without crux, just as Rolfe, does. Sabbah: paulatimque - id per arduum inane - protentus, diu pensilis etc. Sabbah II p.170 wants to preserve V G's text, with the explanation: "**id** marque l'insistance, **inane** est un adjectif substantivé, défini par l'épithète. **arduum:** "l'obélisque est placé en position inclinée et cela au dessus d'un vide impressionnant", hyperbole expressive pour désigner les 32 mètres de cet obélisque gigantesque".

p. 111. 18-19

Although I am usually in favour of maintaining an explicable text, as long as the need for correction (conjecture) has not been clearly demonstrated, S's explanation seems too ingenious to me. Compare also the app.crit. in the edition by Clark. Madvig's version: **in** perarduum inane (with a minimal change from **id** into **in**) seems best to me. For **protentus** cf.Verg.Georg.1.171: huic (buri sc.) ab stirpe **pedes temo protentus in octo** = extended over 8 feet = 8 feet long. Here likewise: stretching out over the very steep empty space (or passively: being stretched out). For **perarduus** cf.Cic.Verr.3.71 (166): Mihi autem hoc **perarduum** est demonstrare; Cassiod. de inst.div.litt.27: opus quidem (ut arbitror) necessarium, sed considerata difficultate **perarduum**, in duobus libris comprehendere velle divinarum et humanarum fontes copiosissimos litterarum (seems to me a Cic. immitation, as is also likely here with Amm., when one accepts M's version). These two passages quoted by Georges, are the only ones from which I know **perarduus.** But this is no proof against the use by Amm., whom we know to use many rare words, some of which are only used by him. With a paraphrase the sentence in Amm. reads: The obelisk is hoisted up and then gives the impression, when one looks **upward,** as if it was stretching itself into empty space, in all its steepness (for the empty space is steep, but this is only noticeable when measured against an object, such as here the tall obeliscus). From a reclining it changes into a vertical position, "floats" for a moment between heaven and earth, as it were, and is then very gently let down on its destined spot.

b   **inane** = air = aer, a real cliché, also in class.lit.

c   **pensilis** Cf.29.1.31: supersistit cortinulae (= small tripod) sacerdos **pensilem** anulum librans, aptum ex carpathio filo perquam levi; 28.4.18: ubi si ... per foramen umbraculi **pensilis** (hanging curtain?) radiolus irruperit solis, queruntur etc.: 31.13.15: cum enim oppessulatas (= locked with bolts) ianuas perrumpere conati, qui secuti sunt, a parte **pensili** domus (balcony) sagittis incesserentur etc. (here t.t.archit.). The adj. not in Claud.Veget.r.m.Arn.adv.nat.Opt.Milev.

p. 111. 19-20   *a*   **tamquam molendarias rotantibus metas.** For the use of **tamquam** + partic. cf. Hofm.-Leum.181.p.603, Zus. α (with lit.); Dederichsus (op.cit. I) p.22 sq.; Riem. (op.cit.I) p.304 sq.; ad 14.1.4 (= I p.58).

b   **molendarius.** extremely rare adj. Cf.Dig.33.7.18.2: Asinam **molendariam** et molam negat Neratius instrumento fundi contineri; ibid. § 5: Idem (Scaevola) consultus de **meta molendaria** respondit ... est autem **meta** inferior pars molae, **catillus** superior (as a variation in the last quotation is given:

molendinaria, which Heum.-Seckel does not include in his dictionary; Clark notes in the appar.critic.: **molendinarias** vulgo, a version taken over by Rolfe. But Seyf. Sabbah: **molendarias**). C.I.L. 6.1711 gives **molendinarius** = miller. Where **molendinum** is late Latin for mill, the variations should not be rejected out of hand. (cf. Souter p.255).

c   **metas.** The **meta** (see above) is the lower part of the mill, ending in a blunt cone. The **catillus** revolves around this cone, propelled by slaves or animals (horse, donkey). The grain is poured into the **topmost** cavity of the catillus, which functions as a funnel, from where it runs down, through holes, until it reaches the **meta,** where it is ground down between this fixed **meta** and the revolving **catillus.** For **mola** and **meta** cf. A.Rich - M.Chéruel[3] Dict. des antiq.rom. et grec. (1883) p.403; 410 sq. (very clear); F.Kretzschmer (op.cit.p.111.12) p.18, 19. For another meaning of **meta** cf. ad 17.4.7, p.110.3-4.

d   For **cranes and levers** cf.F.Kretzschmer (op.cit.17.4.14, p.111.12) p.24 sq.; Sabbah II p.170, note 37, who draws special attention to the images on the base of the obeliscus, erected in the hippodrome of Constantinople and on the Bas-relief on the tomb of the Haterii (with the lit. quoted there). What was involved in the moving and erection of an obeliscus can be read in: **Domenico Fontana,** Della Trasportazione dell' Obelisco Vaticano (1590) - for this Vaticanus 800 labourers, 140 horses and 40 windlasses were needed - and in **James Lees-Milne,** Saint Peter's (1967), p.216 sq. (with illustrations). When one sees the illustrations, one has to conclude that Amm. is not exaggerating.

a **cavea locatur in media. Cavea** = space for the spectators, but here, p. 111. 20 of course, is meant: in the middle of the circus, as the obeliscus is not placed in the midst of the audience (cavea media t.t. = middle circle), but on the **spina.**
b **locatur:** seemingly the main verb. But when one analyses the sentence, one gets the following construction: and after the "mountain" had been attached to it and slowly lifted up, **it remained for a long time in a floating position,** and while thousands of people turned around, it was then put in its place in the middle of the circus. The underlined words contain the main idea.
c for **locare** cf. ad 17.4.13, p.111.2-3*a*.

sfaera. G **sphaera,** similarly Sabbah Seyf. Rolfe. W B: **sphera** (= σφαῖρα) p. 111. 20 = pila, globus. V **sfera.** I see no reason to change V's version, at any rate not in the way Clark does. This **sfera** represents the heavenly globe. For the enormous number of ordinary and extraordinary words borrowed from the Greek cf. Liesenberg (op.cit.I) (1889) p.18 sq. **Sphaera** is at this time already entirely domesticated.
superponitur. Cf.Suet.Oct.Aug.31: Pompeii quoque statuam ... marmoreo **Iano superposuit,** translatam e curia ...; ibid Galba 4: Serv.Galba Imperator ... natus est ... in villa **colli superposita.** With this construction and meaning in general post-class. In judic.lit. linked with **raedae, navigio** = to load into, onto (cf.Heum.-Seckel p.571). For other meanings in late Latin cf. Souter p.404. Three times in Veget.r.m. (and once with the same construction). Not in Claud.Arn.adv.nat.Opt.Milev.

aureis lamminis = gold leaf. p. 111. 21

a **qua confestim vi ignis divini contacta.** Cf. ad 15.1.3 (= III p.9) for p. 111. 21-22 **confestim.**

b **ignis divini** = fulminis. Thus **ignis** is used only for lightning, among others in Verg.Aen.4.167: fulsere **ignes** and Horat.Carm.1.34.5 sq.: ... namque Diespiter.
igni corusco nubila dividens.
For **ignis divinus** Claud. uses twice: **ignis fulmineus.** But similarly as in Amm.26.509 sq (de bello Getico):
... iactata procul dicuntur in hostem
Fulmina, **divinique** volant pro moenibus **ignes:**
Seu coelum, seu Roma tonat.

p. 111. 22 *a* **ideoque sublata.** For **ideo** and **ideoque** cf. ad 16.12.25. p.95.9*a, b;* 16. 12.37, p.97.6*a;* Pighi St.Amm.p.80, 79 (with lit.). Sabbah translates: et **retirée** pour cette raison; Seyf.: und deswegen **beseitigt.** But in my view it has here the meaning of: to destroy, exterminate, Cf.Horat.Carm.3.4.42 sq.:
... scimus, ut inpios
Titanas immanemque turbam
fulmine sustulerit caduco ...
b The sphere on top of the obeliscus has served as lightning conductor, in which capacity it probably was struck off (and partly melted?). Nevertheless, the same thing happened once more. (see following words). The man, of whom it is said: "eripuit caelo fulmen, sceptrumque tyrannis", still had to be born.

p. 111. 22 *a* **facis imitamentum infigitur aereum.** For **imitamentum** cf. ad 16.10.14, p.86.27-28*d.*
b **infigitur** = is fastened on top of it. Not the "normal" meaning of this verb. Compare Dig.33.7.21: Cum fundus sine instrumento legatus sit, dolia molae olivariae et praelum et quaecumque **infixa** inaedificataque sunt fundo legato continentur.
c **aereum** = a(h)eneum. But p.111.21: **aenea.** Without any difference in meaning. Poet., post-class. and often in late Latin. Not in Cic., several times in Liv., not in Caes. Cf. Krebs Antib.I p.117. Not in Claud.Arn. adv.nat.Opt.Milev., though it does occur in Veget.r.m. The variatio is not explained by the necessity of the clausula.

p. 111. 22 **itidem.** Cf. ad 16.12.17, p.93.23-24*b.*

p. 111. 22-23 **auro inbratteatum.** Variatio with p.111.21, without any difference in meaning. Claus.III. For the part.cf. ad 14.6.8 (= I p.92).

a velut ... candentis. For velut + part. cf. ad 17.4.15, p.111.19-20*a*   p. 111. 23
(tamquam).
b candentis. Occurs in Claud. Not in Veget.r.m.Arn.adv.nat.Opt.Milev.

IV, 16
a secutaeque aetates alios transtulerunt. For aetates cf. ad 17.4.9, p.110.9   p. 111. 23-24
(= generations); Krebs Antib.1 p.120 sq.; Claud.26 (de bello Get.)
642 sq.:
 ... Iam protinus **aetas**
Adveniens geminae gentis permisceat ossa,
Et duplices signet titulos commune tropaeum.
(Cimbri and Getae).
b transtulerunt. Cf. ad 17.4.13, p.111.5 (translatio and convecto).

unus in Vaticano, viz. (4)   p. 111. 24
alter in hortis Sallusti, viz. (5) (hortis Sallustianis.

a duo in Augusti monumento, viz. (6) and (7)   p. 112. 1
b erectisunt. Cf. ad 17.4.6, p.110.2.
c Augusti monumento. By this is meant the Mausoleum of the Emperor Augustus, South of the Via de' Pontefici (a side street of the Via di Ripetta), North of the S.Rocco and the S.Girolamo degli Schiavoni. Cf. Richter (op.cit.) p.249 sq.; C.I.L. 884-895. In 1936 the sad remains have been restored. Here the original of the Res gestae Divi Augusti (= Monumentum Ancyranum) is kept. Who are buried here, is described by Richter. **Nerva** seems to have been the last one. (Cf.Sext.Aur.Vict.Epit. 12.12: cuius corpus a senatu ut quondam Augusti honore delatum, in **sepulcro Augusti** sepultum est. Eoque die, quo interiit, Solis defectio facta est).

IV, 17
a notarum textus. Notae = (here) symbols = hieroglyphs. Cf. ad 17.4.   p. 112. 1
8-11, p.110.6*a*.
b textus. Cf.14.6.26; 14.4.7; 15.5.4; 22.15.8; ad 14.6.26 (= I p.101). With the meaning: continuing story, description, contents, "text", late Latin. Often in Amm.Cf. Krebs Antib.2 p.660. Here it **can** have the meaning of: continuing row of symbols but also **"text" consisting of symbols** (= **hierogl.**). In that case a genit.explic. Cf.Arn.adv.nat.5.35 (= Reiffersch. p.205): si enim ad finem a capite **textus omnis expositionis et series obtentionibus** (= concealments) allegoricis clausa sunt etc.,

where **textus** in my view is somewhat abundantly supplemented and explained by **series**. (cf.15.5.4: et peniculo **serie litterarum abstersa**). Not in Claud.Veget.r.m.Opt.Milev. with this meaning.

p. 112. 2 *a* **obelisco** - ... **Circo. Incisus**, also 17.4.8 (notas) quas ei undique videmus incisas (In both places **c.dat.**). Cf.22.15.30: **excisis** parietibus; ad 17. 4.6, p.110.2 (**excisos**) **b**. The constructure of **incidere** with the dativ. is poet. and post-class. Cf. Krebs Antib.1.p.708 sq. With the above meaning not in Claud.Veget.r.m.Arn.adv.nat.Opt.Milev.

b The obeliscus, the text of which is given in a Greek translation in § 18 sq., is called **vetus** and is described as: the one which we saw in the Circus (sc.Maximus). Now (2) and (3) are placed in the Circus Maximus. The transport and erection (§ 12) of **hic recens advectus** (obeliscus) refers to (3). We can hardly suppose that Amm. did not see that one. But it makes the explanation of **videmus** a little harder. In the second place: what does **vetus** mean? (3) is older than (2), as far as the age of the obelisci, as Egyptan monuments, is concerned. **Vetus** (though used somewhat carelessly) may, however, also refer to the obelisci as a Roman monument. In that case this adj. fits (2). Seyf. and Sabbah assume (without further explanation) that the following text refers to (2), perhaps also brought to this assumption by: **veterem principem** (§ 12). Both obelisci mentioned are provided with hieroglyphs. Rolfe² p.327 (note 6) indicates (3) as the obeliscus of the text discussed by Amm.3 modern editors are thus in disagreement. When one looks at the Greek text of Amm., it says in § 19: Ἀπόλλων κρατερός... ὁ ἀγλαοποιήσας Ἡλίου πόλιν and § 21 καὶ ἐκόσμησεν Ἡλίου πόλιν and in §23: ὁ ἀφ' Ἡλίου πόλεως μέγας θεός etc. Thus here **Heliopolis** is mentioned. When taking this as a starting point, only (2) comes into consideration. This also agrees with the inscription on (2); similarly (2) as well as Hermapion's explanation give the name **Ramses** (= Ramses II: 1304-1237 B.C.). The conclusion of **A.Erman** (op. cit.L.XVII bibl.) is: "Somit ergibt sich als sicheres Resultat, dasz Hermapions Obelisk **nicht der Flaminius ist (2)**; es ist ein anderer Obelisk des Sethos und Ramses aus Heliopolis, und es beruht nur **auf einer alten Verwechslung,** wenn Ammian oder sein Gewährsmann ihn für identisch mit dem von Augustus errichteten Obelisken hält" (p.270). **E.Iversen** (op.cit.17.4.8-11, p.110.6-20) is somewhat less critical (p.47). It still seems to me that nobody can give either a judgement on the obeliscus, or an opinion on the hierogl. text, without first very carefully studying the very thorough and analytical dissertation by Erman. **Antique** mistakes concerning obelisci must have occurred more often; cf.Plin.N.H.36.71 (who has the obeliscus of Psammetichus II erected by Augustus on the Circus Maximus, whereas it was really standing on the Campus Martius (1). Thus he confuses (1) with (2); cf. Erman p.249). From the above it is evident that we are not certain at all about the obeliscus of Amm. (§ 17). It may be that the **other obelisk** is one of a **pair** (for they were often erected in pairs) but in any case it is "related" to (2) (cf. Erman p.249).

Very complicated is also the history of the text as it has come down to us (§ 18-§ 23), which in my view is also very important for the relationship between V and M and G. V gives one and a half line of incomprehensible Greek text, after which follows a gap of $1\frac{1}{2}$ pages. The author did not know any Greek himself and has apparently waited in vain for a helper or for a moment when he would be bold enough to copy the Greek characters himself. The Greek text is completely missing in UKTNRSB. FYCWHZPDEA give the "text" by V. The "complete" text is only given by G. Cf. Erman p.246: "Er (the author of V) berechnete dabei die ganze Griechische Stelle auf **2486** Buchstaben, von denen er nur 97 geschrieben hat"; and also ibid. note 1: "Diese Zahlen rgeben sich aus Eyssenhardts Angaben in seiner Edit.Maior des Amm. Der Schreiber hat offenbar die Griechische Stelle seiner Vorlage genau ausgezählt und auf 40 Zeilen zu je 62 Buchstaben und 6 Buchstaben darüber berechnet - **Daraus folgt übrigens wieder dasz der Fuldensis (V) nicht aus dem Hersfeldensis (M) abgeschrieben sein kann, dessen griechisches Stück nur 1574 Buchstaben enthielt.** Und weiter folgt daraus, dasz die Verstümmelung des Hermapionzitates nicht schon von Ammian herrührt, noch die Vorlage jener beiden Handschriften hat es volständig erhalten." Although this is a well-founded argument, I cannot accept the underlined words as conclusive evidence. For we no longer have M, only G, and we therefore do not know exactly in what way this text of M got into G. To the above words Erman adds p.252, note 3 the following: "Da nun aber diese **1574** Buchstaben (viz. of M) 7 Zeilen des Obelisken nebst deren Beischriften entsprechen, so dasz auf jede Zeile mit ihrem Zubehör im Durchschnitt etwa 225 Buchstaben kommen, so entsprechen jene **2486** Buchstaben (of V) etwa 11 Zeilen. Demnach ist es höchst wahrscheinlich, **dasz die Vorlage des Fuldensis (V) und Hersfeldensis (M) noch im wesentlichen die gesamten 12 Zeilen des Obelisken enthalten hat.**" This too I consider somewhat hypothetical. Quite probably M's text will have looked no better than those $1\frac{1}{2}$ lines of V's: chaotic. But Gelenius (and Froben) have tried to put this part into shape in their own way, though quite arbitrarily, when one compares their words with those of V (after having restored them more or less). The **Greek text** of G's is thus very unreliable in relation to the original to which he goes back, and certainly in relation to the original text of Amm. One can only try to reconstruct what is meant by dragging in the hieroglyphic texts of the obelisks and to pay attention, among other things, to the **way in which** these hieroglyphs have been inscribed. Thus the difficulties with Amm. were not caused by the hieroglyphs, but by the unreliable Gr. text, given to us by Gelenius. But the text by **Hermapion** is also unreliable! (we are only supposing that Amm. has taken down this text quite carefully). On this matter Erman gives the following judgement: p.272 sq.: "Man sieht, es ist das keine sorgsame Übersetzung, wie es die ältere der Rosettana war, **sondern ein flüchtiges Machwerk, dessen Autor sich schon am ungefähren Sinn genügen läszt** und der für die Feinheiten der theoretischen beiden Königreiche und der dreiszigjährigen Jubiläen nicht mehr das nötige Verständnis oder den nötigen Respekt besitzt. Bedenkt man dann weiter, was in dieser Übersetzung alles fortgelassen ist und wie auch das ohne Konsequenz geschehen ist, so gewinnt man wirklich den Eindruck, dasz jemand aus den langen Inschriften leichthin dies und jenes herausgenommen hat, was auch einem Nichtägypter verständlich sein konnte. **Hermapion** mag ewta einen Priester, der noch leidlich der alten Schrift kundig war, angesichts des Obelisken gebeten haben, ihm dessen Inschriften zu übersetzen, und der wird dabei so verfahren sein, "**wie es einem Laien gegenüber natürlich war**" (The latter involuntarily brings to mind Herodotus and his contact with Egyptian priests).

c This Gr. text of Hermapion-Ammianus has **now** no longer any significance for the Egyptology, apart from a historical, especially cultural-historical one. But on spite of the miserable Gelenius text the §§ 18-23 could have been of considerable use for the unravelling of the hieroglyphic script. Cf. ad 17.4.8-11, p.110.6-20 (in fine).

d §§ 18-23 will be accompanied by some factual remarks. The author of this comm. does not intend to enter the field of hieroglyphic texts, because he is no expert on this. He will only refer to the works quoted by him (ad 17.4.8-11, p.110.6-20) and especially to the study of Erman. It will be obvious to every reader that linguistic, grammatical or stylistic comments on this Gr. text are quite meaningless, as the Greek is not that of Hermapion-Amm.; or more precisely only partly so.

p. 112. 2 **Hermapionis.** We know nothing of this man. Probably an Egyptian from the Greek period (?). Why H. has included this obeliscus text is not clear. In any case the contents, with its enumeration of royal titles (as Erman says) can hardly have been of interest to **Romans**. The explanation of the name is doubtful. "An eine Zusammensetzung von Hermes und Apis

wird man nicht denken dürfen" (Erman). The name does **not** occur in CIG III 6397, but is there based on a correction. A woman's name ΕΡΜΑΠΙΣ Ditt.Syll. (op.cit.I) I, 11. Cf. Erman p.245, annot.2. **Hermapion** has not come out of nowhere: cf.Sb.p.XLIX (dealing with **Horapollon).** Io ritengo invece che già il primo nucleo dell' opera fosse in greco: in greco erano già stati redatti da **Chairemon** (± time of Nero's reign) i suoi Ἱερογλυφικά, che furono il modello di questo genere di scritti, e in gran parte la fonte del nostro ... E nemmeno è da credere che l'autore del libro creasse di propria iniziativa quelle problematiche spiegazioni dei singoli geroglifici: **esse circolavano già come publica materies insieme coi segni respettivi,** al punto da constituirne la giustifica non solo in Horap. e in Chairemon ma sinanche presso Plutarco, Clemente, Porfirio ecc.
Io ritengo anzi che esistessero liste di semplici segni coi relativi significati, e liste con in più le cagioni delle singole identità". From this one gets some impression of how it will have looked, also with **Hermapion.**

interpretatum: passive! Cf.23.5.7; 24.6.1; 30.5.12. Cf. Krebs Antib.I p.774.   p. 112. 3
The pass. meaning already in Cic. Late Latin is **interpretare** = interpretari (cf. Souter p.216). Thus it is possible that the part. is derived from this verb, though hardly likely, in my view. Means here: translated.
litteris Graecis instead of **lingua Graeca,** in contrast to: **notae ... hieroglyphicae** (§ 8) or **scriptilia elementa** (§ 15).

subiecimus = to let follow, to add. Cf. Claud 36.133 sq. (De raptu Pro-   p. 112. 3
serp.)
... "Procul irrita venti
Dicta ferant", **subicit** Cybele, "Non tanta Tonanti
Segnities, ut non pro pignore fulmina mittat."
(= followed this with, resumed). Thus also 18.358 (In Eutr.I).

Translation inscription: The translated text has its beginning from the   p. 112. 4-5
South onward (= begins with the South). The first row (of hieroglyphs) "reads" as follows: (originally there were 4 × 3 = 12 στίχοι).

IV, 18
a   "Ηλιος ... φιλεῖ: p. 112. 6-7
Erman does not add ΛΕΓΕΙ to the preceding (cf.p.112.4-5), but to the following: λέγει "Ηλιος etc. The beginning as on the bottom row of images of the Flamin. (I, II, III):
"Harachte says, the great god: I have given you..." (Harachte epitheton

of Horus). In the translation the dativus βασιλεῖ Ραμέστῃ has been put in, against the use of these formulas.
For the royal name always stands isolated on these images, as a legend above the sacrificing king (Erman p.267).

b πᾶσαν ... βασιλεύειν:
corresponds with: "I have given you years to all eternity and the kingship of both countries in joy" or "I have given you the kingship of both countries and the years of Horus in joy". or "I have given you a great kingship in joy". (Erman p.267).

c πᾶσαν οἰκουμένην: Cf. ad p.112.8-9; ad p.112.14-15*b*; p.112.22.

p. 112. 6 'Ραμέστῃ = Ramses II 1304-1237 B.C., successor to Sethos I 1318-1304 B.C.

p. 112. 7-8 'Απόλλων κρατερός: the first name of the king = Horus, the strong bull (Erman p.251).

p. 112. 8 φιλαλήθης = loved by the (goddess of) truth. (Erman p.253).

p. 112. 8 *a* υἱὸς Ἥρωνος: According to **Sethe** this would include: 1⁰ son of **Atum**. 2⁰ son of **Pthah Tenen**. 3⁰ son of **Seth** (Seth: god of storms and violence, brother and murderer of Osiris. Rival of Horus. With the Greeks = Typhon. Ptah: god - creator of Memphis, patron of the artisans, with the Greeks = Hephaistos. Tenen = Tatjenen: the original earth god of Memphis. Later equated with Pthah). Cf. Sabbah II p.171, note 40 (with lit.); Woordenboek der Oudheid 2 p.385 (**Atum**. Vergote); ibid.1 p.144 (**Ammon**. Vergote); ibid.6 p.1454 (**Horus**. Vergote).

b Ἥρωνος: Originally a Tracic god. The Tracians assimilated their rider god with Greek gods, especially Apollo. In Egypt introduced in the Ptolemaeic period by Thracic mercenaries. His cultus spread especially in the Fayum. **Afterwards equated with Horus and Atum (Tum)**. Atum is the original sun-god of Heliopolis, later equated with Re, the sun-god of Heliopolis. Horus is the falcon-god, orig. a heavenly god, later equated with the king, during his lifetime. Also considered as the son of Osiris and Isis.

p. 112. 8-9 θεογέννητος κτίστης τῆς οἰκουμένης = Re, who created the gods, who founded the two countries (Erman, p.256).

p. 112. 9 ὃν Ἥλιος προέκρινεν: chosen by Re (Erman p.253).

Ἄρεως Called: row (South) 1,3; (undefined) 3; (East) 1. Within this p. 112. 9
name and the words that go with it, a title of Ramses II is hidden, strong
in truth is Re (?) (Erman p.253).

βασιλεὺς Ῥαμέστης: Son of Re: Ramses, who is loved by Amon p. 112. 9-10
(Erman p.253).

ᾧ πᾶσα ὑποτέτακται ἡ γῆ: Probably here an often-occurring phrase: p. 112. 10
under whose soles (all) countries and (all) foreign countries lie (united).
(Erman p.257).

μετὰ ἀλκῆς καὶ θάρσους: This addition also in an inscription of Ameno- p. 112. 10
phis III (1417-1379 B.C.). (Erman p.258).

IV, 19

ὁ ἑστὼς ἐπ' ἀληθείας = he who is satisfied abouf the truth (Erman p.258). p. 112. 13

δεσπότης διαδήματος = Lord of the upper-Egyptian and lower-Egyptian p. 112. 13-14
diademe. (Erman p.259).

τὴν Αἴγυπτον δοξάσας κεκτημένος: Corrupt text (?) φυλάξας? Perhaps: p. 112. 14
God Month for the country, who protects Egypt. (Month was originally
the local god of Hermonthis, South of Thebe. Later the war-god of the
Egyptian king.) (Erman p.259).

a ὁ ἀγλαοποιήσας Ἡλίου πόλιν etc.: This addition is difficult to p. 112. 14-16
reconstruct. Possibly: (of the Flaminius): "Beautiful on the memorials
at Heliopolis"; "which glorifies H. through large memorials"; "which H.
glorifies for its inhabitant (the god)" (Erman p.259).
b κτίσας τὴν λοιπὴν οἰκουμένην: Probably somewhat like the above
(p.112.8-9): who founded the two countries. λοιπή is not clear: the rest
of the world, i.e. outside Heliopolis? (Erman p.259).
c πολυτιμήσας... ἀνιδρυμένους: No analogous place on the Flaminius.
(Erman p.259).

IV, 20

Ἡλίου παῖς = son of Khepri (the scarabee-god, equated with Re as god- p. 112. 18
creator) (Erman p.253).
παμφεγγής: Incomplete. Probably a comparison of the king with the
sun-god.

p. 112. 19-20 οὗ... καιρῷ: This should not be standing here, but is found on the Flaminius II.2 as the second name of the king **Sethos**: "whose memorials will remain for ever and eternally". Thus these words have got lost here accidentally. (Erman p.260).

p. 112. 20 Ἄμμων = Amun (Amen, Amon): the great god of Thebe, whose origin is not certain. Equated with **Re** as **Amen-Re** (the sun-god of Heliopolis, head of the great enneade, supreme judge; often linked with other gods, who want to achieve universality, e.g. Amun and Sobk (the crocodile-god)).

p. 112. 20-21 πληρώσας... ἀγαθῶν:
The **Phoenix** had in **Heliopolis** a cultus besides that of the sun-god, with whom he was intimately linked. He was considered as an image of the sun-god. The model of the Phoenix is a heron: ardea cinerea, who was seen particularly at the time of the flooding of the Nile. Cf.Flamin.III.3 (Erman p.260).

p. 112.21 ᾧ... ἐδωρήσαντο: Gifted with life, like Re. (Erman p.260). Cf. p.112.11,25 and 113.7 (αἰωνόβιος).

p. 112. 22 βασιλεὺς οἰκουμένης The title was no longer understood: "king of the two Egypts", from an earlier time (Erman p.256).

p. 112. 23 ἀλλοεθνεῖς: This version is based on speculation. Cf.app.crit.edit.Clark.

p. 112. 23-24 ὅν... θεοί: corresponds with a phrase on the Flaminius IV 2: "loved by Atum, Lord of Heliopolis, gifted with life". (Erman p.262).

p. 112. 24-25 δεσπότης... αἰωνόβιος: According to Erman, p.262. these words should not be written here.

IV, 21

p. 113. 1 ΛΙΒΟΣ: λιβός Crönert Seyf. ἄλλος G.Sabbah. I do not dare give a decision on the right version.

p. 113. 2 That **Helios** speaks, is clear. λέγει is not expressed. (Erman p.268).

p. 113. 2 θεὸς... οὐρανοῦ: Titles of the sun-god, exactly thus hieroglyphically (Erman p.268).

δεδώρημαί ... ἀπρόσκοπον: corresponds with the normal phrase: "I have given you life and pleasure" (i.e. a life which always offers pleasure) (Erman p.268). The hieroglyphs vindicate G's version.   p. 113. 2-3

ἀπρόσκοπον: (ἀπρόσκορον G.Norden.Seyf.Sabbah) Dindorf.Clark. Cf. Seyf.1. p.307, note 58. G's version better?   p. 113. 3

κύριος διαδήματος: Cf. ad p.112.13-14.   p. 113. 3

ἀνείκαστος: Clark Seyf.Sabbah. But G Erman: ἀπείκαστος G's version better? Explanation? Cf. Erman p.264.   p. 113. 3

ὅς ... βασιλείᾳ G ᾧ: According to Erman correction of the manuscript by G. (Meaning: for whom the Lord of Egypt has erected statues). The version, as given by Clark, comparable to a phrase on Flaminius IV 3: "who formed the gods in their shapes in the end" (Erman p.264).   p. 113. 4

δεσπότης Αἰγύπτου: According to Erman "nicht unterzubringen".   p. 113. 4-5

καὶ ἐκόσμησεν ... οὐρανοῦ: Is reminiscent of Flamin.II.2: "who glorifies Heliopolis for its inhabitants and cleanses it for Re, its (the town's) Lord."   p. 113. 5-6

συνετελεύτησεν ... αἰωνόβιος Corresponds with the phrase on the Flamin: "he has made (it), the sun of Re, **Sethos,** loved by Ptah". (Erman p.263 sq.).   p. 113. 6-7
βασιλεύς then replaces the royal name itself.

IV, 22

The introduction to the speech of the god as in § 21. θεός instead of θεὸς μέγας: mistaken. For ῾Ραμέστῃ βασιλεῖ cf. ad p.112.6-7a.   p. 113. 9

δεδώρημαι ... ἐξουσίαν: The text by Hermapion probably read: "I have brought you and given you strength **against any country** (against all countries)" (Erman p.168). A more usual formula is: I have given you (every) strength and (every) force (victory). (Erman p.268).   p. 113. 9-10

δεσπότης χρόνων [ὁμοίως] καὶ ῞Ηφαιστος ὁ τῶν θεῶν πατήρ: "Lord of the **Jubilaea,** like his father **Ptah - Tatjenen**" (Rosettana: κύριος τριακονταετηρίων καθάπερ ὁ ῞Ηφαιστος ὁ μέγας). Also Flam.I.1, II.1.   p. 113. 11

p. 113. 11-12 προέκρινεν διὰ τὸν "Αρεα: Cf. ad p.112.9; 112.9-10.

p. 113. 12 βασιλεύς παγχαρὴς: Erman p.265 suspects: βασιλεὺς 'Ραμέστης (§ 18).

IV, 23

p. 113. 15 'Ο ἀφ' 'Ηλίου πόλεως μέγας θεὸς ἐνουράνιος: For μέγας etc. cf. ad p.113-2; ad p.113.9. The first 4 words form the **adjective: "Heliopolitane"**, which belongs to **Atum**. Before it must have been dropped: "Atum, Lord of the two Egypts". (Erman p.269).

p. 113. 16 "Ηρωνος υἱός: Cf. ad p.112.8a, b; p.112.22.

p. 113. 16 ὃν "Ηλιος ἠγάπησεν: Btl.Erfurdt.
ἠγώγησεν G. ἠρώγησεν Gronov. In my view G should not be corrected here. What is meant is a phrase like: "raised, educated by his father Amon", or "raised by Atum" (Erman p.266).

p. 113. 16 ὃν οἱ θεοὶ ἐτίμησαν: Erman does not know what to do with these words. (p.266).

p. 113. 17 ὁ πάσης γῆς βασιλεύων: the king of upper- and lower-Egypt.

p. 113. 17-18 ὃν "Ηλιος προέκρινεν... βασιλεὺς: Cf. ad p.112.9.

p. 113. 18 "Αμμων: Cf. ad p.112.20.

p. 113. 18 παμφεγγής: Cf. ad p.112.18.

p. 113. 19 *a* **et reliqua.** I agree with Seyf. that these final words were very likely those of Amm. himself; not of Gelenius therefore. In this way he indicates that he does **not** give the complete text (cf. ad 17.4.17, p.112.2b). Secondly these words form a kind of apology to his listeners (readers) for inserting such a text (and that in Greek) into his story otherwise written in Latin (he apparently expects that they (readers) can understand this Greek). Thirdly it may be pretended modesty, so as not to look like a schoolmaster who knows everything.
b = and what is said further on, what follows. For the difference between **ceteri** and **reliqui** cf. Krebs Antib.2 p.496.

V. 1

a **Datiano et Cereali consulibus. Datianus** of very low origin. **Notarius** (cf. ad 14.5.6 = I p.128) at the court of Constantinus I (307-337). Remained an influential figure under Constantius II (337-361), who made him **comes** (cf. ad 14.5.1 = I p.125) and **patricius** (Patricius is an honorary title (as **comes** is) which becomes after Constantinus I a life-long personal office, specially presented by the emperor to people who have had the highest functions, giving them the right to first place after the consuls in office and before the praefecti praetorio). Cf. Willems (op.cit.I) p.546. He becomes **consul** (cf. ad 16.1.1 = p.2) in 358 (cf. Seeck Regesten, op. cit.I, p.205). He was a Christian, born in Antiochia, which he embellished with buildings and protected like a patronus. Under Julianus (360-363) he was without influence. But this changed under Jovianus († 364) and under Valentinianus (364-375). That he was not liked in Antiochia, is apparent from the destruction of his possessions near the city during a rebellion, after the death of Jovianus. A delegation sent from Antiochia to Valentinianus at the assumption of the emperorship, also obtained forgiveness for this from Datianus, who at that time, far gone in years, was living in Constantinople, like the court. He must have died soon after; for we hear no more of him. Cf. Festugière (op.cit.XVI bibl.) p.117 sq; Petit (op.cit.XVI bibl.) p.172; p.319 sq; Seeck, B.L.Z.G. (op.cit.I) p.113 sq.

b **Naeratius Cerealis,** brother of **Vulcacius Rufinus** (cf. ad 14.10.4 = II p.100 sq.) and **Galla,** first wife of Flavius Julius Constantius, the halfbrother of Constantinus I. (cf. Stammtafeln I p.43, p.46). **Praefectus annonae** 328 A.D. (Cf. Seeck Reg. p.178). (This important official was sub dispositione praefecti urbi, with the title of clarissimus, and in charge of the supply of victuals to Rome, the price of these victuals, etc. In Constantinople, which did not have a praef.ann., the praefectus urbi of C. had to fulfill this duty).
Praefectus urbi (cf. ad 14.6.1 = I p.131) from Sept.26.352 - Dec.8.353. (Cf. Seeck Regesten p.199, 200). **Consul** 358 (Cf. Seeck Regesten p.205). Cf. et Chastagnol, Les Fastes de la Préfecture de Rome, p.135 sq.

a **cum universa per Gallias studio cautiore disponerentur. universa** = omnia: late Latin. Cf.15.8.1: nullo renitente ad internicionem barbaris vastantibus **universa;** Krebs Antib.2 p.694. Thus often in Veget.r.m.
b **disponerentur.** Cf. ad 17.1.5, p.105.16.
c **per Gallias.** Cf.16.1.2: res magnae quas **per** Gallias ... correxit; 16.6.1: Haec **per** eum annum ... **per** Gallias agebantur (local and temporal

meaning close together); 16.10.1: Haec dum **per** eoas partes et Gallias ... **disponuntur** (see above) etc. **Per Gallias** is as it were a set phrase with Amm. For the numerous examples of this (and comparable places) cf. Reinhardt (op.cit.I) p.22 sq. For **per** = **in c.ablat.** cf.ibid.p.21 sq.

d **studio cautiore.** The comparativus is normal. The two words refer to the capita 2 and 3 of this book.

p. 113. 21 **formidoque praeteritorum** = the "holy" fright for what had happened to them. For the neutr. plur.cf. ad 17.3.2, p.108.12*a* and 17.4.1, p.109.4*a*. **Praeterita** = past (events) also class. and a fairly usual expression.

p. 113. 21-22 *a* **barbaricos hebetaret excursus.** Cf.16.11.10: ad ulteriora necessitudines et fruges opesque **barbaricas** contulerunt (cf.annot.XVI p.159).

As **substant.neutr.** late Latin. Cf.18.2.14: statimque difficultate omni depulsa ponte constrato sollicitarum gentium opinione praeventa visus **in barbarico** miles per Hortarii regna transibat intacta (just preceding this there is a passage somewhat similar to 16.11.10: et indomito furore sedato **necessitudines opesque suas** transferre longius festinabant); Eutr. 7.9: qui (sc.fluvius Albis) **in barbarico** longe ultra Rhenum est; 9.4: Cum biennio ipse et filius imperassent, uterque **in barbarico** interfecti sunt ...; Hist.Aug.Alex.Sev.47.1; N.D.Occ.32, 33. From the last two places can be seen that **in barbarico** has penetrated into the official language.

b **hebetaret.** Cf.Iust.Phil.6.8.2: sic illo, velut mucrone teli, ablato duce Thebanorum, rei quoque publicae vires **hebetatae** sunt. The verb does not occur in Veget.r.m. (and neither does **hebes;** though we do find **obtusus,** in a metaphorical sense) Arn.adv.nat.Opt.Milev. In Claud.22.133 (De laud.Stilich.2):

... Nec te iucunda fronte fefellit
Luxuries praedulce malum, quae dedita semper
Corporis arbitriis **hebetat** caligine sensus
Membraque Circaeis **effeminat** acrius herbis

(where hebetat is further explained by **effeminat).** For **hebiscere** cf. ad 16. 12.54 (= XVI p.274).

p. 113. 22 **excursus.** Cf. ad 17.4.3, p.109.10-11. Not in Claud.Arn.adv.nat.Opt. Milev.

p. 113. 22 **rex Persarum:** Sapor II 310-379 A.D. Cf. ad 14.3.1 (= I p.119); ad 15.1.2 (= III p.7); ad 14.8.5 (= II p.66). From here on we will often refer to, among others, **Pighi,** Nuovi Studi Ammianei (op.cit.XVI) p.131 sq:

La questione orientale nel 358. Cf.et.R.N. Frye. The heritage of Persia, especially **chapter VI (Sassaniden)**; Stein, Spätr. Gesch. (op.cit.I) p.7 sq (with lit.)

rex Persarum - precativam. The following paraphrase may **elucidate** the contents of this sentence: the king of the P. still remained ...; although he had made his peace with the Chionitae and Gelani; and while he intended to return to his own territory, he received etc. p. 113. 22-25

in confiniis. Cf. ad 15.6.2 (= IV p.7). **agens.** Cf. ad 16.2.9 (p.21); 15.6.1 (= IV p.5); Fesser p.23; 15.5.12: Florentius Nigriniani filius **agens** tunc pro magistro officiorum; 15.5.15: **agens** inter haec aput Agrippinam Silvanus ...; etc. Sometimes = to have the command over, to have the power, to act as. Very frequent. Cf.et.Heum.-Seckel p.25.3; Dig.28.5.4.1. p. 113. 22

a **gentium extimarum. Gentes** often used of barbarian, foreign nations. Furthermore in late Latin for heathens (as opposed to Christians and Jews). Cf. Souter p.160.
b cf.17.13.27: variisque discursibus vastabat **extima** limitum; 20.10.2: inquietorum hominum licentius etiam tum percursantium **extima** Galliarum; H.A.Treb.Poll.XXX Tyr.12.13: in Illyrico vel in Thraciarum **extimis** congressus cum Aureolo; Plin.N.H.3.78: **extimis gentibus**; etc. Often in late Latin. Cf.et. Neue-Wagener[3] (op.cit.I) 2 p.192 sq. p. 113. 23

a **Chionitis** = (Chin.) Ye-ta. Cf. Pighi: "si chiamavano propriamente **Qūn**, e il loro capo **qūnxan**; furono poi chiamati **Hephthalitae** dal nome, **Hephthal,** del loro eroe vincitore di Pērōz nel 484" (p.168, with the lit. quoted there). Sabbah II p.172 (note 45) refers to **R.Ghirshman, Les Chionites - Hephthalites,** Mémoires de l'Institut français d'archéologie orientale du Caire, 80, Le Caire, 1948. At this time in Bactriana (?). Cf.et. Pieper Tab.16 **(Chorasan).** Mongolians, enemies of the **Cuseni.**
b **Gelanis.** At the Northern borders of the Persian realm. Cf.R.E.7.1. 1910. p.963 (Kiessling). Gh., quoted above, wants to read **Albanis** instead of **Gelanis.** But, Sabbah says, in that case one might as well read **Segestanis.** Cf.19.2.3: Persae omnes murorum ambitus (sc.Amidae) obsidebant; pars quae orientem spectabat, **Chionitis** evenit, qua funestus nobis ceciderat adulescens (sc.filius Grumbatis regis), **Cuseni** meridiano lateri sunt destinati, tractum servabant septentrionis **Albani,** occidentali portae oppositi sunt **Segestani acerrimi omnium bellatores.** From the p. 113. 23

underlined addition to Segestani one can only conclude, in my opinion, that A.M. repeats a tournure, as so often. Cf.et. **Geli:** R.E.7.1.1910, p.986 (Weissbach).

c **Cusēni:** "Chin.Yue-či = Ἰνδοσκύθαι nel I^p le tribù Yue-či s'unirono sotto la dinastia dei Kūšan, e furono chiamate anche con questo nomine: skr. Kuṣāṇa, lat. **Cusēni**; ne facevano parte i Τοχάροι skr. Tukhāra." (Pighi p.168 with the lit. quoted there). Cf.et. ad 16.9.4 (= XVI p.109). East of Persia **(Ghandara)**, in the upper-Indus valley. Pieper Tab.3.

d Segestani = **(Sacastani)**, East of the Persian realm, but West of the Indus. Pieper Tab.16 **(Sakastene).**

e The above-mentioned nations (a, b, c, d.) are **not** mentioned (by these names) in Tab.Peut.XII 2-5, where they should be placed somewhere.

p. 113. 23 **omnium acerrimis bellatoribus.** See previous note, *b*. For **bellator** cf. ad 16. 12.22, p.213.

p. 113. 23-24 *a* **pignore icto societatis.** In these 3 words Amm. has mixed up foedus ferire and **pignus** dare, ponere; thereby substituting foedus by societas. The whole sentence is equal to: foedere icto **pignore societatis dato.** It seems to me somewhat fruitless to start another argument on the question whether Amm. sometimes did not use Latin expressions correctly, because he did not fully understand them, or because he wanted to be original. Personally I favour the latter point of view. Deviations from the "normal" Latin are to be found more in the syntactic field. But there also one should be very careful with one's conclusions. For the judic. meaning: **contract with collateral security** cf. Heum.-Seckel p.430.

Note. For the meaning pignus = filius cf.19.2.1; 27.6.8; Hagend.St.A. p.32 sq. with lit.

b The period, during which the treaty is concluded and the letter from Tamsapor is received, is ± October/November 357 A.D. (Cf. Pighi p. 135).

c For Amm.'s preference for judicial concepts cf. Pighi note 2, p.178. (with lit. quoted). He shares this preference with many Roman historians.

p. 113. 24 *a* **rediturus ad sua.** In order to place caput **5** in the right context, it is necessary to first read (again) 16 caput **9** (= comm.XVI p.103 sq.). The sequel is to be found in 17.14. The resumption of hostilities on a large scale: 18.4 sq. A very thorough and detailed chronological survey of the years 354 - 359/60 can be found in Pighi p.134 sq., though naturally it has in some places a somewhat hypothetical character.

b **sua** ad 17.1.2, p.104.7-9*d*.

a **Tamsaporis scripta suscepit. Tamsapor:** bitaxš of Assyria and Babylonia. Cf. ad 16.9.3 (= XVI p.106); Pighi p.150. In rank comparable to the praefectus praetorio **(Musonianus).**
b **scripta.** Cf. ad 16.9.4 (= XVI p.109).
suscepit = accepit. Late Latin. Cf. Krebs Antib.2 p.633 (with lit.). Amm. uses this verb for the collecting of taxes: 19.11.3; 26.8.6 (X **offerre);** and the part.perf.pass. substantivised **(susceptus)** with a very special meaning: 30.4.15 = advocate's client (X **patronus).** And furthermore of the reception of the Alamannorum rex Suomarius as supplex 17.10.3 (can be compared with 30.4.15). Cf. et Souter p.408; Georges 2.2974 (both are mistaken with regard to 17.10.3); Heum.-Seckel p.573 sq.; Servius ad Verg.Aen.6.608 sq.: Vult autem intelligi praevaricatores, qui patroni sunt clientium, quos **nunc** susceptos vocamus.
pacem ... precativam. Note the alliteration (p), and the hyperbaton (cf. ad 17.1.6, p.105.21*a*). For **pacem precativam** cf. ad 16.9.4, p.108.

V, 2
ideoque. Cf. ad 16.12.25, p.95.9*a, b*.

non nisi ⟨in⟩ firmato imperii robore temptari talia suspicatus. firmato VEA infirmato Clark Seyf.Rolfe. V's version is also that of Sabbah II p.173 (note 47): "Toutefois, **firmato** peut être la bonne leçon, à condition de voir dans ces tractations un assaut d'hypocrisie: Sapor croit comprendre que de tels sondages sont le signe que l'Empire est renforcé; à ses yeux, c'est parce qu'ils se sentent assez forts pour faire la guerre que les Romains proposent la paix, **non pas pour la conclure mais pour savoir si les Perses la desirent;** une réponse conciliante du roi serait un aveu de faiblesse et produirait la guerre". I agree with this subtile analysis.

temptari talia suspicatus. For **talia** cf. ad 17.3.2, p.108.12*a*. Cf.et. ad 17.4.1, p.109.4*a*. Besides **suspicari** Amm. (and only he) uses with the same meaning **suspectari:** 28.1.8: inpetrarunt ut hi quos **suspectati** sunt ... conpingerentur in vincula.

a **latius semet extentans. Extentare** is one of the many frequentativa or intensiva, often from the sermo poeticus, used so often by Amm. (Cf. Hagend.St.Amm. p.67 sq.). Here it means: to boast. Sabbah: "**et comme il cherchait à s'étendre lui-même plus loin,** il s'empare du mot de paix, mais pour proposer des conditions rigoureuses." I do not agree with the underlined translation. In my view latius ... graves means (paraphrased): he boasted, though he welcomed the name of peace; **but** he made rigourous demands. "So rechnete er mit einem Frieden" (Seyf.) is not correct, I believe. **et** is adversative here (cf. Hofm.-Leum. 231*d* p.660 (with lit)). As regards **extenture** itself, cf.et.22.14.3: ridebatur enim ut Cercops homo brevis umeros **extentans** angustos etc.; Lucret.3.490: **extentat** nervos (said of an epileptic). Extremely rare verb. Not in Claud.Veget.r.m. Opt.Milev.Arn.adv.nat.

b for **semet** cf. ad 16.12.20 (= XVI p.208). Cf.et. **suopte** ad 14.11.3 (= II p.117).

p. 113. 27 **condiciones proposuit.** Cf.Hirt.b.g.8.3: tali **condicione proposita** Bituriges, cum sibi viderent clementia Caesaris reditum patere ... idem fecerunt.

p. 113. 27-28 *a* **missoque cum muneribus Narseo quodam legato.** Cf.17.5.15: imperatoris scripta perferentes **et munera.**

b **Narseo.** Cf.Petr.Patric. (Bonner Corpus I p.131): ὁ δὲ τῆς πρεσβείας ἡγεμὼν Ναρσῆς τὸ τραχὺ τῶν γραμμάτων ὧν ἐπεφέρετο τῇ τῶν οἰκείων ἡμερότητι τρόπων συγκεράσας, ἔδωκε πρὸς ἀνάγνωσιν; Pighi, p.150: "Gli altri duo furono incaricati dell' ambasciata a Constanzo, **Narseo** era il capo, diplomatico ed oratore; una parte analoga fu sostenuta nella prima ambasceria Romano da **Spettato** ed **Eustatio** presi insieme (this **1st** delegation left Sirmium ± March 25.358) e nella seconda da **Procopio** (this **2nd** delegation left ± July 10, 358).

Adace, come **Prospero (1st** delegation) e **Lucilliano (2nd** delegation), era il militare; cadde in battaglia di là dal Tigri, nel 363 (cf.25.1.6: in hac cecidit pugna **Adaces, nobilis satrapa,** legatus quondam ad Constantium principem missus ac benigne susceptus, cuius exuviis interfector Iuliano oblatis remuneratus est, ut decebat." (The Persian delegation left in the middle of November 357. One fixed date is Febr.23, 358, when the Persian delegates pass through Constantinople; cf. Pighi p.156 with lit.)). Cf. et. **Narses** R.E. 16.2.1935. p.1758 (Ensslin). Probably the same Narses is meant in 24.6.12: cum Pigrane et Surena et **Narseo** potissimis ducibus.

c **quodam.** Cf. ad 17.3.6, p.109.1-2*b*.

p. 113. 28 **litteras ad C.dedit.** In the well-known classical sense: wrote a letter to C.

p. 113. 28-29 *a* **nusquam a genuino fastu declinans.** Cf.22.8.26: quam (sc. Panticapaeum) perstringit Hypanis fluvius, **genuinis** intumescens aquis et externis

= congenital (class.). For other meanings in late Latin cf. Souter p.160. The adj. does not occur in Claud.Veget.r.m.Arn.adv.nat.Opt.Milev. Cf. et. Krebs Antib.2 p.621.

b **fastu.** Cf. ad 14.1.1 (= I p.54). Amm. uses the sing. 8 times, the plur. 6 times. The subst. is favoured by writers of the late Latin period. (cf. Hagend.St.A.p.37) Cf. et. 17.13.5: hortante igitur principe **cum genuino fastu** ad citeriorem venere fluminis ripam, ut exitus docuit, non iussa facturi; for the pomp and circumstances of the Persian kings cf.Claud.44 (Eid.1) 83-88.

a **quarum hunc fuisse accepimus sensum.** One should not be surprised p. 113. 29 that with these words Amm. speaks the truth. The style is his own, but the content is historic. This is also true of the following letter from Constantius. For a detailed analysis of both letters cf. Pighi p.181 sq.

b An important source for all details is **Libanius,** who gets his information from one of his relatives, one **Spectatus** (cf. ad 17.5.15) and especially from **Strategius (Musonianus)** (cf. ad 15.13.1 = IV p.78 sq.). Amm. could obtain direct information from **Ursicinus** (cf. ad 14.9.1 = II p.87) and **Cassianus** (cf. ad 16.9.2 (= XVI p.105)), **Prosper** (cf. ad 14.11.5 = II p.118), vicarius of Ursicinus from 354-357 and certainly well-informed on the activities of Strategius and Cassianus, and the philosopher **Eustathius** (cf. ad 17.5.15). Ursicinus, Cassianus and Prosper did **not** correspond with Libanius. From another correspondent, **Clematius** (cf. Seeck B.L.Z.G. p.110; Pighi p.174; not to be confused with the homonym 14.1. 3 = I p.107. He is **not** mentioned in Amm.), agens in rebus, Lib. obtained certainly much information. We are also in the fortunate circumstance that Amm. has a direct Persian informant, viz. **Iovinianus, satrap of Corduene** (cf.18.6.20-18.7.2; Pighi p.151, 152).

c Apart from his role as Amm.'s informant, **Libanius** is also of importance for the other informations he gives us (mainly in the form of letters) of which there are a considerable number. As sources for the Oriental politics, the wars conducted there and the delegations etc., we should also consider **Eunapius** of Sardes (Hist.270-404); **Zosimus** (Hist. 193-410); **Petrus Patricius** (under Justinianus. Hist. from Caesar to Julianus (?)); **Zonaras** (chronicle until 1118); **Philostorgius** (Arian church history until 423); **Photius** ($\pm$ 820-891, Excerpts); **Chronicon Paschale** (until 629); **Hieronymus** (Chronicle until 378); **Theophanes Confessor** (chronicle until 813). Most of the above writings are incomplete or fragmentary. The mutual relation of the sources is given in tables by **Pighi** p.155-157. His distinction into a: tradizione Eunapiana o Anatolica and a: tradizione Ariana o Costantinopolitana seems a little too ingenious to me. However, the last mentioned sources give some very poor material (partly because of the faulty condition and partly because they are mutually dependent). Amm. himself and Libanius remain the principle sources. Finally an important source are the **Oratio I** of **Julianus** (355) and the Oratio II (between 357 and 359), both speeches praising Constantius II (337-361), written rhetorically and with a political purpose (viz. to keep the emperor as his friend), and this in such a way that a critical reader is certainly not fooled. We have to assume that Amm. knew **all** of Julianus' writings. Besides these orationes some **letters by Julianus** can be considered as sources.

V, 3

p. 113. 30-31 *a* **Rex regum Sapor, particeps siderum, frater Solis et Lunae, Constantio Caesari fratri meo. rex regum.** Cf.19.2.11: resultabant altrinsecus exortis clamoribus colles, nostris virtutes **Constanti Caesaris** extollentibus, ut domini rerum et mundi, Persis Saporem **saansaan** appellantibus et **pirosen,** quod **rex regibus imperans** et **bellorum victor** interpretatur. (**Peroz** ruled from 459-484 A.D. This name becomes part of the royal title and means: the invincible. To this day it is one of the titles of the Sjah of Iran (pirouz)). Similarly in modern Persia: šāhinšāh (cf.et. Pighi p.182 sq. and especially note 9, with extensive lit.). As regards the religious titles, cf.23.6.4-5: certatimque summatum et vulgi sententiis concinentibus **astris,** ut ipsi existimant, **ritus sui consecratione permixtus est omnium primus.** Unde ad id tempus reges eiusdem gentis praetumidi appellari se patiuntur **Solis fratres et Lunae,** utque imperatoribus nostris **Augusta** nuncupatio amabilis est et optata etc.

(Of course, Amm. is not aware of the fact that **Augustus,** later a fixed part of the imperial titulatory, was originally a religiously laden word, and, considered as such, could well be compared with the religious titles of the Sassanids. Had he been aware of this, he would have left out the word **praetumidi.** To which can be added, that also in this he was prejudiced, in that he did not realise that the Roman emperors of that era were also worshipped almost like gods, or as their substitutes, or of the one Christian God, on earth). Cf. et Pighi p.183 and notes 2-5, with the lit. quoted there. The king of the Sassanids is of heavenly origin (literally) and a creation of Ahura Mazda. No wonder that he is: Sharer of the stars and brother to Sun and Moon.

b Dilleman (op.cit.XVI) p.97 says: "Ce sont ces relations (viz. with Ursicinus and Iovinianus) et non une hypothétique connaissance de la langue perse, comme l'a laissé entendre Gardthausen (Jahrb.f.class. Philol., Suppl.Bnd.VI, VII, p.511), qui lui ont valu l'importante mission secrète dont il a été chargé à travers la Corduène (18.6.20). Si Ammien est fier de son grec, **il ne dit nulle part qu'il parlait des idiomes orientaux.** Toute la démonstration de son savoir en la matière se limite à la traduction de deux mots perses, **saansan** et **pirosen** (19.2.11) et à l'explication de trois toponymes Syriaques, sans indication de la langue, **Meiacarire** (18.6.16), **Naarmalcha** (24.2.7) e **Zaitha** (23.5.7). Les correspondants latins des deux premiers étaient d'ailleurs d'usage courant, comme le montre la Table de Peutinger." Although Amm. and many of his contemporaries liked to show off their erudition, I am not quite sure that Dilleman is right. It seems very probable to me that Amm. had some knowledge of Persian and/or Arabic, in whatever dialect or form. When reading in the Not.Dign. Orientis, one continually finds added to army divisions of the duces the word: **indigenae.** It is highly improbable that the common man from these divisions spoke much more than his native tongue. All he would probably understand would be some commands. For that reason it is not surprising that a high-ranking officer like Amm. knew an other language besides Latin and Greek. It was perhaps not fashionable in leading circles in Rome, in which Amm. liked to be included, to show off one's knowledge of languages like Persian, Armenian, etc. But it is doubtful whether the "Greeks" in Asia Minor etc. were of the same opinion. Final conclusion: Dilleman gives the **wrong** arguments for this thesis.

c **Constantio Caesari.** This brief indication also in 19.2.11 (see *a*). Officially: Imp.Caes.Flavius Iulius Constantius Aug. (For other additional titles cf. Sandys-Campbell, Lat.Epigr., 1927, p.255). The pompous titles of the imperial chancellary: 17.5.10. Cf.et. Pighi p.182.

d **fratri meo.** Eastern custom, taken over by the Romans. For other places cf. Pighi p.182, notes 7 and 8.

e How little despots can become inflated, can be seen from Sall.Jug. 110.1 (quoted by Pighi): "Nunquam ego ratus sum fore uti **rex maximus** in hac terra et **omnium, quos novi,** privato homini gratiam deberem" (Bocchus).

gandeo - replicasse. Although Sapor's moralising strikes us as rather funny, he probably meant it quite seriously. These Sassanids are rather orthodox and puritan. Therefore the letter by Sapor is the **official** reaction (of Sapor) on the **letter from Tamsapor.** (cf. ad 17.5.1, p.113.23-24*b*; ibid. p.113,24*a*; ibid.p.113, 24-25 and V.2.25-26; ibid. p.113.26*a*). So

p. 114. 1-6

the Romans **have to** reply, somehow. The careful and unofficial contacts of the Romans with the Persians are concluded by **this** letter. The two highest potentates are confronted with each other. Cf.et. Pighi p.173 and 16.9.1-4 (with comm. XVI p.103 sq.) and Pighi p.184: "Con tale principio Šahpuhr ammette d'aver ricevuto delle proposte che presupponevano un riconoscimento della sua ragione e dà quindi al suo scritto il carattere d'una **risposta:** egli è stato officiato, **dunque il nemico riconosce d'aver torto".** The **cupiditas,** which Constantius is reproached with, is found again in the words with which at Ctesiphon **Spectatus** addresses Sapor, according to the words of Libanius (ep.334.4) σκόπει μὴ πλεονεξίαν ἐγκαλῶν αὐτὸς τοῦτο ποιῶν ἐλεγχθῆς (Pighi p.184).

p. 114. 2 *a* **et incorruptum aequitatis agnovisse suffragium.** Cf.Liv.4.6.11: Eventus eorum comitiorum docuit alios animos in contentione libertatis dignitatisque, alios secundum deposita certamina **incorrupto iudicio** esse (the certamina have come into being because of the: comitia tribunis consulari potestate tribus creandis). In my view **suffragium** has here also the meaning of **iudicium,** not **voice** (voix, Stimme), as translated by Seyf. and Sabbah. In any case the use of the subst. here is very striking. In judic. Latin one finds the meaning: intercession, recommandation (with the emperor, for an office) and: support, favour. I do not think these meanings fit here. Cf.Heum.-Seckel p.567; Souter p.399.

b The **cupiditas,** which Constantius is imputed with here by Sapor, is attributed to Sapor by Amm. in 18.4.1: augendique regni **cupiditate** supra homines flagrans. Cf.et.17.4.3: Cambyses, quoad vixerat **alieni** cupidus et immanis (with notes ad l.p.109.12*a*).

c **aequitas** The natural sense of justice, not blinded by, for instance, the pertinax alieni cupiditas. Cf.Dig.41.1.9.3: Hae quoque res, quae traditione nostrae fiunt, **iure gentium** nobis adquiruntur: nihil enim tam conveniens est **naturali aequitati** quam voluntatem domini volentis rem suam in alium transferre ratam haberi; ibid.4.4.1: (Ulpianus) Hoc edictum praetor **naturalem aequitatem** secutus proposuit, quo tutelam minorum suscepit etc. Thus S. reproaches C. for not being a rex **patientior aequi** (= "more inclined to listen to justice and fairness": Stat.Theb.I.190).

p. 114. 3 *a* **pertinax alieni cupiditas quas aliquotiens ediderit strages. aliquotiens** is in Amm. = **saepe** and occurs quite often, e.g. 29.5.22; 29.6.15; 30.2.9; 30.4.16; 30.4.22; 30.7.1; 30.8.3; 30.8.11; 31.2.11; 31.13.19; 31.14.3; Cod. Theod.9.42.15. And probably also Veget.r.m.3.9 (Lang p.87). The adverb does not occur in Claud.Arn.adv.nat.Opt.Milev. nor in the vulgair Mulom.Chir.

b   **ediderit: aor.gnomicus** in the conjunct.orat.obl. (dependent question). Cf. ad 16.12.40, p.97.28 - p.98.1.

c   **quas** = quantas. As so often in the figure of speech called amplificatio, e.g. Stat.Theb.2.303: (Eriphyle) **Quos** optat gemitus, **quantas** cupit impia clades! ibid.1.188: **Quas** gerit ore minas, **quanto** premit omnia fastu! Cf.Heuvel Comm.Stat.Theb.I p.128; Mulder Comm.Stat.Theb.II p.209.

d   **strages.** Cf.Cic. ad Att.1.16.1: quas ego pugnas et quantas **strages edidi** (see also previous note); Cic.leg.3.9.22: Sed ille **quas strages edidit!**

V, 4

a   **quia - replicasse.** Since time immemorial all monarchs and statesmen speak the truth, or so they say, but **not** their enemies or adversaries, or, as Pighi so aptly says: (p.184) "Quanto alla verità et alla sincerità ... essa è l'arma cortese della diplomazia che da millenni s'affila sull' inconsumabile cote dell' ingenuità umana". But here again we have to bear in mind that the destruction of the lie was one of the main points of the doctrine of Zarathustra, and so far Sapor may be "honest" in his own way. p. 114. 3-4

b   The first words mean: because therefore the method (or: the thinking, argumentation) of the truth must be unhindered and free. Cf.Cic. de fato 15(33): illorum **ratio soluta ac libera est** (Fletcher St.Borr.op.cit.II); cf. et. ad 14.10.13 (= II p.110). Cf.et.**Hagend.** abund. (op.cit.I) p.174: **Gudeman** Tac.Dial.² (1914) p.490.

celsiores fortunas. Cf.30.5.3: remissior erga **maiores fortunas** vel verbis asperioribus incessendas. For the personificatio cf. ad 17.2.1, p.107.13. **Celsior**: in official language = higher in rank, "superior". Cf.Cod.Iust. 48.2: Singuli quique **iudices** (cf.XVI p.52) sciant **celsioribus viris** et his, quorum nonnumquam iudicio provehuntur, honorificentiam esse debitam praestandam, nec in subscriptionibus suis **fratres** audeant nominare, apparitione (personnel) multanda, cuius haec cura est (a⁰ 384). Another fine sample of Byzantine bureaucracy. **Celsitudo** is also a title. Cf.Cod. Iust.12.59.3 (to Eusignius praef.praet.): ... Etenim officii **celsitudinis tuae** primiscrinius tres libras auri fisci utilitatibus sine dilatione persolvet etc. (= ± "Excellency". a⁰ 386); ibid.12.3.5: Quis enim patiatur patrem quidem posse per emancipationis modum suis nexibus filium relaxare, **imperatoriam** autem **celsitudinem** non valere eum quem sibi patrem elegit p. 114. 4

137

ab aliena eximere potestate? (here are meant the **patricii**. a⁰ 531-533) = "Your Highness". **Celsitudo** does not occur in this sense in Amm. Cf.et. Claud.29 (Laus Serenae):

patruo te principe **celsam**
Bellipotens illustrat avus ...

(Stilicho was married to Serena, **a cousin of Theodosius** 379-395); ibid.44 (Phoenix) 87 sq. ... tumidusque regendo.

Celsa per famulas acies **dicione** superbit.
(said of the king of the Parths).

p. 114. 5 **in pauca conferam** = I will briefly summarise.

in pauca conferre occurs in Plaut. and Cic., e.g. Plaut.Poen.5.4.54; Cic. pro Cael.6(17): Ut **in pauca conferam,** testamento facto mulier moritur. Cf.et.Veget.r.m.2.3 (= Lang p.37): Cato ille Maior ... plus se rei publicae credidit profuturum, si disciplinam militarem **conferret in litteras.**

p. 114. 6 **reminiscens.** For the acc.c.inf. with this verb cf. Hofm.-Leumann p.586. For the acc.c.inf. in general cf. ad 17.4.13, p.111.5.

p. 114. 6 *a* **haec ... replicasse.** To Constantinus I (307-337) Sapor had sent a delegation in 336, so at this time 22 years ago. Cf. Pighi p.184.

b **replicasse.** Cf. ad 16.12.69, p.102.23-24c (for the contraction). The meaning: to repeat is late Latin. Cf. Krebs Antib.2 p.502; Souter p.351; Amm.30.1.3: (Terentius dux) qui ascitis in societatem gentilibus paucis ob flagitia sua suspensis in metum **scribendo ad comitatum assidue** Cylacis necem **replicabat** et Arrabannis; 28.4.13: poscuntur etiam in conviviis aliquotiens trutinae, ut appositi pisces et volucres ponderentur et glires, quorum magnitudo **saepius replicata** non sine taedio praesentium ut antehac inusitata **laudatur assidue** maxime. For the unrolling of a piece of writing: 20.9.6: **replicatoque volumine** edicti, quod missum est et legi ab exordio coepto.

V, 5-6

p. 114. 6 **adusque - bellorum eventus.** § 5 and § 6 are interesting for the foreign policy of the Sassanids. They pretend to be the heirs of the **Achaemenids.** To them the **Arsacids** do not exist, as it were ($\pm$ 247 B.C. - $\pm$ 228 A.D.).

p. 114. 6 As heirs (of the Achaemenids) they claim their kingdom, at the time when this was largest. Sapor also appeals to the testimony of the Greeks: **anti-**

quitates vestrae. Persian diplomats will undoubtedly have helped him in finding this learned argument. (There were enough Greek-speaking and -reading persons at court and in the capitals). Probably this mainly refers to Herodotus. But S. shows a certain modesty in only claiming the right to **Mesopotamia** and **Armenia,** the most important strategic areas. It is necessary to give here in short a part of past history. **Diocletianus** (284-305) **Augustus** and his **Caesar Galerius** (Caes.293, Aug.305-311), (cf. Stammt.VIII p.50.I), had conquered **Narsāh** (293-302) in 297. "Durch den Frieden von 297 wurde die Römische Provinz **Mesopotamien** bis an den oberen Tigris ausgedehnt, aber auch jenseits von diesem bis an den Arsanias und den Wan-See traten die kleinen Erbfürsten (Satrapen) der **südarmenischen** sogenannten "Satrapieën" unter Belassung ihrer Autonomie in den römischen Reichsverband, wenigstens der Sache nach; denn formell mag auch jetzt noch der König von Armenien als ihre unmittelbarer Lehnsherr gegolten haben. Dieser, der Römerfreund **Trdat**, wurde für den Verlust im Süden durch eine Grenzregulierung auf Kosten der **persischen Provinz Adherbeidschan** entschädigt **und die Römische Suzeränität über Armenien und die nördlich davon gelegene Kaukasuslandschaft Iberien (Georgien) von den Persern feierlich anerkannt.** (Stein p.119 sq.). Soon afterward **Trdat** became a Christian, after which followed the Christianisation of Armenia. Some time later the conversion of the Roman empire followed. Religion and politics became mighty allies. **Sapor II** was not prepared to acquiesce in the defeat of 199 A.D. (**Mesopotamia** conquered by Septimius Severus (193-211) and made into a provincia), nor in the losses of 297 A.D. He continually intervenes in Armenia and further acts in an offensive manner towards the Romans (cf. Pighi p.161). Thus the Romans had to be very wary of this obstinate enemy, who did them considerable harm. "Bisognava prevenire anche un altro pericolo: che cioè il ritorno di Šahpur in Occidente sottraesse **l'Armenia** all' influenza Romana. E proprio in quel tempo la diplomazia di Costanzo diede un utile risultato: il **katholikos d'Armenia Nersēs**, giunse a capo d'un 'ambasceria, mandato dal re **Aršak (III)**; l'antica alleanza tra Romani e Armeni fu rinnovata e confermata da un'alleanza tra i due sovrani: **Olympias**, la vedova di **Constante**, fu mandata sposa ad Arsak. Politica da felix Austria; intanto serviva ad assicurare la sinistra del fronte Romano contro i Persiani". (Pighi p.179 sq).

1) **Note. Olympias** had been engaged to **Constans** (337-350). The marriage was not celebrated. She was a daughter of the former **praef. praetorio Ablabius**, favourite of Constantinus I (307-337) and consul in 331. Constantius II (337-361) had him executed (338). The abovementioned

marriage took place before 357/358. She was still alive in 360, but was later poisoned by the repudiated wife of **Aršak III**.
2) For **Arsaces** etc. cf.20.11.1-3 (this history); 21.6.8; 23.2.2; 24.8.6; 25.7.12; 27.12.1-3 (his death).
3) For **Ablabius** cf.et. Seeck B.L.Z.G. p.35 (homonyms) and p.272.
4) For the spreading of **Christianity** in **Armenia** cf. Pieper (op.cit.II) Tab. 7, and in **Persia** ibid.Tab.16. **Litt.** ibid. p.28 and p.49 sq.; v.Harnack (op.cit.I) p.678 sq. (with lit.): Mesop., Persia, Parthia, India and p.747*B* (with lit.): Armenia, Diospontus, Paphlagonia, Pontus Polemoniacus. Important sources: 1) **Faustus**, annalist from the 4th century A.D., whose annals (fragmentary) only exist in the Armenian translation (Edit.F.H.G. (op.cit.I) 5.2.209 sq.; Lauer, Köln, 1879 (in German)). 2) The extremely valuable **Chronicle of Arbela** ('Εκκλησιαστική) a chronologically ordered series of biographies, such as of the acta marty(ro)rum, covering the period from 100-550 A.D. This chronicle probably dates from the 6th century after Christ. Edit. **Mingana** Sources Syriaques I (1907) in Syrian and French; **Sachau**, in German, with an extensive historical-critical introduction (S.B.Preusz. Akad.1915.6). Detailed review of this work by Harnack (op.cit.I)2. p.683-689. 3) **Chronicon Paschale** (= Chron.Alexandr. = Chron.Constantin.) until 627 A.D., written not long after 629 A.D. Of lesser value than 2) and not very independent. Edit.**L.Dindorf**, Bonn, 1832; **Migne** P.G.92 (1865) c.69-1023. Discussion: **G.Moravcsik**, Byzantinoturcica I, p.122 Budapest, 1942. 4) The **Chronicle of Edessa**, written ± 540 A.D. Edit. **C.S.Chr.Orient.3**, 4; **Haller**, German translation, Texte u. Unters. z.Gesch.d.altchr.Lit.9, 1. (For **Edessa** capital of the province of Osrhoëne, very important early-Christian centre, cf.et.Woordenb.d.Oudheid 4, 1969, p.925 with lit.; Bartelink). Valuable. 5) **Ephrem** (306-373). Edit. **Assemani**, 6 vol., Syrian-Latin and Greek-Latin, 1732, Rome. Born at Nisibis, later living in Edessa. "Topical" are the **Carmina Nisibena** (edit. Bickell, Leipzig, 1866). Cf.et. Woordenboek d. Oudheid, 4, 1969, p.1015, with lit.; Bartelink. Partial translation: Bibl.d. Kirchenväter[2] 37, 1919 (by Euringer and Rücker). Furthermore something can be found with some care in 6) **Joannes Malalas**, chronicle until 563, edit. **L.Dindorf**, Bonn, 1831. A confused, highly popular and uncritical compilation, but sometimes containing valuable material. Extensive lit. **Byzant.** (op.cit.3)) p.184 sq.

p. 114. 6 **adusque**. Cf. ad 14.8.5 (= II p.64); ad 17.2.2 (p.107.20).

Strymona flumen = Struma. Cf.Claud.10 (de nupt.Hon. et Mariae) 309 sq.:
   Dicere nunc possem quae proelia gesta sub Aemo,
   Quaeque cruentarint fumantem **Strymona** pugnae;
ibid.15 (de bello Gild.) 475 sq.:
   Ingenti clangore grues aestiva relinquunt
   Thracia, cum tepido permutant **Strymona** Nilo;
ibid.26.178 sq. (de bello Getico):
   ... facili contemptum **Strymona** saltu,
   et frustra rapidum damnant Aliacmona Bessi.
(viz. the Bessi accuse both of them of not having stopped the Geti).

Macedonicos fines. What is meant, of course, is the **old** Macedonia from early Greek history, made into a great nation by Philippus II and Alexander the Great. For the **later** division cf. ad 17.7.1. The **adj.** also 26.6.20. This same **Macedonia** also referred to 22.8.2: Athos in **Macedonia** mons ille praecelsus **navibus** quondam **Medecis** pervius. In 31.5.16: inflammata **Macedonia** omnis, M. also has a wider meaning than the later more "technical" one from Amm.' time (for here the events are described from the middle of the 3rd century after Christ).

tenuisse maiores ⟨imperium⟩ meos: Clark Seyf.Rolfe. Without **imperium**: V Sabbah, correct, in my view. Cf.Dig.41.2.24: quia, quod ex iusta causa corporaliter a servo **tenetur**, id in peculio servi est et peculium, quod servus civiliter quidem **possidere** non posset, sed naturaliter **tenet**, dominus creditur **possidere**. Cf.et. ad 17.4.5, p.109.18.

tenuĭsse maiores mĕos: clausula III. Cf. Pighi St.Amm.p.54: "Tenere quin absolute pro **pertinere, obtinere** dictum sit, nihil impedit". (with examples). For **simplex pro composito** cf.et. Pighi ibid.p.54 sq. (Comprehensive list with examples from late Roman writers and from Amm.); ad 16.5.6, p.76.12; ad 15.2.5 (= III p.18).

a **ne sit adrogans quod adfirmo.** In the words now following no trace of modesty can be found. Here also nothing new under the sun: cf. Pighi p.185, note 6.
b Note the rhythme and the opening rhyme (**ad-**). Claus.III. **Affirmare**: to state definitely, with certainty (class.). But the **arrogantia** is already partly contained in the **affirmatio** of that which Sapor lets follow.
c Cf.et.17.13.33: postremo ego quoque hostilis vocabuli spolium prae

me fero, secundo Sarmatici cognomentum, quod vos unum idemque sentientes mihi **(ne sit arrogans dicere)** merito tribuistis (from an oratio by Constantius).

p. 114. 9 *a* **splendore virtutumque insignium serie.** Cf.Claud.17 (de Fl.M.Theod. cons.) 14 sq.:

> Accedunt trabeae. Nil iam, Theodore, relictum,
> Quo **virtus** animo crescat, vel **splendor** honore;

ibid.18.29 sq. (In Eutr.I):...

> discrimina quaedam/sunt famulis **splendorque** suus; maculamque minorem/Conditionis habet, domino qui vixerit uno.

(where from the contrast between **splendor** and **macula** the meaning of the first subst. becomes apparent); finally ibid.31.66 sq. (Epith.Pall. et Celer.):

> Per cunctos iit ille gradus, aulaeque labores
> Emensus, tenuit summae fastigia sedis,
> Eoum stabili moderatus iure senatum.
> Hic **splendor** iuveni.

splendor: here: noble parentage of the son from a father, whose eminent career is described (in v.66-68). Thus **splendor** refers to the social position, the splendid style of living, the elevated status. Thus also here in Amm.

b **serie.** Cf. af 16.12.26, p.95,13*b*.

p. 114. 9-10 **vetustis regibus = pristinis regibus.** Cf.Cic.part.orat.11(37): In temporibus autem praesentia et praeterita et futura cernuntur; in his ipsis **vetusta, recentia,** instantia, paullo post aut aliquando futura **(vetusta** here: long ago, **recentia**: recently); quotation by Georges.

p. 114. 10 **antistantem.** The same construction in Cic. de invent.2.1.2: Etenim quodam tempore Crotoniatae multum omnibus (dativ.) corporum viribus et dignitatibus **antistiterunt ... sed ubique ... admisi.** This passage is difficult to interprete. Cf. Pighi p.186: "Se tanto pretendessi sarei nel giusto. Ma un ricordo mi sta a cuore, in ogni caso, sempre; con quello sono cresciuto **ab aduliscentia prima,** e in esso allevato **nihil unquam paenitemdum admisi.**" Ciò è come dire che durante la lunghissima guerra egli non ha mai dubitato del suo diritto, e perciò non ha mai chiesto pace; i Romani, chiedendola - non dimentichiamo che il passo di Strategio era stato per i Persiani una richiesta non già un' offerta (cf. Pighi p. 178), - mostrano di riconoscere il loro torto: è il pensiero che ha suggerito il primo periodo del messaggio (cf. Pighi p.184). E continua: "Per ciò devo ricuperare l'Armenia e la Mesopotamia sottratte al mio avo con voluto inganno". - Questo è il ricordo, il cibo amaro di cui s'è nutrito il rancore di Šāhpuhr fin quasi da momento che il mayupatān mayupat l'incoronava nel seno della madre." Sabbah II p.53 translates: "**Mais en tous les cas** je reste fidèle au souvenir dans lequel j'ai grandi depuis la prime jeunesse, sans jamais rien commetttre dont je doive me repentir" (without further explanation). Seyf.1 p.223 translates: "**Jedoch** liegt mir stets die Erinnerung am Herzen, in der ich von frühester Jugend an aufgewachsen bin und niemals etwas begangen habe, was verwerflich wäre." (An extremely obscure interpretation, in my view. Here neither any further explanation). **ubique** Pighi understands in a temporal sense and refers to Veg.r.m.3.17 (= Lang p.102): Hoc primi Lacones invenerunt, imitati sunt Karthaginienses, Romani postea **ubique** servarunt en Mart. 5.25.-910:

(Hoc, rogo, non melius ...)
Quam non sensuro dare quadringenta caballo
aureus ut Scorpi nasus **ubique** micet?

(Refers to a golden statue which might possibly be erected.) The temp. meaning (= at all time) **can** be defended in both quotations. I add to this Dig.47.2.12.2: sed utrum **semper** creditoris interest an ita demum, si debitor solvendo non est? et putat Pomponius **semper** eius interesse pignus habere quod et Papinianus libro duodecimo quaestionum probat: et verius est **ubique** creditoris interesse, et ita et Iulianus saepissime scripsit (= in all cases or: at all time). Cf.et. Krebs Antib.2 p,687: "Erst die sinkende Latinität macht einen allgemeinen Gebrauch von **ubique**" (with the lit. quoted there); Svennung Pall. (op.cit.II) p.41 (S.319); Ravenn.Cosm.34 (= Schnetz p.110): Etenim **ubique** (= ubicumque) insulas in oceano dilatissimo legimus, ipsas insulas subtilius perscrutantes Christo nobis auxiliante designavimus. When a sentence is difficult or impossible to explain by itself, one should take a look at the periods preceding of immediately following this. It then says: My ancestors possessed a kingdom, stretching as far as the Strymon and the borders of Macedonia. It is proper for me to claim these regions, the more so as I surpass them. (after which our sentence follows). **And therefore I have to reconquer Arm. with Mesop.**, which have been taken from my grandfather (viz. **Narses**) by cunning and deceit. This **therefore (Ideoque)** has to refer to our sentence (sed ubique ... admisi), the contents of which anyhow should mean: but I am satisfied with less, **for I have never overstepped the mark** (nihil umquam paenitendum admisi). Why was that? Because I was: coalitus ab aduliscentia prima **recordationi, (quae) ubique mihi cordi est.** What does this **recordatio** mean? The subst. also occurs in

25.3.17: (last words of Iulianus) nec me gestorum **paenitet** aut gravis flagitii **recordatio** stringit (in the normal class. meaning). **Recordari** means: to bring to mind through one's memory, so that it is present, as it were 1), though the verb may also refer to the future, as in Ovid.Her.10.79: non tantum, quae sum passura, **recordor;** and Iust.5.7: sibi quisque ante oculos obsidionem, famem et superbum victoremque hostem proponentes, iam ruinam urbis et incendia, iam omnium captivitatem et miserrimam servitutem **recordantes.** (This last meaning develops when one brings to memory that of which one thinks that it will agree with what one hopes or fears) 2). From this follows the meaning: to take to heart, to consider seriously. 3) When the last meaning (3) is taken here for **recordatio**, the sentence becomes clear. What does S. say which he takes to heart (and remembers) continuously? In my view this can only mean in the context: the poise, the self-restriction, the moderation in aims and desires, already indicated previously by **aequitas,** as opposed to: **pertinax alieni cupiditas.** So **coalitus** is a participium and **admisi** the verbum finitum in the relative subordinate clause. Nothing should be changed to the construction. From the above can be concluded that I do not agree with Pighi's exposé.

Note. Pighi note 1, p.186 says: "Forse è da leggere **ubique mihi ⟨cordi⟩ est recordatio (sc. rerum):** "dovunque (io sia) il ricordo (con cui sono cresciuto) mi segue." l'errore per **anticipazione** et **posticipazione** non è raro in V: 17.5.3: optima[te]m ...te; 17.5.8: [aetate] **aequitate;** 17.10.2: tageti[ni]cis ... vegonicis; to[res]nitr⟨u⟩um ... fragor**es;** 21.3.4: taciturnum ... eff[ac]icacem; 21.10.6: grati⟨a⟩ ... aemu[ti]la(n)dum (Cf. Hertz Amm. Marc. p.6. op.cit.I). Although both phenomena are of interest to text critics, they are not important here. Amm. deliberately repeats **cor** in **recordatio.** For this **lusus verborum** cf. ad 15.4.2 (= III p.56); Blomgren (op.cit.II) p.128 sq.; Hagend.St.Amm. p.110 sq.; etc. One must not think that such a lusus verborum was restricted to Amm. Very characteristic examples are to be found in **Opt.Milev.** edit. Ziwsa p.290 s.v.

V, 6

p. 114. 11 **ideoque** = ideo.Cf. ad 17.12.25, p.95.9*b*.

p. 114. 12 **Armeniam.** Cf. ad 14.11.14 (= II p.147); ad 17.5.5, p.114.5; Woordenboek der Oudheid 2, 1956, p.306-309 (Nuchelmans-Bartelink), with lit. Here is mainly meant **Armenia maior.**

p. 114. 12 **Mesopotamia.** Cf. ad 14.3.1 (= I p.119); ad 14.8.5 (= II p.64): **Eufratis;** ad 14.9.1 (= II p.85): **Nisibis;** 14.3.3 (= I p.120): **Osdroena;** ad 17.5.5, p.114.5, Opm.4; Pieper Tab.VI and p.27; Pighi p.160 map (**with the borders before and after 363 A.D.**). Here the Roman provincia of Mesopotamia is meant, of the diocesis Orientis, of the praefectura praetorio per Orientem. This province is only part of Mesopotamia, in the broadest sense of the word, but strategically (and economically) highly important. Further mentioned in: 15.13.4; 17.5.11; 17.14.1; 18.6.5; 18.7.3; 18.7.5; 18.8.2; 20.2.4; 20.6.1; 20.7.17; 21.6.2; 21.11.2; 21.13.1; 21.13.8; 23.2.7; 23.6.13; 25.5.3; 25.7.2; 25.8.7; 25.8.16; 26.6.2; 30.2.4. Often mentioned together with **Armenia**: 17.5.4; 17.5.11; 15.13.4. Described by Amm. in a book which has since been lost: 14.7.21: ... per orientales provincias, quas recensere puto nunc oportunum, absque **Mesopotamia,** iam digesta cum bella Parthica narrarentur (cf. ad h.l. II p.51). Indispensable for the geography is the book by **L. Dillemann,** (quoted XVI Bibl.), which gives a very critical analysis of Amm.' sources and the theories about them. In this commentary this work will be quoted several times more as **Dilleman A.M.** I agree with his final conclusion (p.142).

a **avo meo composita fraude praereptam.** avo: Narsāh 293-302 A.D. (cf.17.5.5, p.114.5).

b Cf.Eutr.10.3: Inde ad Gallias profectus est **dolo composito** tamquam a filio esset expulsus (sc. Maximianus by Maxentius; cf.I p.44). Cf.et. ad 16.11.15, p.91.2. Cf.30.1.19; Liv.26.12.16; Fletcher Styl.Borr. (op.cit.II) p.384.

c **praereptam** = snatched (away) (also class.). With the meaning: prematurely snatched away Claud.15.253 (De bello Gild.). Also class. The verb not in Veget.r.m.Arn.adv.nat.Opt.Milev.

d It should be noted here that the Romans had conquered the Persians in 297 A.D. in a "normal" way, viz. in a war and not particularly by cunning and deceit. And the peace treaty of 298 was completely fair, at least in the eyes of the Romans. But (as is usually the case), when the peace treaty of 363 had been concluded, which returned half of Mesopotamia to the Persians, while taking from the Romans the protectorate over Armenia, Sapor observed **this** treaty with great care, **because it was to his advantage.** Cf.27.12.10-18; 29.1.3; Pighi p.187.

(P.praeruptura) Cf. ad 15.5.36 (= III p.123).

illud apud nos numquam in acceptum f⟨e⟩retur: Haupt, Clark. V numquam in acceptum fretus (B fastu). G numquam acceptum fuit. Madvig numquam iri acceptum fretus. Cf. Pighi p.187 annot.1: "Cicerone usa **in acceptum referre** (Verr.II.1.149) e **aliquid acceptum referre** (Caecin.17); i giureconsulti (cf. Kalb Wegweiser in die Röm. Rechtsspr., 1961, p.32,37) conservano **(in) acceptum referre** per significare l'annotazione scritta (cf.Iavol. [Lab.] Dig.32.29.2; Paul.Dig.46.3.101.1) ma hanno **(in) acceptum** o **accepto ferre** (Mac.Dig.48.11.7.2; Paul.Dig.46.4.9,15), col verbo semplice, che spesso nella loro lingua sta in luogo del composto (Kalb Wegweiser p.26), per indicare il contratto verbale. Qui Ammiano segue l'uso della lingua giuridica". Cf.et. Heum.-Seckel p.8. In my opinion this note of Pighi's is sufficient to defend Haupt's version against other conjectures and forced constructions.

p. 114. 13-15 *a* **quod adseritis vos exultantes ... eventus,** Cf. ad 17.5.4, p.114.3-4*a*; Pighi p.187: "Predicava bene, il divino Šahpuhr, con la logica mistica e la mentalità puritana del mazdeismo".

b **adseritis.** Thus also with a partic.praes., which indicates an attendant circumstance 17.11.4 (Pompeium). quorum alterum factitare ut dissolutum, alterum ut novarum rerum cupidum **asserebant** nihil interesse **oblatrantes** ... quam partem corporis redimiret ... = amid invectives. These are the same kind of sentences so often found, for instance, in the N.T.: Ev.sec.Ioan.18.40: Clamaverunt ergo rursum omnes, dicentes: Non hunc, sed Barabbam; Apoc.Ioan.15.2: Et vidi tamquam mare vitreum mistum igne et eos qui vicerunt bestiam ... stantes super mare vitreum, habentes citharas Dei: et cantantes canticum Moysi servi Dei, et canticum Agni, dicentes: ...; Ev.sec.Luc.13.14: Respondens autem archisynagogus, indignans quia sabbato curasset Iesus: dicebat turbae: ... 15: Respondens autem ad illum Dominus dixit; etc. Cf.et. ad 16.12.43, p.98.17-18*b*.
For exultantes cf. ad 16.12.37, p.97.12*a*.

c **nullo discrimine virtutis ac doli.** For the abl. modi cf. ad 14.1.6 (= I p.62); ad 16.8.5, p.81.16; ad 17.4.12, p.110.26*b*. Liesenberg (1890), op. cit.I, p.2 sq. = without making any distinction between courage and cunning. Another moralistic standpoint. But for the rest Sapor blames the Romans for something, which, in theory at least, they refute. Pighi p.188 quotes Liv.45.22.5; 27.44.1; Cic. ad Att.9.7A.1; Ovid.Her.2.85 sq.:
   Exitus acta probat? careat successibus opto
   Quisquis ab eventu facta notanda putat.
Cf.et. ad 17.1.1, p.104.4: **discretio.**

d **prosperos omnes laudari debere bellorum eventus.** Hyperbaton. Cf. ad 17.1.6, p.105.21*a*.

V, 7

p. 114. 15-21 Pighi p.188: "Non solo sarà δίκαιον, in senso assoluto, ma per Costanzo sarà συμφέρον rinunziare a quel territorio, amputare l'Impero di quella parte che, per quanto piccola, è pure stata causa di tanti lutti e ha fatto versar tanto sangue ... L'utilita della rinunzia è esplicitamente dichiarata: **ut cetera regas securus;** con ciò si ritorce la proposta di Strategio: **ut ... latere damni securus, perduelles advolaret adsiduos.**" (16.9.3) and further p.189: "L'argomento dell'**utile** è rafforzato dai due **exempla,** τεχνικόν e παράδοξον del medico e del castoro, entrati nella tradizione Latina fin da Cicerone". (for detailed lit.cf.ibid. note 1 and 2; cf.et.Ev.sec.Matth. 5.29). Where Amm. got his examples from, is difficult to say, as they are well-known and perhaps found by him in writings no longer known to us. Cf.et.Cic. pro Scaur.fr.15 (2.7) p.545 Schoell: quemadmodum castores redimunt se ea parte corporis, propter quam maxime expetuntur (= Orelli II. 2p.260).

a **postremo ... recte. Recte** should be linked with **suadenti!** Hyperbaton. p. 114. 15-16
Morem gerere: construction and meaning as in Terent.Eun.1.2.108; Adelph.2.2.6; Cic. ad Att.2.16.3; Tusc.1.9.17; Terent.Hautont.5.1.74 (mihi); **(voluntati)** Nepos Dat.14.4; **(voluntati)** Cic.Mur.23.46; etc.
b **si ... volueris:** conjunct. **potent.praes.** as a form of politeness. Cf. ad 14.8.8 (= II p.69); ad 14.4.6 (= I p.83); ad 17.4.15, p.111.15-16; ad 17.3.3, p.108.14; ad 17.1.4, p.105.15.

comtemne partem exiguam. Cicero reminiscence. Cf. ad 14.6.8, p.13.22 p. 114. 16 and 14.6.8-9, p.13.17-26 (= I p.92).

semper luctificam et cruentam. For the first adj. and for **luctuosus** cf. ad p. 114. 16 14.5.2 (= I p.84). **Luctuosus** occurs in Veget.r.m.4.12 (= Lang p.136) once, but **luctificus** does not. Both adj. not in Arn.adv.nat.Claud.Opt. Milev.

ut cetera regas securus: instead of **ceteras** (sc. partes). But unconsciously p. 114. 16-17 the neutr.plur. of adjectiva, participia, pronomina is easily selected. Cf. ad 17.3.2, p.108.12*a;* ad 17.4.1, p.109.4*a;* Hofm.-Leum. p.455 sq. (65a).

a **prudenter reputans medellarum quoque artifices. reputans** = tecum p. 114. 17 reputans. For the verb cf. Krebs Antib.2 p.506 (with lit.). I do not believe that the repetition of **p, r, u** and **t** in the two first words is accidental.
b **medellarum ... artifices.** This grand expression only means: doctors, physicians. Lit.: the experts (technicians) of (in the field of) curing (medicine), not, as translated by Seyf. "die gelehrten Ärzte". For **medella**

147

cf. ad 14.8.12 (= II p.79). **Medella** does not occur in Claud.Veget.r.m. Opt.Milev., though we do find **medicina** there. Both words do not seem to occur in Arn.adv.nat. Metaphorically in a law in the Cod.Iust.8.44.17 (a⁰ 290): praeses provinciae in damnis, quae te tolerasse meministi, **medelam iuris** adhibebit. For **artifex** cf. ad 15.3.4 (= III p.40 sq).

p. 114. 18 **et partes corporis amputare.** Note the alliterating p's. Cf.Cic.Phil.8.5(15): In corpore si quid eiusmodi est, quod reliquo corpori noceat, id **uri secarique** patimur, ut membrum aliquod potius, quam totum corpus intereat: sic in rei publicae corpore, ut totum salvum sit, quidquid est pestiferum, **amputetur. Amputare** does not occur in Claud.Veget.r.m. Metaph. in Opt.Milev. The **subst.** in Arn.adv.nat.1.27 Reiffersch., p.18 (metaph.). Cf.et.Cic. de off.3.6 (32): Etenim ut membra quaedam amputantur si ... nocent reliquis partibus corporis etc.; Michael (op.cit.I) p.37.

p. 114. 18 **reliquis.** without difference in meaning with **cetera** (p.114.16). Cf. ad 17. 4.23, p.113.19.

p. 114. 19 **hocque.** et secare et ... amputare ... hocque ... factitare. Cf.16.12.70; 17.12.11; 23.6.45; Blomgren p.29; ad 16.12.69, p.102.23-24*b*. The **copulatio** is important not only for the stylistics, but sometimes also for the correct meaning of a sentence, as well as for the text criticism. Cf.et. ad 15.13.2 (= IV p.80): **asyndeton;** Blomgren passim.

p. 114. 19 **factitare.** Also 14.5.5; 16.5.4; 19.12.12; 27.9.10. For the **intensiva, iterativa, inchoativa** cf. Liesenberg (op.cit.I), 1889, p.1 sq.; ad 14.2.6 (= I p.69).

p. 114. 19-20 *a* **quae cum advertant cur ... capiantur, illud ... amittunt** = quam ob partem ... illam ... In later Latin **cur** and **qua re** are interchangeable, without difference in meaning. This is probably the reason why **illud** can easily refer back to **cur** (= **qua re**). Cf. Krebs Antib.1 p.384 (with lit.).
Note. A peculiar development of **cur** (= **quod**) is found in Dig.38.2.14.1 sq. (Ulp.): neque enim imputare ei possumus, **cur** non deseruit accusationem vel **cur** abolitionem non petierit (cf. Kalb, Wegweiser in die röm. Rechtsspr.², 1961, p.112). (Note the variatio modorum). This meaning definitely does not fit here (according to Kalb cur = quod only in Ulp.).
b **amittunt** = they renounce it.

propia sponte. Cf. ad 17.2.3, p.108.2*b*.

inpavidae. Like the adverbium, since Livius, but here probably used for the sake of the alliteration: propria sponte ... possint inpavidae. Cf. Krebs Antib.2. p.689.

V, 8
a **id sane pronuntio, quod ... venire ... festinabo.** For the constructions of **quod** cf. ad 14.7.5; 14.7.14; 14.10.14; 14.11.7; 14.11.11 (= II, p.22, 41, 111, 120, 123 sq.). Cf.et. ad 14.7.11 (= II, p.35 sq.).
b **si legatio redierit.** Either **conjunct.perf.** (instead of fut.ex.ind. of the or.recta) in the **orat.obl.** (subordinate clause) and then "correctly" used or **fut.ex.ind.** and then less "correct". (As we know, the **conjunct.perf.** often replaces the **conj.fut.ex.**).

pronuntio. As t.t.r.publ., as well as t.t.mil. and t.t.jurid. Here probably the last meaning = I pronounce in a loud voice as my final judgement. Cf. Heum.-Seckel p.469; Veget.3.5 (= Lang p.73): Vocalia dicuntur quae voce humana **pronuntiantur,** sicut in vigiliis vel in proelio pro signo dicitur, ut puta "victoria" "palma" etc.

a **post tempus hiemalis quietis exemptum.** Constructions like: **post tempus exemptum** instead of: tempore exempto are quite usual in late Latin and in Amm. Cf.14.1.4: post hoc impie perpetratum; 15.8.3: post multa ⟨ita⟩que per deliberationes ambiguas actitata; 15.8.15: nemo post haec finita reticuit; 18.2.5: post haec impetrata; 18.3.1: ... quod hae volucres post conpositas sedes opesque congestas fumo pelluntur; 23.6.4: post finitima cuncta ... subacta; etc. Cf. Reinhardt (op.cit.I) p.54; Hofm.-Leum.p.501 and 608 (94 and 185 respect.). Also the **brachylogical use** is typically late Latin. Cf.17.1.2: amor enim **post documenta** flagrantior; etc.
b Cf.Nep.Dat.6: Sed haec propter **hiemale tempus** minus prospere succedebant; Hist.Aug.Vop.Aurel.11.6: tuum est pro virtutibus tuis atque sollertia illic **hiemalia** (= castra hiberna) et aestiva disponere etc.
c **exemptum.** eximere = transigere, late Latin Cf.Pallad.3.17.8: anno deinde exempto; 3.11.15: exemptis quadraginta diebus; Coll.Avell. (367-553) 99.11: exempto anno (all 3 places quoted by Pighi p.190). How it developed into this meaning, can be found, among others, in Dig. (Ulp.) 4.6.26.7: sed cum feriae **tempus eximunt** (take away = let pass = let expire) restitutio dumtaxat ipsorum dierum facienda est, non totius

temporis. For the usual meanings of **eximere** (with constructions) cf. ad 14.2.20 (= I p.78); ad 14.7.12 (= II p.41); ad 17.2.4, p.108.3; Naumann (op.cit.I) p.13 sq. The verb does not occur in Claud.Veget.r.m.Arn.adv. nat.Opt.Milev.

p. 114. 22 **viribus totis accinctus.** This word-combination is not known to me from other sources. Cf.Cod.Iust.9.4: Eorum est scientia punienda et severissimis merito legibus vindicanda, qui **magicis adcincti artibus** ... (a⁰ 321); Verg.Aen.4.493 (c.accus.); Tac.Ann.12.44: Igitur Pharasmanes iuvenem potentiae properum et **studio popularium accinctum** ... metuens ... Linked with **concreta** Veg.r.m.2.15 (Lang p.49). In Claud. not the part. p.p. but other forms of the verb, **without a connection with abstracta or concreta.** The verb does not occur at all in Arn.adv.nat. and Opt.Milev.

p. 114. 22-24 *a* **fortuna condicionumque aequitate spem successus secundi fundante.** That the meaning of these words does not immediately become clear, appears from the following translations: (Sabbah) "et puisque la Fortune et **l'équité des mes conditions** fondent mon espoir d'un résultat favorable"; (Seyf.) "wenn das Glück und **die Gleichheit der Lage** einen günstigen Erfolg mit Sicherheit erwarten lassen"; (Büchele): like Sabbah; (Rolfe): like Sabbah. In connection with the moralistic tone of the letter from Sapor, the translation by Sabbah c.s. seems the best one to me. It also seems somewhat strange to me that Sapor in his letter to his **adversary** would pretend to build his hopes for success on Fortune and "**die Gleichheit der Lage**". That does not seem very confident to me.

b Note the alliterating f in the first and last word of the abovementioned passage and the alliterating s and c in **spem successus secundi.**

c **successus.** Also 17.13.24; 17.13.32; 27.8.9; 21.9.3; 21.9.1;. Often with the addition of adjectiva like **prosper, secundus,** etc. Although already in Varro and later Liv., not strictly speaking a "classical" substantive.

d **condicionumque aequitate.** Cf.20.8.11 (Letter from Iulianus to Constantius): et **condicionum aequiratem,** quam propono, bona fide suscipito cum animo disputans haec statui Romano prodesse nobisque, qui caritate sanguinis et **fortunae superioris culmine** sociamur. (Cf.et.ad 17.5.4, p.114.4).

p. 114. 23-24 **quoad ratio siverit.** Cf. ad 17.4.3, p.109.12. Sabbah: "je me hâterai d'avancer aussi loin que la raison le permettra": thus S. translates **quoad** as: **as far as,** with the explanation (II p.174): "L'ultimatum final contient une double menace: l'attaque sera massive **(viribus totis)** et de grande envergure (**quoad ratio siverit**), S. affirme son intention de renoncer à la tactique monotone de raids limités et de siège, notamment ceux de Nisibe, qu'il a pratiquée depuis 14 ans". But Seyf. translates (I p.223): "**sobald es die Vernunft zuläszt**" and Rolfe (I p.337): "I shall hasten to come on, **so far as reason permits**". Sabbah's opinion is already found in Pighi p.190. Both translations can be justified. But it is the question whether Amm. also uses **quoad** with **local meaning**. Heum.-Seckel does not give this meaning for the judic.lit., while the word does not occur either in Claud.Veget.r.m.Opt.Milev.Arn.adv.nat. The law of probability does not favour the local meaning in this case. It is also important how one wants to translate **ratio** here. Cf. places like Veget.r.m.3.22 (= Lang p.112): Digestis omnibus, quae **ratio militaris** experimentis et arte servavit; 3.6 (= Lang p.78): Ambulante exercitu, ut locorum varietas evenerit, ita **defensionis ratio** variatur; 3.11 (= Lang p.93): **ratio disciplinae militaris**; 3.20 (= Lang p.111): Tantum est, ut electi a duce sapientissimo in his locis, in quibus **ratio** et utilitas postulat, ordinentur; etc.

His litteris diu libratis: Viz. in the **consistorium**. (cf. ad 14.7.11 = II p.34). p. 114. 25
For the **probable** participants to this crown council cf. Pighi p.190.

V, 9
libratis. Cf.22,10.1 (Iulianus) iudicialibus causis intentus ... exquisita p. 114. 25
docilitate **librans**, quibus modis suum cuique tribueret (liberans V E **librans** AG deliberans Corn. Clark Seyf. Rolfe. I am against this classicist correction by Corn. The **clausula** need not be an objection: cf. Blomgren p.93). But in the same book, in the previous caput 22.9.9: verum ille iudicibus Cassiis tristior et Lycurgis, causarum momenta aequo iure **perpendens** (Cic. pro Mur.2.(3)), **suum cuique tribuebat**. Cf.et.Paneg.Nazar. 10.7 (Baehrens p.219): illa igitur vis, illa maiestas fandi ac nefandi discriminatrix, quae omnia meritorum momenta **perpendit librat** examinat (where **perp.** and **librat** are synonymous); Krebs Antib.2 p.21 (who quotes Arnob.adv.nat.Reiff.p.166.16, where, however, is written: si rerum momenta **pendantur**. Not the compositum, therefore). Cod.Theod.8.4.26. With the meaning: to consider, contemplate, late Latin.

a **recto pectore, quod dicitur**. Cf. Otto, Sprichw. (op.cit.I) p.270, with p. 114. 25
comparable expressions, such as: apertum pectus, toto pectore. But **recto pectore** only seems to occur here. Perhaps a Greek expression? Similar expressions do occur in Greek (στέρνον, στῆθος). Cf. et Michael (op.cit.I) p.35; ad fam.10.10.2.

b **quod dicitur.** Cf. ad 17.3.3, p.108.14.

p. 114. 25 **considerate.** Class. Also: 30.1.5: audacter magis quam **considerate.**

V, 10

p. 114. 27 **Victor Constantius.** Cf. Pighi p.191: "Al governo imperiale non restava che sconfessare gli autori dell' infelici trattative e respingere le pretese Persiane". Cf.et.ibid.p.173.

p. 114. 27 *a* **Victor terra marique** versus: **rex regum Sapor.** Cf.15.1.3 (Constantius) confestim a iustitia declinavit ita intemperanter ut **aeternitatem meam** (cf.III p.9) aliquotiens **subsereret** ipe dictando **(subs.**III p.10), scribendoque **propria manu** (III p.10) orbis totius se **dominum** appellaret; 19.2.11: nostris virtutes Constanti Caesaris extollentibus, ut **domini rerum et mundi.** Cf.et. ad 17.5.3, p.113.30-31*c*.
b Pighi p.192: "Le parole victor terra marique alludono in particolare al successo della **guerra Magnenziana** (350-353), ch'aveva confermato l'assoluto dominio di Costanzo, e delle spedizioni navali, con quella guerra connesse, in Sicilia, a Cartagine e ai porti della Tarraconense (Iul. orat.I.40 c; 42 d; 2.74 c); in generale alle **campagne Persiane,** di Costanzo Cesare ed Augusto, e **Alamanniche** di Costanzo Augusto, e **Germaniche** dei collaboratori di Costanzo". P. further quotes C.I.L.3.3705 and C.I.L. 9.1117, with Constantius' many titles. Noteworthy is here the title of **Adiabinicus,** a result of the expedition across the Tigris (343 A.D.).

p. 114. 27 **semper Augustus.** Cf. ad 17.3.4, p.108.17*b* (also for **Dominus),** with the other passages quoted there. Cf.et. ad 17.5.3, p.113.30-31*a*.

p. 114. 27 **fratri meo.** Cf. ad 17.5.3, p.113.30-31*d*.

p. 114. 28 **Sapori regi.** Abbreviated title, instead of **rex regum Sapor.** Cf. ad 17.5.3, p.113.30-31*c*.

p. 114. 29 *a* **Sospitati ... amicus.** Cf.19.4.8: exiguis imbribus disiecto concreto spiritu et crassato **sospitas** retenta est corporum firma. Late Latin Souter p.382. Not in Veget.r.n.Claud.Arn.adv.nat.Opt.Milev. The adj. in Amm. 14.8.3; 18.9.2; 23.6.46; 28.4.19 **(sospitalis);** cf. ad 14.6.23 (= I p.100).
b **si velis.** Constantius is not absolutely convinced of this future friendship, and rightly so, as appears later. Pighi p.193: "Riconosce subito implicitamente che la base, su cui era stato costuito l'edificio diplomatico

Romano, è venuta a mancare: Šahpuhr è ora in pace coi barbari e **può attendere in persona al fronte Mesopotamico**".

a **cupiditatem - insimulo.** Cf. ad 17.5.3, p.114.2*b* and ad 17.5.3, p.114.3 *a-d*.

b **cupiditatem vero semper indeflexam fusiusque vagantem.** Pighi quotes Liv.42.19.2: quod factum tot annis post captam Capuam non fuerat, ut **in vacuo vagaretur cupiditas** privatorum. Cf.et.Claud.18.138 sq. (In Eutrop.I):

Est ubi despectus nimius iuvat. undique pulso
Per cunctas licuit **fraudes** impune **vagari**
Et fatis aperire viam (sc. Eutropio).

ibid.35.355 sq. (de raptu Pros.II):

.... **Mors nulla vagatur**
In terris, nullaeque rogum planxere parentes.

Opt.Milev.3.4 (Ziwsa p.82): tunc Taurinus ad eorum litteras ire militem iussit armatum per nundinas, ubi **circumcellionum furor vagari** consuerat; and ibid.p.81 sq.: nam cum huiusmodi hominum genus ante unitatem per loca singula **vagarentur** ... nulli licuit securum esse in possessionibus suis. Everywhere with the meaning of: to wander around, spreading grief, misfortune; to wander round wrecking, destroying.

c Cf. Cic.Acad.pr.2.20(66): Eo fit, ut errem et **vager latius. Adv.compar.** also in Cic.nat.deor.2.7(20) = diffuse; the same meaning Tusc.4.26(57) **(fuse)**. The adv. does not occur in Claud.Veget.r.m.Opt.Milev.Arn.adv. nat. Cf.et. **profusius** 28.4.26. Cf. ad 16.12.15, p.93.12*b*.

indeflexam. Cf.27.9.4: et, quod erat publice privatimque dolendum, **indeflexa saevitia** punientem gregariorum (= common soldiers) errata, parcentem potioribus. Later and late Latin.

insimulo. Cf. ad 14.5.3 (= I p.85). Pighi p.193: "Costanzo è ..., come lo chiama un'iscrizione di Fano, **defensor pacis** (C.I.L.11.6625): come tale, mette in istato d'accusa l'imperialismo che minaccia la pace Romana". (Cf.et.ibid. note 5).

V, 11

ut tuam. This **ut** = as, like, very often in Amm.Cf.17.1.14: **ut faustus** Caesar exultabat; 17.1.14: magis optabat quam damnatorum sorte **(sicut sperabat) ut** frater Gallus occidi; 17.4.10: non enim **ut** numc; 17.5.10: **ut futurus (si velis) amicus;** 17.5.15: Eustathius ... philosophus ... **ut opifex suadendi;** 17.7.11: **ut opiniones aestimant;** 17.7.13: **ut in Asia**

Delos emersit; 17.7.13: **ut** in Atlantico mari; 17.8.2: sed **ut** est difficultatum ... ratio victrix; etc. Often alternately with **velut, sicut** etc. (For the restrictive meaning **(so far as)** cf. ad 17.2.1 p.107.9*b*.) Cf.et. Schneider (op.cit.I) p.10 sq.; ad 17.4.15, p.111.19-20*a* **(tamquam)**. Sometimes the use of **ut** by Amm. is important for the interpretation and (or) the text criticism.

p. 115. 2 **perindeque** = and likewise = and also = **itemque** (cf. ad 16.12.17, p.93. 23-24). This almost copulative use of this adverb is very striking. To be compared, for instance, with Flor.3.2: Atrox caelum, **perinde** ingenia. The adv. does not occur in Claud.Veget.r.m.Opt.Milev.Arn.adv.nat. For **-que** cf. ad 16.12.37, p.97.6*a*.

p. 115. 2 **suades ... adimere.** This constr. with the infinit., rare in class. Latin prose, though occurring in poetry, frequent in late Latin. Cf. Krebs Antib.2 p.610 (with lit.); ad 15.7.6 (= IV p.18); ad 14.1.3 (= I p.58): **praecipere** and **permittere;** Hassenstein (op.cit.I) p.49.

p. 115. 3 **corpori adimere**: with the dativ a classical construction. Compare **eximere** ad 17.2.4, p.108.3. The verb a well-known t.t.iurid. Pighi reads: **corpore.** (cf.P.St.Amm.p.64 sq.).

p. 115. 3 **quaedam.** Cf. ad 17.3.6, p.109.1-2*b*.

p. 115. 3 *a* **deinceps locetur in solido. Deinceps** = **deinde, postea** is post-class. Cf. Krebs Antib.1 p.409 (with lit.) Cf.22.7.5: Haut multo ⟨de⟩inceps (Wm 2 BG). In Opt.Milev. we find **deinde** (= **atque, praeterea**), but not **deinceps**. In Veget. **deinde,** but not **deinceps.**
b Cf.Verg.Aen.11.426 sq.:
.... multos alterna revisens
Lusit et **in solido** rursus Fortuna **locavit.**

p. 115. 4 **quod † infundendum est potius quam ulla consensione firmandum.** Pighi p.193: "Tu affermi un diritto di proprietà sulla Mesopotamia e sull' Armenia, e a questo titolo le ripeti dal popolo Romano; in secondo luogo suggerisci una diminuzione dell' integrità dell' Impero, col fine specioso della sua salvezza"; dunque una **petitio** e un **consilium** proposti **dolo malo.** "Questi sono **delicta** che si devono perseguire, anzichè favorirne il compimento con alcuna forma d'acquiescenza". Il termine giuridico che riprende **l'insimulo** di prima è un verbo **infendere,** attestato solo nellae

Glossae Latino-Graecae: **infendere** ἐπιτεῖναι ἐγκληματίσαι Dal primo vocabolo, ἐπιτεῖναι appare il senso comune, **urgere;** dal secondo il senso technico: ἐγκληματίζειν che, come il classico ἐγκαλεῖν, significa "perseguire giudicialmente". I have given this quotation in its entirety, in order to show how Pighi places the interpretation of these letters partly in a legal framework. In my opinion he goes too far in this, however ingenious it appears at first sight.

Infendendum would be the best conjecture, if the word would occur in other places besides the **Glossae Latino-Graecae**. Otherwise I do not think there is a solid enough foundation for this.

Refutandum, as given by G seems preferable, also because of the rhyming **-andum. Ref.-firm.** forms a chiasm (cf. Blomgren, op.cit.II, p.20,22,41).

a **Veritatem non obtectam praestrigiis, sed ,perspicuam, nullisque minis inanibus perterrendam.** Pighi p.194: "Qui s'allude ad un altro delictum, la violenza morale, **metus,** su cui tornerà verso la fine (17.5.14: cessent autem quaesso formidines). La verità di Costanzo non ha bisogno di raggiri nè di minacce, ma è perspicua, trasparente". For the legal interpretation see above. Pighi refers to Dig.4.2: quod metus causa (cf.ibid. 4.2.1: Ulpianus 1.XI ad edictum. Ait praetor: "Quod **metus** causa gestum erit, ratum non habebo" ... metus instantis vel futuri periculi causa mentis trepidatio). But I find this leap from civil law to international law (so to say) rather risky and therefore Pighi's reasoning quite twisted.

p. 115. 5-6

b **obtectam** = coated, veiled, as often. Cf.Tac.Ann.4.19: proprium id Tiberio fuit scelera nuper reperta priscis verbis **obtegere;** Cic. ad Att.1. 18.1: nihil fingam, nihil dissimulem, nihil **obtegam.** The verb once in a **literal meaning** in Claud. Not in Veget.t.m.Opt.Milev.Arnob.adv.nat.

c **praestigiis.** Cf.Gell.13.23: quam Graecae istorum **praestigiae** philosophari sese dicentium **umbrasque verborum inanes fingentium** ... ; Cic. Acad.pr.2.14 (45): Sed tamen, ut maneamus **in perspicuis** firmius et constantius, maiore quadam opus est vel arte, vel diligentia, ne ab iis, quae clara sint ipsa per sese, quasi **praestigiis** quibusdam et captionibus depellamur; Cic.nat.d.3.29 (73); Cic.Verr.4.24 (53); Gell.14.1; Georges 2 p.1884. Here, I suppose, appears to be a Cicero reminiscence. The subst. does not occur in Claud.Veget.r.m.Arn.adv.nat., though it is found in Opt.Milev.4.9 (= Ziwsa p.116). Cf.et.Cod.Iust.9.9.27: indignum est enim, ut ultionem pudoris **praestigiae** versuti iuris excludant (a⁰ 295).

d **praestigiis ... perterrendam.** Note the alliterating **p.**

e **perspicuam.** Here with the usual classical meaning. But 28.1.54: magna quaeritabat industria, qua vi senatorem **perspicui generis** interficeret

(= considerable). Cf.et. **perspicaciter (or perspicacitas?)** ad 15.3.2 (= III p.30) and 26.6.1; 29.1.38; **perspicabilis**: 14.8.3 (= worth seeing). The last 3 words rare and late Latin.

e **minis.** For the use of minae (often with Amm. Vergilius imitation) cf. Hagendahl St.A. (op.cit.I) p.10 (Verg.Aen.4.88) and p.25 (with note 2).

f **perterrendam.** Cf. ad 17.1.7, p.105.24*b* **(perterrefactus).**

V, 12

p. 115. 6 **praefectus praetorio: Musonianus (Strategius).** Cf. ad 15,13.1 (= IV p.78). Sabbah II p.175 (note 57) refers to E.Groag, Die Reichsbeambten von Achaia in spät-römischer Zeit (diss. Pannonicae, ser.1, fasc.14), 1946, p.35-36; which is unknown to me.

p. 115. 6-7 *a* **opinatus adgredi negotium publicae utilitati conducens.** For the nom.c. infin.cf. ad 15.7.4 (= IV p.13); ad 15.5.9 (= III p.84 sq.): nom.c.inf. **pass.;** ad 15.6.1 (= IV p.6): **facere** c.inf. **pass.;** ad 17.1.13, p.106.23-24*b* (**esse** and **se** "omitted" in **acc.c.inf.**); ad 17.4.13, p.111.5 (acc.c.inf.).

b **adgredi negotium.** Cf.Claud.8.372 sq. (de IV cons.Honor.):

ne propera. necdum decimas emensus aristas//**aggrederis metuenda** viris. (here used conatively).

Veget.r.m.praef.2 (= Lang p.34): Nec formido iussus **adgredi opus,** quod spontaneum cessit impune; Cic. de off.21: In omnibus autem **negotiis** prius, quam **aggrediare,** adhibenda est praeparatio diligens; Cic. ad Att.2. 14.2: **Magnum quid aggrediamur** et multae cogitationis atque otii.

c 1. **conducens.** The part.praes. has here a futural meaning. Cf. Hofm.-Leum.182*a* p.605. This is seen more often. But since Amm. certainly does not avoid the part.fut., the reason for its use here lies in the metrum: clausula I utilitāti condŭcens: $\underline{}\ \smile\ \underline{}\ :\ \underline{}\ \underline{\smile}$. Cf.et. ad 14.6. 2 (= I p.89): **part.fut. = part.praes.**

2. Cf.Cic. de prov.cons.1.1: nunc vero, patres conscripti, non parva afficior voluptate, vel quod hoc maxime **rei publicae conducit,** Syriam, Macedoniamque decerni, ut dolor meus nihil a communi **utilitate** dissentiat. In connection with *b* (above) the influence of his reading of Cicero here seems very likely to me.

p. 115. 7-8 *a* **cum duce ... pace.** It is clear that Constantius here presents the initiatives of his praef.praet. as some kind of private hobby of the latter, in which he does not have any part at all. By **duce** is meant (16.9.3): **Tampsaporem ducem** (cf. ad 17.5.1, p.113.24*a*). Cf. Pighi p.195.

b **per quosdam ignobiles.** For **quosdam** cf. afd 17.3.6, p.109.1-2*b*. For the adj.cf.15.5.28: ut ipse (sc.Silvanus) quidem per quaestiones familiarium **sub disceptatione** (= trial, law case, examination: late Latin) **ignobili** crudeliter agitatus commississe in maiestatem arcesseretur (= not fitting his position, low, inferior); 22.8.41: insula, quam incolunt **Sindi ignobiles** post eriles in Asia casus coniugiis potiti dominorum et rebus (the meaning is clear from the context: of low origin. **Sindi**: East of the Strait of Kertsj; cf.Iust.2.5.1.-8); 23.6.5: regibus Parthicis, **abiectis et ignobilibus** antea (Hagend.abund.p.177).

c Probably the persons meant by this unflattering adj. are the **emissarii quidam** (cf. ad 16.9.2, p.83.20), also called **speculatores** (16.9.3); and certainly not **Cassianus, dux Mesopotamiae**, since a dux is a vir perfectissimus and after Valentinianus I (364-378), v.clarissimus or v.spectabilis (cf. ad 14.7.7. = II p.23). Nor can **Clematius, agens in rebus** and **Spectatus, tribunus et notarius** (17.5.15) be called **ignobiles**, in my opinion; for the **agentes in rebus**, who, when they had passed through all the ranks, became **principes** with the title of **clarissimi**, as well as the **tribuni et notarii**, who were also **clarissimi**, were too highly qualified for this. Cf.et. ad 17.5.2, p.113.28-29*b*; Pighi 174 sq.

d **me inconsulto.** Completely unbelievable information. See above under **a**. Cf.27.2.9: (Iovinus equitum magister) ... iratus in tribunum animadvertere statuit ausum hoc **inconsulta potestate superiore** fecisse; 20.4.22: quieti stetere paulisper armati et interrogati, quae causa esset **inconsulti motus et repentini** (= ill-considered, unthinking). With the **first** meaning generally post-class. Cf. Krebs Antib.1.p.716; Heum.-Seckel p.257; Cod. Theod.15.1.37: Nemo iudicum in id temeritatis erumpat, ut **inconsulta pietate nostra**, novi aliquid operis existimet inchoandum; 15.15.1: Nulli prorsus, **nobis insciis atque inconsultis**, quorumlibet armorum movendorum copia tribuatur. Cf.et. ad 16.12.10, p.92.15 (**consultam**).

e **sermones conseruit super.** Cf.Curt.Ruf.8.12.9: Coiere, quod ex utriusque vultu posset intellegi, amicis animis: ceterum sine interprete non poterat **conseri sermo**; Fronto the same expression; Stat.Silv.2.1.5 sq.:

cum iam egomet **cantus et verba medentia** saevus

consero, tu planctus lamentaque fortia mavis.

Cf. Krebs Antib.1.338. There is a distinct difference between **s.conferre** and **s.conserere**. The first means: to carry on, to have an interview, a conversation; the second: to **begin, start** an interview, conversation. Post-class. The expression does not occur in Claud.Veget.r.m.Arn.adv.nat. Opt.Milev.

Note: Vollmer's version: **confero** (Stat.Silv.2.1.6) does not seem credible to me.

f **Super.** Cf. ad 14.7.12 (= II p.40 sq.).

p. 115. 8-9 **non refutamus hanc nec repellimus.** Cf.14.11.12: hebetari sensus hominum et obtundi; 15.6.2: nec nominavit nec prodidit aliquem (IV p.7); 15.5.37 (III p.128); 15.5.10 (= III p.86); 14.9.1: discpicere litis exitialis crimina cogebatur, abnuens et reclamans; ad 16.9.2, p.83,20-21; ad 14.11.9 (= II p.122); 16.7.7: colatur a cunctis ordinibus et ametur; 16.12.9: Caesarem hortari vos et orare; etc. And Hagend.abund.p.183 sq. (op.cit., I).

p. 115. 9-10 *a* **adsit modo cum decore et honestate, nihil pudori nostro praereptura vel maiestati.** Cf.Cic. de fin.2.17 (56): adeunda sunt quaevis pericula decoris honestatisque causa; ibid.1.10 (36): ipsius honestatis decore; ibid.2.11 (35): posita in decore tota, id est, in honestate; de off.1.5(17): honestatem et decus conservabimus (examples from Pighi p.195, note 2). With the latter passage P. annotates: "Amm. ha sostituito **decor a decus**: cum decŏre et honestăte" (Claus.III).
b **pudori.** Pighi p.195 (note 3): "Col senso di "fama" **pudor** è proprio della lingua giuridica" (with examples). Cf.et. Heum.-Seckel p.478.
c **praereptura.** Cf. ad 17.5.6, p.114.12-13,*c*.
d **maiestati.** Cf. ad 16.8.1, p.80.24; Scr.H.Aug. (Treb.Poll.) Gall.II. 14.9-11 (quoted by Pighi). Sometimes **maiestas vestra** has more or less the same meaning as our: "Your Majesty" (a) (Veget.r.m.edit. Lang p.33. 8), while it is often connected with **imperator** (b) (Veget.ibid.p.38.19), or we find a combination of (a) and (b) (e.g.Veget.ibid.p.37.20: si provisione maiestatis tuae, imperator Auguste). This **maiestas** is also ascribed to the **signa.** (cf. ad 15.5.16 = III p.96 sq.); cf. Veget.ibid.p.84.14: Prima igitur **signa** locis suis intra castra ponuntur, quia nihil est venerabilius **eorum maiestate** militibus ...

V, 13

p. 115. 10-14 **est enim ... inlibata.** The **deleti tyranni** are Magnentius, Vetranio and Silvanus (cf.I p.41-42; III p.68; III p.8; I p.125). **Quae contrusi etc.** refers to the division of the empire, after the death of Constantinus I (307-337), when Constantius II (337-361) was given the **Eastern territory.** We also find references to the division and the war against Sapor in Julianus Orat. 1.18 C-D. In 348 the Persians end the armistice and the Romans suffer a crushing defeat near **Singara.** But in 338 **Sapor** unsuccessfully lays siege to **Nisibis** (cf.II p.85), as well as in 346. Thus in generally it is true that: **quae ... diu ... servavimus inlibita.** For **contrusi in orientales angustias** the final date is set at 350 A.D.: the murder of **Constans** and the usurpation by **Magnentius** (cf.III p.93). Cf.et.III p.119: **Mursense proelium.** For the sake of completeness, the following **tyranni** should be added: the **Caesar Decentius** (cf.IV p.8 and III p.119) died 353 A.D. and **Nepotianus**, died 350 A.D. (cf.III p.119). But these two are of lesser importance.

absonum et insipiens. V insidiens Nm 2 Btl. Haupt Seyf. Sabbah Rolfe insipiens. Cf.Hagend. abund. (op.cit.I) p.177. **absonus** (metaph.) = absurd. p. 115. 10

nunc cum. V num. Em² BG.cum. Nunc cum Clark Seyf.Rolfe. nam Btl. With Sabbah I prefer G's version: **cum.** I see no grounds for adding **nunc.** For the **indic.perf.** after **cum** cf.16.12.20; 19.7.4; 23.6.7 sq.; Ehrism. p.53. p. 115. 11

gestarum rerum ordines. Here **res gestae** mean not only acts of war, but, as more often, all political and military deeds. (cf.et. ad 16.12.18, p.94.6). For the plur.poet. **ordines** cf. ad 16.12.37, p.97.6c. Furthermore the expression is pleonastic, for g.r.ordines = res gestae. cf.et. ad 16.12.38, p.97.17-21d. p. 115. 11

placatae sint aures invidiae! This version by Clark, Seyf. Sabbah not quite definite. (Haupt (and Rolfe): **aurae).** This is also true of **inluxerunt.** Cf. app.crit.edit. Clark p.115. Pighi does not say anything about this passage. Although with Amm. the personificatio is quite normal. (cf. ad 17.2.1, p.107.13) and sometimes very daring, the sentence: "may the ears of hatred be reconciled" does not strike me as probable. One would sooner expect: **occlusae** sint aures invidiae (dat.)! For **occludere** cf.29.2.14: ut videretur **aures occlusisse** ceris quasi Scopulos Sirenios transgressurus. **Inlucescere** occurs 26.1.7 and 28.4.31. For the version **aurae** cf.et. Michael (op.cit.I) p.22; Cic.Verr.3.41 (98); pro Cluent.56 (153). p. 115. 11

Cum ... orbis ... obtemperat. Cum, purely temporal, c. **indic.praes.** Cf. 15.8.15; 20.3.2 sq.; 21.1.11; 21.1.12; 24.3.8; 25.3.19; 27.9.5; 30.4.20; Ehrism.p.55. p. 115. 12-13

multipliciter. Among others in Sall.Quint.Florus.Gell. Does not occur in Claud.Veget.r.m.Arn.adv.nat.Opt.Milev. Probably a rarely used adverbium. Post-class. and late Latin. Cf. Krebs Antib.2 p.108. p. 115. 12

Contrusi. Cf. ad 17.3.3, p.108.15b. p. 115. 13

p. 115. 13 **orientales angustias,** viz. the Eastern part of the Roman empire. See above. (p.115.10-14). Cf.Cic.Acad.pr.2.35 (112): cur eam (sc.orationem) tantas **in angustias** et Stoicorum dumeta **compellimus?** p.Quint.5.(19): ... qui hunc **in summas angustias adductum** putaret ... ; Opt.Milev.2.11: et tamen deo divitias suas denegastis, cuius hortum **in angustias cogitis** ... ; (and cum variatione) Arn.adv.nat.2.30: frenare ingenitos adpetitus, **cohibere in angustiis vitam** (= Reifersch.p.73).

p. 115. 14 **inlibata.** Cf.Liv.3.61.5: ut, ubi libertas parta esset paucis ante mensibus, eo **imperium inlibatum** referrent; Seneca epist.66.16: Ergo tua quoque virtus non magis laudabilis, si **corpus illibatum** tibi et **integrum** fortuna praestiterit, quam si ex aliqua parte mutilatum (mulcatum). It is possible that Amm. read this last passage somewhere (mutilare, mulcare ∽ **amputare).** Does not occur in Claud.Veget.r.m.Arn.adv.nat.Opt.Milev.

V, 14

p. 115. 14-19 **cessent ... prolapsam.** Cf.Amm.31.5.10-14, a classical passage. in which Amm. impresses upon his readers that the terrible events of these years have occurred often before and that the Romans have always managed to survive them. With the moralistic ending: verum mox post calamitosa dispendia res in integrum sunt restitutae hac gratia, **quod nondum solutioris vitae mollitie sobria vetustas infecta** nec ambitiosis mensis nec flagitiosis quaestibus inhiabat etc. Which was small comfort, for the worst was yet to come. Cf. et Iust.Phil.31.8.8: Africano praedicante neque Romanis, si vincantur, animos minui neque si vincant, secundis rebus insolescere. Captas civitates inter socios divisere Romani, aptiorem gloriam, quam possessiones voluptarias indicantes; Liv.45.8.6; 9.18.9: quod populus Romanus, etsi nullo bello, multis tamen proeliis victus sit, Alexandro nullius pugnae non secunda fortuna fuerit ... ; **Lucil.**26.446 sq. (= Baehrens p.204):

ut Romanus populus victus vi et superatus proeliis

saepe est multis, bello vero numquam, in quo sunt omnia.

Jul.Orat.2.98 B (Pighi suspects, on the basis of this passage: τοῦτο etc., that § 14 does indeed render the original contents of the letter, **because Julianus quotes this passage as being an idea of Constantius.** The oratio must have been written in the beginning of 358 A.D.; cf. Pighi p.197, note 6). Though there are certainly more places dealing with this theme (cf. Pighi p.157), it also fits very well into the antiquarian "fashion" of the late Roman era. Cf.Claud.8 (De IV cons.Honor.) 396 sq.:

Interea Musis, animus dum mollior, insta,

Et, quae mox imitere, legas; **nec desinat unquam
Tecum Graia loqui, tecum Romana vetustas.**

a **cessent autem quaesi formidines, Formidines** here = ± threats with horrifying things. But the sing.17.5.1, p.113.21 in the usual meaning, as well as in 20.9.5: utque id facile **formido intentatorum** efficeret.
b **quaeso.** Cf. ad 14.10.11, p.29.24 (= II p.107).

a **quae nobis intentantur ex more.** For the verb cf. ad 15.4.9 (= III p.61 sq.). Cf.18.6.16: militem qui ... adigente **metu, qui intentabatur,** pandit rerum integram fidem docetque ...
Note. III p.62 ad Tac.ann.3.36: **has** should be scrapped (printing error!). Note the variatio here: cum manus **intentarent** and: minae **intendantur,** in the same caput.
b **ex more.** Cf. ad 17.4.12, p.110.20. Cf.et. Reinhardt (op.cit.I) p.58 sq.

a **cum ambigi nequeat. Non ambigitur c.acc.c.inf.** Liv.10.5.14, Tac.Apul. Amm.etc. Cf. Krebs Antib.1 p.155; Draeger, über Synt.Tac. (op.cit.I) p. 61. **Ambigere** does not occur in Veget.r.m.Arn.adv.nat.Opt.Milev., though it is found in Claud., but not with this construction. But with the meaning: to hesitate, be undecided, not quite dare **c.inf., ambigere** is late Latin. Cf.15.4.12: quo viso omnes e castris effusi, qui **prodire** in proelium cum sociis **ambigebant** ... proterebant etc. Krebs Antib.ibid.; ad 16.12. 35, p.96.24.
b **nequeat.** The verb does not occur in Claud. It is found in Veget.r.m. Arn.adv.nat.Opt.Milev. In Arnob. with a curious pun 5.5 (= Reiffersch. p.177); hanc ... **nequam** incestis Juppiter cupiditatibus adpetivit ... sed cum ... optinere **nequisset** ... Also in judicial literature. (cf. Heum.-Seckel p.366). Cf. Ernout-Meltzer (op.cit.I) p.138, 101, 113; Hoogterp, Vies des pères du Iura p.81 (§ 169); Krebs Antib.2.p.142 (with lit.). Probably various forms of this verb are indeed archaic.

non inertia nos sed modestia pugnas interdum excepisse potius quam intulisse. Note rhythm and rhyme of this sentence. Cf.Tac.Dial.37.12: nam quo saepius steterit tamquam in acie (sc. eloquentia) quoque plures et **intulerit ictus et exceperit** quoque maiores adversarios acrioresque pugnas sibi ipsa desumpserit ...; Ann.3.43: cruppellarios vocant, **inferendis ictibus** inhabiles, **accipiendis** inpenetrabiles; A. Gudeman Tac.Dial.[2] (1914) p.480 (with examples of **inferre** and **excipere ictus).**

p. 115. 16-17 *a* **quotiens lacessimur.** Although in a subordinate clause of a main clause in the acc.c.inf. construction, the indicativus is not so unusual. For the **indicativus iterat.** cf. ad 16.12.21 p.94.18-19*a*. But with the conj.e.g.17.10. 4: et eam (sc.pacem) ... sub hac meruit lege, ut captivos redderet nostros et **quotiens sit necesse,** militibus alimenta praeberet; 16.10.18: quaesitumque venenum bibere per fraudem inlexit, ut **quotiensque concepisset,** inmaturum abiceret partum. Cf.et. ad 16.10.18, p.87.22; ad 14.2.2 (= I p.67); ad 14.2.7 (= I p.70); ad 14.2.7 (= I p.70); ad 14.4.6 (= I p.83); ad 14.1.5 (= I p.60); ad 14.4.1 (= I p.82); Ehrism.p.57.

b The pertaining substantive 19.3.1: aut **lacessitionibus** orebris occuparent obsidioni fortiter adhaerentes; 25.6.11: nam progredientes nos sequebantur, crebris **lacessitionibus** retrahentes. Late Latin. Cf. Souter p.225.

c For the **indicativus in the orat.obl.** in general cf. ad 16.10.17, p.87.15-16*b*.

p. 115. 16 **nostra.** Cf. ad 17.1.2, p.104.7-9*d*.

p. 115. 17 *a* **fortissimo † benevolentiae spiritu defensare.** V Clark Sabbah Seyf. **bonae conscientiae** Novák Rolfe. Novák refers to 16.7.7: comitem circumferens **conscientiam bonam** and 21.5.7; 15.8.2; 29.2.11; 29.5.27; 30.2.12; 17.13.2. Mommsen: ⟨licet⟩ benevolentiae Pet. p⟨l⟩enae potentiae. Both conjectures should be rejected, in my opinion: the first one is far-fetched and improbable, the second, though ingenious, also unlikely. Pighi refers for V to Aug.epist.3, 138.2, 14: ipsa bella sine benevolentia non gerentur, ut ad pietatis iustitiaeque pacatam societatem victis facilius consulatur (p.196, note 6). Also defended by Meurig Davies Class. et Med. (op.cit. XVI) p.183. But nowhere in the Amm. text is **benevolentiae** supported, in contrast with **bonae conscientiae,** Novák's conjecture. Translation: with the courageous inspiration, given by a clear conscience. This fits very well into the context. But to who(m) does **benevolentiae** refer? Pighi explains (not acceptably, in my view): **perchè noi amiamo fortissimamente i nostri sudditi.** In spite of August. I do not find this suitable here: especially not the combination of **fortissimo spiritu** and **benevolentia.** And if **benevolentiae** does not refer to the own subjects, can it then relate to the Persians or their king? Even in general to enemies? This seems very strange to me. (Translation: with the (powerful), courageous inspiration, given by benevolence (generosity)). For mercy can only be granted to the enemy when he has challenged (defied, attacked) us, **after he has been conquered.** How does that happen in **bella** and **proelia?** Preliminary conclusion:

Novák's conjecture is to be preferred, because the version of V can not be satisfactorily explained.

b **defensare.** Cf.14.5.8; 19.6.6; 20.11.12; 26.7.9; 30.4.22. Archaic, poetic, post-class. Whether it still has here an intensifying meaning, is to be doubted. Also used by legal authors. With Sallust. archaism? Not in Veget.r.m.Opt.Milev.Arn.adv.nat., though used by Claud.

id experiendo legendoque scientes. For the use of the **gerundium** cf. ad 14. 1.6 (= I p.61) = by experience (my own) and reading. "More ordinary": id experti scientes et legendis libris, or: legendo. Apparently Amm. avoids **legentes** here, because he does not consider this perfective enough besides **experti** (although the **part.praes,** is sometimes used perfectively by him) (cf. ad 17.1.12, p.106.16-17*a*). Hence the 2 gerundia here. *p. 115. 17-18*

quibusdam. Cf. ad 17.3.6, p.109.1-2*b*. *p. 115. 18*

raro rem titubasse Romanam. Note the alliterating **r.** Used in this way to describe the faltering of the **state** etc., not known to me from other sources. Cf.Cod.Iust.7.63.5 § 1c. eundem diem fatalem non observari et lites exspirare et huius modi luctuosis infelicitatibus **patrimonia hominum titubare.** Found in Claud., not in Veget.r.m.Opt.Milev.Arn.adv.nat. Also used by legal authors (see above). The adv. **titubanter** 24.4.28, with lit. meaning. *p. 115. 18*

Summa ... bellorum = end result, complete result. Cf.Veget.r.m.3.1 (= Lang p.65): ... ut haec, in quibus peritia certaminum et **victoriae summa** consistit ... intellegerentur celerius. *p. 115. 19*

ad deteriora prolapsam. V deteriorem G deteriora Sabbah II p. 175 (note 60): "V donne **ad deteriorem prolapsam,** qui peut être une hellénisme (comparer 19.10.1: maris casus asperiores solitis) et n'est donc pas nécessairement une faute".

V, 15

a **Hanc ... suadendi.** For the 1st and 2nd legation cf. ad 17.5.2, p.113, 27-28*b*. Cf.et. ad 17.5.2, p.113.29*b*. As regards the persons mentioned in this passage: for **Prosper** cf.II p.118 (14.11.5), for **Musonianus** cf.IV p.78 sq. (15.13.1). *p. 115. 20-23*

b **Eustathius** was a heathen philosopher, Cappadocian and a pupil of Iamblichus. Married to the prophetess **Sosipatra,** with whom he had 3 sons. During the winter of 355/356 in Antiochia. From there he tra-

163

velled to Egypt. Also mentioned in Amm.17.4.1. The emperor Julianus invited him to his court (cf.ep.76 = 34 Bidez). His wife survived him. Cf.B.L.Z.G. Seeck (op.cit.I) p.147 (with lit.).

Eustathius and **Prosper** are apparently no longer of importance after the 1st legation.

c **Spectatus.** From Antiochia. A relative of **Libanius,** whose uncle **Phasganius** was also his uncle. From a high-ranking family. Tribunus et notarius (cf. ad 14.5.6 = I p.128). In 355 he is in Antiochia, from where he returns to court. In 356 he is back in his own country, for the negotiations with the Persians. Immediately thereafter he goes back to the court. He remains there from the end of 356 to the beginning of 357, when he again travels to Antiochia, though soon after he returns to court. Also mentioned in 17.14.1. After this 1st legation (358) he returns to court via Antiochia and remains there from the end of 358 until the beginning of 360. In 361 he becomes suspect and loses his influence at court. In 363 he is in Paphlagonia. Like **Ursicinus** and **Musonianus** (cf. Pighi p.198), he has probably fallen victim to the failure of the peace negotiations and failure of the Oriental policy. Cf. Seeck B.L.Z.G. p.281 sq.; **Petit, Lib.** (op.cit.XVI) p.178, 215. 330, 367 (note 7).

p. 115. 20 **nullo impetrato** = nulla re impetrata. In general post-class. and late Latin. Cf. Krebs Antib.2.p.172; Nipperdey-Andresen Tac.[11] (1915) I.p.242; Hofm.-Leum.p.489 (84). Cf.et. ad 14.1.4 (= I p.59).

p. 115. 20-21 **effrenatae ... cupiditati.** Cf.Cic. pro domo 44 (115): At videte hominis intolerabilem audaciam cum proiecta quadam et **effrenata cupiditate.** For the substant.cf. ad 17.5.3, p.114.2*b*.

p. 115. 21 **amplius** often has the meaning of **plus** (here) or **plures.** Cf.Veget.r.m.2.2 (= Lang p.35): Romani legiones habent, in quibus singulis sena milia armatorum, interdum **amplius** (= **plures**) militare consuerunt; 2.23 (= Lang p.59): Postremo sciendum est in pugna usum **amplius** (= **plus**) prodesse quam vires. Amplius occurs quite often in Veget.r.m. Cf.et. Heum.-Seckel p.31 (Very frequent in legal writings).

p. 115. 21 **potuit** = one could have had, **potentialis of the past,** in the indic., according to the class. rule.

p. 115. 21-22 **post ... tribunus.** The alliterating p's, together with the emphasis given to the 2 proper names, is not accidental, in my opinion.

itemque. Cf. ad 16.12.17, p.93.23-24*b*.

philosophus. The fact that the philosophi of these days are quite different figures from, for instance, Plato, Aristoteles, c.s., is so well-known, that we need not dwell on it. Nevertheless, it should be noted that the influence of these philosophi, at least on the heathen public, is greater, than one would expect, at least as far as the "classical" idea of philosophy is concerned. For Amm. **philosophus** is a name of honour. Cf.23.6.19 apud Asbamaei quoque Iovis templum in Cappadocia, ubi **amplissimus ille philosophus Apollonius** traditur natus **(Ap.v.Tyana)**.
That a person of high rank like **Musonianus** (according to our terminology a kind of viceroy) thinks it **normal** to introduce to the emperor a philosopher (though known to him), as being a suitable member of so important a legation, shows quite clearly that the position of many philosophers was quite high. To which should be added the considerable influence they had through their teaching on the sons of the "haute bourgeoisie". Cf. J.Vogt, The decline etc. (op.cit.XVI) p.130 sq. and p.320 (literature). Though there is a great difference in appreciation between the Greek-speaking Eastern half of the empire and the West.

opifex suadendi. Cf.30.4.3 (professionem oratorum forensium) Tisias suasionis opificem esse memorat assentiente Leontino Gorgia; 14.11.11: advenit post multos Scudilo ... velamento subagrestis ingenii, **persuasionis opifex** callidus (note the variatio in these 3 places); Prud.Psychom. 259 sq.:

Fraus, detestandis vitiorum e pestibus una,
Fallendi versuta opifex ...

Quint.2.15.4: esse rhetoricen **persuadendi opificem;** Cic. ad fam.7.25: ... a stilo: is enim est **dicendi opifex.** Possibly a reminiscence of Quint.

scripta ... et munera. Cf. ad 17.5.2, p.113.27-28*a*.

a **enisuri ... arctoae.** On March 25, 358, the delegates leave from Sirmium, to which they return on July 10 358. (Pighi p.136). Very worthwhile, as far as this legation is concerned, is **Eunap.Vit.Soph.466,** where the eloquence of **Eustathius** is highly praised. According to Eunapius **Eust.** with his words, cast a spell, as it were, on **Sapor.** The latter even invited him to his table. But the **magi** intervene and tell the king that the philosopher is a magician. How grossly he over-estimated himself, is shown at the end of the caput, which also contains a eulogy of his wife

Sosipatra, end 466-468, one of the many fairy-tales of that period. How this legation ended, is told by Amm. in 17.14.1-2. Cf.comm. ad h.1.
enisuri = with instructions to do their best.
apparatum. Cf. ad 16.5.9, p.76.23-25*b*. With an other meaning 14.5.1: ludos circenses ambitioso editos **apparatu.**
b **suspendere** = to cause delay, to slow down. Cf. Krebs Antib.2 p.634. This meaning in general poet. and post-class. With **this** meaning also Veget.r.m.4.24 (= Lang p.145). Derived from **this** meaning Tert. **suspendium** = delay (but in Amm.19.11.3: ad usque proscriptiones miserorumque **suspendia** pervenerunt, the subst. is used literally). Cf. Souter p.408, also for derived subst.adj.adv. With the meaning: dismiss: Bened.Reg. 25: Is autem frater qui gravioris culpae noxa tenetur, **suspendatur** a mensa simul et ab oratorio. Finally as an example of the first meaning Panegyr.lat.12.9 (= Baehrens p.279): sic agrestes Curii, sic veteres Coruncani, sic nomina reverenda Fabricii, cum induciae bella **suspenderant,** inter aratra vivebant.

p. 116. 2 ⟨**ne**⟩ Clark Rolfe Seyf. **ut** B G. **dum** Btl. Sabbah. The latter notes in II p.176 (note 62): "Clark en introduisant **ne** dans le texte et Rolfe en traduisant: to stay Sapor's preparations, so that **his** northern provinces might not be fortified beyond the possibility of attack, sont dans l'erreur. Puisqu'il manque un mot dans V, il faut suivre B G, qui ajoutent **ut**; ou, mieux encore, suppleér **dum,** sous sa forme abrégée (Lindsay, notae Latinae, p.364) qui a pu être interprétée comme un **d** annulé par la barre qui traverse la partie supérieure de la haste (**dum** est attendu après **interim)**". Clark Seyf. Rolfe take the sentence to mean that by **provinciae** are understood provinciae **Saporis**; Sabbah as provinciae **imperatoris (Romani).** For, Sabbah says, the delegates have to delay Sapor's military preparations for as long **as it takes Constantius to bring his Northern provinces to a sufficient state of defense against possible attacks by the Alamanni (cf.cap.6).** Only then could Constantius turn his attention to the Persians without risk. This last view does not seem to me to be altogether in agreement with the policy followed by Constantius (cf. Pighi p.163), who prefers to use diplomacy, keeps his troops in reserve and avoids a military-offensive behaviour. S. arrives at this view because **arctoae,** placed near **provinciae,** would always mean **Illyricum** (14.11.11; 19.11.3; 26.7.12; 31.16.7). But in 14.11.11 the meaning is much less restricted; 19.11.3 can be considered like that, just as 26.7.12; but not, in my opinion, 31.16.7. I assume that by **Illyricum** S. means the **praefectura praetorio Illyrici etc.,** although he does not say so. But the **dioecesis Thraciarium** is not part of this praefectura, at least not in 390 A.D. And in any case this dioecesis is **arctoa** (or its provinciae).

But **arctous** occurs 13 times in Amm., also with words other than provinciae. In 30.4.1 it says: Haec **per Gallias** et **latus** agebantur **arctoum**. The previous chapter deals with the war against the **Alamanni,** carried on by **Valentianus,** of whom it is said, towards the end, that he moves into his winter quarters in **Trier.** Thus here Sabbah's explanation does not fit at all. And in 31.4.2, where it is said: novos maioresque solitis casus versare **gentes arctoas** rumores terribiles diffuderunt: per omne, **quidquid ad Pontum a Marcomannis praetenditur et Quadis,** multitudinem barbaram ... circa flumen Histrum vagari (The Marcomanni and Quadi reside to the East of the Alamanni), the **gentes arctoae** are not only North of the borders of **Illyricum.** Finally one should be wary of drawing conclusions from the use of words like **arctous,** which are used for stylistic reasons, in order to avoid technical, too impersonal expressions. The arguments just mentioned here are also contrary to **ut** of B G, when **provinciae (imperatoris)** is meant, **situated in "Illyricum".** Therefore two possibilities remain: 1⁰ provinciae (Saporis) and **ne;** 2⁰ provinciae (imperatoris) and **ut** (in Northern Mesopotamia and the region of the upper reaches of the Tigris). The regions in question are: Zabdicene, Corduene, Arzanene, Rehimene, Moxoene with the cities Nisibis, Bezabde, Singara (Nisibis and Singara are situated more in N.E. Mesopotamia), as well as Sophanene (with Amida and Nararra). These are the regions which, except for Sophanene, had to be ceded to the Persians under the peace treaty of 363, a bufferzone in which and about which there was constant fighting. Of 1⁰ and 2⁰ I prefer 2⁰. Amm. wants to say that **Sapor** has to be kept dangling, so that the Northern provinces, the endangered provinces therefore, (see above) could be reinforced **supra humanum modum** (cf. ad 14.11.3 = II p.115; ad 16.11.3, p.88.22; Fesser p.23), a hyperbolic expression, which in ordinary language means, insofar as was humanly possible. For an attack by Sapor of **these** regions was to be expected as it had been his policy from the beginning of his rule, to reconquer **these** regions. **Sapor,** however, does not have to strengthen **his** border regions especially, as his policy is an offensive one, against which the Romans only have a defensive answer. For the catastrophe of the late Roman empire is, that the quantity as well as the quality of its armies is no longer sufficient to protect all its borders. A question of priorities, therefore, as here. Often at the expense of other border districts. Cf.et. ad 17.5.5, p.114.5; Dussaud (op.cit.II) map XV; Pighi (map) p.160.

Note. For **Illyricum** cf.et. ad 15.3.7 (= III p.44 sq.); ad 14.7.9 (= II p.31); 16.10.20, p.88.3 sq. (= XVI p.141 sq.).

p. 116. 3 **arctoae**. Poet., in prose late Latin. Cf. Hagendahl St.Amm.p.71 (with lit.)

VI, 1

p. 116. 4 *a* **Inter quae ita ambigua**. For **inter** cf.17.4.1, p.109.4*a*. **ambigua**: also 16.5.5; 19.11.1; 26.5.9.
b In this caput the **bellum Alamannicum** V is described. For the first 4 b. Alam.cf.XVI p.1. The first 2 take place during the years 354-355, the 5th in the summer of 358.

p. 116. 4 *a* **Iuthungi Alamannorum pars**. For the Alamanni cf. ad 14.10.1 (= II p.96 sq.); Woordenboek der Oudheid I (1965) p.95 (Nuchelmans); G.J. **Wais**, Die Alamannen in ihrer Auseinandersetzung mit der römischen Welt² (1942); **K.F. Stroheker**, Germanentum etc. (op.cit.XVI) p.30 sq. (Alamannen im Reichsdienst), with lit.; E. **Neuscheler**, Amm. Marc. als Quelle für die Alam.gesch., Festschr. K. Bohnenberger, 1938, p.40 sq.
b For the **Juthungi** cf. Stroheker ibid.p.32 sq.: "Bereits vor der Kaisererhebung **Aurelians** (Frühjahr 270) waren die **Juthungen** nördlich der oberen Donau, die damals noch einen selbständigen Stamm bildeten und erst später völlig in den **Alamannen** aufgingen, zum Römischen Reich in ein Vertragsverhältnis getreten und hatten sich gegen Jahrgelder zur Stellung von Hilfstruppen verpflichtet.... Mit **Aurelian**, der 270 gegen die verbündeten **Juthungen** und **Alamannen** schwere Kämpfe zu bestehen hatte, wobei zahlreiche Gefangenen in seine Hand fielen, wird die Bildung der ersten nach diesen Stämmen benannten regulären Truppenkörper des Reichsheers in Verbindung gebracht" (with lit.). A cohors quarta **Iuthungorum, Affrodito** is mentioned in N.D. Or.28 (Egypt); ibid.33 an ala prima **Iuth., Salutaria** (Syria); Laterc. Veron.13: **Iothungi** (enumerated under the gentes barbarae etc.). A cohors nona **Alamannorum, Burgo Severi** mentioned in N.D.Or.31 (Egypt); An ala prima **Alam., Neia** and a cohors quinta **pacata Alam., Oneuatha** ibid. 32 (Phoenicia); Laterc.Veron.13: **Alamanni**.
Bucinobantes are mentioned N.D.Or.6 (Seeck p.16, 17); **R(a)etobarii** ibid.5 (Seeck p.12, 14). For the last 2 tribes, belonging to the **Alam.**, cf. Stroheker ibid.p.40 (with lit.). **B.** are mentioned 29.4.7 A.M., **R.** not mentioned; **Iuth.** only here in A.M. Cf.et.R.E.10.2 (1919) 1347-1348 (Schönfeld): **Iuthungi**.

c It is remarkable how the **Alamanni** (and the gentes belonging to them) are mentioned in the N.D. only in the **Orient**, together with the **Franci, Quadi, Gothi, Vandali, Saxones** etc. This clearly reflects a certain military policy, to keep certain "barbaric" elements separate so as not to promote tribal consciousness. Cf. Stroheker ibid.p.34 sq.

a **Italicis conterminans tractibus. Conterminans** = **contiguus** (cf.16.2.10, p.73.20; 16.9.3, p.84.1-2*b*). The verb late Latin. In Amm.: 14.2.5; 14.8.5; 23.6.45. Cf. Souter p.76. Not in Claud.Veget.r.m.Opt.Milev.Arn.adv.nat. p. 116. 4-5
b **tractus**. Cf. ad 16.3.1, p.74.8-9; ad 17.1.10, p.106.10.

obliti pacis et foederum. See previous note (p.116.4*b*). p. 116. 5

a **quae adepti sunt obsecrando**. The gerund. **obsecrando** makes their disloyalty even worse. But, as has been said before: the Germans do not have Ammianus' sympathy. Cf. ad 16.2.4, p.91.20. p. 116. 5
b **adipiscor** = (here) **impetro**.
The part. **adeptus** occurs pass.: 18.6.1: Sabinianus **adepta** repentina potestate (cf. Fesser p.35).
c For the **gerundium** cf. ad 17.5.14, p.115.17-18.

Raetias. Cf. ad 15.4.1 (= III p.54). p. 116. 6

turbulente. Cf. Dig.48.19.28 § 3: Solent quidam, qui volgo se iuvenes appellant in quibusdam civitatibus **turbulentis** se adclamationibus popularium accommodare ... exilio puniendi sunt, nonnumquam capite plectendi, scilicet cum saepius **seditiose et turbulente** se gesserint (Callistratus. ± 200-250 A.D.). An interesting example of action against "different" opponents. From the above quotation it is clear that here **turbulente** means: violating the quiet, peace. The same combination as above Veget.r.m.3.4 (= Lang p.72): si qui **turbulenti vel seditiosi** sunt milites. Cf.et.Opt.Milev.4.2 (Ziwsa p.4): Quae **pax** si, ut data erat, sic integra inviolataque mansisset nec ab auctoribus scismatis **turbaretur**. The adverbium not in Claud.Veget.r.m.Arn.adv.nat.Opt.Milev. p. 116. 6

a **adeo ut etiam oppidorum temptarent obsidia praeter solitum**. The barbarians often avoid the siege of towns, or do not bring them to a close. Cf.31.15 sq.: Hadrianopolis, Perinthus, Constantinopolis. Cf.16.2.12: audiens itaque Argentoratum Brotomagum Tabernas Salisonem etc. civitates barbaros possidentes, **territoria** earum habitare **(nam ipsa oppida** p. 116. 6-7

ut circumdata retiis busta declinant) and comm.ad.h.l.XVI p.25 sq. As residences the cities are also avoided by the (not-romanized) barbarians, which fact is also known to us from other sources.

b **adeo ut + conjunctivus:** class. and post-class. Cf. Hofm.-Leum.p.760; Krebs Antib.1 p.87. Cf.Veget.r.m.1.3 (= Lang p.8): Quod **usque adeo** verum est, **ut** aranti Quinctio Cincinnato dictaturam constet oblatam; 2.23 (= Lang p.58): Missibilia quoque vel plumbatas iugi perpetuoque exercitio dirigere cogebantur **usque adeo, ut** tempore hiemis ... tegerentur.

c **obsidium.** Also 18.6.3; 19.13.1; 20.6.5; 20.7.3; 21.12.3; 21.12.16; 22.8.49; 24.2.9; 24.2.22; 24.4.6; 24.5.4; etc. Less often with him **obsidio:** 19.3.1; 20.11.7; 20.11.12; 23.5.20; 25.8.18; 28.4.12. **Obsidium,** the older form, may be an archaism with Amm.Cf.Fesser p.53 (with lit.). Veget. r.m. only has **obsidio.**

d **praeter solitum.** Cf. Fesser p.23; ad 16.11.3, p.88.22.

VI, 2

p. 116. 7 *a* **cum valida manu missus Barbatio.** For **valida manu** cf. ad 15.4.1 (= III p.55).

b For **Barbatio** cf. ad 14.11.19 (= II p.132).

p. 116. 8 **in locum Silvani peditum promotus magister.** For **Silvanus** cf. ad 15.5.2 (= III p.68 sq.); for **peditum magister** cf. ad 14.9.1 β (= II p.88). Mentioned: 15.5; 16.2.4; 16.11.2; 18.3.2; 18.4.2; 22.3.11. The name **Silvanus** further occurs: 25.9.4: **Silvanus** quidam causarum defensor (an inhabitant of Nisibis); 28.4.19: dein cum a **Silvani lavacro** vel Mamaeae aquis ventitant sospitalibus. (cf.S.H.A.Alex.Sev.9-10).

p. 116. 8 *a* **ignavus sed verbis effusior.** He is also called **ignavus** 16.11.7. This adjective disqualifies the soldier. Cf.Veg.r.m.1.2: Constat quidem in omnibus locis et **ignavos** et strenuos nasci (= Lang p.6); 1.7 (= Lang p.11): Quid enim prodest, si exerceatur **ignavus,** si pluribus stipendiis moretur in castris?; 3.18 (= Lang p.103): Imperitorum enim vel **ignavorum** est vociferari de longe, cum hostes magis terreantur, si cum telorum ictu clamoris horror accesserit; etc. The same is true of the substant.; cf.3.8 (= Lang p.84): Opus vero centuriones **decempedis** (measuring-staffs of 10 feet) metiuntur, ne minus foderit aut erraverit alicuius **ignavia** (a fine example of personificatio); 3.12: Tunc inimicorum **ignavia** vel error ostendendus est (viz. in the **adhortatio ducis).**

b **effusior.** Cf.Krebs Antib.1 p.494: "Noch beachte man, dass **effusus** auf eine Person bezogen, **verschwenderisch,** auf eine Sache angewendet **über-**

mässig, übertrieben, und zwar beides bei Cicero, bedeutet" (and the lit. quoted there). The adverbium **effuse:** 20.7.15; 23.5.3. Cf.et. ad 16.12.15, p.93.12*b*. **(fusius).**

alacritate militum vehementer erecta: causal, in contrast with: ignavus ... effusior. For **erigere** cf. ad 16.12.37, p.97.8; ad 17.2.1, p.107.13; ad 17.4.6, p.110.2. p. 116. 9

exigua portio = exigua pars. **Portio** actually means the share in something, intended for, measured out to everyone. But the distinction is not always observed, especially in post-class. Latin. Cf.Krebs Antib. I p.326 sq. (with lit.); Veget.r.m.4.31: Praecepto maiestatis tuae, imperator invicte, terrestris proelii rationibus absolutis, navalis belli residua, ut opinor, est **portio** (= pars). p. 116. 10

dilapsa. Cf.Curt.Ruf.7.4.20: (Bactriani) postquam adventare Alexandrum compertum est, **in suos quisque vicos dilapsi.** Bessum reliquerunt; Iust. Phil.16.4.17: Igitur Clearchus sexaginta senatores comprehensos (nam **ceteri in fugam dilapsi erant)** in vincula compingit; ibid.2.12.18: qui cum deserto bello **ad sua tuenda dilabi vellent;** ibid.13.5.17: Graecorum quoque **copiae,** finibus Graeciae hoste pulso, **in urbes dilapsae.** Almost a t.techn. mil.

quae periculi metu se dedit⟨in⟩fugam. This version of G's also Clark Seyf. Sabbah Rolfe. V metus edidit fugam. EB metus edidit fugam **NA metu edidit fugam.** When V is not quite clear, one should pay attention to G. and others. But though G's version is "better" Latin, it is further removed from V. The version given by N A seems preferable to me, The meaning, however, is the same as that in G's version. And its unusual character is no reason for correction, to my view. **Edere** further in 21.15.6 (another unusual combination); 22.15.26; 29.1.31; 29.1.43. Perhaps unconsciously Amm. has had in mind the very frequent expressions such as ἄγερσιν ποιεῖσθαι = ἀγείρειν (Herod.7.5); ἅμιλλαν π. = ἀμιλλασθαῖ (Isocrates 4.85); θήραν π. = θηρᾶν (Xenophon Anab.5.3.10); μάχας π. = μάχεσθαι (Soph.El.294); etc.

a ⟨la⟩**res suos non sine lacrimis reviseret et lamentis.** res suas AG. **lares suos:** Nm₂Em₂. The latter correction could be defended by the alliteration (here connected with rhyme), and in the use of **lares** by Amm. (cf. ad 16.7. 1, p.78.24; ad 16.10.13, p.86.13*b*; 16.11.7, p.89.13). But I see no objection at all against **res suas** as given by G (V has **suos),** which is also that of Sabbah. The version **lares suos** also that of Seyf. Rolfe. p. 116. 10-11 *b* Cf.Tac.Germ.27: **lamenta ac lacrimas** cito, dolorem et tristitiam tarde ponunt; Cic.Tusc.2.21 (48): si se **lamentis** muliebriter **lacrimisque** dedet.

VI, 3

p. 116. 11-12 *a* **Nevitta postea consul.** Mentioned 21.8.1; 21.8.3; 21.10.2; 21.10.8; 21.12.25; 22.3.1; 22.7.1; 24.1.2; 24.4.13; 25.5.2. Here he is **equestris praepositus turmae,** For **turma** cf. ad 15.4.10 (= III p.64). Usually a **turma** is under the command of a **tribunus** (for **tribunus** cf. ad 14.5.8 (= I p.129)). Since **praepositus** is a t.t.mil., it is unlikely here that Amm. would use the word in a general sense, viz. commander. In rank the **praepositus** is below the **tribunus.** In the N.D. **praepositi** numeri, militum, equitum are mentioned (cf. N.D.Seeck p.306). Elsewhere we find **praep.** scholae, legionis, cohortis, militum, auxilii, equitum, though sometimes the division of the troops is not mentioned: Amm.26.6.7: ex praeposito Martensium militum; and elsewhere. Cf. Grosse Mil.p.144 (op.cit.I), with lit. There is also **praep.limitis** (cf. N.D.Seeck p.306) who had the military command in a part of the limes in Africa. They were under the command of the comes Africae, the dux Mauretaniae and the dux Tripolitanae; a praep.limitis Thebaidos; a **praepositus laetis** (instead of a praefectus laetorum et gentilium), a **praepositus classi** (instead of a praefectus classis), a **praepositus castri** (instead of a praefectus castrorum). Cf. Grosse ibid.p.144 sq. A **praepositus fabricae** (= **tribunus fabricae**): Amm.29.3.4 (**Tribuni fabr.** are mentioned 14.7.18; 14.9.4; 15.5.9 (for **tr.fabr.** cf. ad 15.5.9 = III p.85)). "Trotzdem hat die Charge auch in der Spätzeit einen auszerordentlichen Charakter, den einer Aushilfe, gehabt; denn die Führer der **numeri** heiszen durchweg tribuni oder auch tribuni et praepositi, sehr selten findet sich praepositus allgemein angewandt" (Grosse ibid.p.144). For this general meaning cf.S.H.A.Sev.Alex.46.4: dabat **praepositituras** locorum civilium non **militum;** ibid.Gord.24.3: neque enim quisquam ferre potuit datas eunuchis suffragantibus **militum praepositituras** (quoted by Grosse).

b Amm.21.8.1 (361 A.D.): Discedens inter haec **Iulianus** a Rauracis peractis, quae docuimus dudum, **Sallustium** praefectum promotum remisit in Gallias **Germaniano** iusso vicem tueri **Nebridii,** itidemque **Nevittae** magisterium commisit armorum, **Gomoarium** proditorem antiquum timens, quem, cum **Scutarios** ageret, latenter prodidisse **Veteranionem** suum principem audiebat. In this passage we are informed of the fact that **Nevitta** becomes **magister equitum per Gallias.** (cf. Enßlin, Zum Heerm. amt etc., op.cit.I, p.113: **Gomoarius;** p.117: **Nevitta).** [For **Veteranio** cf. ad 15.1.2 (= III p.8); for **scutarii** ad 14.10.8 (= II p.105); For **Nebridius** ad 14.2.20 (= I p.118); For **Sallustius** cf.21.8.1; 23.1.1; 23.1.6; 23.5.4; for **Germanianus** 26.5.5]. It appears from 26.5.1 that he has a successor: et **Valentiniano** quidem, cuius arbitrio res gerebatur, **Iovinus** evenit, dudum promotus a **Iuliano, per Gallias magister armorum** (a⁰ 364). In 362 he was consul with the praef.praet. **Mamertinus.** He serves as a general during the Persian war: 24.1.2; 24.4.13. And he plays an important part in the election of the emperor **Iovianus:** 25.5.2: contra **Nevitta et Dagalaifus** proceresque Gallorum virum talem ex commilitio suo quaeritabant (a⁰ 364). What then is his position? According to Enßlin ibid.p.118 sq., on the basis of his consulate, among other things (in 362), from which it is clear that he was very highly thought of by Iulianus, he was a **magister equitum praesentalis**, and appointed as such by Iulianus before the Persian war. An adverse criticism by Amm.21.10.8: **Mamertino** in consulatu iunxit **Nevittam,** nec splendore nec usu nec gloria horum similem. quibus magistratum amplissimum detulerat **Constantinus,** contra inconsummatum (uncultivated) et subagrestem et quod minus erat ferendum, celsa in potestate crudelem. According to Enßlin (ibid.p.120), one should not conclude from 25.5.2 that **Nevitta** was a Gallian, as is assumed by v.Nischer. According to Bidez (La Vie etc., op.cit.I p.209) he was a Goth (on which grounds?) which belief is shared by Enßlin (Kaiser Jul.Ges.werk, op.cit.I p.112). Schönfeld (op.cit.I p.172) sub voce, does not give a definite conclusion. In any case a German. The suffix **-itta** is Gothic. Cf.et.Förstemann (op.cit.I 1160 sq.; 1162). With the unfavourable judgement of Amm. on **Nevitta** one should always take his Anti-Germanism, and his antipathy of "barbarians" in general into account. He was a member of the military tribunal in **Calchedon** (361), about whose judges Amm. gives his opinion: causas vehementius aequo bonoque spectaverunt praeter paucas, ubi veritas reos nocentissimos offerebat (22.3.2). Hence: crudelis? Cf.et.R.E.17.1 (1936) 156-158 (Enßlin); Brok (op.cit.XVI) p.97.

1. **Note.** It is essential to consider carefully the critical remarks by Enßlin (z.Heerm.amt) regarding v.Nischer (Hermes, 63, 1928) and v.Borries (R.E.X, 1919, p.26-91).
2. I do not know of any **systematic** study on the feelings of rancour and inferiority of civil and military authorities of German descent, but I am sure there must have been some.

a **et adfuisse et fortiter fecisse firmatur.** A striking alliteration with rhyme. For **fortiter fecisse** cf. ad 15.5.33 (= III p.120): **fortia facta** etc.; ad 15.5.35 (= III p.122): **fortiter facientes;** ad 16.12.29, p.95.27.

p. 116. 12-13

b **firmatur** = confirmatur: simplex pro composito. Cf. ad 16.5.6, p.76.12. Here metri causa: claus I.

c For the **nom.c.infin.pass.** Cf. ad 15.5.9 (= III p.84); ad 14.7.5 (= II p.20); and for the nom.c.infinit. (general, not only c.infinit.pass.) Reiter (op.cit.I) p.38-39.

firmari with nom.c.inf. does not occur very often (cf.Pallad.10.3.1). **firmari** with acc.c.inf. is also found in Pallad. (3.29.3; both examples quoted by Georges). **firmare with acc.c.inf.** occurs more often (such as in Pallad.) and Amm.28.1.29; 28.1.37. Cf.et.Veget.r.m.3 praef. (= Lang p.64): Primi (Athenienses) denique experimenta pugnarum de eventibus colligentes **artem proeliorum scripsisse firmantur** usque eo, ut rem militarem, **quae** virtute sola vel certe **felicitate creditur contineri** etc.; ibid. 3.6 (= Lang p.75; locus classicus for the use of the **itineraria** by military commanders): usque eo, ut sollertiores **duces itineraria** provinciarum, in quibus necessitas gerebatur, non tantum adnotata sed etiam picta **habuisse firmentur** etc.

VII, 1

p. 116. 14 *a* **isdem diebus.** Cf.16.7.1; 26.10.1; 22.9.15. **terrae motus horrendi.** The earthquake, which is described here, takes place on August 24 358 (according to the Julian calendar), In 7.1-8 the earthquake itself is described; in 7.9-14 the theories on earthquakes. The last paragraphs form the 2nd great **digressio** in book XVII (the first deals with the obelisci and hieroglyphicae). The description of the catastrophe is masterly, both as regards the contents and the style. But Amm.'s stylistic qualities also reveal themselves in the "learned" discussion. However, one should bear in mind that the author is not a modern physicist or geologist, but a historian of Antiquity, who is also an artist and who therefore does not write only ad usum lectorum, but also as delectationem. His "ignorance" is the ignorance of those days; just as our knowledge will soon be condemned as ignorance in the future. Furthermore the antique historian fulfills a role, which is nowadays (and not yet for so very long) fulfilled by the scientific journalist. In those days this was the only way to give information to a cultured public on physics, geography, astronomy etc., as this public did not itself have enough time, inclination or power of concentration to study the detailed and difficult sources themselves. Finally these digressiones formed a welcome change for readers or listeners in the ever-continuing historical tale, with its many facts, events and places. Socrates 2.39.2 also mentions the earthquake in **Nicomedia,** in connection with a council, which was to be held there, but had to be moved to another place

because of the catastrophe. Cf.et.ibid.2.38.4 and Hussey adnot.III p.211. Also Camus, Amm.Marc. (1967) p.232 (with lit.).
b A **second** earthquake is described by Amm. in 26.10.15. This took place on July 21 365. This one was mainly a sea-quake, in which **Mothone** (in South-Messenia) was badly damaged

a From the time of Cic. onward **terrae motus** is the standard expression p. 116. 14
for: earthquake. Also for Amm., who uses the term 17.7.14: tria genera **terrae motuum;** and 17.7.13: **terrarum motus,** a variatio. But 17.7.9 (with the same meaning): **de terrae pulsibus.**
b **motus.** Cf. ad 14.2.1 (= I p.67). Other places: 14.2.9; 14.6.1; 16.12. 14; and others.

per Macedoniam Asiamque et Pontum. For **per** cf. ad 17.5.1, p.113, 20-21*c*. p. 116. 14-15
Because of the vastness of the stricken area, I think that we should assume that following areas are meant here, viz.: 1⁰ the **dioecesis Macedoniae** (of the praefectura praetorio Illyrici Italiae et Africae); 2⁰ the **dioec.Asiana** (of the praefectura praetorio per Orientem). 3⁰ **the dioec. Pontica** (of the same praef.). For **Nicomedia** lies in the provincia Bithynia, which, according to N.D.Or.25, belongs to the **dioeces.Pontica,** together with the provinciae Helenopontus and Pontus Polemoniacus. The rest of **Asia,** (in the old, not the technical sense) is formed by the **dioec.Asiana.** For it would be strange indeed if Bithynia would be hit by the earthquake and Hellespontus not (which lies next to it and opposite Macedonia, used both in a narrower and in a wider sense). And Hellespontus belongs to the **dioeces.Asiana.** While it would also be strange that this earth- and sea quake would only touch the provincia Macedonia and not equally the prov. Achaia, Thessalia and Creta. All 4 of these belong to the **doiec. Macedoniae.** If one does not accept this explanation, one has to assume that here the author has expressed himself very inaccurately and incompletely, and that he indicates **roughly** the stricken areas by **old** geographical terms.

assiduis pulsibus. Cf.17.7.9: terrae **pulsibus;** 31.12.12: **pulsuque** minaci p. 116. 15
scutorum. Cf.Gell.9.13: quem locum ex eo libro Favorinus philosophus cum legeret, non minoribus quati afficique animum suum **motibus pulsibusque** dicebat, quam si ipse coram depugnantes eos spectaret. Veget.r.m. 4.43 (= Lang p.162) has: **remorum pulsu** (like Cic. and Liv.). The subst. further occurs in Claud. Not in Opt.Milev.Aın.adv.nat. Cf.et. ad 15.4.2 (= III p.55), with other examples.

175

p. 116. 15 **oppida multa concusserunt et montes.** Note the hyperbaton and the clausula (I). For **oppidum** cf. Madvig 2.p.4. **Oppidum** is not an exact concept: it can be a big city (e.g. Antiochia, though hardly ever Rome) and does not necessarily have to indicate a country town. But often completely equal to **urbs.** Cf.Claud.1 (In Prob. et Olyb.cons.) 161 sq.:

.... Medisque subactis
Nostra Semiramiae timeant insignia turres;
Sic fluat attonitus **Romana per oppida** Ganges

(here used metri causa); ibid.3 (In Rufin.I) 193 sq.:

.... orbisque rapinas
Accipit una domus. populi servire coacti
Plenaque privato succumbunt **oppida** regno.

(again metri causa; one should also note the alliterating p's); ibid.7.121 sq. (De III cons.Honor.):

Gaudent Italiae sublimibus **oppida** muris
Adventu sacrata tuo ....

But of Constantinople Claud. says in 5.54 (In Rufin.II):

Urbs etiam magnae quae dicitur aemula Romae;

as of Rome: dilecta **urbs** (28.79). He also speaks of **urbes** 24.141 sq. (De cons.Stilich.III):

Innumeras uno gereret cum tempore pugnas,
Hispanas caperet, **Siculas** obsideret **urbes;**

(metri causa) and ibid.8.602 (De IV cons.Honor.):

Hoc si **Maeonias** cinctu graderere per **urbes.**

Veget.r.m. has **oppidani,** but not **oppidum** (though on the other hand, he often has **civitas;** and **urbs** or **urbes,** though less often). **Oppidum** does not occur in Opt.Milev. (though **civitas** and **urbs** both occur, such as twice in connection with **Roma).**

p. 116. 15-16 *a* **inter monumenta tamen multiformium aerumnarum.** In my view the genitivus is here explicativus. And the curious combination = inter multiformes aerumnas quae monumentis (muniments, history books) tradita sunt. Cf.24.4.5: hacque gloria posteritati sunt **commendati.** non invidemus: accedat hoc quoque **monumentis veteribus** facinus pulchrum (cf.Cic.ad fam.5.12.1: ut cuperem quam celerrime res nostras **monumentis commendari tuis).** Note the alliterating m's.

b **multiformis.** Cf. ad 16.3.5, p.108.29.

c **aerumna.** Cf.III p.62; ad 16.3.1, p.108.9.

p. 116. 16-17 *a* **eminuere Nicomédiae cládes.** For the **poet.pluralis** cf. ad 17.2.1, p.107.

14-15*b*. Gr.: Νικομήδεια. As so often with Amm., the Greek accent is preserved. Claus.I.
b Cf.Itiner, Ant.Aug.Wessel.p.140; Hierocl.Synecd.Wessel.p.691, 692; Itiner.Burdig.Wessel.p.572, 575; Tab.Peut.IX,2; Anon.Rav.Schnetz.p.31; Guid.geogr.Schnetz p.134; Amm.22.8.5: et Astacum (?) secuto tempore Nicomediam a rege cognominatam **(Nicomedes I in 264 B.C.** moved the population of **Astacus,** which was completely destroyed, to the newly-founded **Nicomedia);** 22.9.3: praetercursa Chalcedone et Libyssa, ubi sepultus est Hannibal Poenus, Nicomediam venit (sc.Julianus), **urbem antehac inclutam,** ita magnis retro principum amplificatam impensis (especially Diocletianus and Constantinus I), ut aedium multitudine privatarum et publicarum recte noscentibus **regio quaedam urbis aestimaretur aeternae** (For Roma was divided into regiones). Further on, in § 4 and § 5 Amm. tells how deeply touched **Julianus** was by the catastrophe to the town, and the poverty of its erstwhile so prosperous inhabitants. He gives a large sum for repairs (this happens about 4 years after the earthquake, for which Amm. uses here the term **terrae tremor);** and the complete tragedy 22.13.5: et quartum ... (?) Decembres, vergente in vesperam die, **reliqua Nicomedia conlapsa est terrae motu,** itidemque Nicaeae portio non mediocris (362 A.D.). And this was not the last earthquake to ravage the town. In his youth **Julianus** had several times stayed for longer periods in Nicomedia and was very well-known there. **Libanius,** who had also lived in Nicomedia, has devoted **Orat.61** to this town. For its location cf.adnot.ad p.116.14-15 (3⁰). Cf.et.R.E.s.v. (Ruge) 17.1.1936. 468-492; Pieper (op.cit.II) tab.7 (Metropolis) and p.30 (with lit.).

a **Bithyniae urbium matris.** Also mentioned: 14.11.6; 22.8.7; 22.8.14; 22.8.16; 25.10.12; 26.1.3; 26.4.1; 26.8.3; 26.8.7; Anon.Vales.I.3.5. For the location cf. ad p.116.14-15 (3⁰).
b **urbium matris = metropolis** (late Latin). Cf.et.26.1.3: progresso **Nicaeam** versus exercitu, quae in Bithynia **mater est urbium** (this information does not agree with p.116.17, nor with the actual situation. **Nicaea** is not a metropolis and only a bishop's seat). Cf. Krebs Antib.2 p.79. Amm. is more of a purist here than many of his contemporaries: for μητρόπολις will have sounded quite familiar to his ears.

a **cuius ruinarum eventum vere breviterque absolvam.** This sentence has to mean: I will tell truthfully and briefly **how it happened** that it collapsed = vere breviterque absolvam quomodo evenerit ut rueret. **ruinae** does

not mean here: ruins, rubble, caved-in houses, but is a **plur.poet.** The genit. is **explicativus.**
b **absolvam.** Cf. ad 15.1.1 (= III p.5).
vere breviterque. The veritas is safe with our author (insofar as this is possible with a historian). But **our** ideas on **brevitas** are somewhat different. Cf.et. ad 16.12.10, p.92.16-17.

VII, 2

p. 116. 19 **primo lucis exortu.** For the substant. cf. ad 17.1.5, p.105.16*a*. And for the enormous variation in indicating the break of day cf. ad 15.5.31 (= III p.117).

p. 116. 19 **diem nonum kal.Septembrium** = (in "correct" Latin) ante diem nonum Kalendas Septembres. Cf.15.8.17: Haec diem octavum iduum Novembrium gesta sunt, cum Arbetionem consulem annus haberet et Lollianum (here **year,** month and day are indicated); 26.10.15: diem duodecimum Kalendas Augustas, consule Valentiniano primum cum fratre (just as in the previous place); 22.7.1: adlapso itaque Calendarum Januariarum die; 22.13.5: et quartum ... (?) Decembres; 23.3.3: diem secutum, qui erat quartum decimum kalendas Aprilis, observari debere pronuntiabant; 23.3.7: diem sextum Kalendas ⟨Apriles⟩, quo Romae Matri deorum pompae celebrantur annales; 25.6.9: cumque hinc Kalendis Iuliis stadiis triginta confectis; etc. This kind of indications of time unfortunately does not occur often in Amm. It would certainly be a help with the often uncertain chronology, if this were the case. Note also the variatio and the formulation which often deviates from the class. Latin. This same deviating formulation also in Veget.r.m., e.g.4.29 (= Lang p.157). Cf. et. **Svennung Pall.** (op.cit.II) p.238 sq. (Zur Datierung der Römer, extensive and important).

p. 116. 19-20 **concreti nubium globi nigrantium.** Cf.Stat.Theb.2.106:
Tu, veluti magnum si iam tollentibus austris
Ionium **nigra** iaceat **sub nube** ...
(with notes p.96 comment.Mulder); Lucret.6.495 sq.:
Nunc age, quo pacto pluvius **concrescat** in altis
nubibus umor et in terras demissus ut imber
decidat, expediam.
Verg.Aen. 4.120 sq.:
His ego **nigrantem** commixta grandine **nimbum**
desuper infundam.

Nigrare occurs a few times in Claud. (besides **niger**); not in Veget.r.m. Opt.Milev.Arnob.adv.nat. An unusual word: Varro Lucr.Verg.Stat.Tert. Poetism? As regards **globus** cf.Lucan.4.73 sq.:
   ... (nubes) vetitae transcurrere **densos**
   involvere **globos** ...
For another meaning of **globus** cf. ad 16.12.49, p.99.11. The adverbium **globatim**: 27.9.6 (does not seem to occur anywhere else, except in Glossaria).

a **laetam paulo ante caeli speciem confuderunt.** For **laetus** (Xtristis, dirus) cf. Phaedr.edit. Burmann[4] p.130 ad 2.5.14; Veget.r.m.4.41 (= Lang p.160): **Laetus** orbis (sc.lunae) ac lucidus serenitatem navigiis repromittit ... Sol quoque exoriens vel diem condens interest utrum aequalibus **gaudeat** radiis an **obiecta nube** varietur, utrum solito **splendore** fulgidus etc.; Curt.Ruf.5.4.8: amnis presso in solum alveo delabitur, imminentque colles, ipsi quoque frondibus **laeti**; Enk ad Gratt.Cyn.v.1 (1918).   p. 116. 20

b **speciem.** Cf. ad 17.4.7, p.110.5*a* + *b*.

c **confuderunt.** Cf.Curt.Ruf.8.3.13: **Confuderat** (= effecerat ut confunderentur) oris exsanguis notas (= lineamenta oris) pallor, nec quis esset nosci satis poterat; Iust.3.5.11: ut, si omnes adversum proelium consumpsisset et temporis spatio **confusa corporum lineamenta** essent, ex indicio titulorum tradi sepulturae possent; Claud.17.133 sq. (de Flav. Mall.Theod.cons.):
   (Ut) cognovitque Deam: vultus veneratus amicos
      occurrit, scriptaeque notas **confundit** arenae
(Gesner: Dum festinat, vestem trahit vel pedibus adeo calcat et sic **confundit** arenam, sive pulverem humi sparsum, in quo cursus aethereos signaverat v.126); Veget.r.m.3.23 (= Lang p.115): Sed genus animalium (sc. camelorum), harenis et tolerandae siti aptum, **confusas** etiam in pulvere vento vias absque errore dirigere memoratur; ibid.2.12 (= Lang p.46): Sed antiqui, quia sciebant in acie commisso bello celeriter ordines aciesque **turbari atque confundi**; etc.

a **amendato solis splendore.** For **amendare** cf. ad 16.12.15, p.93.15*b*; ad 16.12.58, p.101.8*c*. Translation: and after they had **banished** sun's lustre: unusual and poetic diction.   p. 116. 20-21

b for **splendor** cf.116.20*a*. Every reader of Amm. is struck by the large number of substantiva verbalia ending in **-or**, which indicate a situation, mood, sound, etc. Liesenberg (1888) p.24 gives a concise list of these words. In general its use does not deviate from that by prose-writers and poets of silver-Latin.

179

p. 116. 21 *a* **nec contigua vel adpŏsita cernebăntur.** For **contigua** cf. ad 16.2.10, p.73. 20; ad 16.9.3, p.84.1-2*b*. **adposita.** Cf.Tac.Ann.2.7: ipse audito castellum **Lupiae flumini adpositum** obsideri, sex legiones eo duxit; Curt.Ruf.4.1.26: regionem quoque **urbi appositam** dicioni eius adiecit; ibid.10.10.4: Pithon Mediam, Lysimachus Thraciam **appositasque Thraciae** Ponticas gentes obtinere iussi; (metaphorical) Cic.Inv.2.54. (165) audacia non contrarium, sed **appositum** est ac propinquum. Also in Quint.4.3.11 (quoted by Georges, also metaph): iudicis quoque noscenda natura est, iuri magis an aequo sit **appositus** (= whether he is attracted more to severe justice or to fairness). In general post-class. = vicinus, propinquus. Not in Claud.Veget.r.m.Opt.Milev.Arnob.adv.nat. The adject. has been preserved in Italian (apposito), but only in a metaphorical sense.

b Clausula III. The choice of the adject. is explained by the claus. and the search for a rhythmic parallel with **contigua**, which also has the accent on the antepaenultima.

p. 116. 21-22 *a* **oculorum optutu praestricto.** Cf.17.8.5: humi prostratis sub **obtutibus eius** pacem ... tribuit; 21.6.2: et mementote quod siquid admisit huius modi, **sub obtutibus** meis conscientiae ipsius sententia punietur (§ 2 and § 3 are both fine examples of arrogant self-exaltation); 20.3.12: sciendum est siderea corpora nec occidere nec oriri sed ita videri **nostris obrutibus** constitutis in terra; 24.6.8: ut lamminis cohaerenter aptati corporum flexus splendore **praestringerent occursantes optutus** (describes equites catafracti). Although the meaning: **glance, sight,** would fit everywhere here, one could just as well have written **oculi** in the 4 quoted places. This use is restricted to late Latin, however.

obtutus without the genit. **oculorum** poet. and late Latin. Cf. Krebs Antib.2 p.193, with lit. The subst. does not occur in Claud.Veget.r.m.Opt. Milev.Arn.adv.nat.

b **praestricto.** Cf. ad 16.10.13, p.86.14-15*b*; 25.10.5; 31.3.7 (both places = to pass by (closely)). With the meaning to blind, to darken, to paralyse: 29.6.9; 30.6.2; 31.7.7 etc. Cf.et. ad 16.9.2, p.83.20-21.

p. 116. 22 *a* **humo involutus crassae caligini squalor insedit.** Cf.19.1.9: aegre defensum **caligine tenebrarum** extrahitur corpus (cf.Verg.Aen.11.187: conditur in tenebras altum **caligine** caelum); 31.13.12. Cf.et.Cic. post red. in Sen.3 (5): ex superioris anni **caligine et tenebris;** Claud.3 (In Rufin.I) 12:

    Sed cum res hominum tanta **caligine volvi**
    Adspicerem ......

The subst. does not occur in Veget.r.m. A similar kind of abundancy as in 19.1.9 Arn.adv.nat.7.29 (= Reiffersch.p.263): debet omne quod geritur causam sui habere perspicuam nec **caliginis** alicuius **obscuritate** contectam (with rich alliteration!)

b V crassae caliginis. Similarly Sabbah Seyf. Rolfe. The conjecture by Corn., endorsed by Clark, is wholly superfluous (see under *a*); Sabbah's explanation II p.177 incorrect.

c **squalor.** Cf. ad 17.1.8, p.106.2.

d The dat. **humo** belongs to **involutus** as well as to **insedit**. The part. is used medially. Cf.Verg.Aen.XII 292 sq.

VII, 3

a **dein ... manubias. Numine summo.** Cf. ad 16.12.18, p.94.7; ad 16.12. 52, p.99.26-p.100.1, *c*, *d*,*e*. p. 116. 22-23

b **1 fatales manubias.** Cf.19.11.15: quos impetus conculcaverat vehemens aut furori resistentes hostili lateraque nudantes intecta **ordo fatalis** absumpsit. (Cf.Seyf.II p.192 (113): **ordo fatalis** bedeutet lediglich phrasenhaft den Tod (Cf.W.Seyf. Klio 43-45, 1965, 291-306)). My only objection is against the incorrect term: **phrasenhaft.**

27.5.10: Valens Constantinopolim redit, ubi postea Athanaricus proximorum factione genitalibus terris expulsus **fatali sorte** decessit et ambitiosis exsequiis ritu sepultus est nostro. Cf.et. ad 16.1.1, p.71.1, *a b c;* ad 14.1.1 (= I p.53).

2 manubiae is t.t. of the sermo auguralis. Cf.Sen.nat.quaest.1.41: In illo dissentiunt (sc.Etrusci et philosophi), quod fulmina dicunt a Iove mitti et tres illi **manubias** dant. **Prima** etc. (From this it follows that **here** the singularis occurs). In **this** meaning also in Fest.Serv.Mart.Cap. (cf. Georges 2.804). Thus truly an exceptional word. The meaning is: stroke of lightning, thunderbolt. Very probably Amm. will not have found this word in the **libri fulgurales** themselves (for this entire matter cf. C.O. **Thulin**, Die Etruskische Disziplin, 3 vol., Göteborg, 1905-1909; Enßlin, Zur Gesch.schr. etc. (op.cit.I) p.83 sq.) but from some archaising writer or 4th century commentator. His interest in omens, fortune-telling, etc. is shared by his heathen (and often also Christian) contemporaries. The subst. does not occur in Veget.r.m.Claud.Opt.Milev.Arn.adv.nat. Cf. et.Serv. ad Verg.Aen.11.259 sq.: (scit triste Minervae sidus) Re vera autem constat Graecos tempestate laborasse aequinoctio vernali, quando **manubiae Minervales,** id est fulmina, tempestates gravissimas commovent.

c **contorquente** = slinging. flinging, hurling. With this meaning, connected with telum, hasta etc., also among others in **Verg.Ovid.** Curt. Quint.Flor.**Stat.** Cf.Veget.r.m.4.22 (= Lang p.144); tanto maiora saxa

fulminis more contorquet (In Veget. the verb occurs 3 times). Found in Arn.adv.nat., but not in Claud.Opt.Milev. The verb is here used because of the clausula (IV): cŏntorquente manŭbias (Not a dialusis).

p. 116. 23-24 *a* **ventosque ab ipsis excitante cardinibus. Cardo** is a t.t. of astronomy: the point around which something revolves. Cf. Varro r.r. 1.2.4: nam intus paene sempiternae hiemes, neque mirum, quod sunt regiones inter circulum septemtrionalem et inter **cardinem caeli**, ubi sol etiam sex mensibus continuis non videtur; Cic.nat.deor.2.41 (from Aratus):

Extremusque adeo **duplici de cardine** vertex
Dicitur esse polus;

Ovid. ex ponto 2.10.45:

(45) Ipse equidem certe cum sim **sub cardine mundi**
(48) Et tecum **gelido** saepe **sub axe** loquor.

From the meaning: axis of the earth, (North-, South-)Pole, the meaning: **heavenly zone**, evolved. Cf.Flor.4.12.4: sed omnes **illius cardinis** populos ... perpacavit; Lucan.4.670:

.... non fusior ulli/terra fuit domino: qua sunt longissima regni/**cardine ab occiduo** vicinus Gadibus Atlas/terminat, **a medio** confinis Syrtibus Hammon; ibid.5.71 sq.:

Hesperio tantum quantum summotus **eeo/cardine** Parnasos gemino petit aethera colle;

Quint.12.10.67; Veget.r.m.: Veteres autem iuxta positionem **cardinum** tantum **quattuor ventos principales** a singulis caeli partibus flare credebant (4.38 = Lang p.154); ibid.4.38 (= Lang p.155): A verno itaque solstitio, id est **ob orientali cardine,** sumemus exordium, ex quo ventus oritur apheliotes ... **meridianum** autem **cardinem** possidet notus, id est auster; ibid.4.38 (= Lang p.156): **Septentrionalem** vero **cardinem** sortitus est aparctias sive septentrio (in all these places of Veget. the winds are associated with **cardines**); Arnob.adv.nat.4.5 (= Reiffersch.p.145): si orientem solem respexero, **cardo** mihi **frigoris** et septentrio fit laevus; Claud.36.428 sq.: (de raptu Proserp.):

Qua te parte poli, **quo te sub cardine** quaeram?
ibid.5.274 sq. (In Rufin.II):

Tu licet **occiduo** maneas **sub cardine** Solis,
Tu mihi dux semper ......

Thus also often in Claud.Amm. can therefore have borrowed this word from the literature, though it is possible that the term was also used in the army. Cf.et.Gell.2.22 (where the word **cardo** does not occur, but in which caput a detailed explanation on the winds etc. is given).

b **excitante.** Cf.28.4.5: ut nec Epimenides ille Cretensis, si fabularum ritu **ab inferis excitatus** redisset; 21.16.11: ita ille quoque **ex minimis causis,** malorum congeries **excitabat.** Cf.et. **excitus** ad 16.12.19, p.94.10*c*.

magnitudo furentium incŭbuit procellārum. Magnitudo = multitudo, also p. 116. 24 class. For **incubuit** cf. ad 17.4.5, p.109.21. Hyperbaton. Clausula III.

a **cuius inpetu pulsorum auditus est montium gemitus** (Hyperbaton) et p. 116. 24-25 **elisi litoris fragor.** Cf.16.10.9 (c.adn.p.85.23).
b Cf.14.1.10: ad vertenda opposita instar rapidi fluminis irrevocabili **impetu** ferebatur; 14.7.16: et eodem **impetu** Domitianum praecipitem per scalas itidem funibus constrinxerunt.
c Cf.14.8.5: orientis vero limes ... laeva Saracenis conterminans gentibus, dextra **pelagi fragoribus** patens; 16.10.9: non montium litorumque intonante **fragore;** Claud.passim. Not in Veget.r.m.Optat.Milev.Arn. adv.nat.
d **elidere** = to smash, shatter; strangle. Cf.28.6.30: Remigius quoque digressus ad otium, **laqueo vitam elisit;** Veget.r.m.3.20 (= Lang p.108): In hoc genere cavendum est, ne inimicorum cuneis transversa tua acies **elidatur;** ibid.3.24 (= Lang p.117): sed crescente audacia postea collecti plures milites pariter pila, hoc est missibilia, in elefantos congerebant eosque vulneribus **elidebant;** ibid.4.2 (= Lang p.130): Murus autem ut numquam possit **elidi,** hac ratione perficitur; ibid.4.22 (= Lang p.144): Saxis tamen gravioribus per onagrum destinatis non solum equi **eliduntur** et homines sed etaim hostium machinamenta **franguntur** (From these places in Veget. it is evident, in my opinion, that **elidere** is a normal word to "soldiers" of that period); Optat.Milev.2.21 (= Ziwsa p.57): Quando posset turba hominum stare, quae rectorem suum a vobis **elisum** (= exstinctum) esse conspiceret?; Claud.5.433 (In Rufin.II):
   Nec minus assiduis flagrant **elidere** saxis
   Prodigiale caput ....;
(Literally) ibid.5.220:
   His dictis omnes una fremuere manipli:
   Quantum non Italo percussa Ceraunia fluctu,
   Quantum non madidis **elisa tonitrua** Cauris. (= N.W. winds)
Similarly Claud.49.64 (Aponus). Not in Arn.adv.nat. Cf.et. ad 16.12.13, p.93.1*b* **(inlidere);** ad 16.12.43, p.98.16 (idem).

haecque. Cf. ad 16.12.17, p.93.23-24*b*; ad 16.12.37, p.97.6*a*; ad 16.12.25, p. 116. 25 p.95.9*b*.

p. 116. 25-26 *a* **tyfones atque presteres.** τυφών: a kind of whirlwind. Cf.Val.Flacc. 3.130 sq.:

Quantus ubi immenso prospexit ab aethere **Typhon**
Igne simul ventisque rubens ....

Plin.n.h.2.49: "Praecipua navigantium pestis, non antennas modo, verum ipsa navigia contorta frangens". Apul. de mundo 15: Si ignitum non fuerit fulmen, Typhon vocatur; Plin.ibid.: Maiore vero illati pondere incursuque, si late siccam rupere nubem, **procellam** gignunt, quae vocatur a Graecis **Ecnephias.** Sin vero depresso sinu, arctius rotati, effregerint sine igne, hoc est sine fulmine, vorticem faciunt, qui **Typhon** vocatur, id est, vibratus Ecnephias (c.annot.Franzii edit.Franz., a⁰ 1778, I, p.338-339).

b πρηστήρ: a fiery whirlwind. Cf.Plin.n.h.2.50: Quod si maiore depressae nubis eruperit specu, sed minus lato quam procella, nec sine **fragore Turbinem** vocant, proxima quaeque prosternentem. Idem ardentior, accensusque dum furit, **Prester** vocatur, amburens contacta pariter et proterens; Seneca Nat.Quaest.5.13: Hic ventus circumactus, et eundem ambiens locum et se ipsa vertigine concitans, **turbo** est. Qui si pugnacior est ac diutius volutatur, inflammatur et efficit quem πρηστῆρα Graeci vocant; Lucret.6.245 sq.; 6.423 sq. All this learned talk is, of course, drawn from Greek sources. For us it is important to know that Amm. is familiar with the works of **Seneca** and **Plinius n.H.** (cf.Fletcher, Rev. de philol.63, 1937, p.387-388).

Note. It may seem somewhat strange that in discussing the written sources of Amm., one has mainly the **Latin** sources in mind. And indeed, I believe that he knows, for instance, Livius and Tacitus well, though perhaps Polybius. Dionys. Halic., Thucyd. not at all or only superficially, although originally he speaks Greek. This applies not only to the historians, but also to the literature in an narrower sense. Exceptions are, of course, contemporary Greek sources as Julianus, Libanius etc. But Latin dominates. It is therefore not accidental that Amm. does **not** write in Greek, (like Claudianus), while Zosimus, and many other great church writers do. He does not see himself as a successor in the line of Thucyd. etc., but rather in that of Livius, Tacitus, etc. The choice is deliberate.

p. 116. 26 *a* **cum horrifico tremore terrarum.** Cf.29.2.21: **coetus** furiarum **horrificus;** 31.10.8: proinde **horrifico** adversum **fragore** terrente; 31.13.2: caelum ... **clamoribus** resultans **horrificis.** Poetism. Cf.Hagend.St.A.p.59.

b **tremore terrarum.** A variatio. Cf. ad 17.7.1, p.116.14*a*.

p. 116. 26 **civitatem.** Cf. ad 17.4.12, p.110.21-22*c;* ad 17.7.1, p.116.15 **(oppida).**

p. 116. 26 **suburbana.** Cf. ad 16.10.14, p.86.22.

funditus everterunt. Cf.Cic.de fin.2.25 (80): Ratio ista, quam defendis, praecepta, quae didicisti, quae probas, **funditus evertunt** amicitiam.

VII, 4

et quoniam - concidebant. The words are not quite clear. I believe that here is meant: **the houses standing on the slopes of the hills,** fall downwards, because these slopes slide down and thus come down on lower-lying houses. Thus the effect of the earthquake is even greater.
vehebantur = devehebantur = were dragged down.
adclivitate = because of the slope; **thus no abl. separativus** without preposition. For the houses are not dragged down the hills but collapse with them and then fall down.

adclivitate. Also 16.2.14; 14.2.13. This place is reminiscent of Caesar b.g.2.18.2: Ab eo flumine pari **acclivitate collis** nascebatur adversus huic et contrarius. The subst. occurs in Caes.Colum.Amm. Certainly a rare substantive. Not in Claud.Veget.r.m.Opt.Milev.Arn.adv.nat.

a **vehebantur.** Therefore simplex pro composito. (Cf. ad 16.5.6, p.76.12). This could be compared with Arnob. **ducere** = **traducere** (5.38; 5.45. Cf. et.Hagend., op.cit.II, p.161 sq.); **tendere** = **extendere** (4.17: cf.Hagend. ibid.p.163, especially annot.3); **sacrare** = **consecrare** (sacrare is poetical and archaising): 2.41; 6.13; 6.21; 5.19; (cf.Hagend.ibid.p.162); **structus** = **obstructus** (3.43; cf.Hagend.ibid.p.163 sq.); **suadere** = **persuadere** (1.64; 2.60; 4.16; cf.Hagend.ibid.p.160); etc. The reasons for this phenomenon are mostly metrical (clausula). Also here in Amm. metri causa: claus.III, with dialusis (Cf.Pighi St.A.p.46). Cf.et. ad 16.12.46, p.99.3-4.
b One should expect here an aoristic perfectum (cf. ad 16.12.39, p.97. 25-26). See under *a*. Cf.et. ad 14.2.14 (= I p.75); ad 14.11.32 (= II p.143); Ehrism.p.14 sq., with, among others, these examples of **imperf.pass.** instead of **perf.pass.**: 16.12.36; 16.12.37; 16.12.43; 17.1.5. Far less often we see the **imperf.act.** instead of **perf.act.** (Ehrism ibid.p.16).

concidebant. The appropriate verb for the collapse of buildings. But the clausula (III) also plays a part in the choice of the verb.

reclangentibus cunctis. Reclango probably only in Amm. = to resound. For **cunctis** cf. ad 17.3.6, p.109.2.

sonitu ruinarum immenso. Note the sound-picture in: reclangentibus -

185

immenso. For **ruinarum** cf. ad 17.7.1, p.116.17-18*a*. Besides the class. **sonitus** Amm. uses **sonus**. (cf. ad 14.6.18 = I p.99).

p. 117. 2-4 **interquae ... constringunt. Clamoribus** governs the genit. quaeritantium (for the **substantivisation** of the **part.praes.** cf.Hofm.-Leum.p.457, 66*a;* Hoogterp Et. sur le lat. du cod. Bob. des Evangiles p.212 sq.), though the syntactic "role" of this participium is a different one: viz. that of a **Greek genitiv. absolutus,** where, as we know, its subject, e.g. ἄνθρωπος or an indefinite neutrum, can easily be left out, while the fixed rule of the **lat.abl.abs.** is not strictly adhered to, viz. that the aforesaid subject may not occur in a different case in the main clause (example Xenoph.Anab. 4.4.11; ibid.1.2.17; Thucyd.1.7.1; ibid.1.74.1). The **genit.abs.** occurs in Latin, but very rarely, in the Itala and with church-writers, and should here be considered a Grecism. As the 2 first examples Bell.Hisp.14.1 and 23.5 can be counted (cf. Hofm.-Leum.p.449).

p. 117. 2 **inter quae.** Cf. ad 17.4.1, p.109.4*a*.

p. 117. 2 **celsa culmina**: alliteration. From the context (as well as from the adject. **celsus**?) it is clear that the tops of the mountains are meant here, although Claud.40 (Epist.II) 41 sq. uses the same word for houses: (Non ego promisi)
    Nec quod nostra Ceres numerosa falce laboret,
    Aurataeque ferant **culmina celsa** trabes;
but ibid.17 (De Fl.Mall.Theod.cons.) 206 sq.:
    .... sed ut altus Olympi

p. 117. 2 (207)
    Vertex (= culmen), qui spatio ventos hiemesque relinquit,
(209)
    Celsior exsurgit pluviis etc. Cf.et.ibid.37 (Gigantom.) 72 sq.:
    Subsidit patulis Tellus **sine culmine** campis
    In natos divisa suos ....
(sine culmine = sine montibus).
for **culmen** cf.et. ad 14.1.1 (= I p.54); ad 15.5.17 (= III p.99); ad 16.6.1, p.78.12*c*. The meaning **ridge, top of a roof** is also found quite clearly in Opt.Milev.2.18 (= Ziwsa p.51 sq.): ubi cum contra inportunitatem suam viderent basilicam clausam, praesentes iusserunt comites suos, ut ascenderent **culmina**, nudarent **tecta**, iactarent tegulas. **Culmen** does not occur in Veget.r.m.Arn.adv.nat. Fairly often in Claud.
For the subst. **celsitudo** cf. ad 16.10.14, p.86.26-27*b*.

resultabant. Cf.14.6.18; 19.2.11; 19.6.10; 20.11.21; 29.1.23; 30.1.20; p. 117. 2
31.1.2; 31.13.2: **resultabant** canes ululantibus lupis (= the dogs answered
the howling wolves). This meaning: to resound, cause an echo, in general
poet. and post-class. Cf. Krebs Antib.2 p.512 (with lit.); Verg.Aen.5.149
sq.:
> Consonat omne nemus vocemque inclusa volutant
> Litora; **pulsati colles clamore resultant;**

Stat.Theb.2.714:
> ... oranti nox et **iuga longa resultant;**

Claud.1.174 sq. (In Prob. et Olyb.cons.):
> Extemplo strepuere chori, **collesque** canoris
> Plausibus **impulsi** septena **voce resultant;**

ibid.36.389 sq. (De raptu Proserp.III):
(Megaerae)
> Dant tenebrae Manesque locum, plantisque **resultant**
> Tartara ferratis; etc.

The verb does not occur in Veget.r.m.Opt.Milev.Arn.adv.nat.

quaeritantium. Cf. 14.4.3; **ad** 14.7.7 (= II p.25); 15.11.16; 17.7.4; 25.5.2;
28.1.54 (with indirect interrogative sentence); 29.1.35; 31.10.16; 26.1.3. p. 117. 3
Not in Claud.Veget.r.m.Opt.Milev.Arn.adv.nat.

coniugium = marriage partners; as in Verg.Aen.2.579 (spouse) and ibid.
3.296; 7.433 and 11.270 (consort, spouse (female)). Cf. Claud.29.26 sq. p. 117. 3
(Laus Seren.):
> .... terrae pelagique labores
> Et totidem saevi bellis, quot fluctibus, anni,
> **Coniugii** docuere fidem

(viz. of Penelope to her husband);
Aur.Vict.Caes.1.7: Felix adeo (absque liberis tamen simulque **coniugio**)
ut Indi ... legatos mitterent ... (sc. Augustus). (for **absque** cf.I p.81). The
subst. was probably also chosen because of the clausula (III); for this
exerts some influence not only on the choice of verbs and verb-forms,
but also on the choice of other word species.

a **et siquid necessitudines artae constringunt.** Btl. Haupt Clark Seyf. p. 117. 3-4
Sabbah Rolfe. V siquid necessitudinis arte constringunt G constringit.
Sabbah II p.177: "Il paraît cependant plus simple et plus prudent de
supposer **deux fautes habituelles de V (confusion e/i et e/ae)** et d'adopter la
correction de Bentley et Haupt". I do not agree with the explanation (and

possible defense) of V's version by Sabbah (ibid.). The version given by G can be easily explained if one remembers to separate the object of **constringit** from **quaeritantium**; translation: while they searched diligently for their husbands, wives and children, and whoever was linked to **them** closely by kinship. **Siquid necessitudinis** is object of **quaeritantium.**
b Cf.Horat.Epod.15.5 sq.:
   Artius atque hedera procera **adstringitur** ilex
   Lentis adhaerens bracchiis.
Claud.26 (de bello Getico) 491 sq.:
   Sed numquam Mavors adeo **constrinxit in artum**
   Res, Alarice, tuas.
artius astringere and **artissime constringere** both occur in Cic. Cf.et.III p.125 sq. **(arte** and **artus).**

VII, 5

p. 117, 5 **aer iam sudus.** Although occurring, among others, in Cic. and Verg., it is still probably a farfetched word, and just a little archaic. Not in Claud. Veget.r.m.Arn.adv.nat.Opt.Milev. Here, as so often: dry and cloudless. An extremely rare adverbium: **sudum** in Prudent.cath.7.80.

p. 117, 5 **funereas strages.** Pluralis poet. For the adject. cf.26.10.12; 29.5.46; 31.7. 16. Cf.Hagend.St.Amm.p.40: "Adjectivum a Verg. quod sciam primum admissum, sensu latiore i.q. funestus, exitialis epicis potissimum familiare, sero in prosam orationem transiit" (with lit. and examples). Here = corpora prostrata. Somewhat abundant Claud.35 (de raptu Proserp.) 357 sq.:
   Navita non moritur fluctu, non cuspide miles.
   Oppida **funerei** pollent immunia **leti.**
The adj. does not occur in Veget.r.m.Arn.adv.nat. and Opt.Milev., who writes in 1.13 (Ziwsa p.15): (tempestas persecutionis) nonnullos **funestam** prostravit in **mortem** and apparently avoids **funereus.**

p. 117, 5 **retexit.** Cf.Verg.Aen.4.119 sq.:
   In nemus ire parant, ubi primos crastinus ortus
   Extulerit Titan radiisque **retexerit** orbem;
ibid.9.459 sq.; Lucan.7.787 sq.:
   postquam **clara dies Pharsalica damna** retexit/nulla loci facies revocat
   feralibus arvis/haerentes oculos.
The verb several times in **Claud.** Not in Veget.r.m.Arn.adv.nat.Opt.Milev. Probably a poetic word.

a **superruentium ruderum.** Cf.16.12.53 pars ⟨per⟩ limosum et lubricum p. 117. 6
solum, in sociorum cruore lapsi, intactis ferro corporibus, **acervis superruentium obruti** necabantur; Apul.met.1.16: atque ego de alto recidens
Socraten - nam iuxta me iacebat - **superruo** cumque eo in terram devolvor
(= fall down on top of S.); ibid.2.26: et statim **corpori superruens** (=
throwing oneself on). No places are known to me from other sources. In
any case a very rare verb. (and not in Claud.Veget.r.m.Arn.adv.nat.Opt.
Milev.).
b **ruderum. Rudus (n.)** collectivum and **rudera (pl)** for: rubble, caved-in
buildings, etc. found in Tac.Suet. and others, but far from generally used.
Here it means: **collapsing** buildings, what seems indeed very rare to me =
aedificia, tecta, muri, quae efficiunt rudera. Comparable Stat.Theb.2.562:
immanem quaerens librare **ruinam** = saxum ruinam efficiens (cf.comm.
Mulder ad h.l.p.301 sq.).

constipati. Cf.19.11.14: et antequam exsatiaret caedibus barbaricis manus, p. 117. 6
acervi constipati sunt mortuorum. Here of living persons and also among
others in Cic. and Caes. Several times in **Veget.r.m.** Not in Claud.Arn.
adv.nat.Opt.Milev. The subst. **constipatio** 24.8.5; 26.6.14. (Late lat.).

Sub. Cf. ad 17.4.13, p.111.6*b*. p. 117. 6

nonnulli ... quidam ... alii ... conplures ... quosdam. Note the variety in p. 117. 5-10
the pronomina. Cf. ad 17.8.5, p.120.5-7.

collo tenus. Cf. ad 16.8.3, p.81.6; Liesenberg (1890), op.cit.I, p.16 sq. Not p. 117. 7
in Claud.Veget.r.m.Arn.adv.nat. Once in Opt.Milev. Cf.et. Krebs Antib.
2 p.654 sq. (with lit.) In Amm. only with the ablat.!

aggeribus. Here = masses of rubble = ± rudera. This meaning occurs p. 117. 7
more often. In Veget.r.m. only the t.t.mil. (= thrown-up dam, bank).

siqui iuvisset. Qui in a substantive sense after **si** occurs more often, also p. 117. 7
in class. Latin, instead of **quis** (just as instead of **qui, quis** may be used
adjectively).
Note. Thus Amm. uses **siqui** in accordance with the classical rules, which
in late Latin is certainly no longer the general custom: **Aliquis** drives out
quis after si, ne, num. etc. and penetrates into negative sentences. Cf.
Hofm.-Leum. 82*a*, p.483. Cf.et. ad 17.4.12, p.110.25*c;* ad 16.11.8, p.89.
19-20.

p. 117. 8 *a* **auxiliorum inopia necabantur.** Although the imperf.pass. can be explained here, one should always remember that Amm.c.s. avoid **compound passive forms.** Cf. ad 17.7.4, 117.1*b*.

b **auxiliorum** = auxilii, poet.plur. The combination of **inopia** with **auxilium** is not known to me from other sources. Comparable with this Tac.Ann.13.57: (describing peat, moor-fires) neque extingui poterant, non si imbres caderent, non fluvialibus aquis aut quo alio humore, donec **inopia remedii** et ira cladis agrestes quidam eminus saxa iacere etc. (= fire extinguisher = help in fighting the fires).

p. 117. 8-9 *a* **alii ... pendebant. lignorum** = **trabum.** fixi = transfixi. pendebant = dependebant. (In both cases: simplex pro composito; cf. ad 17.7.4, p.117. 1*a*). For **pendere** cf. ad 16.12.53, p.100.8.

b **exstantium:** to stick out, protrude, viz. from the collapsed piles of houses. Cf.Tac.1.70: permiscentur inter se manipuli, modo pectore, modo **ore tenus extantes,** aliquando subtracto solo disiecti aut **obruti;** Ovid. Metam.11.358:

Nant alii **celsoque exstant** super aequora **collo.**

c **acuminibus.** Cf. ad 16.12.54, p.100.11*a*; Arn.adv.nat.3.10 (Reiffersch. p.118): illas telis gravibus et **dolorum acuminibus fixas** heiulare. The subst. does not occur in Opt.Milev.

VII, 6

p. 117. 9 **uno ictu** = by one stroke **simultaneously.**

p. 117. 9-10 *a* **paulo ... cernebantur.** Translation: And what had previously been human beings, were then seen as piles of corpses, which could not be identified (lit.: who could no longer be distinguished). **Promiscae strages** is therefore the nominal part of the predicate.

b Cf.23.2.4: Cumque eum profecturum deduceret **multitudo promiscua** itum felicem reditumque gloriosum exoptans oransque (promiscua Wm2NG).

Promiscus of § 6 also in Varr.Liv.Tac.Gell.Cypr. The two adjectiva do not occur in Claud.Veget.r.m.Opt.Milev.Arn.adv.nat. V reads: **promisce** (for the error in writing e/ae cf. ad 17.7.4, p.117.3-4*a*).

c **strages.** Repeated after few lines (§ 5). But here, in my opinion, a normal pluralis = ± acervi).

p. 117. 10 **quosdam.** Cf. ad 17.3.6, p.109.1-2*b*.

inclinata fastigia. Inclinare here, as so often, used intransitively (or, perhaps medially). Although the transit. meaning also fits here: caused by the earthquake to sway and cave in. Cf.Cic.de orat.2.44 (187): Sed tantam vim habet illa, quae recte a bono poeta dicta est ... oratio, ut non modo **inclinantem excipere aut stantem inclinare**, sed etiam adversantem et repugnantem ... capere possit. (The underlined words contradict each other, as Georges rightly remarks).

intrinsecus. Cf.23.4.13; 24.4.22; 31.15.6. Among others in Cato, Colum. Cels.Auct.b.afric. (with **this** meaning = internal, within). Further late Latin and quite rare. Cf.Krebs Antib.1 p.778; Souter p.217; **Keil, Comm. in Cat. de agricult.p.48.** Not in Claud.Arn.adv.nat.Opt.Milev. **Often in Veget.r.m.** For other adverbia ending in **-secus.** cf. Liesenberg (1889) p.15.

servabant N.Btl.Nov. Clark Rolfe. **ferebant** B G Sabbah. **serebant** V. **serabant** E Haupt Seyf. **ferebant** does not seem recommendable to me, because of the meaning, nor **serebant.** Of the 2 remaining versions the best one seems to me the extremely rare verb **serabant.** (= lock with a bolt), for which Georges quotes Venant.Fort.vit.S.Menard.6; Arn. in psalm. 147 (Another meaning in Varro l.lat.7.108 (ad Naev.b.Punic.53 sq. = Baehrens p.51: ∪ ⏑ ∪ ⏑ quod brúti|néc satís **sardáre** queúnt.): in bello Punico "nec satis sardare" ab **serare** dictum, id est **aperire;** hinc etiam **sera;** qua remota fores panduntur (= Goetz-Schoell p.123)).

intactos Cf.16.12.53: **intactis** ferro corporibus.

a **angore et inedia consumendos. Angor** does not occur in Claud.Veget. r.m.Arn.adv.nat.Opt.Milev. For **inedia** cf. ad 14.7.5 (= II p.20); 14.2.19: **inediae** propinquantis aerumnas exitialis horrebant. The last subst. is found in Veget.r.m. and Arn.adv.nat. Not in Claud. and Opt.Milev.
b **consumendos.** Cf. ad 16.12.22, p.94.26*b*. Cf.Cic.ad fam.16.10.1: Gravissime aegrotasti: **inedia** et purgationibus et vi ipsius morbi **consumptus es.**

inter quos. For the frequent and varied use of **inter** cf. ad 17.6.1, p.116.4*a;* Liesenberg (1890) p.15; ad 17.4.1, p.109.4*a;* Reinhardt (op.cit.,I) p.55 sq.

Aristaenetus. Bithynian. Heathen. From **Nicaea.** Studied in Athens. Came into contact with **Libanius** when the latter was teaching in **Nicomedia.** In 355 his wife died, whom he mourned for a long time. Was asked for many offices, which he refused. Only in the summer of 358 did he decide to accept an office, but one which allowed him to remain in Bithynia. He became **vicarius** of the newly-founded **dioecesis Pietas.** Through this he came into close contact with the praef.praet. **Hermogenes.** He was killed in the earthquake of August 24th 358, and buried in **Nicaea.** Libanius wrote a monody on him. Cf.Seeck B.L.Z.G. (op.cit.I) p.85 sq. (he is not to be confused with **Aristaenetus,** son of Bassianus, relative and pupil of Libanius; cf.ibid.p.87 sq. The latter is a native of **Antiochia.**).

[Hermogenes was the successor of **Musonianus (Strategius)** in 358 (cf. ad 15.13.1 = IV p.78). Cf. ad 19.12.6: **Hermogenes** enim **Ponticus** ea tempestate praefectus praetorio.

For **vicarius** cf. ad 14.5.7 (= I p.128).]

Cf.et. Petit (op.cit.XVI) p.35.383; Festugière (op.cit.XVI) p.428 sq.

p. 117, 12   *a* **affectatam recens dioecensim curans.** V **regens.** This is unnecessary besides **curans.** Lindenbr. **recens** and also Clark Sabbah Seyf. Rolfe. L.XVII was written before 389 and after 383. **Eusebia** died in 361 A.D. (cf. Stammt.I p.48). In view of these dates it is clear that **recens** refers to a date **later than** 361 A.D., otherwise **recens** is meaningless. The **dioecesis** "Pietas" is not mentioned in the Not.Dign. In any case, A. resides in **Nicomedia.** This "honorary" dioecesis will probably have included the **provincia Bithynia** and part of the **dioecesis Pontica.** For **recens** cf. ad 17.4.12, p.110.23.

b These 3 words are rendered by Wagner with: "paullo ante institutam provinciam", who refers for the meaning of **affectare** here to Liv.1.46.2: neque ea res Tarquinio spem **adfectandi regni** minuit (Weissenborn-Müller": die Hoffnung auf Erreichung (eigentlich auf erfolgreiches Streben nach) der Herrschaft. Cf.et.ibid.1.50.4: **adfectare eum imperium;** 2.7.6: **regnum** eum **adfectare;** 29.6.2. spes autem **adfectandae eius rei.** But these passages in Liv. are no argument for the translation: **institutam.** For we are here concerned with the titling of a new dioecesis in old Roman territory. And indeed, one expects here: **newly founded.** But I know of no places where **this** meaning is elucidated; not even in legal writings. At any rate one should here with Amm. assume a very much broadened meaning. Cf.14.1.10 (= I p.66); Liesenberg (1889) p.1; Krebs Antib.1 p.123 sq. (with lit.).

c 1. **curare** = to be in command of. Cf.18.5.5; 24.4.13; 29.4.3; 31.8.3: equestris exercitus ... **cura** commissa; Fesser p.9; Thes.IV s.v.; Heraeus ad Tac.hist.2.24; Heum.-Seckel p.114. Almost the same words 17.11.5: Romae Artemius **curans vicariam praefecturam.**

2. Cf. **regere** ad 16.10.21, p.88.12; ad 16.11.6, p. 89.6; Georges 2.2283*b* (with lit.). The **part. praes.** as **substantive** (= **regent, monarch**): Claud.8 (de IV cons.Honor.) 299 sq.:

.... componitur orbis
Regis ad exemplum, nec sic inflectere sensus
Humanos edicta valent, ut vita **regentis;** ibid.

21 (de laud.Stilich.I) 167 sq.:

.... (ut) placidi servirent legibus enses.
Scilicet in vulgus manant exempla **regentum**
Utque **ducum** lituos, sic **mores,** castra sequuntur;

Seneca Clement.1.22.3: Verecundiam peccandi facit ipsa clementia **regentis;** ibid.1.19.1: excogitare nemo quicquam poterit, quod magis decorum **regenti** sit quam clementia; Tac.Dial.41: ... sic minor oratorum honor obscuriorque gloria est inter bonos mores et in obsequium **regentis** paratos (cf. Gudeman[2] comm.p.505). All these examples given by Georges. Cf. ad 15.5.14 (= III p.91).

d **dioecensim.** The spelling **diocensis** only given by the **laterculus Veronensis** (= edit. Seeck N.D. p.247 sq.).

Pietatis. Not only the faithful and loving wife is called **pia**, but the blessed in the Elysium are also called **pii.** Cf.Claud.35 (de raptu Pros.II) 365 sq.:

Exsultant cum voce **pii,** Ditisque sub aula
Talia pervigili sumunt exordia plausu.

Previously it was told in 562 sq.:

Ducitur in thalamum virgo. Stat pronuba iuxtu
Stellantes Nox picta sinus.

a **cognominarat** = nominarat (as very often). Cf.18.9.4; 21.1.8; 22.8.23; 22.9.7; 23.6.23; 23.6.72; 27.3.7; 27.4.8; 29.6.19; 30.7.2; 31.2.13; 31.11.2. Cf.et. ad 15.5.4 (= III p.75); ad 15.12.5 (= IV p.77); ad 14.5.8 (= I p.88): **cognomentum;** Blomgren (op.cit.II) p.89 (annot.2) ad 31.3.1 **(cognominare).**

b For the contracted form cf.Hagend. Prose métr. (op.cit.II) p.176-197 (with lit.). Here not in the clausula, metri causa, as nearly always.

animam exhalavit. Cf. Seneca Ep.101.14: Invenitur aliquis, qui malit inter supplicia tabescere et perire membratim et toties per stillicidia **amittere animam,** quam semel **exhalare?** Verg.Aen.2.562: vitam exhalantem; Ovid.Met.7.579 sq.; Sil.It.10.153 sq. Poet.lat. geneially. Does not occur in Claud.Veget.r.m.Arn.adv.nat. Cf.et.Opt.Milev.1.27 (= Ziwsa p.30): Iamdudum opinionis incertae et inter caligines, quas livor et invidia **exalaverat,** latere veritas videbatur; Amm.14.9.1: occultis Constantium litteris edocebat implorans subsidia, quorum metu tumor notissimus Caesaris **exhalaret.**

p. 117. 14 **Cruciatam diutius** = either: too long already or = **positivus.** The latter possibility most likely. Cf. ad 14.6.12 (= I p.96).

VII, 7

p. 117. 14-15 **alii subita magnitudine ruinae oppressi.** E ruine (cf. ad 17.7.4, p.117.3-4a). VAG om. Clark, Seyf. Rolfe follow E. Sabbah follows V. In any case **subita** is logically linked to **ruinae.** For the collapse is sudden, not the size. But to me it suggests that **ruinae** is an explanation, which somehow got into the text, of **magnitudo,** which is used pregnantly here: = magnitudo decidens, irruens.
mōlibus contegŭntur: claus.III. Hence the compositum.

p. 117. 15 **conlisis quidam capitibus. Quidam** = nonnulli. cf. ad 17.3.6, p.109.1-2b. **Collidi** is the t.t.med. for: be crushed, badly damaged. Thus also in Celsus and judicial writers. Cf.Claud.17.82 sq.;

Hi vaga **collidunt** caecis primordia plagis.

(primordia = elementa, atomos; plagae = the colliding of atoms; caecus = fortuitus). The verb does not occur in Veget.r.m.Arn.adv.nat. Opt.Milev.

p. 117. 16 **praesectis.** Cf.Caes.b.c.3.9.3: et **praesectis** omnium mulierum crinibus tormenta effecerunt; Horat.Ars Poet.294; Varro Liv.Ovid.Colum.Vitruv. Plin.N.H. Seneca Apul. Not in Claud.Veget.r.m.Arn. adv.nat.Opt. Milev. Here in Amm. = ± "pinched off".

p. 117. 16 **inter vitae mortisque confinia.** Cf. ad 15.6.2 (= IV p.7); Thes.IV s.v. And in very refined style Claud.44 (Phoenix) 69 sq.:

Qui fuerat genitor, natus nunc prosilit idem
Succeditque novus. **Geminae confinia vitae**
Exiguo medius discrimine separat ignis;

Arn.adv.nat.5.9 (= Reiffersch.p.182): suspensis per formidinem gressibus et **inter media constitutus sollicitudinis speique confinia** palpabat res intimas; (singularis) Opt.Milev.5.3 (= Ziwsa p.123): dum se **in confinio senserit mortis.** Not in Veget.r.m.

a **aliorum adiumenta paria perferentium implorantes** Note the alliteration. "Ordinary" Latin: alios implorantes ut se adiuvarent. Cf. ad 14.7.9 (= I p.27); 15.7.5: tribuliumque **adiumentum** nequicquam **implorante**; 27.3.12: Damasus et Ursinus ... asperrime conflictabantur, adusque mortis vulnerumque discrimina **adiumentis** utriusque progressis (= fellow party members, supporters).

b **paria.** Cf. ad 17.3.2, p.108.12*a;* ad 17.4.1, p.109.4*a*.

a **cum obtestatione magna deserebantur.** Paraphrase: they begged others for help, although these were suffering a similar fate, but, **in spite of their urgent appeals (supplications),** they were nevertheless abandoned (for the part. = verbum finitum cf. ad 17.3.5, p.108.20*a*). **cum obtestatione** is really an ablat.modi. Cf.Hofm.-Leum.51*b* **Zus.**p.430.

b **deserebantur.** Claus.III. Cf. ad 17.7.5, p.117.8*a*.

c **obtestatio** = urgent appeal, also in Cic.Nepos.Liv.Tac. The subst. does not occur in Claud.Veget.r.m.Opt.Milev.Arn.adv.nat.

VII, 8

a From this § we see, what was already known, that in most cases fires, caused by calamities, could not really be fought. A **fire brigade,** if there was one, did not possess the appropriate means, especially because the modern fire-pump had yet to be invented. Hence the calamitous nature of every local fire and the, to us moderns, sometimes exaggerated fear of fire, which persists far into the Middle Ages. Cf. L.Bréhier, Les Instit. de l'Empire Byzant. (1949) p.192: Les services urbains; Willems, Dr. publ.rom.p.488 sq. (with litt.).

Added to this, of course, is the fact that earthquakes not only cause a panic fright, but also often disturb or block the water-supply. Cf.et. **P.Baillie Reynolds,** The Vigiles of Imperial Rome (1926); Calza-Becati[4], **Ostia,** p.24,81; p.117.19-20 (with some technical details).

b Also a **well-organised fight against disasters,** set up either by the government or on a private level, is totally lacking in Antiquity. Thus the impact of a serious earthquake like this one in **Nicomedia** can hardly be exaggerated.

a **potuit ... exuss⟨iss⟩ent.** Irr.hypoth. period of the past, constructed according to the classical rules. Cf. ad 14.3.2 (= I p.79); ad 15.6.3 (= IV p.8).

b **Vexussent.** E A G exussissent. B excussisset. Seyf. Sabbah Clark

Rolfe follow G. For the claus ᷉ ∼ ∼ ∼ ᷉ ∼ cf. Blomgren (op.cit.II) p.9 sq. V's version should not be changed, in my opinion.

p. 117. 18 **sacrarum et privatarum. Sacrarum** is not the opposite of privatarum, which is the case, however, with **profanarum**. Public buildings, such as thermae palaestrae, etc., should be mentally added, as the latter are certainly not **aedes privatae.**

p. 117. 19 *a* **palantes abrupti flammarum ardores. Abrupti** Clark Seyf. Sabbah Rolfe. Seyf. translates: "wenn sich nicht **eine plötzliche Feuersbrunst** ausgebreitet hätte"; Sabbah: "**les flammes déchainées** des incendies". Obviously **abrupti** is considered as participium of **abrumpi**, in the meaning: to break loose, to erupt (1). But in that case one would sooner expect: **erupti.** (Cf.Cic.Verr.IV.48.(106): dicitur inflammasse taedas iis **ignibus** qui ex Aetnae vertice **erumpunt;** Lucr.1.724: faucibus **eruptos** iterum vis ut vomat **ignis;** etc. This verb occurs more often in Amm.: cf. ad 17.2.2, p.107.18*a*). The **adject. abruptus** (= repentinus, subitus) Cod.Theod.10. 10.28: abrupto periculo (= sudden(ly)). (2). **Abruptus** does not occur at all in Arn.adv.nat. and Opt.Milev. Several times in Claud. and more often in Veget.r.m., but **not** with the meaning as in the Cod.Theod. So, although **abrupti**, with the meaning (2) can not be entirely rejected, however rarely used, I think it is better to read **abrupte** here (for the confusion e/i cf. ad 17.7.4, p.117.3-4*a*). This adverbium is found more often in Amm.: cf.14.1.8: regina, quae **abrupte** mariti fortunas trudebat in exitium praeceps; 15.2.9: tenues vero, quibus exiguae vires erant ad redimendam salutem aut nullae, damnabantur **abrupte;** 20.5.5: velut incitatos torrentes hostes **abruptius** inundantes superastis; 26.6.12: Procopius aerumnis diuturnis attritus ... aleam periculorum omnium iecit **abrupte.** Liesenberg (1889) translates 17.7.8: an einzelnen Punkten, hier und da; 26.6.12: jäh, überstürzt, hastig; 20.5.5: jählings, ungestüm. I can certainly endorse the 2 last translations. I cannot find more evidence for the first translation. Still, L. points the way, in my view: **palantes abrupti** = **suddenly flaring up here and there.** This also fits the situation. The caved-in masses prevent an unhindered city fire. The fire, however, spreads (palari) and suddenly is seen in various places. That is why the fire lasts for such a long time. **Abrupte** therefore belongs to the concept: **to come forward, to appear,** which is enclosed in **palari**. Brachylogia is often found in Amm., among others with prepositions (cf. Blomgren, op.cit.II, p.169 sq.; cf.et. Persson, Eran.20 p.28 sq.). "Ordinary" Latin: nisi flammae ardentes **abrupte prosilirent** et palarentur.

b **ardores.** Plur.poet. (cf. ad 17.2.1, p.107.14-15*b*). Claus.I.

per quinque dies et noctes. V reads: L.quinquaginta E A G. In connection with the above remarks 5 days (quinque Gdt; likewise Clark Seyf. Rolfe) seem too little to me; 50 probably too much. I can also recommend the very good annotations by Sabbah II p.177.**71,** in connection with **Lib. orat.** 61.15 and **Plin.Epist.10.33:** Cum diversam partem provinciae circumirem, **Nicomediae** vastissimum incendium multas privatorum domos et duo publica opera ... absumpsit. Est autem latius sparsum **primum violentia venti, deinde inertia hominum ... et alioqui nullus usquam in publico sipho** (= fire-pump), **nulla hama** (fire-bucket), **nullum denique instrumentum ad incendia compescenda.** Et haec quidem, ut iam praecepi, parabuntur. Plin. then proceeds to ask the emperor if he will establish a **collegium fabrorum** of "only" 150 men. (Traianus had partly abolished the **collegia,** and placed others under strict supervision; cf.Dig.47.22.1: Marcianus). Thus these **fabri** will serve as fire brigade. Which **siphones** are meant here by Plin., is not quite clear. When one studies Isid.Orig. 20.6.9: **siphon** vas appellatum quod aquas sufflando fundat; utuntur enim hoc orientales; nam ubi senserint domum ardere, **currunt cum siphonibus plenis aqua et exstinguunt incendia.** Sed et camaras expressis ad superiora aquis emundant; then they can only be very primitive tools. But there is also a **sipho,** constructed according to the same principles as the **ctesibica machina** (by Ctesibius of Alexandria, described by Vitruvius 10.7), probably manufactured by **Heron,** a pupil of Ctes., because this agrees with the instructions which he gives himself (de Spirit.p.180). This machine is a predecessor of our fire-pump, as designed by **van der Heyden.** But though there were water pipes, there were no **fire-hoses,** so that the practical effect of this ingenious machine was very small (if they were used for fires at all). According to Dig.33.7.2.18 (§ 16 Pegasus ait **instrumentum domus** id esse, quod tempestatis arcendae aut incendii causa paratur; but then, this is said of a rich household!), the following tools belong to the **instrumentum domus:** Acetum quoque, quod exstinguendi incendii causa paratur, item centones (patch quilts) **sifones,** perticae quoque et scalae, et formiones (mats) et spongias et amas (= hamas) et scopas (brooms) contineri plerique et Pegasus aiunt. From this it appears that rich men who wanted to be on the safe side, organised the fire extinction in their own homes themselves. Thus the fire-fighting in a town like **Nicomedia** can not have been too effective, although perhaps not as bad as in the days of Plinius.

p. 117. 20 **quicquid consumi poterat.** Cf. ad 16.12.21, p.94.18-19.

VII, 9-14

In this note we will discuss the sources which Amm. may have used, or at any rate, will have known. Cf.et. ad 17.7.1, p.116.14a and *b;* ad 17.7.3, p.116.25-26*b* (with remark).

a **Seneca** in L.VI Nat.Quaest. describes the earthquakes, with the inevitable moralisations, so typical of him. As authorities in this field he mentions: Thales, Anaxagoras, Anaximenes, Aristoteles, Theophrastus, Metrodorus, Democritus, Posidonius. Cap.12: Spiritum esse qui moveat, et plurimis et maximis auctoribus placet. Archelaus antiquitatis diligens ait ita: Venti in concava terrarum deferuntur: deinde ubi iam omnia spatia plena sunt, et in quantum aer potuit, densatus est, is qui supervenit spiritus, priorem premit et elidit ac frequentibus plagis primo cogit, deinde perturbat. Tunc ille quaerens locum omnes angustias dimovet et claustra sua conatur effringere. **Sic evenit, ut terrae, spiritu luctante et fugam quaerente moveantur.** etc. Cap.21: mentioned: **Thera, Therasia.** Cap.25: Si velis credere, aiunt aliquando **Ossam Olympo cohaesisse, deinde terrarum motu recessisse** et scissam unius magnitudinem montis in duas partes. Tunc effugisse Peneum, qui paludes quibus laborabat Thessalia, siccavit, abductis in se quae sine exitu stagnaverant aquis (rational explanation of the myths). Cap.26: mentioned: **Helices et Buris** eversio.cap.32: **Helicen Burinque** totas mare accepit: ego de uno corpusculo timeam?

b **Plinius** N.H. 2.81-2.96. Mentioned as authorities: Anaximander, Pherecydes. c.81: ventos in causa esse non dubium reor ... neque aliud est in terra tremor, quam in nube tonitruum: nec hiatus alius quam cum fulmen erumpit, **incluso spiritu luctante et ad libertatem exire nitente.** cap.83: Factum est semel, quod equidem in **Etruscae disciplinae voluminibus** inveni, ingens terrarum portentum ... in agro Mutinensi.c.87: Clarae iam pridem insulae, **Delos et Rhodos,** memoriae produntur enatae. Also mentioned there: **Anaphe, Thera, Therasia, Hiera.**c.92: In totum abstulit terras, primum omnium ubi Atlanticum mare est, si Platoni credimus, immenso spatio **(Atlantis).** cap.94: (abstulit) **Elicen et Buram in sinu Corinthio,** quarum in alto vestigia apparent ... Similiter **in Boeotia et Eleusina.**

c **Gellius.** Cap.2.28: Quaenam esse causa videatur, quam ob rem terrae tremores fiant, **non modo his communibus hominum sensibus opinionibusque compertum non est, sed ne inter physicas quidem philosophias satis constitit, ventorumne vi** accidant specus hiatusque terrae subeuntium, an **aquarum**

198

subter in terrarum cavis undantium fluctibus pulsibusque, ita ut videntur existimasse antiquissimi Graecorum, qui **Neptunum** ἐννοσίγαιον καὶ σεισίχθονα appellaverunt, an cuius alius rei causa, alteriusve dei vi ac numine, nondum etiam, sicut diximus, pro certo creditum ... (Romani) ubi terram movisse senserant, nuntiatumve erat, ferias eius rei causa edicto imperabant; sed dei nomen, ita uti solet, cui servari ferias oporteret, statuere et edicere quiescebant; **ne, alium pro alio nominando, falsa religione populum alligarent.**
... idque ita **ex decreto pontificum** observatum esse M.Varro dicit: quoniam et qua vi et per quem deorum dearumve terra tremeret incertum esset.

d **Macrobius** 1.17.22: Nec mirum si gemini effectus variis nominibus celebrantur, cum alios quoque deos ex contrario in eadem re duplici censeri et potestate accipiamus et nomine, **ut Neptunum, quem alias** Ἐνοσίχθονα, **id est terram moventem,** alias Ἀσφαλίωνα, id est stabilientem vocant.

e **Cicero** de divin. 1.33(72): Quae vero aut coniectura explicantur, aut eventis animadversa et notata sunt, ea genera divinandi, ut supra dixi, non naturalia, sed artificiosa dicuntur: in quo haruspices, augures coniectoresque numerantur. Haec improbantur a Peripateticis; a Stoicis defenduntur. Quorum alia sunt posita in monumentis et disciplina; **quod Etruscorum declarant et haruspicini, et fulgurales et tonitruales libri, vestri etiam augurales.** (Seneca names Ep.108: **libri augurales** and a little further on: **libri pontificiales.** This is intended as an addition, not as an indication of a possible source).

f The Greek authors mentioned by Amm. have not, I believe, been read by him personally: Aristoteles, Anaxagoras, Anaximander. For him these are **indirect** sources, and I suspect that these 3 gentlemen have been brought forward ornatus causa. On the other hand, I think it quite likely that Amm. consulted **Strabo** and **Pausanias,** this in connection with his geographical hobbies, although he does not mention them by name (and not only here). Another work with which Amm. may have been familiar, is the compilation by **Diogenes Laërtios,** also because excerpt literature was then very fashionable. Cf.et **Finke** (op.cit.I). p.70. But first of all one should think of the Latin literature on this subject: Julius Obsequens, Solinus., Rufius Festus, Pompeius Festus, Aurelius Victor e.a.

g Herz (op.cit.I) p.277 says: "Die Gellianische Stelle über das Erdbeben 2.28.1 ff. ist bei Amm.17.7.9ff. mit einer anderen **contaminirt** worden, die die Meinungen der griechischen Philosophen in ganz ähnlicher Weise wie Sen.nat.quaest.VI.4ff. zusammenstellte, **doch nicht mit dieser selbst**".

It is clear that this simple way of source analysis is not the right one (as well as being obsolete). Amm. does not contaminate one source with another, but gets his material from many and manifold sources, which he then **reconstructs and composes in his own style.** This view of Herz here is shared by Seyf.I p.309, note 89.

h For the rational explanation of myths cf. Camus, Amm.Marc. (1967) p.230 sq. (with lit.); Eßzlin, Zur Gesch.schr. etc. (op.cit.I) p.58 sq.

VII, 9

p. 117. 21 **terrae pulsibus.** Cf.31.12.12: pulsuque minaci scutorum; ad 17.7.1, p.116. 14a; ad 17.7.1, p.116.15.

p. 117. 22 *a* **coniectura veteres conlegerunt.** Seyf.: "**die Theorien** ... die die Alten über die Erdbeben gesammelt haben". Sabbah: "de résumer **les hypotheses** qu'ont émises les Anciens ...". **Coniectura** is almost a t.t. for: to explain, to account for omens. Thus also in Amm.21.1.12: somniorum autem rata fides et indubitabilis foret, ni ratiocinantes (= ± explainers) **coniectura** fallerentur interdum. But with its usual meaning 31.3.6: Huni enim, ut sunt in **coniectura** sagaces, multitudinem esse longius aliquam suspicati etc.

The meaning "theory", hypothesis fits well here. But Seyf. and Sabbah translate as if there was written here **coniecturas,** although, like Clark, they give **coniectura** in their edit. It does not become clear from their translation that they have noticed the **brachylogia.** The complete text should have been: pauca dicere quae de terrae pulsibus **veteres coniecerunt** et quales coniecturas conlegerunt. But the first subject **veteres** are the natural scientists themselves, the second subject **veteres** are the compilators! This explanation is not ingenious, for "what the elders ... **collected through conjecture (hypothesis)**" is nonsense. For they collected conjectures (by others), not **through** conjectures. Cf. ad 17.7.8, p.117.19*a*.

b **quae ... veteres conlegerunt.** Words which are typical of Amm. and his time. Cf.17.7.9-14*f*.

p. 117. 22 **veritatis arcana.** Amm. here uses a word (**arcana**), which often has a religious meaning. In spite of a certain level-headedness, which he certainly possesses, he is still a child of his time. The **veritas** is here veiled, hidden, from the ignorant masses, as well as from the quarrelling **physicists.** It should have to be revealed by other methods than purely scientific ones. Because these fail, the people have to submit to the rules laid down in the **libri rituales et pontificii,** under the supervision of priests.

But they do not give any explanations, but only prescribe expiatory sacrifices **(piacula)**, in order to pacify the wrathful divine powers (§ 10).

a **vulgaris inscitia.** The adj. has no pejorative meaning. Cf. Krebs Antib. 2 p.755: "**Vulgaris** bedeutet aber nur **gewöhnlich, alltäglich,** nicht niedrig, von gemeiner Herkunft, und ist nur Beiwort von Sachen, nicht von Menschen". Though the meaning is definitely unfavourable in Arn.adv. nat.7.24 (= Reiffersch.p.257): polimina porro sunt ea quae **nos** proles (plur.) verecundius dicimus, a **volgaribus** autem adsolent cognomine testium nuncupari (polimina = ± proles = ± testes). And similarly of persons: Dig.26.4.5.1: si autem patroni persona **vulgaris** vel minus honesta sit (vulgaris X honesta); ibid.48.5.14.2: Sed et in ea uxore potest maritus adulterium vindicare, quae **volgaris** (= common prostitute) fuerit. The adj. does not occur in Claud.Veget.r.m.Opt.Milev.
b Cf.26.1.2: Proinde **inscitia vulgari** contempta ad residua narranda pergamus. I do not believe that here **vulgaris** has an unfavourable meaning either. The ignorance is that of the lower classes who have no knowledge of the way in which history should be written, but who expect of her: similia plurima (sc.inania) praeceptis historiae dissonantia discurrere per negotiorum celsitudines assuetae (ibid.).

sed ... penetrarunt. The ornateness of these words is somewhat at odds with the clarity, as often; although one can **feel** what is being meant: sed ne longae quidem lucubrationes fysicorum penetrarunt quamquam sempiterna iurgia eorum nondum exhausta fuerunt. For the fact that the physici are unable to penetrate the **arcana** is due not so much to their eternal quarrels as to the insufficiency of their studies. For the **personificatio** cf. ad 17.2.1, p.107.13.

sempiternus: also class. But the subst. (= aeternitas) late Latin (not in Amm.).

fysicorum. Some of which are mentioned in §§ 11 and 12. Cf.7.9-14*a* and *b* (before this). Also spelled: **physicus:** Cic.nat.deor.1.30(83): non pudet igitur **physicum, id est speculatorem venatoremque naturae,** ab animis consuetudine imbutis petere testimonium **veritatis?** Cf.et. Cic. de orat. 1.10(42), with the notes by Courbaud (1905) p.41. **iurgia** = **disceptationes.** Iurgia penetrarunt: Claus.III.Cf. ad 17.7.6, p.117.13*b*.

201

VII, 10

p. 117. 24-
p. 118. 2
unde ... caute. V pontificiis obtemperantur optemperantibus sacerdotiis (sine lacuna). Clark assumes a lacuna after **pontificiis** and then reads: **obtemperatur observantibus sacerdotiis caute.** Likewise Seyf. and Sabbah (though the latter without lacuna). Novák's version: unde **et in ritualibus et pontificio sacerdotio obtemperantibus** ⟨libris super auctore motus terrae nihil dicitur⟩ caute, ne etc. (followed by Rolfe) I find violent and incredible (Wiener Stud.33, 1911, p.309 sq.). A G **et** (instead of **ut**). I think it is better to keep **et** (as given by A G) and from V **obtemperantur** (= obtemperant. Cf. ad 16.12.22, p.94.24; ad 17.4.5, p.109.19-20c. I have no evidence for obtemperari = obtemperare. But one should bear in mind πείθομαι). I consider **obtemperantibus** a dittography; a **lacuna** need not be assumed. Thus my suggestion is: **unde et in ritualibus et pontificiis obtemperantur sacerdotiis caute.** Translation: so that they **obediently follow the priests** with the libri rituales as well as with the libri pontificii, in a careful way, so as not to etc. (or: taking care that etc.). However, this suggestion does not completely satisfy me either.

p. 118. 1
a **ritualibus et pontificiis.** Cf. ad VII.9-14 (before this) *e* and *c* (in fine). **(Libri) pontificii** occurs in Cic.Cf.nat.deor.1.30(84): Deinde nominum non magnus numerus ne in **pontificiis** quidem nostris, deorum autem innumerabilis. The adj. is also found (with other subst.) in Cic.Sen.Gell. Solin.Arn.adv.nat.2.65 (Reiffersch.p.100 sq.): ut enim dii certi certas apud vos habent tutelas licentias potestates **neque eorum ab aliquo id quod eius non sit potestatis ac licentiae postulatis,** ita unius **pontificium** Christi est dare animis salutem et spiritum perpetuitatis adponere (cf. Cod.Theod.16.5.13 **pontificium** = pontificatus); Symm.

b Cf.Cic.1.33(72) (quoted VII.9.14): et **rituales** libri (But, I believe, a better version here: **tonitruales**); Festus 285 M.; Censor.17.5. Extremely rare adject. The **adverbium ritualiter** 29.1.29: construximus ... mensulam ... **ritualiter** consecratam (a little further on we find the adject. **arcanus:** quotiens super rebus arcanis consulebatur; cf. ad 17.7.9, p.117.22).

p. 118. 1-2
sacerdotiis: abstractum pro concreto = sacerdotibus. And also **plur. poet.** (cf. ad 17.2.1, p.107.14-15*b*). For **abstr. pro concr.** cf. Hassenstein (op.cit.I) p.13 sq.; Hagendahl Strena etc. (op.cit.I) p.82 adnot.1; Blomgren p.85 adnot.1 (op.cit.II); ad 14.8.13 (= II p.80).

p. 118. 2
ne ... nominato. Cf. ad VII 9-14*c*. The **partic.** again gives the main point (cf. ad 17.3.5, p.108.20*a*). Translation: so that they would not call upon

one god instead of another, while performing their sacrificial rites. For the great care exercised in invoking the gods, cf. **K.Latte,** die Religion der Römer, 1927, p.1-4 **(Tab.Iguv.VI A B);** Horat.Sat.2.6.20; Carmen Saec. 14 sq.; etc.

concutiat. Cf.Claud.33 (de raptu Proserp.I) p.138 sq.: p. 118. 3
Hinc latrat Gaetula Thetis, Lilybaeaque **pulsat**
Bracchia consurgens; hinc dedignata teneri
Concutit obiectum rabies Tyrrhena Pelorum.
(cf.7.1, p.116.14). Ibid.48 (Eid.Magnes) p.5 sq.: (Quisquis ... rimatur):
Unde fluant venti, trepidae quis viscera terrae
Concutiat motus ....
ibid.36 (de raptu Pros.III) 66:
Dixit (Juppiter) et horrendo **concussit** sidera motu.

abstruso. Cf.19.8.5: in **abstrusa** quadam **parte** oppidi cum duobus aliis latens; Plaut.Poen.341 sq.:
Invendibili merci oportet ultro emptorem adducere:
proba mers facile emptorem reperit, tametsi in apstruso sita est.

piacula = expiatory sacrifices. With another meaning 23.6.35: **eratque** p. 118. 3
piaculum aras adire vel hostiam contrectare, antequam magus etc. (= nefas erat). I do not agree with Seyf.'s translation: "und es soll kein Frevel begangen werden" (cf. ad 7.10.p.118.2. My views are shared by Sabbah). **Committere** is not only used with bellum, pugnam, proelium, etc. but also in wider sense, as in Curt.Ruf.9.4.27: Iam admovebat rex, cum vates monere eum coepit ne **committeret** aut certe differret **obsidionem;** Cic. ad Q.fr.3.4.6: Haec scripsi a.d.IX Kal.Nov., quo die **ludi committebantur,** in Tusculanum proficiscens ...; Vell.Paterc.2.64.4: sed tribuni sanguine **commissa proscriptio,** Ciceronis velut satiato Antonio paene finita; Liv.2.36.1: Ludis mane servum quidam pater familiae **nondum commisso spectaculo** sub furca caesum medio egerat circo; **coepti inde ludi** etc. ... Cic.pro Sex.Rosc.Am.5(11): longo intervallo **iudicium** inter sicarios hoc primum **committitur,** cum interea caedes indignissimae maximaeque factae sint. The meaning: **to begin,** is present everywhere, But with this passage, one should not think first of all of: committere scelus, delictum, noxam, dolum, iniuriam etc. Cf.et.Seyf.I p.309 annot.92, with the lit. quoted there.

VII, 11
For the contents of this § cf.VII.9-14*a, b, c*.

p. 118. 4 *a* **ut opiniones aestimant inter quas Aristoteles aestuat et laborat.** For the **personificatio** cf. ad 17.2.1, p.107.13. But here it is indeed carried to a great length! **Aristoteles** is on a par with the **opiniones** of others (= Aristotelis opinio). The rhythmics of the sentence illustrate the bobbing up and down: claus.III.Cf.et.Gell.6.2.15: Chrysippum quoque philosophum non expedisse se in ea refert, his verbis: **Chrysippus aestuans laboransque,** quonam pacto explicet et fato omnia fieri et esse aliquid in nobis, intricatur hoc modo (Fletcher).

b Cf.Cic. ad Att.7.13a.1(5): iam intellexi tuum aenigma; Oppios enim de Velia saccones dicis. in eo **aestuavi** diu; ad fam.7.18.1: Quae ego paulisper in te ita desideravi, non imbecillitate animi tui, sed magis, ut desiderio nostri te **aestuare** putarem; Verr.2.23(55): Quod ubi auditum est, **aestuare** illi, qui pecuniam dederant; putare nihil agi posse absente Epicrate; Arn. adv.nat.5.11 (= Reiffersch.p.183): **Aestuatum** est in conciliis deorum, quibusnam modis posset intractabilis illa feritas edomari.

c Cf.Tac.Ann.4.39 edit. Nipperdey[11] I, p.345 (note 11): "... **aestimare** wird nur vom Wert gebraucht, und daher entweder der Gen. oder Abl. des Wertes oder ein die Weise des Schätzens bezeichnendes Adverb dazugesetzt; von der Beurteilung der Beschaffenheit stets **existimare,** und dieses musz daher stehen, so oft ein auf das Object bezügliches Adjektiv **(aliquid bonum exist.)** oder Adverb **(largiter honoris,** nämlich esse, **exist.)** hinzugefügt wird. Hiervon weichen nur wenige Dichterstellen ab "(with examples). Cf.et Krebs Antib.1 p.118 sq. (with lit.). But here im Amm. **opiniones aestimant** = **opinantur (sc. physici).** Claud.28 (de VI cons. Honor.) p.39 sq.:

Non alium certe decuit rectoribus orbis
Esse larem, **nulloque magis se colle potestas**
Aestimat, et summi sentit fastigia iuris.
(sc. Palatino).

Aest. = **putare** in Opt.Milev. The verb not in Veget.r.m. or Arn.adv.nat. (though both have **aestimatio).**

d Which image Amm. has in mind with these words, is obvious among others from Caes.b.c.2.6.5: illae (naves) adeo graviter inter se incitatae conflixerunt, ut vehementissime **utraque ex concursu laborarent.**

e **Aristoteles.** Cf. ad VII 9-14*f.* Cf. Sabbah II p.178 note 72: "Sur les tremblements de terre, Ammien se réfère à Aristote, **qu'il cite nommément** (de mundo: 4.30; 4.32)". Περὶ κόσμου, however, is not by Arist. and was probably written in the 1st cent.B.C. For lit. on A.cf. Woordenboek der Oudheid, 2, 1966, p.300 sq. (Verbeke); **Capelle**, Neue Jahrb.f.d. Klass. Alt.15, 1905, p.529 sq. (de mundo). Earthquakes are also dealt with in Aristoteles' Μετεωρολογικά.

a **in cavernis minutis terrarum.** Cf.Cic.nat.deor.2.9(25): atque etiam ex puteis iugibus (= never running dry) aquam calidam trahi et id maxime hibernis fieri temporibus, quod magna vis **terrae cavernis** continetur caloris. p. 118. 5

b **minutis.** In general this adj. means: very small, minute. Since it is used here for **cavernae,** which are called σῦριγξ by the Greeks, it may here be completely equal to **parvus.** For a σῦριγξ may be a rift in the earth, a cave, or a mine; even the subterranean burial grounds of the Egyptian kings near Thebe were called thus. So Amm. will not have imagined the **cavernae** as being too small. The adj. not in Claud.Veget. r.m.Arn.adv.nat. In Opt.Milev.1.6 (= Ziwsa p.9) in a metaph. sense: quinto, ut **minuta** (= trifles) praetermittam, dixisti de oleo et sacrificio peccatoris.

quas Graece σύριγγας **appellamus.** Cf. ad 14.11.18 (= II p.129); 22.15.30: Sunt et **Syringes** subterranei quidam et flexuosi **secessus** (cf. ad 17.7.11, p.118.10*b*). p. 118. 5

a **inpulsu crebriore aquis undabundis.** Cf.14.7.6: famis et furoris **impulsu** Eubuli ... domum ... inflammavit (sc.vulgus); 26.6.4: postremae necessitatis **impulsu** deviis itineribus ad Calchedonos agrum pervenit (sc. Procopius); 31.8.5: ne subita multitudo ut **amnis immani impulsu (?)** undarum obicibus ruptis emissus convelleret levi negotio cunctos (cf.app. crit.Clark II p.576; Seyf.4 p.270; Blomgren p.15 annot.1; ad 15.4.2 = III p.55). Cf.et. ad 17.7.1, p.116.15 **(pulsus)**. **crebriore** = crebro. Cf. ad 14.6.12 (= I p.96). p. 118. 5-6

b **aquis undabundis.** One should expect a genitivus here. The ablat. is either **absolutus,** in which case it indicates the attendant circumstances (= with the waters waving) or it is, like **impulsu,** an **abl.** instrum., in which case it further explains **impulsu crebriore** (= viz. as a result of the waving waters). The translation by Sabbah II p.58: "sous la pression répétée des **eaux de source qui les inondent**" was not clear to me from our text. For that matter, it does not say **inundantibus** (cf.p.74.16 Cl.). The adj. very rare. In Gellius 2.30: sed mare est etiam atque etiam **undabundum** (the word-usage in this caput is interesting in connection with Amm.) Not in

Claud.Veget.r.m.Arn.adv.nat.Opt.Milev. For adj. ending in **-bundus** cf. **fremebundus** (22.8.24); **vitabundus** 30.1.13; **vastabundus** (31.8.6). Hofm.-Leum.172 X p.226 sq. (with lit.); Fesser p.10; **Paucker Hier.** (op.cit.1) p.65 sq. (with list); **Roensch It.** (op.cit.I) p.138 sq.; Hagend.St.A.p.44. Claus.III with dialysis.

p. 118. 6 **Anaxagoras.** Cf. ad VII 9-14*f.* Fragments in Diels-Kranz, Die Fragmente der Vorsokratiker,[5] 1936, 1-44. Cf.et. Woordenboek der Oudheid 1, 1965, p.160, with lit. (Nuchelmans).

p. 118. 7 **Subeuntium ima terrarum.** Cf.Verg.Aen.6.140:
Sed non ante datur **telluris operta subire.**
For **ima terrarum** cf. ad 17.3.2, p.108.12*a;* ad 17.4.1, p.109,4*a.*

p. 118. 7-8 *a* **qui cum soliditatibus concrustatis inciderint ... partes convibrant ... quas subrepserint.** For **cum iterat.** cf. ad 14.2.7 (= I p.70); 14.2.2 (= I p.67). **Subrepserint** in the relative sense is a **fut.exactum,** not distinguishable in form from the **conjunct.perf.inciderint,** and for that reason probably written here, as well as because of the claus.(II), although the preceding time could have been expressed "correctly" by the **indic.perf.**
b **soliditatibus concrustatis.** Liesenberg: "feste, mit einer Rinde überzogene Massen" = solidis terrae structuris crusta tectis. Abstractum pro concreto. But the subst. has a techn. meaning. Cf.Vitr.7.3 (**soliditates** = tectoria calce, arena et marmore solidata), which may have been known to Amm. The subst. occurs among otheis in Cic.Pallad. **Chalc.Tim.277** (= **the fixed vault of heaven**). Non.Vitruv.Ambros.Cod.Iust. With the meaning: firmness, strength, in Veget.r.m.3.7 and 4.8; metaph. Arn.adv. nat.7.22 (Reiffersch.p.255): ... cum ipsum illud primum, a quo defluit secundum, inanissimum esse reperiatur et vacuum et **nulla soliditate firmatum?** Not in Claud. (though **solidare** and **solidus**) and Opt.Milev.
c Cf.30.6.5: arefactis ideo membris, quod meatus aliqui, quos haemorrhoidas nunc appellamus, obserati sunt **gelidis frigoribus concrustati.** Seems to occur only in Amm. Simplex: 15.10.5: humus **crustata** frigoribus; 24.2.14: portam ... hostilem. crasso ferro **crustatam.**

p. 118. 8 *a* **eruptiones nullas repperientes.** Note the alliterating **r** and **p**. The usual meaning: raid, sally: 24.4.13: ineundis autem conflictibus et defendendis ab incendio vel **eruptionibus** machinis praeerat imperator. But here the subst. has the meaning of: **vias erumpendi** (way out, escape routes). Many substantiva verbalia ending in -io have the meaning: **the possibility of, -to**. Thus here also.

b **repperientes** = reperientes. The doubling of the **p** in the praesens is unusual. Probably a vulgar analogy formation (perf.repperi).

convibrant. Cf.Apul.Flor.12 (v.d.Vliet p.161): discit (sc.psittacus) autem statim pullus usque ad duos aetatis suae annos, dum facile os, uti conformetur, dum tenera lingua, uti **convibretur**. Not in Claud.Veget.r.m. Arn.adv.nat.Opt.Milev. Extremely rare verb. p. 118. 8

quas subrepserint. The construction c.accusat. and without preposition, also in Horat.Sat.2.6.99 sq.:

   ambo propositum peragunt iter, Urbis aventes
   moenia nocturni **subrepere.**

The verb used fairly often by poets, also in Claud. Not in Veget.r.m. Arn.adv.nat.Opt.Milev.

V **umidi.** Gdt.Clark Seyf. Rolfe: **tumidi**. Sabbah maintains V's version with the translation: "chargés d'humidité". But I would like to know where this humidity comes from in Anaxagoras' theory. I am inclined to accept the version of Gdt, which does not cause any palaeographical objections. p. 118. 9

unde = and therefore, for that reason. This meaning post-class. and late Latin. Cf.S.Bened.Reg.7 (Linderb.p.29): Cavendum **ergo ideo** (abundantia!) malum desiderium, quia mors secus introitum dilectationis posita est, **unde** Scriptura praecipit dicens: "Post concupiscentias tuas non eas"; ibid.3 (Lind.p.23): convocet abbas omnem congregationem et dicat ipse, **unde** agitur (= de qua re); Heum.-Seckel p.601; Krebs Antib.2.691 sq. (with lit.); Souter p.447 (with still other meanings). Cf.et.Veget.r.m.1.20 (= Lang p.23): Sic dum exercitium laboremque declinant, cum maximo dedecore trucidantur ut pecudes. **Unde** enim apud antiquos murus dicebatur pedestris exercitus; 2.23 (= Lang p.56): exercitium ... **unde** ... exercitus nomen accepit (= **a quo**); ibid.3.12: sed hoc remedio formido lenitur, si, antequam dimices, frequenter exercitum tuum locis tutioribus ordincs, **unde** et videre hostem et agnoscere consuescant (= with the result that, for which reason; but a local meaning is also possible here); ibid.4.40 (= Lang p.159) = with the result that; fairly often in Opt. Milev. with the meaning: **itaque, igitur** and **de(ex)quo**; Arn.adv.nat.1.10 (Reiffersch.p.10): pestilentias morbos fames atque alias suggerit malorum exitiabiles formas: **unde** tibi est scire, ne quod exuberat sic tollat ut per p. 118. 9

207

sua dispendia modum rebus luxuriantibus figat? (= from which (where), because of which).

p. 118. 10 **spiramina.** Cf. ad 14.7.15 (= II p.42). Hagend.St.A.p.36: "Sive de loco, per quem aliquid exspiratur, sive de spiritu dicitur a poetis aevi imperatorii ... **in prosa oratione ab Arn.adv.nat.** (7.28 Reiffersch.p.261: interclusis **spiraminibus** = naribus)". Also in Veget.r.m.4.38 (= Lang p.156): Nam secundo **spiramine** (= vento) optatos classis invenit portus; ibid. 4.42 (= Lang p.161): Elementum pelagi tertia pars mundi est, quae praeter ventorum **flatus** (cf. ad 14.6.22 = I p.99) suo quoque **spiramine** motuque **vegetatur** (an example of unnatural diction); Claud.48.36 (Eid.V). Not in Opt.Milev. (which does have **spiritus**).

p. 118. 10 *a* **quod in ultimis eius secessibus occupantur.** The incredibility of this statement (viz. of the lull in the wind, which precedes earthquakes) is quite obvious, even when taking the knowledge of that time into account. *b* **secessibus.** Cf. ad 16.1.5, p.72.6-7*c*. This meaning also in Verg.Aen. 1.159; 3.229; Tac.ann.14.62: magna ei praemia et **secessus amoenos** promittit (with the latter meaning also in Suet.Aug.72, Calig.45; Juven.3.5). Not in Claud.Veget.r.m.Arn.adv.nat.Opt.Milev. Cf.et Souter p.369 (other meanings); Heum.-Seckel p.530.

VII, 12

p. 118. 11 **Anaximander.** Cf. ad VII 9-14*f.* Fragment: Diels-Kranz, Die Fragm. der Vorsokratiker I⁵, 1934, 81-90. Cf.et. Woordenboek der Oudheid, 1, 1965 (with lit.; Nuchelmans).

p. 118. 11 **arescentem.** Cf.18.7.9: unde ad Constantiam usque oppidum, quod centesimo lapide disparatur, **arescunt** omnia siti perpetua.

p. 118. 11 **nimia aestuum siccitate.** Cf.19.4.2: **Nimietatem** frigoris aut caloris, vel umoris aut **siccitatis**, pestilentias gignere philosophi et illustres medici tradiderunt; 19.4.1: pestilentia tot malis accessit ... **vaporatis aestibus** varioque plebis languore nutrita. For the plur.poet. cf. ad 17.2.1, p.107. 14-15*b*. Cf.et Auct. ad Herenn.4.6(9): Isti cum non modo dominos se fontium, sed se ipsos fontes esse dicant et omnium rigare debeant ingenia, non putant fore ridiculum, si, cum id polliceantur aliis, **arescant ipsi siccitate** (quite a striking resemblance!). The lit. meaning: dry weather, drought (of the soil, as here), among others in Cic.Liv.Cels.Plin.N.H.

Of trees Veget.r.m.4.26 (= Lang p.153). Not in Claud. (who has **siccus**) nor in Opt.Milev. (who gives **siccari**). But it is found in Arn.adv.nat.

madores imbrium. Madores: plur.poet. (see previous note). This subst. rare; among others in **Sall.hist.fr.** Apul.Mart.Cap. (Cf. Georges 2.753). Does not occur in Claud.Veget.r.m.Opt.Milev. In Arn.adv.nat.5.40 (= Reiffersch.p.209): ... Iovis et Cereris dicere atque appellare concubitum et cum deorum criminibus **labem imbris** (= rainfall) e caelo et **telluris** significare **madorem?** p. 118. 11-12

rimas pandere = to develop clefts. fissures. But usually this is expressed by: **rimas agere**, – ducere, -facere (the underlined words in Cic.). Cf. Veget.r.m.4.36 (= Lang p.153): Nam quae virides conpinguntur (sc. trabes), cum nativum umorem exudaverint, contrahuntur et **rimas faciunt** latiores. p. 118. 12

pandere grandiores = p. maiores, without difference in meaning. Claus. III. But gradually **grandis** drove out **magnus** and passed into the Romance languages. Cf. Krebs Antib.1 p.629 sq. (with lit.); Grandgent (op.cit.I) p.9. This use of **grandis** is very evident, for instance, in Veget.r.m.I.6 (= Lang p.10), where grandes = proceres = magnos and 3.1 (= Lang p.67), where grandes = magnos. p. 118. 12

Supernus aer. Cf.19.7.5: tamen quia hostiles ballistae ferratis impositae turribus **in humiliora ex supernis valentes** ... nostra multo cruore foedabant ... p. 118. 12
Supernus = of the world above ground, i.e. the earth. Similarly used by Claud.35.239 sq. (De raptu Proserp.2):
.... Quae te fortuna **supernis**
Abstulit et tanto damnavit sidera luctu?
(Gesner: **Siderum** luctus est, quod non vident amplius in terris **Proserpinam**). Ibid.36.104 sq. (de raptu Pros.3):
Quod si non omnem pepulisti pectore matrem
Si tu nota Ceres et non me Caspia tigris
Edidit: his oro miseram defende **cavernis**
Inque **superna** refer. (defende = "vi hinc aufer" G.)
The adj. does not occur in Veget.r.m.Opt.Milev. It is found, however, in Arn.adv.nat. Comparable with 19.7.5 Gell.9.1.2: cum proclivior faciliorque iactus sit ex **supernis** in infima, quam ex infimis in **superna.**

p. 118. 13 **spiritu.** Cf.p.118.10: **spiramina.** Variatio. **spiritu quassatam:** claus III, with dialysis. The verb used literally and metaphorically by Amm.14.5.2; 19.8.2; 24.3.9; 24.5.12; 31.4.5. The verb **quassare** also in Claud.Veget.r.m. Opt.Milev., though not in Arn.adv.nat. (who has **quassatio).**

p. 118. 13-14 **cieri propriis sedibus.** For **propriis** cf. ad 14.5.8 (= I p.88); Souter p.328. **Sedibus** = fundamentis (14.8.14; 14.6.5).

p. 118. 14 **terrores** = catastrophes. Cf.Liv.29.27.14: ceteros omnes caelestes maritimosque **terrores.** With another meaning 14.11.30: Dionysium **gentium** quondam **terrorem** (= "terror" of). Cf.Iust.Phil.3.1.1: Xerxes rex Persarum, **terror** ante **gentium.**

p. 118. 14 **vaporatis temporibus.** Vaporatus = glowing, hot. Cf.18.9.2: vaporatis aestibus; 26.7.2: vaporatis aestibus; 28.4.18: vaporato tempore; 25.4.10: in pulvere vaporato Persidis. Cf.24.4.17 (adverbium): aestus in meridiem crescens **effervescente vaporatius sole** ... (For other words derived from **vapor,** with similar meanings, cf. Souter, p.435). The above meaning of **vaporatus** only in late Latin, as far as I know. (For e.g. Pers.Sat.1.126: inde **vaporata** lector mihi ferveat **aure, vaporata** does not mean: warm, glowing, but: cleansed with hot water; cf.Comm. v.Wageningen, 1911, p.27). Seyffarth's translation is incorrect, therefore. (1.p.229).

p. 118. 15 *a* **nimia aquarum caelestium superfusione. Superfusio** = inundation, flood: late Latin. In Ambros.Serv. Cf. Georges 2.2939; Souter p.403. Not in Claud.Veget.r.m.Opt.Milev.Arn.adv.nat.
b **caelestium.** For this adj.cf. ad 15.8.10 (= IV p.34, 35). Cf.et. ad 16.12. 13, p.93.2-3*d* **(caelestes).**

p. 118. 15 **aquae caelestes** is a frequently occurring expression for rain ("water from heaven"), also in prose.

p. 118. 15 **ideoque.** Cf. ad 16.12.25, p.95.9*b*.

p. 118. 16 *a* **umentis substantiae potestatem.** The adj. **umens** (= umidus): postclass. and poet. With Amm. probably a poetism. **Claud.** also has it. Not in Veget.r.m.Opt.Milev.Arn.adv.nat.
b The words are reminiscent of 14.11.25: **(Nemesis)** vel ut definiunt alii, **substantialis tutela** generali **potentia** partilibus praesidens fatis en 21.1.8: et **substantiales potestates** ritu diverso placatae, velut ex perpetuis fontium

venis, vaticina mortalitati subpeditant verba, quibus numen praesse dicitur **Themidis.** Liesenberg translates: "Beherrscher des Meeres". Better is Seyf.: "Gebieter des feuchten Elements". Likewise Sabbah. The word **potestas,** however, is hard to translate. For Neptunus is no longer the "classical" god of the sea and earthquakes, pictured with a trident, etc., but in the neo-platonic concept he has become an abstract (although dynamic) **power** of the humid element of the world. So one should certainly not imagine a concrete god (of course, this does not apply to the popular belief). Only the name still reminds one of the old sea-god. **umens substantia** = umens **elementum** (= στοιχεῖον), one of the 4 arch-elements: earth, water, air, fire. But on the other hand, one could also call this Neptunus a **substantialis potestas** (καθ' ὑπόστασιν), because he represents the essence of humidity (**substantia** = ὑπόστασις). Cf.et.Galletier-Fontaine Amm.I p.229 (note 139, 140); Enßlin, Zur Gesch.schr. etc. (op.cit.I) p.66 sq. (with lit.; not quite clear in my view); Souter p.396; Bauer, Wörterb.N.T.², 1928, 1353 (ὑπόστασις); (for the concepts: οὐσία, ἰδέα, παράδειγμα, ὑπόστασις) **Mau** (op.cit.I) p.56 sq.
Note. The meaning, which we find frequently in legal lit., of: **state of wealth, inventory,** does not occur in Amm. Neither that of: **livelihood, provisions.** Cf.Heum.-Seckel p.563.

poetae veteres et theologi. The old poets, are, for instance, Homer, p. 118. 16-17
Hesiodus, Pindarus (and others). Cf. Galletier-Fontaine Amm.1, p.230, note 141: "Référence aussi vague que celle aux "**theologicae doctrinae**" en 16.5.5, ou aux "**theologi**" en 21.14.3. A. fait problablement allusion aux traditions religieuses anciennes et complexes que les hommes du IVe siècle plaçaient sous le patronage des chantres mythiques **Musée, Orphée et Linus,** justement désignés par **Augustin,** Cité de Dieu 18.14 sous le titre de "poetae, qui etiam theologi dicerentur" (cf. les notes ad.loc. dans la Bibliothèque augustinienne, Oeuvres de saint Augustin, t.36, Paris, 1960). **Porphyre** fait aussi allusion à plusieurs reprises aux "traditions des théologiens" (τα τῶν θεολόγων). Déjà **Cicéron** recourait dans nat.deor. 3.21.53, à l'insérende vague "ii qui theologi nominantur" pour introduire des développements de caractère éuhémériste ... Et **Arnobe** devait parler avec mépris, en s'adressant auc païens, de "vestri theologi" (adv.nat.3.11)". In this last quotation Arn. mentions besides **theologi** also **poetae** (without the addition **veteres).** The word **theologi** also occurs in Amm.21.1.8: **theologi veteres.** It seems to me that the explanation of Gall.-Font. (above) is not entirely accurate. For the **theologicae doctrinae** in 16.5.5 are neo-Platonic doctrinae, whereas the **theologi veteres** (21.1.8) do belong to the

poetae veteres. Nor are the **theologi** in 21.14.3 only **theologi veteres.** When one reads the curious enumeration of persons there (c.14.4-5), this becomes quite clear.

p. 118. 17 **theologi nuncuparunt.** Claus.III. For the **contractio** etc. cf. ad 16.12.69, p.102.23-24c; ad 16.12.19, p.94.11-12; Hagendahl Perf.formen (op.cit.I) p. 29 sq.

VII, 13

p. 118. 18 **Fiunt.** Note the **variatio**: accidunt (§ 11), contingunt (§ 12).

p. 118. 18 **brasmatiae** (βρασματίαι). Only in Amm.? Derived from βράσσω = to bubble, boil.

p. 118. 19 **qui humum more ⟨aes⟩tus i⟨mi⟩tus suscitantes.** Cl.Her.Seyf.Rolfe. Sabbah: qui humum intus suscitantes. **intus** G. molestius Wm2 BA. **imitus Haupt.** imo de situ intus Seguine. funditus Nov. The text is very corrupt. Probably the version of Cl.c.s. renders the sense of the words best. (For **imitus** cf. Cass.Var.3.47.(55) = Migne I, 1865, p.602: Memorant autem aevi pristini servatores (Juret., forte scrutatores, vel observatores) hanc insulam (sc. **Vulcanus**) ante aliquot annos, undarum rupto terrore, **ignitus** (Juret. **imitus**) erupisse; Apul.Met.4.12; Gell.). Sabbah apparently assumes a dittography (comp. the textcrit.app.edit.Cl.p.118), and also gives a reasonable sentence, but is further removed from V's text. I do not think the conjectures by Sequine and Novák should be accepted. I suggest that **intus** as given by G should be maintained, while **imitus** should not be introduced. Perhaps e.g.: qui humum **more aestus intus** suscitantes?

p. 118. 20 **Delos emersit.** Cf.22.8.2: Aegaeum, quod paulatim fusius adulescens, dextra (qua late protenditur) per Sporadas est insulosum atque Cycladas, ideo sic appellatas quod omnes ambiunt **Delon partu deorum insignem**; 22.12.8: Iulianus ... venas fatidicas Castalii recludere cogitans fontis ... circumhumata corpora statuit exinde transferri eo ritu, **quo Athenienses insulam purgaverunt Delon.** In Amm.'s days the island **Delos** is only a shadow of what it once was, famous from myth and history, but otherwise of no real significance, unless as the seat of a bishop. (Cf.Pieper Tab.9). Cf.et. ad VII 9-14*b*.

p. 118. 20 **Hiera et Anaphe:** Cl. Rolfe Sabbah. Seyf.: **Thera et Anaphe. Hiera and Anaphe** also mentioned in Plin.N.H. (Cf. ad VII.9-14*b*). Seyf. here follows a suggestion by Wagner (= Comm.I p.276). The enumeration here in Amm. makes it very clear, to my view, that with Hiera we should not think of: 1⁰ **Hiera** of the **Aegates Insulae**. 2⁰ **Hiera** of the **Liparaeae Insulae**; both situated near Sicily. **Anaphe** lies close to **Thera**; in which neighbourhood we should also place **Hiera**.

a   **Rhodus - perfusa.** Cf.VII 9-14*b*; Claud.24 (= de cons.Stilich.III, 226):   p. 118. 21-22
   Auratos Rhodiis imbres, nascente Minerva,
   Indulsisse Iovem perhibent ....
The origin of this legend probably Hom.Il.2.670 (cf.annot. **Leaf** ad l.). A literal rain of gold in Pind.Ol.7.34,50. Cf.et. Ameis-Hentze³, 1896, I, p.149 (with lit.).
b   **Ofiusa** = ὀφιοῦσ(σ)α = rich in snakes. These snakes are fought by the **deer:** hence the many pictures of these animals. Cf.Plin.N.H.5.36; Strabo 14, 2.7.
Although Plin. mentiones several names of **Rhodos, Pelagia** is not one of them. Nor is this the case with Strabo, who also gives several names. The name may have been derived from the shape of the island **(pelagia = pelagia concha).**
c   **Rhodus** also mentioned: 23.4.10 (siege by Demetrius Poliorcetes). Rhodii:22.16.10-11 (Pharos under obligation to pay taxes to the Rhodians). The golden age of the island is already long past, but commerce and shipping still maintained a reasonable degree of prosperity. The city of Rhodus is the seat of an archbishop. (Pieper Tab.7).

dictitata = dicta, nominata. Cf. ad 14.6.8, p.13.26 (= I p.93). **Fesser's**   p. 118. 21
words, quoted there, are not in agreement with my views on the use of **intensiva** by Amm.

Eleusin in Boeotia. The addition: in Boeotia, makes it clear which town   p. 118. 22
of **Eleusis** is meant here, viz. the one that was situated near lake **Kopais.** It was not destroyed by an earthquake, but engulfed by a flood. Period of great prosperity of the town in the Mycene age. Cf. Strabo 9.2.18; Paus.9.24.2.

apud Tyrrenos Vulcanos. Vulcanus is one of the **insulae Liparaeae,** which,   p. 118. 22
according to Julius Obsequens, (quoted by Sabbah) emerged in 571 (Roman dating). **Tyrr(h)eni** are at this time called **Tusci** (14.11.27; 15.5.14) and the country **Tuscia** (21.5.12; 28.1.6; 27.3.1). **Tyrr(h)enus** (cf. Tyrrenum mare 15.10.2; 29.6.17) is a literary name, no longer in use in the

living language. N.D.Occ. also has **Tuscia** (The Laterculus Polem.Silv., on the other hand: in mari **Tyrrheno**). Cf.et. ad 15.5.14 (= III p.91).

p. 118. 23 **climatiae** = κλιματίαι = epicliniae. Only in Amm.?

p. 118. 23 *a* **limes.** limis = **limus.** Cf.20.9.2: **limibusque** oculis. Also comparable: non **indecoribus** barbis (23.6.75); **inquies** Persa (19.5.1), **inquies** homo (29.1.5) (cf.Fesser p.57); **infirmium** (20.6.6); **saevium** tyrannorum (15.9.6), suppliciorum **saevium** (29.5.48; cf. Blomgren op.cit.II, p.118 note 1). The adj., often linked with **oculi,** also in Plaut.Terent.Ovid.Horat.Plin. Quint., far from general. Not in Claud.Veget.r.m.Arn.adv.nat.Opt. Milev.
b **limes ruentes et obliqui.** For this abundantia cf.Hagend.abund. (op. cit.I) p.173 sq., with numerous examples. Clark wants to read cursus causa: **atque.** But the claus. $\sim\sim\sim\sim\sim\sim$ occurs more often in Amm. (cf. Blomgren p.9 sq.).

p. 118. 24 **conplanant.** Also in legal lit.: to smooth, to level, to bring to a par. Pregnantly: to destroy.

p. 118. 24 **chasmatiae** (χασματίας). Apul. de mundo 18 (quoted by Georges). Derived from χάσμα (= chasm), which occurs, among others, in Sen. and Plin.

p. 118. 24 **Voratrina** = chasm, abyss. Extremely rare subst. With **this** meaning not known to me from other sources. Not in Claud.Veget.r.m.Arn.adv.nat. Opt.Milev.

p. 119. 1-2 *a* **ut in Atlantico mari, Europaeo orbe spatiosior insula.** Here is meant **Atlantis** (Plato, Timaeus, 24e-25a). **Atlanticum mare** in Amm. only here. The adj. has a much more restricted meaning than our Atlantic, viz. around and near the Atlas mountains, like here in Amm. **Europaeus** (adj.) also in 22.8.42.
b Besides the provinciae Thracia, Haemimontus, etc. a **prov.Europa** (N.D.Or.XXVI) also belonged to the **dioecesis Thraciarum.** A **consularis Europae** ibid.I. This province further mentioned ibid.II, Laterc.Veron. IV, Laterc.Pol.Silv.VI. This **Europa** mentioned in Amm.27.4.12.

p. 119. 1 **spatiosior.** Adj. post-class. Also in Claud. Not in Veget.r.m.Arn.adv.nat. Opt.Milev.

Crisaeo sinu Helice et Bura. The s.Cris. is part of the Corinthian Gulf, bordered on its Eastern shore by Phocis, named after **Crisa,** a town situated between Delphi and Cirrha, which lies on the Gulf. But here s.Cris. equals s.Corinthiacus. **Helice** and **Bura** both were towns in Achaia, East of Aegium and West of Aegae. **Helice** was destroyed in 373 B.C., just as **Bura** probably. Cf. Strabo 8.7.5; Seneca Nat.Quaest.7.5.2; Ovid. Met.15.293 sq.:

Si quaeras **Helicen et Burin,** Archaidas urbes,
Invenies sub aquis; et adhuc ostendere nautae
Inclinata solent cum moenibus oppida mersis.

From this it is already apparent how proverbial this catastrophe had become.

et in Ciminia Italiae parte oppidum Saccumum. In S.-Etruria the **mons and lacus Ciminius** (Lago di Vico) were situated. Cf.Tab.Peut.V.2. Of the town of **Saccumum,** which used to lie in this neighbourhood, practically nothing is known.

ad Erebi ... occultantur. One can see from this how the facts are embellished poetically.

a **Erebi profundos hiatus.** Cf.Claud.35 (de raptu Proserp.II) 258 sq.:
Quod conata nefas, aut cuius conscia noxae
Exsul ad **immanes Erebi** detrudor **hiatus?**
Erebus only here in Amm.

b The subst. **hiatus** also 23.6.17: in his pagis **hiatus** quoque conspicitur terrae, unde halitus letalis exsurgens...; 29.5.42: qui Caesaream mitti dispositus (sc.Mazuca) ... dilatato vulneris **hiatu** discessit (= died); 29.1.19: admovente stimulos avaritia et sua et eorum, qui tunc in regia versabantur, **novos hiatus** aperientium (cf.Tac.Hist.4.42).

aeternis tenebris. Cf.Claud.20 (In Eutrop.II) 229 sq.:
.... Sic fata repente
In diram se vertit avem, rostroque recurvo
Turpis et **infernis tenebris** obscurior alas
Auspicium veteri sedit ferale sepulcro.

VII, 14
inter haec tria genera ... mycematiae ... audiuntur: μυκηματίας (derived from μυκάομαι).

In Amm. only here. But only in Amm.? It should be clear by now that the **mycematiae** are the 4th kind of earthquakes. The meaning of **inter** does not differ here from **ad** (= with which, with). The translation by Seyf. is either obscure or incorrect: "**Bei diesen drei Arten von Erdbeben** hört man ein Dröhnen mit drohendem Laut, **wenn die Elemente entfesselt sind und gewaltig anstürmen ...**". The last underlined words are translated correctly by Sabbah: "lorsque l'assemblage des éléments se disloque **et qu'ils bondissent de leur mouvement propre**" (ultro).

p. 119. 5 **compagibus.** Cf. ad 16.12.44, p.98.20c; Fesser p.24.

p. 119. 7 *a* **taurinis reboare mugitibus.** The adj. is post-class. and poet. The subst. in general exactly the same. For **taurinus** cf.et.Claud.24 (de cons.Stil.III) 364 sq.; ibid.45 (Eid.II) 38; Stat.Theb.2.78 (c.comm. Mulder p.80). For **mugitus** cf.Claud.34 (de raptu Pros.II) 33 sq.: (praef.) Te neque Dictaeas quatiens **mugitibus** urbes // **Taurus**, nec Stygii terruit ira canis;
Ibid.II.7 sq.:
.... ter conscia fati
Flebile **terrificis** gemuit **mugitibus** Henna;
and passim.

b **reboare** Cf. Hagend.St.A.p.72: "Lusus quidam inest, quasi e **bove** hoc verbum originem trahat. Sed est, nisi fallor, e Graeco verbo ἀντιβοάω ductum. Soli fere adhibent poetae, plerumque de inanimis" (with examples and note).

c The 3 above-mentioned words not in Veget.r.m.Arn.adv.nat.Opt.Milev.

p. 119. 7 **fragores fremitusque terrenos.** Alliterating (f)r. For **fragor** cf.17.7.3, p.116.24-25c. For **fremitus** cf.15.8.10: quia igitur vestrum quoque favorem adesse **fremitus** (= approval) indicat laetus; 26.7.17: et pro ... **terrifico fremitu**, quem barbari dicunt barritum, nuncupatum imperatorem (sc. Procopium) ... reduxerunt ad castra.

p. 119. 7 *a* **sed hinc ad exorsa.** Cf. ad 14.6.26 (= I p.101); ad 15.12.6 (= IV p.78); ad 15.11.16 (= IV p.70).

b **exorsa** = ± theme, subject (on which one has started). A different nuance of **exorsa** is given in 14.11.26: (Adrastia) voluntatumque nostrarum **exorsa** interdum alio quam quo contendebant **exitu** terminans (exitu X exorsa). Here ± the aim of all our desires. Not in Claud.Veget.r.m. Arn.adv.nat.Opt.Milev.

VIII, 1

The war described here (May-August 358), in the §§ 8-11.4, is the 3rd p. 119. 8
German war. The 1st and 2nd have been described in book XVI (Comm.
p.1).

Parisios. The information on the winterquarters in Paris corresponds p. 119. 8
with 17.2.4. For **Parisii** cf. ad 15.11.3 (= IV p.60). Cf.et.Pieper Tab.13;
Not.Gall.4.8: civitas Parisiorum; Not.Occ.42.22 sq.: In provincia Lugdu-
nensi Senonia (= prov.Lugd.IV): Praefectus classis Anderetianorum,
Parisius. At this time the names of the tribes (Parisii) are beginning to
drive out the names of cities (Lutetia, Luticia).

Alamannos. Cf. ad 14.10.1 (= II·p.96); ad 17.6.1, p.116.4*a*, *b*, *c*. p. 119. 8

nondum ... et saevos. As was already apparent from cap.6, the **Alamanni** p. 119. 9-10
are far from being definitely beaten, in spite of their considerable defeat
after the battle of Strasbourg. This is shown already from these words
alone. At this late stage the Roman empire is no longer able to properly
defend all its frontiers, a situation which can not be altered even by
important military successes.

insaniam V. **ad** insaniam A Nov. Cl.Seyf.Rolfe. **in** insaniam Lind. **insania** p. 119. 9
Wm2 G Sabbah.
The version as given by G seems preferable to me: by their insane rage.

a **post Argentoratum**: short and "incorrect" for: post cladem ad Arg. p. 119. 10
acceptam. For **post** with temp. meaning cf. ad 17.4.1, p.109.4*a*.
b cf.XVI.12.

a **operiensque Iulium mensem.** Instead of: mensem Iulium, metri causa. p. 119. 10
Claus.I.
b For **operior** used intrans. cf.21.7.7; 27.3.9; Blomgren (op.cit.II) p.169.
The verb does not occur in Claud.Veget.r.m.Arn.adv.nat.Opt.Milev.
c Cf.Wagner (p.278) ad h.l.: "Galliae tum inclementius coelum erat,
nec suscipi aliquid poterat, nisi, uti Amm. paulo post ait": aestatis remissione, solutis frigoribus et pruinis"; Cassiod.Var.1.24: atque ideo per
Nandium Saionem nostrum admonendum curavimus, ut ad expeditionem, in Dei nomine, more solito, armis, equis, rebusque omnibus neces-
sariis sufficienter instructi, **octavo die cal. Iuliarum proxime veniente**,
modis omnibus. Deo favente, moveatis (quoted by Lindenbr.).

p. 119. 11 *a* **unde sumunt Gallicani procinctus exordia.** Cf.Cic. de fin.5.7(18): ut illa prudentia, quam artem vitae esse diximus, in earum trium rerum aliqua versetur, **a qua totius vitae ducat exordium;** ad Herenn.2.30(47): Quapropter **initium** enumerationis **sumendum** est a divisione; ibid.3.6(11): In huius modi igitur causa **principium sumetur** ... ; ibid.4.13(19): repetitio est, cum continenter ab uno atque eodem verbo in rebus similibus et diversis **principia sumuntur;** invent.1.20(28): brevis erit, si, unde necesse est, **inde initium sumetur;** Amm.26.1.9: tertius a prima vigilia **sumens exordium** ad horam noctis extenditur sextam. For these and similar exprescf. Krebs Antib.1 p.549 (with lit.). Cf.et.Veget.r.m.1.20: a quibus pugnandi **sumebatur exordium** (= Lang p.23); ibid.4.38: a verno itaque solstitio ... **sumemus exordium** (= Lang p.155);

b **Gallicanus.** The adj. also: 15.5.36; 17.9.6; 20.4.1; 22.3.7; 25.10.8; 25.4.13; 25.10.10; 23.5.25; 29.6.16; 30.10.3; 30.10.1; 31.12.6; 27.1.1; 27.8.5. **Gallicanus** in Amm. only with reference to the trans-Alpine Gallia, never to the **provincia Gallica,** which is mentioned, among others, by Cic. and Varro, and which lay in Italia. Cf. et. Krebs Antib.1 p.618 (incomplete). The adj. does not occur in Claud.Veget.r.m.Arn.adv.nat.Opt. Milev. As so often, it is difficult to determine whether we are dealing here with an archaism, or whether the word is still part of living language, and was used, for instance, by soldiers.

c **procinctus.** Cf. ad 16.11.6, p.89.7.

p. 119. 11 **diutius angebatur.** Claus.III. The comparat. is probably used metri causa. For the **comp.** = **posit.** cf. ad 14.6.12 (= I p.96).

p. 119. 11-13 *a* **nec enim ... annona.** Cf.18.2.3: (4th German war, 359 A.D.; cf. ad 17.8.1, p.119.8): id inter potissima mature duxit implendum, ut ... **horrea** quin etiam exstrueret pro incensis, **ubi eondi possit annona a Britaniis sueta transferri;** Zosim.3.5.2: (Iulianus) ὀκτακόσια κατεσκεύασε πλοῖα μείζονα λέμβων, ταῦτά τε εἰς τὴν Βρεττανίαν ἐκπέμψας κομίζεσθαι σῖτον ἐποίει· Καὶ τοῦτον τοῖς ποταμίοις πλοίοις ἀνάγεσθαι διὰ τοῦ Ῥήνου παρασκευάζων etc. Iul. ad Athen.279d-280*a;* Liban.orat.18.83 (= edit. Foerster 2 p.271); Bidez, La vie de l'Emp.Iul. (op.cit.I) p.156; Sabbah Amm.II p.179, note 75.76. Amm. has already told us that the regions of the upper- and middle Rhine are pacified. The region of the lower Rhine should now follow. Hence the campaigns against the **Salii** and the **Chamavi.** The aim of these operations is to restore the connections with **Britannia,** which are badly needed for the provisioning of the garrisons along the Rhine. From 17.8.1 it appears that grain is still being imported from

Aquitania. But in 18.2.3 we read that this is no longer the case. Britannia is closer. This import of grain from Br. is now insured after the submission of the **Salii** and the **Chamavi** and after the construction of a river fleet of 600 ships (told by Iul.). Sabbah rightly remarks that the above is **indirectly** reported in Amm. By a combination with other authors the aim of Iulianus' campaigns becomes clear.

b Cf.18.2.1: **Egressurus** autem ad **procinctum** urguentem, cum Alamannorum pagos aliquos esse reputaret hostiles. **Egredi** well-known t.t.mil.

c **antequam.** Cf. ad 14.6.23 (= I p.100).

d **Aquitania.** Cf. ad 14.10.2 (= II p.97); ad 15.11.1-18 (= IV p.58); Woordenb. der Oudheid 2 p.238 with lit. (Nuchelmans).

Correction: II p.97 last line should read: **Occ.22,** all 3 etc.

e **aestatis remissione.** Cf.Cic. de orat.2.17(72): qui tamquam machinatione aliqua tum ad severitatem, tum ad **remissionem animi,** tum ad tristitiam, tum ad laetitiam est contorquendus (severitas X remissio: example by Georges). Here = softening, gentleness. The subst. does not occur in Claud.Veget.r.m.Arn.adv.nat. It is found, however, in Opt. Milev. with a meaning which it has in many Eccl., viz.: **forgiveness** (e.g. **remissio peccatorum, -delictorum).** For the meaning in jud.lit. cf. Heum.- Seckel p.505.

f **Solutis frigoribus et pruinis.** Cf.Veget.r.m.3.2 (= Lang p.68): ne saeva hieme iter **per nives ac pruinas** noctibus faciant (= ripe); Claud. 24.255 sq. (de cons.Stil.III):

.... Divas nemorumque potentes
Fecit **Hyperboreis** Delos praelata **pruinis.**

(= snow, ice). **In Claud. only the plur.** The meaning is the same for sing. and plur. Both occur in both prose and poetry. With Amm. here the same meaning as in Claud. Both pluralia metri causa: claus.III. For the **plur. poet.** cf. ad 17.2.1, p.107.14-15*b*.

Solvi = to melt, as in Ovid., Lucret. and others. Cf.Claud.26.266 sq. (de bello Getico):

Frigida ter decies nudatum frondibus Aemum
Tendit hiems vestire gelu; totidemque **solutis**
Ver **nivibus** viridem monti reparavit amictum;

ibid.24.234 sq. (de consul.Stilich.):

.... Si **solveret** ignis,
Quas dedit immanes vili sub pondere **massas.**

g Cf.Veget.r.m.3.3 (= Lang p.69): In omni expeditione unum est et maximum telum, **ut tibi sufficiat victus,** hostes frangat inopia. Ante igitur quam inchoëtur bellum, de copiis expensisque sollers debet esse tractatus

(= inspection, examination), ut pabula frumentum ceteraeque annonariae species, **quas a provincialibus consuetudo deposcit,** maturius exigantur **et in oportunis ad rem gerendam ac munitissimis locis** amplior semper modus, quam sufficit, **adgregetur.** Quod si tributa deficiunt, prorogato auro comparanda sunt omnia. (cf.Amm.18.2.3).

VIII, 2

p. 119. 13-14 *a* **sed ut est difficultatum paene omnium diligens ratio victrix:** careful consideration. Cf.Cic. pro lege Man.7(17): quorum vobis pro vestra sapientia, Quirites, **habenda est ratio diligenter.**
b **victrix.** Cf. ad 16.12.12, p.92.27-28*d*. For the feminina ending in **-trix,** some of which occur only in Amm., cf. Liesenberg (1888) p.7 (op.cit.I).

p. 119. 14 **multa mente versans et varia.** Note the placing of the words. For the **hyperbaton** cf. ad 17.1.6, p.105.21*a*.

p. 119. 14-15 **id tantum repperit solum. tandem** N A Clark Seyf. Rolfe. **tutum** Schneider Momms. **tantum** V Hagend. Sabbah. V's version should be adhered to. Cf. Hagend. Strena phil.f.P.Persson (Upps.1922) p.74 sq.: "Wir haben es hier mit einer im Spätlat. häufig vorkommenden **pleonastischen Verbindung** zu tun, welche vor einigen Jahren Löfstedt mit etwa einem Dutzend Beispiele und unter Hinweisung auf ital. **soltanto** nachgewiesen hat (Krit. Bem. zu Tertull.Apolog. Lunds Univ.Ärsskr.N.F.Avd.1.Bd.14 Nr.24. Lund 1918.p.37 sq.). Die Anzahl läszt sich nicht unerheblich vermehren .... Überhaupt ist darauf zu achten, dasz eine pleonastische Verstärkung des Ausdrucks bei den Begriffen "**nur**", "**blosz**" im Spätlat. besonders beliebt gewesen ist". For the **abundantia** in general cf.Hofm. Lat.Umg.spr. (op.cit.I) p.92 sq. And for the **pleonasm** Hagend.abund. (op.cit.I) p.209 sq.; Oder, Mulom.Chiron.p.310 sq.

p. 119. 15 **anni maturitate.** Instead of this unusual word-combination, which is not quite accurate either, **adulto vere** (cf. ad 14.2.9 = I p.71) would have been better. **Maturitas** is used metaphorically in 14.1.10: Thalassius ... considerans incitationem eius ad multorum augeri discrimina non **maturitate** vel consiliis mitigabat (mature judgment, experience). Cf.et. Krebs Antib.2 p.62 sq. The subst. does not occur in Claud.Veget.r.m.Opt.Milev., though it is found in Arn.adv.nat.

p. 119. 15 **insperatus.** Cf. ad 16.2.7, p.73.11. Cf.et.Liesenb. (1889) p.17 sq.; Hagend. St.Amm.p.45 sq. (for the adj. and part. composed with **-in**). The adj. is also class.

firmatoque consilio. Cf.28.1.26: Lollianus ... exploratius causam Maximino spectante convictus codicem noxiarum artium **nondum per aetatem firmato consilio** descripsisse (= established view). And here, quite rightly. Büchele: "sobald er darüber mit sich im Reinen war". The translations by Sabbah: "ayant renforcé ses dispositions tactiques" and Seyf.: Dieser Plan fand Billigung", are in my opinion incorrect. Cf.et. Cic.Verr. 3.1.3: Atque ille iis praesidiis ingenii fortunaeque munitus, tamen hac cura continebatur, quam sibi, **nondum confirmato consilio,** sed ineunte aetate, susceperat (cf. Michael, op.cit.I, p.46). Cf.et. ad 17.1.12, p.106. 18-19; Michael p.22.

a **XX dierum ... libentium militum. Bu(c)ce(l)latum** is a kind of "ship's biscuit", soldiers' bread in the form of biscuits. Only in late Latin. Cf. Souter p.33; Heum.-Seckel p.50; Georges I p.872. It is derived from **buc(c)ella** (a small mouthful), which is in its turn a diminutive of **bucca** (vulgar Latin = a mouthful). In Cod.Theod.14.17.5 **buccella** means: a small loaf of bread which was distributed among the poor: Civis Romanus, qui in viginti **panibus sordidis** (qui nunc dicuntur **Ardiniensis**) quinquaginta uncias comparabat, triginta et sex uncias in **bucellis sex mundis** sine pretio consequatur: Ita ut ius in his nullus habeat officialis, nullus servus, nemo qui aedificiorum percipiat panem (cf.14.17.1 ibid.). This law dates from 369 A.D. In a law of 360 A.D. one reads about **buccellatum:** Repetita consuetudo (= study of past practice) monstravit expeditionis tempore **buccellatum ac panem** ... milites nostros ita solere percipere: **biduo buccellatum, tertio die panem** ... (Cod.Theod.7.4.6). Cf.et. Cod.Theod.7.5.2: In excoctione (= baking) **buccellati** quod devotissimis (soldier's titel = ± loyal, devoted). militibus convenit praeparari, in translatione etiam **annonae** nullius excipiatur persona videlicet ut ne nostra quidem domus ab his habeatur immunis (404 A.D. This demonstrates the care, at any rate theoretically, for the provisioning of the soldiers). Vegetius r.m. does not use the term.

b For the period during which the soldiers had to carry **umeris** (suis), the store of bread cf. ad 16.11.12, p.90.12; Cod.Theod.7.4.5: Expeditionalem annonam **ex horreis** milites viginti dierum debent suscipere ut eam transvehant **propriis in expeditione necessitatibus** profuturam (359 A.D.) For the care of the soldiers in general cf. ad 16.3.3, p.74.19; Müller Mil. (op.cit.I) p.621 sq.; Grosse Mil.p.241 sq. (with lit.), op.cit.I.

c **sedibus.** Cf. ad 14.2.12 (= I p.115); Souter p.370; Georges II p.2571; Veget.r.m.3.4: quod (sc.tumultum) hi praecipue faciunt, qui **in sedibus** otiose delicateque vixerunt (= Lang p.71); ibid.Lang p.71 line 11; line 22;

p.72 line 3; ibid.3.5 (= Lang p.74): Quae omnia **in sedibus itineribus** (asyndeton) in omni exercitatione castrensi universi milites et sequi et intellegere consuescant; Cod.Theod.6.24.2 (364 A.D.): Quaternas enim annonas eos (sc.filios domesticorum vel propinquos parvos) quos armis gestandis et procinctibus bellicis idoneos ad huc non esse constiterit, in **sedibus** iubemus adipisci.

d   **ad usus diurnitatem excoctum.** Cf.23.6.38: oleum usus communis herba quadam infectum condiunt harum rerum periti **ad diuturnitatem servantes** et coalescens; 25.4.15: remissa debita multa **diuturnitate** congesta. Here = ad usum diuturnum. Cf.et.20.5.5: vos vigore **ususque diuturnitate fundati**; Sall.Hist.3.87: **ad diuturnitatem usus** (Fletcher).

e   **excoctum. Excoquo** = (here) baking (of bread). Just as **panis excoctio** in Cod.Theod.11.16.15 = the baking of bread. With **this** meaning late Latin. The compos. does not occur in Claud.Arn.adv.nat.Veget.r.m. Opt.Milev. Cf.et.*a*,

f   **umeris.** Cf.17.1.13: frugesque portaturos **humeris** (c.annot.).

g   **libentium militum.** We would prefer to express this negatively: those who did not oppose this, who did not grumble about this.

p. 119. 18   **hocque subsidio fretus.** For **fretus** cf. ad 16.12.13, p.93.2-3*f.* Seyf. translates **subsidio** with "Hilfe", Sabbah by: "réserve", Rolfe: "supply". The last translations are correct, in my opinion.

p. 119. 19   **secundis (ut ante) auspiciis profectus.** The vague indication of time probably refers to the capita 1 and 2 of this book, broadly speaking.

p. 119. 19-20   **intra mensem quintum vel sextum.** Seyf.: "im Mai oder Juni"; Sabbah: "qu'en moins de cinq ou six mois"; Rolfe: "within the fifth or sixth month"; Büchele: "innerhalb fünf oder sechs Monaten". **Intra** with temporal meaning also, for instance 23.5.6: intra praestitutum diem; 25.9.4: intra triduum. The meaning here is unequivocal.
Cf. Krebs Antib.1 p.765: "**Inter** decem annos bedeutet während zehn (voller) Jahre, zehn Jahre hindurch, im Verlauf von zehn Jahren, aber **intra** steht von der Zeit, sowohl in ihrer Dauer, als bevor sie zu Ende ging, also **sowohl = wahrend als vor dem Ablauf eines Zeitabschnittes**". (with lit.) The meaning **during** seems impossible to me; for it seems highly unlikely that 2 expeditions can be accomplished in one month. The translations by Büchele (and Sabbah) are correct. And **intra** + **subst.** + **ordinale**, as it is used here, is often found in Latin.

consummari = to finish, complete. In Amm. also 29.6.3; 30.7.11. Cf. Krebs Antib.1 p.349 (with lit.). The verb does not occur in Claud.Veget. r.m.Arn.adv.nat.Opt.Milev. Cf.et. Souter p.75; Heum.-Seckel p.101; ad 16.11.11, p.90.9.

p. 119. 20

VIII, 3
quibus paratis. Cf. ad 17.4.14, p.111.7-8.

p. 119. 21

a **Francos ... Salios.** For the **Franci** cf. ad 15.5.11 (= III p.86 sq.); Woordenboek der Oudheid 5 p.1148, 1970 (with lit.B.Stolte); **W.J. de Boone**, De F., from their first appearance until the death of Childerik (1954); **D.Blok**, The F. Their actions in the light of history (1968) (both works in Dutch). Schönfeld (op.cit.I) p.89; Heum.-Seckel p.220.
[**Correction.** Read III p.87: Or.**31** ...; ibid.**32**; ... N.D.Or.**5**; ... N.D. Occ.**42**.]
b **Salii.** The S. are mentioned in the N.D.: Or.5.10,51 (belonging to the auxilia palatina); Occ.5.29,177 (belonging to the aux.palat.); Occ.5.62: **Salii Gallicani** (cf. ad 17.8.1, p.119.11*b*); similarly 5.210; Occ.7.129: **Salii iuniores Gallicani.** Though the **Salii** live in Germania II, W. of the Meuse (± the Dutch provinces of Limburg, Brabant, Zeeland), their residence must originally have been more to the North, which is shown from the name **Salland** (in the province of Overijssel), a region named after them. Cf.et. Schönfeld, p.197 sq.

p. 119. 21

videlicet. Cf. ad 17.3.6, p.108.29-p.109.1*b*.

p. 119. 21

quos consuetudo Salios appellavit. For the **personificatio** cf. ad 17.2.1, p. 107.13. Salios appellavit: claus.III. The use of the perfectum is very striking here: in my view a perf. or plq.perf. does not fit **consuetudo**. And as far as the contents are concerned, neither an imperf.: for the **Salii** were still called this, not only in the past. Hence **appellavit** should mean: those whom the common usage has called Salii up to now **and still calls them thus** (= **Gr. perfectum**). Cf.et.Plin.m.8.7: **appellat ... consuetudo ...** dentes (Fletcher); 19.8.9; 21.13.8; 31.3.1 (Blomgren p.89).

p. 119. 22

in Romano solo. These words have a stronger emotional value than, for instance, intra fines Romanos, intra limites imperii. Because in the above and similar connections **solum** often means: native soil.

p. 119. 22

p. 119. 22-23 *a* **apud Toxiandriam locum.** For **apud** cf. ad 14.11.21 (= II p.137); Krebs Antib.1 p.190 sq. (with extensive lit.).

b The addition of **locum** makes it quite clear that here is meant a place (town), viz. the capital of the **Toxiandri**. Therefore these **Toxiandri** are not the same people as the **Salii**, who have settled in their territory, as happened so often in these days in the border districts. That this happened "illegally", is apparent from Amm.'s words: **ausos ... praelicenter.** Sabbah and Seyf. seem to consider **Toxiandria** a region, and do not translate **locum.**

Cf. A.W. Bijvanck, Nederland in de Romeinse tijd (the Netherlands in the Roman era), II (1943) p.490,634, 648, 670, 676, 678, 695, 708.

p. 119. 23 *a* **habitacula sibi figere praelicenter.** Cf.14.8.6: ex **agrestibus habitaculis** urbes construxit multis opibus firmas et viribus. Late latin = domicilium, habitatio. Cf. Krebs Antib.1 p.643 (with lit.).

b **praelicenter.** Cf. ad 16.5.3. p.75.20-21. And for the **place of the adverb** cf. ad 17.11.1, p.123.24.

c **figere.** Cf. ad 16.11.8, p.89.14-15; ad 16.7.7, p.79.27-28.

p. 119. 23 **Tungros** = Atuatuca Tungrorum in Germania II. Once again the popular name has driven out the official Roman name. (cf. ad 8.1, p.119.8: **Parisios).** = Tongeren Cf. ad 15.11.7 (= IV p.62); Seeck N.D. Index p.300, 315, 327; Pieper Tab.13 and p.46; **Byvanck** (op.cit.8.3) passim. It was situated on the road from Cologne to Paris.

p. 119. 24 **occurrit** = came to meet him. But in 8.2. (p.119.15) t.t.mil. = to march against someone.

p. 119. 24 **legatio praedictorum (sc.Saliorum).** Cf. ad 16.2.1, p.72.10*b;* ad 16.12.21, p.94.17; ad 14.3.4 (= I p.81); ad 16.11.14, p.90.25. The use of **praedicti**: substantive in the plural, is quite remarkable here.

p. 119. 24-25 *a* **opinantium repperiri imperatorem etiam tum in hibernis** = se posse repperire. The infin. is used conatively. **etiam tum** = then still. **tum** EAG Seyf. Sabbah, Clark, Rolfe. **dum** V. It is doubtful whether the version by V should be altered: it is unnecessary for the sake of the meaning. Cf. Krebs Antib.1 p.527 (with lit.); Plaut.mil.992:

Dissimulabo, hos quasi non videam neque **esse hic etiamdum** sciam; Pseud.956 sq.:

Minu'malum hunc hominem esse opinor quam esse censebam coquom
Nam nihil **etiam dum** harpagavit praetor cyathum et cantharum;

224

a Rud.1381; Ter.heaut.229:

Hoc ego mali non pridem inveni, neque **etiam dum** scit pater;
Ter.Eun.568 sq.:

..... forte fortuna domi

erat quidam eunuchus, quem mercatus fuerat frater Thaïdi,

neque is deductus **etiamdum** ad eam.

All examples (by Georges) in negative sentences. Probably we are dealing here with an archaism of Amm., and not with a vulgarism. For in later vulgar Latin **etiam** disappears completely. (Cf. Grandgent, op. cit.I, 11, 14 = p.8 sq.).

b **hibernis:** in Paris (8.1). Cf. ad 14.10.16 (= II p.112).

a **pacem sub hac lege praetendens** = sub hac condicione (very frequent p. 119. 25
and well-known meaning). Cf.20.4.4: qui relictis laribus transrhenanis **sub hoc** venerant **pacto**, ne ducerentur ad partes umquam transalpinas. For **sub c.ablat.** cf. ad 17.4.13, p.111 6*b;* ad 15.3.11 (= III p.52).

b **praetendens** = proponens: therefore not falsely suggesting, **pretending,** but with a favourable meaning. Only in Amm.? Cf. ad 16.11.14, p.90.22-23*a, b.*

a **ut ... nec lacesseret quisquam nec vexaret** = ("correcter") ne lacesseret p. 119. 25-26
quisquam **neve** vexaret. But **ut** can be easily explained here, for the sentence = **ut quiescerent temquam in suis neve ... neve.** (cf. ad 17.3.5, p.108.20*a*).

b **quiescentes.** Here: to live undisturbed, quietly. 14.4.5: to rest, make a halt; 21.1.12: altius quiescentis = to be fast asleep, in a deep sleep.

c for **tamquam** cf. ad 17.4.15, p.111.19-20*a*. Mentally can be added: habitantes.

d **in suis.** Cf. ad 17.1.2, p.104.7-9*d*.

e Cf.Veget.r.m.4.31 (= Lang p.150): Nemo enim **bello lacessere** aut facere audet inuriam ei regno vel populo etc.; Aur.Vict. de Caes.6.1: At Galba ... ubi Romam ingressus est ... rapere, trahere, **vexare,** ac foedum in modum vastare cuncta et polluere; Iust.Phil.18.2.11: Post haec legati Siculorum superveniunt, tradentes Pyrrho totius insulae imperium, quae adsiduis Carthaginiensium **bellis vexabatur.** Both verbs are almost t.t. mil. Compare for **vexare** also Gell.2.6, a rather nice piece of prose.

a **negotio plene digesto.** Cf.Veget.r.m.4 praef. (= Lang p.129): rationes, p. 119. 27
quibus vel nostrae civitates defendendae sint vel hostium subruendae, ex diversis auctoribus **in ordinem digeram;** ibid.4.30 (= Lang p.149): Quae

225

ad obpugnandas vel defendendas urbes auctores bellicarum artium prodiderunt vel quae recentium necessitatum usus invenit, pro publica, ut arbitror, utilitate **digessi** ...; 2.23 (= Lang p.56): Legionis ordinatione **digesta** ad exercitium revertimur; 3.26 (= Lang p.124): **Digesta** sunt, imperator invicte, quae nobilissimi auctores ... memoriae prodiderunt; 3.22 (= Lang p.112) **Digestis** omnibus, quae ratio militaris experimentis et arte ser\avit; Opt.Milev.1.4 (= Ziwsa p.6): frater meus igitur Parmenianus, ne ventose ac nude ut ceteri loqueretur, quidquid sentire potuit, non solum dixit sed etiam **in scriptura digessit**. But with another meaning Claud.28 (de VI cons.Hon.) 589 sq.:

> gestarum patribus causas ex ordine rerum
> eventusque refert veterumque exempla secutus
> **digerit imperii** sub iudice **facta** senatu.

(= to rule, settle).
Cf.et. ad 15.4.1 (= III p.54).

b **plene.** Cf. ad 16.12.14, p.93.5-6*b* (**plenus**); Imhof (quoted by **Mulder** p.300): "quidquid non mancum est aut dimidiatum, sed **totum et integrum,** ita ut nil desit aut desideretur"; Ovid ex P.2.7.77:

> Sustineas ut onus, nitendum **vertice pleno** est
> Aut flecti nervos si patiere, cades.

The **adv.** is rarely found in class.Latin. Confusion with **plane** occurs in manuscripts. Cf. Krebs Antib.2 p.308. With the aforeside meaning **plenus** and **plene** occur fairly often in judicial literature (cf. Heum.-Seckel p.433). The late Latin **pleniter** does not occur in Amm. Cf.et.Claud.18 (In Eutr.I) 494 sq.:

> .... quae iam connubia prolem,
> Vel frugem latura seges? Quid fertile terris,
> Quid **plenum** sterili possit sub consule nasci?

(although other explanations of **plenus** are possible here).

p. 119. 27 **oppositaque condicionum perplexitate.** Cf.18.6.19: his ob **perplexitatem nimiam** aegerrime lectis consilium suscipitur prudens (= obscurity); 31.2.12: veteres Massagetas, qui unde sint vel quas incolant terras, quoniam huc res prolapsa est, consentaneum est demonstrare **geographica perplexitate monstrata** etc. (correct, in my opinion, Büchele: "die geographische Begriffsverwirrung"). Cf.et. ad 15.1.1 (= III p.5); Souter p.298; Heum.-Seckel p.424 **(perplexus).** The subst. and adj. do not occur in Claud.Veget.r.m.Opt.Milev.Arn.adv.nat.

p. 119. 27- p. 120. 1 *a* **ut in isdem tractibus moraturus dum redeunt. ut** c.part.fut. = Gr. ὡς c.

226

part.fut. = as if he intended to stay (awhile) = tamquam si moraretur. Cf.Hofm.-Leum.p.603 (Zus. α); **Riemann** (op.cit.I) § 139, p.304 sq. Cf. et. ad 15.5.3: **ut quasi** (= III p.71); Schneider (op.cit.I) p.10 sq. **(ut =** as can be expected, because of); ad 17.4.15, p.111.19-20a **(tamquam);** ad 14.1.4 (= I p.58 sq.: **tanquam);** ad 17.2.1, p.107.9b (restrictive: insofar as).
b Cf.14.3.2: Mesopotamiae **tractus** omnes. Also class. = district, region. With this meaning also in Claud. Not in Veget.r.m. Opt.Milev. Arn.adv.nat. Also in the Cod.Theod.10.19.8; 11.5.3; 7.4.33. As far as I know, not a t.t. of the administration or of the government.
Cf.et. ad 17.6.1, p.116.4-5b; ad 15.8.1 (= IV p.27).

dum redeunt. For the constructions of **dum** cf. ad 17.4.4, p.109.14. p. 120. 1

a **muneratos absolvit. Absolvere** = to let go. Cf. **vita absolvi:** 25.3.23; p. 120. 1
27.11.1 (= ἀπολύεσθαι = discedere. Cf.Hagend.St.Amm.p.101, note 1). The above meaning: **to send away, to let go,** several times in Plaut. In view of another meaning of this verb in Amm. (cf. ad 15.1.1 = III p.5), it seems likely that here it is an archaism.
b **muneratos.** Cf. ad 14.7.4 (= II p.19).

VIII, 4
dictoque citius - suscepit. A sample of immoral conduct, which was, how- p. 120. 1-5
ever, considered quite permissible towards barbarians like the Germans. Very revealing for this way of thinking 28.5.2 sq.; 31.16.8. The conduct of the Romans can often be compared with the extermination policy of the whites towards the American Indians, though unfortunately (for the Romans, that is!) with less success.

dictoque citius. Cf.Verg.Aen.1.142: p. 120. 1
Sic ait, et **dicto citius** tumida aequora placat; Liv.23.47.6; Horat.Sat.2.2. 80; Petron.131.5; Hom.Il.19.242; etc.

a **Severo duce misso per ripam.** For Severus cf. ad 16.10.21, p.88.7b; p. 120. 2
ad 16.2.8, p.73.16b **(Marcellus).**
b **per ripam.** In view of the dwelling-places of the **Salii** the **Meuse** must have been intended here.

Cunctos. Cf. ad 17.3.6, p.109.2. p. 120. 2

a **tamquam fulminis turbo perculsit.** For **tamquam** cf. ad 17.8.3, p.119. p. 120. 3

25-26c. Though we are struck by the repetition of the same word after a few lines, this happens quite often with Amm., e.g. in this same cap.8 § 2: **repperit** and § 3 **repperiri**.

b Sabbah: "un tourbillon foudroyant". Seyf.: "die er wie ein Donnerwetter überraschte". **Turbo** also used of persons Cic. pro domo: 53 (137); Oros.3.7.5, with the meaning: tornado. Here too, this meaning seems to fit. Compare, however, Verg.Aen.12.531 c.annot.Forbig: "turbine, i.q. iactu, adiuncta tamen rotationis notione"; and Stat.Theb.2.565.

c **perculsit**. This same perf. form also 25.8.13. Veget.r.m. does not have this typical military term.

p. 120. 4 *a* **in oportunam clementiae partem effectu victoriae flexo** = prospero effectu (27.2.4) victoriae flexus est (reflex.) in clementiam, quae pars oportunior erat, quae pars tunc videbatur oportunior esse (sc. quam hostem delere plene). For **effectus** cf. ad 14.3.4 (= I p.81); 18.2.7; 19.11.2; 27.2.4. The words explained here are far from clear and hardly logical.

b **flexo**. The part. gives the main point. Cf. ad 17.3.5, p.108.20*a*. The same is true of **adgressus**. The two perfecta **perculsit** and **suscepit** carry less weight than the afore-mentioned participia.

p. 120. 5 *a* **suscepit**. Also a military term: **to take under one's protection**, to admit, said of those who have subjected themselves. Thus it is more than: to accept the subjection of (Sabbah, Seyf.). Cf.Veget.r.m.3.26 (= Lang p. 121): In sollicitandis **suscipiendisque hostibus,** si cum fide veniant, magna fiducia est, quia adversarium amplius frangunt **transfugae** quam perempti.

b Cf.Zos.3.8.1 (= Mendelss.p.121): Ταῦτα οὕτως διαθεὶς ὁ καῖσαρ Σαλίους τε καὶ Κουάδων μοῖραν καὶ τῶν ἐν τῇ Βαταουίᾳ νήσῳ τινὰς τάγμασιν ἐγκατέλεξεν, ἃ καὶ νῦν ἐφ' ἡμῶν ἔτι δοκεῖ περισώζεσθαι Cf.et. Bidez, La vie etc. (op.cit.I) VI p.156 sq. (with lit. p.381 sq.); L. **Schmidt**, Aus den Anfängen des salfränkischen Königtums, Klio 16, 1941, p.306-327 (quoted by Seyf.).

VIII, 5

p. 120. 5 **Chamavos**. Originally the **Ch.** lived in the Eastern part of the Dutch province of Gelderland and the adjoining German territory. Later they conquered part of the land of the **Bructeri** (between the rivers IJssel and Lippe). In the 4th century they made an attempt to invade the Roman empire, but were resisted by Constantine the Great. Under Julianus they drove the **Salii** (cf. ad 17.8.3, p.119.21*b*) from the Betuwe (province of

Gelderland). The Medieval district of **Hamaland** was named after them. Although often mentioned together with the Franks, the **Chamavi** are not Franks. In the N.D. the **cohors undecima Chamavorum,** Peamu(?) is mentioned (sub disp.v.spect. ducis Thebaidos) (Seeck p.65); and probably Laterc.Veron.13 (= Seeck p.251): **Camari** (Muellenh.: **Chamavi**) also mentioned. The Ch. live outside the borders of the Roman empire. Cf.et. Woordenboek der Oudheid 3 (1967a) p.625 (Stolte); Schönfeld (op.cit.I) p.125 (with lit.). Also mentioned Amm.17.9.2.

itidem. Cf. ad 16.12.17, p.93.23-24*b*. Besides **similia** the adverbium is abundant here.   p. 120. 5

similia = eadem. Amm. uses **similia** particularly in the connection: **haec et similia** (cf. ad 14.1.8 = I p.63; ad 15.3.2 = III p.30), but then with its normal meaning, For the first-mentioned meaning cf.Opt.Milev.6.1 (= Ziwsa p.144): et tamen cum omnium vestrum una sit coniuratio, in hoc titulo **simili** (= eodem) **errore** dissimiliter deliquistis; ibid.3.7 (= Ziwsa p.89): ergo videtis a Moyse et Phinee et Helia et Macario **similia** (= eadem) esse facta, quia ab omnibus unius dei praecepta sunt vindicata; and thus more often. Cf.et.Inst.2.13.5: lege antiqua XII tabularum omnes (masculos et feminas sc.) **similiter** (= eodem modo) ad successiones ab intestato vocabantur ... ideo simplex ac **simile** (= idem) ius et in filiis et in filiabus. ...; ad 14.6.26 (= I p.101).   p. 120. 5

adortus, varying with **adgressus,** (§ 4), previously, and without difference in meaning.   p. 120. 5

partim ... partim ... alios. Cf. ad 14.1.4 (= I p.59); ad 16.11.8, p.89.15-17; ad 15.9.7 (= IV p.51); Krebs Antib.2 p.247 (with lit.); Hofm.-Leum.236 p.664.   p. 120. 5-7

conpegit in vincula. Cf.26.7.4: in vincula conpinguntur; 28.1.8: ut ... conpingerentur in vincula; 26.10.5: in custodiam conpegerunt. Our expression: to put in irons, throw into jail. These meanings not very frequent. Cf.Cic. de orat.1.11 (46): (oratores) excludi ab omni doctrina rerumque maiorum scientia ac tantum in iudicia et contiunculas tamquam in aliquod pistrinum **detrudi et compingi** videbam (both verbs are forceful expressions; cf.edit. Courbaud, 1905, p.47 ad h.l.); Hirt.b.G.8. 5.2: Caesar ... in oppido Carnutum Cenabo castra ponit atque in tecta partim Gallorum partim quae coniectis celeriter stramentis tentoriorum   p. 120. 7

229

integendorum gratia erant inaedificata, **milites conpegit** (= packed together, crowded closely together); Plaut.Amph.155:

quid faciam nunc si tresviri me **in carcerem compegerint?**

ibid. Menaech.942:

et ob eam rem **in carcerem** ted **esse compactum** scio.

ibid.Rud.1146 sq.:

tum tibi hercle deos iratos esse oportet, quisquis es,

quae parentes tam **in angustum** tuos **locum compegeris.**

Cic. ad Att.8.8: urbem reliquerat, Picenum amiserat culpa, **in Apuliam se compegerat** (= ± hid himself), ibat in Graeciam etc.; Pomp.com.; Fronto. The verb does not occur in Claud.Veget.r.m.Opt.Milev. With a different meaning in Arn.adv.nat.7.33: obscenas **compingere cantiones.** Archaism or vulgarism?

p. 120. 7 *a* **alios praecipiti fuga repedantes ad sua.** Cf.Caes.b.G.2.24: **praecipites fugae** sese mandabant; Curt.Ruf.5.13.2: ibi transfugae nuntiant **praecipitem fuga** Bactra petere Darium; Stat.Theb.2.194: **praecipiti** convulsa **noto** (c.comm. Mulder ad h.l.p.148). The adj. occurs, among others, in Amm.26.7.11: et electi quidam **stoliditate praecipites** (= ± with much daring for lack of brains) ad capessendum Illyricum missi sunt; 29.1.21: inde factum est, ut clementiae specie penatibus multi protruderentur insontes **praeceps in exilium acti** (= head over heels); 14.1.8: quae abrupte mariti fortunas trudebat **in exitium praeceps.**

b **repedantes.** Cf. ad 17.2.4, p.108.4. **trepidantes** VEAG; Conj.Bentl.Cl.; Sabbah Seyf. also have **trepidantes**. Probably **Hagend.** Strena phil.f. P. Persson p.77 is right to defend **trepidantes,** a version also given by previous editors.

c **Sua.** Cf. ad 17.1.2, p.104.7-9*d*. 17.2.4 almost the same words: repedavit ad sua. This repetition of the same "**formulas**", seemingly in conflict with the **variation** is often seen in Amm. Cf.et. ad 17.4.1, p.109.6*b*.

p. 120. 8 *a* **spatio longo** = ± longo itinere. Cf.Caes.b.c.1.78: Tarraco aberat longius; **quo spatio** plures rem posse casus recipere (= admittere) intellegebant (= on the long way there (thither)); b.g.4.10: Rhenus autem oritur ex Lepontiis ... et **longo spatio** per fines Nemetum ... citatus fertur (= longo cursu); b.g.4.35: Quos **tanto spatio** (= tam longo itinere) secuti equites, quantum cursu et viribus efficere potuerunt (cf.comm. Meusel ad h.l., 1920, p.342, note 3); Nep.Eum.9: **Dimidium** fere **spatium** (= iter) confecerat, cum ... suspicio allata est ad Eumenem hostem appropinquare; Verg.Aen.10.219; **medio in spatio** (= itinere); Veget.

r.m.3.11 (= Lang p.94): Observatur autem, ne **longo spatio fatigatum** militem neve lassos post cursum equos ad publicum proelium cogas; multum virium **labore itineris** pugnaturus amittit (The only place in Veget.r.m. with **this** meaning); etc. This and other places give the impression that **spatium** often is the equivalent of **iter,** particularly in the soldiers language.

b The **plur.** occurs several times in connection with **amplus.** Cf.31.4.8: **spatia ampla camporum;** 17.13.22: spatia ampla camporum; 31.3.3: camporum ampla spatia; 17.12.3: spatia amplissima; 22.8.12: amplissima spatia; 14.6.16: ampla spatia; 14.7.16: ampla spatia; 24.3.12: spatia ampla; 27.2.5: spatiis amplioribus; 25.2.6 **amplitudine spatiorum;** Blomgren (op.cit.II) p.170 sq. Another example of formula-like expressions (cf. ad 17.4.1, p.109.6*b*).

defatigaret. The verb chosen metri causa: claus.I. Cf.Caes.b.g.5.16.4: p. 120. 8 accedebat huc ut ... alios alii deinceps exciperent, **integrique et recentes defatigatis** succederent; (7.25.1: ... semperque ipsi **recentes defessis** succederent); 1.40.8: diuturnitate belli **defatigatis** Gallis; Caes.b.c.3.85.2: et insolitum ad laborem Pompei exercitum cotidianis **itineribus defatigaret;** Curt.Ruf.9.2.11: militem, **labore defatigatum,** proximum quemque fructum, finito tandem periculo, expetere; ibid.8.4.6: multique, prius metu quam **labore defatigati,** prostraverant humi corpora; ibid.4.16.16: gravesque armis, et **proelio ac fuga defatigati,** gurgitibus hauriebantur; etc. The verb, and especially the part.perf.pass., seem to be part of the language of soldiers or military authors. Not in Claud.**Veget.r.m.** Opt. Milev.Arn.adv.nat.

a **abire interim permisit innocuos.** For the construction of the **verba per-** p. 120. 8 **mittendi** cf. ad 14.1.3 (= I p.58). Cf.et. ad 17.4.13, p.115.5; ad 17.1.2, p.105.1*d*.

b For the variatio cf. ad 15.5.14 **(abiit innoxius)** = III p.91.

c **innocuus.** Cf.25.6.13; 29.1.36. With pass. meaning. Cf. Krebs Antib.1 p.747 (with lit.); ad 14.1.2: **insons** (= I p.57); ad 16.2.6, p.73.9*c*.

d **interim** = provisionally. This meaning probably only post-class, and late Latin. Cf. Krebs Antib.I p.771 (with lit.); Souter p.215; Heum.-Seckel p.281; ad 17.4.11, p.110.14-15*a*.

precatum consultumque. For the **supinum** cf. ad 14.6.12 (= I p.95); ad p. 120. 9 14.11.4 (= II p.117); ad 14.6.23 (= I p.100).

p. 120. 9 *a* **humi prostratis.** For the **locat.** cf. ad 17.4.13, p.111.4. For the **ablat. loci** cf. ad 14.2.12 (= I p.74); Liesenb. (1890) p.3 (op.cit.I); ad 14.11.21 (= II p.137). **Humi** not in Claud.Veget.r.m.Arn.adv.nat.Opt.Milev.
b Cf.Curt.Ruf.8.2.5: Ille humi prostraverat corpus; ibid.8.5.12: semet ipsum ... prostraturum humi corpus; ibid.8.5.6: prosternentes humi corpora; ibid.8.4.6: prostraverant humi corpora; ibid.4.10.21: ut prostratam humi vidit; Liv.25.37.9: strati humi; ibid.9.20.2: legati ... humi strati; ibid.9.6.4: corpora humi prostraverunt; 38.21.11: prosternunt corpora humi; 45.20.9: prostraverunt se omnes humi; etc. A flower of speech which was probably known to Amm. from his reading.

p. 120. 10 *a* **sub obtutibus eius.** Cf. ad 17.7.2, p.116.21-22*a*. Cf.Prud.Hymn.II (Laurent.) 277 sq.:
Tunc, si facultas subpetat
Coram tuis obtutibus
Istos potentes saeculi
Velim recensendos dari.
b **sub.** Cf.16.12.18; 18.3.6; 21.6.2; 30.4.15.

p. 120. 10 **pacem hoc tribuit pacto.** Cf.14.4.4: uxoresque mercennariae conductae ad tempus **ex pacto;** 16.12.26: armatorumque milia ... partim mercede, partim **pacto** vicissitudinis reddendae quaesita. With the usual meaning = condition, treaty = lex, condicio. With **this** meaning not in Veget.r.m., though once **quo pacto** = in which way (IV.13 = Lang p.137).

p. 120. 10-11 **ut ad sua redirent incolumes.** Note the **variatio** with p.120.8. For **sua** cf. ad 17.8.5, p.120.7*c*.

IX, 1
p. 120. 12 **cunctis igitur ex voto currentibus.** Note the alliterating c. For **cunctus** cf. ad 17.3.6, p.109.2. For **ex voto** cf. ad 14.10.3 (= II p.100): **ex usu;** ad 15.1.2 (= III p.8): **ex more;** ad 15.5.4 (= III p.72): **ex re(publica);** Reinhardt (op.cit.I) p.58 sq. Did Amm. have in mind Tac.Hist.3.48: Laetum ea victoria Vespasianum, **cunctis super vota fluentibus,** Cremonensis proelii nuntius in Aegypto adsequitur? **(J.W. Meyer,** in his excellent Dutch translation, compares: "everything goes on swimmingly"). Cf.et. Krebs Antib.2 p.754 sq. (does not discuss: **ex voto).** with lit.

p. 120. 12 **studio pervigili.** Similarly: 18.2.10; 22.15.22. Cf. ad 14.8.13 (= II p.80).

a **utilitatem fundare provinciarum.** Sabbah: **d'assurer les avantages ob-** p. 120. 13
tenus par les provinces; Seyf.: das Wohl der Provinzen fest zu begründen;
Rolfe: to put the well-being of the provinces in every way on a firm
footing. I do not understand this translation by Sabbah. For the meaning
of **utilis** and **utilitas** cf. Anon.Val.12.61: Dixit ... item: Romanus **miser**
imitatur Gothum et **utilis** Gothus imitatur Romanum (= dives); Greg.
Tur.4.3; Legal authors: especially **utilitas publica** = general welfare, the
common good (e.g. in Heum.-Seckel p.610); Bened.Reg.7 (Linderb.28):
Nam ut sollicitus sit circa cogitationes suas perversas, dicat semper
utilis (= bonus) **frater** in corde suo "Tunc ero immaculatus coram eo,
si observavero me ab **iniquitate** mea"; ibid. **inutilis** 48 (= Linderb.56 sq.):
et videant ne forte inveniatur frater acediosus (= listless), qui vacat otio
aut fabulis et non est intentus lectioni et non solum sibi **inutilis** est, sed
etiam alios distollit (= distract the attention of) = worthless, bad, In
my opinion the translations by Seyf. and Rolfe are correct.
b Cf.15.5.25: namque convena undique multitudine trepide **coepta
fundante** (c.comm. ad h.l. = III p.109)..

a **munimenta ... Mosae.** It is difficult to say which forts are meant here; p. 120. 13-14
but the words: **subversa dudum obstinatione barbarica** remind one of the
two forts mentioned in 17.2.2 (cf. ad 17.2.1, p.107.11*d*). Unfortunately
there is a gap in 17.2.2 (Clark p.107.18-19), which it is very important
for the localisation to fill up (cf. ad 17.2.2, p.107.18-19*a*). Cf.et. **C.Jullian**
(op.cit.II) 7, p.200, note 3; **J.Vannerus,** Le limes et les fortifications gallo-
romaines de Belgique, enquête toponymique, 1943, Mém. de l'Ac.Royale
de Belgique, 2e série, tome 11, fasc.2), p.241, note 2. (both works quoted
by Sabbah).
b **munimenta.** Cf. ad 16.12.58, p.101.6-7*d*.
c **recta serie.** Series is a continuing, unbroken row. Thus used e.g.
17.5.5 (For a different meaning cf. ad 16.12.26, p.95.13*b*).
Recta has to mean: in a straight line (hard to find in non-canalized
rivers). But perhaps this straight line can best be found on the stretch of
the **Meuse from Maastricht to Liège.** For the localisation this adj. **recta**
should not be neglected. Unless we assume that **recta** has been written
down rather thoughtlessly by Amm., which does not seem very likely
to me. It will probably have been in his sources.
d **superciliis.** Almost homonymous 14.10.6: supercilia fluminis Rheni.
Cf.et.14.8.5: supercilia ... Nili; etc. Cf. ad 14.2.9 (= I p.71); ad 16.12.19,
p.94.9. For a different meaning cf. ad 16.12.4, p.91.19-20*d*.

p. 120. 14 *a* **subversa dudum obstinatione barbarica.** Cf.16.2.2, p.107.21-22: **destinatis** barbarorum animis incredibili **pertinacia** reluctantibus. Barbarians are by nature: obstinate, stubborn, rebellious, etc., in Roman eyes, of course. Cf.et.16.11.11: conversus hinc Iulianus ad **reparandas** Tres Tabernas (**munimentum** ita cognominatum) **haut ita dudum obstinatione subversum hostili** (The underlined words also in 17.9.1). With its real meaning **obstinatio** e.g. 15.6.4. (personificatio); 19.2.10; 16.12.48. Comparable the following utterances of Amm. about the barbarians: 16.12.2: barbara feritate certaminum **rabiem** undique concitante; 16.12.3: fastus barbaricos; 16.12.31: hi sunt barbari quos **rabies** et inmodicus furor ... coegit; 16.12.44: sed violentia iraque inconpositi barbari; 16.12.61: utque nativo more sunt barbari humiles in adversis, disparesque in secundis. And, as has been noted before, the **Germans** are pre-eminently barbarians.

b **dudum** = iam dudum, iam pridem. Cf. ad 16.12.58, p.101.7; Krebs Antib.I p.479. In Veget.r.m. **probably** used as here praef.2 (= Lang p.34). He also has **iam dudum** 4.31 (= Lang p.150), and once **dudum** with its usual meaning, viz.1.17 (= Lang p.20).

p. 120. 15 **pro tempore.** Cf.15.5.25: coactisque copiis multis **pro statu rei praesentis** id aptius videbatur ut; ad 14.11.4 (= II p.118); Reinhardt (op.cit.I) p.60.

p. 120. 15 *a* **et ilico sunt instaurata. Ilico** does not occur in Claud.Veget.r.m.Arn. adv.nat. In Opt.Milev.1.21 (= Ziwsa p.24). Cf. Krebs Antib.I p.681 (with lit.); W.Kalb Jur.lat.p.80; Bourciez (op.cit.II) p.120, 122*b*.

b **instaurata.** Cf.29.6.19: (praef. urbi Claudius): et **instauravit** vetera plurima = reficere, renovare = to restore. Late Latin. Cf.Paneg.lat.4 (Eumen.) 3 (= Baehrens p.118): ut ... iuxta cetera quae **instaurantur** opera ac templa **reparentur** (both verbs are synonymous); Krebs Antib.1 p.757. In **this** meaning **instauratio** also late Latin; e.g. Veget.r.m.3.25 (= Lang p.120): Sed quocumque eventu colligendi sunt superstites ... et **armorum instauratione** refovendi; Paneg.lat.4.4 (= Baehrens p.119): huius quoque **operis instauratione;** Paneg.lat.5.21 (= Baehrens p.148): devotissima vobis civitas Aeduorum ... nunc exstructione veterum domorum et **refectione** operum publicorum et templorum **instauratione** consurgit (both subst. synonymous). The verb does not occur with **this** meaning in Claud.Veget.r.m.Arn.adv.nat.Opt.Milev. Cf.et. Souter p.211; Heum.-Seckel p.273 sq.

p. 120. 15-16 **procinctu.** Cf. ad 16.11.6, p.89.7.

IX, 2

consilium prudens. cf. ad 17.8.2, p.119.16. The expression also in Cic. ad Att.9.7. A § 1; 10.8.2. Cf.et.b.Alex.24.7: superl. p. 120. 16

a **ex annona decem dierum et septem, quam ⟨in⟩ expeditionem pergens vehebat cervicibus miles.** The number of 17 days is not in agreement with the 20 days in 17.8.2. **For it is not a new expedition which is described here.** Furthermore 20 days was the normal period (cf. ad 17.8.2, p.119. 16-18*b*). It is possible that **after** the events of 17.8.3-5 the soldiers received additional rations. But this is not mentioned anywhere. Moreover, it appears from 17.9.2-3 that the estimated store of grain was by no means reassuring. The scene of battle is not too far from Paris. The victories are quickly accomplished (17.8.4-5). Thus there is no need to assume a long period of time. I believe the solution to the dilemma to be as follows: the rations which the soldiers carry on their backs, are part of the grain **quod erat in sedibus consumendum.** The relation between the two parts is not known, but probably the portion of 20 days should at least be one half. Probably the soldiers did not at first, out of self-preservation, use up their own rations, but lived instead from what was in store. This explains 17.9.2: **portionem subtractam in isdem condidit castris.** But when the march **goes on,** the system breaks down. There are not enough reserves and the soldiers have used up the larger part of their own. For Iulianus believed that he could complement the **portio subtracta** with grain **ex Chamavorum segetibus,** and the soldiers have relied on this. This policy of the commander has, therefore been very reckless. For 1⁰ the stores in Gallia have not been sufficiently or not at all assessed and 2⁰ the expectations of the crops did not have a solid foundation. The cause: the desire of Iulianus to achieve quick successes against the Germans and consolidate the borders. With this in mind, caution has been thrown to the winds. p. 120. 17-18

The soldiers are rightly angry, for of the rations that they took with them, **(i.e. what is left of them, 17.9.2)** one portion has been taken off for reserves in the **3 munimenta** (17.9.1). The number 17 is either an error in Amm.'s source(s) or his own mistake, caused by the fact that of the **original** portion of 20 days, a portion of 3 days per man, was taken away. Though one should bear in mind that no soldier any longer had a ration for (20 or) 17 days, **expensis quae portabat, nusquam repperiens victus.** (Cf. et.Hist.Aug.Sev.Alex.47.1: Milites expeditionis tempore sic disposuit, **ut in mansionibus annonas acciperent nec portarent cibaria decem et septem, ut solent, dierum nisi in barbarico** etc.). Cf.et. C. von Clausewitz, Vom Kriege, edit. W. von Scherff, 1880, p.272 sq.

235

b 1. ⟨in⟩expeditionem pergens. These words obviously refer back to 17.8.2.

2. ⟨In⟩expeditionem Cl.Seyf.Rolfe Em2.G.A ad. Not in V. Sabbah follows V's version, and rightly so, in my opinion. In the first place there are enough examples in earlier Latin, especially with composita; but in Apul. Amm., etc. one should always be alert to a literary, "archaically" coloured use, or to a Grecism. Cf.Hofm.-Leum.p.386,20 (with examples); Curt. Ruf.ed. Dosson-Pichon Rem.87, 204; Stat.Theb.I comm.Heuvel p.157.

c cervicibus. Variatio of 17.8.2: umeris. Cf.et.17.1.13.

p. 120. 18 *a* portionem = partem, as often. Cf. Krebs Antib.2 p.326 sq.

in isdem castris = in isdem munimentis (17.9.1). For castra cf. Grosse Mil. (op.cit.I) p.66 sq. Cf.et.23.3.7: et paulisper detentus, ut omen per hostias litando firmaret, Dauanam venit castra praesidiaria, unde ortus Belias fluvius funditur ⟨in⟩Eufraten; 25.9.12 Proinde extractis civibus et urbe tradita missoque tribuno Constantio, qui munimenta praesidiaria cum regionibus Persicis optimatibus assignaret ... (The underlined substant. synonymous); ad 16.12.3, p.91.16-17*b*.

b for isdem cf. ad 15.5.19 (= III p.103).

IX, 3

p. 120. 20 longe autem aliter accidit. Cf. ad 15.6.1 (= IV p.6).

p. 120. 20 nondum etiam maturis. Cf. ad 17.1.13, p.106.22*a*. Pleonasm. Hagend. abund.p.209; Oder Mulomed.Chir.p.310 sq.

p. 120. 21 victus. Cf.14.2.12; 14.4.3; 14.4.6.

p. 120. 21 extrema minitans. Cf.27.10.5: ultima minitantium; 25.9.5: mortem ... minitantibus. For the construction cf. Krebs Antib.2 p.86.

p. 120. 22 *a* Iulianum conpellationibus incessebat et probris. In the eyes of the soldiers Iulianus had apparently all of a sudden become an unreliable "Easterner", a glib-talking "Greek". But I believe one should also read the true description of his character by Bidez: La vie de l'Emp.Jul.p.350 (Conclusion). But Julianus had the disadvantage of his outward conduct, his uncontrolled behaviour which was not in agreement with the image of an emperor in the late Latin and Byzantine era. He was a truly unconventional type.

b Cf.23.2.4: nondum ira, quam ex **compellationibus et probris** conceperat, emollita.

Asianum. Here curiously used. For the term does not refer to the oratorical art of Julianus, but to his entire personality, which is also expressed in his way of talking. Cf. Quint.inst.or.12.10.17: p. 120. 22
Asiana gens tumidior alioqui atque iactantior, vaniore etiam dicendi gloria inflata est; **Norden** Ant.Kunstpr. (op.cit.I) I p.251 sq.; A. Gudeman Tac.Dial.[2] (1914) p.69, 313, 394.

Graeculum. Cf.Tac.Dial.3: etiam si non novum tibi ipse negotium importasses, ⟨ut⟩ Domitium et Catonem, id est nostras quoque historias et Romana nomina, **Graeculorum fabulis** adgregares (c.comm. Gudeman p.203); Cic. de or.1.11 (47): Verbi enim controversia iam diu torquet **Graeculos homines,** contentionis cupidiores quam veritatis; ibid.1.22 (102): Quid? mihi vos nunc, inquit Crassus, tamquam **alicui Graeculo otioso et loquaci** et fortasse docto atque erudito quaestiunculam, de qua meo arbitratu loquar, ponitis?; etc. **Graeculus** is used with the same sort of disdain as **Asianus.** p. 120. 22-23

specie sapientiae stolidum. Note the **alliteration**(s). Cf. ad 15.2.4 (= III p.17); Blomgren (op.cit.II) p.130; Petschenig Philol.56 p.556 sq. p. 120. 23

utque. Cf. ad 17.8.3, p.119.27-p.120.1*a*. p. 120. 23

quidam. Cf. ad 17.3.6, p.109.1-2*b*. = **nonnulli.** p. 120. 24

armatos = milites. In the same way **Veget.r.m.** uses **armati:** 4.18 (= Lang p.140.10); 4.19 (= Lang p.141.15); 2.1 (= Lang p.35.13); 2.1 (= Lang p.35.11); 2.6 (= Lang p.40.13); 3.3 (= Lang p.70.2); 3.6 (= Lang p.77.8); 3.21 (= Lang p.111.7); etc . p. 120. 24

a **verborum volubilitate conspicui.** Note the alliterating consonants **v** and **b**. In these 3 words one can hear the gentlemen talking rapidly. p. 120. 24
b **volubilitate.** Cf.25.9.3: tum Sabinus fortuna et genere inter municipes clarus **ore volubili** replicabat etc. Adj. also class. Adverbium 20.11.26: (about the rainbow) halitus terrae calidiores et umoris spiramina ... **supinantur volubiliter** contra ipsum igneum orbem irimque conformant.

Late Latin. The subst. is also class. Cf.Cic.Planc.25(62): Virtus, probitas, integritas in candidato, non **linguae volubilitas,** non ars, non scientia requiri solet; De orat.1.5(17): Est enim et scientia comprehendenda rerum plurimarum, sine qua **verborum volubilitas** inanis atque irridenda est (sc. eloquentia), c.comm.edit. E.Courbaud (1905) p.19, notes 5 and 6. The subst. does not occur in Claud.Veget.r.m.Arn.adv.nat.Opt.Milev.
c **conspicui.** Cf. ad 16.12.24, p.95.5-6.

p. 120. 24-25 **haec et similia.** Cf. ad 17.8.5, p.120.5.

p. 120. 25 **strepebant.** Cf.31.16.6 (accusat.adverb.): subraucum et lugubre strepens; de cothurno strepere tragico; ad 17.11.1, p.123.18.

IX, 4
p. 120. 25 **meliorum.** Cf. ad 17.3.2, p.108.12*a;* ad 17.4.1, p.109.4*a.*

p. 120. 26 **perpessu asperrima.** Cf.Cic.Tusc.2.8 (20):
O multa dictu gravia, **perpessu aspera**
Quae corpore exanclata atque animo pertuli! (Fletcher).
For the **supinum II** cf. ad 14.11.4 (= II p.117); for the **supinum I** cf. ad 14.6.12 (= I p.95); ad 14.6.23 (= I p.100).

p. 120. 26-27 *a* **per nives tolerantes et acumina crudelium pruinarum.** For the **plut.poet.** cf. ad 17.2.1, p.107.14-15*b.* For **pruinae** cf. ad 17.8.1, p.119.11-13*f.* **Acum.crud.pruin.** = acrium cr.pr. = biting cruel frost (cf. Blomgren, op.cit.II, p.171). For **acumina** cf. ad 17.8.5, p.117.8-9*c;* ad 16.12.54, p.100.11*a.*
b **per.** here temporally used. Examples cf. Reinhardt (op.cit.I) p.31 sq.

p. 120. 27 **pro nefas! Nefas** as a parenthetic exclamation also in Verg.Horat.Cat., and others. For **pro** cf. Krebs Antib.2 p.385 (with lit.). In Claud.3,55 (= In Rufin.I) **pro dolor.** Similarly in Opt.Milev.7.4 (= Ziwsa p.175). This expression is late Latin with the meaning of: ah! alas!. Undoubtedly Amm. uses here a very literary flower of speech. Cf.et.Stat.Theb.I Heuvel p.90; eiusd.II Mulder p.88 (with lit.). Fairly frequent in Statius, Cf. ad 16.12.70, p.103.9.

p. 120. 27 **cum ultimis hostium fatis instamus.** Cf.Sil.It.1.266 sq.:
Et quoties campo rapidus fera proelia miscet
Qua sparsit ferrum, latus rubet aequore limes.

> Ergo instat fatis et rumpere foedera certus,
> Quo datur, interea Romam comprendere bello
> Gaudet ....

(quotation of Fletcher).

ignavissimo: a term full of contempt in the mouths of soldiers. Cf. ad 17.6.2, p.116.8. p. 120. 28

tabescentes. Cf.25.8.15: adeo enim atroci **tabuimus** fame ...; 14.3.4: suorum indicio proditus, qui admissi flagitii metu exagitati ad praesidia descivere Romana, absque ullo egressus effectu deinde **tabescebat immobilis.** p. 120. 28

IX, 5

nequi. Cf. ad 17.7.5, p.117.7. p. 120. 28
turbarum: mutiny, rebellion. With **this** meaning not in Veget.r.m. Cf.et. **turbamentum**: 25.7.12; 26.7.8, with somewhat the same meaning.

concitores. Cf.14.10.5: Eusebius praepositus cubiculi missus est Cabyllona aurum secum perferens, quo per **turbulentos seditionum concitores** occultius distributo etc. Not in Veget.r.m. Post-class.subst. In Iust.Phil.2.9. 21; 5.1.1, linked with **bellum.** p. 120. 29

pro vita loqui sola testamur. Hyperbaton. Cf. ad 17.1.6, p.105.21*a*. p. 120. 29

contrectare. Cf. ad 17.4.12, p.110.24. p. 121. 1

a **nobis ... confutatis** = velut si ... confutati essemus. The sentence structure is highly artificial: quae ... **nobis negata, velut ... confutatis.** For **confutare** cf. ad 14.9.6 (= I p.91); 19.12.12: Demetrius ... philosophus ... **sacrificasse aliquotiens confutatus;** 26.3.1: ut veneficos ... captos postque agitatas quaestiones **nocuisse quibusdam apertissime confutatos;** 29.5.43: et quosdam alios per secretiora consilia **temeratorem quietis iuvisse confutatos aperte** flammis absumpsit .... The verb not in Claud. Veget.r.m.Opt.Milev.Arn.adv.nat. p. 121. 1-3
b The partic. construct. indicated above metri causa: Claus.III.

IX, 6

querellarum. Cf.20.4.11: quo textu ad comitatum perlato lectoque Iulianus contemplans **rationabiles** (= justified = ± iustas) **querellas** ...; 30. p. 121. 3

9.1: ad **querellas** in eos (sc. duces potiores) motas aliquotiens obsurdescens (= complaints, objections, criticism). Hence the expression: **sine querella** = blameless, irreproachable. (cf. Souter p.338), not in Amm.

p. 121. 3-4   *a*   **inter tot enim rerum probabilium cursus.** For **temporal inter** cf. ad 17. 4.1, p.109.4*a*.
b   **probabilium** = **laudabilium**, as seen more often, also class. Latin. The adj. does not seem at this time to be so general any more. Not in Claud. Veget.r.m.Arn.adv.nat.Opt.Milev.
c   **cursus.** Cf.14.6.17; 16.1.4: **bellorum gloriosis cursibus** Traiani simillimus; 16.12.36.
Cursus publicus (= government post): 20.8.22; 21.9.4. Cf.et. ad 16.2.6, p.73.6-7; ad 16.12.37, p. 97.9.

p. 121. 4   **articulosque necessitatum ancipites.** For **articulus** cf. ad 16.12.37, p.97.6*c*. For **necessitates** cf.19.11.17: Constantius Sirmium redit ... et maturatis quae **necessitates temporis** poscebant **instantes** (= what the circumstances of that time made urgently necessary). The above expression is somewhat pleonastic, though (cf. ad 17.1.13, p.106.22*a*). For **articulus** is a decisive, critical, dangerous period of time. But **anceps** also means: critical, dangerous. And **necessitatum** is almost a genit. identitatis (cf. ad 17.4.8, p.110,6*a*). Translation: and during critical periods which were precarious and full of distress.

p. 121. 4-5   **sudoribus Gallicanis miles exhaustus.** Cf.14.2.14: (Seleucia) quam comes tuebatur Castricius tresque legiones **bellicis sudoribus** induratae. Cf.et. ad 17.2.1, p.107.10*a*. For **Gallicanus** cf. ad 17.8.1, p.119.11*b*.
exhaustus. Cf. ad 17.4.5, p.109.18.

p. 121. 5   **nec donativum meruit nec stipendium.** A **donativum**, given to the soldiers by Silvanus in Constantius' name, must be meant 15.6.3: **donatum stipendio** militem Constantii nomine allocutus est (for **personal** gifts to soldiers e.g. **coronae**, cf. Müller Milit. (op.cit.I) p.620 sq.). According to Seeck Unterg. (op.cit.I) II p.254, 539, the soldiers would in the 4th century no longer receive regular pay, but instead a kind of pay in natura, alternated with gifts of **donativa**. I agree with Müller that this idea can not be correct. Because of all sorts of circumstances, the **stipendium** was paid rather irregularly, but an army which would be satisfied with just being provided with food, clothing, etc., with now and then a **donativum**, seems highly unlikely to me in those days. This view does not tally either with

Amm.'s words. Cf.20.8.8; 22.9.2; 29.5.37; 31.11.1; 28.6.12; 28.6.17. **(stipendium)**. Cf.et. Müller ibid.p.622 sq.; Grosse Mil. (op.cit.I) p.243 sq., 312 (with lit). The **donativa** tend to become fixed parts of the soldiers' pay and then are no longer voluntarily given. They remain in use until the 6th century A.D. (cf. **Fiebiger**, s.v.R.E.5.2.1542 sq.). But part of the pay certainly consisted of **annona**, which agreed with the "Naturalwirtschaft" of the late Antique economy. Though later this was replaced, first partly and later entirely by the **adaeratio** (cf.R.E. I 340 sq.s.v., Seeck), i.e. payment in cash. This begins already in the 4th century. Thus in 445 A.D. the **annona** was fixed at 4 **solidi**. Besides the **annona** there was the **capitum** for pack- and riding animals, which like the **annona,** was fixed annually. That officers, etc. received larger allocations of **annona** and **capitum,** goes without saying.

Summarising, one can say that the soldiers' pay was made up of the following parts: **annona** (this also included clothing and fuel), **donativa, stipendium,** and when necessary, **capitum** (cf. Seeck s.v.R.E. III.2.1543 sq.). Because of the importance of the **donativa** (always paid out in cash) during various periods of time, **stipendium** sometimes seems to be equal in meaning to **donativum**. But every text should be looked at separately, while deliberate (= stylistic!) and accidental inaccuracies of the authors should also be taken into account.

iam inde ut Iulianus illo est missus. Iam ut c. coniunct. is often found in   p. 121. 5-6
the late Latin, e.g. Itin.Aether.3.6: **iam ut exiremus** de ecclesia, dederunt nobis presbyteri loci ipsius eulogias (= small presents, gifts); Hofm.-Leum. 320 p.758 (with lit.). **(Iam) inde a principio, (iam) inde ab eo tempore** are well-known combinations, though the above combination of Amm. is not known to me from other places. Cf.et. Krebs Antib.1 p.720 sq. **(inde)**. Cf.et.Apul.Met.10.9: Sic inductus signavit pecuniam, quam **exinde, ut iste repraesentatus est** iudicio, iussi ... adferre ...; ibid.1.24: "Mi Luci" ait "sat pol diu est quod intervisimus te, at hercules **exinde cum a Clytio magistro digressi sumus. ...**"; ibid.2.13: Sed vicissim tu quoque, frater, mihi memora quem ad modum **exinde ut de Euboea insula festinus enavigasti ...**"; B.J.de Jonge, Apul.Met.II comm.p.64 (with lit.).

a **erogari ... permittebat.** For the construction cf. ad 14.1.3 (= I p.58).   p. 121. 7
b **erogare** is also a t.t. For instance, in the expression: erogare annonam; **erogatio** militaris annonae (= distribution); **erogatio** per susceptores (= collectors of taxes) facta; etc. (cf.Heum.-Seckel p.174 with examples). Cf.et. Souter p.128.

p. 121. 7 **more solito.** Cf. ad 15.1.2 (= III p.8).

IX, 7

p. 121. 7-8 **hocque.** For -que cf. ad 16.12.37, p.97.6*a;* ad 16.12.17, p.93.23-24*b;* ad 16.12.25, p.95.9*a* and *b*. The construction is: exinde claruit ... hoc committi, quod ... adpetitus est ...

p. 121. 8 **exinde** = in consequence of, from which, as more often. Cf.et. ad 17.9.6, p.121.5-6.

p. 121. 8 **claruit.** Cf. ad 17.1.14, p.107.8.

tenacitas = avarice. Cf.22.3.7: cum enim Caesar in partes mitteretur occiduas **omni tenacitate stringendus.** Liv.34.7.4. Only in **this** meaning in Liv. and Amm.? Cf.et. Krebs Antib.2.651.

p. 121. 9 **idem Caesar.** For this use of **idem** cf. ad 15.5.19, p.51.16-19 (= III p.103). Cf.et.24.5.2: in **hac eadem** regione; **hocque idem** ut faciat uxor, urget maritus. (for **hocque** see above); ad 16.12.21, p.94.19-20*a*.

p. 121. 9 **petenti ex usu gregario cuidam.** For **ex usu** cf. ad 14.10.3 (= II p.100). For **gregario** cf. ad 15.1.2 (= III p.8). The adj. does not occur in Veget. r.m.Claud.Opt.Milev.Arn.adv.nat. Cf.et. Souter p.166. **Gregarii milites:** Cod.Iust.12.39.4.

p. 121. 9 *a* **ut barbas detonderet.** Cf.Apul.Met.4.31.6: adsunt Nerei filiae chorum canentes et Portunus **caerulis barbis hispidus** ...; Petr.Sat.99.5: Adhuc loquebatur, cum crepuit ostium impulsum stetitque in limine **barbis horrentibus** nauta ... = heavy beard. Both places quoted by Georges.

b Cf.Claud.18.382 sq.:

... bellorum alios transcribit in usus,
Militet ut nostris **detonsa Sicambria** signis.
(= with cut-off hair).
ibid.28.388 sq.:
... Iam flavescentia centum
Messibus **aestivae detondent** Gargara **falces.**
Sen.Ep.92.28: Sed ut **ex barba capillos detonsos** negligimus; Curt.Ruf. 10.5.17: Persae, **comis** suo more **detonsis** ...; Pers.4.38: inguinibus qua re **detonsus gurgulio** (= penis) exstat? ibid.3.54: porticus, insomnis quibus et **detonsa iuventus**//
invigilat ....

("Stoici enim barbam promittebant, sed capillos radebant" v.Wageningen); Cato de agricult.96.1.: postea cum **detonderis** (oves); Colum.7.4.7 (oves); Ovid.Fast.3.237:

Arboribus redeunt **detonsae frigore** frondes;

Prop.4.8.15: huc mea **detonsis** avecta est Cynthia **mannis** (pony); Mart. 8.52: (of a tonsor puer)

(Dum)

expingitque cutem facitque longam

detonsis epaphaeresin **capillis,**

barbatus mihi tonsor est reversus; etc.

On the basis of the last poem it might be said that **detondeo** is a **phrase used by hair-cutters** (and by **cattle-breeders,** as evidenced by the passages quoted above). But when one studies the **authors** in whose work the word occurs, one must define it as: archaic, poetic., post-class. **Here,** however, it seems to be a normal word in the soldiers' language and not a literary reminiscence.

aliquid vile: a small coin. We would very much like to know: how much? p. 121. 10 Obviously the garrison's hairdresser was not expensive. It is also characteristic that the Caesar Iulianus can be approached by a common soldier with such a "minor" request.

contumeliosis calumniis. Note the alliteration. Cf.23.2.3: sed **Antiochensi-** p. 121. 10 **bus** avaris et **contumeliosis** huiusmodi iudicem convenire. As we know, **calumnia** is a t.t.iurid.: false charges, distortion of justice, etc. Here the meaning of the word is loaded, because this infamous criticism by the notarius could have dangerous consequences for Iulianus, especially under the rule of the highly suspicious Constantius.

Gaudentio tunc notario. Cf. ad 15.3.8 (= III p.47 sq.) for Gaud. For p. 121. 10-11 **notarius** ad 14.5.6 (= I p.128). In 15.3.8 and 16.8.3 Gaud. is: **agens in rebus** (cf.III p.48). The new function is a promotion. The **notarius** is **clarissimus.**

a **ad explorandos eius actus.** These activities are often part of the duties p. 121. 11 of the **notarii;** just as they are of the **agentes in rebus.**
b Cf.14.1.8: in Gordianorum actibus; 14.4.2: in actibus principis Marci; 21.8.1: in actibus Magnenti; 22.13.3: in actibus Magnenti; 22.15.1: in actibus Hadriani et Severi principum; 22.9.6: in actibus Commodi; 25.8.5: Traianus et Severus principes ... in eorum actibus; 28.3.8: in

243

actibus Constantis; ad 14.1.8 (= I p.109). For the judic.lit. Heum.-Seckel p.10 (some meanings are comparable). Cf.et. ad 17.1.14, p.107.8.

p. 121. 11 **per Gallias.** Cf. ad 17.5.1, p.113.20-21*c*.

p. 121. 11-12 **quem ... competenti.** Cf.22.11.1.

p. 121. 12 *a* ⟨ut⟩**loco monstrabitur competenti. ut** EG Cl.Seyf.Sabbah. Although G's version is worthy of consideration, a **contaminatio** seems more probable to me here: **quem postea interfici** (eo iubente/ut ipse iusserat) loco **monstrabitur** competenti and: **qui postea interficitur** eo iubente **ut** loco **monstrabitur** competenti. Other examples of contamination in Blomgren (op.cit.II p.55,64). Sometimes one tends to rationalise a text too much.
b **Conpetens.** With this meaning (= idoneus, iustus, verus, legitimus) late Latin, among others in Paneg., Eccl., and later legal authors. Cf. Krebs Antib.I p.311; Heum.-Seckel p.83 sq. (both also deal with the **adverbium**); Souter p.65. The adv. **competenter** 31.12.2: quoniam ... cognitum est cogitare hostes ... itinera claudere, per quae commeatus necessarii portabuntur, occursum est huic conatui **competenter.** (= in a suitable manner). The adj. in Arn.adv.2.30 (= Reiffersch.p.73): causa competens; Opt.Milev.3.4 (= Ziwsa p.83): annonam conpetentem; 7.1 (= Ziwsa p.164): conpetentibus poenis; 3.4 (= Ziwsa p.84): (metatores) contra apostoli praecepta **conpetenter** suscepti non sunt; Veget.r.m.2.18 (= Lang p.52): Quidvis enim efficit sollertia, si **conpetentes** non denegentur expensae; 3.7 (= Lang p.80): acies ... intervallis **conpetentibus** separatae; 4.7 (= Lang p.132): defensionum obpugnationum ... genera, quae locis **conpetentibus** inseremus; not in Claud.

X, 1

p. 121. 13 *a* **Lenito ... vario. Blanditiae** is a dangerous way to put down a mutiny, particularly for a Caesar and future Augustus. One should read Veget. r.m.3.4 (= Lang p.72) on the way in which one should deal with **seditiosi milites**, which impresses me as being very reasonable and sensible.
b Cf.Liv.6.16.6: iamque haud procul **seditione** res erat. cuius **leniendae** causa ...; Amm.27.3.9: eaque vi territus ipse, primitiis crebriscentis **seditionis** in maius, secessit ad Mulvium pontem. ... ut **lenimenta** ibidem **tumultus** operiens, quem causa concitaverat gravis (a.l.: adlenimenta; lenimenta, without **ut**).
c For **lenitudo** (= gentleness, mildness) cf.18.10.4; 30.8.6.

a **contextoque navali ponte.** Cf.14.2.10: **contextis** cratibus; 21.12.6: cratesque ... **textas;** 23.3.9: totidemque (naves) ad **compaginandos** necessariae pontes; 25.8.2: ratibus ... **textis;** 31.5.3: ratibus ... **contextis;** 23.3. 9: naves ... ex diversa trabe **contextae** (contectae V); ad 14.2.10 (= I p.73); Fesser p.12; app.crit. ad h.l. Clark Seyf.; Veget.r.m.2.25 (= Lang p.60): quatenus **contextis** isdem, sicut dicunt, monoxylis.
b **pons navalis** = ship's bridge. This term does not occur in Veget.r.m. But to me it seems to belong to the soldiers' language. Usually the term is circumscribed. Late Latin. Cf.17.1.2: flumine **pontibus constratis** transmisso.

Rheno transito. Cl. (in edit.) Seyf. Sabbah. **transito Rheno** Cl.Nov. Rolfe. Heraeus: Rheno ⟨flumine⟩ transito. A transposition metri causa does not seem necessary. Cf. Blomgren p.93 sq. (op.cit.II), with examples of an almost similar clausula.

terris Alamannorum calcatis. For Al. cf. ad 17.6.1, p.116.4; ad 14.10.1 (= II p.96 sq.). The verb **calcare** fairly often in Amm. with the meaning: to set foot on: 31.10.13; 31.4.13; 27.2.8; 27.5.9; 30.8.5; 31.13.6; to trample on, to mock, despise: 23.6.53; 25.3.18; 27.12.1; 29.5.54; ad 16. 12.38, p.97.17-21*g*.

Severus. Cf. ad 16.10.21, p.88.7. For **magister equitum** cf. ad 14.9.1 (= I p.88).

bellicosus. For the numerous adiectiva ending in -*osus* cf. Liesenberg (op. cit.I) 1888 p.27 sq. Here the adj. means: **martial, brave,** as often (and not: bellicose, which the adj. also often means.). Said very clearly of a general in Veget.r.m.3.18 (= Lang p.103): In sinistra parte exercitus tertius esse dux debet, satis **bellicosus et providus,** quia sinistra pars difficilioɪ est et velut manca in acie consistit.

ante haec = antea. Post-class. Cf. **inter haec** = interea (ad 14.6.1 = I p.89).

conmarcuit. Cf.31.12.13: et ut miles fervore calefactus aestivo siccis faucibus **commarceret.** Only in Amm.?

X, 2
universos ... et singulos. Universi, combined with **singuli,** as here, or

dispersi, unus et alter etc., also in "correct" and class. Latin; but **universi** = **omnes** only late Latin. Cf.et. Krebs Antib.2 p.694 (with lit.).
Note also the **hyperbaton** (17.1.6, p.105.21a).

p. 121. 16 **ad fortiter faciendum.** Cf. ad 15.5.35 (= III p.122); ad 15.5.33 (= III p.120); ad 16.12.29, p.95.27.

p. 121. 17 *a* **tunc dissuasor pugnandi contemptus videbatur et timidus.** Here one has a choice between an **asyndeton bimembre** (diss. on a par with the adj. cont. and tim.) and an undivided sentence, in which the adj. belong with diss. **The asyndeta** in Amm. are many and frequently used. Cf. Blomgren (op.cit.II) passim.
b **contemptus** = despicable. Also class. The late Latin adj. **contemptibilis** does not occur in Amm. Cf. Krebs Antib.1 p.350 (with lit.).

p. 121. 18 **adventantem.** This verb also: 22.15.30; 15.3.7; 15.8.20; 16.2.12; 21.12.10; 21.14.1; 24.6.17; 25.5.6; 26.8.4; 27.2.2; 27.5.2; 28.4.26; 28.5.6; 30.1.7; 31.1.1; 31.3.8; 31.7.3; 31.15.10. With accusativus without praepos.: 14.10.11; 18.2.11; 21.12.22; 24.6.5; 30.5.1.

p. 121. 18-19 *a* **ut in Tageticis libris legitur⟨vel⟩ Vegoicis.** Cf.21.1.10: Extis itidem pecudum attenti **fatidicis** in species converti suetis innumeras accidentia sciunt. **Cuius disciplinae Tages** nomine quidam monstrator est, ut fabulantur, in **Etruriae** partibus emersisse subito visus e terra: Cic.divin.2.23 (50): **Tages** quidam dicitur **in agro Tarquiniensi,** cum terra araretur et sulcus altius esset impressus, exstitisse repente et eum affatus esse, qui arabat. Is autem **Tages,** ut **in libris est Etruscorum,** puerili specie dicitur visus, sed senili fuisse prudentia ... tum illum plura locutum multis audientibus, qui omnia eius verba exceperint **litterisque mandaverint**: omnem autem orationem fuisse eam, qua **haruspicinae disciplina** contineretur; eam postea crevisse **rebus novis cognoscendis et ad eadem illa principia referendis;** Ovid.Met.15.552-559:

Hand aliter stupuit, quam cum **Tyrrhenus arator**
Fatalem glaebam mediis aspexit in arvis
Sponte sua primum nulloque agitante moveri,
Sumere mox hominis, terraeque amittere formam,
Oraque **venturis** aperire recentia **fatis:**
Indigenae dixere **Tagen, qui primus Etruscam**
Edocuit gentem casus aperire futuros.

Macr.5.19.13: Sed Carmini **(Carminius,** according to Servius, author of a treatise: **de elocutionibus)** curiossissimi et docti verba ponam, qui in libro **de Italia** secundo sic ait: "prius itaque et **Tuscos** aeneo vomere uti, cum conderentur urbes, solitos, **in Tageticis eorum sacris** invenio et in Sabinis ex aere cultros, quibus sacerdotes tonderentur"; Serv.ad Aen.2.781: Constat namque **illic a Tage aruspicinam repertam,** ut Lucanus meminit (sc. in Lydia = Etruria); ibid. ad Aen.8.398: Sed sciendum secundum aruspicinae libros et **sacra Acherontia, quae Tages composuisse dicitur,** fata decem annis quadam ratione differri; Luc.1.635 sq.:

.... "Di visa secundent,
et fibris sit nulla fides, sed **conditor artis**
finxerit ista **Tages**". Flexa sic omina **Tuscus**
involvens multaque tegens ambage canebat.

Cf.et. ad 17.7.10, p.118.1*a, b;* R.E. (Weinstock) 4 A 2, 1932, 2009 sq.; Cens. de die nat.4.13; Arn.adv.nat.2.69 (= Reiffersch.p.103): Antequam **Tages Tuscus** oras contingeret luminis, quisquam hominum sciebat aut esse noscendum condiscendumque curabat, an **fulminum casibus aut extorum** aliquid significaretur in venis? **Tages** is not mentioned in Opt. Milev.Claud.

b **Vegoia (Vegoe, Begoe).** Cf. Servius ad Aen.6.72: libri **Begoes nymphae, quae artem scripserat fulguritorum apud Tuscos;** Amm.25.2.7: **Etrusci haruspices** accersiti ... **ex Tarquitianis libris in titulo de rebus divinis** id relatum esse monstrantes, quod face in caelo visa committi proelium vel simile quidquam non oportebit. Cf.et.R.E. (Weinstock) 8 A 1, 1955, 577 sq.; **Camus, Amm.Marc. (1967)** p.206 (and the entire cap.13 p.200 sq.: Divination et Magie), with lit.; **Enszlin, Zur Gesch.schr.** etc. (op.cit.I) p.83 sq.; Woordenboek der Oudh., 5, 1970, 1320 sq. with lit. (Janssen).

c To mention the names discussed under *a* and *b* is not a special antiquarian hobby of Amm. Together with all sorts of miracle workers, "prophets" and "philosophers", these characters fit into the late Heathen era, where they experience a re-birth, as it were.

a **fulmine mox tangendos.** For the gerundivum cf. ad 16.12.22, p.94.26*b*. p. 121. 19 For **tangere** cf.Ovid.Trist.2.144: (Ulmus) Quae fuerat saevi **fulmine tacta** Iovis; Cic.div.2.21(47): (statua) **de caelo tacta;** Liv.25.7.7: **tacta de caelo** multa; ibid.29.14.3: murum **de caelo tactum;** Plin.h.n.36.4.1: quod e **caelo** ... **tactum est;** Verg.Buc.1.17: **de coelo tactas** quercus; Plin.h.n.2.54 (used absolutely): **tacta** Iunonis aede; etc. The verb is, as it were, the t.t. for the stroke of lighting.

b Cf.26.3.4: verum haec similiaque tum etiam ut **coercenda mox** cavebantur; 31.12.4: cum litteris ipsum quoque **venturum mox** indicantibus. Cf.et. ad 16.10.19, p.87.24-25*b*.

p. 121. 19 **hebetari.** Often used of the senses and the mind. Cf.Verg.Aen.2.605 (visus); Plin.N.H.20.21 (oculorum aciem); ibid.18.30 (sensus); etc. In general post-class. and poet. Cf.et.Claud.22 (de laud.Stil.) 131 sq.:
         .... Nec te iucunda fronte fefellit
         Luxuries praedulce malum, quae dedita semper
         Corporis arbitriis **hebetat caligine sensus.**
Souter p.170 **(intrans.:** late Latin); ad 16.12.54, p.100.11*b* **(hebisco);** Iust.6.8.2: Sic illo, velut mucrone teli, ablato duce Thebanorum, **rei quoque publicae vires hebetatae sunt.** Not in Arn.adv.nat.Opt.Milev.Veget. r.m.
tonitruum. Genit. of **tonitrus** (decl.IV). Thus also 25.3.12. But 21.1.11: **tonitrua** (of **tonitruum**). Cf. Krebs Antib.2 p.666 (with lit.). Cf. ad 14.6.18 **(sonus)** = I p.99. But uncertainties concerning the declinations are quite frequent in late and vulgar Latin, as can be seen, for instance, from the examples in **Oder** Mulom.Chir.p.304 of the **4th declination.**

p. 121. 20 *a* **maiores aliquos ... fragores.** Obviously **maiores** does not have a comparative meaning here. It probably means no more than just: large (or: fairly large). Cf. ad 14.6.12 (= I p.96).
b for **aliquos** cf. ad 17.4.12, p.110.25*c*; ad 16.11.8, p.89.19-20.
c **fragores.** Cf. ad 17.7.3, p.116.24-25*c*.

p. 121. 20 *a* **iter ignaviter egerat. Ignaviter:** a rather unusual adverbium. Nonclass. Vulgarism? Archaism? **Hirtius** (in Cic. ad Att.15.6.2): An ego, cum omnes caleant, **ignaviter** aliquid faciam?; **Luc.**537 Marx; **b.Afr.**81.1; Quadr.Gell.Apul. Not in Veget.r.m. (who does have **ignave),** Claud.Opt. Milev.Arn.adv.nat. Cf.Krebs Antib.1 p.676.
b The usual expressions are: **iter facere, conficere.** Thus also several times in Veget.r.m. Also compare ibid.3.6 (= Lang p.76): Securum **iter agitur** quod **agendum** hostes minime suspicantur; ibid.1.23 (= Lang p.26): (Porta praetoria) ... aut, **si iter agitur,** illam partem debet adtendere, ad quam est profecturus exercitus. Though there is probably a small difference in nuance in both places.
c For other meanings of **agere** ad 16.12.69, p.103.1.

p. 121. 20-21 **praeter solitum.** Cf. ad 16.11.3, p.88.22.

a **ductores viarum praeuntes.** What are meant here are the units marching in front, who have to **reconnoitre** the road. But not guides (scouts) in the actual sense of the word, as they do **not** know the way themselves (ni ... se loca **penitus ignorare** firmarent). Behind terreret should be added mentally: **et quae fecisset.** The idea is as follows: **Severus,** who has suddenly(?) become afraid, does not want to march hastily, when he might get involved in dangers and fights. But the **ductores viarum** do not act according to his wish, pushing on **alacri gradu.** Then the general, afraid and panicky, threatens them with severe punishment if they do not slow down. And he would certainly have carried out these threats, if they had not assured him unanimously, that they did not know the way, i.e. had denied that they had **deliberately** taken a direction known to them, so as to get quickly in contact with the enemy. After this threat by S. they keep quiet. I wonder if Seyf. and Sabbah in their translations have meant the same thing as I believe Amm. to have meant.

b For **ductor** cf.et. ad 16.2.11, p.73.25; ad 14.2.17 (= I p.76); Veget.3.5 (= Lang p.74); ductor = dux.

c Which t.t. is hidden behind **ductores viarum** is not clear, but it may be either **Superventores,** or **Praeventores** (mentioned in Amm.18.9.3) or **Exploratores;** all three groups are mentioned in the Not.Dign. Cf. Seeck N.D. p.322, 325, 326; Grosse Mil. (op.cit.I) p.29,54.

ultima minitando. Cf. ad 17.9.3, p.120.21. The verb does not occur in Veget.r.m. Claud.Arn.adv.nat.Opt.Mil. Cf. ad 14.11.8 (= II p.121).

a **conspirantes in unum** = agreeing on this one point. Thus also with favourable meaning Claud.5.119 (= In Ruf.II).

    Et quamvis praesens tumor, et civilia nuper
    Classica, bellatrix etiam nunc ira caleret,
    In ducis eximium **conspiravere favorem.**

Cf.et. ad 15.4.9 (= III p.62): **conspiratus;** ad 16.3.3, p.74.18-19.

b Cf.et. **conspiratio** ad 16.12.34, p.96.19-20.

penitus ignorare. Cf.Cic. ad Att.8.12.1: explicari mihi tuum consilium plane volo, ut **penitus intellegam;** de orat.1.5 (17): et omnes animorum motus, quos hominum generi rerum natura tribuit, **penitus pernoscendi;** ibid.1.12 (53): penitus perspexerit; ibid.1.20 (92): penitusque perspectis; ibid.1.51 (219): penitus perspexerit. One should bear in mind, however, that in late Latin **penitus** = omnino and **penitus** with negation = **omnino non.** Cf. Kalb Jur.Lat. (1961) p.80; Krebs Antib.2 p.272; Veget.r.m.1.7

(= Lang p.10 sq.): Sequitur, ut, cuius artis vel eligendi vel **penitus repudiandi** sint milites, indagemus; ibid.1.20 (= Lang p.21): Sed in hac parte antiqua **penitus** consuetudo **deleta est.**

p. 121. 23 **interdicti ... auctoritatem.** Of course, the **auctoritas** refers more to the person issuing the prohibition, than to the prohibition itself. Amm. considers **auctoritas** important and it is one of the few good qualities which he ascribes to **Gallus.** (14.11.28). Cf.et. ad 15.9.8 (IV p.53); ad 16. 8.2, p.81.3-4; ad 17.4.8. p.110.7-8c.

X, 3

p. 121. 24 **Inter has tamen moras.** For **inter** cf. ad 17.4.1, p.109.4.
Moras is clearly a plur.poet.cf. ad 17.2.1, p.107.14-15b.
Alamannorum. Cf. ad 17.8.1, p.119.8.
rex Suomarius. Cf. ad 16.12.1, p.91.3-5.

p. 121. 24-25 **cum suis** = cum **satellitibus** (cf. ad 16.12.58, p.101.5-6b) = cum **comitibus** (cf. ad 16.12.60, p.101.18).

p. 121. 25 *a* **Saeviensque in damna Romana.** For this in finale cf.14.10.5; 15.5.15; 15.8.2; 16.3.3; 24.1.12; 26.5.8; ad 16.3.3, p.74.18-19; ad 15.8.2 (= IV p.27); Reinhardt (op.cit.I) p.61.
b **damnas Romanas et** V. **damna romana, sed (set):** Val.Cl.Seyf.Sabb. Rolfe. It is, of course, quite a clever intervention in the text to read **romanas et** as: **romana set.** Anyone can sense that in that case **damnas** should be **damna** before **Romana.** But there are 2 objections against this text correction: 1⁰ **et** often has an adversative meaning in Latin (cf. Hofm.-Leum. p.660 231d) and therefore does not have to be changed into **set,** as happens so often, 2⁰ It is a very frequent phenomenon in vulgar Latin (and also in late Latin), that **neutr.plur.** develop into **femin.sing.** Cf. Grandgent (op.cit.I) p.146 sq. (351-353). This mistake may be blamed on the copyist, but that is not at all certain. Thus one finds: brachias, armentas, membras, etc. And the influence of the spoken language can not be denied by even the most avid purist. Cf.et.Mulom.Chir.Oder p.300 sq.

p. 121. 26 **insperatum.** Cf. ad 16.2.7, p.73.11.
si propria retinere permitteretur. For **proprius** cf. ad 14.5.8 (= I p.88). For the construction of the **verba permittendi** cf. ad 14.1.3 (= I p.58). Cf.et. ad 15.7.4, p.57.5; ad 15.7.6, p.57.12 (= IV p.15, 18); ad 15.6.1, p.55.16 (= IV p.6); ad 16.10.11, p.86.7.

a **Vultus incessusque supplicem indicabat.** These words are reminiscent of Veget.r.m.3.12 (= Lang p.95), quoted ad 16.12.7, p.92.2. For **incessus** cf.ibid.   p. 121. 27

b Cf.Cic. pro Archia 28: Atque ut id libentius faciatis, iam me vobis iudices, **indicabo** et de meo quodam amore gloriae nimis acri fortasse, verum tamen honesto vobis confitebor.

susceptus ... iussus ... The main point is expressed in the participia, especially the first one. Cf. ad 17.3.5, p.108.20*a*.   p. 121. 27- p. 122. 1

bono ... placido. Hyperbaton. Cf. ad 17.1.6, p.105.21*a*. Often metri causa. Here Claus.II. For the **homoioteleuton** cf. ad 15.10.4 (= IV p.56). Cf.et. ad 15.4.2 (III p.56) **(annominatio).**

nihil arbitrio suo relinquens. Arbitrium is the unrestrained judgment, the free choise, one's own discretion. This is thus given up by **Suomarius,** which is a symbol of submission, of the surrender of his independence.   p. 122. 1

pacem genibus curvatis oravit. The expression: **genibus curvatis** is probably a Vergilius reminiscence and/or his imitators, which poet fairly often uses the word **curvatus.** More usual combinations seem to be: genua flectere, ponere (alicui), submittere; genibus nixus etc. Cf. ad 16.12.65, p.102.10.   p. 122. 1-2

X, 4

a **cum concessione praeteritorum. Concessio** = forgiveness. Cf.Cod.Iust. 2.2.2: cum igitur confitearis patroni tui filium sine permissu praesidis in ius vocasse, **poenam** edicto perpetuo praestitutam rescripto tibi **concedi** temere desideras. The subst. not with this meaning in judicial Latin. Cf. et.Arn.adv.nat.7.8 (Reiffersch.p.243): hoc est enim proprium numinum, liberales venias et concessiones habere gratuitas. Not in Opt.Milev.Claud. Veget.r.m. In Amm. also: 14.10.14: Alamannorum reges et populi formidantes per oratores, quos videtis, summissis cervicibus **concessionem praeteritorum** poscunt et pacem.   p. 122. 2

b For the **neutr.plur.** cf. ad 17.3.2, p.108.12*a;* ad 17.4.1, p.109.4*a*.

sub hac ... lege. Cf. ad 17.8.3, p.119.25*a*.   p. 122. 2

ut captivos redderet nostros. A normal condition. For the rest one does not read too much about these prisoners of war, who probably were not   p. 122. 3

251

p. 122. 3 **et quotiens sit necesse.** For the **repraesentatio** cf. ad 14.7.9 (= II p.31). The conjunct. is of the subordinate clause of the oratio obliqua, but it can also be a **conjunct.iterat.** For the latter conjunct. cf. ad 14.2.2 (= I p.67); ad 14.2.7 (= I p.70, 71); ad 14.1.5 (= I p.60 sq.); ad 14.4.6 (= I p.83); Ehrism. p.57; ad 16.10.18, p.87.22; ad 16.12.21, p.94.18-19*a;* etc.

p. 122. 3-5 **militibus ... flagitandum.** For **alimenta** cf. ad 16.3.3, p.74.19; ad 16.11.12, p.90.12.

p. 122. 4 *a* **susceptorum vilium.** For **susceptor** cf. ad 15.5.3 (= III p.69); ad 16.5.14, p.77.17-19*c, d;* Willems (op.cit.I) p.599 (with lit.). For **securitas** cf.ibid. Thus the **susceptores** are the **collectors** who get **receipts** for the **annona** they hand in. **Securitas = pittacium authenticum.** Fraud, which apparently occurred quite often, was greatly feared. Cf.Cod.Theod.7.4.11; 12.6.19; 12.6.21 (c.comm.Gothofr.). In 19.11.3 the **susceptores** are called **suscipientes,** as opposed to the **offerentes,** the tax-payers. This entire passage (19.11.3) clearly illustrates the fiscal abuses. **Inferre** and **inlatio** are t.t.: e.g. inferre vectigal, inferre pecuniam fisco, aerario; illatio capitalis (= capitationis; cf. ad 16.5.14, p.77.17-19*a);* etc. Cf. Heum.-Seckel p.264 sq. **Offere** is also a t.t. of the legal literature. Cf. Heum.-Seckel p. 387. Similarly **oblatio.**
b **vilium.** So **viles** the **susceptores** certainly are not, generally speaking, for after all, they are **curiales** (town-councillors), elected by the town council **(curia).** Thus they belong to the privileged, but also, in these days, heavily taxed class of the towns. But in the eyes of the emperor they are subaltern subjects, at any rate compared to a **rex,** even if he was a German. Like the susceptores, he has to collect receipts, which makes him a kind of civil servant.

p. 122. 4-5 **quas ... flagitandum.** Oratio obliqua. Or.recta: quas si non ostenderis (fut.exact) ... scias te etc.

p. 122. 5 **eadem flagitandum.** Pet. Niemeyer Clark Seyf. Rolfe. **clade fatigandum:** C.F.W. Müller Sabbah. **ea defatigandum:** VEAG. **Defatigare** is a verb which occurs, among, others, fairly often in Cic., also in a metaph. sense. The verb does not occur in Claud.Veget.r.m.Arn.adv.nat.Opt.Milev.

Here the verb means: to cause trouble, to bother with. Cf.S.Aur.Vict. Epit.48.5: Nam Hunnos et Gothos, qui **eam** (sc.rem publicam) sub Valente **defatigassent,** diversis proeliis vicit (sc.Theodosius). **Ea** is accusat. of content. The fact that with **this** meaning and **this** construction the verb does not occur elsewhere, is no reason, in my view, to reject V's version. Translation: then he had to know that once again he would have to be troubled with these deliveries (**ea** = inlata). Cf.et. Sabbah II p.180, note 83, with whose remarks I do not agree; ad 16.7.8, p.80.9c.

X, 5

a For **disponere** cf. ad 16.12.23, p.94.27; ad 16.12.27, p.95.18. **Inpraepe-** p. 122. 6
dite: 17.10.5; 21.10.5; 22.12.7; 26.6.11; 27.10.2. The formulary style of Amm. is apparent once more from 21.10.5: imperator revertitur Naessum ... quo **inpraepedite** cuncta **disponeret,** suis utilitatibus profutura. Late Latin. Only in Amm.? The **adject.**21.5.6; 30.2.4. Late Latin. Only in Amm.? The latter passage another example of the above formula-like style: (30.2.4) et, ni Sauromaci praesidia militum impertita principio sequentis anni, **ut dispositum est, impraepedita** reverterint. Cf.et. ad 17.4.1, p. 109. 6*b*.

b **quod ... conpleto.** The construction gives rise to problems. V completo. BG completum. **quo ... disposito et ... completo Haupt.** The last correction expresses the meaning correctly. Cl., Seyf. Sabbah Rolfe follow the same version by V. One can either (1) accept this sentence-part with its "faulty" syntax, as it stands, (which can be defended), or (2) one can take over G's version and consider **quod ... completum** as an **accus.absolutus.** Cf.Hofm.-Leum.p.449; Svennung Pall. p.166, 176, 179, 187, 199, 228, 392 (op.cit.II); IJ.M.Biese, Der spätlat. Akkus. absol.u.verw. (Helsingfors 1928, dissert.); Oder Mulom.Chir. p.313 sq.; Rufus de podagra 21 (= Mørland p.29); S.Bened.Reg.18 (= Linderbauer p.38.20); etc. It should also be pointed out that the **accusat.absol.** is a not uncommon phenomenon in Greek. Personally I prefer solution (2).

Hortari. Cf. ad 16.12.1, p.91.3-5*f.* His territory was situated South of p. 122. 6
the river Main, near Vangiones (Worms) and Lopodunum (Ladenbourg). Cf. Sabbah p.181. Whereas the territory of **Suomarius** was to the North of this river.

pagus. Amm. uses a word here which does not really fit the land, or even p. 122. 7
kingdom of a German monarch. Cf. ad 16.2.8, p.73.14 **(civitas);** ad 16.2.

12, p.73.27-p.74.1 (**territorium**); ad 16.12.59, p.101.9 (**territorium**). Normally **regnum** should have been written here.

p. 122. 8 **ductores** = guides. Cf.et. ad 17.10.2, p.121.21*a*, *b*.

p. 122. 8 **Nesticae.** In connection with Julianus' instruction and the fact that **Charietto** is a barbarian, definitely not a Roman either. Only mentioned here in Amm. and not known from other places. **tribunus Scutariorum.** For **tribunus** cf. ad 14.5.8 (= I p.129); ad 15.3.10 (= III p.50). For **scutarii** ad 14.7.9 (= II p.27); ad 14.10.8 (= II p.105); Sabbah p.181.

p. 122. 8 **Charietto.** A barbarian of tremendous strength and size, who from **Trier** carried out a private guerilla against Germans who invaded Gallia. He offered his services to **Julianus** and was a considerable help to the latter. He later became a **comes per utramque Germaniam** (for **comes** cf. ad 14.5.1 = I p.125). He was killed in 365 in the war against the **Alamans** (27.1). Cf.et. Zos.3.7, where he is highly praised.
Note. For **comes** cf.et. Grosse Mil. (op.cit.I) p.152-180; 182; and particularly p.155 sq.: "Jeder **dux** war zugleich auch **comes** inferior, deshalb werden beide Benennungen gelegentlich als gleichbedeutend gebraucht. Erhielt er aber als persönliche Auszeichnung die **comitiva primi ordinis**, so nannte er sich mit vollem Titel **comes et dux**".

p. 122. 8-9 **fortitudinis mirae.** For the **genit.qualitatis** cf. ad 16.4.12, p.110.26*b*.

p. 122. 9-10 **ut ... captivum.** The main point is contained in the two participia. Cf. ad 17.3.5, p.108.20*a*.

p. 122. 10 **offerrent** = would bring to him, before him. Just as **duci** (= to lead before ...), almost synonymous, the technical terms for these actions.
et = and thus, in this way, and indeed.
correptus. The difference with **comprehensus** is very small. The last partic. has more the meaning of: imprisoned, the other: caught, collared.

p. 122. 11 *a* **pacto optinendae salutis pollicitus.** Note the alliterating **p** and **t**, probably not accidental. Cf. ad 17.9.3, p.120.23.
b Cf.Iust.8.5.3: Victi igitur necessitate, **pacta salute** se dediderunt. It seems to me that Amm. expresses himself in a contrived manner, instead of, for instance, **pacta salute** or **condicione optinendae salutis (proposita).**

X, 6

hoc progresso ... vetabatur. Translation: **while he was leading the way,** p. 122. 12-13
the army followed, but was obstructed etc. The partic. here has the
meaning of a **partic. praesens**, as often (cf.Hofm.-Leum.184 p.607, with
lit.). Instead of the **imperf. vetabatur** one would expect an **aoristic perf.**
The **perf.pass.**, however, is avoided by Amm. (cf. ad 14.2.14; 14.11.32;
ad 17.7.4, p.117.1*b*). Clausula III.

circuitus. With the same meaning **circumitus**: 18.7.10; 23.6.20 (E B G have p. 122. 13
in the latter place: **circuitus**). Without difference in meaning.

flexuosos. Cf.14.2.9: per **flexuosas** semitas; 24.4.10: nam accessus undique p. 122. 14
rupibus anfractu celsiore discissis, **flexuosisque excessibus** (meaning
uncertain here) ob periculum anceps.
Subst.neutr.27.5.4: quae (sc.familiae) antequam ad dirupta venirent et
flexuosa capi potuerunt per plana camporum errantes. For other places:
ad 15.11.17 (= IV p.73). Not in Claud.Veget.r.m.Arn.adv.nat.Opt.
Milev.

ira ... percitus. Cf.Plaut.Casina 3.5.627 sq.: p. 122. 14
   cave tibi, Cleustrata, apscede ab ista, opsecro,
   ne quid in te mali faxit **ira percita.**
Liv.6.5.4: percitum ira. Cf.et. ad 14.2.17 (= I p.76).

armatorum. V armorum. G armatorum, also Seyf.Cl. Rolfe Sabbah: p. 122. 14
armorum. Cf.31.10.5: cum quadraginta **armorum** milibus; ad 16.12.7,
p.92.3-4*b*.

⟨**et**⟩ **pecora diripiebat et homines.** For the hyperbaton cf. ad 17.1.6, p.105. p. 122. 15
21*a*. Claus.II. Probably here also an **asyndeton**: urebat agros, pecora
diripiebat. Cf.Blomgren p.40.

resistentesque = who offered resistance; the correct translation in my p. 122. 15
view. Thus also Seyf. Sabbah: malgré leur résistance; which does not
seem fitting here.

sine ulla parsimonia. Cf.29.6.8: quos necopinantes **sine ulla parsimonia** p. 122. 15-16
deleverunt; 15.4.8: et **sine parsimonia** ... configebant; 25.3.10: (miles)
sine parsimonia ruebat in ferrum; 31.13.6: exanimata cadavera **sine**

parsimonia calcabantur (= ἀφειδῶς). Cf.et. ad 17.4.1, p.109, 6*b*. With variatio 17.1.7: nulli parcendo.

p. 122. 16 **parsimŏnia contruncăbant.** Claus.III. The compositum is deliberately chosen. Plaut. Otherwise late Latin. Archaism? Vulgarism? For the **constructio ad sensum** cf. Blomgren (op.cit.II) p.46 sq., with examples.

X, 7

p. 122. 16 **perculsus.** I can not understand why the version by V **percussus** should be rejected in favour of **perculsus** (E B G Cl. Seyf. Rolfe; but Sabbah like V). Cf.Verg.Georg.2.476: ingenti **percussus amore;** Aen.9.197: **magno** laudum **percussus amore;** Horat.Epod.11.2:
   Petti, nihil me sicut antea iuvat
   Scribere versiculos **amore percussum gravi**
   Amore etc.
To name only a few of the many examples.

p. 122. 16-17 **rex cum multiplices legiones. regiones** VEAG. **legiones** Hadr.Val.Cl. Sabbah Rolfe. **regionum direptiones** Her. **regionum** Seyf. I do not agree at all with note 132, Amm.Marc.Seyf.I p.311. It is incomprehensible to me why **legiones** would not give the right meaning. The king is faced with two distinct problems: the ruins of burnt-down villages plus **a large hostile army.** He therefore is afraid to lose his last possessions as well, if he continues the war. So out of sheer necessity he submits himself. Cf.et. Blomgren (op.cit.II) p.137, especially note 2.

p. 122. 16 **multiplices** = numerous = complures, multas. As is sometimes also the case in class. Latin. Wholly equal here to **multas,** in my opinion.

p. 122. 17 **vicorumque.** Cf. ad 16.2.8, p.73.14*b;* Heum.-Seckel p.623. Amm. here uses a word **not** suitable for the conditions in Germania, outside the Roman empire. For there were not towns which the Germans feared and avoided. (cf.16.2.12). Vicus is used of all non-fortified settlements, not belonging to the urbes, oppida, civitates, municipia and castella, munimenta, castra, can(n)abae etc. But a **vicus** is included in the organisation. **(territorium:** 16.2.8; 16.2.12; 16.12.59). A German "village" is quite a different matter. It is quite well possible that Amm. knows the Germ. word for this, but does not use it for stylistic and chauvinistic reasons.

exustorum. The compositum, though well suited here, also chosen metri, causa: claus.III.

fortunarum: possessions, property; as is apparent from the context.

iacturas: loss. **Plur.poet.** (cf. ad 17.2.1, p.107.14-15*b*). The plural form may have been occasioned by the "plurale tantum" **fortunae.** Cf.29.6.7: evenisset profecto tunc inexpiabile scelus numerandum inter **probrosas** rei Romanae **iacturas;** 25.3.8 (Epaminondas) et qui animam intrepidus amittebat, **iacturam clipei** formidavit; Cic.fin.bon.2.24.(79): Quid? si (amicitia) non modo utilitatem tibi nullam afferret, sed **iacturae rei familiaris** erunt faciundae...

contemplatus. The partic. has here the meaning of a **praesens.** Cf. ad 17. 10.6, p.122.12-13.

oravit ipse quoque veniam. Cf.Verg.Aen.4.435:
  Extremam hanc oro veniam (miserere sororis),
  Quam mihi cum dederit, cumulatam morte remittam.

a **facturum ... promisit.** After **exsecratione** Her.Cl. assume a lacuna. Although Seyf. in his text indicates a lacuna, he assumus (I p.311 note 133) following in Pighi's steps (Aevum 1937, p.397 sq.) that we have an **asyndeton** here, as apparently Sabbah in his edit. also does. The asyndeton is very frequent in Amm., in many forms. Rolfe reads: ... facturum se imperanda iurandi exsecratione **promisit** ⟨Captivos⟩ restituere universos -id enim cura agebatur impensiore- ⟨iussus fidem non praestitit⟩. With this text by Rolfe the meaning of the passage is given very well, in my view. But for the rest it is too good to be true. (Cf.Rolfe I p.362; Clark app.crit.I p.122). In my opinion the rhythm of the sentence resists the assumption of an asyndeton; so that I am inclined to adopt Haupt's conjecture: **facturum**⟨que⟩. Cf.et. ad 15.13.2 (= IV p.80).
b for **promisit c. infin.praes.** cf. Hofm.-Leum.170 p.586 sq. Also occurring in class. Latin. Here probably easily explained by the preceding partic. fut. **facturum.**

exsecratione. Cf.26.7.9: cum essent omnes in unum quaesitae iamque exercitus species apparebat **promissis** uberrimis inhiantes **sub exsecrationibus diris** in verba iuravere Procopii.

universos = omnes. Late Latin.

p. 122. 19-20 **id enim cura agebatur inpensiore.** Id = restituere captivos. Cf.Ovid.Met. 2.405 sq.:

> ... Arcadiae tamen est **inpensior** illi
> **Cura** suae ....;

Tac.Hist.1.31: quod eos a Nerone Alexandriam praemissos atque inde reversos longa navigatione aegros **impensiore cura** Galba refovebat; Gell.20.1: **impensiore** damno. **Impensior(e) cura** in Amm., among others in 17.10.7; 19.6.6; 19.11.17; 20.8.1; 26.1.1; With **variatio:** 20.10.3: pleniore cura; 22.6.4: perpensiore cura; 27.12.5: intentiore cura; 28.2.4: vehementior cura; 29.5.46: altiore cura; 30.2.3: studio curatiore; 31.2.19: sollicitior cura; Fesser p.24.

p. 122. 20 **detentisque. -que:** adversative. = retentisque.

X, 8

p. 122. 21 **erectus.** Cf. ad 16.12.65, p.102.11; ad 16.12.37. p.97.8. Cf.24.3.3: cum eos parvitate promissi percitos (alliteration!) tumultuare sensisset, **ad indignationem plenam gravitatis erectus** (cf.et. ad 17.4.1, p.109.6*b*.).

p. 122. 21-22 *a* **cum munerandus venisset ex more:** = ut muneraretur = in order to receive his reward, gift (as was the custom). In our eyes a not very nice habit of these German monarchs, whose proud independence and unselfishness should not be overestimated.

b **ex more.** Cf. ad 14.10.3 = II p.100; ad 15.1.2 (= III p.8); af 15.5.4 (= III p.72): **exusu, ex more, ex re (publica).**

p. 122. 22 **comites.** Cf. ad 16.12.58, p.101.5-6*b*. (For another meaning of **comes** cf. ad 14.5.1 = I p.125; ad 17.12.5, p.122.8).

p. 122. 22 **ope et fide.** Used to indicate, I believe, the typical Germanic "Treue" of these followers.

p. 122. 23 **non ante ... dum** = non ante ... quam. The construction used here is the "regular" classical one with negative main clauses (cf.Caes.b.g.1.53.1) in the past tense. (for **ante ... quam** cf. ad 14.6.23 = I p.100). For **dum** cf. ad 17.4.4, p.109.14.

p. 122. 23 **rediere.** For the ending **-ere** cf.Hagend.Perf. formen (op.cit.I) p.29 sq. and particularly p.45.

X, 9

ad colloquium ... premebatur ... = postquam ad colloquium tandem accitus est a Caesare **eum adoravit trementibus oculis** et (of sed) victoris superatus aspectu condicione difficili **pressus est** (= **passus est se premi**). For the partic. **adorato** (= verbum finitum) cf. ad 17.3.5, p.108.20*a*. For the imperf. **premebatur** (= pressus est) cf. ad 17.7.4, p.117.1*b*. p. 122. 23-
p. 123. 2

colloquium = "Audience" (with the emperor and other royal persons such as here the Caesar Julianus). Thus also used in Cassiod. In class. Latin and otherwise the word used for audience is: **aditus**. Cf. ad 15.5.27 = III p.112. p. 122. 23

trementibus oculis. This partic. reminds one of Cassiod.Var.6.6. (formula magisteriae dignitatis): Per eum senator veniens nostris praesentatur obtutibus; **admonet trepidum,** componit loquentem, sua quinetiam verba solet inserere, ut nos decenter omnia debeamus audire. This formula is worth reading for its almost hieratic style. p. 123. 1

adorato. Cf. ad 15.5.18 (= III p.100, 101); ad 15.5.27 (= III p.112). p. 123. 1

condicione ... hac. With the same meaning 17.8.3; 17.10.4: sub hac lege. Cf. ad 17.10.3, p.122.2. p. 123. 2

a **quoaniam consentaneum erat.** "Normally" one would expect here a conjunctivus of the oratio obliqua. For these 3 words belong, as a subordinate clause, to the words of the **condicio** posed by Julianus to Hortarius. For the **indic.** in the or.obl. cf. ad 16.10.17, p.87, 15-16*b*. It seems improbable to me that **quoniam ... reparari** would be an observation by Amm. and would therefore be written in the indic.
b **consentaneum est,** c.inf. and c.acc.c.inf., often in Cic., so that it may be a reminiscence here. For the construction cf. Krebs Antib.I p.336. The adj. does not occur in Claud.Veget.r.m.Arn.adv.nat.Opt.Milev. For a typical late Latin nuance cf. Souter p.73. p. 123. 2-3

civitates. Cf. ad 17.4.12, p.110.21-22*c*. p. 123. 3

vi barbarorum. Amm. either has Julianus make a rude remark here, or he forgets for a moment that he is supposed to be a historian, who should report another person's words, instead of his own. p. 123. 3-4

259

p. 123. 4 **carpenta et materias.** The carpenta are two-wheeled wagons, intended in the first place to: transport the wood (tree-trunks) and secondly: for transport in and around the building-sites. What is not written in Amm., but what he apparently considers self-evident, is the "delivery" of wagoners and helpers, who will have to stay for a long time in the towns under repair. The king has to draw upon his own domain, and the possessions of his fellow-countrymen. What is demanded here of **Hortarius**, signifies a considerable blow to a simple agrarian community, which had already been badly stricken by the war (17.10.6-7). **Materia (materies)** is lumber as building- and construction material (for the **plur.poet.** cf. ad 17.2.1, p.107.14-15*b*.), as opposed to **lignum (ligna)**: firewood. They are mentioned together in the well-known passage in Tac.Ann.1.35: ac propriis nominibus incusant vallum, fossas, **pabuli materiae lignorum adgestus.** (To procure the 3 last-mentioned matters was part of the soldiers' task). **Lignum** is not mentioned here, though the Romans will certainly have needed that also, for their brick-works **(tegularia)** which the legions exploited themselves, as well as for other things. The reconstruction of the tens of destroyed towns required an enormous organisation, and had to be finished quickly, because of the permanent state of war at the borders. A complete reconstruction could not always be realised, for the work on the defenses (walls, ramparts, canals, forts, etc.) had priority, of course. Cf.et.18.2.5-6.

p. 123. 5-6 **inprecatusque ... supplicia.** Oratio recta: et mihi inprecor (si perfidum quicquam egero) mihi luenda esse cruore supplicia. **egisset** is therefore the conjunct. of the orat.obl., quite according to the classical rules. For **imprecari** cf. Krebs Antib.I p.698 (with lit.). The construction as it is used here (gerundivum in the acc.c.inf.) seems very unusual to me. I know of no other examples. (Compare the acc.c.inf. with **precari** and **deprecari**); cf. Hofm.-Leum.170 p.585; Ovid.Ep.18.81 sq.).

p. 123. 6 **cruore** = suo sanguine = sua vita. Amm. uses **cruor** and **sanguis** rather arbitrarily. Cf.19.2.14: ubi enim quiescendi nobis tempus est datum, exiguas, quae supererant vires continuus cum insomnia labor absumpsit **sanguine** (= cruore) et pallente exspirantium facie perterrente ... (15) cum quidam graviter saucii **cruore** (= sanguine) exhausto spiritus reluctantes efflarent; 16.12.52 (= Clark I p.100.3-5); 14.5.9 (in these last two places used "normally"); 14.7.3: et in circo sex vel septem aliquotiens deditus certaminibus pugilum vicissim se concidentium perfusorumque **sanguine** (= cruore) specie ut lucratus ingentia laetabatur; Krebs Antib.1

p.378. It is remarkable how **cruor,** which occurs rather frequently with Claud., is completely absent in Veget.r.m.

supplicia. Cf.Curt.Ruf.4.7.27 (the priest in the temple of Ammon to Alexander the Great) Sacerdos parentem (by **parens** the sacerdos means: Jupiter, Alexander: Philippus) eius negat ullius scelere posse violari, Philippi autem omnes (sc.interfectores) **luisse supplicia.** p. 123. 6

ad propria remeare permissus est: ad territoria sua (16.12.59). For the constructions with the **verba permittendi** cf. ad 14.1.3 (= I p.58). Cf.et. ad 15.6.1, p.55.16; ad 15.7.4, p.57.5; ad 15.7.6, p.57.12; ad 16.10.10, p.86.7. For **proprius** cf. ad 14.5.8 (= I p.88). p. 123. 6

annonam ... daretur. For **annona** cf. ad 17.9.6, p.121.5; ad 16.5.14, p.77. 17-19c, d; ad 14.7.11 (= II p.36). p. 123. 6-8

transferre. One would sooner expect another compositum here (cf. ad 17.10.4, p.122.4a). p. 123. 7

ad internicionem: often in Liv. Cf.Sall.fragm. (Ep.Cn.Pomp. ad sen.) Eussner p.131: Hispaniam citeriorem, quae non ab hostibus tenetur, nos aut Sertorius **ad internecionem vastavimus;** ad 15.8.1 (= IV p.26). p. 123. 8

regione. With unintentional contempt for a region which was a German **regnum.** Amm. is, after all, a Roman citizen. Rome and Constantinople were divided into **regiones** (and subdivided into **vici**); in Italy there are the **regiones (sub)urbicariae** (important for the civil and criminal jurisdiction of the **praefectus urbi** and the **vicarius urbis Romae**). The word is also used in the judicial literature for: district, region, landscape etc., often without a noticeable difference with **pagus** etc. Cf.et.17.1.3. p. 123. 8

nihil inveniri poterat quod daretur. Whether this kind of destruction was wise from a strategical point of view, is to be doubted. In the first place the stores could not be profited from (and the providing with food of the Roman soldiers in far-away places was not always so very good), while in the second place the population was brought to despair and hatred. And the often dubious loyalty of the kings after they had suffered defeats, did not mean that their compatriots were also loyal. At the most they resigned themselves for the time being until their rulers were either driven p. 123. 8

away or dead. It may therefore be not without reason, that in the chauvinistic flourish of § 10 he did not write **populi**, but **reges**.

X, 10

p. 123. 9 *a* **tumentes quondam immaniter.** For **tumere** cf. Heuvel Stat.Theb.I comm.p.171; Mulder ibid.II comm.p.100; Claud.3.165 (= in Rufin.I):
...... Sic rex ad prima **tumebat**
Maeonius, pulchro cum verteret omnia tactu;
Tac.Dial.18.8 (Cicero): inflatus et **tumens** nec satis pressus; Mart.4.49: Musa nec insano syrmate nostra **tumet**; etc. Usually the verb is not used absolutely, as here in Amm. Occurs several times in Claud., as do **tumor, tumidus** and **tumescere**. With the meaning: swollen, puffed up, conceited, largely a voc poetica. Cf.et. ad 15.8.7 (= IV p.32): **detumiscere.**
b for **immaniter** cf.18.7.5; 26.2.4; 27.4.9; 27.8.9; 31.7.8; 31.13.1; 29.1.1; 29.2.9; 30.8.13; 24.7.5. Late latin. Among others Gell.Amm.August.

p. 123. 9 **rapinisque ditescere.** In class. Latin also often in the plur. Therefore not a plur.poet. Cf. Krebs Antib.2 p.473 sq. The verb is poet. Latin and late Latin.

p. 123. 10 **Romanae potentiae.** Cf.Claud.5.4 sq. (In Rufin.II)
Iamque tuis, Stilicho, **Romana potentia** curis,
Et rerum commissus apex.
Ibid.1.191 sq. (In Prob. et Olybr.cons.):
Sic Proba praecipuo natos exornat amictu,
Quae decorat mundum, cuius **Romans potestas**
Foetibus augetur.
(**Proba** is the mother of the brothers Probinus and Olybrius.
Potestas is metri causa, without any difference with **potentia**).

p. 123. 10 **Subdidere colla iam domita.** Cf.Sil.Ital.10.216 sq.:
Ingens ferre mala et **Fortunae subdere colla**
Nescius, adversa fronte incurrebat in arma.
iam = now finally, only now.

p. 123. 11 **tributarios.** Cf.14.8.15: (Cyprus) **tributaria** facta est. Cic.Plin.Suet.Iust. Judicial Latin. = taxable. Also a subst. The **coloni** (the predial farmers, bound to the soil) were also called **tributarii** (cf. Willems p.618, with lit.).

p. 123. 11 **nati et educati.** For the homoioteleuton cf. ad 15.10.4 = IV p.56.

obsecundabant. The verb, which also occurs in Cic., seems to me to be a p. 123. 11 real flower of speech, for it is rarely used. Also the meaning is really more like: to resign onself to, to oblige. Here, however, it is equal to: **oboedire.** For the various shades of meaning compare the well-known passage in Cic. pro lege Manil.16 (48). In late Latin the verb occurs as deponens.

ingravate. Also in 18.2.6. Late Latin. Also in August. = **ingravanter.** p. 123. 11 (also late Latin, not in Amm.). Cf. Souter p.206. The adj. **ingravatus** (= ungrudging) occurs in Symm.Epist. Cf. Souter ibid. For the placing of the adverbium cf. ad 17.11.1, p.123.24.

a **stationes. Statio** has here a general meaning = ± garrison, as is p. 123. 12 evident from the context. For the soldiers are going to their winter quarters, like Julianus. (For the t.t. **statio** cf.ad 14.3.2 (= I p.120); Heum.-Seckel p.553 s.v.). They are spread out: 1° in order to avoid crowding, which might lead to disturbances and riots etc.
2°. because the space inside the castra, castella, munimenta, etc., was very limited. There every inch of space was utilized, at least as far as the common soldier was concerned. Numerous excavations have given us a fairly exact idea of te situations in camps and forts. The **stationes** may have been part of the **limes,** or lain close to them. The distance between them will not have been too great, so as to ensure a fast mobilisation. For another meaning of **statio** cf. ad 15.8.14 (= IV p.38).
b Cf.et.26.8.5: qui ubi **Dadastanam** tetigit, **in qua statione** perisse diximus Iovianum.

milite consuētas. Claus.III and u should either be considered as a vocal, p. 123. 12 or the less common claus. $\overset{x}{\sim} \sim \sim \sim \overset{x}{\sim} \sim$ which is nevertheless used by Amm., where the u is a consonant. Cf. Blomgren (op.cit.II) p.9.

XI, 1
comitatu. Cf. ad 14.5.8 (= I p.129). p. 123. 14
subinde. Here, as so often: immediately thereafter.
subinde noscerentur. Another claus.ex. p.123.12 (above). And a **simplex pro composito** (cf. ad 16.5.6, p.76.12), although the compositum **(cognoscerentur)** would have allowed a "normal" clausula. (claus.III).

erat enim ... scientiam. For the position of the Caesar towards **Constan-** p. 123. 14-16 **tius** cf. ad 17.3.2, p.108.10*a, b;* ibid.p.108.11 (ex conquisitis); 17.1.14; ad

16.12.67, p.102.16-17; ibid.p.102.17; ad 16.12.69, p.103.2-3; ad 15.2.7 (= III p.19; before Julianus became Caesar); ad 15.8.3, p.58.18-p.61.3*a;* ad 15.8.16, p.60.23-24; 15.8.18-20.

p. 123. 15 **tamquam apparitorem.** For **tamquam** cf. ad 17.4.15, p.111.19-20*a*. Cf. et. **velut** (p.123.11); Hofm.-Leum.181 p.603 Zus. What is said here about this kind of words with **participia**, is true in general also of their function with **substantiva**. Cf.et. ad 17.8.3, p.119.27 - p.120.1*a*.
For **apparitor** cf. ad 15.5.36 (= III p.125); ad 15.7.3 (= IV p.12)*b*.

p. 123. 15 *a* **super omnibus gestis.** Cf. ad 16.12.70, p.103.9-10*b;* ad 17.4.1, p.109.6*a*.
b For **gesta** = **res gestae** cf. ad 16.12.18, p.94.6; Krebs Antib.1 p.625. Fairly often with the panegyrici. For a special late Latin meaning (= acta) in the **judic.lit.** cf. Souter p.161; Heum.-Seckel p.229.
Completely different meaning **gestus** (IV) (cf. ad 16.12.43, p.98.14), at least in Amm.Cf.et. Souter p.161.

p. 123. 16 **referre scientiam.** Cf.16.12.67: in palatio Constanti quidam Julianum culpantes ut princeps ipse delectaretur, inrisive **Victorinum** ideo nominabant, **quod verecunde referens quotiens imperaret** ... (cf. ad 16.12.67, p.102.17). This passage can also serve as an explanation for 11.1: **omnes ... accidit.**

p. 123. 16 **ad Augusti referre scientiam** (= referre ea quae sciebat ad Augustum) is a "strange" combination, as **referre** by itself, with the meaning of: to inform, report is already sufficient. But it is also found in legal texts: **referre ad scientiam principis,** for instance Cod.Iust.7.61.1,2; 12.35.11. From the verb in **this** meaning is derived: **referendarius** (subst.): "a court or papal official whose business is with reports, petitions etc." (Souter p.345). This subst. only in use from the 5th century onwards, hence not in Amm. Cf.et. Heum.-Seckel p.498. Cf.et. ad 16.11.7, p.89.11 **(relatio);** ad 15.5.13 (= III p.90).

p. 123. 16 **omnes qui plus poterant in palatio.** Note the **alliteratio.** For these influential persons cf. ad 16.8.11, p.83.4.*b, c:* **potentes in regia.** For **palatium** cf. ad 14.5.8 (= I p.129); Heum.-Seckel p.402; Souter p.283. **Comitatus** and **palatium** are used (as so often) without any difference in meaning, and that so closely together.

p. 123. 16-17 **adulandi professores iam docti.** Just as in the literature one finds professores sapientiae, eloquentiae, litterarum, liberalium studiorum, etc., thus Amm. invents a new kind of professors, viz. professors in the art of flattery, who were already long schooled in that (**iam** docti: **iam** in the very frequent meaning of **iam dudum**). Cf.22.4.1: non ut philosophus **veritatis indagandae professor** (= not as a philosopher who pretends only to search for the truth).

a **recte consulta prospereque conpleta.** For adject. and partic.neutr.plur. cf. ad 17.3.2, p.108.12*a;* ad 17.4.1, p.109.4*a*. Note the alliterating **c** and **p**. Translation: the right decisions and their succesful conclusions. Cf. et.16.12.8: utilitati securitatique **recte consulens** Caesar.   p. 123. 17
b Cf.18.7.4: et imperatis sine mora **conpletis**. Thus also in Veget.r.m. Lang p.17.11; p.36.1: **iussa conplere**; p.27.4; p.36.22.

vertebant in derididulum. Rare archaic adject. In Varro Plaut.Terent. Not in Cic.Caes. In Liv.39.26.4 (?). Similarly once in Quint. Furthermore: Tac. **Gell.Apul.** Also in Lucret. Cf. Krebs Antib.I p.423 (with lit.). Not in Claud.Veget.r.m.Opt.Milev.Arn.adv.nat. For **archaism** cf. ad 14.7.10 (= II p.33); Hagend.Arn. (op.cit.II) p.118; p.169 sq.; Hagend.St.Amm. p.108 note 1 (op.cit.I). Cf.et. Gudeman Tac.Dial.² (1914) p.308 sq.; 338 sq.   p. 123. 17-18

talia. Cf. ad 17.3.2, p.108.12*a*.   p. 123. 18

strepentes. Cf.17.9.3: haec et similia multa **strepebant**; 16.7.2: (Marcellus) mox venit Mediolanum, **strepens** et tumultuans (ut erat vanidicus et amenti propior); 31.16.6.; 19.11.7; etc.   p. 123. 18

insulse. Although found in **Cic.Eutr.Apul.**, it seems probable to me that this little flower was picked from **Gellius** (16.12.6; 12.2.6 (superlat.)), because just before the last-quoted passage Gellius has: **derididulos versus.** So this may be a case of either an unconscious reminiscence or of a deliberate one ("hidden" quotation, a literary puzzle which authors of that period often gave their readers). Not in Veget.r.m.Claud.Opt.Milev. Arn.adv.nat. For the **place of the adv.** cf. ad 17.11.1, p.123.24.   p. 123. 18

in odium venit. Cf.Cic. de fin.2.24(79): ne **in odium veniam**, si amicum destitero tueri. The expression replaces the passivum. which is lacking of **odi** as we find also in Cic. pro Vat. 3(9): sic ego **te** ... tamen dico esse **odio civitati**: Nep.Lys.1.3: ut eius opera **in maximum odium Graeciae**   p. 123. 18

Lacedaemonii **pervenerint.** But the activum is also circumscribed "unnecessarily", e.g. Opt.Milev.1.3: quamvis ... omnibus notum sit, quod nos **odio habeant** et execrentur et nolint se dici fratres nostros (= Ziwsa p.4); ibid. Ziwsa p.5; ibid.4.4 (= Ziwsa p.106): **odio nos habetis,** fratres utique vestros, nec apostolos imitari voluistis.

p. 123. 19 **capella:** lit. kid, young goat. One would have expected here **hircus (hirculus).** The use of the term of abuse is explained by **hirsutus,** referring to **Julianus'** philosopher's beard.

p. 123. 19 **hirsutum.** Cf.Ovid.Met.12.765 sq.:
Iam rigidos pectis rastris, Polypheme, capillos,
Iam libet **hirsutam** tibi falce recidere **barbam.**
ibid.2.30:
Et glacialis hiems **canos hirsuta capillos.**
Curt.Ruf.9.10.9: prominent ungues nunquam recisi, **comae hirsutae et intonsae sunt;** Claud.1.214 sq. (In Prob. et. Olybr.cons.):
Illi (sc.Tiberino) glauca nitent **hirsuto** lumina **vultu**
Caeruleis infecta notis, reddentia patrem
Oceanum.

p. 123. 19 **carpentes:** berating (class.) of **persons,** also used, e.g. in Caes.b.g.3.17: ut iam non solum hostibus in contemptionem Sabinus veniret, sed etiam nostrorum militum vocibus nonnihil **carperetur.**

p. 123. 20 **loquacem talpam.** Wagner: "quam cum olim, falso tamen, plane caecam esse crederent, hoc voluisse videntur cavillatores, Iulianum de rebus, quas plane non intelligeret, garrire temere et iudicare". Probably Wagner has in mind Verg.Georg.1.183:
Aut **oculis capti** fodere cubilia **talpae.**
Or Sen.Nat.Quaest.3.16: pleraque (sc.animalia) ex his caeca, ut **talpae** et subterranei mures, quibus deest lumen, quia supervacuum est. Although W's explanation sounds plausible, I suspect that the **loquax talpa** stems from some fable, unknown to me.

p. 123. 20 **purpuratam simiam:** not an emperor in purple, but a purpled monkey, imitating comically a real emperor (or Caesar). Here, too, a fable or farce as the origin of the expression is not impossible, in my view.

p. 123. 20-21 **litterionem Graecum:** Greek school-master. Seyf.: "Federheld", a beautiful translation, like Wagner's "Sylbenstecher". Cf. Krebs Antib.2

p.29, who, like Georges s.v. II 686, wrongly quotes 28.4.14, where this word does not occur. Though it says in 28.4.13: ut deesse solus magister ludi litter⟨ar⟩ii videretur (a version which is also found in Seyf. and Rolfe, of W.A.G. But V:

litterii). Ludus litterarius is a normal combination, post-class. Cf. Krebs ibid.p.28. I see no reason here to read **litterio.**

The subst. further occurs in August. (cf. Krebs ibid.p.29). According to Heraeus Arch. L.L.G (op.cit.I) 12 p.273 (1902): die Römische Soldatensprache, it is a word taken from the soldiers's language for the scholar, erudite (= **litteratus** in Cic.et.al.), but then with a mocking or contemptuous meaning; just as "das Militär" has expressed on other occasions his contempt for intellectuals and artists. This is, however, not at all true of Amm., who rather takes an entirely opposite standpoint and values a cultural education very highly.

Note. For "**castrensis sermonis reliquiae**" cf.et. Pighi St.Amm. (1935) p.173, with a list which should be studied critically, in my view.

et his congruentia plurima. Class. Besides this: **congruus.** Cf. ad 16.12.12, p.92.27b.   p. 123. 21

a **atque u⟨t tin⟩tinnacula principi resonantes.** V atque utinnacula. BG   p. 123. 21-22
atque vernacula. The version given above by Cl. also that of Sabbah. Seyf. atque ut **tinnacula** (Löfst.). Rolfe atque ut **tintinnabula** (R.Unger). For further versions cf.Cl.app.crit.p.123. **Tintinnaculum** and **Tintinnabulum** are synonymous (cf. Souter p.421; Georges II 3132). But since **tintin(n)are** and **tintinnire** occur besides **tinnire** and **tinnitare,** it seems logical to me to assume here a verbal stem, from which **tinnaculum** is derived, and thus to maintain V's version. Then we only need to correct the haplographia. BG gives an unfortunate "correction" of a misunderstood version of the manuscripts. For **tinnire** Cf.31.1.2: et querulum quoddam nocturnae volucres **tinniebant** et flebile.

b **resonantes**: resounding in the ears of the emperor, ... filling the ears with their jingling. **Principi** = auribus principis. It seems a nice find to present the empty flattery as the jingle of bells, gratifying to the ears.

gestienti. The verb is stronger than **cupio. C.inf.** also class. It occurs   p. 123. 22
several times in Arn.adv.nat., once in Veget.r.m. Not in Claud.Opt.Milev. In the Cod.Iust.3.29.1. Cic. reminiscence?

obruere. Here this verb has (as happens more often, cf.Cic.Tusc.2.27(66)),   p. 123. 22

the meaning of **obnubilare** (cf. ad 16.1.5, p.72.1) or **obumbrare** (cf. ad 17. 12.70, p.103.10-11).

p. 123. 23 **ut.** Cf. ad 17.8.3, p.119.27-p.120.1*a*.

p. 123. 23 **segnem ... timidum.** The first adj. means: lax, cowardly, the second: timid. But both adjectives do not fit Julianus, who is sooner **audax** and **fortis atque strenuus.** The meaning of these qualifications is, of course, to deny the Caesar his unmistakably soldierly characteristics.

p. 123. 23 **incessentes.** The verb does not occur in Claud.Veget.r.m.Arn.adv.nat. Opt.Milev. Cf.et. ad 16.11.8, p.89.18*b*.

p. 123. 23 *a* **umbratilem.** Again the same contempt for the "intellectual", the scholar. See above ad 17.11.1, p.123.20-21.
 b Cf.Cic.Tusc.2.11(27): vitamque **umbratilem**; ibid. de orat.34(157): Educenda deinde dictio est ex hac domestica exercitatione et **umbratili** medium in agmen, in pulverem, in clamorem (c.annot. in ed.**Courbaud,** 1905, p.125); orat.19.64: Mollis est enim oratio philosophorum et **umbratilis** (cf.et.Brut.9(37); de leg.3.6.(14)). Georges quotes Colum.1.2: quae non sit mora **segnis,** non **umbratilis.** Colum., as well as Amm. will have had Cicero as their source. With Amm. the adj. is used in a contemptuous sense: ± a pale bookworm, who shuns the daylight.
 c The adj. further occurs: 18.6.2: memores, quod relictus ad sui tutelam cum **inerti et umbratili milite** nihil amiserat per decennium (sc.Ursicinus); 21.16.21: quae et alia horum similia eidem Ioviano imperium quidem, sed et cassum et **umbratile** ut ministro rerum funebrium portendebant; 26.8.5: (Arintheus) et dedignatus hominem superare certamine despicabilem (sc. Hyperechium) ... ipsis hostibus iussit suum vincire rectorem; atque ita **turmarum antesignanus umbratilis** comprensus suarum est manibus. The meanings in the 3 examples are respectively: 1. weak, spineless, dull; 2. shadow-authority, pseudo-authority; 3. shadow warrior. (Thus 3 different nuances of meaning than in *b*).
Note. for **antesignanus** cf.16.12.18, p.94.5; 1. for **turma** ad 15.4.10 (= III p.64).
2. One should also compare **umbraticus** 30.4.15: qui cum semel **umbraticis lucris** et inhiandae undique pecuniae sese dederint (= obscure profitable practices, - which shun the light of day).

p. 123. 24 *a* **gestaque secus.** Cf. ad 15.5.38 (= III p.129). For the curious placing of the **adverbia,** at the end of sentences or parts of sentences, cf. Blomgren p.108 sq. (with numerous examples). This occurs very frequently in Amm. **and (this time) usually not metri causa.** This habit is not always understood and causes editors soemetimes to make errors, as, for instance, Clark here and there.

b for **gesta** cf. ad 17.11.1, p.123.15*b*.

a **verbis comptioribus exornantem.** With the literal meaning: **(to decorate)** p. 123. 24 e.g. Cic. ad fam.7.23.2. Metaph. e.g. Cic.Tusc.2.5(12): Nonne verendum est igitur ... ne philosophiam **falsa gloria exornes?** Cic. de orat.3.38(152): Tria sunt igitur in verbo simplici, quae orator afferat **ad illustrandam atque exornandam orationem:** aut inusitatum **verbum,** aut novatum, aut translatum; Tusc.2.14(33): si nulla est (sc.patientia doloris), quid **exornamus philosophiam** aut quid eius nomine **gloriosi sumus** (= ea gloriamur)? Also in connection with **gloria,** following immediately upon the words explained above, I suspect that we are dealing here with a Cic. reminiscence.

b Cf.Cic. de sen.9(28): facitque persaepe ipsa sibi audientiam diserti senis **compta** et mitis **oratio;** Tac.Hist.1.19: Inde apud senatum non **comptior** Galbae, non longior quam apud militem **sermo;** Quint.10.1.79.

primitus. Archaism. = primum, primo. Occurs in several late Latin p. 123. 24 authors. Cf. Krebs Antib.2 p.376 (with lit.). The adv. occurs several times in Opt.Milev., not in Claud.Veget.r.m.Arn.adv.nat. For the **adverbia ending in -itus** cf. Liesenberg (op.cit.I), 1889, p.15; ad 14.1.9 (= I p.65).

XI, 2

namque ... invidiae etc. Another moralistic contemplation, with the p. 123. 25 sq. required **exempla.** Cf. Naudé (op.cit.XVI) Amm.Marc.p.81 sq. (with lit.); D.A.Pauw, Characterisation of Amm.Marc. (in Dutch) (1972) p.50 sq. (with lit.). Lindenbr.: "Vetus dictum est: Τοῖς διὰ τοῦ ἡλίου πορευομένοις ἕπεται κατ' ἀνάγκην σκιά, τοῖς δὲ διὰ τῆς δόξης βαδίζουσι ἀκολουθεῖ φθόνος."

Cf.et.Claud.24.43 sq. (de cons.Stil.3):

 Est aliquod meriti spatium, quod nulla furentis
 Invidiae mensura capit.

ibid.29.228 sq. (Laus Serenae):

 ....: dum gentibus ille (Stilicho)
 Confligit, vigili tu prospicis omnia sensu,

Ne quid in absentem virtutibus obvia semper
Audeat **invidiae rabies,** neu rumor iniquus.
And finally the last 2 lines of the epigram 91 (In sepulcrum speciosae):
Hic foimosa iacet Veneris sortita figuram,
Egregiumque decus **invidiamque** tulit.

p. 123. 25 **obiecta ... invidiae.** Obiectus = subject to, exposed to, etc., fairly often in Cic. Cf.Tusc.1.46(111): fortunae obiectum; pro Mur.40(87): Obiicitur enim concionibus seditiosorum ... ; pro Vat.9(23): qui consulem morti obieceris ... ; pro domo 57(145): si in illo paene fato rei publicae obieci meum caput pro vestris caerimoniis; etc. Resembling our place Plin. N.H.29.8: Non deseram Catonem tam ambitiosae artis **invidiae** a me **obiectum.** Cf.et.Claud.26.115 sq. (de raptu Proserp.III):
(me Cererem sc.) revocat tandem custodia cari
Pignoris (sc.Proserpinae) et **cunctis obiecti fraudibus** anni.
(anni = aetatis suae).

p. 123. 26-28 **legimus ... offensam.** Personificatio. Cf. ad 17.2.1, p.107.13.

p. 123. 26 **duces.** Here generally used: general. For the t.t. cf. ad 14.7. 7 = II p.23.

p. 123. 27 **etiam si inveniri non poterant.** For the **indicat.** in the or.obl. cf. ad 16.10. 17, p.87.15-16*b*.

p. 123. 27 **malignitatem:** malignity. Plaut.Liv.Sen.Tac.Prud. and others. Also in judic.lit. For the meaning: **sin, impiety,** cf. Souter p.240. The subst. does not occur in Claud.Veget.r.m.Arn.adv.nat., though it is found in Opt. Milev., in the first-mentioned meaning.

p. 123. 27 **spectatissimis actibus.** For the subst.cf. ad 17.11.7, p.121.11*b*. The adj.: outstanding, spectacular, class.; also in judic.lit. Not in Claud.Veget. r.m.Opt.Milev.Arn.adv.nat.

p. 123. 28 **offensam.** With this same active meaning also, e.g. Iust.Phil.1.9: sed (Cambyses) **offensus superstitionibus** Aegyptiorum Apis ceterorumque deorum aedes dirui iubet. Not in Claud.Veget.r.m.Opt.Milev.Arn.adv. nat.

XI, 3

p. 123. 28 **Cimonem.** The well-known Athenian statesman, 504-449 B.C. The battle of the Eurymedon took place in 469 B.C. The Persians were beaten here on land and at sea. Cf.R.E. (Swoboda) 11.438-453; Woordenboek d Oudh.3, 1967, 659 (Nuchelmans), with lit.; Bury, Hist. of Greece (1924) p.335-359 (passim); Zimmern, The Gr.Commonwealth[4] (1924) p.333-p.409 (passim); Beloch II.2 (1916) p.65-176 (passim). Amm. will sooner have gained his knowledge from **Nepos' biogr. (V)**, than from the biogr. of Thucyd. and Plutarchus. Cf.et. Sabbah A.M. II p.181 (note 88).

a **insimulatum ... saepe ante.** Gardth.Cl.Seyf. assume a gap. Rolfe: insimulatum **incesti (Lind.), qui** saepe ante et. Sabbah: insimulatum saepe ante, **qui** prope. B.G. ante **qui** prope. **V sine lac.** In my opinion Sabbah's version is the best. But another conception of V's text is still possible, namely that: The **accus. Cimonem ... insimulatum** is caused by: finxisse malignitatem ... **in** veteres duces. Strictly speaking it should have been: **ut in** Cimonem etc. But Amm. has in mind: **ut Cimon insimulatur.** Where, however, he wants to express the contrast between **envy** and **achievements**, he expresses the latter by the verbum finitum **(delevit)** and the main point, as so often, by the part. **(insimulatum,** Cf. ad 17.3.5, p.108.20*a*). The accusativus construction of § 2 is continued "by the feel of it" into § 3, which causes an erroneous construction of the sentence. With this view **saepe ante et** belongs with **delevit** (so that **saepe ante** should not be linked to **insimulatum!**) Cf.et. Blomgren (op.cit.II) p.46 sq. Viri arte grammatica imbuti will perhaps raise objections against this kind of exegeses; but one should not lose sight of the fact that our texts (and especially the latter ones) have often been needlessly smoothed out.

b For the constructions of the **verba accusandi** cf. ad 14.5.3 (= I p.85).

p. 123. 28-29

innumerum. Cf. ad 17.4.8, p.110.6*b;* Opt.Milev.2.5 (Ziwsa, p.42): igitur cum manufestum sit ... nos cum tot **innumerabilibus populis** esse et tot provincias nobiscum; 7.1 (Ziwsa p.159): revera sufficiebat sibi ecclesia catholica habens **innumerabiles populos** in provinciis universis; Krebs Antib.1 p.748. Delevit innumerum: claus.II.

p. 124. 1

a **coegitque gentem insolentia semper elatam.** V sem relatam. Sem⟨per⟩ **elatam**: Lind.Cl.Seyf. Sabbah Rolfe. **Saepe elatam?** Cl. in app.crit. The Lind. version is to be preferred, in my opinion.

b **insolentia** here, of course, insolence. But 24.1.2: utque ductor usu et docilitate firmatus metuens, ne **per locorum insolentiam** insidiis caperetur occultis (= unfamiliarity with). Both meanings are class.

c These words, "natural" in the mouth of a Roman patriot, hide the

p. 124. 1

271

annoyance at the position of the most powerful competitor of the Romans, viz. the Persians (c.q. Sassanids). They possess **insolentia**, because their policy against the Roman empire is often an agressive one. But the Persians' opinion of the Romans, who possessed a large part of the former Persian realm, will have been no different (with perhaps more justification). It is advisable to re-read **Sapor's** letter: 17.5.3 sq. Cf.et. **Brok** (op.cit.XVI) p.2-8 (with lit.).

d **elatam.** With this metaph. meaning also: 15.7.7: Athanasium episcopum ... ultra professionem **altius se efferentem**; 26.8.13: Ea victoria ultra homines sese Procopius **efferens.**

p. 124. 1-2 **obsecrare suppliciter pacem.** For this verb cf. Krebs Antib.2 p.188. I doubt whether **pacem obsecrare** occurs very frequently. The verb does not occur in Claud.Veget.r.m.Opt.Milev.Arn.adv.nat.

p. 124. 2 *a* **Aemilianum itidem Scipionem.** Refers to **P.Cornelius Scipio Aemilianus Africanus Minor,** the son of L. Aemilius Paulus, adopted by P.Corn. Scipio, son of **P.Corn. Scipio Africanus Maior.** Born in 184/185, died (murdered?) in 129 B.C. The destroyed cities are **Carthago** (146 B.C.) and **Numantia** (133 B.C.). The information **obstinatae-excisae** is not quite accurate: 1⁰ because in 149 B.C. (beginning of the 3rd Pun.war) Carthago was no longer a threat to Rome. 2⁰. because **Numantia** was certainly not in a position to threaten the Roman sovereignty. It was the capital of the Arevaci, who in 143 B.C. took the side of **Viriathus,** leader of the **Lusitanians.** Though Viriathus was dangerous, this was only to the Spanish districts (died 139 B.C.). 3⁰. because both cities could not bracketed together, viz. the one a metropolis of the world trade and the other a fortified, but also primitive town in the Spanish province. The simplification is that of the exempla literature; but characteristic for the late "Roman", to whom this all happened a long time ago (for Amm. more than 500 years!). For **Viriathus** cf. ad 14.11.33 (= II p.144). Cf. Ihne III.5 (1872) p.273 sq. (passim); IV.6 (1876) p.230, 267; Mommsen[13] (1921) II.p.15 sq.; Hohl[5] (1923) Grundr.d.röm.Gesch. p.161 sq. (with lit.).

Also mentioned: 23.5.20; 24.2.16-17; 25.10.13. For other **Scipiones** cf. ad 14.6.11; 15.10.10; 25.9.10; 31.13.17; 22.9.5; 21.14.5; **24.4.27** (cf. Finke, op.cit.I, p.65). For the sources used by Amm. for **17.11.3 etc.** cf. Finke p.45, p.44.

b For **itidem** cf. ad 16.12.17, p.93.23-24*b*.

p. 124. 2 **somniculosus.** With this pass. meaning also in Cic.Colum. (late Latin are

somnolentus and **somnolentia**). The adj. not in Claud.Veget.r.m.Opt. Milev.Arn.adv.nat.

a **incusari**: fairly soon after **insimulatum** p.123.28 as variatio, but with the same meaning. **Incusare** is not used for a legal indictment. (**Accusare** can be used for both: judicial and non-judicial indictment). **Insimulare** can also be used for a judicial indictment, but it often has an unfavourable meaning: (to bring false charges). Both verbs occur in the judic.lit. (Cf. Heum.-Seckel p.259. 272). p. 124. 3

b The **acc.c.inf.** is caused by **legimus**. Cf. ad 17.11.3, p.123.28-29*a*.

a **malivolentia**. Although it has a slightly different meaning than **malignitas**, the first subst. is used here only variationis causa. Here we now have claus.IV. When one reads **malignitate**, one has claus.III. p. 124. 3

b for the spelling (= malevolentia) cf. Georges II 779-780, with the lit. quoted.

inpetrabili vigilantia. For the adj. cf. ad 14.8.5 (= II p.67). "**Energisch**" by Seyf. is less correct. Better Sabbah: "**efficace**" or "**anstellig**" by Büchele. Of course, the subst. here means: vigilance, literally. Cf.Cic. ad fam.7.30.1: Nihil tamen eo consule mali factum est: fuit enim mirifica **vigilantia**, qui suo toto sonsulatu somnum non viderit. p. 124. 3

a **obstinatae in perniciem**. Cf.Tac.Hist.3.56: (Vitellius) acerrimum **militem** et usque **in extrema obstinatum** trucidandum capiendumque tradidit; ibid.2.101: Caecina legiones adsecutus centurionum militumque **animos obstinatos pro Vitellio** variis artibus subruebat. But **obstinatus**, linked with **ad.c.acc.** or with the **infinit.** is more common. Cf. Krebs Antib.2 p.190 sq. p. 124. 3

b Cf.Veget.r.m.4.28 (= Lang p.148): oppidani ... prorumpunt ... omniaque **in perniciem suam** fabricata opera subvertunt; 3.10 (= Lang p.92): Nam civile odium **ad inimicorum perniciem** praeceps est, ad utilitatem suae defensionis incautum.

excisae: t.t.mil. for: destroy entirely, does not occur in Veget.r.m. (though **excidium** does). Class. p. 124. 4

XI. 4

nec non etiam. Cf.28.4.33: ut ... et iudicibus celsis, itidemque minoribus, **nec non etiam** matronis ... clametur assidue ... Cf.et.Hagend.abund. (op.cit.I) p.214 (with lit.).

Pompeium: Cn. Pompeius Magnus 106 - 48 B.C. Cf. Drumann-Groebe p. 124. 4

(op.cit.I) IV² (1908) p.332 sq. (with lit.); Niese-Hohl⁵ (1923) p.204 sq. (with lit.); Ihne VI (1886) 8 p.118 sq. (passim); VII (1890) 9 p.1 sq. (passim); Mommsen III¹² (1920) p.12 sq.; p.98 sq.; ad 14.8.10 (= II p.74 sq.); ad 14.8.12 (= II p.78); ad 16.7.10, p.80.14-17; ad 14.11.32 (= II p.144); 22.16.3; 23.5.16; 29.5.33; **Finke** p.48 (ad 22.16.3); ibid. p.57 sq.; ibid.p.68 sq. (ad 17.11.4).

p. 124. 5 **obtrectatores.** Cic.Suet.Iust. Not in Claud.Veget.r.m.Opt.Milev.Arn. adv.nat.

p. 124. 5 **scrutantes.** Used concessively. The substant.20.3.3; 22.8.10 (?); Cl. scitatores.

p. 124. 5-6 *a* **cum nihil unde vituperari deberet inveniretur. unde** = from where = because of which, hence. Cf.Caes.b.g.5.53.4: atque **unde** (= a quibus) initium belli fieret, explorabant; Cic. pro Flacco 26 (62);' Cic.Verr.3.70 (165); etc. etc. Cf.et. Heum.-Seckel p.601; Kalb, Röm.Rechtsspr. (1961) § 53 p.55. For the post-class. and late Latin **conclusive unde**ᵢ (often used by lawyers, etc.) cf. Krebs Antib.2 p.691 sq. (with lit.); ad **16.7.11, p.118.9.** Note. **unde** = **ubi (qua)** and **inde** = **ibi (ea)** do not seem to occur in Amm. Cf. Svennung Pallad p.615 sq. (with examples and lit.).
b **deberet:** conjunct. consecut.

p. 124. 6 **observarunt.** One would expect here an **imperfectum**. Cf. ad 14.5.2 (= I p.84).

p. 124. 6 **ludibriosa et inrita.** Cf.29.2.3: qui ... incantamenta quaedam anilia vel **ludibriosa** subderent **amatoria** ad insontium perniciem concinnata. Also Gell.August. = ridiculous. **inrita** = with which they had no success, without result = of no value whatsoever. With this last meaning also Gell.11.2.

p. 124. 6-9 For the sources of this passage cf.Plut.Pomp.48.7; Seneca Contr.7.4.7; Val.Maxim.6.2.7. But it seems more probable to me also here, that Amm. has **not** made **direct** use of Plutarchus (cf. ad 17.7.9-14f). Cf.et. **Finke** p.68; Sabbah A.M.II p.181 (note 89); Seyf. I p.312 (note 139), who refers to Otto Sprichw. (op.cit.I) 116 sq.; A.M.ed. Wagner Comm.I p.285.

p. 124. 6-7 **genuino quodam more:** with a kind of innate habit. Very good Seyf.: In einer bestimmten charakteristischen Art". Cf.22.8.26: Hypanis fluvius,

genuinis intumescens **aquis** et externis (= its own water and that flowing in from outside).

digito uno scalpebat. This act was considered to be effeminate. Very clearly Iuven.p.130 sq.:   p. 124. 7
> Ne trepida, numquam pathicus tibi derit amicus
> Stantibus et salvis his collibus: undique ad illos
> Convenient et carpentis et navibus **omnes**
> **Qui digito scalpunt uno caput.**

quodque ... gestabat ... insign. Symbol of royal dignity. Cf. Suet,Iul.Caes.   p. 124. 7-11
79.1: Cum ... quidam e turba **statuae eius (sc.Caes.) coronam lauream, candida fascia praeligatam, imposuisset** et tribuni plebis ... coronae fasciam detrahi hominemque duci in vincula iussissent, dolens seu **parum prospere motam regni mentionem** etc.

aliquandiu: during a certain period of time. Probably a flower of speech,   p. 124. 7
although, not quite frequent, in class.Latin. Cf.Thes.s.v. Not in Claud. Veget.r.m.Opt.Milev.Arn.adv.nat., though it is found in Dig.7.1.57 = aliquantum temporis.
Cf. **aliquantisper** 31.3.3 and Fesser p.42 (with lit.), also an unusual word.

a   **tegendi ulceris causa deformis.** For the **hyperbaton** cf.17.1.6, p.105.21*a*.   p. 124. 7-8
For **causa c. gerundi(v)o** cf.Hofm.-Leum.177, 178 p.596, 598 (with lit.).
b   **deformis.** Here = dirty, soiled; with which one can not really show oneself.

fasciola candida. Cf. ad p.124.7-11. The subst. is rare, but is found, among   p. 124. 8
others in Varro L.L.5.130; Cic. de har. resp.21(44); Horat.Sat.2.3.255. Further post-class. and late Latin. The demin.neutr. **(fasciolum)** occurs in Veget.mulom.2.57.1 (= Lommatzsch p.149); Mulom.Chir.64 (= Oder p.23).

a   **candida crus colligatum gestabat.** Note the alliteration. The version of   p. 124. 8
the last 2 words is doubtful. The version given above is that of Her. (which is based on Val.Max.6.2.7: Cui (sc.Pompeio) candida fascia crus alligatum habenti Favonius ...), which is followed by Seyf.Rolfe. G Sabbah **colligabat.** V collibatam, a corrupt version. Novák: **colligatum habebat.** Colligare is a t.t.; thus one finds colligare crura, vulnera, etc. I believe that G's version is to be preferred.

b **gestabat** (conjecture). This verb also 14.10.8; 23.6.6; 24.6.8; 26.9.7; 25.1.15; 26.6.15; 20.4.19; 25.10.2; 22.9.1; 28.2.8; (conjecture?). Cf.et. ad 17.4.4, p.109.16*a*.

p. 124. 9 **factitare.** Also used: 14.5.5; 16.5.4; 19.12.12; 27.9.10 (V factibat).

p. 124. 9 **dissolutum.** With this meaning: thoughtless, dissolute, unrestrained, etc. fairly often in Cic. The adj. does not occur in Claud.Veget.r.m.Opt. Milev., but is found in Arn.adv.nat. Cf.1.59 (Reiffersch.p.40): enimvero **dissoluti** est **pectoris** in rebus seriis quaerere voluptatem; 6.12 (Reiffersch. p.223): Liber membris cum mollibus et languoris feminei **dissolutissimus laxitate**, Venus nuda et aperta, tamquam si illam dicas publicare etc. Cf.et. Krebs Antib.1 p.462.

p. 124. 9 **adserebant.** With the meaning: to assert, to assure, post-class. and late Latin. Cf.Thes.s.v.; Krebs Antib.1 p.207. From this the late Latin **assertio** is derived (not in Amm.). Cf.et. ad 16.12.17, p.93.29.

p. 124. 10 **nihil interesse oblatrantes.** Cf.14.9.1: (Ursicinus) dispicere litis exitialis crimina cogebatur, abnuens et reclamans **adulatorum oblatrantibus turmis.** Cf. Seneca de ira 3.43.1 (c.dat.). Also in Suet.Sil.Ital.August.Ambros. Prudent.Lact.Post-class. and late Latin.

p. 124. 10-11 **nihil interesse ... quam partem ... redimiret.** Construction and modus according to the classical rules.

p. 124. 10 *a* **argumento subfrigido.** The subst., with another meaning 28.4.1: vitium ... in alto iudice maculosum, quod citeriorem vitam paene omnem vergentem in luxum per **argumenta scaenica** (= plais) amoresque peregerat ...
b **subfrigido** = somewhat weak, without strong evidence. The adj. only in Amm.? The adv. **subfrigide** in Gell.2.9. Only there?

p. 124. 11 *a* **regiae maiestatis insigni.** Cf.Cic. pro Sext.26 (57): cum purpura et sceptro et illis **insignibus regiis**; Curt.Ruf.4.4.11: **regio insigni** et armis fulgentibus conspicuus; ibid.7.4.11: magnum onus sustines capite, **regium insigne**; ibid.8.12.14: Omphis, permittente Alexandro et **regium insigne** sumpsit et ...; Iust.Phil.10.1: (Artaxerxes) sinceriusque gaudium ex procreatione capturus, si **insignia maiestatis suae** vivus in filio conspexisset; Aur.Vict.Caes.3.13: His elatus dominum dici atque **insigne regni** capiti nectere tentaverat; etc.

b **regiae.** Cf. ad 16.12.17, p.93.24; ad 16.8.11, p.83.4*c*.

amantior ... patriae. Cf.Cic. ad Att.9.19.3: et boni cives, **amantes patriae,** mare infestum habebimus; ad Q.fr.1.1.5(15): ... si quem forte **tui** cognosti **amantiorem;** Hofm.-Leum.31 p.406; ad 17.4.3, p.109.12*b*.

p. 124. 11-12

a **ut documenta praeclara testantur.** Attention should be paid, while reading out loud, to sound and rhythm. **Documenta** here = proof, evidence.

p. 124. 12

b Cf.14.2.8: cum (latrones sc.) se impares nostris fore congressione stataria **documentis frequentibus** scirent (instructive example = experience) 14.7.6: post cuius (sc.consularis Syriae Theophili) lacrimosum interitum in unius exitio quisque **imaginem periculi sui** considerans **documento recenti similia** formidabat (note the abundantia. The sentence would have meant exactly the same if **documento recenti** had been left out). Here the meaning is also: instructive example. Cf.et. ad 17.1.2, p.104.10-p.105.3*b*.

XI, 5

In this § Amm. suddenly follows again the **town chronicle,** from where he passes in cap.12 to the Sarmatae and Quadi. Actually the importance attached to Roman city events is anachronistic. For Rome is no longer the principal city of the late Roman empire. But ennobled by its illustrious past and a long tradition, it preserves an "ideal" place in historiography. For the town chronicle cf. **Naudé** Amm.Marc. (op.cit.XVI) p.59-60; p.123-124; **Seeck,** "Die Reihe der Stadtpräfecten bei Amm.Marc." Hermes 18, 1883, p.289 sq.; **Christa Samberger** "Die Kaiserbiographie in den Res Gestae des Amm.Marc." Klio 51, 1969, p.349 sq. (of this p.382-385); **Kohns** (op.cit.XVI) p.25 sq. (with lit.); **Enszlin,** Zur Gesch.schr. etc. (op. cit.I) p.25 sq.; Klein (op.cit.I) p.48 sq.

p. 124. 13-16

Dum haec ita aguntur. Cf. ad 15.3.1, p.41.14 (= III p.27). For **dum** cf. ad 17.4.4, p.109.14. For the **variatio aguntur ... agebat** (14) cf. ad 14.10.1 (= II p.95). For the **praes.hist.** cf. Ehrism. (op.cit.I) p.8 sq.; ad 14.11.32 (= II p.143); (after **dum**) Ehrism.p.47 sq.; Reiter (op.cit.I) p.63 sq. Note. for other **formulary expressions** cf. ad 17.4.1, p.109.6*b* 1.

p. 124. 13

a **Artemius curans vicariam praefecturam.** Cf. Seeck, R.E.II.2.1444 s.v.; **Kohns,** p.122 sq. (with lit.). He has temporarily taken over the **prefectura urbis** since Aug. 25th 359 A.D., on which day **Iunius Bassus** died (cf. Seeck Regesten p.206). For **praef, urbi** cf. ad 14.6.1 (= I p.131, with the correc-

p. 124. 13-14

tion: Willems p.563 sq.). Artemius is **vicarius urbis Romae**. The **dioecesis Italiae** is divided between 2 **vicarii**. One has his seat in Milan and his territory extends over the 7 Northern provinces of the dioec. This one is called **vicarius Italiae**. The other **(v.u.R,)** rules over the 10 other provinces of the dioec., i.e. middle- and South Italy, with the exception of the capital "Cependant, à Rome même, le **vicarius** exerce, concurremment avec le **praefectus urbi,** la juridiction civile et criminelle, de même que le **praefectus urbi** a la juridiction civile et criminelle, concurremment avec le **vicarius** et les gouverneurs respectifs, dans les parties des provinces du diocèse situées dans un rayon de 100 milles autour de Rome, et qui s'appellent **regiones urbicariae** ou **suburbicariae**" (Willems p.579 sq. with lit.). **Note.** A **vicarius praefecturae urbis** is mentioned under Constantine the Great. But even if this function would still exist (or be temporarily restored), it seems highly unlikely to me that such a functionary would be meant here. Cf. Willems p.564 note 2. Cf.et. **Sabbah** Amm.II p.181 note 90 (with lit.).
b **curans** = administrans (17.4.1: **administrante** secundam adhuc Orfito praefecturam). **Curare** the well-known t.t.: to order, lead, govern., etc.; said of military functions as well as high state officials. Cf. ad 17.7.6, p.117.12*c*.

p. 124. 14 *a* **pro Basso quoque agebat.** Bassus succeeded **Orfitus**. (cf. ad 14.6.1 = I p.130 sq.). Cf.et. **Kohns** p.121; **Sabbah** Amm.II p.182 note 91; Seeck R.E.III 1.108. He entered upon his duties after March 25, 359 A.D.
b **agebat.** Cf. ad 16.12.69, p.103.1. Cf.et. Fesser p.19; ad 17.5.1, p.113.22.

p. 124. 14 **recens promotus.** For **recens** cf. ad 17.4.12, p.110.23. For **promovere** cf. 26.5.2: et Valentiniano quidem, cuius arbitrio res gerebatur, Iovinus evenit **dudum promotus** a Juliano per Gallias **magister armorum**; Veget. r.m.2.8 (= Lang p.42): Vetus tamen consuetudo tenuit, ut ex primo principe legionis **promoveretur centurio** primi pili, qui non solum aquilae praeerat etc. The construction with **in** or **ad** c.accus. is seen more often: cf.Veget.r.m.2.21 (= Lang p.55): ita ut ex prima cohorte **ad gradum quempiam promotus** vadat ad decimam cohortem etc.; Curt.Ruf.6.11.1: Bolon quidam ... vetus miles, ab humili ordine **ad eum gradum,** in quo tunc erat, **promotus.** This meaning **(to promote)** post-class. and late Latin. Cf. Krebs Antib.2 p.399 (with lit.); Lagergren, de vita et elocutione C.Plin. ... (1871) p.126; Heum.-Seckel p.469; ad 16.12.8, p.92.4-5; ad 16.12.19, p.94.8.

p. 124. 15 *a* **fatali decesserat sorte.** Cf.27.5.10: ubi postea Athanaricus ... **fatali**

sorte decessit; 19.11.15: quos ... **ordo fatalis absumpsit** (with variatio). (**fatum** = **fata** = mors; cf.Comm. Heuvel Stat.Theb.I (1932) p.258; Comm. Mulder Stat.Theb.II 1954 p.305).
b For **decedere** cf. Krebs Antib.1 p.396 (with lit.); Heum.-Seckel p.123.

cuius administratio ... dignum. Cf. Kohns (op.cit.XVI) p.123: "Dann liegt es nämlich nahe, dasz seit dem Tode des **Bassus** Rom sich in Versorgungsschwierigkeiten befand, die sowohl unter **Artemius** als auch unter dem auf ihn folgenden praefectus urbi **Tertullus** Unruhen zur Folge hatten". This conclusion is made very plausible by Kohn ibid. Amm. does not give any reasons for this. Though these were not riots, but **seditiones turbulentae.** It is clear from the context that these **seditiones** were not **memorabile aliquid, quod narrari sit dignum.** because he does not tell us anything about them (for that reason Seyf.'s translation: "sonst aber nichts merkwürdiges" is not right, in my view). p. 124. 15-16

administratio. Cf.27.3.11: Advenit successor eius (sc. **Lampadii,** praef. urbi) ex quaesitore palatii **Viventius,** integer et prudens Pannonius, cuius **administratio** quieta fuit et placida (= government, rule, duration of office). Cf. ad 17.11.5, p.124.13-14*b;* Heum.-Seckel p.15. Late latin the meaning is: **diaconatus,** not in Amm. p. 124. 15

a perpĕssā ēst tūrbūlēntās. Claus.III. Without synizesis. The choice of the verb is not accidental. p. 124. 15-16
b Cf.30.4.13: tertius eorum (sc.iuris peritorum) est ordo, qui, ut in **professione turbulenta** (= a turbulent profession) clarescant etc.
c For the **verb** cf. ad 16.10.3, p.84.19-20*a*.

sit: conj.consecut. According to the class. rule. Cf. ad 17.11.4, p.124.5-6*b*. p. 125. 16

XII.

In this chapter and the next one the **first war against the Sarmats** (and the Quads) is described, during April-June 358. The **second war against the Sarmats** is told in book XIX. This takes place during the months of April/May - Oct./November 359. For the chronology cf. **Pighi** N.Stud.Amm. (op.cit.XVI) p.136; eiusd. (op.cit.IV) p.XXVI, with improved chronol.; **Seeck** Regesten p.205, 206. Cf.et. Stein Spätr.Gesch. (op,cit.I) p.224, with lit.; p.198, with lit. p. 124. 17-
p. 128. 10

XII, 1

p. 124. 17 **Augusto.** Obviously put in front to indicate that we are now in the region where Constantius Augustus operates.
inter haec. (Cf. ad 17.4.1, p.109.4*a*) = interea. Cf. ad 14.6.1 (= I p.89); Reinhardt (op.cit.I) p.55.

p. 124. 17 **quiescenti.** Here with a special meaning: to reside; linked with **per hiemem** = hibernating. This meaning evolved from: to keep quiet = not make, start a war. In 14.4.5: nulla copia **quiescendi** permissa, the verb means: to find rest, to rest; in 21.1.12: animantis **altius quiescentis**, the meaning is: to sleep deeply.

p. 124. 17 **per hiemem.** For the numerous examples of **per temporale** cf. Reinhardt p.29 sq.

p. 124. 17 **apud Sirmium.** For **apud** cf. ad 14.11.21 (= II p.137); Reinhardt p.51; Hofm.-Leum.92 p.499 (with lit.); Heum.-Seckel p.37 (2); ad 15.3.7 (= III p.46).

p. 124. 17 **Sirmium.** Cf. ad 15.3.7 (= III p.45).

p. 124. 18 **permixtos Sarmatas et Quados.** For these two peoples cf. ad 16.10.20, p.88.3-4; Stroheker (op.cit.XVI) p.324: Index; Expositio totius mundi et gentium edit. Rougé, 1966, p.17 sq.; Sabbah Amm. II p.182, note 93.

p. 124. 19 **armaturae:** armament. In 14.6.17 **leves armaturas** means: the light-armed; 14.11.3 per multiplicem **armaturae scientiam**: tactics; in 25.3.5 is **armatura**: armed forces. For other meanings cf. ad 14.6.17 (= I p.142); ad 15.5.6 (= III p.82).

p. 124. 19 **Pannonias.** Cf. ad 15.3.7 (= III p.44 sq.); Expositio (op.cit.) p.196, 309, 310; Pieper Tab.14.

p. 124. 19-20 **Moesiarumque alteram.** In view of the dwelling-places of the Quads and the Sarmats at that time, **Moesia I** must have been meant. Cf. ad 16.10.20, p.88.4; Expositio (op.cit.) p.196, 309; Pieper Tab.14.
Note. Sabbah Amm.II p.182 (note 94) is mistaken in informing this: **Moesia** I, with the capital **Naissus**. See above.

p. 124. 20 *a* **cuneis dispersis.** For **cunei** cf. ad 16.11.5, p.88.29; Cod.Iust.6.62.2 (a⁰

347): Universis tam legionibus quam vexillationibus (cf.III p.98) comitatensibus (cf.II p.129) seu **cuneis** insinuare debebis (= to inform, to announce), ut cognoscant etc.

b Seyf.: in **getrennten** Abteilungen. Sabbah: par bandes **dispersées**. It seems to me that Amm. means: scattered over a large area. For why, if they were **permixti,** would they attack separately? The part.perf.pass. fairly often in Veget.r.m.

incursare. Also 14.3.1; 16.10.20; 26.4.5; 27.12.15; 29.6.16. p. 124. 20

XII, 2
aperto habilibus Marti. Cf.Ovid.Met.13.207 sq.: p. 124. 21
Post acies primas urbis se moenibus hostes
Continuere diu, nec **aperti** copia **Martis**
Ulla fuit.

hastae sunt longiores = — longae. Compar. = posit. (cf. ad 14.6.12 = p. 124. 21
I p.96).

a **loricae ex cornibus rasis et levigatis** etc. A description in Paus.1.21.6. p. 124. 21-22
Cf.et.Veget.r.m.4.9 (= Lang p.135): Cornua quoque vel cruda coria proficit colligi ad catafractas texendas aliaque machinamenta sive munimina.
b for **loricae** cf. ad 16.12.46, p.99.3-4*b*.
c lēvigatis. Cf. ad 17.4.7, p.110.6*a;* Min.Fel.3.6; 22.4.

plumarum specie. Cf.24.4.15: et primi Romani hostem undique **lamminis** p. 124. 22
ferreis in modum tenuis plumae contectum fidentemque, quod tela rigentis ferri lapsibus impacta resiliebant ... lacessebant; 24.2.10: tum defensores ... resistebant **ferrea nimirum facie omni,** quia lamminae singulis membrorum liniamentis cohaerenter aptatae fido **operimento totam hominis speciem** contegebant. **Fesser** compares with this p.21 Sall.Hist.4.66: equites catafracti **ferrea omni specie** and ibid.4.65: equis paria **operimenta** erant, namque **linteo ferreas lamminas in modum plumae adnexuerant.** Imitatio coupled with variatio are very obvious here.

a **linteis indumentis.** Cf.23.4.14: sagitta est cannea ..., quae in muliebris p. 124. 22
coli formam, quo nentur **lintea stamina;** 29.1.31: ac **linteis** quidam **indumentis** amictus calciatusque itidem **linteis soccis** torulo capiti circumflexo verbenas felicis arboris gestans etc.; I p.64 **(adject. ending in -eus).**

p. 124. 22   *b*   for the substant.cf. ad 14.7.20 (= II p.49) and before this (a). Cf.et. **indutus:** 24.2.5; 30.7.4; Fesser p.52; Veget.r.m.3.5 (= Lang p.74). Not in Claud.Arn.adv.nat.Opt.Milev.

p. 124. 22   **innexae.** Probably a poetism. Also fairly often in post-class. prose. Often in Claud.

p. 124. 22 sq.   **equorumque etc.** It appears from the following words in § 2 and § 3 that these Sarmats and Quads are first and formost horsemen, at least in a war. This is clear from the context. During the later periods of the empire the Romans are faced more and more with enemies who fight on horseback; which was, of course, of considerable influence on the Roman army itself, which had to adapt itself to this. Hence the increasing share of the cavalry in the army, with the attendant reduction in infantry. Cf. Grosse (op.cit.I) p.15 sq.; p.314 sq.; p.324 sq. In this mobile warfare, which often resembles a guerilla, the legionarius of old times can no longer play a part.

p. 124. 23   **plurimi** = plerique. Very frequent, "incorrect" use. Joined to this development: **plurimum with positivus** = superlativus (cf.Hofm.-Leum.p.464 (73)); Mulomed.Chir.Oder p.229: quam rem **plurime salubrem** (= superlat.). Both late Latin.

p. 124. 23   **ex usu.** Cf. ad 14.10.3 (= II p.100). Cf. et. ad 15.1.2 (= III p.8); ad 15.5.4 (= III p.72).

p. 124. 23   *a*   **castrati.** With Cic. (cf. Quint.8.6.15) this verb does not suit a proper style; cf.de orat.3.41 (164): Nolo morte dici Africani **castratam** esse rem publicam; nolo **stercus curiae** dici Glauciam: quamvis sit simile, tamen est in utroque **deformis cogitatio similitudinis.** Plaut.Cato.Varro.Colum. Plin.N.H.Curt.Vitr.Prud.: with lit. and metaph. meaning. Not in Veget. r.m.Arn.adv.nat.Opt.Milev.Mulom.Chir. Apparently it is a professional term, which (understandably) strikes us as being somewhat vulgar. Therefore a castrate was not called **castratus** in "decent language, but **eunuchus** or **spado** (cf. ad 14.6.17 = I p.143). But the deformitas is no longer felt by Claud., for instance, who uses **castrandus** (literally) 18.45. (In Eutrop. I) and **castrat** (metaph.) ibid.18.194. **Hieron.** also uses the verb (metaph.). **Note. But Curt.Ruf.** has **castrati hominis** (6.3.12) and **castratum** (subst.10.1. 37). Cf.et.Heum.-Seckel p.57.

b Concerning the **castration** itself cf. Varro r.r.2.7.15; Xenoph.Inst. Cyri 7.5.62.

feminarum = equarum. **visu**: post-class. and late Latin with the meaning: sight, view.
visu exagitati: claus.III. The choice of the compositum is deliberate. The verb also: 14.3.4; 14.10.4; 15.8.1; 27.3.8; 27.6.14; 30.5.6; 31.7.16; 31,12.1 (cf.et. ad 14.3.4 = I p.81).

p. 124. 23

raptentur: in order that they will not let themselves be dragged along (dynamic medium). The verb also 14.7.16; 15.12.4; 22.16.3; 31.10.7.
Note. In 14.4.3 Clark has **reptantes** (similarly Seyf. Gallet.-Fontaine. Rolfe). But Gardth. ⟨se⟩**raptantes**.

p. 124. 23

a **in subsidiis ferocientes**. The subst., a well-known t.t.mil., (= rearguard, reserves) can mean here **ambush** (= **insidiae**, a word also used by Amm.). For in my opinion the first two meanings are not satisfactory here.
b **ferocientes**: behaving impetuously, wildly. Also used (always as part. praes.): 21.12.5; 25.1.15; 27.8.9; 29.5.41; 30.1.20. Apul.Gell.Paneg.Tert. Cypr. and others. Thus in general late Latin. Not in Claud.Veget.r.m. Arn.adv.nat.Opt.Milev.

p. 124. 24

hinnitu. Cf.23.6.36: septem (sc.magi) ... imperitandi initium **equino** **hinnitu** sortiti.

p. 124. 24

densiore: dense, unbroken. Compar. = posit. (cf. ad 14.6.12 = I p.96). Not used metri causa.

p. 124. 24

Vectores. Cf. ad 16.12.51, p.99.25*b*. Cf.et.Claud. 17.181 sq. (de Fl.Mal. Theod.cons.):
    Terribiles rursum lituos veteranus adibo,
    Et desueta **vetus** tentabo caerula **vector?**
(= navigator, captain, helmsman). The subst. not in Veget.r.m.Arn.adv. nat.Opt.Milev.

p. 124. 24

XII, 3

a **et per spatia discurrunt amplissima**. Cf.17.13.22: per spatia ampla camporum; 31.4.8: spatia ampla camporum; 31.3.3: per camporum ampla spatia; 22.8.12: per haec **amplissima spatia**; 14.6.16: per ampla

p. 124. 24-25

283

spatia urbis; 24.3.12: per spatia ampla; 27.2.5: spatiis amplioribus occupatis; 25.2.6: **amplitudine spatiorum;** Blomgren p.170 sq.

b for **discurrere** cf. ad 16.2.10, p.73.21; ad 16.12.21; p.94.19-20*b*.

c Compare with this § 3 the description of the **Saraceni** in 14.4.4 (cf.I p.82), especially 14.4.3: sed errant semper per spatia longe lateque distenta etc.

p. 124. 25 **sequentes - vertentes.** Like the Parths. Cf.Claud.8.530 sq. (de IV Cons. Honor.):
Scis quo more Cydon, qua dirigat arte sagittas
Armenius, **refugo** quae sit fiducia **Partho.**
Amm.19.8.10: Romanum agmen ... quod **persequebatur** multitudo Persarum, **incertum unde impetu tam repentino terga viantum adgressa.**

p. 124. 26 **insidendo velocibus equis et morigeris.** For the hyperbaton cf. ad 17.1.6, p.105.21*a*. **Insidēre equo** seems to be the standard expression; cf.Liv.7.6.5; 8.38.15; etc. **Morigerus** is arch. and late Latin. (cf. Krebs Antib.2 p.102, with lit.). Cf. et **B.J. de Jonge** Comm.Apul.Met.II (1941) p.33 (5.(29.9 H.)); Claud.Epigr.51 (de mulabus Gallicis):
Adspice **morigeras** Rhodani torrentis **alumnas**
Imperio nexas, imperioque vagas.
Dissona quam varios flectant ad murmura cursus,
Et certas adeant voce regente vias.
The adj. does not occur in Veget.r.m.Opt.Milev.Arn.adv.nat. **equis et morigeris:** claus.IV with dialysis.

p. 124. 26-27 **trahentesque ... binos** etc. Cf.Val.Flacc.Argon.6.161:
... Comitumque **celer mutator equorum**
Moesus et ingentis frenator Sarmata conti.
Liv.23.29.5: nec omnes Numidae in dextro locati cornu, sed quibus, **desultorum** in modum, **binos trahentibus equos** inter acerrimam saepe pugnam in recentem equum ex fesso **armatis** transsultare mos erat: tanta velocitas ipsis, **tamque docile equorum genus est;** ibid.44.9.4 **(desultor);** Manil.5.85 sq.; Suet.Caes.49 **(equos desultorios).**

p. 124. 27 *a* **permutatio.** Cf.15.1.2: **equorum permutatione** veloci, ut nimietate cogendi quosdam exstingueret (sc.Apodemius; cf. ad h.l.III p.6 sq.); 14.11.19: itineribus rectis per **mutationem iumentorum** emensis; 26.6.9: et votis, licet obscuris et tacitis, **permutatio status praesentis** ... concordi gemitu poscebatur. **Permutatio** is a t.t. of the trade language (not in Amm.)

Probably **permutatio** is also the normal word for: a change (of horses) and is **mutatio** a variatio in this. Veget.r.m. does not know the subst. The adj. **permutabilis** occurs 31.2.11 (only in Amm.?); **mutabilis** 14.11.30, without difference in meaning.

b **iumentorum.** Cf. ad 16.12.22, p.94.25-26*b*.

vigor. Post-class. Cf. Krebs Antib.2 p.740 (with lit.). Used by poets since p. 124. 27
Verg. Cf.25.3.8: arma poscebat et equum ... **eo vigore** ... **quo** Epaminondas ... saucius ... quaerebat ... scutum; 16.12.11: **quo vigore** ... membris marcentibus occurramus? Not in legal writings, though **vigere** is. Cf. Heum.-Seckel p.624.

integretur. Affected word for: **recreetur, reficiatur,** etc. Perhaps a flower p. 124. 27
of speech, originally from Cic. (de inv.1.17(25)), but borrowed from Gell. (15.2.5)? Though the latter has: **refici integrarique** animos. In prose postclass. Not in Veget.r.m.Claud.Opt.Milev., though 3 times in Arn.adv. nat. Cf.et.Heum.-Seckel p.276.

XII, 4

Aequinoctio itaque temporis verni confecto. Cf. Mela 3.5 (37): ubi sol non p. 125. 1
cotidie ut nobis sed primum **verno aequinoctio** exortus, autumnali demum occidit.Amm. also used **vernalis** (26.1.10), in prose late Latin (= **vernus**). The adj.: **aequinoctialis** 22.15.31: apud Meroen, Aethiopiae partem **aequinoctiali circulo** proximam (= aequator). **Aequinoctialis circulus** also in Varro L.L.9.18 (= Goetz-Schoell p.151). On **aequinoctium** itself cf. ibid.p.60 sq. (6.8); p.96 (7.14). As subst. **vernum:** 15.10.4: et haec, ut diximus, **anni verno** contingunt.

coacta militum valida manu. Cf. ad 15.4.1 (= III p.55). p. 125. 1-2

a **ductu laetioris fortunae profectus.** Cf.26.7.15: et secundioris **ductu** p. 125. 2
fortunae: 26.9.5: (Arbitio) orabat, ut se ac si parentem magis sequerentur **felicissimis ductibus cognitum,** quam profligato morem gererent nebuloni (sc.Procopio); 21.12.17: **aquarum ductibus** intersectis (= water works); 31.4.7? (cf.app.crit.Cl.II p.565; Seyf.IV p.254).
b For **fortuna** cf. ad 15.5.1 (= III p.67 sq.); ad 16.12.64, p.102.5-6; Naudé, Fortuna etc. (op.cit.XVI.X).

a **flumen Histrum exundantem pruinarum iam resoluta congerie.** The p. 125. 3-4
Hister (Danube) also mentioned 21.8.2; 21.10.3; 22.7.7; 24.3.9; 27.4.6;

27.5.2; 27.6.12; 29.6.2; 31.2.13; 31.3.3; 31.3.8; 31.4.2; 31.4.12; 31.8.1; 31.8.6.

b 16.4.2: ira **exundante** substridens; ad 16.4.2, p.74.26-27. With slight difference in meaning 15.4.2: Rhenus ... copiis **exuberans** propriis (cf. et.18.4.4; 22.15.14; 23.6.50; 23.6.65). The last verb occurs frequently in late Latin. Cf.et.Veget.r.m.1.10 (= Lang p.14): Saepe repentinis imbribus vel nivibus solent **exundare** torrentes; 4.42 (= Lang p.161): more torrentium fluminum nunc **exundat** in terras ...; Opt.Milev. 4.9 (= Ziwsa p.115): in deo perennis maiestas **exundat,** sicut in fonte aqua largiter fluentibus venis **exuberat.** The verb also occurs in Claud.

c Cf.15.10.4: cum liquente gelu **nivibusque solutis** flatu calidiore ventorum per diruptas utrimque angustias et **lacunas pruinarum congerie latebrosas** descendentes etc. For **pruinae** cf. ad 17.2.3, p.107.25-26*a*. For **congeries** cf.24.2.15: telorum **congerie;** 20.1.1: praeteritarum cladium **congerie** fessas. Poetism, as asserted by Krebs 1 p.329?

d Cf.Ovid.Trist.3.10.14 sq.:
Nix iacet, et iactam ne sol pluviaeque **resolvant,**
Indurat Boreas perpetuamque facit.
Alternating with **solvere:** 15.10.4 (before this). Cf.et.17.7.14: cum **dissolutis** elementa **conpagibus** ultro adsiliunt etc.

p. 125. 4 **super navium foros ponte contexto transgressus.** Cf.21.7.7: per Capersanam Eufrate **navali ponte transcurso;** 27.5.2: **ponteque contabulato supra navium foros** flumen **transgressus est** Histrum; ad 17.1.2, p.104.7-9*c;* ad 17.1.2, p.105.4; ad 16.8.10, p.83.2; ad 16.12.63, p.102.4; ad 17.10.1, p.121.14*a, b;* 29.4.2: tacite quantum concessit facultas, nequi **conserendo** officeret **ponti, iunxit navibus Rhenum.**

p. 125. 4-5 **populandis barbarorum incubuit terris.** Note the **hyperbaton** (cf. ad 17.1.6, p.105.21*a*). For the constructions cf. Krebs Antib.1 p.718. **C.dat.** in general post-class. But the above construction **(c.dat.gerundivi)** is certainly unusual and rare.

p. 125. 5-6 *a* **qui ... cernentes** = itaque **eos praevenit** itinere festinato, ut (so that) cernerent catervas ... iugulis suis imminere, etc. (cf. ad 17.3.5, p.108.20*a*). For the constructions of **praevenire** cf. Krebs Antib.2 p.372 (with lit.).

b For **festinare** cf. ad 14.7.10 (= II p.32).

p. 125. 6 **catervas.** Cf. ad 16.2.6, p.73.5*a*. Here said of the **Roman** army!

p. 125. 6 **bellatoris.** Cf. ad 16.12.22, p.94.21. Here adject. = martial. In general the adj. is poet. Claud. had the subst.24.12 (de cons.Stil.III), but 3 times the **adject.bellatrix** (which also occurs in Cic.Tusc.4.24 (54)).

iugulis suis imminere. The somewhat drastic expression reminds one of Curt.8.1.20: et Rhosacis **manum, capiti regis imminentem,** gladio amputavit. Cf.et.**17.12.16;** Cic. in Catil.3.1.2; Phil.14.9.25; in Pis.2.5: Michael p.25.

per anni tempus: because of the time of year. For this causal meaning of **per** cf.Reinhardt (op.cit.I) p.44. (whose examples of **per causale** are not always accurate, in my opinion).

posse rebantur. Claus.I. **Reor** arch.-poet. Cf.Cic. de orat.3.153; Quint.8. 3.26; Fesser p.41; Krebs Antib.2 p.507. (both with lit.). It should be noted that the choice of an arch. or poet. word is sometimes prompted (consciously or unconsciously) by the **clausula:** e.g.19.11.7: quod rebătur inexplicăbile (claus.IV); 20.11.24: quod secus atque rebătur evĕnit. (claus.I); 21.7.1: Illyriis percursis et Itălia (ut rebătur) (claus.III); 22.12. 3: quos audita referre ad imperatorem pŏsse rebăntur (claus.I. Note the formulary style; cf. ad 17.4.1, p.109.6*b*); 23.5.19: ominibus secŭndis (ut rĕor) (claus.I); 24.5.6: obscurior (ut ĭpse rebătur) (claus.I); 25.3.20: aut nominatum quem hăbilem rĕor (claus.I); 27.10.1: Valentiniano ... (ut rebatur ĭpse) profĕcto (the verb not in the claus.; compare 24.5.6); 31.3.6: longe aliter quam rebătur evĕnit (claus.I; compare 20.11.24). Cf.et. ad 15.6.1, p.55.17 (= IV p.6).

sed vitantes exitium insperatum. The part.praes. has a **conative** meaning (as so often). Cf. ad 17.5.12, p.115.6-7*c*. For **insperatus** cf. ad 16.2.7, p. 73.11. For the **imperf. de conatu** cf. ad 14.10.2 =(II p.99).

a **Semet omnes effuderunt in fugam.** For **semet** cf. ad 16.12.20, p.94.14*c*.
b Cf.Liv.40.40.10: Tunc vero Celtiberi omnes **in fugam effunduntur** (medial): ibid.28.15.9; Curt.Ruf.4.15.29: laevumque cornu **in fugam effusum;** 4.16.20: omnes hostes aut **in fugam effusos;** 8.2.38: barbari **in fugam effusi.** For the constructions etc. cf. Krebs Antib.1 p.493 (with lit.). For the use by poets cf.et.Stat.Theb.II **Mulder** p.77 sq.; ibid.I **Heuvel** p.201 (fusus = effusus).

XII, 5
stratisque plurimis. It is somewhat remarkable that Veget.r.m. does not

use the simplex, neither does he use **consterno,** in contrast to **prosterno.** When one traces the use of **sterno,** it seems as if this verb in the meaning: **to throw down, -on the ground violently, hostilely,** is in general post-class. and poet.

p. 125. 9   *a*   **quorum gressus vinxerat timor:** poetically coloured words.
      b   **gressus.** Also 14.2.6; 15.10.4; 17.12.21; 27.10.8; 28.2.13. Post-class. and poet. Fairly often in late Latin = gradus, incessus, ingressus.

p. 125. 9-10   **siquos exemit celeritas morti ... videbant.** The indic. after **si iterativum** is "correct" according to the classical rule; but according to the same rule the **preceding time** should have been expressed: **exemerat** (for perfectum = plusquamperf.cf. ad 14.3.4 = I p.81; ad 16.12.15, p.93.10-p.93.23). For the **indicativus iterat.** cf. ad 14.4.1 (= I p.82); ad 16.12.21, p.94.18-19. Cf.et.15.4.12: proterebant barbaram plebem, **nisi quos fuga exemerat morte** (correct tense used!); 21.12.11: obtriti sunt saxis immanibus, praeter paucos **quos morte** (Clark morti) ... **velocitas exemerat pedum;** 31.11.4: ut praeter paucos **quos morte velocitas exemerat pedum,** interirent reliqui omnes (for formulary expressions cf. ad 17.4.1, p.109.6*b*); 29.3.7: Sallustius **morte exemptus** est; ad 17.2.4, p.108.3.

p. 125. 10   *a*   **inter latebrosas convalles montium occultati.** For **latebrosus** cf. ad 14.2.2 (= I p.67); 14.2.2: loca petivere mari confinia, per quae ⟨a?⟩viis **latebrosis** sese **convallibusque occultantes;** 15.10.4: per diruptas utrimque angustias et lacunas, **pruinarum congerie latebrosas** (cf. ad 17.12.4, p.125. 3-4*c*). Cf.et.Plaut.Trinum.II.2.2: (Lysit.) ... pater, adsum, impera quidvis, //neque tibi ero in mora neque **latebrose** me aps tuo conspectu **occultabo.** The adj. occurs among others in Plaut.Cic.Liv.Verg.Sil.It.Lucan.Sen.phil. Min.Fel.Claud. Also in late Latin prose (cf. Souter p.227). Not in Veget. r.m.Opt.Milev.Arn.adv.nat.
      b   **convallis** is not synonymous with **vallis.** It is a valley, surrounded on all sides by mountains; or it can mean the elevation enclosing the valley. Although it also occurs in Cic. and Caes.Plin.N.H. and others, as well as Varro, Apul. and **Gromat.,** I think that with Amm. the word may be a poetism. (Cf.Verg.Georg.2.186; Claud.36.85; 37.22; Val.Flacc.2.515).
      c   **occultati.** Cf. Krebs Antib.2 p.198: "Statt **occulere** brauchen Caes. und Sallust nur **occultare,** was auch bis ins Spätlat. dann bevorzugt wurde" (with lit.). For the constructions cf.ibid. The verb does not occur in Veget.r.m.Opt.Milev.Arn.adv.nat., though it is used by Claud.

videbant patriam ferro pereuntem. Concerning the difference between the **partic.constr.** and the **acc.c.inf.** with verbs expressing an observation, cf. Hofm.-Leum. § 182 p.605: "dasz bei der Partizipialkonstruktion **der Nachdruck auf der sinnlichen Perzeption** einer im Verlauf begriffenen Handlung oder eines Zustandes liegt, während beim A.c.I. mehr **der Inhalt der Verbalhandlung** unter Zurücktreten der Sinneswahrnehmung (daher z.B. regelmäszig bei **video** = **intellego**) betont wird (vgl.z.B. die unter **audio** Thes.II 1268, 40 sq. 1269, 32 sq. verzeichneten Belege)". This part. constr. occurs in the Latin language at all times. However, it is quite well possible that Amm. has been led here by his affinity with the Greek language. Cf.Thyc.7.47.1; 2.51.4 (nomin. of the part.); etc. These constr. occur frequently with, among others, ὁρῶ, ἀκούω, αἰσθάνομαι.
Note. For the **nominat. of the part.** after the abovementioned verbs, frequent in late Latin, and developed under influence of the Greek, cf. Hofm.-Leum. § 172, p.589 (with lit.).

quam vindicassent ... si ... restistissent. Irr.hypoth. sentence of the past. Normal construction. For the **irrealis** cf. ad 15.6.3 (= IV p.8); ad 14.3.2 (= I p.79 sq.).

profecto = in my sure and certain opinion. Cf. Krebs Antib.2 p.391 (with lit.). Cf.16.12.21, p.94.20.

vigore. Cf.16.12.11: **quo vigore** inedia siti laboreque membris marcentibus occurramus?; 25.3.8.

discesserant = fugerant. With almost the same meaning: Veget.r.m.3.22 (= Lang p.114.4,8): to retire, to retreat, etc.

XII, 6
Sarmatiae. For the **Sarmatae** cf. ad 17.12.1, p.124.18.
Sarmatia: only here with Amm.

secundam ... Pannoniam. Cf. ad 16.10.20. p.88.4-5; 17.12.1, p.124.19.

prospectat. With the meaning of: attingere, contingere, post-class. and poet.

Valeriam. Cf. ad 16.10.20, p.88.3. Also mentioned: 19.11.4; 28.1.5; 28.3.4; 29.6.3; 29.6.12. Cf.et. Pieper Tab.14.

p. 125.14 **opes**: goods and chattels, possessions.

p. 125.14 **urendo rapiendoque.** The choice of the simplicia instead of the composita is not accidental, in my opinion. Veget.r.m. only knows **exurere**, but does not have **rapere** and **diripere** (= to ransack) at all. Claud. only has **rapio**, with the above and other meanings, And furthermore **exustas** (metri causa) 50.46; for the rest **uro** several times. For **simplex pro composito** cf. ad 16.5.6. p.76.12. Cf.et.17.10.6: **urebat** agros⟨et?⟩ pecora **diripiebat** et homines ...; ad 17.10.7, p. 122.17: **exustorum.**

p. 125.14 *a* **occurrentia militaris turbo vastabat.** For participia (and adjectiva) neutr.plur.cf. ad 17.3.2, p.108.12*a;* ad 17.4.1, p.109.4*a* (cf.et. ad 17.4.14, p.111.7-8: neutr.plur.pronomina). **Occurentia** means: what fell into their hands, came up before them (object of urendo rapiendoque). Probably Grecism: παρατυγχάνω?

b Cf.17.6.1: Iuthungi ... Raetias **turbulente vastabant.** Cf.Claud.24.199 sq. (de cons.Stil.III):

...... solio seu fultus eburno

Cingas iure forum: **densi** seu **turbine vulgi**

Circumfusa tuae conscendant rostra secures.

Although it seems far-fetched, it is not impossible that we are faced here with a "hidden" quotation, viz. Ovid.Amor.3.15.5 sq. (though context and meaning are completely different!);

Siquid id est, usque a proavis vetus ordinis heres

Non modo **militiae turbine** factus eques.

(cf.Trist.4.10.7 sq.).

c as regards the **personificatio** cf. ad 17.8.4, p.120.3*b;* ad 17.2.1, p.107.13.

XII, 7

p. 125.15 *a* **immensitate permoti.** Cf.20.5.4: cum ... **cladis immensitas** persultaret. Cic. reminiscence? Cf. de nat.deor.1.54; 2.98 (quoted by Georges). **It is found in Eccles.** not in Claud.Veget.r.m.Opt.Milev.Arn.adv.nat. Cf. Souter, p.185; Cod.Theod.8.4.6.

b **permoti** instead of **moti** several times metri causa: claus.I. To which can be added that composita do not always (and this was also formerly the case) still have an intensified meaning.

p. 125.15 **posthabito latendi consilio:** They subordinated their plan to keep hidden to all other matters, such as their safety = they abandoned that plan.

The main point is once more contained in the partic. (cf. ad 17.3.5, p.108.20a).

Sarmatae ... fugam. Langen Mommsen assume a lacuna after **cogitarunt.** Similarly Cl.Seyf. **V. does not give a gap. A ut after cogitarunt.** Which is followed by Rolfe. Sabbah: nec expedire tela, **ne vim vulnerum declinarent,** nec etc. (does **not** assume a gap, therefore). It should also be pointed out that V reads **declinarent,** A E G **declinare.** The solution given by Sabbah Amm.II p.182 sq. (note 96) is complicated and improbable, in my opinion. The translation by Seyf.: "hatten aber im Sinne, **die Unsrigen in drei Heeresabteilungen mit gröszerer Sicherheit angreifen zu können**" seems untenable to me (cogitarunt securius aggredi = cogitarunt securius **se posse** aggredi, could if necessary, be defended; cf. ad 17.1.3, p.106.23-24b). I would like to suggest the following explanation: **agentes** accus., belonging to **nostros.** Subject of **possent:** Romani. And **ut** should be inserted after cogitarunt. The context is then as follows: It is evident from the previous 4, 5, 6, that the Romans are complete masters of the sitation. Over a wide area they march through enemy territory in 3 columns, **agentes securius** (without care, unconcerned: a normal meaning, also with military authors, as, for instance, Veget.r.m. Comparativus is probably positivus: cf. ad 14.6.12 = I p.96. (For **agere** cf. ad 16.12.69, p.103.1). The Sarmats now try with the courage born of desperation to raise themselves from their defeat, to regroup themselves from their hidingplaces **and to attack the Romans suddenly, so that they neither,** etc. This regrouping is accompanied with a ruse: petendae specie pacis. Therefore **tripertito agentes** can never in my opinion refer to the Sarmats. For when they would form themselves into 3 groups, how could the Romans then assume that they would ask for peace? For this would clearly be an **offensive** military tactic! One should also bear in mind that the number of surviving Germans and Sarmats will have been somewhat greater than one would deduce from §§ 4, 5, 6. Some rhetoric exaggeration is, after all, part of such stories. And another point: the enemies of the Romans often follow guerilla tactics. In any case the Sarmats, in spite of the help given them by the Quads, are beaten for the second time, as well as their allies: **sed ne eos ... aperta.** However, the Romans have acknowledged the risk they have run; so that, when the campaign is continued, **iunctis densius cuneis,** they hastily march toward the **regna Quadorum.**

p. 125. 15-
p. 125. 18

specie. Cf. ad 17.4.7, p.110.5b. Cf.17.1.3: a similar stratagem!

p. 125. 16

p. 125. 16 **agmine tripertito.** Cf.Caes.b.g.6.6.6: Caesar partitis copiis cum Gaio Fabio legato et Marco Crasso quaestore celeriterque **effectis pontibus adit tripertito:** 7.67.2: equitatum **tripertito divisum** contra hostem ire iubet; 8.33.1: **tripertito** cohortibus **divisis** trina ... castra fecit; Cic.Tusc.5.13 (40).

p. 125. 16-17 **ădgredi cogitărunt.** Claus III. The abbreviated ending of the verb in the clausula = adgredi se posse cogitarunt.

p. 125. 17 **expedire tela.** Either (in general): to bring out, or (as t.t.mil.) to prepare for battle. With the meaning: to liberate from: 16.4.3; 18.8.8.

p. 125. 17 **vim vulnerum.** Here, as so often, the subst. has the meaning of: gash, cut, thrust; (in general): being wounded. In Liv. and fairly often with poets. The borderline between the meaning of **being wounded** and **wound** can not always be clearly determined. Cf.Claud.5.64 sq. (In Rufin.II):
 Vinctas ire nurus, hunc in vada proxima mergi
 Seminecem, hunc **subito percussum vulnere** labi,
 Dum fugit ....
ibid.20.2 sq. (In Eutr.II):
 ...... certae non augure falso
 Prodigii patuere minae, **frustraque peracto**
 Vulnere monstriferi praesagia discitis anni.
(frustra = ± too late). Cf.et.Stat.Theb.II Comm. Mulder p.285.

p. 125. 17 **declinare.** Cf.Veget.r.m.3.21 (= Lang p.111): ubi animus semel territus non tam **tela hostium** cupit **declinare** quam vultum; Cic.orat.68 (228): nec satis recte (sc.oratio) **declinat impetum**, nisi etiam in cedendo, quid deceat, intelligit. Probably a t.t. of the language of the gladiators. Cf.et. Claud.21.286 sq. (de laud.Stilich. I):
 .... velut arbiter alni,
 Nubilus Aegaeo quam turbine vexat Orion,
 Exiguo clavi flexu **declinat aquarum**
 Verbera, nunc recta, nunc obliquante carina;
ad 17.1.3, p.105.8*b;* ad 16.12.49, p.99.16*b.*

p. 125. 18 **in rebus artissimis.** Cf.Tac.Hist.3.69: misso ... nuntio, qui circumsideri ipsos et, ni subveniretur, **artas res** nuntiaret; Obid.ex Ponto 3.2.25 sq.:
 Pars estis pauci melior, qui **rebus in artis**
 Ferre mihi nullam turpe putastis opem;

Claud.26.491 sq. (de bello Getico):
Sed numquam Mavors adeo **constrinxit in artum**
Res, Alarice, **tuas**.

ultimum: the ultimate, last way out. Cf.Liv.10.31.6: illinc ad **ultimam** iam p. 125. 18
dimicantibus **spem**; 5.37.1: civitas, quae ... **ultima** experiens **auxilia**
dictatorem multis tempestatibus dixisset ...; ad 14.2.6 (= I p.69); ad
16.12.14, p.93.10; ad 15.3.8 (= III p.49); ad 14.11.8 (= II p.121); 29.5.3:
ultimorum metu iam trepidans. The subst.sing. also 19.2.5: a sole itaque
orto usque **diei ultimum**.

XII, 8

ilico. Cf. ad 17.9.1, p.120.15*a*. **Sarmatis ... Quadi**: cf. ad 16.12.1, p.124.   p. 125. 19
18.

periculorum ... participes. Cf.Curt.Ruf.7.1.3: omnium **periculorum** eius p. 125. 19
particeps. Note the alliteration.

noxarum: crimes = raids, robberies. Cf.16.12.61: claudente **noxarum** p. 125. 19
conscientia linguam; Caes.b.g.6.16.5: Supplicia eorum, qui in furto aut
latricinio aut aliqua **noxia** sint comprehensi. Veget.r.m. does not have
the subst. at all. Whether it is here with Amm. a t.t. or whether by the use
of this word the author condemns the raids of the Q. and S., can not be
determined. Cf.et.Heum.-Seckel p.374.

indiscreti. Cf. ad 16.12.33, p.96.14-15*b*.   p. 125. 20

prompta ... audacia: determined boldness. The subst. often in Veget.r.m., p. 125. 20
sometimes with the meaning: **pugnacity**. Regarding the adj. cf.Veget.r.m.
3.3 (= Lang p.70): ita ut urbes atque castella ab his militibus, qui minus
prompti inveniuntur **in acie** ... defendantur; 4.31 (= Lang p.150): Nemo
enim bello lacessere aut facere audet iniuriam ei regno vel populo, quem
expeditum et **promptum ad resistendum vindicandumque** cognoscit; 1.1
(= Lang p.6): Etenim in certamine bellorum exercitata paucitas **ad
victoriam promptior** est; 1.2 (= Lang p.6): Contra septentrionales populi
... sunt **ad bella promptissimi**. One should also compare the use of **audere**,
e.g. Amm.16.12.46.

a **in discrimina ruentes aperta**: Because they threw themselves blindly p. 125. 20-21 into undisguised dangers. For **discrimina** cf.17.1.10, p.106.9*a;* ad 16.12.55, p.100.16*b*.

b For **aperta** cf. ad 14.5.7 (= I p.87).

XII, 9

p. 125. 21-22 **pars quae potuit superesse**: curious turn of phrase = the part which managed to escape with their lives.

p. 125. 22 **eventu**. Often linked with **secundus, prosper**. Very frequent in Amm. Cf. 14.1.1; 14.6.26; 16.6.1; 16.11.15; 16.12.65; 16.12.67; 31.8.3; etc. Often linked with **secundus, prosper**.

p. 125. 23 *a* **iunctis densius cuneis**. For the reason why the Romans did this, cf. ad 17.12.7, p.125.15-18. For **cunei** cf. ad 16.11.5, p.88.29; ad 16.12.8, p.92.8; ad 16.12.20, p.94.14*d*.

b Cf.16.12.20: **densantes** semet in **cuneos**. Cf.et. ad 14.2.10 (= I p.73).

p. 125. 23 **ad Quadorum regna**. Towards the North. Cf. Sabbah Amm.Marc.II p.183, note 97. We can not come to any closer localisation. From the next §§ of this chapter the mixing of the **Quadi** and **Sarmatae** is evident. Added to this is the fact that Amm. does not know these regions by sight, while the tribes living there hardly have any fixed residences.

p. 125. 24 **ex praeterito casu** = ex praeterita clade. For the meaning of **casus**, which is very frequent in Amm., cf. ad 15.5.1 (= III p.67). Cf.et. ad 17.10.4, p.122.2; 14.10.14.

p. 125. 24 **impendentia** = that which **could** threaten them. Cf.et. ad 17.5.12, p.115. 6-7*c*. For **impendentia** subst.neutr.cf. ad 17.3.2, p.108.12*a;* ad 17.4.1, p.109.4*a;* ad 17.4.14, p.111.7-8.

p. 125. 24 **formidantes**. Although this verb, which expresses a much stronger fear than **timere**, fits very well here, the metrum can also have been of some influence: claus.III. Cf.Curt.Ruf.4.16.17: quippe ubi intravit animos **pavor**, id solum **metuunt** quod primum **formidare** coeperunt. Claud. has **formidatus** (cf.Stat.Theb.II Comm.Mulder p.54, with lit.) and **formidandus**. Cf.et.Veget.r.m.3.1 (= Lang p.66): Quod si casu acies verterint tergum, necesse est multos cadere de multis et illos qui effugerint, ut semel **territos** postea **formidare** conflictum; 4.6 (= Lang p.131) **formidatur, ne** multitudo ... occupet ...; 2 praef. (= Lang p.34): nec **formido** iussus **adgredi opus,** quod spontaneum cessit impune; etc.; ad 16.12.7, p.92.3-4*a* **(formidabilis);** ad 16.12.24, p.95.5*a;* 14.10.14; 17.12.9: **formidantes;** 16.12.24; 15.12.3: **formidandus;** 14.2.15; 17.13.27.

a **rogaturi suppliciter.** For the part.fut.cf. ad 16.12.33, p.96.14-15*a;* ad 17.1.8, p.106.4*a*.
b Cf.Ovid. ex Ponto 1.10.43 sq.:
Qui meritam nobis minuat, non finiat iram,
Suppliciter vestros quisque **rogate deos.**
Cf.et. ad 16.12.15, p.93.16.

p. 125. 24

fidentes: confident (viz. of the mercy of the emperor). For the verb cf. ad 16.12.50, p.99.19-20*b*. For **simplex pro composito** cf. ad 16.5.6, p.76.12. Here the metrics are no reason to use the simplex, though this is sometimes the case in other places. I do not see much difference between **fido** and **confido** in Amm.

p. 125. 24

conspectum. Cf. ad 16.12.18, p.94.6.

p. 125. 25

a **erga haec⟨et⟩similia lenioris.** For **erga** cf. ad 14.1.8, p.3.4-5 (= I p.63); Krebs Antib.I p.510 (with lit.); Heum.-Seckel p.173. For **haec et similia** cf. ad 14.1.8 (= I p.63); ad 17.8.5, p.120.5; ad 15.3.2 (= III p.30); ad 14.6.26 (= I p.101); ad 16.12.29, p.95.26.
b The insertion of **et** is problematical. Cf. ad 15.5.33 (= III p.119 sq.); ad 15.13.2 (= IV p.80); 14.8.9, p.24.16: Emissa Damascus; 14.8.11, p.24. 24: Ascalonem Gazam; 14.7.9: blande hortaretur verecunde (p.20.16); 14.6.17, p.16.5-6: ita praepositis urbanae familiae suspense digerentibus sollicite (?); 14.6.18, p.16.18-19: vocabili sonu, perflabili tinnitu fidium resultantes; etc.
c **lenioris:** compar. with the usual meaning: rather mild.

p. 125. 25

dictoque die. Cf.Cic.harusp.4(7); Verr.1.57(149): in Caecil.20(67). Alternating with **praestituere.** Cf.Tusc.1.39(93): At ea (sc.natura) quidam dedit usuram vitae, **tamquam pecuniae, nulla praestituta die** (cf.Amm.18.5 2: adlapsuro iam **praestituto die solvendae pecuniae).** Well-known t.t. iurid. But still the influence of Cic. reading?

p. 125. 25-26

statuendis condicionibus: sc. deditionis (cf.Curt.Ruf.7.11.27; 9.8.12). Instead of **statuo** Liv.29.12.13 says: P.Sempronius condiciones pacis

p. 125. 26

295

dixit. Cf.et.14.10.10: cum pacem oportere **tribui** quae **iustis condicionibus** petebatur ... sententiarum via concinens adprobasset.

p. 126. 26   Eyss. Clark Seyf. assume a gap after **condicionibus.** V does not have a gap. V G have **modo**, which is scrapped by Lindenbr., Her.⟨pari⟩modo, and Rolfe, Nov. ⟨quoquo⟩ modo. Sabbah A.M.II p.183, note 98, has a dittography in mind: **modo ... more** (p.125.26), caused by the abbrevation m̊ (= modo), which the copyist found in his model. But when **modo** is maintained, it should be included with the **preceding** words, with the meaning of: just, only (suggested by Sabbah). I think this solution is the best one. The context is then as follows: the prince **Zizais**, afraid as he is for too harsh conditions, because **only** a period had been fixed for the **conditions** of the surrender, but the surrender itself had not yet been accepted, lined up the ranks of the Sarmats, not for battle, this time, but **ad preces,** although they keep their weapons with them, which they only throw down **later,** at a sign of the reassured **Zizais** (p.126.9). To our minds all this seems like a primitive theatrical show. The fact that at first they were allowed to keep their arms, (except for **Zizais**, that is, p.126.1), seems to me to be a sign of suspicious caution on the part of the **Sarmats,** who under these precarious circumstances have to wait and see what happens. To us the attitude of the prince seems to be exaggerated. But it is hard to imagine the mentality of these "barbarians". Though it is very probable that Amm. exaggerates too: ad maiorem gloriam Romanorum! Furthermore, a comma should be placed after **quoque** and after **regalis.**

p. 125. 26   **quoque** = also in actual fact (as it often means).

p. 125. 26   **etiam tum:** then still. Cf.16.11.13 (Iulianus): rudis **etiam tum** ut existimabatur; ad 16.12.25, p.95.7-8*b*.

p. 125. 26   **regalis.** Cf. ad 16.10.16, p.87.8. But in 17.13.30 **Zizais** appears to be **rex.**

p. 125. 27   **ardui corporis.** V apud vi. For this last, incomprehensible version Nov. gives **ardui**, which is taken over by Cl.Seyf.Rolfe. G.Sabbah: **haud parvi,** the correct version, in my opinion. One should also read the ingenious explanation by Sabbah A.M.II p.183, note 99.

p. 125. 27
p. 126. 1   **ad preces** = ut precarentur. **Ad** with final meaning. Cf.23.5.11; 29.2.1; 29.2.9 etc.; Reinhardt (op.cit.I) p.51; Hofm.-Leum.p.498.90*c;* Grandgent (op.cit.I) p.44.90; Krebs Antib.1 p.81.

Cf.17.10.3,4 (p.121.26 - p.122.2); 17.10.9 (p.122.23 - p.123.2); 17.1.12 p. 126. 1-
(p.106.16 - p.106.18); 16.12.61 (p.101.20 - p.101.25); ad 16.12.61, p.101. p. 126. 6
20-21*a*.

pectore ... stratus. Note the effect of the alliterating **p** and **s** and the 2 p. 126. 1-2
successive clausulae II and I.

stratus. Simplex pro composito, metri causa. See also previous note. Cf. p. 126. 2
16.5.6, p.76.12; ad 17.8.5, p.120.9.

a **et amisso vocis officio prae timore.** Cf.16.12.61: claudente noxarum p. 126. 2
conscientia linguam; ad 16.12.61, p.101.22-23. A rather elaborate way of
saying. Free translation: and because, on account of his fear, his voice
refused to serve him.
b For **prae** cf.15.5.30; 18.6.16; 27.10.4.

tum cum. V dum cum. Cf.29.4.7: **dum cum** hostium disiecta frangeret p. 126. 2
timor. (Cl. tum cum; Seyf. dum cum; Rolfe tum cum). In my view the
version as given by V should be adhered to in both places. Cf. Löfstedt,
Beiträge zur Kenntnis der späteren Latinität, Diss. Uppsala 1907, p.32;
Hagend.abund. (op.cit.I) p.213 sq.

a **conatus ... poscebat.** Translation: (he roused greater pity) while he p. 126. 3-4
(because he), **although** he was allowed to explain what his demands
(wishes) were, had tried this fairly often, **but not enough,** because his sobs
prevented him from doing this. The translations by Sabbah, Seyf.,
Büchele, Rolfe are not quite clear and accurate, in my opinion. Attention
should be paid to the crowding of the participia.
b **permissus.** For the construction cf. ad 14.1.3 (= I p.58). Cf.et. ad
15.6.1, p.55.16; 15.7.4, p.57.5; 15.7.6, p.57.12 (all these notes in IV).
c Note the alliterating **p**. Deliberate, it seems to me (5 times). And before: maiorem misericordiam movit.
d Cf.22.16.7: paenuria calcis ad momentum **parum** repertae (for the
tautologia cf. Hagend.abund., op.cit.I, p.216.)

XII, 10

recreatus: medial = having recovered himself. Cf.16.4.4: quies ... **ad** p. 126. 4
recreandas tamen sufficiens vires ....

297

p. 126. 4-5 **denique tandem.** Cf. ad 17.1.13, p.106.22. Note once again the crowding of the participia. The main point is contained in **recuperato.**

p. 126. 5 *a* **iussusque exsurgere.** The prince had already received permission to speak, but he was still laying on the ground. Now, after he has his nerves under control, he is ordered to stand up, or at least to raise himself.
b for **exsurgere** cf.16.5.5 (ex); 23.4.5 (ab); (with ablat.): 22.8.11; (with adverb.): 23.6.17; 27.4.7.

p. 126. 5 **genibus nixus.** Cf. ad 17.10.3, p.122.1-2.

p. 126. 5-6 *a* **concessionem delictorum etc.** For **concessio** cf. ad 17.10.4, p.122.2. For **delictorum** cf.14.10.9: optimates misere, **delictorum veniam** petituros et pacem. **Delicta** (= offenses) is a weak expression for what he calls in 17.12.8: **noxae;** 17.12.13: **facinora gravia;** 17.13.1: **multa et nefaria;** 17.13.2: **criminum magnitudo;** 17.13.23: **exitiale scelus;** etc.
b **concessionem ... tribui supplicavit et veniam.** Hyperbaton. Cf. ad 17.1.6, p.105.21*a*.
c **veniam.** Unless this word is practically synonymous with **concessio,** it **can** mean here: complying with their wishes. But the first seems more probable to me, when one reads 14.10.9. Cf. et. 17.12.21: et adepti **veniam** iussa fecerunt (but here: mercy); 17.13.11; 17.12.19: post impetratam **veniam** recepti in fidem; 17.10.7: oravit ipse quoque **veniam** (annot. ad p.122.18); 16.12.65: gentilique prece **veniam** poscens; etc.
d **tribui.** Cf. ad 17.12.9, p.125.26.
e Again we are struck by the almost similar and **formulary expressions** (cf. ad 17.4.1, p.109.6*b*), used by Amm., when enemies beg for peace and forgiveness and these are granted to them.

p. 126. 6 *a* **eoque etc.** Here a new main clause really begins: and the crowd, which had also been admitted there, in order to utter its appeals .... **manus precibus dederunt** (constructio ad sententiam, sensum). Cf.14.6.17: **multitudo spadonum** a senibus in pueros desinens, **obluridi** distortaque liniamentorum conpage **deformes;** ad 17.10.6, p.122.16.
b for the sentences joined together with **-que** cf.16.12.17, p.93.23-24*b;* 16.12.25, p.95.9*b;* 16.12.37, p.97.6*a;* 16.12.35, p.96.22.

p. 126. 6 **ad precandum admissa.** Admittere is a t.t. of the language of the court. Cf. ad 15.5.12 (= III p.89); ad 15.5.18 (= III p.100). **Admissio** is the permission for an audience with the emperor; **admissionalis** is the chamberlain who announces to the emperor the person requesting the audience. But thus also often in Curt.Ruf., e.g. 4.1.25; 8.3.11; 7.6.5; 3.12.10; etc. Cf.et. Nepos Con.(9) 3; Suet.Nero 13; Aug.53.

cuius ora formido muta claudebat. Cf. ad 17.12.9, p.126.2*a*. For the **personificatio** cf. ad 17.2.1, p.107.13. Note the effect of the alliterating m's. (**admissa ... muta**).   p. 126. 7

a **periculo adhuc praestantiŏris ambĭguo:** as long as the danger threaten-   p. 126. 7-8
ing their leader had not yet found a definite end (lit. was still undecided, precarious). The placing of **adhuc** is noteworthy, as it belongs to **ambiguo**. (= **etiam tum** (ad 17.12.9, p.125.26), usque ad id tempus, etc.: cf. Krebs Antib.1 p.90 sq.). The reason, I believe, is not the clausula (now II, otherwise IV), but the melodiousness: a factor which should often be taken into account.
b **praestantioris** = regalis. Here the word means ± leader, commander. The comparativus, used of **persons,** also in Verg.Aen.6.164; Ovid.Met. 2.724; Pers.6.76. A poetic reminiscence seems unlikely to me. But we should remember the late Roman forms of address: **praestantia** is a title (= Your Eminence; cf.Heum.-Seckel p.452; Souter p.318) as wel as **praestantissimus.** (cf. Souter p.318).
c For the adject. **ambiguus** cf. ad 16.5.5, p.76.4-6*e*. (For the verb **ambigere** cf. ad 16.12.35, p.96.24).

ubi ... monstravit. For **ubi temporale** cf. ad 14.2.20 (= I p.78). For **ubi**   p. 126. 8-9
iterativum cf. ad 14.2.7 (= I p.70). As so often, **ubi** is here completely equal to **simul(atque), ut** (c.indic.perf.) = as soon as.

solo iussus attolli. Cf.Ovid.Metam.2.448:   p. 126. 8
    Vix oculos **attollit humo** ....
(c.ablat.separ.). But without **solo (humo)** Curt.Ruf.6.9.32: Philotas ... non **attollere oculos,** non hiscere audebat. Cf.et.Claud.28.42 (de VI cons. Honor.):
    Attollens apicem **subiectis** Regia **Rostris**
    Tot circum delubra videt ......
Attolli = **se attollere** (used medially), fairly frequent. Claud. uses the verb quite often. Only once in Veget.r.m. and then with the meaning of: to raise a shout 3.18 (= Lang p.103).

exspectantibus diu: who had waited for that for a long time.   p. 126. 8

299

p. 126. 8-9 **dīu monstrăvit.** Claus.I. Simplex pro composito. Cf. ad 17.4.9, p.110.10-11.

p. 126. 9 **omnes**: modification of **multitudo**. Cf. ad 17.12.10, p.126.6a.

p. 126. 9 *a* **clipeis telisque proiectis. Now** they throw away their weapons. Cf. ad 17.12.9, p.125.26. There is hardly any difference with **abiectis** (p.126.1).
b For **clipeus** cf. ad 16.12.57, p.100.25-26 - p.101.2. Cf.et. ad 14.10.8 (**scutum, cetra, parma**) = II p.105. In any case, Amm. uses once more a **Roman** military t.t. for a German weapon, which will probably have looked somewhat different from the Roman one.

p. 126. 9 **manus prĕcibus dedĕrunt.** Claus. ⌣́ ⌣ ⌣ ⌣ ⌣́ ⌣. For this claus.cf. Blomgren p.9 sq. I consider attempts to construct a more normal clausula (Cl. de⟨di⟩derunt; Nov. dederant) wholly superfluous. When one reads out the sentence aloud, one does not hear anything disturbing. The expression itself is far-fetched for: they stretched out their hands to plead, pleadingly. Cf.Liv.24.16.10: (cum) nunc **manum ad caelum tollentes** bona omnia populo Romano Gracchoque ipsi **precarentur.**

p. 126. 10 *a* **plura excogitantes:** inventing still **more** (ways to plead) (than the prince). I therefore do not agree with Sabbah and Seyf., who consider **plura** as **complura**, a meaning which we often find in post-class. Latin (cf. Krebs Antib.2 p.311, with lit.). In this late era **plures** may also mean: numerous.
b This verb, which is also class., not in Claud.Opt.Milev.Arn.adv.nat. It is found, however, in Veget.r.m. and in judic.lit. (cf.Heum.-Seckel p. 186). Here claus.I.

p. 126. 10 *a* **humilitate supplicandi.** The substant. also (with a lit. meaning) 15.10.4: praecelsum ... iugum ... e Galliis venientibus **prona humilitate devexum**; 21.10.4: latus ... **prona humilitate deruptum**. The meaning here: submissive, abject attitude, contrasting with **superbia, arrogantia**, a state of mind characterising these "barbarians", so long as they have not been chastised, at least according to Amm. (cf. ad 16.12.4, p.91.20; 17.10.10; 17.10.3; 17.1.13 etc.). Cf.et.17.1.12: precibus et **humilitate suprema** petiere ... pacem.
b The verb **humilitare** 29.2.15: horret mens reminisci, **quo iustitio humilitati** tot rerum apices visebantur; 30.4.2: **ad humilitandam celsitudinem potestatis** negotiorum examina spectanda instituisse arbitratus.

XII, 11

duxerat ... subregulos. The persons mentioned here are otherwise unknown, just as **Zizais**. Except for Zizais they are called **subreguli** (vassal "rulers"?). This word only occurs in late Latin (cf. Souter p.395). As the **Alamanni**, for example, already have several **reges** (cf.16.12.1), **reguli** and **subreguli** can not amount to much. Although **reguli** are not mentioned as such, they must have been there; otherwise the **subreguli** would not make sense! Unless, of course, Amm. once again expresses himself untechnically as he often does. Sabbah A.M.II p.183, note 101, devises a sort of political organisation of the **Sarmats** and the **Quads**. **Optimates** is a term indicating the upper class (aristocracy or nobility) of these barbarians (cf. ad 16.12.26, p.95.13*a*). But one should also take into account a tribal organisation and the different tribes making up this organisation (which one should not imagine too large).

duxerat. The **plq.perf.** is used correctly. Note the tenses in the preceding § (10).

pavor. V patior, which does not make sense. Although the conjecture by Her. is acceptable. I believe that the version remains doubtful. Cf.et. ad. 15.8.16 (= IV p.41).

a **cum impetrandi spe similia petituros** = sperantes similia petituros se (ea) impetraturos esse. For **similia** cf. ad 17.12.9, p.125.25*a*. (= eadem). For the **part.fut.** cf. ad 17.12.9, p.125.24*a*.
b Cf.24.4.10: imperator ... oppidum ... **spe patrandri incepti** maximis viribus oppugnabat (without **cum**).

a **qui licet elati gaudio salutis indultae.** For **licet** cf. ad 14.1.5 (= I p.59); ad 16.10.11, p.86.5-6*a*. It appears indirectly from these words that their lives were saved by the emperor. The idea is as follows: and although they rejoiced in the saving of their lives, which had been granted to them, (they kept these feelings under control, and) promised to recompense the hostile deeds they had done (by the burden of conditions, lit.), by taking upon themselves severe conditions. These conditions are mentioned in: **seque ... offerent**. These, therefore, are conditions which they impose upon themselves. This is apparent from: **praevaluit tamen** etc.
b for **elatus** cf. ad 16.12.4, p.91.20; 16.12.69: magniloquentia **elatus** adulatorum; 21.4.7: hoc casu **elatior** Iulianus (= bolder, prouder); ad 17.11.3, p.124.1*d*.

p. 126. 13 *a* **condicionum sarcina** = molestis, gravibus condicionibus. The metaph. meaning of **sarcina** fairly often in Ovidius; cf.ex Ponto 3.7.14; 1.2.147; Tristia 5.6.5; Heroid.7.107; 8.9.4 = onus. Cf.et. Propert.4.3.45 sq.:
Romanis utinam patuissent castra puellis!
essem militiae **sarcina** fida tuae.
b Derived from this verb: **consarcinare.** Cf. ad 14.5.6 (= I p.87); Krebs Antib.1 p.333; Souter p.73.

p. 126. 14 **inimice facta.** Another weak expression; cf. ad 17.12.9, p.126.5-6*a*.

p. 126. 14 *a* **pollicebantur.** Constructed with the **infin.praes.** instead of the **infin.fut.** For other examples cf. Krebs Antib.2 p.318 (with lit.). For this use of the **infin.praes.**, fairly common in late Latin, cf. Hofm.-Leum.p.586 sq. 170 B δ. Cf.et. ad 14.7.11 (= II p.35); ad 14.5.7 (= I p.87); Kalb, Das Juristenlat. (1961) p.44 sq.
b For the **nominat.c.infinit.** ad 15.7.4 (= IV p.13); Hofm.-Leum.p.588 sq. (172, 173); Kalb, Röm.Rechtsspr. (1961), p.81 (78); Linderb.Reg. Bened.33, p.46, line 10.
c For the difference between **promitto** and **polliceor** with legal authors, cf. Kalb, Das Jur.Lat. (1961) p.61 (with notes 1 and 2).

p. 126. 14 **seque.** Cf. ad 17.12.10, p.126.6*b*.

p. 126. 14 **facultatibus:** "means" = property. Class. Usually pluralis. Also often in legal lit. Nevertheless the use of the substant. here is noteworthy.

p. 126. 15 **ambitu.** Cf. ad 16.2.1, p.72.12. **Singularis:** 16.2.1; 18.6.10; 19.2.14; 20.7.2; 20.11.6; 26.8.7; and **15.1.4.** resembling our place here (± size, extent).

p. 126. 15 **terrarum suarum ambitu** is far-fetched and poetical. For the **abstractum pro concreto** cf. ad 17.7.10. p.118.1-2.

p. 126. 15 **Romanae potentiae.** Cf. ad 17.10.10, p.123.10.

p. 126. 16 **offerent.** This conjunctivus can best be viewed as an **irrealis.** The context is then as follows: libenter **obtulissent,** nisi **praevaluisset.** An irr. of the past, therefore, For the **irrealis** cf. ad 14.3.2 (= I p.79); ad 15.6.3 (= IV p.8). The two sentences are asyndetically connected. The indic.perf., suddenly appearing, makes the story livelier. The "shifting" of the tenses is not uncommon. (conj.imp. instead of conj.plq.perf.).

praevaluit. The verb is post-class. For constructions etc. cf. Krebs Antib.2 p.372 (with lit.); Souter p.320; Heum.-Seckel p.455. The verb does not occur in Claud.Veget.r.m.Opt.Milev.Arn.adv.nat. p. 126. 16

aequitas: righteousness. Particularly the alleviation of the severe laws, in agreement with the natural sense of justice (this nuance here; cf. Heum.-Seckel p.22; for in the eyes of the **Romans** the barbarians really deserved other punishment, according to the harsh laws). In Val.Max. we see the **aequitas** Caesariana as opposed to the **violentia** Sullana. p. 126. 16

benignitas: leniency, mercy (× **severitas**). This subst. also in judic.lit. with the meaning of: leniency with regard to the application of regulations of the law; cf. Heum.-Seckel p.48. Though the meaning: generosity, charity would also fit here. Perhaps with these words Amm. had in mind Cic. de off.1.14(42): videndum est enim ... deinde ne maior **benignitas** sit quam **facultates** ... p. 126. 16

inpavidi. Cf. ad 16.12.27, p.95.18-19. Since Livius in prose. Not in Veget. r.m.Opt.Milev.Arn.adv.nat. In Claud.50 (Eid.VII)14: horror ... **inpavidus** ... sui. Cf.et.18.2.15. p. 126. 17

reddidĕre capt^{i}vos. Claus.I. Cf. ad 16.12.19, p.94.11-12. Cf. ad 17.10.4, p.122.3; 17.10.8. p. 126. 17

duxeruntque, Cf. ad 17.12.10, p.126.6*b*. p. 126. 17

obsides postulatos. Cf.17.12.13: obsides **imperatos;** 17.12.16: filios **obsidatus sorte** ... obtulerunt; 17.12.21: sobolemque suam **obsidatus pignore** ... tradiderunt; etc. p. 126. 17

oboedire ... spoponderunt. For the construction cf. ad 17.12.11, p.126.14*a, b*. Whether Amm. senses much difference between **polliceor** and **spondeo,** seems doubtful to me. I believe that these two verbs in this § have only been used variationis causa. While with the choice of words in this sentence the alliteration will certainly also have played a part. (p, pr, pt) as well as the play of sounds in **promptissime spoponderunt** (cf. ad 15.4.2 = III p.56). Another construction than (acc.c.) inf. with **spondeo** 24.1.8: p. 126. 18

303

qui ... multa sibi **de lenitudine** Romana **spondebant.** (Cf.Cic. ad fam.15. 21.1; Just.3.4.1; both places quoted by Georges).

p. 126. 18 **promptissime.** The positivus of the adverbium e.g. 27.10.12; 28.1.35.

p. 126. 18 **oboedire praeceptis.** Cf.17.12.19: imperator... nulli nisi sibi ducibusque Romanis **parere praecepit** (no difference here, in my view, between **oboedire** and **parere**); 17.10.10: **obsecundabant imperiis** ingravate (cf. ad p.123.11). Cf.et. ad 15.13.4 (= IV p.82).

XII, 12

p. 126. 19 **clementiae.** More or less the same as **benignitas** in § 11.

a **regalis ... Araharius.** For **regalis** Cf. ad 16.10.16, p.87.8. This prince of the **Quadi** is not otherwise known to us, nor the Sarmat **Usafer.** This **Usafer** appears to be a sort of vasal of **Araharius** (particeps inferior: 17.12.14). A. rules as regalis over **part** of the Quads, East of Bregetio and the bend of the Danube; and furthermore over a **part** of the **Transiugitani**, who live on the other side of the mountains ("other" in the eyes of the Romans and Sarmats, that is). **Transiugitani** appear to be mentioned only here in Amm. They are not mentioned in the Not.Dign. Cf.R.E. VI A II 2158 (Polaschek, 1937). (Names of peoples composed with **trans**: **Transtigritani** 19.9.2; **Transtigritanae gentes** 18.9.2; Not.Dign. **Transtigritani**: Or.VII 22,58).

b In connection with the following §§ I refer to: 1⁰ the works by **Patsch** quoted in the Comm.II p.12. 2⁰ Amm.M. **Sabbah** II p.184, note 103 (with lit.). 3⁰ **Seyf.** A.M. I p.313, note 156 (with lit.). 4⁰ **Stein Spatr.Gesch.** (op. cit.I) p.224 (with lit.); ibid.p.198 (with lit.). 5⁰ **Anon.Vales. I Westerhuis** (1906), § 31, p.49 sq.; § 32, p.51 (with extensive bibliography and also with **numismatic and epigraphical data**). 6⁰ Vulić (op.cit.II). The group of **Sarmatae**, of whom **Araharius** is protector, belong to the **Sarmatae liberi**, or **Argaragantes**, who in 334 were conquered and driven away by their slaves from the Banaat, where they lived. These slaves are the **Limigantes**, who now settled in the Banaat. Their masters fled to the North, up to the **Victohali** (17.12.19). But many of them submitted to the Romans and were given dwelling-places in depopulated areas of the Balkan peninsula and Italy. For the chronology cf. Seeck Regesten p.182. (334 A.D.) and ibid.p.205 **(358 A.D., in which year the events described here took place)** and p.206 **(359 A.D. destruction of the Limigantes)**; Goyau (op.cit.I) p.424, 475, 477.

c The name **Argaragantes** does not occur in Amm., nor in the Not.Dign.

and does not seem to occur anywhere else. **Limigantes** are mentioned in Amm., but not in the Not.Dign. For **Araharius** cf. Schönfeld p.23 (op. cit.I).

inter optimates excellens. For **optimates** cf. ad 17.12.11, p.126.10 - p.126. 12. For **excellens** cf. 16.12.23: Chnodomarius et Serapio, **potestate excelsiores ante alios reges;** 19.1.3; 30.5.10; ad 17.5.4, p.114.4 **(celsior).** p. 126. 20

agminum gentilium duces. Duces here of course, in the general meaning: leader, commander; not a t.t. (cf. ad 14.7.7 = I p.23). For the various meanings of **gentiles** cf. ad 14.5.6 (= III p.81). Here = barbarorum. Cf. et. ad 16.12.65, p.102,11. p. 126. 20

quibusdam. Cf. ad 17.3.6, p.109.1-2*b*. p. 126. 21

confiniis. Cf. ad 15.6.2 (= IV p.7); ad 17.7.7, p.117.16. Note the alliterating **f**, also in the next line. The subst. **feritas** also in 20.4.6: barbara feritas; 29.1.10. p. 126. 22

iunctissimis. The superlat. of this part.perf.pass. in general post-class. and poet. p. 126. 22

plebem. Cf. ad 16.12.17, p.93.28*b*; ad 16.12.34, p.96.21. p. 126. 23

plebem veritus imperator, ne ... consurgeret: prolepsis. More often in Amm. Cf. Blomgren (op.cit.II) p.99, note 2; ad 17.5.3, p.114.3*c*. p. 126. 23-24

a **ferire foedera simulans.** The class. construction is acc.c.inf. The **infinit.constr.** is poet. and post-class. Cf. Krebs Antib.2 p.580. Cf.et. ad 17. 12.11, p.126.14*b*. Cf.et.17.1.3: **simulata** pacis petitione.
b Here Amm. uses the old solemn expression: **foedus ferire,** although there is no mention of a **foedus** in the actual sense of the word, since the **Quades** and **Sarmates** submit themselves almost completely and are dediti. In this way he uses this expression also: 17.12.13, p.127.2. Cf. Willems (op.cit.I) p.345 sq. (with lit.); **Täubler, Imperium Romanum I (1913). Die Staatsverträge und Vertragsverhältnisse** (passim). p. 126. 23

in arma repente consurgeret. Cf.Verg.Aen.10.90 sq.:
... Quae causa fuit **consurgere in arma**
Europamque Asiamque et **foedera** solvere furto?
Cf. Fletcher, Rev. de Phil.LXIII, 1937, p.382. p. 126. 23-24

p. 126. 24 *a* **discreto consortio.** These words express the main point. Cf. ad 17.3.5, p.108.20*a*. For **consortium** cf. ad 16.5.11, p.77.5*a;* Heum.-Seckel p.97; ad 16.12.38, p.97.17-21 **(consors).**

b For the basic meaning: **to separate** Amm. uses in 18.8.12 and 28.5.3: **discriminare. se discernere** = to remove oneself; to leave: 26.6.3; 29.5.54. To decide (= reveal): 23.5.9 (said of oracles). Cf.et.16.11.14: Barbationem ... Gallico vallo **discretum;** ad 16.12.33, p.96.14-15*b* **(indiscretus).**

p. 126. 24 **pro Sarmatis obsecrantes.** For the **substantivation of the part.praes.** cf. Hofm.-Leum.66, p.457 (*a*); Hoogterp, Et. sur le lat. du Cod.Bob. des Evang. (1930) 417, p.212 sq.; Blomgren p.88 (op. cit.II). The expression is similar to: the spokesmen of the Sarmats. For **obsecrare** cf. ad 14.5.7 (= I p.87).

p. 126. 24 **paulisper.** On the difference between **parumper** and **paulisper** cf. Krebs Antib.2 p.250 (with lit.). For **parumper** cf. ad 14.2.16 (= I p.76).

p. 126. 25 **abscedere.** c.ablat.: 16.12.3; 19.9.5; 30.2.3. With **ex:** 18.8.6.

p. 126. 25 *a* **dum ... spectaretur.** Conjunct. in the subordinate clause of the oratio obliqua. But the conjunct. is also found after **dum** = **as long as.** Cf. ad 17.4.4, p.109.14.

b **spectare** = (here) to judge, investigate. With this meaning not in legal writings. More or less the same meaning also in Claud.26 (de bello Getico) p.113 sq.:

Non illis (sc.Romanis) vani ratio ventosa favoris,
Sed **graviter spectata salus** (sc.patriae),
ductorque placebat.

(The **ductor** is **Stilicho).** In Veget.r.m. only with the meaning of: be directed towards (with indication of place). With the meaning: to look back on, to pay attention to: Arn.adv.nat.2.11. (= Reiffersch.p.55): nos ea quae proferuntur a Christo audire et **spectare** nolitis? Not in Opt. Milev.

XII, 13

p. 126. 26 **reorum ritu oblati.** For **oblati** cf. ad 16.12.65, p.102.10. Attention should also be paid to the alliteration. For **ritus** cf. ad 17.1.7, p.105.27*c*.

p. 126. 26 **curvatis corporibus.** Cf. ad 17.10.3, p.122.1-2.

facinora gravia. Cf. ad 17.12.10, p.126.5-6*a*. For **facinora** cf.14.11.25 (= I p.138).

purgare. Cf.Curt.Ruf.7.5.39: Ille, **facinus purgare** non ausus, regis titulum se usurpare dixit, ut gentem suam tradere ipsi (sc.Alexandro) posset.

a **ultimae sortis infortunia metuentes.** For **ultimae** cf. ad 17.12.7, p.125.18.
b Cf.19.7.8: rex ... Persarum ... his **turbinum infortuniis** percitus. The substant.plur.poet., later and late-Lat. Cf. Krebs Antib.1 p.739 (with lit.); Heum.-Seckel p.266. The subst. does not occur in Claud.Veget.r.m.Arn. adv.nat.Opt.Milev.

pignera foederis: guarantee. But sometimes **pignus** has the meaning of: hostage. Cf.Livius 33.22.9; Suet.Aug.21. And here, too, the word is equal to: **obsides.** Cf.et. ad 16.12.25, p.95.10*b*.

exhibere. Exhibere is a t.t.iurid., just as **exhibitio**, and means, among other things, to take a person to court, in order to interrogate him or call him to account; cf.Dig.2.4.6: Qui duos homines **in iudicio sisti** promisit, si alterum **exhibet**, alterum non, ex promissione non videtur eos stetisse, cum alter eorum non sit **exhibitus**; Heum.-Seckel p.189 sq., special 5. Thus one says, for instance, testem exhibere, pupillum-, debitorem exhibere etc.; Amm.28.6.29: isque (sc.Romanus) Merobaudis favore susceptus **necessarios** sibi plures **petierat exhiberi**; 29.2.10: irremisse ab extremis regionum intervallis **exhibitis** omnibus, quos solutus legibus **accusator perduci** debere profunda securitate **mandarat**; 29.1.25: modo non ab extremo Atlante magnorum criminum **arguendos poscens aliquos exhiberi.**

conpulsi. For the construction cf.15.5.14 (= III p.91).

XII, 14

a **his ex aequo bonoque compositis.** For the **neutrum of the pronomina** cf. ad 17.4.14, p.111.7-8.
b **aequum** and **bonum** are often linked in Latin lit. But we are probably dealing here with a Sallustius reminiscence. Cf.Sall.b.Iug.35.7: fit **reus** magis **ex aequo bonoque** quam **ex iure gentium** Bomilcar...
c For **ex** linked with **neutra of the adiectiva** = adverbium, cf.14.4.4: ex pacto; 14.10.7: ex improviso; 15.2.10 and 15.5.11: ex confesso; similarly 21.1.3; 26.4.6: ex integro; 29.3.9: ex professo; 17.13.10: ex adverso; similarly 20.1.3; 21.6.3; etc.

p. 127. 3 **Usafer in preces admissus est.** For **Usafer** cf. ad 17.12.12, p.126.19-20*a*. **in preces** = ut precaretur. (cf. ad 17.12.9, p.125.27 - p.126.1). For this **in finale** cf. ad 17.10.3, p.121.25*a*. For **admissus** cf.17.12.10, p.126.6.

p. 127. 3-6 **Arahario - consueto.** Cf. ad 17.12.12, p.126.19-20*a, b*.

p. 127. 4 *a* **pertinaciter obstrepente.** The adv. also 21.13.11; 22.15.15; 25.8.17; 29.5.30. Does not occur in Claud.Veget.r.m.Arn.adv.nat.Opt.Milev. (for **pertinax** cf. ad 17.12.36, p.97.4).
b **obstrepente**: protesting loudly. The verb does not occur in Veget. r.m.Opt.Milev.Arn.adv.nat. Though several times in Claud. (besides **obstrepitare** (35.355: de raptu Pros.II)). Cf.et. **strepere**: 17.11.1, p.123.18; 17.11.4, p.124.10: **oblatrare**.

p. 127. 4 *a* **firmanteque pacem quam ipse meruit. Indic.** in the relative subordinate clause of the **orat.obl.** Cf. ad 16.10.17, p.87.15-16*b;* Reiter (op.cit.I) p.58 sq., 64.
b **meruit**: to acquire, obtain (and no more), thus not: "to merit" (on the basis of "merits"). Cf.17.10.4: (pacem) et eam ... sub hac **meruit** lege. Cf. Krebs Antib.2 p.75; Georges II 889 A 1, 2, with lit.
c **firmante.** With the same meaning: to state, assure, and with the same acc.c.inf.constr. also: 28.1.29; 28.1.37 (with "incorrect" construction).

p. 127. 5 *a* **ut participi licet inferiori.** For **ut** cf. ad 17.8.3, p.119.27 - p.120.1*a;* Schneider p.10. For **licet** cf. ad 14.1.5 (= I p.59); further: ad 14.6.6 (= I p.91); ad 14.11.6 (= II p.119); ad 16.10.11, p.86.5-6.
b **particeps**: partner, comrade; here, as often, almost: **socius.** Cf.Curt. Ruf.6.7.6; 6.8.10; 6.6.36; there more often. With Amm. **particeps inferior** (= lower in rank) indicates the relations among the vasals, of which he does not know or does not want to name the native term. **Particeps** does not occur in Claud.Veget.r.m.Opt.Milev. In Arn.adv.nat.3.40 (= Reiffersch.p.138): sed eos (sc.Consentes et Complices) summi Iovis consiliarios ac **participes** existimari (= socios).

p. 127. 5-6 *a* **et obtemperare suis imperiis consueto.** For **obtemperare** cf. ad 17.12.11, p.126.18. Also Caes.b.g.4.21.5: **imperio** populi Romani **obtemperare.** In Veget.r.m. the verb is used in particular to indicate the "obedience" of the soldiers (passim).
b For the construction of **consuetus** (c.inf.) cf. Krebs Antib.1 p.346 (with lit.); Hofm.-Leum.p.579, 166*a*.

XII, 15

verum - clientes. The partic. **iussi.** contains the main point. Cf. ad 17.3.5, p.108.20*a*. p. 127. 6-7

a **quaestione discussa:** after the "question" had been investigated. This general meaning: subject, theme, question, also class., is required here. p. 127. 6
b **discutere** (and **discussio**) with the above meaning, only in late Latin. Cf. Souter p.108; Krebs Antib.1 p.456 (with lit.); Heum.-Seckel p.151. For other meanings cf.15.5.13; 25.1.3.

aliena potestate eripi. For the first 2 words cf. ad 17.12.12, p.126.19-20. For the verb **eripere** (here constructed **c.abl.**) cf. Naumann (op.cit.I) p. 17; ad 15.5.36 (= III p.123); ad 16.12.45, p.98.24*a, b*. p. 127. 6

Sarmatae, i.e. only the part which was under the protection of **Araharius.** p. 127. 6

a **ut semper Romanorum clientes** = because they had always been protégés of the Romans. (for **ut** see previous remarks p.127.5). In class. Latin the above should be: ut qui semper Romanorum clientes fuissent. Cf. Terent.Andr.175: p. 127. 7

    Mirabar hoc si sic abiret, et **eri semper lenitas**
    Verebar quorsum evaderet.

Hofm.-Leum.p.467, 76*b*. But quite probably it is here the influence of the Greek, where the **adverbium pro adjectivo** occurs frequently.
b **clientes.** Used thus of **peoples** in Caes.b.g.6.4.5 (**clientela**) and 6.12.2 (**clientelae**); 1.31.6 (**clientes**), with note 6, p.140 Comm. Kraner-Dittenberger-Meusel I (1913). Cf.et. Grosse Mil. (op.cit.I) p.284 sq.; ad 16.12. 58, p.101.5-6.

a **quietis vincula conservandae:** as ties (= pledges) to keep the peace (cf. ad 17.12.11, p.126.17; ad 17.12.13, p.127.2) = pacis pignora conservandae. For **vinculum** cf.Liv.8.28.8: victum eo die ob inpotentem iniuriam unius **ingens vinculum fidei** (credit) = guarantee; Dig.26.7.39.5: Curatores adulescentis mutui periculi gratia cautionem invicem sibi praebuerunt et in eam rem **pignora** dederunt: cum officio deposito solvendo fuissent, irritam cautionem esse factam et **pignoris vinculum solutum** apparuit; ibid.41.2.46: ut enim eodem modo **vinculum obligationum** solvitur, quo quaeri adsolet; etc. Heum.-Seckel p.625. p. 127. 7-8
b **quies = pax.** Cf.Sall.Cat.31.1: ex summa laetitia atque lascivia, quae **diuturna quies** pepererat, repente omnis tristitia invasit; Tac.Germ.14:

309

si civitas, in qua orti sunt, **longa pace et otio** torpeat, plerique nobilium adulescentium petunt ultro eas nationes, quae tum bellum aliquod gerunt, quia et **ingrata genti quies** ... ; Ovid.ex Ponto 2.2.77 sq.:
Adde triumphatos modo Paeonos, adde **quieti**
Subdita montanae **brachia Dalmatiae.**

p. 127. 8 *a* **gratanter amplexi sunt.** For the adv.cf. ad 16.10.21, p.88.9; Heum.-Seckel p.231. Does not occur in Claud.Veget.r.m.Opt.Milev.Arn.adv. nat.

b **amplexi**: They have lovingly applied themselves to that, - have eagerly taken hold of. Cf.Cic.Cat.4.4(7): alteram (sententiam sc.) C.Caesaris, qui mortis poenam removet, ceterorum suppliciorum omnes acerbitates **amplectitur;** pro Flacco 18(43): sed cum **rem publicam nimium amplecteretur,** peculatus damnatus et bona et senatorium nomen amisit (Ernesti annot.: **amplecti r.p.** est ambigue dictum; nam est curare r.p. et ei consulere et pecuniam publicam ad se rapere); ad fam.4.8.2: **nobilitatem** vero **et dignitates** hominum, quantum ei res et ipsius causa concedit, **amplectitur.** And thus often in Cicero and others.

XII, 16

p. 127. 8 *a* **Ingerebat autem se post haec:** advanced upon, threw himself forward. Cf.Mela Chor.7 (65) (= Randstr.p.58): et quibus ars studiumque sapientiae contingit non exspectant eam (sc.mortem), sed **ingerendo semet ignibus** laeti et cum gloria arcessunt; Iust.Phil.11.14.5: Alexander autem periculosossima quaeque aggrediebatur, et ubi confertissimos hostes acerrime pugnare conspexisset, **eo se semper ingerebat**... This meaning is far from general. **Se ingerere** with the above meaning not in Claud.Veget. r.m.Arn.adv.nat.Opt.Milev. For late Latin meaning cf. Souter p.205 (also: **ingestio**, not in Amm.).

b **post haec.** Cf. **post hoc:** 28.1.29; **post haec:** 14.7.1; 14.7.5; 14.7.15; 14.9.7; **post quod:** 17.14.3; **post quae:** 21.3.4; 21.15.4; 31.5.9; etc.; Reinhardt (op.cit.I) p.54; ad 14.1.1 (= I p.53); ad 17.8.1, p.119.10*a;* and for a comparable usage of **inter** ad 17.4.1, p.109.4*a;* ad 14.6.1 (= I p.89). Cf.et. Krebs Antib.2 p.333 (with lit.); Hofm.-Leum.p.501, 94.

p. 127. 9 **maximus numerus catervarum confluentium nationum et regum.** For **caterva** cf. ad 16.2.6, p.73.5*a*. But here the subst. is used zeugmatically; for the **reges** will in any case not come in **catervae**, however numerous the tribes with their kings may be (for **reges** cf. ad 16.12.17, p.93.24). For **nationum** cf. ad 16.12.26, p.95, 14; Heum.-Seckel p.359.

a **suspendi a iugulis suis gladios obsecrantium.** Cf. ad 17.12.4, p.125.6.   p. 127. 9-10
In spite of the notes by Lindenbr. and Wagner (edit.Wagner-Erfurdt II p.289 sq.) and the annotations by Rolfe, (I p.376) I believe that here **suspendere** means: to remove, take away (to withdraw), as Seyf. and Büchele take it to mean. The translation by Sabbah is not clear to me: qui suppliaient les Romains de **ne pas abattre leurs glaives** sur leur gorge. Lindenbr., Wagner and Rolfe refer to their view to 21.5.10: iussique universi in eius nomen iurare sollemniter **gladiis cervicibus suis admotis** sub exsecrationibus diris verbis iuravere conceptis omnes pro eo casus, quoad vitam profuderint, si necessitas adegerit, perlaturos (one of the many barbarian abuses which sneaked into the Roman army cf. Müller Mil. (op.cit.I) p.629). But this passage is here beside the point (for the **oath** cf.et Grosse Mil. (op.cit.I) p.217.250; Veget.r.m.II.5 = Lang p.38 sq.).

b In legal writings the meaning of: to leave undecided –, unfinished –, unexecuted, occurs fairly frequently (cf. Heum.-Seckel p.574). Closer to our meaning are: Bened.Reg.25 (Linderb.p.42): Is autem frater qui gravioris culpae noxa tenetur, **suspendatur a mensa** simul et ab oratorio; Cass.Var.5.36.2 (Theod.rex illum (sc.Starcedium) ob membrorum debilitatem ab expeditione bellica eximit; et permisit ut deinceps vitam remissam ... exigat): nec aliquis tibi imputabit desertoris opprobrium, quando illi quos contigerit **a militia morbi causa suspendi,** ex prioribus factis habendi sunt iure reverendi; Souter p.408.

obsecrantium. This participium is joined with **nationum et regum,** but the   p. 127. 10
subject of the following **compererat** is **multitudo.** Although **compererant** would h_ave better satisfied the metrics of the clausula (III), viz. $\acute{-}\cup\acute{-}$: $-\cup\acute{-}\underset{\smile}{\cup}$ in its "normal" form; but not completely either. For the verb **obsecrare** cf. ad 17.11.3, p.124.1-2.

postquam...conpererat. For the use of the tenses and modi after **postquam** cf.   p. 127. 10
Hofm.-Leum.p.734, 297; 14.2.12: **postquam abierat** timor, vicos opulentos adorti... digressi sunt; (c.conj.) 30.7.11: inter quae illud elucere clarius potuit, si Macrianum regem ... vivum capere potuisset, ut industria magna temptarat, **postquam** eum evasisse Burgundios ... **didicisset** .... (according to Ehrismann attraction; but the conj. after **postquam** does occur in vulgar Latin). One also finds in Amm. the perf.indic. Cf. Ehrism. (op.cit.I) p.69.

inpune ... abscessisse. Cf.Cic. ad Herenn.4.39(51): Nam si istum **impuni-**   p. 127. 10-11
tum dimiseritis etc.

p. 127. 11 **et pari modo ipsi quoque adepti pacem.** Cf.18.2.19: pacem **condicionum similitudine** meruerunt; 17.12.21: et **adepti veniam** iussa fecerunt.

p. 127. 12 **accitos ex intimis regni. Accire:** to send for, to summon: in the usual classical meaning. For the adj.cf.Cic. ad fam.13.29.4: Itaque abdidit se **in intimam Macedoniam** quo potuit longissime a castris; Vell.Pat.2.40.1: nationes, quae dextra atque **intima Ponti** incolunt. **Intima** (n.pl.) is seen more often like this. For **adj. and part.neutr.plur.** cf. ad 17.3.2, p.108.12*a;* ad 17.4.1, p.109.4*a*.

p. 127. 12 **procerum filios. Proceres** = **optimates** (cf. ad 16.12.26, p.95.13). Also class. and post-class. Cf.Cic. ad fam.13.15.1: Audiebam enim **nostros proceres** clamitantes ...; Liv.1.45.2: **proceres Latinorum;** ibid.10.28.7: **proceres iuventutis;** Tac.ann.14.53: egone, equestri et provinciali loco ortus, **proceribus civitatis** adnumeror?; Cass.Var.4.3.1: Tales enim provehere principem decet, ut quoties **procerem suum** fuerit dignatus aspicere, toties se cognoscat recta iudicia habuisse (the king's court, collect.); ibid.9.24.8: Quoties ille te **grandaevis proceribus** imputavit, dum non sufficerent ad primordia tua, quos tanta longaevitas aetatis instruxerat? (courtiers); Souter p.324; Cod.Iust.1.14.2: Quae ex relationibus vel suggestionibus iudicantium per consultationem in commune **florentissimorum sacri nostri palatii procerum auditorium** introducto negotio statuimus; Heum.-Seckel p.462 (for **relatio** cf.II p.34; III p.90; ad 16.11.7, p.89.11; for **palatium** cf. ad 17.11.1, p.123.16; **auditorium** = imperial court of justice).

p. 127. 12 **obsidatus sorte.** Cf. ad 16.12.25, p.95.10*a, b*.

p. 127. 12 **opinione celerius.** Cf.Cic. ad fam.14.23: et ipse **opinione celerius** venturus esse dicitur; Caes.b.g.2.3: eo cum de inproviso **celeriusque omni opinione** venisset; Sall.Iug.53.5.; quod Metellus **amplius opinione** morabatur; ibid. 85.3: domi forisque omnia curare ... **opinione, Quirites, asperius est;** Cic. ad fam.10.31.6: Quod familiarem meum in tuorum numero habes, **opinione** tua mihi **gratius est;** Cic. de orat.35(164): Formam enim totius negotii **opinione maiorem, melioremque** video; Plaut.Mil.4.6.23 (1238): istuc curavi, ut **opinione** illius **pulchrior** sis; etc. The ablat.comparationis **opinione** linked with comparativi of adj., or adv. occurs very frequently throughout Latinity, so that there is no need to look for certain reminiscences.

itidemque. Cf. ad 16.12.17, p.93.23-24*b*.

captivos. Cf. ad 17.10.4, p.122.3. The frequent mentioning of the **captivi** of the Romans among the barbarians may be a sign that the (guerilla)war against the "barbarians" all too often was only partially successful.

ut placuerat: sc. imperatori. As we know, the dat. is often omitted with the **impersonale placet.**

a **quos haut minore gemitu perdid****ē****re quam s****ū****os** (sc. obsides: their own people). It is possible that these Sarmats have grown used to these **captivi,** also perhaps because many of the "Roman" soldiers, especially in the border districts, did not have one drop of Roman blood in their veins. I do not think it likely that Amm. would impute faked lamentations to these Sarmats. Neither do I think that Amm. means that the **economical loss,** caused by the return of these captivi, made the Sarmats complain (see above).
b For **haut** cf. ad 14.2.17 (= I p.77). **Gemitus** also 16.12.50: auditoque occumbentium **gemitu** crebro.
c **perdid****ē****re.** Cf. ad 16.12.19, p.94.11-12. Claus.I. But this clause does not have any influence here. Metric.model: $-\cup-:\stackrel{\prime}{-}\cup$

XII, 17 sq.
The contents of the §§ 17-20 are not quite clear. Cf. ad 16.12.12, p.126. 19-20. I believe that we should distinguish here between 3 groups of **Sarmatae liberi.** 1⁰ Those S., who are under the rule of **Usafer,** under protection of **Araharius.** 2⁰ A larger group of S., who have fled to the North, further than group 1⁰. 3⁰ the displaced group of 300.000. (the 3rd group is not mentioned by Amm.). The 2nd group appears to be under the protection of the **Victohali (defensores).** Group 1 had already been ordered (§ 15) to dissociate themselves from the **aliena potestas (sc.Quadorum).** Now group 2 gets similar orders (§ 19): **nulli** nisi sibi ducibusque Romanis parere praecepit (sc.imperator). And to complete the **restitutio libertatis** (§ 20), he appoints **Zizais** as **rex,** in my opinion of both groups 1 and 2. This **libertas** is, of course, restricted. For the Roman emperor and the generals still have to be obeyed **(parere).** We are not informed on the nature of the relationship between **Usafer** and **Zizais.** He probably becomes a **subregulus** of **Zizais.** (cf. ad 17.12.11, p.126.10-12). These details either do not sufficiently interest Amm. or his sources were not accurate enough.

p. 127. 15 **quibus ordinatis:** after these settlements. For the various meanings of **ordinare,** also in late Latin, cf. Krebs Antib.2 p.226 sq.; Souter p.279 Heum.-Seckel p.397.

p. 127. 15 **translata est in Sarmatas cura:** lit.: one shifted one's "cares" to the Sarmats. But **cura** and **curare** are often almost t.t. Cf. ad 17.7.6, p.117.12*c;* ad 14.7.19 (= II p.47); Souter p.85.

p. 127. 15 **miseratione.** Here pity, as often. But in 19.10.3: lamentations.

p. 127. 16 **simultate.** Thus also said of states, e.g. Iust.Phil.2.6.16: Erant inter Athenienses et Dorienses **simultatum** veteres offensae. The subst. does not occur in Opt.Milev. or Claud. It is found, however, in Arn.adv.nat. and Veget.r.m.3.10 (= Lang p.92): Nulla enim quamvis minima natio potest ab adversariis deleri, nisi **propriis simultatibus** se ipsa consumpserit (where **simultas** has its original meaning).

p. 127. 16-17 *a* **quibus incredibile quantum prosperitatis haec attulit causa.** Cf.16.5.6: incredibile quo quantoque ardore; ad 15.8.15 (= IV p.39).

b For **prosperitas** cf. ad 17.4.6, p.110.1*a*. **causa:** circumstances; here not, I believe, cause of reason.

p. 127. 17-18 **ut verum ... vel fieri.** p.127.17 V **opinatur,** Sabbah. opinantur: E. Vales Seyf.Rolfe. This last version seems preferable to me, because this statement has been made by more than one person. Unless (which is, possible) Amm. is making a covert attack on a contemporary. Although a firm believer in the hierarchy of the Roman state and the elevated position of the emperor, **fatum vinci ... fieri** does certainly not express Amm.'s views. Cf.15.5.37: post quas ita completa, Constantius **ut iam caelo contiguus casibusque imperaturus humanis,** magniloquentia sufflabatur adulatorum; 19.12.16: unde blanditiarum taetra commenta, Palatina cohors exquisite confingens, **immunem eum fore malorum communium** adserebat, **fatum eius vigens semper et praesens,** in abolendis adversa conantibus eluxisse .... But not only the adulatores (imperatoris) speak like this, others too; Cf.Manil.Astron.1.391 sq.:

Cetera non cedunt: uno vincuntur in astro

Augusto, **sidus nostro qui contigit orbi;**

Caesar nunc terris, **post caelo maximus auctor.**

Paneg.XII 27 (= Baehrens p.295): quin ego, si fas piumque mortalibus aestimare **caelestia,** nullam maiorem esse crediderim **principum felicitatem** quam fecisse felicem et intercessisse inopiae **et vicisse fortunam et dedisse homini novum fatum** ...; Claud.8.118 sq. (= de IV cons.Honor.):

Magnarum largitor opum, largitor honorum;
Pronus et in melius gaudens convertere fata.
(121) sq.) .... hoc nobilis ortu
Nasceris, aequaeva cum maiestate creatus,
Nullaque privatae passus contagia sortis.
(126 sq.)
Membraque, **vestitu nunquam temerata profano**
In sacros cecidere sinus (sc."augustorum parentum").

Veget.r.m.2.5 (= Lang p.38): Iurant autem per Deum et Christum et Sanctum Spiritum et per maiestatem imperatoris, **quae secundum Deum generi humano diligenda est et colenda** (very close indeed to the Holy Trinity); I praef. (= Lang p.4): ... quia neque recte aliquid inchoatur, **nisi post Deum faverit imperator;** II.6 (= Lang p.39): Haec (sc.cohors) imagines imperatorum, hoc est **divina et praesentia signa,** veneratur; Firm. Mat.2.30.3-6; Enßlin, Zur Gesch.schr. etc. (op.cit.I) p.77 sq. For **fatum** cf.15.3.3 (another example of imperial conceit): Constantius, **quasi praescriptorum fatorum ordinem convulsurus,** recluso pectore patebat insidiantibus multis; ad 15.5.1 (= III p.67): **fortuna;** ad 16.1.1, p.71.1; Camus, Amm.Marc. (1967) p.173 sq.

Fatum Vinci Principis Potestate Vel Fieri Alliteration! p. 127. 18

aestimaretur. Cf. ad 17.7.11, p.118.4*c;* Heum.-Seckel p.23; ad 17.1.8, p.106.1. p. 127. 17

quidam. Cf. ad 17.3.6, p.109.1-2*b*. p. 127. 17

XII, 18

a **potentes – regni.** huius regni sc. **Sarmatarum liberorum.** For they constitute the upper class. The subjected nations are mainly the **Sarmatae Limigantes (servos),** whose further history is told in 17.13. p. 127. 18-19
b **potentes.** Cf.16.8.11, p.83.4.
c **nobiles:** noble. **Nobiles** in the original sense of the word no longer exist under the monarchy. The members of the **ordo senatorius** (1) could be called thus, but their title is **clarissimus** (2). Another category which might be called nobiles, are the **honorati** (3), i.e. those citizens who have fulfilled military or civil functions, effectively as well as in name only, which gave them at least the title of **clarissimus.** The **ordo decurionum** (4)

315

could also be called nobiles, because of its hereditary status. This **ordo**, however, is lower in rank than the two first-mentioned groups. Finally, the title of **nobilissimus** (5), which is borne only by members of the imperial family. From this can be concluded that of course, the monarchy has its nobility (and a very proud one at that!), but that the terminology is a different one. Constitutionally speaking, **nobilitas** and **nobiles** are obsolete terms. Cf. for 1, 2, 3, 4, 5 respectively, Willems (op.cit.I) p.575 sq.; p.547 sq.; p.548; p.583 sq.; p.543 (all with lit.). Probably **nobiles** has here in Amm. more or less the same meaning as **optimates** (cf. ad 16.12.26, p.95.13a). But I am not entirely sure of that. Nobilis is also mentioned, in the judic.lit., when it means: esteemed, noble (but here it is not a t.t.). Cf.Cod.Just.6.23.19: Omnium testamentorum sollemnitatem superare videatur, quod insertum mera fide precibus **inter tot nobiles probatasque personas** etiam conscientiam principis tenet. (the n.p. personae are the members of the consistorium; cf. ad 14.7.11 = II p.34). Nobilitare is also used in this way: cf.Cod.Iust.12.1.13: Mulieres honore maritorum erigimus, **genere nobilitamus** et forum ex eorum persona statuimus et domicilia mutamus; Heum.-Seckel p.368. Veget.r.m. has **nobilitas** and **nobilissimi** (3.26 = Lang p.124) only as: excellent, famous. Cf.et.Claud.1.1.13 sq. (In Prob. et Olyb.cons.):

.... Quemcumque requires

Hac de stirpe virum, certum est de consule nasci.

Per fasces numerantur avi, **semperque renata**

Nobilitate virent, et prolem fata sequuntur.

ibid.20(2)79 sq. (In Eutr.II):

Subter adulantes tituli, nimiaeque leguntur

Vel maribus (= even for real men) laudes: **claro quod nobilis ortu;**

Cum vivant domini? (sc.Eutropii servi)

(subter = on the pedestal).

The subst. in Amm.16.10.13: adlocutus **nobilitatem** in curia; 29.1.12: plures a disiunctissimis regionibus trahebantur, **dignitatibus et nobilitate conspicui.**

p. 127. 19 **indigenae:** × **advenae.** Native, indigenous residents, who belonged there because of their descent (although they, too had once come there as strangers). The subst. does not occur in Veget.r.m.Opt.Milev.Arn.adv. nat. Several times in Claud. as adj., e.g. 28.8 (De VI cons.Honor.):

Indigenas habitus nativa Palatia sumunt.

In the Cod.Theod. **indigena** occurs also with the above meaning. Thus the word does not have the same meaning as **incola** (Cf. Willems op.cit.I, p.501, 583). In the N.D.Or. 23 the following are mentioned: equites promoti **indigenae**, equites sagittarii **indigenae**, equites Saraceni **indigenae** (all sub dispositione v.spect. ducis Foenicis). Apparently natively recruited troops. (For the **promoti** cf. Grosse Mil. p.16 sq., 49 sq., 52 sq.; ad 15.4.10 = III p.65).

a **coniuratio clandestina ... armavit in facinus,** For the personificatio cf. ad 17.2.1, p.107.13. The adj., although class. and used, among others, in Cic.Caes.Liv.Lucr.Plaut., does not seem to be very common. It is not found in Veget.r.m.Claud.Opt.Milev.Arn.adv.nat. Though Veget. does have in 4.26 (= Lang p.146) the arch. or vulgar **clanculo** (cf. Krebs Antib.1 p.287), which is remarkable. p. 127. 19-20

b For the construction cf.Liv.39.16.3: Necdum omnia, **in quae coniuraverunt**, edita **facinora** habent; Curt.Ruf.7.1.6: Eundem **in** Philippi quoque **caedem coniurasse** cum Pausania pro comperto fuit. For **in finale** cf. ad 17.10.3, p.121.25*a*.

For **facinus** cf. ad 14.11.25 (= II p.138). In Amm.16.11.9; 18.6.6; 19.6.4; 22.8.34; 24.4.5; 24.4.20; 24.4.24; 26.8.10; 27.6.9; 30.3.6; 31.12.1. Here with an unfavourable meaning: reckless crime. The fact that the **servi** may have had some cause for rebellion, does not enter the author's mind. Rebellions against "authority" (even the "barbarian" one) are not in his line. However honest he may have been, he favours the established order of the time. Though this does not mean that he does **not,** as we have repeatedly seen, offer criticism on the persons in charge.

a **atque ut ... adsuevit.** Here again Amm. expresses himself in a typically Roman way. The barbarians are incapable of living in a constitutional state. Justice and laws are and were introduced by the Romans. It reminds one of the famous words in Verg.Aen.6.851 sq.: p. 127. 20

Tu regere imperio populos, Romane, memento;
Hae tibi erunt artes, **pacique imponere morem,**
Parcere subiectis et debellare superbos.

b **in vīribus adsuĕvit.** Claus.III. **adsuevit:** 4-syllabic. The choice of the word is not accidental. Special attention should also be paid to the curious placing of **esse.**

c For **ut** cf. ad 17.8.3, p.119.27 - p.120.1*a*.

d **ferocia** of persons also 31.10.21.

praeminentes. Rare verb, among others in Tac. and Sen.Rhet. Cf. Souter p.314. Does not occur in Claud.Veget.r.m.Opt.Milev.Arn.adv.nat. p. 127. 21

Literally in August.Conf.6.9(14): ingressus est ad cancellos plumbeos, qui vico argentario desuper **praeminent.**

XII, 19

p. 127. 21-22 *a* **confundente metu consilia.** Similar sentences with **personificatio** 17.12.5, p.125.9; 17.12.10, p.126.7; 16.12.49, p.99.17; 17.1.2, p.104.10; Blomgren (op.cit.II) p.87 sq. (with more examples).
b for the verb cf. ad 17.7.2, p.116.20*c*.

p. 127. 22 *a* **ad Victohalos discretos longius confugerunt.** Cf.Eutr.8.2: (Traianus) Daciam Decebalo († 106 A.D.) victo subegit, provincia trans Danubium facta in iis agris, **quos nunc Taiphali habent, Victoali et Thervingi.** (Eutropius' breviarium continues untill the death of Iovianus in 364 A.D. and is published in ± 369 A.D.; this gives us at least one date of these **Victohali**); Hist.Aug.M.Ant.14.1: Profecti tamen sunt paludati ambo imperatores (sc.**M.Aurelius**, 161 - 180 A.D. and **Lucius Verus**, 161 - 169 A.D.) et **Victualis et Marcomannis cuncta turbantibus**, aliis etiam gentibus, quae pulsae a superioribus barbaris fugerant, nisi reciperentur, bellum inferentibus. (This campaign takes place in 167 A.D.); ibid.22.1: Gentes omnes ab Illyrici limite usque in Galliam conspiraverant, ut **Marcomanni** Varistae Hermunduri et **Quadi Suebi Sarmatae** Lacringes et Buri hi aliique (?) cum **Victualis** Osi Bessi etc. (This takes place in 172 A.D.). (For the **Sarm.** and **Quadi** cf. ad 17.12.1, p.124.18; for the **Suebi** ad 16. 10.20, p.88.3; the **Marcomanni** are mentioned: 22.5.5; 29.6.1; 31.4.2). Cf.et R.E.VIII A 2, 2087 (Gutenbrunner); Schönfeld (op.cit.I) p.262, also for the variety in the spelling.
b **discretos longius**: belongs together. For **discretus** cf. ad 17.12.12, p.126.24. Cf. et **discretim**: 28.1.36; 29.6.13; **discretio**: 23.6.67; 26.6.7.
c **lŏngius confugĕrunt.** Although in my opinion the compar. is not a positivus here, as so often, yet the choice of the compar. and of the compositum is caused by the clausula (III).

p. 127. 22-23 *a* **obsequi defensoribus (ut in malis) optabile, quam servire mancipiis arbitrati.** The meaning of **obsequi** is more: to adapt oneself to someone, to listen to someone, rather than: **to obey.** This last meaning is required here, I believe. But in Eutr.1.12 one has the same meaning: Eodem anno etiam magister equitum factus est, qui **dictatori obsequeretur.** (However, in 7.10: **to pay homage to**: Multi autem reges ex regnis suis venerunt, ut **ei obsequerentur** (sc.Octaviano). Both examples quoted by Georges). But it has been noted before that Amm. makes free use of the various

Latin verbs for **to obey**; cf. ad 17.10.10, p.123.11; ad 17.12.11, p.126.18. Perhaps the same applies to the verbs meaning: **to promise.** (cf. ad 17.12.11, p.126.18).

b for **defensor** cf. ad 16.12.15, p.93.12*b;* Heum.-Seckel p.128; Souter p.91.

c for **ut** cf. ad 17.8.3, p.119.27 - p.120.1*a*.

d **optabile** = magis optabile. The **positivus followed by quam,** as used here, is also found in earlier Latin, though its use increases in late Latin. Cf.Hofm.-Leum.p.730 sq. (295). With Amm. it **may** be a Grecism. Also several times in Cic., e.g. in Pison.14(33): Atque, ut tuum laetissimum diem cum tristissimo meo conferam. utrum tandem bono viro et sapienti **optabilius** putas, sic exire e patria ... an ...?; de orat.2.83(334): Ergo in suadendo nihil est **optabilius** quam dignitas; pro Mil.11(31): certe **optabilius** Miloni **fuit dare** iugulum P.Clodio ... **quam** iugulari a vobis.; Claud.8.430 sq. (de IV cons.Honor.):

Adspice, completur votum. iam natus adaequat
Te meritis, et, quod **magis est optabile,** vincit
Subnixus Stilichone tuo.

Optabile in Veget.r.m.3.4 (= Lang p.72). The adj. does not occur in Opt. Milev.Arn.adv.nat. Perhaps Cicero reminiscence? (it is also found in among others Ovid.Sen.Fronto).

e **mancipiis** = servis. Probably metri causa. Claus.III: **mancĭpiis arbĭtrāti. Servis** would produce the claus. $\stackrel{x}{\smile} \sim \sim \sim \stackrel{x}{\smile} \sim$ which is less common (cf. Blomgren p.9 sq.). In the strictly legal sense the **Limigantes** are not **mancipia.** But the subst. is also used thus (= servus) in the Digests with the incorrect explanation Dig. 1.5.3.4: **Servi** ex eo appellati sunt, quod imperatores **captivos** vendere ac per hoc **servare(!)** nec occidere solent: **mancipia** vero dicta, quod ab **hostibus** manu capiantur (both subst. are clearly synonymous here). Cf.et. ad 17.12.12, p.126.23*b;* Heum.-Seckel p.330 (s.v.**3).**

quae deplorantes. Group 2 is concerned here. (cf. ad 16.12.17 sq., p.127.15 sq.). Cf.Cic. de senect.3.7: **quae** ... nostri fere aequales, **deplorare** solebant.

a **post impetratam veniam recepti in fidem.** The main point is expressed in the first partic. The **2nd. group** has, either in connection with the first group, or together with the **Victohali,** been guilty of hostile actions against the Romans. For this they ask and receive forgiveness from the Romans, after which they come under Roman protection **(recepti in fidem,** the standard expression for this). Their new situation, the relative independence, is called by them **libertas**. But, not satisfied with this, they demand guarantees **(praesidia)**. This presumptious attitude is not appreciated by the emperor **(iniquitate rei permotus)**.

b For **post** cf. ad 17.12.16, p.127.8*b;* ad 17.4.1, p.109.4*a*.

p. 127. 25 **praesidia.** The nuance: security, guarantee, is required here, because they had already received **protection (fides)**. I cannot find satisfactory parallel places for this.

p. 127. 25 **iniquitate.** Cf.14.9.6: (Eusebius) et ducebatur intrepidus **temporum iniquitati** insultans imitatus Zenonem, illum veterem Stoicum ... (cf.Cic. Rosc.Amer.29.81: Sex.Roscio **temporis** illius acerbitatem **iniquitatemque** obiicient; Curt.7.7.6: Terrebat eum non hostis sed **iniquitas temporis;** Liv.35.17.11: **temporum iniquitate** pressi). In 17.12.19 the meaning is: unfair, i.e. exaggerated and presumptious demands.
permotus. Cf. ad 17.12.7, p.125.15*b*.

p. 127. 25-26 **inspectante omni exercitu.** Cf. Kraner-Hofm.-Meusel[11] ad Caes.b.c.2.20. 4: "Das Verb kommt im klass. Lat. nirgends in einem Tempus finitum, sondern nur ... im **abl.abs.** vor. Nur Brutus in Cic.ep. ad Brut.1.4.5 hat **inspectare** ...".
Inspectante exercitu also occurs in Sisenna fr. and Cic., so that here it is probably a reminiscence.

p. 127. 26 **verbis molliŏribus imperător.** Claus.III. The comparat. probably metri causa. **mollis** = merciful, mild. Cf. Krebs Antib.2 p.95 sq. (with lit.).

p. 127. 27 **parere praecepit.** For the verbs of **to obey** cf. ad 17.12.19, p.127.22-23*a*. For the construction of **praecipere** cf. ad 15.7.6 (= IV p.18); ad 15.7.4 (= IV p.15); ad 15.7.2 (= IV p.10).

XII, 20

p. 127. 27 **restitutio libertatis.** Cf. ad 17.12.17 sq., p.127.15 sq.; ad 17.12.19, p.127. 24*a*.

p. 127. 28 **dignitatis.** Cf.29.1.12: plures ... **dignitatibus** et nobilitate **conspicui;** 24.5. 10: et imperator ira gravi **permotus** reliquos ex ea cohorte, qui abiecte sustinuerant impetum grassatorum, ad pedestrem compegit militiam, quae onerosior est, **dignitatibus imminutis.** (= by which they were degraded).

augmentum. Cf. ad 17.3.5, p.108.20-21*b*. **Zizaim.** Cf. ad 17.12.11, p.126. 10-12; ad 17.12.17 sq., p.127.15 sq. _{p. 127. 28}

isdem. Seemingly the last-mentioned group, but actually group 1 and 2, in my view (cf. ad 17.12.17 sq., p.127.15 sq.). For the meaning of **isdem** cf. ad 15.5.19 (= III p.103). _{p. 127. 28}

a **conspicuae fortunae tum insignibus aptum profecto (ut res docuit) et fidelem.** For **conspicuae** cf. ad 16.12.24, p.95.5-6; 16.12.13, p.93.1-2*b*. **tum,** of course belongs to **aptum,** a good example of a hyperbaton (cf. 17.1.6, p.105.21*a*). **fortuna** is not "Glück" here (Seyf.) or "fortune" (Sabbah) but: position, dignity (as often). _{p. 127. 28-29}

b Cf.Cic.Verr.1.58(152): Quod ornamentum pueritiae pater dederat, **indicium atque insigne fortunae,** hoc ab isto praedone ereptum esse, graviter et acerbe homines ferebant. Cf.et. ad 17.11.4, p.124.11*a*; ad 17.11.4, p.124.7-11.

c **tum ... aptum.** Cf.p.126.7-8: adhuc ... ambiguo; p.125.26: etiam tum regalis; p.116.11-12: Nevitta, postea consul; p.89.5: Valentinianus postea imperator; p.81.9: consularem Pannoniae tunc Africanum; p.81.17: Mavortius tunc praefectus praetorio; p.70.2: abiecte ignavus; p.41.20: Eusebius cubiculi tunc praepositus; etc. **Adverbia (especially of time) linked with adjectiva and substantiva** are found fairly often in Amm. Cf. et.Hofm.-Leum.p.467,76*b*.

ut res docuit. Cf.17.2.1: ut postea claruit; 17.3.3: ut docebitur postea, etc. Cf.et. ad 17.3.2, p.108.11; ad 17.3.3, p.108.14. _{p. 127. 29}

nec ... quisquam. The pronomen used "correctly". Cf. ad 17.3.6, p.109. 1-2*b*. _{p. 127. 29 / p. 128. 1}

discedere ... permissus est. For the construction cf. ad 14.1.3 (= I p.58). Cf.et. ad 15.6.1 (= IV p.6); ad 16.10.11, p.86.7; ad 15.7.4 (= IV p.15); ad 15.7.6 (= IV p.18); ad 17.12.11, p.126.14*b*; ad 15.5.14 (= III p.91). _{p. 128. 1}

post haec gloriose gesta. For **post** cf. ad 17.12.16, p.127.8*b*. For **gloriose** cf. ad 16.12.70, p.103.9-10*a*; ad 16.10.3, p.84.24. For **gesta** = res gestae cf.16.12.69: cum **gestis** non adfluisset; Krebss Antib.1 p.625 (with lit.). _{p. 128. 1}

p. 128. 1-2 **antequam ... remearent.** For the construction cf. ad 14.6.23 (= I p.100).

p. 128. 2 **ut placuerat.** Cf. ad 17.12.16, p.127.13; ad 17.12.20, p.127.29; 17.1.13: quia id **nostris placuerat.**

p. 128. 2 **remearent.** Apart from this place also 17.10.9; 18.6.20; etc. Cf. Fesser p.41: "Wohl ein Wort höheren Stiles, wie der Vergleich mit **meare, permeare, intermeare, praetermeare** zeigt". (with litt.) Cf. **repedare** ad 17.2.4, p.108.4.

p. 128. 2 **captivi.** Cf. ad 17.12.16, p.127.13.

XII, 21

p. 128. 2 *a* **his in barbarico gestis.** After **post haec ... gesta** just previously, the repetition is quite remarkable, even though the abl.abs. is used. **in barbarico** also 18.2.14: visus **in barbarico** miles per Hortarii regna transibat intacta. Thus Eutr.7.9; 9.4; Hist.Aug.Alex.Sev.47.1; Not.Dign.Occ.32.41; 33.48. **Barbaricum** as subst. is late Latin.

b The adject. **barbaricus** in general poet. and post-class. in prose. In Amm.16.11.11: et victum ... ex **barbaricis messibus** ... collectum. Cf.et. Krebs Antib.1 p.232 sq.

p. 128. 3 *a* **Bregetionem castra commota sunt.** The place is also mentioned 30.5.15. According to N.D.Occ.33, the following is sub dispositione v.spect. **ducis provinciae Valeriae ripensis**: praefectus legionis primae adiutricis cohortis quintae partis superioris, **Bregetione** (For **Valeria** cf.III p.44, ad 15.3.7). In the Itiner.Anton.Aug. it is mentioned on p.263,265 edit. Wesseling. **Bregetio** was a garrison town as well as a base of the Danube fleet. The town was situated opposite the country of the **Quadi**, on the river's right bank. Cf.Tab.Peut.V.3: **Brigantio** (either an error or a mistake in spelling, for the location between **Aquincum** and **Carnuntum** is correct); Patsch R.E.3.847-851; Mommsen C.I.L. III p.539; **F.Pichler, Austria Romana** (1904) II-III, p.125,268; R.Chevalier, Les voies Romaines (1972) p.198, 199. Pieper Tab.14 (op.cit.II) does not mention the place (from which may be concluded that it was not an ecclesiastical centre?).

b Cf.Cic.Verr.5.37(96): Posteaquam ... praetorem **commovisse** ex eo loco **castra** senserunt. The verb is a t.t.mil. and sacr. (cf.Verg.Aen.4.301) and a general verb for: to shift, move (of objects and persons). It is not always recognised as such, e.g. (in my view) Caes.b.g.3.15.3: ut se ex loco **movere** non possent (version by Kraner, Dittenb., Meusel I 1913[17],

p.265; but α: **commovere**, which is explained by the editors as a dittography: Anhang p.423). For the moving of a camp etc. the following verbs are generally used: **movere, promovere, proferre**. The reason for the use of the **compositum** may have been: alliteration + clausula (II; metric model) $-\cup-:-\cup\underaccent{\smile}{}$).
Cf.et. ad 17.12.7, p.125.15*b*.

a **belli Quadorum reliquias**. Cf. ad 17.12.12, p.126.19-20*a*. Apart from the **Quadi of Araharius** more (or even all?) parts of this nation seem to have gone to battle. These parts (tribes) are called **populi**.   p. 128. 3
b **reliquias**. Cf. ad 17.2.1, p.107.10*c*. (**sudorum reliquias**).

a **circa illos agitantium tractus**. **Agitare** here with the meaning of: to act, undertake actions; here better not: to find oneself (cf. ad 16.2.8, p.73.17; ad 16.12.69, p. 103.1). The verb is found very often in Amm. (cf. Liesenberg, 1889, p.3 sq.), with various meanings. Though sometimes the meaning can be entirely colourless, as is apparent from 22.8.26: Quorum post terga Cimmerici agitant incolae Bospori (= vivunt). Thus **agitare praesidium** in 29.5.18 means: to be garrisoned at, probably also 29.5.27 (although here another meaning is also possible).   p. 128. 4
b **tractus**. Cf.14.3.2: Mesopotamiae **tractus** omnes. Cf.et. ad 15.8.1 (= IV p.27); ad 17.8.3, p.119.27 - p.120.1*b*. With **this** meaning the subst. does not occur at all in Veget.r.m. or Opt.Milev.; in Arn.adv.nat.2.61 (= Reiffersch.p.97): **per tractum temporis** (= paulatim); in Claud. often with this and other meanings.

exstingueret. Obviously a Cic. reminiscence; cf. ad fam.10.25.1: Si interest, id quod homines arbitrantur, rei publicae te, ut instituisti atque fecisti, navare operam rebusque maximis, **quae ad exstinguendas reliquias belli pertinent**, interesse...   p. 128. 4

regalis Vitrodorus. For **regalis** cf. ad 16.10.16, p.87.8. He is the son of king **Viduarius**. Both are unknown to us. (of whom **Zizais** is a son, Amm. does not say. His father must alo have been a **rex**, in my opinion.). For **Vidu-arius** (= Δορί-μαχος) cf. Schönfeld p.264; for **Vitrodorus** ibid.p.270, 239, 262 (both with lit.).   p. 128. 5

Agilimundus. For this see Schönfeld p.4. Otherwise unknown.   p. 128. 5

subregulus. Cf. ad 17.12.11, p.126.10-12.   p. 128. 5

323

p. 128. 6 **optimates.** Cf. ad 17.12.11, p.126. 10-12.

p. 128. 6 **iudices.** For **iudex** cf. ad 16.5.13, p.77.11-14c. Here, too, a term is being used (as is the case with **optimates**), which can really only be used for Roman situations. Either Amm. does not know the foreign terms or he chooses not to use them.

p. 128. 6 **populis.** Cf. ad 17.12.21, p.128.3a. Thus, tribes, or tribal relations, but **parts of the Quadi.**

p. 128. 6 **praesidentes.** The use of this verb by Amm. is no accident. For **praesides** is a general name for governors of the smaller provinces. (cf. ad 14.10. 8 = II p.106). Cf.et.Heum.-Seckel p.452. For the verb cf.Heum.-Seckel ibid.

p. 128. 6-7 *a* **viso exercitu in gremio regni solique genitalis.** Cf.Verg.Aen.3.509:
Sternimur **optatae gremio telluris** ad undam.
Cic. pro Cael.24(59): cum Q. Metellus abstraheretur e sinu **gremioque patriae,** Sil.Ital.3.677 sq.:
Nam cui dona Iovis non divulgata per orbem
In gremio Thebes geminas sedisse colombas?
ibid.12.204 sq.:
Talesne e **gremio Capuae** tectisque sinistris
Egredimur?
ibid.2.573 sq.:
.... tandemque supremum,
Nocte obita, **Libyae gremio** captiva iacebo.
Paneg.Genethl.Maxim.3,4 (Baehrens p.105): repente in **medio Italiae Gremio** apparuistis.
b For **genitalis** cf. ad 16.12.25, p.95.11; ad 16.10.16, p.87.9. **(gentilis).** Cf.et.Ovid.Metam.8.184: **loci natalis** amore; Vell.Paterc.2.7.7: **genitali solo;** Hist.Aug.Aurel.3.2: **solum genitale;** Ovid.ex Pont.1.3.35: **natale solum;** Krebs Antib.2 p.586.

p. 128. 7 *a* **sub gressibus iacuere militum** †, The usual expressions are: adcidere, abicere, proicere, prosternere se ad pedes alicuius; provolvere se, provolvi ad pedes alic. Comparable with this place Cic.Verr.5.49(129): (mater) mihi **ad pedes** misera **iacuit;** Ovid.Trist.1.8.15 sq.:
Illud amicitiae sanctum et venerabile nomen
Re tibi pro vili **sub pedibusque iacet?**
Ibid.Met.14.489 sq.:

.... sors autem ubi pessima rerum
Sub pedibus timor est, securaque summa malorum.
I do not share Clark's objection to the cursus (and neither do Sabbah, Seyf.). Clark, Novák, Rolfe: **militum iacuere** c.c., superfluous, in my opinion.
b **gressibus.** Cf. ad 17.12.5, p.125.9*b*.

et adepti veniam iussa fecerunt. Cf. ad 17.12.16, p.127.11; ad 17.12.10, p.126.5-6*c*.; 30.6.1. p. 128. 7-8

sobolemque suam obsidatus pignore. For **soboles** cf. ad 16.10.19, p.87.25. p. 128. 8
For **obs.pignore** cf. ad 17.12.16, p.127.12.

ut obsecuturi condicionibus impositis. For **obsequi** cf. ad 17.12.19, p.127. p. 128. 8-9
22-23*a*. **ut** causally used (cf. ad 17.8.3, p.119.27 - p.120.1*a*.).
a **eductisque mucronibus.** Cf.Verg.Aen.10.651 sq.: p. 128. 9
   Talia vociferans sequitur, **strictumque** coruscat
   Mucronem (and ad 14.5.8 = I p.88). Cic.Cat.2.1.2:
Quod vero non cruentum **mucronem,** ut voluit, **extulit.** But also Cic. de invent.2.4.(14): **gladium** propter appositum e **vagina eduxit** .. **gladium** cruentatum **in vaginam recondidit** With this meaning **educere** does not occur in Veget.r.m.; but it does occur in the same meaning as in Amm. 16.12.7: pedestres copiae ... **educuntur** (sc. e castris) and 16.12.41: educta acie. Cf.et. ad 16.12.36, p.97.5.
b for **mucro** cf. ad 16.12.46, p.99.2*a*; ad 14.5.8 (= I p.88).

⟨**quos**⟩ **pro numinibus colunt.** quos E W m2 B G Cl., Rolfe, Seyf. V om. p. 128. 9-10
quos. Similarly Sabbah. The last version is, I believe, the correct one:
pro numinibus colunt is one of the numerous inserted explanations and additions which characterise Amm.'s style. Cf. Blomgren (op.cit.II) p.154.

iuravere se permansuros. For the "omission" of **esse** cf. ad 17.1.13, p. 128. 10
p.106.23-24*b*.

XIII, 1
a **His (ut narratum est) secundo finitis eventu.** The addition between p. 128. 11
brackets is, strictly speaking, wholly superfluous. But see previous note.
The number of these additions in the last §§ is remarkable. Cf. p.127.7; p.127.13; p.127.23;p.127.29; p.128.2; p.128.8.

b Cf.17.10.9: post tot **secundos eventus;** ad 17.12.9 p.125.22; 16.6.1: haec per eum annum spe dubia **eventu** tamen **secundo** per Gallias agebantur. This sort of expressions which conclude a description of events or introduce a description of new events, is very frequent in Amm.

p. 128. 11 **his.** Cf. ad 17.4.14, p.111.7-8.

p. 128. 11 **Limigantes etc.** Cf. ad 17.12.18, p.127.19-20; ad 17.12.17 sq., p.127.15 sq.; ad 17.12.19, p.127.22-23*e;* ad 17.12.12, p.126.19-20*b, c.*

p. 128. 12 **ocius.** Comparat. = posit. Cf. ad 14.6.12 (= I p.96).

p. 128. 12 *a* **utilitas publica** = the national interest. Cf.et.Cic.pr. lege Man.6.14: Itaque haec vobis provincia (sc.Asia), Quirites, si et **belli utilitatem** et pacis dignitatem sustinere vultis, non modo a calamitate, sed etiam a metu calamitatis est defendenda. Also here in Amm. the **b.utilitas** is concerned, which is, of course, the **utilitas publica** as well; Veget.r.m.Lang 128: In his (sc.homines agrestes incultique) nomen rei publicae repperit **communis utilitas;** ibid. Lang p.135: magna **urbis utilitas;** Lang p.5: pro **utilitate Romana;** Lang p.37: pro **utilitate rei publicae;** Lang p.149: Quae ... auctores bellicarum artium prodiderunt ... **pro publica ... utilitate** digessi; Lang p.150: Romanus autem populus pro decore et **utilitate magnitudinis suae** (a flower of speech): In Veget. **utilis** and **utilitas** also often have the meaning of: useful, practical, appropriate for the **conduct of war.**
b **publicus** is also a t.t.mil. Cf.Veget.3.26 (= Lang p.124): Boni duces **publico certamine** numquam nisi ex occasione aut nimia necessitate confligunt (= proelium-, pugna-, Mars publicus).

p. 128. 12 **signa transferri** = to shift, transfer the war, the hostilities. (But in Caes. b.c.1.60.4, for instance, it has a different meaning: **Transit** etiam cohors Illurgavonensis ad eum cognito civitatis consilio et **signa ex statione transfert** = transit). **Signa transferre** does not occur in Veget.r.m. For **signa etc.** cf. ad 15.5.16 (= III p.96 sq.).

p. 128. 12 **nefas ... nefaria.** A kind of play upon words. Cf. ad 15.4.2 (= III p.56). The combination: **admodum nefas (est)** is not otherwise known to me. Cf.et. ad 16.8.1.

p. 128. 12-13 **quos ... perpetrasse.** The emphasis is on **inpune.** Translation: for it would be a great sin, that they had committed many felonies **without having been punished for them.**

nefaria. Cf.29.5.22: **nefariis ... proditoribus.** p. 128. 13

perpetrasse. Cf. ad 16.8.1, p.81.1. p. 128. 13

nam velut obliti priorum: viz. they had driven their masters **(the Sarmatae** p. 128. 13-14 **Liberi)** from their land (cf. ad 17.12.12, p.126.19-20*b*, *c*.).

velut. For **velut** + **partic.** cf. ad 17.8.3, p.119.27 - p.120.1*a;* Hofm.- p. 128. 13 Leum.p.603, 181 Zus α.

tunc erumpentibus Liberis. This refers to 17.12.1 sq. For **erumpere** cf. ad p. 128. 14 17.2.3, p.107.26*c* . The three words quoted here are equal to: **tunc, cum erumperent** Liberi (sc.Sarmatae), ipsi quoque ... perrupere ... It should be noted here that in vulgar Latin **cum ... tunc** disappears and that **tunc** is used increasingly at the expense of **tum** (because it is part of the popular language). Cf. Svennung (op.cit.II) p.412 sq. (important for the relation between **tum** and **tunc**); Grandgent (op.cit.I) p.41(82).

ipsi quoque: belongs to **perrupere.** The combination often seen in Amm., p. 128. 14 e.g. 17.12.16.

tempus aptissimum nancti: because they had (in their opinion) had a p. 128. 14-15 very good (apt) opportunity.

limitem: The military frontier, often mentioned in the Not.Dign.e.g.Or. p. 128. 15 28.1: Comes **limitis** Aegypti; Occ.1.38,39: duces **limitis** Mauritaniae Caesariensis, **limitis** Tripolitani; Occ.5.126 sq.: Comites **limitum** Italiae, Africae, Tingitaniae etc.; Occ.37.24; Extenditur tamen tractus Armoricani et Nervicani **limitis** per provincias quinque; etc. For the soldiers guarding the frontiers **(limitanei)** cf. Grosse (op.cit.I) p.63-70, p.275 sq. (with lit.); N.D. Occ.25.20; 26.12; Heum-Seckel p.317; Hist.Aug. passim. **Not** mentioned in Amm.

perrupere. For the verb cf.21.9.1; ad 16.11.9, p.90.2. The verb is in the p. 128. 15 clausula (I). Metric model: $-\cup-:-\cup$. Cf. ad 16.12.19, p.94.11-12.

p. 128. 15 **fraudem**: infamous deceit, treacherous attack. Cf. ad 17.12.8, p.125.19 (**noxa**); ad 17.12.10, p.126.5-6 (**delictum**).

p. 128. 15-16 **dominis suis hostibusque**: the Sarmatae Liberi.

p. 128. 16-
p. 128. 19 **criminum ... scelerum.** See above: **fraudem.** All these terms fit into the ideology of the Roman "imperialism", which Amm. also firmly believes in. It is not for us moderns to criticise him too harshly for this. Unfortunately little has changed in this respect.

XIII, 2

p. 128. 16 **deliberatum.** In the **consistorium** (cf. ad 14.7.11 = II p.34).

p. 128. 16 **id**: eam fraudem.

p. 128. 17 *a* **hactenus ultione porrecta.** Translation: while one only **wanted** to extend the revenge to this point. The underlined word is important, because the punishment could not take place until **after** the **Limigantes** had declared themselves in agreement. It appears from the next passage that they were not in agreement.
b In connection with **lenius** the above translation of **hactenus** seems the right one to me. But in late Latin it may also mean: in the following way. Cf. Krebs Antib.1 p.645 (with lit.); Heum.-Seckel p.234.

p. 128. 17 *a* **porrecta.** This metaphorical meaning of the verb in general post-class. and poet. Cf.Ovid.Trist.3.11.5 sq.:
   Quis gradus ulterior. **quo se tua porrigat ira,**
   Restat? quidve meis cernis abesse malis?
Iust.Phil.39.5.3: Iam enim **fortuna Romana porrigere se** ad Orientalia regna, non contenta Italiae terminis, coeperat; Arn.adv.nat.2.21 (Reiffersch.p.65): (describes the drinking of pure water) fiet enim familiaris e more consuetudo in naturam versa **nec adpetitio porrigetur ulterius,** esse amplius nesciens quod petatur. The verb does not occur in Opt. Milev. at all; in Claud. and Veget.r.m. only with the literal meaning.
b The **adverbium porrecte,** only in late Latin, in Amm. (only compar.): 20.3.10; 21.9.1; 25.2.6; 29.5.48. Cf. Souter p.309.

p. 128. 18 *a* **ut ad longinqua translati amitterent copiam nostra vexandi.** This explains the 3 preceding words. But the main point is once more expressed in the participium **translati** = ut ... transferrentur sic ut amitterent etc.

b **longinqua.** This neutr.plur. also 21.4.7; 21.7.1; 20.8.15; 23.6.7; 24.1.13; 25.8.12; This also found in Tac., Sall. and others.

c Cf.16.12.58: rex Chnodomarius reperta **copia discedendi.**

d Cf.Aur.Vict.de Caes.6.1.: At Galba ... rapere, trahere, **vexare** (to rob, ransack; to ill-treat, ravage) ac foedum in modum vastare cuncta et polluere. Fairly often in Claud., not in Veget.r.m.

e **nostra.** Cf. ad 17.1.2, p.104.7-9*d*.

quos ... commissorum. This relative clause has a causal meaning. But it would have been more "correct" if instead of **monebat** he would have written: **moneret** (conjunct.obl.). For these words express the thoughts of the emperor and his advisers. Translation: for the awareness of the crimes which they had committed for too long, urged them to fear the dangers (viz. those still awaiting them from the Romans) **as they believed** (sc. the emperor c.s.). For they have no intention of fulfilling the principal demand of the Romans. (§ 3: abnuere parati **si iuberentur aliorsum migrare**). Cf.et. ad 14.3.4 (= I p.81). p. 128. 18-19

formidare. A little further on (§ 5) the verb is iused again. For this verb and its derivativa cf. ad 17.12.9, p.125.24. p. 128. 19

scelerum conscientia ... commissorum. Note the alliteration and the hyperbaton. p. 128. 19

diutius. Here the comparat. has its full meaning. But the clausula (III) also exerts some influence, as so often. Cf.Hagend.St.Amm.p.130 sq. p. 128. 19

XIII, 3

ideoque. Refers back to the **2nd sentence of § 1.** Cf.et. ad 16.12.25, p.95.9*a* and *b*. p. 128. 19

pugnae molem. The substantive is often used for: a mass of soldiers, an armed crowd; and further for military- and siege implements. Here: weight, heaviness of the battle. Cf.Tac.Hist.1.61: Germanorum auxilia e quibus Vitellius suas quoque copias supplevit, **tota mole belli** secuturus; Ann.6.36: mox Artabanus **tota mole regni** ultum iit; Liv.26.6.9: Apud alios nequaquam tantem **molem pugnae** inveni, plusque pavoris quam certaminis fuisse; Veget.r.m.3.1 (= Lang p.66). p. 128. 20

p. 128. 20 **suspicati**: presential. Cf. **suspectare** 24.2.22 and **suspectari** (deponens) 28.1.8.

p. 128. 21 **aspectu primo.** The subst. also 15.4.5; 16.2.10. The expression also in Caes.b.g.7.56.4; Cic.de orat.3.25 (98); in which § has the same meaning: **prima specie.** (on this use of **primo** cf.Caes.b.g. Meusel[17] ad loc.II p.372).

p. 128. 21 **tamquam.** Cf. ad 17.8.3, p.119.27 - p.120.1*a*.

p. 128. 21 *a* **fulminis ictu perculsi.** The subst. also: 17.7.6; 21.9.4; 20.7.2; 29.6.14; 31.13.1. In Claud.36.60 (de raptu Proserp.) also: **ictum fulminis (ictus** is used fairly often by him). Also frequently occurring in Veget.r.m.Cf.et. ad 16.12.45, p.98.21.
b Cf.Cic. de nat.deor.3.35(84): Hunc igitur nec Olympius Iuppiter **fulmine percussit** nec Aesculapius misero diuturnoque morbo tabescentem interemit; Curt.Ruf.6.11.17: postquam ... **ictus nudis ossibus incussos** ferre non poterat; Liv.10.31.8: plerosque **fulminibus ictos** nuntiatum est; etc. The forms **perculit, percussit; percussus** and **perculsus** are often mixed up by the copyists. The meanings, too, are often interchangeable. Hence G **percussi** (which might even be the correct version). Cf.et. ad 17.8.4, p.120.3; ad 17.10.7. p. 122.16.

p. 128. 22 **ultimaque cogitantes.** For **ultimus** cf. ad 14.2.6 (= I p.69); ad 16.12.14, p.93.10; ad 17.10.2, p.121.21; ad 17.12.7, p.125.18; ad 15.3.8 (= III p.49); ad 14.11.8 (= II p.121).

p. 128. 22-23 **vitam precati ... spoponderunt**: They begged for their leves promising ... The main point is again contained in the partic. **(precati)** (presential, like **suspicati).** Cf. ad 17.3.5, p.108.20*a*.

p. 128. 22-23 *a* **tributum annuum dilectumque validae iuventutis et servitium.** The word **tributum** is used, among others, in 16.5.14, p.77.17; 31.14.2, p.593.8; 17.3.1, p.108.9. It is not a real t.t. for the various forms of taxes (cf. ad 17.3.1, p.108.9; ad 16.5.14, p.77.17-19; ad **17.3.1, p.108.9-10a;** ad 17.3.2, p.108.10*a*). Cf.et. ad 16.5.15, p.77.22-23*c* **(res tributaria);** ad 17.10.10, p.123.11 **(tributarii).** What is meant here by Amm. is probably: an annual tribute, not defined in detail, such as grain, wood, skins, etc.
b Cf.19.11.6-7; 30.6.1; 31.4.4. The army consisted for a considerable part of Romanised and non-Romanised "barbarians" and every offer of

recruits is eagerly accepted. (cf.19.11.7: **aurum** quippe gratanter provinciales ⟨pro(?)⟩**corporibus** dabunt, quae spes rem Romanam aliquotiens adgravavit; Amm.Marc.II Sabbah p.219, note 282; **Cod.Theod.7.13: de tironibus** (c.comm.Gothofr.)).
On the recruiting in general, a rather complicated and sometimes obscure matter in these days, cf. Grosse (op.cit.I) p.198 sq. (with lit.). particularly p.206 sq.; ad 16.11.4, p.88.24-25 **(Laeti barbari)**; ad 15.5.6 = III p.81 **(gentiles)**; Veget.r.m.I.1-19; 26 (deals with the recruiting; training etc. of the **tirones**).

c Probably by **dilectus** are meant here: **tirones** (abstractum pro concreto; cf.17.7.10, p.118.1-2).

d **validae iuventutis**. For the adjective cf. ad 15.4.1 = III p.55.

e **servitium**. It is not clear what the **Limigantes** mean by this term (cf. ad 17.12.19, p.127.22-23*e*). **Servi** of the Romans? (But towards the emperor all **subiecti** are **servi** = δοῦλοι; cf.Procop.Anecd.30.26. So that would not be anything special). And **servi**, in the strict sense of the world, is certainly not what the L. will have meant. Thus nothing else is left but: servi of the **Sarmatae liberi**. This would mean a restoring of the old submissiveness. Quite an extreme offer of the **Limigantes**.

f **spoponderunt**. Cf. ad 17.12.11, p.126.18; ad 17.12.19, p.127.22-23*a*.

abnuere. The object forms the sentence: **si ... migrare**. p. 128. 23

si iuberentur: conj.obl. For the constructions of **si** cf. ad 14.1.7 (= I p. 128. 23-24 p.62); ad 14.3.2 (= I p.79); ad 14.4.6 (= I p.83); Hassenstein (op.cit.I) p.43 sq.

aliorsum. Also among others 21.12.10; 28.2.2; 30.1.14; 31.7.6. Also used p. 128. 24 metaph. = **alio**, which Amm. does not use (Novák Cur.A. (Op.cit.I) p.45). Arch., vulgar and late Latin. Not in Claud.Veget.r.m.Opt.Milev. Arn.adv.nat.

ut. Cf. ad 17.8.3, p.119.27 - p.120.1*a*. p. 128. 24

gestibus. Cf. ad 16.12.43, p.98.14; Krebs Antib.1 p.625; **Cic. de off.1.36** p. 128. 24 **(130)**: probably the source of 14.6.18.

ut ... voltibus. Note the rhythm of the sentence, expressing the liveliness p. 128. 24 of gestures and facual expressions.
Cf.17.10.3: et quia **vultus** incessusque supplicem **indicabat**.

331

p. 128. 25 **confisi.** Cf. ad 17.12.9, p.125.24 (**fidentes**). Cf.27.10.9: **locorum** gnaritate **confisi**; 30.1.12: idem; Fesser p.17.

p. 128. 25 *a* **ubi lares post exactos dominos fixere securi.** For the contents of the sentence cf. ad. 17.12.12, p.126.19-20*b*.
  b For **lares** cf. ad 17.6.2, p.116.10-11*a*.
  c For **post** with temp. meaning ad 17.12.16, p.127.8*b*.
  d **exactos.** Cf. ad 16.12.62, p.101.26-27*b*.
  e **fixere.** Cf. ad 17.4.12, p.110.26 - p.111.1*c;* ad 16.7.7, p.79.27-28*a;* ad 16.11.8, p.89.14-15.

XIII, 4

p. 128. 26 *a* **Parthiscus** = Tisia: flows near **Acimincum** into the **Danubius** (which further on is called **Hister**, without difference in meaning; but correctly used, the river is called **Danubius** from its origin to the waterfall near **Orsova**; the lower reaches until the mouth of the river are called **Hister**). The **Danubius** is mentioned 22.8.44; 29.6.6; 31.3.7; 31.4.1; 31.4.5; 31.11.6.
The **Hister** is mentioned: 19.11.4; 21.8.2; 21.10.3; 27.6.12; 29.6.2; 31.3. 8; 31.4.2; 31.8.1; 31.8.6. The **Parthiscus** is only mentioned here. The Danube forms the natural and also strategic frontier of the Roman empire in the North, after the loss of **Dacia** ($\pm$ 270 A.D.). There were 2 river fleets: the **classis Pannonica** and the **classis Moesica**. In the N.D. the **praefecti** of the classes are mentioned: Or.41; Or.42; Occ.32; Occ.33; Occ.34. For the **Danuvius** cf. Woordenboek der Oudheid, 4, 1969, p.796 (Nuchelmans); **Pichler, Austria Romana** (1904) II p.155 (Ister), 139 (Dan.); Brandis, R.E.IV.2.2103-2133. For the abovementioned **Acimincum** cf. **Pichler** ibid.p.103 (with the many deviating spellings of the name).
For the **Parthiscus** cf. Pichler ibid.p.174. For **Bregetio**, which will be mentioned in the next §§ (but not by Amm.) cf. ad 17.12.21, p.128.3.
  b The acts of war against the **Limigantes**, as described in the §§ 4-23, are not quite clear. Though the names of the **Amicenses** (1). **Picenses** (2) and **Taifali** (3) (§§ 18-20) give us some indication. If we now knew where exactly (1) and (2) and (3) could be found, we might be able to throw some light on Amm.'s text. However, this is not the case. On the map by Sabbah A.M.II (Camp.d.Const. sur le Dan.) the **Acimicenses** (Amm. **Amicenses**) (1) are situated between the **Danuvius** and the **Tibiscus**, which flows into the **Danuvius** a little to the East of **Singidunum**, on a terrain which forms as it were a peninsula, pointing towards the South. He places the **Pincenses** (2) East of the **Tibiscus** and North of the **Danuvius**. And

East again of (2) the **Taifali** (3). The **Pincenses** (2) are probably named after the river **Pincus,** which flows into the **Danuvius** near **Pincum,** East of **Viminacium.** (Amm. **Picenses**). **Pichler** ibid. (map) places the **Pi(n)censes** (2) **South** of the Danube, in the basin of the river **Pincus,** which seems logical enough. He situates the **Amicenses** (1) in the neighbourhood of **Viminacium,** thus in any case **East** of the **Tibiscus** (p.112). Sabbah wants to make the **Amicenses** equal to the **Acimicenses,** who should have been named after **Acimincum** (and then should have to live in the vicinity). However, one should be very careful with names. The last equalisation is not certain (nor is it absolutely certain that the **Pincenses** are the same as the **Picenses;** that is to say, which of the two forms is the right one). From the context it seems probably (though not quite certain) that the **Amicenses** and **Picenses** are tribes (peoples) belonging to the **Limigantes.** Cf.et.Sabbah II notes 106-109 (with lit.); Seyf.I p.314, notes 171, 172 (with lit.). The **Amicenses** and the **Picenses** are only mentioned here in Amm. The **Taifali** here (§§ 19-20) and 31.3.7; 31.9.3-5. (1) and (2) are not mentioned in the Not.Dign., contrary to the **Taifali** (3).

Note. Acimincum (Pichler p.103) should not be confused with **Aquincum** (= **Acincum**: Amm.30.5.13, 14; Woordenb. der Oudheid 2, 1966, p.237, with lit., Nuchelmans; Tomaschek R.E.2.333; **Pichler** p.115 (with many other spellings of the name)).

c The scene of battle is along the Danube and the Tibiscus and Parthiscus in the border regions of the **provinciae Pannonia II and Moesia I** (and perhaps also part of **Dacia ripensis),** which, according to Amm., is a rather watery and swamp-like terrain. For the prov. cf. ad 16.10.20, p.88.4; ad 15.3.7 (= III p.44). We know for certain that the Romans marched from **Bregetio** (17.12.21) to the South. The mention of the **Parthiscus** (17.13.4, line 26) and of the **Danubius** (17.13.4, line 29) more or less defines the area of the first confrontation, which was probably the abovementioned peninsula (b). Also probably they cross the Danube near **Acimincum** (cf.19.11.8). It seems logical to assume that a part of the troops (or the impedimenta) were sent by ship **downstream** from **Bregetio.**

The **further** scene of battle should be sought more to the East and North, mainly North of the Danube. No more is to be found in Amm.'s text, in my opinion.

a **inruens obliquatis meatibus. Inruens** c.accus., like **incursare** (cf. ad p. 128. 26 17.12.1, p.124.20).

b Cf.30.1.9: praeruptos undarum occursantium fluctus **obliquatis meati-**

bus declinabant; 28.4.10: osculanda **capita** in modum taurorum minacium **obliquantes;** 25.8.2: **undarum occursantium fluctus obliquis meatibus** penetrabant. (cf. ad 17.4.1, p.109.6*b*). The verb is poet. and post-class. Cf.et. ad 16.12.57. p.101.1.

c The subst. also 23.6.65; 25.8.2; 28.2.2; 30.6.5. Post-class. and poet. Cf. Krebs Antib.2 p.64 (with lit.); ad 16.1.5, p.72.8.

p. 128. 27 **licentius fluit.** Comparat. = posit.Claus I. Note the alliteration (s and l) in **solus ... lata.**

p. 128. 27 **spatia longa et lata.** Cf. ad 17.12.3, p.124.24-25*a*.

p. 128. 27 *a* **sēnsim praeterlăbens.** There are no grounds for objections against the claus. by Cl.Nov. For this claus. ⌣̆ ⌣ ⌣ ⌣ ⌣̆ ⌣ cf. Blomgren (op.cit.II) p.9 sq.

b The verb is rather uncommon and probably a Verg. reminiscence. Cf.15.11.16; 21.12.8; 22.8.4; 28.2.2; ad 17.2.2, p.107.18-19*c*.

p. 128. 28 *a* **et ea coartans prope exitum in angustias.** Cf.Liv.28.5.8: Thermopylarum saltum, ubi **angustae** fauces **coartant** iter; ad 15.11.16 = IV p.72 **(artans).** Cf.et. Souter p.56; Heum.-Seckel p.73 (for the late Latin meaning: to coerce). The **subst.** 29.2.11 **(coartatio).**

b **exitus.** Cf. ad 16.12.13, p.93.3.

p. 128. 28 Cf.15.4.3: (Rhenus) lacum invadit ... quem Brigantiam **accola Raetus** appellat.

p. 128. 28 **impetu.** The subst. among others, also 14.1.10: instar rapidi fluminis, inrevocabili **impetu** ferebatur; 14.7.16: et eodem **impetu** Domitianum praecipitem per scalas itidem funibus constrinxerunt; 15.11.16: (Rhodanus) et proclivi **impetu** ad planiora degrediens ... viam sibi **impetu** veloci molitur.

p. 128. 29 **alveo.** For this subst.cf. ad 16.11.9, p.89.25*b;* ad 16.12.57, p.101.2-3*b*. (In late lat. **alveus** is sometimes equal to **alvus;** cf. Blomgren, op.cit.II, p.151, with examples).

p. 128. 29 **Danubii defendit.** This name for the Danube probably chosen for the sake of the alliteration. Blomgren (op.cit.II p.55): "Nimirum non potest **Parthiscus** alveo Danubii, sed suo tantum accolas defendere". What

334

exactly Amm. meant, can be guessed as rather than proved. Cf. et. ad. 17.13.5, p.129.3.

a **barbaricis excursibus.** The adject. is chosen from a Roman point of view, to whom **Limigantes** and their possible enemies are **all** barbarians. But to the **L.**, of course, the attackers inside their own country are not **barbari**. p. 128. 29
b For the substant. cf. ad 17.4.3, p.109.10-11; ad 17.5.1, p.113.22.

a **Suo tutos praestat obstaculo.** For the hyperbaton cf. ad 17.1.6, p.105. 21*a*. Claus.II. Metric model: $-\cup-:-\cup\underline{\cup}$. p. 128. 29-30
b Cf.Cic.pr.Planc.41(97): **iter** mihi **tutum**, multis minitantibus, magno cum suo metu **praestiterunt**; ibid.pr.Flacc.13(31): Quam multi orae maritimae clarissimi viri praefuerunt, qui ... **mare** tamen **tutum praestiterunt**; Krebs Antib.2 p.365 (with lit.).
c Cf.21.10.4: utrubique spatiosa camporum planities iacet ... ut nullis habitetur **obstaculis**. The subst. also Senec.nat.2.52.1. But for the rest late Latin. Cf. Krebs Antib.2 p.190; Heum.-Seckel p.383. Not in Claud. Veget.r.m.Opt.Milev.Arn.adv.nat.

pleraque. Cf. ad 17.4.14, p.111.7-8. p. 128. 30

umidioris soli. Cf.Colum.4.19: **humidius solum**, humidioresque venti. p. 128. 30

incrementis fluminum. Cf.Dig.43.12.1.5: nemo denique dixit **Nilum**, qui **incremento suo** Aegyptum operit, ripas suas mutare vel ampliare ... si tamen naturaliter creverit, ut **perpetuum incrementum** nanctus sit, vel alio flumine admixto vel qua alia ratione ... In Amm.14.6.3; 14.11.26; 28.6.5. p. 128. 30

redundantia. The standard verb for flooded rivers, lakes, etc. Cf.Lucr. 6.712: p. 128. 31
    Nilus in aestatem crescit **campisque redundat**
    Unicus in terris, Aegypti totius amnis,
Claud.47 (Eid.IV)7:
(Aegyptus) Gaudet aquis, quas ipsa vehit, **Niloque redundant.** (= quaeque Nilo redundant).
Veget.r.m.: 4.5 (= Lang p.131) et, cum **aquis** coeperint **redundare** (sc. fossae); Krebs Antib.2 p.487 (with lit.); Heum.-Seckel p.498.

p. 128. 30-31 **flūminum redundăntia.** Claus.IV. The choice of the part.praes.neutr.plur. of this verb is probably deliberate.

p. 128. 31 **stagnosa.** Cf.Sil.Ital.6.653 sq.:
Hic dum **stagnosi** spectat templumque domosque
Literni ductor.
Also in Apul. and others. Extremely rare adj. Not in Claud.Veget.r.m. Arn.adv.nat.Opt.Milev.

p. 128. 31 **referta.** c.ablat. with objects, normal construction, also in late Latin. Cf. Krebs Antib.2 p.490 (with lit). Of **persons** c.ablat.e.g.Cod.Iust.11.48.13.1: possessione **referta** cultoribus.
salicibus. Cf.Ovid.Metam.10.96:
Amnicolae simul **salices** et aquatica lotos.

p. 128. 31 **ideoque.** Cf. ad 16.12.25, p.95.9*a, b*.

p. 128. 31- **perquam.** Cf. ad 15.2.4 (= III p.16); Krebs Antib.2 p.285 (with lit.).
p. 129. 1 Not in Claud.Veget.r.m.Arn.adv.nat.Opt.Milev

p. 129. 1 **gnaris.** Often linked with **perquam**: 18.2.2; 27.5.3; 28.1.7. Cf.et. ad 16.2. 10, p. 73.21 **(gnaritas).**

p. 129. 1 **super his.** Cf. ad 17.4.1, p.109.6*a;* ad 16.12.70, p.103.9-10*b*.

p. 129. 1 *a* **insularem anfractum.** For the adject. cf. ad 15.7.2 (= IV p.10). Souter p.212 also quotes Cassiod.Var.12.24.3.
b for the subst. cf. ad 17.1.9, p.106.7. The attendant **adject.** arch. and late Latin, in Amm.29.5.37: tumulos, per **anfracta** undique **spatia** in sublime porrectos.
c The entire phrase is of course, far-fetched = insulam quam suis anfractibus efficit (sc.Danuvius).

p. 129. 1-2 **aditu ... contiguum.** For **aditus** cf.14.2.18; 15.5.27; 24.2.15; 29.6.16. As a **t.t.**: ad 15.5.27. For the **adject.** cf. ad 17.7.2, p.116.21*a*. That **aditus** means **mouth** here, is clear from the context.

p. 129. 2 **amnis potior**: the larger of the two rivers, i.e. the Danube.

p. 129. 2 **ambiens.** With this literal meaning also in Curt.Ruf.4.2.9: **muros** turresque

urbis praealtum **mare ambiebat;** 4.7.16: Tandem ad sedem consecratam deo ventum est ... undique **ambientibus ramis** ... contecta est; Claud.1 (In Prob. et Olyb.cons.):
(267) O consanguineis felix auctoribus anne.
(273) Pratis te croceis pingat. te messibus aestas
   Induat, **autumnusque madentibus ambiat uvis.**
ibid.22.365 (de laud.Stilich.II):
   Tunc habiles armis **humeros** Dea vestibus
   ambit Romuleis.
Vell.Paterc.2.101.1: in insula **quam** amnis **Euphrates ambiebat;** Arn. adv.nat.3.35: universam istam molem mundi, **cuius** omnes **amplexibus ambimur,** tegimur ac sustinemur; Heum.-Seckel p.29. For the subst. **ambitus** cf. ad 16.2.1, p.72.12*b*. Not in Veget.r.m.Opt.Milev. Cf.et. ad 17.12.11, p.126.15.

terrae consortio: the communion with the continent. Very affected. for **consortium** cf. ad 16.5.11, p.77.5*a;* ad 17.12.12, p.126. 24*a*.   p. 129. 2

XIII, 5
genuino fastu. For the two words cf. ad 17.5.2, p.113.28-29*a*, *b*.   p. 129. 3

a **ad citeriorem venere fluminis ripam.** Hyperbaton. Cf. ad 17.1.6,   p. 129. 3
p,105.21*a*. Where **ripa citerior** is said from a Roman point of view, it can not mean here: this, i.e. **the Roman side of the Danube.** For in that case the Limigantes would have surrendered completely; which they obviously do not want (yet). When we assume that the Romans crossed near **Acimincum,** the only river which can be considered is the **Tibiscus** (not the **Parthiscus,** therefore). For the Romans are on the **East bank** of the Danube (and perhaps of the Parthiscus?), after they have crossed.
b Amm. often uses the **plur.poet.** Cf. ad 16.12.57, p.101.2. This use is also very striking in **Pomp.Mela** (cf. Index edit. Ranstrand p.111).

ut exitus docuit. Cf. ad 17.12.20, p.127.29. This small sentence explains   p. 129. 4
the 3 following words. For the subst. cf. ad 16.12.13, p.93.3.

non iussa facturi, sed ne viderentur ... formidasse. Note the variation in   p. 129. 4-5
the construction = non ut iussa facerent, sed ne etc. Cf.Hagend.St.Amm. (op.cit.I) p.127 sq.; 16.11.13, p.90.19-21; Blomgren (op.cit.II) p.55 sq. Although the **infinit.perf.** can be explained, it seems to me that we here have another example of the **aoristus** (cf. ad 16.12.40, p.97.28 - p.98.1).

337

For the claus. (III) it makes no difference whether the infin.praes. or the perf. is used.

p. 129. 4 **iussa.** Cf.17.12.21, p.128.8 (annot. ad 1.). Further on, p.129.6: **iubenda;** ad 17.11.1, p.123.17b.

p. 129. 4 *a* **militis praesēntiam formidāsse** = militis conspectum. **praesentia** is being used more freely in later Latin. Of course, the subst. fits very well here in the clausula. Cf.Veget.r.m.1.13 (= Lang p.17): nec ante eis in tritico redderetur annona, quam **sub praesentia praefecti legionis,** tribunorum vel principiorum ... ostendissent (= praefecto ... praesente, etc.); Opt.Milev.3.4 (= Ziwsa p.83 sq.): et facerent, quidquid illis dementia sua dictasset, nisi **praesentia armati militis** obstitisset; ibid.5.10 (= Ziwsa p.140): cum **praesentia multorum** (= conspectu multorum) gaudeat et de aliquorum absentia contristetur; Krebs Antib.2 p.363. Its use in judic.Latin is also in agreement with the above; cf.Heum.-Seckel p.451. (The adject. **praesens** may in late Latin have the meaning of **praesentalis** = employed at the imperial court).
b For **formidare** cf. ad 17.12.9, p.125.24.

p. 129. 5 **stabantque contumaciter.** Although it can be explained, the use of the adverbium is nonetheless very **remarkable** here. Cf.17.13.10: cadentes **insuperabili contumacia barbari;** Veget.r.m.3.4 (= Lang p.72): Numquam enim ad **contumaciam** pari consensu **multitudo** prorumpit, sed incitatur a paucis. Those resisting the "established order" (e.g. common soldiers, "barbarians", etc.) are quickly marked with the adject. **contumax.**

p. 129. 5 **ideoque.** Cf. ad 17.13.4, p.128.31.
propinquasse: sc.se.Amm. makes use exclusively of the simplex, never of **appropinquare.** Cf. Fesser p.25 (with lit.). For the **nomin.c.infin.** cf. ad 17.12.11, p.126.14b; ad 17.1.13, p.106.23-24b.

p. 129. 5 **monstrantes.** In the claus.(I). Cf. ad 17.12.10, p.126.8-9.

p. 129. 6 **repudiarent.** Used as said by Cic.pr.Quint.14(46): **conditionem** aequissimam **repudiet.** Veget.r.m. has the verb in the meaning: to refuse, reject **tirones** (1.7; 1.8). In Arn.adv.nat. and Claud. the verb does not occur, though several times in Opt.Milev.

338

The contents of §§ 6 and 7 should be viewed very critically, in my opinion. Also in connection with § 5 they impress me as giving a justification of the Roman behaviour. There is no question of negotiations: the Romans want to do things their way, especially with regard to the **migratio** (read: deportation to somewhere else: § 13.3).

p. 129. 6-
p. 129. 13

The barbarians are pictured as being especially clever, as well as martial. The inclusion of the **Limigantes** already leads them to the slaughter beforehand, if they are not obedient. The agression of these primitive barbarians is deliberately provoked. Though the soldier A.M. is forced to praise their heroic courage shown at their downfall. (§§ 10, 11).

p. 129. 6

XIII, 6

contemplans. C.acc.c.infin. also 17.13.28; 18.5.1: cum iurgando contra potentes se magis magisque **iniustitia frangi contemplaretur.** The partic. perf.pass. of the verb **contemplare:** 16.8.6(?); 31.5.9; 31.15.6(?). The verb does not occur in Veget.r.m. (who has **contemplatio:** 4.35) Claud., Arn. adv.nat.Opt.Milev. The subst. **contemplator:** 19.1.7 (someone standing guard, on the look-out). Cf. Souter p.76. Cf.et. ad 17.10.7, p.122.18.

p. 129. 6

agmina. Here, groups, columns. The adverbium **agminatim** also has this same meaning: in crowds, in groups: 18.6.23; 22.8.47; 31.4.5.

p. 129. 7

celeritate volucri. Cf.14.11.26: velocitate **volucri;** 19.4.7: **volucri** velocitate; 30.2.6: festina celeritate; 27.1.3: festina(?) celeritate; 18.6.11: agilitate **volucri;** 31.7.7: aliti velocitate; ad 16.12.58, p.101.5-6.

p. 129. 7

morantes. VEAG migrantes. Cl.Rolfe follow the conjecture by Nov.: **morantes.** Pet. **pigrantes.** Her. **mirantes.** Sabbah follows V (with the translation: pendant qu'ils étaient en mouvement; an impossible explanation, in my view. **migrantes** could only mean: they who (continuously) are on the move (to other regions)). Blomgren (op.cit.II) reads: ⟨Li⟩**migantes** (p.137: Constat autem singulas syllabas in textu Ammianeo saepius interisse, et hoc ipso loco forsitan **li-** post **ri** ideo facilius exciderit, **quod r et l litterae in codice Fuldensi non ita raro inter se commutatae sunt**"); (with many examples).

p. 129. 7

acies clausit. Simplex pro composito. Claus.I Cf. ad 16.5.6, p.76.12. Though the use of **claudere** for the composita: **includere, concludere,**

p. 129. 8

339

intercludere is fairly common. Note the alliterating **c** in the sentence: celeritate ... clausit.

p. 129. 8 **stansque in aggere celsiore.** Cf. ad 15.8.4 (= IV p.31); ad 16.12.8, p.92.8; 17.13.25. The **tribunal** is formed by the **agger celsior.** The emperor is standing on an elevated platform, not only so as to be heard better, but also in order to impress the **Limigantes.**

p. 129. 9 **Stipatorum praesidio:** body-guards. Also 24.4.4. The subst. occurs several times in Cic. Cf.et.Iust.Phil.13.4: **Stipatoribus regis** satellitusque Cassander filius Antipatri praeficitur. Thus **stipatus** occurs fairly often in Curt.Ruf., e.g. 10.7.17: et rex quoque irruperat, **stipatus satellitum turba,** quorum princeps Meleager erat. It is a word with a general meaning; with Amm. it is not, I believe, a term techn. The **stipatores** are, of course, picked men.

p. 129. 9 **ferocirent.** For this verb cf. ad 17.12.2, p.124.24*b*.

p. 129. 9 **lĕnius admonĕbat.** Compar. = posit. (cf. ad 14.6.12 = I p.96). Metri causa: Claus.III. Cf.et. ad 17.12.9, p.125.25*c*. These **comparativi of adverbia** occur rather often in Amm., often in the clausula (cf. Liesenberg op.cit.I, 1889, p.13 sq.).

XIII, 7

p. 129. 10 **fluctuantes.** With the same meaning as in Verg.Aen.10.680: Haec memorans animo, nunc huc, nunc **fluctuat** illuc; ibid.12.486 sq.: (perhaps Amm. remembers this passage).

Heu, quid agat? Vario nequiquam **fluctuat** aestu
Diversaeque vocant animum in contraria **curae;**

Catull.65.4:

Nec potisest dulces Musarum expromere fetus
Mens animi (tantis **fluctuat** ipsa malis;

ibid.64.62:

Prospicit et magnis curarum **fluctuat** undis.

The verb also occurs in Claud.Veget.r.m.Arn.adv.nat., though not in Opt.Milev. Cf.et. Krebs Antib.1 p.599 (with lit.); ad 16.12.57, p.100.24-25*b* (**fluitare**).

p. 129. 10 **ambiguitate mentium.** Generally the substantive means: ambiguity. But here, with **mentium:** by the hesitant, uncertain attitude of their mind

(hearts); with the added meaning of: false, unreliable, which the adject. **ambiguus** often has. Cf.et. **(ambigere)** ad 16.12.35, p.96.24.

in diversa: in completely different directions, viz. battle or submission. p. 129. 10
But 14.4.3: per **diversa** reptantes (?): various, different.

rapiebantur. Amm. often uses the intensivum **raptare** (cf. ad 17.12.2, p. 129. 10
p.124.23).

furori mixta versutia: abl.abs. The 2nd subst. occurs in Liv., 42.47.7, p. 129. 10-11
but is for the rest late Latin (though the adject. **versutus** is class.). Not in
Claud.Veget.r.m.Arn.adv.nat.Opt.Milev.

temptabant cum precibus proelium. Note the alliterating **pr.** The terse, p. 129. 11
pregnant words mean: on the one hand they (apparently) tried to beg,
while on the other hand they prepared for battle.

vicinumque. Here: (from) nearby, pro adverbio. p. 129. 11

excursum. Cf. ad 17.4.3, p.109.10-11; ad 17.5.1, p.113.22. The attendant p. 129. 12
subst. **excursator:** 24.1.2, 25.1.2 (= skirmisher) seems to occur only in
Amm.

consulto. Well-known class. adverb. Cf. ad 16.12.10, p.92.15 **(consultus).** p. 129. 12

a **lŏngius scŭta.** Claus.I. **Longius** here probably = rather far, somewhat p. 129. 12
far. Cf. ad 17.12.19, p.127.22c.
b For **scutum** cf. ad 14.10.8 (= II p.105); ad 16.12.57, p.100.26 - p.101.2
(clipeus).

sensim. Also used shortly before this: 17.13.4, p.128.27. Often in Amm. p. 129. 13
Veget.r.m.3.22 (= Lang p.112) linked with **cessim** (an archaic. and late
Latin adverb). **Sensim** not in Claud.Arn.adv.nat.Opt.Milev.

sine ullo fraudis indicio: without showing ⟨in some way⟩ that they were p. 129. 13
practising deceit.

spatia: terrain, clear passage. For the **plural.** cf. ad 17.12.3, p.124.24-25a. p. 129. 13

p. 129. 13 **furarentur**: (so that) they would win furtively. Lit.e.g. 16.8.4. Cf.et. ad 16.9.1, p.83.14 **(furta)**.

XIII, 8

p. 129. 14 *a* **vergente in vesperum die. In vesperum** is the usual form. For **vesper** and its declinations cf. Krebs Antib.2 p.730 sq. (with lit.). This accusat. also 26.8.13: et ignorans quod quivis beatus, versa rota Fortunae, **ante vesperum** potest esse miserrimus.

b Cf.Curt.Ruf.4.7.22: Est et aliud Hammonis nemus: in medio habet fontem - Solis aquam vocant ... **inclinato (sc.die) in vesperam** calescit ... **quoque nox propius vergit ad lucem,** multum ex nocturno calore descrescit...

p. 129. 14 **moras rumpere** Cf.Verg.Georg.3.42 sq.:
.... En age, **segnis**
Rumpe moras; vocat ingenti clamore Cithaeron.
ibid.Aen.4.569 sq.:
Eia age, **rumpe moras.** Varium et mutabile semper
Femina. Sic fatus nocti se immiscuit atrae.

p. 129. 14-15 *a* **lux moneret excedens** For the verb **excedere** cf. (1) (with the praep. **ex** in the formula **excedere e vita):** 14.5.8; 14.11.27; 21.1.6; 23.6.44; (2) c.abl.: 26.9.11 (excessit vita Procopius); 17.1.3; 19.9.5; 22.15.26; 22.15.31; 25.7.8; 25.9.4; (3) c.accusat.: 14.9.9; 22.15.32; 23.6.17; 30.1.13; 31.2.1. Cf.et. Krebs Antib.1 p.534 sq. (with lit.). Here: the receding (fading) light **(exc.sc. e caelo).**

b **lux.** Especially with poets = **sol; dies.** Cf.Stat.Silv.edit. Vollmer 3.3. 54 p.410 (comm.); ibid.Theb.2.120 (= edit. Mulder p.102); 2.184 (= Mulder p.142); 2.272 (= Mulder p. 198).

p. 129. 15 **erectis vexillis.** For **vexillum** cf. ad 15.5.16 (= III p.96 sq.). For **erigere** cf. ad 17.4.6. p.110.2.

p. 129. 15 *a* **igneo miles impetu ferebatur.** For the hyperbaton cf. ad 17.1.6, p.105. 21*a*. Said in Veget.r.m.4.41 of the sun.

b Cf. (Valentinianus) 30.6.3: tamquam ictus e caelo vitalique via voceque simul obstructa **suffectus igneo lumine** cernebatur. (stroke). For this, also class.adject. cf. Krebs Antib.1 p.676. For the numerous **adj. ending in -eus** cf. Liesenberg (1888) p.32; Hagendahl St.Amm. p.38 sq. and particularly **p.39 note 2** (in which Liesenb. is complimented and corrected); Paucker Vorarb. (op.cit.I) I p.105 sq. (of the 277 adject.

ending in -eus, which he enumerates, 87 only occur with the posteriores).
c Cf.Liv.38.27.2: pars maior ... **qua quemque impetus tulit**, fugerunt. Veget.r.m. does not have the pass. (med.) with this meaning, though it is quite common both in prose and poetry. Cf.et. ad 17.13.4, p.128.28.

conferti. Cf. ad 16.12.21, p.94.19*b*. Cf.et. ad 17.13.4, p.128.31 **(refertus)**; 27.1.3. p. 129. 15-16

densiore. Cf. ad 17.12.9, p.125.23*b*. Adject. pro adverbio. p. 129. 16

contracta. Another well-known t.t.mil., said of the concentrating of troops, ships, etc. But is does **not** occur with **this** meaning in Veget.r.m. p. 129. 16

adversus. Thus 24.2.13; 27.7.5; 31.5.9. Adverbium: **(adversum)** 31.10.8 (= **exadversum:** 23.6.72). p. 129. 16

ut dictum est. § 9, p.129.19. immediately following this, is not repeated very elegantly. For this kind of expressions cf. ad 17.12.20, p.127.29. p. 129. 16-17

impetum contulerunt: they concentrated their attack. p. 129. 17

incessentes. The verb also: 14.7.6; 15.7.2; 17.9.3; 17.11.1; 21.1.6; 21.12.10; 24.2.11; 27.1.3. Cf.et. ad 17.11.1, p.123.23. p. 129. 17

truculentis. Also: 20.6.1; 25.1.14; 29.5.48. Cf.Plaut.Asin.2.3.21(401): **truculentis oculis;** Tac.Ann.1.25: **vocibus truculentis.** Coincidence or deliberate reminiscence? o. 129. 18

XIII, 9
a **furoris.** Cf. ad 16.12.36, p.97.4*b*. For the **genitivus identitatis** cf. ad 15.10.4 (= IV p.55); ad 16.5.9, p.76.24*a;* ad 17.4.8, p.110.6*a*.
b A Cic. reminiscence is likely here. Cf.Cic.pr.S.Rosc.22(62): neque audacia solum, sed **summus furor atque amentia;** Verr.II.1.3(7); ibid.II.4. 17(38); **Hagend.abund.** (op.cit.I) p.195, with more examples. p. 129. 18

exercitus ira ferre non potuit. For the personificatio cf. ad 17.2.1, p.107.13. Further on, on p.129.20, another example: quem habitum caput porci **simplicitas militaris** appellat (cf.16.5.5, p.76.5). Another pers. with **ira** 22.3.8: praetendens quod eum **militaris ira** delevit (= milites irati). Thus one finds 28.6.5: **barbaricus tumor** (= barbari tumentes). p. 129. 18

343

p. 129. 19 **imperatori ... acriter imminentes.** Cf.29.5.52: ut ... popularibus suis **acriter immineret.** In both cases claus.III.

p. 129. 19-20 **desinente in angustum fronte.** These words are an explanation of the following: **quem ... appellat.** The 4 words are equal to: desinente exercitu **in frontem angustam.** For this use of **in c.accus.** cf.16.2.13: in bicornem figuram acie divisa; 20.3.1: (solem) primo adtenuatum in lunae corniculantis effigiem, deinde in speciem auctum semestrem, posteaque in integrum restitutum; 22.8.9: (mare) in aequoream panditur faciem; 22.8. 13: Inachi filia mutata ... in bovem; 24.8.7: multiplicato scutorum ordine (?) in orbiculatam figuram; 29.5.52: eosque adsiduitate pugnandi mutaret in metum; Reinhardt (op.cit.I) p.61. Cf. et. ad 17.10.2, p.121.25a.

p. 129. 20 **habitum.** Here = ± formation, (battle)-array. But 14.2.17: (miles) hastisque feriens scuta, qui **habitus** iram pugnantium concitat et dolorem (= behaviour, attitude); 25.2.5: Erat autem nitor igneus iste, quem **diaissonta** nos appellamus ... fit autem **hic habitus** modis compluribus (= this appearance). For other meanings in late Latin cf. Souter p.168; Heum.-Seckel p.234. The subst. does not occur in Veget.r.m.Arn.adv. nat.; though fairly often in Claud. and Opt.Milev.

p. 129. 20 **caput porci.** Cf.Veget.r.m.3.19 (= Lang p.105): Cuneus dicitur multitudo peditum, quae iuncta cum acie **primo angustior** deinde latior procedit et **adversariorum ordines rumpit** .... Quam rem milites nominant **caput porcinum.** (for the reverse formation in V-form cf. ad 16.11.3, p.88.23). For **cuneus** cf. ad 16.11.5, p.88.29. Cf.et Seyf. I p.314, note 166 (with the lit. quoted there).

p. 129. 20 **simplicitas militaris** = the simple soldiers' language. (as opposed to the technical terms of the professional military language). The word has here a favourable meaning (= unadorned) as in Curt.Ruf.8.12.10: Laetus (Alexander) **simplicitate barbari** rex et dexteram fidei suae pignus dedit et regnum restituit (= integrity, honesty). With an unfavourable nuance Veget.r.m.3.3 (= Lang p.70): Praecipueque vitetur, ne adversariorum dolo atque periuriis decipiatur **provincialium incauta simplicitas** (X the dexterity and smartness of city folk).

p. 129. 21 *a* **impetu disiecit ardenti.** Cf. § 8, p.129.15: **igneo impetu,** without any difference in meaning. Another striking aspect is that in the lines 14-21 **impetus** occurs 3 times.

b **disiecit** is a well-known t.t.mil. Does not occur in Veget.r.m.

dextra pedites ... equites laeva: Chiasm. (Cf. ad 16.8.2, p.81.1-4*b* 3). Cf. Blomgren (op.cit.II) p.20, 22, 41. The stylistic effect is enhanced by the repetitions **pedites ... peditum** and **equites ... equitum**. p. 129. 21-22

catervas, Cf. ad 16.2.6, p.73.5*a*. p. 129. 21

p̆editum obtruncăbant. Claus.III. Cf. Claud.15.394 sq. (De bello Gild.): p. 129. 21
    Et quos ipse sinu parvos gestaverat, una
    Obtruncat iuvenes, inhumataque corpora vulgo
    Dispulit et tumulo cognatas arcuit umbras.
The non-class. verb, found among others in **Sallust.Liv.Vell.Tac.Curt. Fronto** Iust., gives the impression of being an archaic flower of speech. Does not occur in Veget.r.m.Arn.adv.nat.Opt.Milev. Cf.et. ad 17.10.6, p.122.16 **(contruncare).**

turmis. Cf. ad 15.4.10 (= III p.64). p. 129. 22

agilibus. Cf.23.5.1: tendens imperator **agili gradu** Cercusium principio mensis Aprilis ingressus est; ad 16.11.5, p.88.28-29; Veget.r.m.2.14: (= Lang p.47): Praeterea sicut centurio eligendus est magnis viribus ... qui omnem artem didicerit armaturae, vigilans sobrius **agilis** etc.: apparently a highly recommendable quality for a soldier. Cf.et. ad 16.12.19, p.94.12. p. 129. 22

se turmis ... infuderunt. Cf.14.1.1: fortunae saevientis procellae **tempestates alias rebus infudere communibus;** 14.5.6: (Paulus notarius) fluminis modo **fortunis** complurium **sese repentinus infudit;** Curt.Ruf.5.6.1: Hinc (sc.Persepoleos) illa immensa **agmina infusa:** hinc Darium prius ... **Europae** impium intulisse bellum; ibid.7.9.8: barbari quoque ingentem vim sagittarum **infudere ratibus;** ibid.8.9.19: Gemmas margaritasque mare **litoribus infundit;** (ibid.3.12.20: sed nondum **fortuna se animo eius superfuderat;** with comparable meaning); Flor.3.21.6: Esquilina Collinaque porta geminum **agmen urbi infudit;** Verg.Aen.5.551 sq.: p. 129. 22
    .... Ipse omnem longo decedere **circo**
    Infusum populum et campos iubet esse patentis.
Here = pushed their way in = ± pounced upon. For the constr. of **infundere** cf. Krebs Antib.1 p.740. **Se infundere** with the above meaning not in Veget.r.m. Cf.et. **se effundere** ad 17.12.4, p.125.8*b*.

XIII, 10

p. 129. 22-23 **cohors praetoria.** According to Müller Milit. p.579 (op.cit.I): "alte Terminologie" (cf. ad 16.12.20, p.94.15*a*). Here it is certainly an archaic flower of speech. Veget.r.m. does know **praetoria porta** (Lang 26.2) and the **praetorium** (Lang 26.7, 84.15) with the familiar meaning, but he does not mention a **cohors praetoria.**

p. 129. 23 **ex adverso.** Cf. ad 17.12.13, p.127.2-3*c;* Hofm.-Leum. p.529 sq., 119 (with lit.).

p. 129. 23 **Augustum cautius stipans.** For **Augustus** cf. ad 17.3.4, p.108.17*b*. The comparat.adverbii is here certainly used metri causa (= positivus): Claus.I. For the verb cf. Verg.Aen.4.136:

Tandem progreditur, **magna stipante caterva;**

Claud.35 (de raptu Proserp.) II.55 sq.:

Tali luxuriat cultu: comitantur euntem

Naïdes et **socia stipant** utrimque **corona;**

ibid.8.582 sq. (de IV Cons.Honor.):

Illustri te prole Tagus, te Gallia doctis

Civibus, et **toto stipavit** Roma **Senatu.**

(and thus frequently in Claud.). With this meaning (surround closely, encircle) also class., the verb does not occur in Veget.r.m.Opt.Milev. Arn.adv.nat. Derived from this **stipatores** (= body-guard); cf. 24.4.4: scutum, quo contectus ... unius lateri ferrum infixit, alterum **stipatores** ... occiderunt; Iust.13.4.18: **stipatoribus regis** satellitibusque Cassander filius Antipatri praeficitur; etc. (also class.).

p. 129. 23-24 **resistentium pectora ... terga fugientium.** For the **chiasm** cf. ad 17.13.9, p.129.21-22, just preceding this one. For the **substantivisation of the part. praes.** cf. ad 17.12.12, p.126.24. **Incidere** (= to pounce upon) here constructed with the accusat. The usual constr. is: **in c.accus. or dativ.** (Cf. Krebs Antib.1 p.709). Veget.r.m. only has **in c.accus.** (though not of persons). Cf.et.Tac.Hist.3.29.1: obruitque **quos inciderat** (sc. ballista); Lucr.4.568: at quae pars vocum non **auris incidit ipsas** (here: to fall down upon, find oneself in); B.J. de Jonge, Apul.Met.II, Comm.p.61 (with examples from Apul.). Curt.Ruf. also has **incidere c.dat.** of **c. in c.acc.**

p. 129. 24 *a* **insuperabili contumacia.** Cf.15.10.11: indeque exorsus aliud **iter** antehac **insuperabile** fecit (= insurmountable, impossible to accomplish, im-

passable). Found among others in Liv.**Verg.Ovid.** Seneca Front.Plin. epist.Gell. Cf.et.Claud.15.459 sq. (de bello Gild.):
> ... **caput insuperabile rerum**
> Aut ruet in vestris, aut stabit **Roma,** lacertis.

Not in Veget.r.m.Opt.Milev.Arn.adv.nat.

b For the **subst.** cf. ad 17.13.5, p.129.5.

a **horrendo stridore.** For **stridor** cf. ad 16.12.13, p.92.29 - p.93.1*a*. For the **stridor umbrarum** cf.Claud.3.126 (In Ruf.I); Stat.Theb.II Comm. Mulder p.65 sq.   p. 129. 25

b Cf.27.10.10: hinc impatientia militis perterrente, inde **horrenda circumsonantibus Alamannis.** A "hidden" quotation? Cf.Verg.Aen.12.669 sq.:
> (pater Aeneas) ... opera omnia rumpit
> **laetitia** exultans, **horrendumque intonat** armis

and ibid.6.287 sq.:
> et centumgeminus Briareus ac belua Lernae
> **horrendum stridens,** flammisque armata Chimaera.

The adject., as well as the combination of the 2 words, is poetical.

monstrabant. Cf. ad 17.12.10, p.126.8-9.   p. 129. 26

et iacentes ... perferebant. For a correct understanding of this passage one should bear in mind that Amm. distinguishes 2 main groups: 1⁰ those who fall, are killed in battle; 2⁰ **those lying on the ground, who are still alive and who,** because of their serious injuries or because they are trampled on and can no longer be seen, **cannot flee** and await their end **alto silentio,** in spite of their pain. This **second** main group is split up into **three parts,** characterised by: *a.* succisis poplitibus; *b.* dexteris amputatis; *c.* superruentium conlisi ponderibus. Although syntactically **ideoque adempto fugiendi subsidio** belongs to *a*, it belongs logically to *a*, *b*, and *c*, which again can be differentiated by plurimi, alii and nonnulli, respectively. The **common predicate** is **cruciatus ... perferebant,** the common subject **iacentes** (sc.barbari).   p. 129. 26-29

absque. Cf. ad 14.3.4 (= I p.81). The preposition occurs often in Amm.; **4 times in Veget.r.m.,** not in Claud.Opt.Milev.Arn.adv.nat.   p. 129. 26

succisis poplitibus. Cf.Liv.22.51.7: quosdam et **iacentis vivos succisis** feminibus **poplitibusque** invenerunt; Veget.r.m.1.11 (= Lang p.16): ut ...   p. 129. 26

347

nunc a lateribus minaretur, interdum contenderet **poplites** et crura **succidere** (sc.tiro).

p. 129. 27 **ideoque adempto fugiendi subsidio**. For **ideoque** cf. ad 16.12.25, p.95.9*a* and *b;* for **fugiendi subsidio** cf. ad 17.1.7, p.105.24-25*b*, *c*. Bur here the 2 words do not mean: refuge to flee to, but: expedient consisting of flight (**a genit.explicat.**, therefore). Freely translated: after the possibility to seek help in flight had been taken away from them.

p. 129. 27 **dexteris**: right **arms** (as often).

p. 129. 27 **amputatis**: Cf.Suet Galba 7.9. Nam et numulario, non ex fide versanti pecunias, **manus amputavit** mensaeque eius adfixit. (here: of course, hands); ibid.20: donec gregarius miles ... **caput ei** (sc. Galbae) **amputavit**. The verb does not occur in Claud.Veget.r.m., though it is found in Opt. Milev. The subst. in Arn.adv.nat.1.27 (Reiffersch.p.18): ... accipiamus innocentiae voluntatem et ab omni nos labe **delictorum omnium amputatione** purgemus; Curt.Ruf.4.6.16: **manum amputat;** 8.1.20 (likewise); 3.8.16: **amputaverat manus;** 5.5.6: alios pedibus, quosdam **manibus** auribusque **amputatis;** 4.15.17: quippe **amputata** virorum **membra** humi iacebant; 9.1.32: **crus ... amputare** coepit; Sil.Ital.3.552 sq.:
  Nec pestis lapsus simplex: abscisa relinquunt
  Membra gelu, fractosque asper rigor **amputat artus.**
The verb impresses me as **not** having originated from the soldiers' language of Amm.Marc.

p. 129. 28 **ferro intacti**. Cf.16.12.53: pars ... **intactis ferro corporibus** acervis **superruentium** obruti necabantur.

p. 129. 28 **superruentium**. Cf. ad 17.7.5, p.117.6.

p. 129. 28 *a* **conlīsi pondĕribus**. Claus.II. Although the **pluralis** is "correct" here according to Latin usage, the influence of the metrum is very clear.
b For the **partic.** cf. ad 17.7.7, p.117.15; Krebs Antib.1.297.
c Cf.Veget.r.m.4.22: Onager autem dirigit lapides, sed pro nervorum crassitudine et magnitudine **saxorum pŏndera iaculătur** (Claus.III).

p. 129. 28 **cruciatus**. Cf.14.9.6: qui ita evisceratus ut **cruciatibus** membra deessent (= tortures, lit.). The verb with the meaning of: **to crucify** late Latin. The subst. **cruciarius** (= ripe for the gallows, - the cross) 29.2.9.

a silēntio perferēbant. Claus.III = they bore to the end. But the choice of the compositum is, as so often, also influenced by the metrum.
b Of the **subst**. Amm. uses the **ablat.plur.** in 23.6.33 (cf.Hagend.St.Amm. p.97 sq.). This seems to be exceptional.

XIII, 11
quisquam. "correctly" used. Cf. ad 16.8.2, p.81.1-4, c.3.

diversa. Cf. ad 17.13.7, p.129.10. The substant.14.6.22 (**diversitas**).

supplicia = ways of executing, - of killing. Unless here it means: fatal tortures.

exoravit = urgently begged to.

a **iugiter.** Cf.19.4.6: animalia praeter homines cetera **iugiter prona** (= because they continuously walk head downwards); 20.3.1: et a primo aurorae exortu adusque meridiem **intermicabant iugiter** stellae; 26.3.6: Sub hoc tamen Aproniano ita **iugiter** copia necessariorum **exuberavit**. Late lat. Also in Veget.r.m.4.16 (= Lang p.139). Not in Claud.Opt. Milev.Arn.adv.nat. Cf.et. Krebs Antib.1 p.805 (with lit.); Fesser p.57.
b The adj. **iugis** in Amm.21.5.3: populandique **iugem licentiam**; 27.11.3: praefecturis, quas **iugi familiarum licentia** capessere cogebatur; 28.1.1: clades ... quas obliterasset utinam **iuge silentium**; 30.4.11: qui ... **iugi silentio** umbrarum sunt similes propriarum; 20.11.25: et super his **iugi fragore** tonitrua fulgoraque mentes hominum pavidas perterrebant; 28.4.5: quae probra aliaque his maiora **dissimulatione iugi neglecta** ita effrenatius exarserunt. According to Marx (op.cit.I) p.440, this is an archaism, although it occurs in class. Latin, but rarely and often in standard connections. Cf.Fesser p.53.

licet adflicti. For **licet** cf. ad 14.1.5 (= I p.59 sq.). The partic. is a t.t.mil.: thrown down, thrown onto the ground. Thus also Caes.b.g.6.27.2. Not metaph. here, therefore.

minus ... potius ... quam. A contaminatio of: **minus** criminis aestimabant alienis viribus **quam** conscientiae suae iudicio vinci and **optabant ut potius** alienis viribus **quam** conscientiae suae iudicio **vincerentur**. For the **contam.**, cf. ad 17.11.7, p.121.12.

p. 130. 1 **aestimabant.** For the **nom.c.infin.** cf. ad 17.12.11, p.126.14*b*. (for the **accus.c.infin.** ad 17.4.13, p.111.5; ad 17.1.2, p.105.1*d*).

p. 130. 2 *a* **mussantesque.** Cf. ad 14.6.8 (= I p.93). To the words quoted there by Fesser should be added that with the use of intensiva one should also pay attention to the sentence rhythmics and the clausula. The idea that Amm. "ohne inneres Gefühl die Sprache handhabt", is of course, no longer believed in.
b The sentence means: and sometimes they were heard to mumble (grumble, growl) that that which had happened to them was due to fortune (blind fortune), and not their fault.
c **mussantes audiebantur:** here we have a Greek partic. construction, in my opinion, as for instance, in Thucyd.1.24.1; Isocr.Trapez.23 (one should also compare the **nomin.c.infinit.** with the **passivum** of the **verba declarandi et sentiendi:** Hofm.Leum.p.589(173)).
audire c. partic. occurs several times in Opt.Milev.; cf.2.5 (= Ziwsa p.40): nec audierunt spiritum sanctum dicentem in psalmo ...; 2.23 (= Ziwsa p.59): O sacrilegium inpietati commixtum, dum homines per vos iurantes libenter auditis; etc.

p. 130. 3 **fortunae non meriti:** genit.possess. Cf.Hofm.-Leum.p.394 (23*b*).

p. 130. 3 **q̆uod ev̆enit.** Dialysis. Claus.I.

p. 130. 3-4 **in semihorae curriculo.** Cf.Cic. pro Rabirio perduellonis reo 2.6: quoniam ... meque ex comparato et constituto spatio defensionis **in semihorae curriculum** coegisti; Amm.18.8.7: Quae dum **in curriculo semihorae** aguntur. The 2nd subst. also 26.3.2: in **amphitheatrali curriculo** (= the races in the amphitheatre).

p. 130. 4 **discrimine proeliorum emenso.** For **proelia** cf. ad 16.12.37, p.97.6*c*. The linking of the 2 substantiva also 25.3.5: inter prima **discrimina proeliorum**. For the **partic.** cf. ad 17.1.8, p.106.1. For **discrimen** ad 17.1.10, p.106.9*a*.

p. 130. 5 **declararet.** In the original sense of the verb: to clarify.

XIII, 12
p. 130. 6 *a* **vixdum populis hostilibus stratis.** It is obvious from § 19 that the **populi** concerned are the **Amicenses;** Cf. ad 17.13.4, p.128.26*b*. When the

Amicenses belong to the **Limigantes** (which is probably the case) he means by **populi**: tribes, families. (cf. ad 17.12.21, p.128.6).
b **hostilibus** = **hostium**. Although here an adject., **hostilis** is also used substantively = **hostis**. Cf.31.13.14; 15.8.13; 24.1.16; Blomgren p.157; Fesser p.14.
Note. 31.13.14 V **hostilibus**. E A Cl. **hostibus,** incorrect, in my opinion.
c **stratis**. The simplex metri causa: claus.I. Cf. ad 17.12.9. p.126.2.

gregatim. Cf.29.1.25: aliisque gregatim post illum occisis. Does not occur in Claud.Veget.r.m.Opt.Milev.Arn.adv.nat. Although also found in Cic.Colum.Plin. et al., nevertheless with Amm. probably a literary flower of speech. p. 130. 6

peremptorum: no difference in meaning with **caesorum** (130.9) **necati** (130.20). The subst. **peremptor** 25.6.6. p. 130. 6

a **necessitūdines ducebăntur**: claus.III. The simplex (= abducebantur) is selected metri causa. p. 130. 7
b The substant. = **relatives**, post-class. and late Latin. With the same meaning also 21.16.20; 24.5.3; 31.5.5.

extractae. Cf.15.4.8: **periculoque** praesidio tenebrosae noctis extracti; 15.5. 31: Silvanum extractum aedicula; 17.13.13: nec quemquam casa ... **periculo mortis** extraxit; 18.6.16: hoc extracti **periculo;** 24.5.4: Nabdates ... quem extractum cum octoginta(e)latebris expugnatae docui civitatis (e rest.Cl.); 25.1.2: extrahere pugna; 27.6.4: vixque se **mortis periculo** contemplans extractum; 29.6.14: ni **periculo mortis** aliquos citum extraxisset effugium; 26.9.9: e frutectis ubi latebat extractus; 19.6.2: (munimenta) **unde** hominum milia extracta complura. Attention should be paid again to Amm.'s preference for **formulary expressions**. (cf. ad 17.4.1, p.109.6*b*). p. 130. 7

tuguriis: not houses, but poor huts made of clay, straw, thatch, etc. with roofs reaching down to the ground (**humilis**). Deminut. **teguriola** Veget. r.m.4.26 (= Lang p.146), a sentry-box on walls and on towers for the **vigiles**. That the "barbarians" sometimes lived in a different style, is apparent from 17.1.7 (cf.annot.p.105.27). p. 130. 7

aetatis sexusque promiscui = of all ages and sexes = aetate sexuque promiscui. The adj. also 23.2.4: cumque eum (Julianum sc.) profecturum p. 130. 7-8

351

deduceret **multitudo promiscua** (cf.Tac.Ann.12.7). Cf.et.Veget.r.m.4.25 (= Lang p.146): Tunc enim de fenestris ac tectis **omnis aetas ac sexus** inrumpentes obruit saxis (with the same meaning); **ad 16.11.9, p.89. 26-27.**

p. 130. 8-9 **et fastu ... servilium:** very poetically coloured.

p. 130. 8 **fastu.** Cf. ad 14.1.1 (= I p.54); ad 16.12.3, p.91.16. **fastu ... abolito.** Cf. 17.9.4: spe meliorum abolita.

p. 130. 8 *a* **ad infimitatem obsequiorum venere servilium.** Cf.29.2.1: Palladius ... ipsa **sortis infimitate** ad omnia praeceps. late Latin. cf. Souter p.204.
b **obsequiorum.** For the meaning cf. ad 17.12.19, p.127.22-23*a*. The pluralis is poeticus. The meaning is more or less: they found themselves in the lowly position of servile obedience.

p. 130. 9 **exiguo temporis intervallo decurso.** For **intervallum** cf. ad 17.1.12, p.106. 19. **Decurrere** = expire, elapse also 22.15.9; 24.3.10; 24.6.2; 31.12.11; 31.13.7 (22.15.9 B G **decursa**; V Corn.Cl. **decussa**). With other meanings 18.6.5; 20.11.22; 21.1.14.

p. 130. 9-10 **caesorum aggeres et captivorum agmina cernebantur.** For the **alliteration** cf. ad 17.9.3, p.120.23. For the **lusus verborum** ad 15.4.2 (= III p.56).

XIII, 13

p. 130. 10 **incitante itaque fervore certaminum.** Cf.16.12.2: barbara feritate **certaminum rabiem** undique concitante (cf.annot.p.91.12). For the **pluralis poeticus** cf. ad 17.13.11, p.130.4 **(proelia)**; Hagend.St.A.p.93.

p. 130. 11 **fructuque vincendi:** the fruit, result of the victory. In connection with the gerundium: not the present result, but the future one; i.e. the fruit of the complete victory and destruction. The word-combination seems rather unusual to me.

p. 130. 11 *a* **consurrectum est in perniciem eorum. Consurgere:** to prepare for battle, to break up camp, t.t.mil. Cf.Liv.10.13.4: itaque suis sociorumque viribus **consurgere** hostes **ad bellum.** Curt.Ruf.7.9.9: Iamque terrae rates applicabantur, cum **acies** clipeata **consurgit** et hastas certo ictu ... mittit e ratibus (the basic meaning is still clearly visible here); Iust.Phil.12.15.11: Hac voce veluti bellicum inter amicos cecinisset ... ita omnes **in aemula-**

tionem consurgunt et ... favorem militum quaerunt; ad 17.12.12, p.126. 23-24.

b For **in finale** cf. ad 17.10.3, p.121.25*a*.

c For **pernicies** cf. ad 17.1.12, p.106.16; ad 17.11.3, p.124.3*b*.

a **qui deseruĕre prŏelia** † (Cl.; he suggests reading **deseruerant** c.c.). But p. 130. 11-12
the clausula ⌣̆ ⌣ ⌣̆ ⌣ occurs more often and **-ia** can be read per synizesin; Cf.14.11.33: horruĕre gĕntes; 20.7.9: exultatiŏne măgna; 22.8.17: interlăbens lŭcos; 22.14.3: in inmĕnsum tŏllit; etc. Blomgren (op.cit.II) p.93 sq.

b There need be no objection against the **perfectum**: Cf. ad 16.12.15, p.93.10 - p.93.23; and a "shifting" of the tempora occurs frequently in late Latin and in Amm., both because of the evolution of the language itself, as for reasons of metrum or variatio.

a **vel in tuguriis latitantes occultabantur.** The alliteration is not accidental. p. 130. 12
in my opinion. Claus.III.

b **latitare** also 22.7.5. Cf.Cic. pro Cluent.13(39): extrahitur **domo latitans** Oppianicus a Manilio.

c Cf.Sall.Jug.12.5: cum interim Hiempsal reperitur **occultans se tugurio** mulieris ancillae. **Occultare** is used more than **occulere,** also in late Latin. Cf. Krebs Antib.2 p.198 (with lit.).

ad loca: sc. the tuguria, mentioned above. p. 130. 12

barbarici. Cf. ad 17.12.21, p.128.2*a, b*. p. 130. 13

a **disiectis culmis levibus.** Definitely a Vergilius reminiscence. Cf.Aen. p. 130. 13
8.652 sq.:
  In summo (sc.clipeo) custos Tarpeiae Manlius arcis
  Stabat pro templo, et Capitolia celsa tenebat.
  Romuleoque recens horrebat regia culmo.
Cf.et.Horat.Oden 2.15.17. sq.:
  Nec fortuitum spernere **caespitem** (viz. for roof-covering)
  leges sinebant etc.
Verg.Buc.1.69:
  Pauperis et **tuguri congestum cespite culmen.**
Sidon.Ep.7.17.21-22.

b Here lit.: to tear apart, to destroy. But often used as t.t. for the destruction of walls, fortifications, buildings, etc. Cf.et. ad 16.12.42, p.98.10.

p. 130. 13 **obtruncabant.** Cf. ad 17.13.9, p.129.21.

p. 130. 14 *a* **vel trabibus conpacta firmissimis.** Thus there were also wooden houses and not only lowly **tuguria.**
b Cf.Verg.Aen.12.674 sq.:
Ad coelum undabat vertex, turrimque tenebat,
Turrim, **compactis trabibus** quam eduxerat ipse;
Mart.12.72:
Iugera mercatus prope busta latentis agelli
Et **male compactae** culmina fulta **casae.**
Cf.et. ad 17.8.5, p.120.7; ad 16.11.8, p.89.20; ad 17.1.2, p.104.7-9c.

p. 130. 14 **periculo etc.** Cf. ad 17.13.12, p.130.7 (extractae).

XIII, 14

p. 130. 15 **inflammarentur.** Cf.15.3.9: **eumque** ad suspiciones ... mollem et penetrabilem, ita acriter **inflammavit.**

p. 130. 15 **nullus.** Cf. ad 14.7.5 (= II p.22); Liesenberg (1890, op.cit.I) p.8, with more examples. Compare the use of **ullus** (ad 14.2.2 = I p.68) = quisquam. Cf.et. ad 17.2.3, p.107.26b.

p. 130. 15 **latere:** without any difference in meaning with **latitare** (p.130.12).

p. 130. 16 *a* **cunctis vitae praesidiis circumcisis.** For **cunctus** cf. ad 17.3.6, p.109.2. Translation: after all means, expedients (= all means to save life) had been cut off on all sides. Cf.et 17.7.5, p.117.8b (for a comparable expression); 17.13.10, p.129.27.
b For **praesidium** with various meanings cf. ad 17.2.1, p.107.12-13b, c; ad 17.12.19, p.127.25.

p. 130. 16-18 **peribat ... sternebatur.** The subject **(quisque)** should be separated from **nullus.**

p. 130. 16 **obstinate (obstinatius).** Cf.22.5.4; 24.4.15; 25.7.9; 29.5.51. Cf. ad 17.11.3, p.124.3a; ad 16.12.48, p.99.9-10b.

p. 130. 16 **o.igni peribat absumptus:** hyperbaton (cf. ad 17.1.6, p.105.21a), and that 2 times. **Absumere** does not differ in meaning from **consumere,** (cf. ad 17.7.6, p.117.11b; 15.13.1: Domitiano crudeli morte **consumpto).**

aut incĕndium vĭtans. The simplex probably metri causa: claus.I. p. 130. 17

egressusque = emerged. For the verb cf. ad 17.1.4, p.105.15. p. 130. 17

uno = altero. **Unus** = **alteruter** late Latin (cf. Souter p.449; thus the p. 130. 17
information by Krebs Antib.2 p.695 is not quite correct: N. L.). Cf.
et **unus alterum**, often in late Latin (Hofm.-Leum.78, p.472, γ); but cf.
also Caes.b.c.3.108.6.

supplicio. Cf. ad 17.13.11, p.129.29. p. 130. 17

declinato. The verb also among others occurs: 15.1.3; 16.12.49; 16.12.57; p. 130. 17
17.5.2; 22.9.5; 22.14.2; 30.4.22; 30.1.9. Cf. ad 16.12.57, p.101.1*a;* ad
17.12.7, p.125.17.

a **ferro stĕrnebatur hostĭli.** Simplex metri causa: Claus.III. p. 130. 17-18
b Cf.Liv.30.35.8: ac, si nihil aliud, vulneribus suis **ferrum hostile** hebetarent (Fletcher, Rev. de philol.LXIII, 1937).

aliqui. Cf. ad 17.4.12, p.110.25*c;* ad 16.11.8, p.89.19-20. For the following p. 130. 18
description compare 16.12.55 t/m **57.**

a **amnis vicini se commisere gurgitibus, peritia nandi ripas ulteriores** p. 130. 19
occupare posse sperantes. Cf.16.12.55: quidam **nandi peritia** eximi se
posse discriminibus arbitrati **animas fluctibus conmiserunt;** 16.12.55: ne
... nostrorum quisquam **se gurgitibus committeret** verticosis; 16.12.57:
nandi strenuis; 16.12.57: ad **ripas ulteriores** post multa discrimina pervenire.
b For **gurges** cf. ad 14.2.10 (= I p.73); for **ripas** 16.12.57, p.101.2;
17.13.5, p.129.3*b*. **Sperantes:** c.nomin.c. infinit.; cf. ad 17.12.11, p.126.14*b*.
(posse is "correct": it replaces the **infinit.fut.** according to the class. rule).
c For **peritia** cf.19.8.5: **peritia locorum** (Sall.Iug.46.8: nam in Iugurtha
tantus dolus tantaque **peritia locorum** et militiae erat). It also occurs elsewhere **c.gerundio.** The subst. is post.-class. with the exception of Sall.
Cf.et. Krebs Antib.2 p.282.
d **conmisĕre gurgĭtibus.** Cf. periĕre confĭxi (p.130.21). Claus.II and Claus.
I. Cf.et. ad 16.12.19. p.94.11-12.

summersi: because they were drowned. Not transitively used! p. 130. 20

355

p. 130. 20-21 *a* **alii iaculis periere confixi.** Cf.16.12.56: ut marginibus insistentes (sc. Romani) **confoderent telorum varietate** Germanos.

b **confixi**: probably here equal to **transfixi** (p.100.5). G confixi V **confixis**. This last version can be reasonably defended, in my opinion. Cf.et.20.7. 11; 26.8.8.

p. 130. 21-22 *a* **adeo ut abunde cruore diffuso meatus fluminis spumăret inmĕnsi.** V spumare timens B G spumaret, tumens. N Vales i⟨n⟩mens⟨i⟩. The version of Vales. is to be preferred metri causa: claus.I.

b Cf.16.12.57: **spumans** denique **cruore** barbarico, decolor alveus insueta stupebat augmenta.

c For **spumans** cf. ad 16.12.57, p.101.2-3*a*. For **meatus** cf.16.12.57. p.101.1*b*; for **abunde** (adv), also class. cf. Krebs Antib.1 p.59 **(with lit.);** Heum.-Seckel p.6. The adv. does not occur in Claud.Veget.r.m.Opt. Milev.Arn.adv.nat.

d For **cruor** cf. ad 17.10.9, p.123.6.

p. 130. 22 *a* **per elementum.** For **per** cf. ad 14.11.1 (= II p.113); 17.12.4, p.125.7.

b for **elementum** cf. ad 15.4.4 (= III p.59). Of the 4 **elementa**: water, fire, air and earth, the first 2 are meant here. Cf.Veget.r.m.4.42 (= Lang p.161): **Elementum pelagi** tertia pars mundi est; Claud.33.246 sq. (de raptu Proserp.I):

Hic **elementorum seriem** sedesque paternas
Insignibat acu (sc. Proserpina) etc.

ibid.8.284 sq. (de IV cons.Honor.):

Nonne vides, operum qui se pulcherrimus ipse
Mundus amore liget, nec vi connexa per aevum
Conspirent **elementa** sibi?

S.Opt.Mil.4.9 (Ziwsa p.116): nam et per Esaiam prophetam idem dei dolor est, dum in hoc **duo** testatur **elementa,** dum dicit: audi, **caelum** et percipe auribus, **terra**: filios generavi et exaltavi. ipsi autem me dereliquerunt. Arn.adv.nat.1.2 (Reiffersch.p.4): Numquid in contrarias qualitates **prima illa elementa** mutata sunt, ex quibus res omnes consensum est esse concretas? ibid.1.29 (R.p.20): Quis, ne fixa pigritiae stupore torpescerent **elementa vitalia,** solis ignes constituit ad rerum incrementa futuros?

p. 130. 22 **vincentium** = victorum. For the **substantivisation of the part.praes.** cf. ad 17.12.12, p.126.24.

ira virtusque. Compare the combination **ira-dolor** (ad 14.2.17 = I p.76).   p. 130. 23

XIII, 16

post hunc rerum ordinem: lit.: after this chain of events. Far-fetched for   p. 130. 24
e.g.: his rebus gestis. One should also compare, however, Verg.Aen.
7.44 sq.:
  ... **maior rerum** mihi nascitur **ordo,**
  maius opus moveo.
Cic. harusp. 9(19): Etenim quis est tam vecors, qui aut cum suspexerit in
caelum, deos esse non sentiat, et ea, quae tanta mente fiunt, ut vix quisquam arte ulla **ordinem rerum** ac necessitudinem (?) persequi possit, casu
fieri putet?
For **post temp.** cf. ad 17.12.16, p.127.8*b*.

placuerat. Here = placuit. Cf. ad 16.5.12, p.77.9-11*c*. But here not metri   p. 130. 24
causa. For the reverse "transposition" cf. ad 16.12.15, p.93.10 - p.93.23.
The **plusq.perf. can** be defended, in view of the next sentence: et ...
colligi.

cunctis adimi spem. For **cunctus** cf. ad 17.3.6, p.109.2. For **adimere** cf. ad   p. 130. 24
17.13.10, p.129.27.

vitaeque solacium: sc. servandae.   p. 130. 25

post lares incensos. For **post** see the sentence immediately before this.   p. 130. 25
For **lares** cf. ad 16.7.1, p.78.24; ad 16.10.13, p.86.13*b;* ad 16.11.7, p.89.13.

navigia iussa sunt colligi. Cf.Liv.28.39.19: **Locus** inde **lautiaque** legatis   p. 131. 1
praeberi iussa. Although "correct", **non-personal** subjects do not occur
very often with iubeor, vetor, etc., especially when these are concrete
objects. An intermediary form Veget.r.m.2.6 (= Lang p.40): maior
autem interdum esse consuevit (sc. **legio**), si non tantum unam cohortem
sed etiam alias miliarias **fuerit iussa suscipere.**
Cf.et.Opt.Milev.2.16 (= Ziwsa p.51): eadem voce vobis libertas est
reddita, qua voce idolorum **patefieri iǔssa sunt těmpla** (claus.I).

ad indagandum. A hunter's term, very suitable here. Also class., lit. as   p. 131. 1
well as metaph. (cf.e.g.Cic.Tusc.5.23(64); de finib.2.13(39)). The verb
occurs once in Veget.r.m. (metaph.): 1.7 (= Lang p.11). Not found in
Claud.Opt.Milev.Arn.adv.nat.

p. 131. 1 **eos⟨quos⟩.** This version E W m2 Momms.Cl.Seyf.Rolfe. V **eos.** N A G Sabbah **quos.** The last version is to be preferred, in my opinion. The antecedent is often omitted. Cf.e.g.14.1.9; 14.1.6; 14.10.16; 26.6.11.

p. 131. 2 *a* **ulterior discreverat ripa.** For the localisation cf.17.13.5, p.129.3*a*.
b for **discernere** cf. ad 17.12.12, p.126.24*b*.

XIII, 17

p. 131. 2 **alacritas:** pugnacity. Thus used also 16.12.14 (p.93.5). Thus also **alacer** 16.2.9 (p.73.19).

p. 131. 2 **intepesceret.** Cf. ad 17.4.14, p.111.8*c*.

p. 131. 2-3 **pugnatorum.** Cf.18.8.10: Inter quos dux ipse agnitus **pugnatorumque mole circumdatus** ... abscessit. The subst. is found, among others, in Verg.Liv. Suet.Plin. In Veget.r.m.3.15 (= Lang p.99) **pugnatores** = **milites.** Similarly ibid.3.9 (= Lang p.86). Not in Claud.Opt.Milev.Arn.adv.nat. The **adj. pugnatrix:** 23.6.28 (natio), late Latin.

p. 131. 3 **inpositi luntribus.** For **luntres** cf. ad 16.11.9, p.90.1. Imponere t.t.naut. = to embark.

p. 131. 3 **inpositi ... ducti.** The main point is expressed in these 2 participia. (cf. ad 17.3.5, p.108.20*a*).

p. 131. 3 **abdita.** Cf. ad 17.3.2, p.108.12*a;* ad 17.4.1, p.109.4*a;* ad 17.4.14, p.111.7-8.

p. 131. 3 **velites expediti.** Cf. ad 17.2.1, p.107.12*b* (**velites**). The addition of the adject. is almost superfluous.

p. 131. 3 **occuparunt.** Cf. ad 16.12.19, p.94.11-12. Here not metri causa.

p. 131 .4 **latibula.** Cf.24.4.12: **terrarum latibula concava** oblongis tramitibus alibi struebantur (a kind of subterranian passages). Also class. Not in Claud. Veget.r.m.Opt.Milev.Arn.adv.nat. Probably a rarely used word for: **latebrae.**

p. 131. 4 **aspectus.** Also among others 15.4.5; 16.2.10; 17.10.9.

a **gentiles lembos.** For the adj. cf.15.5.6 (= III p.81); 16.10.16, p.87.9; 16.12.65, p.102.11.

b Apparently Amm. uses here **lembus** without any difference in meaning with **lunter,** for there has been no changing of boats. A **lembus** is a small, low and fast vessel, with many oars and tapering to a point. But Amm. himself says of the **luntres** in 16.11.9: nanctique **vacuas lintres,** per eas **licet vacillantes** evecti, etc., so that one gets the impression of their being very simple boats.

But perhaps the diligent reader of Vergil, which Amm. is, has had in mind Georg.1.201?: Non aliter quam qui **adverso** vix **flumine lembum // Remigiis** subigit.

Cf.et Liv.24.40.2: nuntiantes Philippum primum Apolloniam tentasse, **lembis biremibus** centum viginti **flumine adverso** subvectum; Curt.Ruf. 4.5.18: **piratici lembi** (also 4.5.21). The subst. is further found in Plautus, and others. Cf.et Claud.17.330 sq. (de Fl.M.Theod.cons.):

Lascivae subito confligant aequore **lembi**
Stagnaque remigibus spument immissa canoris.

(describing a naumachia). Ibid.21.358 sq. (de laud.Stilich.):

Praedonem lembo profugum, ventisque repulsum
Suscepit merito fatalis Tabraca portu.

c **Linter** also occurs in Claud. But the two names of boats not in **Veget. r.m.** Arn.adv.nat.Opt.Milev.

a **nota remĭgia conspicăntes. Remigia** = remos, as so often, though not in classical prose. Veget.r.m. uses **remigium,** but not with this meaning. For that he uses **remi** (and **remiges).**

b the active form (= **conspicari**) only late Latin? It is not certain whether Amm. uses here the deponens. Cf. ad 17.4.5, p.109.19-20*c;* ad 16.12.22, p.94.24. And it should also be borne in mind that which various authors **conspicari** occurs as a **passivum.** Here the verb has been used metri causa: claus.III.

XIII, 18

ubi ... senserunt. For **ubi temp.** cf. ad 14.2.20 (= I p.78). For **ubi iterat.** cf. ad 14.2.7 (= I p.70).

quod verebantur. For **quod** cf. ad 17.13.16, p.131.1.

propinquare. Amm. never uses **appropinquare.** In this he is compared by Fesser p.25 with Tacitus, who uses mainly **propinquare.** It may be possible;

p. 131. 6 *a* **suffugia locorum palustrium.** Cf.17.13.29: alios periculi declinatio adegit **suffugia** petere **latebrarum palustrium.** The subst. is post-class. and is often used by Tac. The combination **loci palustres** occurs more often, among others in Veget.r.m.3.6: at vero **in locis** silvestribus vel montuosis sive **palustribus** pedestres magis formidandae sunt copiae (in this short sentence 3 adj. ending in **-ter).** Cf.et.ibid.3.2: nec perniciosis vel **palustribus aquis** utatur exercitus; Amm.16.12.59: lacunam **palustribus aquis** interfusam circumgrediens ut transiret.

b For the **genit.explic.** cf.16.12.59: ad **subsidium vicini collis** evasit.

pl 131. 6-7 ⟨se⟩**contulerunt.** Contulerunt: V Sabbah Seyf. **se c.**: N G Cl.Rolfe. But the clausula already supports the version by V: palŭstrium contulĕrunt (claus.III). Otherwise **conferre** = **se conferre** is late Latin. And in old, vulgar and late Latin one finds many examples of verbs, where the **activum** has a **reflexive meaning.** Cf.Hofm.-Leum.p.546 sq. (140), with lit. Just as sometimes the activ. has a **passive meaning.**

p. 131. 7 **secutus infĕstius mĭles.** The compar. = posit., metri causa. Cf. ad 14.6.12 = I p.96. Claus.I. The compar. of the adv. occurs several times in Liv. Cf.28.29.8: de nullis enim, quam de vobis, **infestius** aut inimicius consuluerunt. The adv. does not occur in Claud.Veget.r.m.Opt.Milev.Arn. adv.nat.

p. 131. 7-8 **victoriam repperit.** Here the verb has the meaning of: to acquire, as seen more often.

p. 131. 8 *a* **caute ... consistere ... credebatur.** Note the alliteration (c). As regards the construction: the subject of the nomin.c.infin. is "omitted", viz. aliquis or quisquam. (for the **nomin.c.infin.** cf. ad 17.12.11, p.126.14*b;* ad 15.7.4, p.57.3; ad 15.7.6, p.57.12). The omission of the pronomen can be easily explained by the preceding **miles.** The **pron.indef.,** however, is also often omitted in Greek in infin. constructions.

b The also class. adv. occurs a few times in Veget. Not in Claud.Arn. adv.nat.Opt.Milev.

p. 131. 8 **consistere.** Seyf.: "wo sie nicht vorsichtig Fusz fassen konnten". A correct translation, as the verb means here: to keep one's foothold. to obtain a firm footing. Not only wrong, but also not suitable here, is Sabbah's translation: "en des lieux où l'on croyait imprudent **de faire halte**".

XIII, 19

post ... Amicenses ... Picenses. For these two peoples cf.17.13.4, p.128. 26b, c. For **post temp.** ad 17.12.16. 127.8b. p. 131. 9-10

absumptos. Cf. ad 17.13.14, p.130.16; Veget.r.m.4.44 (= Lang 163): Inter tanta tamen mortium genera qui acerrrimus casus est, **absumenda** piscibus insepulta sunt corpora. Ibid.2.20 (= Lang p.54) with the meaning of: to consume, spend, run through. p. 131. 9

diffusos. The verb is more or less synonymous with **disicere**. (cf. ad 17.13. 9, p.129.21). p. 131. 9

ex regionibus appellati. Ex = (called) because of = after. For **ex, causally** used cf. ad 14.6.11 (= I p.94). p. 131. 10

conterminis. The adj. is post-class. It occurs in legal literature, not in Claud.Veget.r.m.Opt.Milev.Arn.adv.nat. Probably a less commonly used word. Cf.14.8.5: laeva Saracenis **conterminans** gentibus. This verb late Latin. Cf. Souter p.76; Krebs Antib.1 p.353. p. 131. 10

quos tutiores fecere sociorum aerumnae. Tutus has here the not so usual active meaning of: being on his guard, taking care, cautious. The examples quoted by Georges from Liv. ((9.32.3 and 22.38.13) are not so convincing, in my view. A good example is Horat. de art.poet.28: p. 131. 10-11

    serpit humi **tutus nimium** timidusque procellae.

fecere. Cf. ad 16.12.19, p.94.11-12. Here not metri causa. p. 131. 10

aerumnae. Cf. ad 15.4.10 (= III p.62); ad 16.12.51, p.99.22; ad 17.3.1, p.108.9 **(aerumnosus)**. p. 131. 11

rumorum adsiduitate conpertae. Cf.22.8.18: Adtritis **damnorum assiduitate** finitimis; 23.6.3: cui **victoriarum crebritas** hoc indiderat cognomentum (personificatio); 25.2.6: amplitudine ... spatiorum; 31.12.13: amplitudine camporum; 31.3.8: amplitudine fluentorum; 14.9.1: ruinarum varietates; 24.3.9: negotiorum magnitudines; 17.13.22: spatia ampla camporum; p. 131. 11

16.10.3: proeliorum ardor (personif.); 14.10.10: sententiarum via concinens; etc.

p. 131. 11-14 **ad quos opprimendos ... auxilium ... adsumptum est.** For the **accus. gerundii and gerundivi after prepositions** cf. Hofm.-Leum.178 III p.599 and ad 14.1.8 (= I p.63): **erga.** For **ad finale** cf. ad 17.12.9, p.125.27 - p.126.1.

p. 131. 12 **per diversa conspersos.** For **per div.** cf. ad 16.2.2, p.72.19. The verb **conspergere** means: to strew, sprinkle. But here = **dispergere**.

p. 131. 12-13 **inprudentia viarum arcente.** For the **personif.** cf. ad 17.2.1, p.107.13. **Inprudentia** = unfamiliarity with, ignorance. Thus also in Liv.Sallust. and others. With this meaning also in judic.lit. (cf.Heum.-Seckel p.252). The subst. does not occur at all in Claud.Veget.r.m.Opt.Milev.Arn. adv.nat.

p. 131. 13 **Taifalorum.** Cf. ad 17.13.4, p.128.26*b, c;* Patsch (op.cit.II) 1928 III.1 p.37 sq. (with lit.); ibid. Map 2; Schönfeld (op.cit.I) p.219, with lit. Before the **West-Goths** and the **Taifalians** moved out of Transdanuvia, the T. were living South of the Transsylvanian Alps in the "**Kleine Walachei**".

p. 131. 13 *a* **Liberorum adaeque Sarmatarum.** For the **Sarm.Lib.** cf. ad 17.12.12, p.126.19-20*a, b;* 17.12.17, p.127.15 sq.
b for **adaeque** cf.16.12.63, p.102.1*a*.

XIII, 20

p. 131. 14-16 **Cumque separaret ... elegit ... obtinebant ... occupaverant.** According to the rules, one should expect in **all** 3 cases after **separaret** a perfectum. Cf. ad 17.7.4, p.117.1*b;* ad 16.5.12, p.77.9-11 *c;* ad 16.12.15, p.93.10 - p.93.23. S$\bar{e}$dibus obtin$\bar{e}$bant: Claus.III.

p. 131. 14 **locorum ratio.** Sabbah: "la configuration du terrain". This meaning intended here. **ratio** = condition, state; several times with this meaning in Cic. and others.

p. 131. 14-15 **tractus contiguos.** For the **subst.** cf. ad 17.1.10, p.106.10. For the **adject.** ad 17.7.2, p.116.21.

p. 131. 15 **Moesiae.** Cf. ad 16.10.20, p.88.4; ad 17.13.4, p.128.26*c*.

a **proxima.** For **prope** cf. ad 16.12.27, p.95.17. For **proximus c.dat.** p. 131. 15
(normal in post-class. Latin). etc. cf. Krebs Antib.2 p.419 (with lit.). For
the **neutr.plur.** cf. ad 17.3.2, p.108.12*a;* ad 17.4.1, p.109.4*a;* ad 17.4.14,
p.111.7-8.
b Cf.Terent.Haut.54: ... cum agrum **in proxumo** hic mercatus est.

e regione = directly opposite, c.dat. and c.genit. Cf.20.3.11: **e regione** p. 131. 16
vero cum normaliter steterit (sc.luna) contra (sc.solem), lumine pleno
fulgebit. Fairly often in class. Latin. Cf.Caes.b.g.7.36.5: erat **e regione
oppidi** collis sub ipsis radicibus montis; ibid.7.35.1.
(it is doubtful whether the version of β should not be maintained here;
cf. Meusel[17], 1920, II p.584, who includes Klotz' conjecture into the text,
needlessly, in my opinion); Cic.Acad.pr.2.39 (123): Dicitis etiam, esse
e regione nobis, e contraria parte terrae, qui adversis vestigiis stent contra
nostra vestigia, quos Ἀντίποδας vocatis.
The dativus **sibi** depends both on **e regione** and on **oppositas.**

XIII, 21

a **Quae Limigantes ... territique subactorum exemplis.** Cl.Seyf. **Quae** p. 131. 17
perpessi (Pet.) Limigantes territique subactorum exemplis. Rolfe. **Quae
contemplantes** Limigantes, Günther. **Limigantes territique** subactorum
exemplis et prostratorum, Sabbah. V does not have a gap after **Limigantes.** A G **territi.** Sabbah gives the following translation of his version:
"**Mais** les L., **même terrifiés** par les exemples de ceux qui avaient été
soumis ou abattus". This translation seems somewhat forced to me and
difficult to defend. The simplest solution seems to me provisionally:
"**Quae Limigantes territi** subactorum etc. **territus** is then the partic. of
terreri = to let oneself be frightened = to be afraid of.
A shifting of activum and passivum occurs frequently in late Latin. And
the Greek Amm. may also have been influenced by φοβέομαι (c.accus.),
as well as by the Latin **vereri.** Cf.17.13.3, p.128.20; ad 17.13.17. p.131.5*b*.
b **terreo c. infinit.**27.7.9: (quidam principes) **inimicos loqui terrent** amplitudine potestatis.
c By **Limigantes** the **Picenses** must have been meant here, as well as
the remainder (if any) of the **Amicenses** (§ 19: post absumptos **paene
diffusosque** Amicenses); and perhaps some other tribes of these **Limigantes,** not mentioned by Amm.?

a **subactorum ... prostratorum.** The substantivisation of the **part.perf.** p. 131. 17

pass. increases in late Latin and occurs very frequently in Amm. Cf. Hofm.-Leum.66*b*, p.457 sq.

b Cf.Cic.pr.Font.12(26): ut velint isti aut quiescere, id quod victi ac **subacti** solent aut etc.

p. 131 17-18   **exĕmplis et prostratŏrum**: Claus.III. Homoioteleuton and clausula support the version **subactorum etc.**

p. 131. 18   **haesitabant.** This verb also 18.7.2; 20.4.22; 29.2.19.

p. 131. 18   **ambiguis,** Cf. ad 17.6.1, p.116.4*a*.

p. 131. 18   **oppeterent.** Here with the nuance: to seek Death. The verb also 29.3.5; 30.3.7; 31.7.13; 31.13.18; 31.16.2; 16.5.17 (cf. ad 1., p.78.7); 17.1.14; 19.7.1; 21.12.13; 24.5.6; 26.8.10; 27.1.5; 20.4.8; 28.1.16; 15.5.32; cf. et. **Hagend.St.Amm.** p.64.

p. 131. 18-19   **oppĕterent an rogărent.** Claus.III. The choice of the **first** verb may have been influenced by the claus.

p. 131. 19   **rogarent** = to beg for mercy. This pregnant meaning also in 21.4.8 with **orare.** Further examples in Hagend. **zu A.M.** (op.cit.I) p.78 sq.

p. 131. 19   The verb **suppetere** class. and very frequent. In Amm. we also frequently find the subst. **suppetiae** (cf. ad 16.4.3, p.75.1-3), which is non-class. and does not occur in judic.lit., nor in Claud.Veget.r.m.Opt.Milev. (In Arn. adv.nat.3.10).

p. 131. 19   **documĕnta non lĕvia** = d.gravia = weighty, instructive examples, Claus.II.

p. 131. 19-20   **vicit ... consilium.** "Néanmoins, **sous la pression du conseil des anciens,** le projet de se rendre finit par triompher" (Sabbah); "Dennoch fand der Rat Anklang sich zu ergeben, **obwohl die Versammlung der Alten zum Äuszersten drängte**" (Seyf.); "Finally, however, **the urgency of an assembly of the older men prevailed,** and the resolve to surrender" (Rolfe). The difficulty lies in **ad ultimum,** which may mean: finally, as well as: to the utmost, to the very end (cf. ad 17.12.7, p.125.18). It seems to me that Rolfe gives the best translation, in spite of Seyf.'s objections (I p.314).

p. 131. 20   **dedĕndi se consĭlium** † Cl. There need be no objections against the claus.

364

here: ◌̆ ◌ ◌ ◌ ◌̆ ◌ the conjecture se⟨se⟩ by Her. is superfluous (cf. Blomgren, op.cit.II, p.9 sq.). -ium is pronounced per synizesim.

a **variaeque palmae victoriarum.** An example of abundantia. Cf.25.3.13: cuius posteritatis ultimus Catalina **claras gloriarum adoreas** sempiternis maculis obumbravit. Other similar examples in Hagend.abund. (op.cit.I) p.197. "Normal" prose: variis victoriis. p. 131. 20-21
b Veget.r.m.3.5 (= Lang p.73) mentions under **vocalia signa**: victoria, **palma,** virtus, Deus nobiscum etc.; so that the word may be a fairly ordinary equivalent of **victoria.**

supplicatio. Here "unconditional surrender". For the meaning: written request to the emperor, cf. Souter p.406; Heum.-Seckel p.572. p. 131. 21

qui armis libertatem invaserant = who had violently seized their freedom. The constructions **c.accus. without in** seem to dominate after Livius (cf. Krebs Antib.2 p.781, with lit.). The above meaning also occur in Cic. and others. Cf.Suet.Caes.9.1: ut ... **dictaturam** Crassus **invaderet;** Iust. Phil.16.4.6: Sed Clearchus exsilio facinorosior redditus et dissensionem populi occasionem **invadendae tyrannidis** existimans. p. 131. 21-22

et reliqui eorum cum precibus. G Seyf. Sabbah Rolfe V reliqui ore cum. Gelenius' version seems reliable to me, although the repetition of **eorum** causes obscurity, as well as lack of style. By the first **eorum** the **Limigantes** are meant, as a whole, which is apparent from the relative clause **qui ... invaserant;** by the second **eorum** the same people, but then in particular those that were left (cf. ad 17.13.21, p.131.17*c*). By the **dominos** p.131.23, the **Sarmatae liberi** = **Argaragantes** are meant (cf. ad 17.12.12, p.126. 19-20*b*, *c*). The **fortiores** (p.131.23) are, of course, the Romans. p. 131. 22

ut: causally used. Cf. ad 17.8.3, p.119.27 - p.120.1*a*. p. 131. 23

inbelles. The emotional content of the word is found very clearly in Veget.r.m.4.7 (= Lang p.133): **Inbellis quoque aetas ac sexus** propter necessitatem victus portis frequenter exclusa est, ne penuria obprimeret **armatos,** a quibus moenia servabantur. Cf.et.Stat.Theb.edit. Mulder II p.335 sq. (ad v. 664 sq.) p. 131. 23

fortioribus visis = eis qui fortiores sibi visi sunt. A rather drastic ex- p. 131. 23

365

p. 131. 23 ample of **substantivisation** of the part.-perf.pass. (cf. ad 17.13.21, p. 131.17*a*).

p. 131. 23 **inclinavere cervices.** Cf.17.10.10, p.123.10: Romanae potentiae iugo subdidere colla iam domita.

XIII, 22
p. 131. 23-24 **accepta itaque publica fide.** Rolfe: "And so, having received a **safe-conduct**". Well-known t.t.: personal guarantee, safe-conduct.

p. 131. 24 **montium propugnaculo**: genit.explicat. The 2nd. subst. also in 24.4.10: et **proclivis planities** ... propugnaculorum firmitate muniebatur. For the t.t. cf. ad 16.4.2, p.74.26.

p. 131. 25 **convolavit**: to fly, - rush nearer. Also in judic.lit. (cf.Heum.-Seckel p.108). Several times in Cic. Sabbah: "et la plupart **volèrent se rassembler** aux abords du camp romain". But it is the question whether **con-** has this meaning here; because this prefix often gives an intensified meaning to composita of which it is a part. Thus also here, in my opinion.

p. 131. 25 **diffusa per spatia ampla camporum.** For the part. cf. ad 17.13.19, p.131.9. Here it is reflexive. For **spatia ampla** cf. ad 17.12.3, p.124.24-25*a*.

p. 131. 26 **opumque vilitate** = opibus vilibus. Cf. ad 15.4.4 (= III p.58).

p. 131. 26- p. 132. 1 *a* **quam eis celeritatis ratio furari permisit.** For the construction of the verba permittendi cf. ad 14.1.3 (= I p.58); ad 16.10.11, p.86.7 **(datur)**; ad 15.7.6 (= IV p.18): **praecipere**; ad 17.12.11, p.126.14*b* **(nom.c.infin.)**.
b For the **personificatio** cf. ad 17.2.1, p.107.13. For the personif. of celeritas cf. ad 16.12.56, p.100.21-22. at first sight **celeritatis ratio** seems somewhat obscure. The explanation is as follows, I believe: **c.r.** = **celeris fugae ratio** = the circumstances of their hasty flight.
c **furari** here (and more often) = to grab together hastily. Amm. does not inform us whether part of their possessions became the booty of the Romans. It was not, of course, in the Romans' best interests, after this final victory without bloodshed, to leave the **Picenses c.s.** without any possessions and thus bring them to despair, viz. those whom they forced to **solum vertere**.
Whether the military leaders had any further plans for these **Limigantes**,

is not mentioned by Amm. But it does not seem impossible to me. Cf.et ad 17.13.7, p.129.13.

XIII, 23

et qui ... putabantur: and of whom one would have thought, a well-known Latinism. Very striking is: (qui) **putabantur cogi** solum vertere. More "normal" would have been: et **quos** animas **amittere** potius quam **cogi** solum vĕrtere putăbant. But in that case we would have had the less usual clausula ⌣́⌣⌣⌣⌣́⌣ Whether this has been an unconscious reason, is hard to say. An even more remarkable example of the coupling of passive forms 20.4.6: (Caesar) quid de residuis **mitti praeceptis** agi deberet... For **animam amittere** cf. af 17.3.2, p.108.12-13a. p. 132. 1-2

solum vertere. Cf.Cic.Paradoxa 4.31: omnes scelerati atque impii ... quos leges exilio adfici volunt, **exules sunt, etiam si solum non mutarunt**; Sall. Jug.44.4; nam Albinus ... plerumque milites stativis castris habebat, nisi cum odor aut pabuli egestas **locum mutare** subegerat; Curt.3.7.11: Erat in exercitu regis Sisenes Perses. Quondam a praetore Aegypti missus ad Philippum, donisque et omni honore cultus **exsilium** (= foreign country) **patria sede mutaverat** (= exsilio patriam sedem mutaverat). The normal word for exchanging residences etc. is **mutare**; while **solum, terram vertere** is a t.t. of the agriculture: to turn, plough the land, the soil (with the plough, etc.). p. 132. 2

a **dum licentem amentiam libertatem existimarent. licens** = unrestrained, licentious, as often. When one does not want to be harnessed to the Roman foreign policy, one is very quickly attributed with **amentia licens**.
b **dum + conjunct.** Cf. ad 17.4.4, p.109.14; ad 17.10.8, p.122.23. p. 132. 2-3

a **parere imperiis et sedes alias suscĭpere sunt adsēnsi.** Note the alliterating **s**. Not accidental, in my opinion. Claus.III, which explains the placing of **sunt**.
b For **assensus sum** and **assensi** cf. Krebs Antib.1 p.207 (with lit.).
c **Infinitive constr.** with **assentior** are not very frequent. In Cic. de orat. 2.10(39); ad Att.14.19.1 (both quoted by Georges).
d for **parere** cf. ad 17.12.19, p.127.27.
e **suscipere = accipere**: late Latin. Cf. **susceptor** (ad 17.10.4, p.122.4a). Note the combination on p.122.4: **susceptorum** vilium more, securitates **accipiens** pro inlatis (while **acceptor** occurs: cf. Heum.-Seckel p.7 and Georges 1 p.54). p. 132. 3

p. 132. 4 *a* **nec bellis vexari nec mutari seditionibus possint** = possent. Cf.Ehrism. (op.cit.I) p.17 sq. "In enuntiatis consecutivis affirmativis **possit** per repraesentationem pro **posset** legitur; in **negativis** autem sententiis recte **imperfectum** ponitur, uno excepto loco (sc.17.13.23)". In order to restore the "aequabilitas", E. also wants to read **possent** here. But that is quite unnecessary, in my view. Examples of the first category 19.2.13; 21.12.8; 25.1.12; 19.1.5.
b for the **chiasm** cf. ad 16.8.2, p.81.1-4*b* 3.

p. 132. 5 **isdemque ... acceptis**: isdemque sc. **imperiis** or ex sententia: **condicionibus**. For **isdem** cf. ad 15.5.19,20 (= III p.103). For -**que** cf. ad 17.12.10, p.126.6*b*.

p. 132. 5 **ex sententia**: according to their feeling = with their approval. Cf. for **ex** ad 14.10.3 (= II p.100); ad 15.1.2 (= III p.8).

p. 132, 5 **ut credebatur.** Cf. ad 17.12.20, p.127.29.

p. 132. 5 **quievere**: they kept quiet. The verb also, among others, in 14.4.5; 21.1.12. Cf. ad 17.12.1, p.124.17.

p. 132. 5 **paulisper.** Cf. ad 17.12.12, p.126.24 = a little while. "Correctly" used, therefore.

p. 132. 5-6 **post ... erecti.** Participium instead of a verbum finitum. The sentence is linked **asyndetically** with the main clause **quievere paulisper** (translation: but after that ... they have etc.). For the **asyndeton** cf. ad 17.12.9, p.125. 25*b*.

p. 132. 6 *a* **feritate nativa.** Cf.20.4.6: cum hinc **bărbara fĕritas** inde iussorum ŭrguet (V) auctŏritas (twice the same claus.II and homoioteleuton); 29.1.10: **prodigiosa feritas** (sc.Valentis) in modum ardentissimae facis fusius vagabatur (alliteration!).
b cf.24.1.13: (Iulianus) licentiores militum per longinqua discursus **affabilitate nativa** prohibendo vel minis (= innate affability).

p. 132. 6 *a* **in exitiale scelus erecti.** Cf.Verg.Aen.6.511 sq.:
sed me fata mea et scelus exitiale Lacaenae
his mersere malis; illa haec monimenta reliquit.
(cf. Fletcher, Rev. de Philol.LXIII. 1937).
b **erecti.** Cf. ad 17.10.8, p.122.21; ad 17.4.6, p.110.2.

ut congruo docebitur textu. For the adj. cf. ad 16.12.12, p.92.27*b*. For textus cf. ad 17.4.17, p.112.1*b*. For the **formulary expression** cf. ad 17.7.14, p.119.7*a*.

XIII, 24

a **hoc rerum prospero currente successu.** In connection with the ending -e of the participium this must be an **ablat.absol.** Literal translation: because this (favourable) course of events **ended succesfully** (so that the adject. is used predicatively). **Prospero** is somewhat abundant. Similar expressions e.g. 16.12.62: Quibus ita favore superni numinis **terminatis;** 16.12.67: His tot ac talibus **prospero** peractis **eventu** (alliteration); 17.9.1: cunctis igitur ex voto **currentibus** (cf. ad 17.9.1, p.120.12); 17.10.5: quod ... conpleto (doubtful version); 17.13.1: his (ut narratum est) **secundo** finitis **eventu;** 16.11.15: et ille tamquam expeditione **eventu prospero terminata.** ... ad comitatum ... revertit; 16.6.1: haec per eum annum spe dubia **eventu** tamen **secundo** ... agebantur; 18.3.1: haec dum in Galliis caelestis corrigit cura; 24.2.9: Quo negotio itidem **gloriose** perfecto; 24. 4.31: post quae tam **gloriosa;** 24.6.4: proinde **cunctis** ex sententia **terminatis;** 27.2.4: hoc **prospero** rerum **effectu;** 28.5.8: post haec ita **prospere** consummata; etc. Cf.et. ad 17.13.1, p.128.11*b*.
b for **prospero** cf. ad 16.4.5, p.75.10*b*.
c for **successus** cf. ad 17.5.8, p.114.22-24*c*.

Illyrico. Cf.II p.32.

a **tutela ... competens. Tutela** here with its basic meaning: protection = praesidium. Cf.Veget.r.m.3.10 (= Lang p.90): Dux ergo ... cuius fidei atque virtuti possessorum fortunae, **tutela urbium,** salus militum ... creditur; ibid.4.31 (= Lang p.150): Apud Misenum igitur et Ravennam singulae legiones cum classibus stabant, ne longius a **tutela urbis** abscederent. **Tutela** occurs with a very special meaning 14.11.25: (Nemesis = Adrastia) vel, ut definiunt alii, **substantialis tutela** generali potentia partilibus praesidens fatis.
b **Competens:** fitting, appropriate. Late Latin = iustus, idoneus, verus, legitimus etc. Cf.Heum.-Seckel p.83; Souter p.65. The late Latin adverb 31.12.2: occursum est huic conatui **competenter** (= with appropriate measures). Cf.et. Krebs Antib.1 p.311 (with lit.).

gemina ... ratione = duplici ratione = duobus modis. For there are 2 different ways in which the **tutela Illyrici** is achieved, not one with 2 facets. A good example of this artificial use of **geminus** Cod.Iust.1.3.4: Quod si clandestinis artibus putaverint (sc. officiales rationales) inrependum (sc. in ecclesiam), **duas** concedant liberis, aut, si proles defuerit, propinquis e propria substantia (= fortune) **portiones** tertiam sibimet retenturi: si vero propinquorum necessitudo defuerit, **geminae** (= duae) **portiones** officiis (= offices) in quibus militant (= are at work, fulfil their offices) relinquantur, portione tertia tantummodo retenta. Cf.18.2.9: gemina ... ratione; 19.11.2: **gemina consideratione** alacrior; 19.12.8: Scythopolis, **gemina ratione** visa magis omnibus oportuna; 25.7.12: quod ratione gemina cogitatum est.

p. 132. 8 **ratiŏne firmăta.** The simplex metri causa: claus.I.

p. 132. 8-9 **cuius negotii duplicem magnitudinem imperator adgressus utramque perfecit.** Another example of the way in which Amm. and his contemporaries express concrete matters abstractly, sometimes at the expense of clarity. = et eius **tutelae firmandae laborem,** magnum et duplicem, imperator adgressus **perfecit.** Grammatically **utramque** belongs to **magnitudinem,** but logically to **duplicem**: the twofold task of the strengthening of the protection of Illyricum. This twofold duty of the emperor is described in the next 2 sentences of § 24.

p. 132. 9-11 *a* **infidis ... exules populos (licet mobilitate suppares) acturos tamen paulo verecundius ... conlocavit.** Cl.Seyf. sine lac. Sabbah. **suppares** Haupt Cl. Seyf. Sabbah. **populus** V. populos E A G. Sabbah translates: "il parvint à ramener et à rétablir dans les résidences de leurs aïeux les peuples exilés, qui, **tout en ressemblant par leur versatilité aux infidèles,** devaient montrer cependant un peu plus de retenue". By the **populi** are meant the tribes of the **Sarmatae liberi** (= **Argaragantes**), (for **populi** cf. ad 17.12.21, p.128.6). The **sedes avitae** are the Banate (cf. ad 17.12.12, p.126.19-20*b*). The **Argaragantes** are **exules,** because they had been driven from their homeland by the **Limigantes.** But it seems to me to be a tour de force, even for Amm., to link **infidis** with **suppares.** The first part of the sentence is corrupt and a gap is very likely here.

b The adject. substantivically also in Plaut.Mil.1015: Mi. quo argumento? Pa. **Infidos celas:** ego sum tibi firme fidus.

c **exules populos.** Cf.Claud.8.73 sq. (de IV cons.Honor.):
  Per varium **gemini** scelus erupere tyranni (= duo)
  Tractibus occiduis. hunc (Maximum) saeva Britannia fudit;
  Hunc (Eugenium) sibi **Germanus** famulum delegerat **exul** (Arbogastes).

Opt.Milev.1.12 (= Ziwsa p.14): Haeretici vero **veritatis exules,** sani et verissimi symboli desertores (= alienati a). The word occurs several times in **Claud.,** not in Arn.adv.nat. or Veget.r.m.
For the adj. **exularis** cf. ad 14.5.1 (= I p.83); ad 14.5.3 (= I p.126); 15.3.2.
d **mobilitate** = instability (X **constantia**), changeability. Cf.Cic.Phil. 7.3(9): Quid est inconstantia, **mobilitate,** levitate cum singulis hominibus, tum vero universo senatui turpius?; Sall.Iug.88.6: **mobilitate** ingeni; Tac. Hist.5.8: **mobilitate** vulgi; etc.
e **suppares.** The adj. which also among others occurs in **Cic.** and **Vell.,** and others, must be considered in Amm. to be an archaic flower of speech. The adj., which is far from general, does not occur in the judic.lit. or Claud.Veget.r.m.Opt.Milev.Arn.adv.nat.
f **acturos tamen paulo verecundius:** of whom one might expect that in future they would conduct themselves with more respect (towards the Romans) or: more modestly (in relation to the Romans). = quos sperabant tamen paulo verecundius acturos esse or: qui possent (conj.orat.obl.) t.p.v. agere. **acturos - verecundius** replaces a relative clause in the potentialis. **verecundius** is another typical example of the attitude of the Romans towards barbarians. For these are by nature immodest and insolent. Cf. Dig.1.12. 1.8: si **verecunde** expostulent: said of **slaves** who utter complaints about their **domini** to the **praefectus urbi.** Cf.et. ad 16.12.67, p.102.17*a*.
g **reductos:** the partic. expresses the main point. Cf. ad 17.3.5, p.108.20*a*.
e **avitis.** The adj. is often linked with agri, bona, possessiones, etc. Cf. Claud.3.190 sq. (= In Ruf.I): ... metuenda colonis//fertilitas. Laribus pellit (sc.Rufinus), detrudit **avitis//Finibus,** aut aufert vivis, aut occupat heres.

isdemque. Cf. ad p.132.5 (13.23). p. 132. 11

a **ad gratiae cumulum.** Sabbah: "et pour mettre un comble à **leur grati-** p. 132. 11 tude". This translation is incorrect. Better Seyf.: "Um **seine Gnade** voll zu machen". For **gratia** is here: a mark of one's favour, benevolence, **mercy.** For the last meaning cf.Min.Fel.27.7; Aug.Conf.6.3.4; Heum.-Seckel p.231 s.v.**2;** Souter p.165.
b The 2nd substant. often with the above meaning in **Cic.** Cf. ad Att. 16.3.3: Sed eas litteras Curium mihi spero redditurum: qui quidem, etsi per se est amabilis a meque diligitur, **tamen accedit magnus cumulus commendationis tuae.**
ibid.1.16.5: Iam vero ... etiam noctes certarum mulierum atque adules-

371

centulorum nobilium introductiones nonnullis iudicibus **pro mercedis cumulo** fuerunt; ad fam.16.21.1: ... tum vero iucundissimae tuae litterae **cumulum mihi gaudii** attulerunt; Ovid.Metam.11.205 sq.:
   Stabat opus: pretium rex infitiatur, et addit,
   Perfidiae cumulum, falsis periuria verbis.

p. 132. 11 **ignobilem.** Cf.15.5.28: sub **disceptatione ignobili** (= dishonourable, shameful); 22.8.41: insula, quam incolunt **Sindi ignobiles** (= little known).

p. 132. 11 **quĕmpiam rĕgem:** Claus.I. Cf.Hofm.-Leum.p.484,82c: "Es scheint schon zu Plautus' Zeit ein Archaismus gewesen zu sein, **wie sein häufiges Vorkommen am Versschlusz** und das Fehlen eines Plurals (erst seit Cic. und selten) schlieszen läszt; in der Volkssprache war es jedenfalls schon zu Ciceros Zeit ausgestorben, es fehlt z.B. bei Trogus. Petron und im Spätlat. bei Filastr. u.a.". The pronomen has probably found its way into the late Latin archaic lit. via **Cic.**

p. 132. 12 **regalem.** Cf. ad 17.12.9, p.125.26 and 17.12.20: **Zizaim regem isdem praefecit.**

p. 132. 13 **bonis animi corporisque praestantem.** Cf.17.12.20: conspicuae fortunae (sc.regis) tum insignibus aptum profecto ... et fidelem.

XIII, 25

p. 132. 13 **tali textu recte factorum.** Cf.16.1.1: fatorum ordine contexto versante; 17.5.13: gestarum rerum ordines. Note the alliterating **t.** For **textus** cf. ad 17.4.17, p.112.1*b* = series.
For **factorum** cf. ad 17.3.2, p.108.12*a*.

p. 132. 14 **iam metuente sublimior,** For the **substantivisation** of the **part.praes.** cf. ad 17.12.12, p.126.24. Translation: C. already beyond all fear. For the **adject.** cf. ad 16.12.24, p.95.4-5*b*.

p. 132. 14 **militarique consensu.** Cf.Liv.5.47.7: Luce orta vocatis classico ad concilium militibus ad tribunos, cum et **recte** et perperam **facto** pretium deberetur, Manlius primum ob virtutem laudatus donatusque non ab tribunis solum militum, sed **consensu** etiam **militari**; ibid.31.2.10: ceteri in castra metu compulsi, inde sine certo duce **consensu militari** proxima nocte, relicta magna parte rerum suarum, ad consulem per saltus prope invios pervenere; Fletcher, Rev. de philol. LXIII. 1937.

secundo Sarmaticus appellatus. Sarmaticus Max.335. Sarm.Max.II 358.   p. 132. 14-15
For further titles of Constantius II (332-361) cf. Sandys-Campbell, Lat. Epigr.², 1927, p.255; Cagnat, Cours d'épigr.lat.³, 1898, p.219.

a   **ex vocabulo subactorum.** For **ex** cf. ad 17.13.19, p.131.10; and also II   p. 132. 15
p.100; III p.8; III p.72; 17.12.14, p.127.2-3*c;* I p.94.
b   for the 2nd substant. cf. ad 17.13.21, p.131.17.

for **vocabulum** cf. ad 17.4.11, p.110.15-16.   p. 132. 15

iamque discessurus. For the **part.fut.** cf. ad 17.12.9, p.125.24*a*.   p. 132. 15

convocatis ... potestatum. Cf.15.8.4 (IV p.30 sq.); Sabbah Amm. II p.186,   p. 132. 16-17
note 112. Though the names **cohortes, centuriae** and **manipuli** sound very familiar, they mean something quite different at this time, after the enormous changes in the organisation of the army by **Diocletianus** and **Constantinus I** and their successors. Our exact knowledge is limited, for mirabile dictu, a military author like **Vegetius** is archaising as often as **Amm.** a professional soldier. Cf. Grosse Mil. (op.cit.I) p.23 sq., particularly p.35 sq.; Stein Spätröm.Gesch. (op.cit.I) p.106 sq (with lit.); p.186 sq. (with lit.); p.362 sq. (with lit.); ad 14.2. 12 (= I p.115.).

tribunali insistens. Thus Kellerb.Nov.Cl.Seyf.Rolfe. **tribunal** V Sabbah   p. 132. 16
E A G. There can be no objection, in my view, against the accusat.constr. Cf.Apul.Metam.2.21.5: (Senex) **Insistebat lapidem** claraque voce praedicabat, siqui mortuum servare vellet, de pretio liceretur.

a   **signisque ambitus et aquilis.** For **signa** and **aquilae** cf. ad 15.5.16 (=   p. 132. 17
III p.96 sq.).
b   **ambitus.** Somewhat far-fetched for: **circumdatus.** Cf.Verg.Aen.10.243; Ovid.Metam.1.36 sq.:
   Tum freta diffundi rapidisque tumescere ventis
   Iussit et **ambitae circumdare litora terrae.**
Tac.Ann.1.68; Curt.Ruf.4.2.9; 4.7.16; etc. For the **substant.ambitus** cf. ad 16.2.1, p.72.12*b*. Cf.et.Claud.22.365 sq. (de laud.Stil.II):
   Tunc habiles armis **humeros Dea vestibus ambit**
   Romuleis (a Verg. reminiscence?).
Thus several times in **Claud.**

p. 132. 17 **multiplicium potestatum.** Potestates = **Potentiores:** cf. ad 16.8.11, p.83.4*b;* Heum.-Seckel p.443, 1*a* (with this meaning fairly often in legal lit.): authorities, persons vested with power. Cf.et. ad 14.10.10 (= II p.107).

p. 132. 17 **his.** Cf.15.8.5; 21.5.1; 21.13.9; Pauw p.39, note 15. It seems plausible what P. says, viz. that Amm.'s speeches are neither his own creation, nor do they give the literal content. He aims at a **reliable rendering of the general tenor** of what was really said, but **language and style are Ammianus' own work.**

p. 132. 18 **adlocutus est:** t.t. For the **adlocutio** cf. ad 16.12.29, p.95.23-24*e;* **Grosse Mil.** (op.cit.I) p.249; **D.A. Pauw, Character sketches in Amm.Marc.** (Dutch) (Thesis, Leiden 1972), p.37 sq. (with lit.).

p. 132. 18 **ore omnium favorabilis:** amidst general applause (as usual). Cf.23.5-16: talia ore sereno disseruit, **favorabilis** studio concordi cunctorum.

p. 132. 18 The adj. also 26.7.3; 26.10.5. Post-class. = ± **gratiosus.** (the act. meaning: granting favours, etc. is rare). Cf.et. Krebs Antib.1 p.583. (with lit.). The adj. does not occur in Veget.r.m.Claud.Arn.adv.nat.Opt.Milev. though it is used in judic.lit.

p. 132. 18 **ut solebat.** Cf. ad 17.12.20, p.127.29.

XIII, 26

p. 132. 19 For the speeches in Amm. cf. et. **C.P.T.Naudé,** A.M. in the light of the antique historiography (in Afrikaans) (op. cit.XVI) p.99 sq. (with lit.). When reading this, one should pay attention to "the background of the theory", certainly in my opinion.
One should also bear in mind that an author of Antiquity should be read aloud, and especially his speeches. The literary fashions in style of one's own time are certainly not a final criterium when judging, for instance, the now following prose.

p. 132. 19 Cf.25.3.17: nec me gestorum paenitet aut gravis flagitii **recordatio** stringit; ad 17.5.5, p.114.10-11. For the **personificatio** cf. Blomgren (op.cit.II) p.90.

p. 132. 19 **rerum gloriose gestarum.** Cf. ad 17.12.20, p.128.1.

iucunditate. Cf. ad 17.1.2, p.104.9-10*d*. p. 132. 19

ad modum verecundiae. Cf. ad 17.13.24, p.132.9-11*f.* = verecunde. vere- p. 132. 20
cŭndiae replicăre: claus.III. (no synizesis).

replicare. Cf. ad 16.12.3, p.91.13*c;* ad 16.12.34, p.96.17. p. 132. 20

a **divinitus delata sorte vincendi.** Cf.Verg.Aen.9.18 sq.: Iri, decus caeli, p. 132. 20-21
quis te mihi nubibus actam//**Detulit** in terras? This meaning **deferre** has
more often: to bring down to earth from heaven. Here also: literally
therefore.
b Cf. **caelitus:** 22.9.7; 25.2.5; Souter p.34 (late Latin). In Veget.r.m.2.20
(= Lang p.54): Illud vero ab antiquis **divinitus institutum est,** ut ex donativo, quod milites consecuntur, dimidia pars sequestraretur apud signa
(a fine example of the deification of institutions of Antiquity). The adverbium does not occur in Claud.Opt.Milev.Arn.adv.nat. It is not impossible
that we have here, with **this** meaning, (= by the will of God, -gods) a
Cic. reminiscence.

proelia ... pugnarum. Alliteration. The two substant. do not differ in p. 132. 21-22
meaning.

correximus: to have "corrected", set things to rights, restored to the old p. 132. 21
condition. Cf.16.12.12: et statum nutantium rerum ... aliquotiens divina
remedia **repararunt.**

fervore. Cf.18.2.3: ante **proeliorum fervorem;** 17.13.13: **fervore certaminum.** p. 132. 21

Romanae rei fidissimi defensores. Note the alliterating **r** and **f.** For **defen-** p. 132. 22
sor cf. ad 16.12.15, p.93.13*b.* For **Rom.rei** cf. ad 16.11.7, p.89.10.

quid enim tam pulchrum tamque posteritatis memoriae iusta ratione p. 132. 22-23
mandandum. A sentence with alliteration, **homoioteleuton** (cf. ad 15.10.4 =
IV p.56) and **anaphora** (cf. Blomgren, op.cit.II, p.21, 44, 45; Hagend.,
Eranos 22.4. 1924, p.190). Other examples of **anaphora:** 14.4.3; 17.13.32;
18.2.1 and Hagend.ibid.

posteritatis memoriae, Cf.Caes.b.c.1.13.1: proinde habeat **rationem** p. 132. 23
posteritatis et periculi sui; Cic.Phil.2.22(54): O miserum te, si intelligis!
Miseriorem, si non intelligis, hoc **litteris mandari,** hoc **memoriae prodi,**

375

huius rei ne **posteritatem** quidem omnium saeculorum unquam **immemorem fore** ... (this quotation must have been known to Amm.); Ovid. ex Pont.3.2.29 sq.:

... et illa meae superabit tempora vitae,
Si tamen a **memori posteritate** legar.

The **memoria posteritatis** is a heathen theme rather than a Christian one and not very suitable in the mouth of a "Christian" emperor. Cf.et.14.6.17, p.16.15-16; 17.4.9.

p. 132. 24 *a* **strenue factis.** For the adject.cf. ad 16.12.24, p.95.6; ad 16.12.51, p.99.23*b*.

b Cf.Plaut.Bacch.444 sq.:
... "eho senex minimi preti,
ne attigas puerum istac caussa, quando **fecit strenue**".

Sall.Jug.22.3: ceterum, quo plura bene atque **strenue fecisset** ... ; Gell. 15.4: tum quia ... deinceps civili bello mandata sibi pleraque impigre et **strenue fecisset**; Veget.r.m.2.5 (= Lang p.39): Iurant autem milites omnia se **strenue facturos**, quae praeceperit imperator (the adv. only occurs once, in this connection, in Veget.).

c Cf. ad 17.13.25, p.132.13 **(recte factorum).**

p. 132. 24 **ductor.** Cf. ad 16.2.11, p.73.25; ad 14.2.17 (= I p.76); ad 16.12.18, p.94.6.

p. 132. 24 **prudenter consultis** = wise decisions. Cf. ad 16.12.10, p.92.15; 17.13.7, p.129.12; ad 14.11.3 (= II p.116): **consulto consilio;** ad 17.9.2, p.120.16: **consilium prudens,**

p. 132. 24 **exultet.** Cf. ad 16.12.37, p.97.12*a*, Cic.Tusc.4.6(13). The adverbium **exultanter** 23.5.8 (in the comparat.); cf.Plin.Ep.3.18.10. Cf.et. ad 17.1.14, p.107.4-5*a*.

XIII, 27

p. 132. 24-25 **persultabat Illyricum furor hostilis.** For the verb cf. ad 16.12.6, p.91.22-23. For the **personificatio** cf. ad 17.2.1, p.107.13. Blomgren p.83. For **furor** ad 16.12.31, p.96.6; ad 12.46, p.99.1. For **Illyricum** cf. II p.32. **hostilis** = hostium: very frequent **(hostilis = hostis substant.:** 15.8.13; 24.1.16). Cf. et. ad 17.13.12, p.130.6*b*.

p. 132. 25 **absentiam nostram** = nos absentes. For the **abstractum pro concreto** cf. ad 17.7.10, p.118.1-2.

inanitate tumenti. Cf. ad 15.4.9: strictis mucronibus discurrebant, frendendo **minas tumidas intentantes.** For the partic. cf. ad 17.10.10, p.123.9*a*. The subst. = stupid, vain conceit. Cf.Gell.13.8.2: non quae libri tantum ac magistri per quasdam **inanitates verborum** et imaginum, tamquam in mimo aut somnio, dictitaverint; Cic.Tusc.3.2(3): **in summa inanitate versatur,** consectaturque nullam eminentem effigiem, sed adumbratam imaginem gloriae. With the meaning: vanity = insignificance, futility: 26.2.2: cumque multorum taedio, quos **votorum inanitas** cruciabat, tandem finita nocte lux advenisset ... Cf.et.Arn.adv.nat.7.3 (= Reiffersch. p.239): quidquid enim geritur, debet habere causam sui neque ita esse ab ratione seiunctum, ut in operibus geratur **cassis et in vacuis ludat inanitatis erroribus** (very much abundant!). **in** is here = **through, by** (cf. ad 17.4.11, p. 110.14-15*a*). The adv. **inaniter:** 16.4.2 (cf.Cic.Tusc.4.6(13); Gell. 9.11.6 (?)). p. 132. 25

I do not share the objections of Fletcher, Class.Quart. 24(1930) p.194. He wants to replace **leviores iacturas** by **saeviores** (cf.Tac.Ann.2.26.3: gravia et **saeva** damna). Like Seyf. and Sabbah, I adhere to the version as given in the manuscripts. I also consider the version **qua,** for **quae** of Lindenb., and accepted by Cl., Rolfe, Seyf. and Sabbah, to be superfluous, however attractive the "improvement" may be. Finally I would like to keep **vetari** by V, instead of accepting the conjecture of Corn. **vitari,** as is done by Cl. Rolfe and Seyf. (Sabbah also **vetari**). Cf.Comm. ad 11. p. 132. 24-
p. 133. 7

Italos. For Amm. the **Itali** will have been the inhabitants of the **dioecesis Italia,** which was larger than what we think of as Italy. p. 132. 26

Cf. ad 14.7.9 (= II p.31 sq.). Thus he will mean by **Galli** the inhabitants of **Septem Provinciae.** Cf. ad 14.11.1-18 (= IV p.57 sq.). But this is not absolutely certain. Cf.et. ad 14.7.9 (= II p.32), in fine. p. 132. 26

dum ... tueremur. Cf. ad 17.13.23, p.132.2-3*b*. p. 132. 26

discursibus. Cf. ad 16.12.37, p.97.9; 17.13.28, p.133.14: in the same meaning as here. p. 132. 26

extima limitum = extimos limites. Cf. ad 14.3.4 (= I p.81).Cf.20.10.2: extima Galliarum; Hist.Aug.Tyr.XXX 12.13: in Thraciarum extimis; Lucr.4.647: extima membrorum; etc. Old-fashioned and solemn for p. 132. 26-27 the more ordinary **extremus.** Often in late Latin. Cf. Neue-Wagener[3] (op.cit.I) II p.192 sq. This superlat. does not occur in Claud.Veget.r.m. Opt.Milev.Arn.adv.nat.

p. 132. 27 **nunc ... aliquotiens.** Amm. favours non-corresponding concepts, such as **partim ... partim, alii ... alii** etc. Cf. ad 16.2.6, p.73.5*b*. Cf.16.9.1: non-numquam ... aliquotiens ... interdum; ad 17.8.5, p.120.5-7.

p. 132.27 *a* **cavatis roboribus.** Cf.Caes.b.g.3.13.3: **naves totae factae ex robore** ad quamvis vim et contumeliam perferendam; Cic.Acad.pr.2.31(100): (Sapiens) non enim est e saxo sculptus aut **e robore dolatus...** Robur is used of any kind of hard wood and is often = **truncus.** In Verg.Aen.2.230 **sacrum robur** is: the wooden horse.
b Cf.Liv.21.26.8: novasque (sc. **lintres**) alias primum Galli inchoantes **cavabant ex singulis arboribus:** deinde et ipsi milites, simul copia materiae simul facilitate operis inducti, **alveos informes** ... raptim faciebant.

p. 132. 27 **peragrans.** Cf.22.8.4: et Abydon, unde iunctis pontibus Xerxes **maria pedibus peragravit.** Cf.Cic. de fin.2.34(112): non ut illum (sc.Xerxem) **maria pedibus peragrantem;** Michael (op.cit.I) p.32.

p. 132. 28 **non ... nec ... aut.** Cf. ad p.132.27 before this passage. For **neque ... aut** cf.Hofm.-Leum.p.674, 247*b*. One should also remember that here **aut** does not exclude, but enumerates (= **et**), as happens frequently in vulgar Latin. Cf.Hofm.-Leum. ibid. **c** (with lit. and places). Cf.et.Thes.II 1568, 4 sq.

p. 132. 28 **congressibus.** Cf.29.6.15: Sarmatas Liberos ... aliquotiens expulit et afflixit **congressibus densis** attritos ...; ad 16.5.9, p.76.24.

p. 132. 28 **fretus.** Cf. ad 16.12.13, p.93.2-3*f*. In this § the personification is carried to great lengths.

p. 132. 28 **latrociniis.** Cf.17.12.2: (Sarmatas et Quados) ... quibus ad **latrocinia** magis quam **aperto** habilibus **Marti** hastae sunt longiores; Sall.Iug.97.5: pugna **latrocinio** magis quam **proelio** similis fieri; Flor.3.2.4: durum atque velox genus ex occasione magis **latrocinia** quam **bella** faciebat; Liv.21.35.2: inde montani pauciores iam, et **latrocinii** magis quam **belli** more, concursabant (and thus more often in **Liv.**; cf.comm.Drakenb.VI p.176, ad 21.

35.2). The subst. does not occur in Claud.Veget.r.m.Opt.Milev.Arn.adv. nat. Cf.et. ad 16.9.1, p.83.14.

astu et ludificandi varietate. Similarly 31.12.9. For the subst. cf. ad 15.5.5 (= III p.80). **Lud.var.** = ludificationibus variis. The gerundium can be of **ludificare** or of **ludificari**. Cf.Krebs Antib.2 p.38 (with lit.). Neither verb occurs in Claud.Veget.r.m.Arn.adv.nat.Opt.Milev., though **ludificare** is found in judic.lit. p. 133. 1

a **iam inde ab instituta gente** = iam inde ab incunabulis huius gentis. But the emperor (or the author) expresses himself inaccurately. There are at least 2 peoples involved here: the **Sarmats** and the **Quads.** Thus in my view it should have been: **harum gentium.**
For **gens** (= **natio;** cf. ad 16.12.26, p.95.14). cf. ad 16.12.65, p.102.11; ad 16.10.16, p.87.9; ad 15.5.6 (= III p.81).
b **instituere** is here used very curiously indeed: Amm. probably means: creation, formation: i.e.: from the moment when these **gentes** could be recognised as such, viz. as nations with their own characteristics, etc. One can **instituere** civitatem, leges, etc., but **not populum, gentem, nationem.** p. 133. 1

formidatus. Cf. ad 17.12.9, p.125.24. p. 133. 2

a **quae longius disparati ... tulimus** = and, because we were rather far away, we have endured the circumstances (tolerated), **which could be borne (by us),** because we hoped that because of the successful activities of our generals **slighter losses** (= even if they were slight losses) could be brought to a halt. The relative clause **quae ferri poterant** is explained by the causal subordinate clause **leviores ... sperantes.**
b **disparati.** Cf.24.1.3: ut decimo paene lapide postremi **dispararentur** a signiferis primis; 24.2.3: unde amne transito miliario septimo disparata; 15.11.18: Ad gradus, ab Arelate octavo decimo ferme lapide **disparatum;** 20.3.7: sustinet luna defectum, cum ... ab eius (sc.solis) orbe centum octoginta partibus ... **disparatur;** ad 16.12.70, p.103.6c. Not in Arn.adv. nat.Opt.Milev. p. 133. 2-3

iacturas. Cf. ad 17.10.7, p.122.18. The subst. also occurs in Claud.Opt. Milev; Not in Veget.r.m.Arn.adv.nat. p. 133. 3

efficacia. Cf. ad 14.8.5 (= II p.67); ad 16.12.25, p.95.8*a*. p. 133. 3

p. 133. 3 **vitari posse.** "Construction normal". **Vetari:** there are many examples in lit., where **vetare** = to obstruct, prevent; e.g. Horat.Sat.1.10.56:
> quid **vetat** et nosmet Lucili scripta legentis
> quaerere num ... negarit;

Ovid.Am.3.7.35:
> Quid **vetat** et nervos magicas torpere per artes?

(Cf.et.ibid.Fasti 1.295); Tac.Ann.3.26; et ubi nihil contra morem cuperent, nihil per metum **vetabantur;** Stat.Theb.12.558:
> **Quos vetat igne** Creon Stygiaeque a limine portae;

S.Aur.Vict.Caes.33.34: Quia primus ipse, metu socordiae suae, ne imperium ad optimos nobilium transferretur, **Senatum militiā vetuit,** etiam adire exercitum (in the last two examples = to keep away from).

XIII, 28

p. 133. 3-5 **ubi ... erepsit.** Cf. ad 14.2.20 (= I p.78). And for **conj.iterat** ad 14.2.7 (= I p.70).

p. 133. 5 **erepsit.** The verb among others, in Plaut.Varro Horat.Suet.Sen.Juven. Stat. Cf.Stat.Silv.2.2.30:
> Inde per obliquas **erepit** porticus arces,
> urbis opus, longoque domat saxa aspera dorso.

(c.annot.Vollmer p.343). Varro r.r.3.15.1: (Glirarium) ... tota levi lapide aut tectorio intrinsecus incrustatur, ne ex ea **erepere** possit (sc.glis); Horat. Sat.1.5.77 sq.:
> incipit ex illo montis Apulia notos
> ostentare mihi, quos torret Atabulus et quos
> nunquam **erepsemus,** nisi nos vicina Trivici
> villa recepisset lacrimoso non sine fumo.

p. 133. 4 **scandens in maius.** Cf. ad 16.4.1, p.74.22; Fesser p.6 sq. Simplex pro composito (cf. ad 16.5.6, p.76.12).

p. 133. 4 **funestas ... clades.** Cf. ad 17.7.5, p.117.5 **(funereus).**

p. 133. 4-5 **clades erĕpsit et crĕbras:** hyperbaton (cf. ad 17.1.6, p.105.21a). Claus.I.

p. 133. 5-6 **communitis ... post terga.** Of the 3 ablativi absoluti the first 2 are linked by **-que.** The 3rd is joined **asyndetically** (for the **asyndeton** cf. Blomgren, op.cit.II, p.21 sq.), and has the value of a consecutive subordinate clause: so that we left nothing behind, which might frighten us.

380

communitis. Cf.17.1.12: quod castra ... apparatu deberent välido com-   p. 133. 5
munīri (claus.III).

aditibus. Cf.16.11.4: clausis **aditibus** repercussi; 17.4.2: portarum centum   p. 133. 5
quondam **aditibus** celebrem; 14.2.18: obseratis undique portarum **aditibus.**
Also (sing.): 24.2.15; 29.6.16. For the t.t. cf. ad 15.5.27 (= III p.112).
Cf.et. ad 17.4.2, p.109.7-8.

Raeticis. Cf. ad 15.4.1 (= III p.54); ad 14.7.9 (= II p.31).   p. 133. 5

tutelaque pervigili. For the adj. cf. ad 14.8.13 (= II p.80). For **tutela** cf.   p. 133. 5
ad 17.13.24, p.132.7*a*.

a **Galliarum securitate fundata.** For **Galliae** cf. ad 15.11.1-18 (= IV p.57   p. 133. 6
sq.); ad 17.13.27, p.132.26 **(Gallos).**
b Cf.Dig.22.1.33: si non parient (sc.debitores usuras) prospicere **rei
publicae securitati** debet praeses provinciae, dummodo non acerbum se
exactorem nec contumeliosum praebeat; ibid.39.1.5.11: cum **publicae**
salutis et **securitatis** intersit et cloacas et rivos purgari (both quotations
are from Ulpianus). For the t.t. cf. ad 17.10.4, p.122.4*a;* Heum.-Seckel
p.531 (s.v.) *c.*

a **terrore:** here it means, as so often, something that causes fright, panic.   p. 133. 6
b Cf.21.7.1: in id flexus est (Constantius) ut finito propiore bello (sc.
cum Parthis gesto) vel certe mollito, **nullo pos terga relicto quem formidaret** Illyriis percursis et Italia (ut rebatur) Iulianum ... caperet. **Terga**
also used 16.2.10; 19.11.17; 30.1.15. Cf.Hagend.St.Amm. (op.cit.I) p.83
(with lit.): "Constat autem **terga,** ubi ad **nomen collectivum** spectat, iam
a scriptoribus optimae Latinitatis ac summo quidem iure poni" (and in
a certain sense **Caesar, rex Persarum, Papa** and **Constantius** are collectiva).
For the pluralis poet. **terga** cf.18.8.5; 19.6.9; 22.15.16(?); ad 15.7.4 (= IV
p.14); Hagend.ibid.p.82. In this place not metri causa.

Pannonias. Cf. ad 17.12.1, p.124.19; ad 16.10.20, p.88.4-5.   p. 133. 7

(si) placu(er)it numini sempiterno. Btl.Cl.Seyf.Rolfe. **V placuit** G ut pla-   p. 133. 7
cuit. V's version is followed by Sabbah. When the **last** version is maintained **placuit numini semperiterno** is an intermediary sentence, with the
meaning: and it has ⟨as has become evident⟩ pleased the eternal deity.
This can well be defended. But the combination of **part.fut.** with sentences

beginning with si, is quite frequent in Amm., so that it may be possible that si is omitted by the copyist. **Placuit** then does not need to be changed. The train of thought of Const. is in orat. recta as follows: **si placuit** (= fut. exact.) numini sempiterno labentia firmabimus. There can be no objection against this, at any rate in late Latin.

p. 133. 7 **labentia firmaturi.** Cf.Sen. de ben.6.31.9: praeterea, quae una rebus salus est, occurrere ad primos rerum impetus et inclinatis opem ferre non poteris, nec fulcire ac **firmare labentia;** Fletcher, Rev.de philol.LXIII, 1937, p.387.
For the **part.neutr.plur.** cf. ad 17.3.2, p.108.12*a* and ad 17.4.1, p.109.4*a*.

p. 133. 7-8 **cunctisque.** see above. For **cunctus** cf. ad 17.3.6, p.109.2.

p. 133. 8 **parătis ut nŏstis:** Claus.I. For these abbreviated verb forms cf.Hofm.- Leum.p.335,244. Nosti similarly in claus. Veget.r.m.3.20 (= Lang p.108): Tuam autem aliam exercitus partem, in qua deteriores bellatores habĕre te nŏsti (claus.I) ... separa. Veget. also has the abbreviated forms **nosse** and **norunt.** Nosse and nosti also occur in Opt.Milev. and **nosse** also in Claud. Cf.et. ad 16.12.69, p.102.23-24*c*. Cf.et.17.13.1, p.128.13: et nefăria perpetrăsse (claus.III); 17.13.5, p.129.4-5: praesĕntiam formidăsse (claus. III); 14.1.8, p.3.8: ăctibus factităsse (claus.III); 14.5.5, p.11.1: prĭncipes factitărunt (claus.III); 14.6.10, p.14.12-13: cuncta superăsse virtŭte (claus.I); 14.7.18, p.22.6: tribunos fabricărum insimulăsset (claus.III); 14.9.4, p.26.20: culpăsse tribŭnos (claus.I); 14.9.5, p.27.1: cum nec vidisset qŭidquam nec audĭsset (claus.III, with dialysis); 14.10.10, p.29. 20-21; sententiarum via cŏncinens adprobăsset (claus.III); etc.

p. 133. 8 *a* **vere adulto egressi.** Cf.14.2.9 (= I p.71); Tac.Ann.13.36. For similar expressions cf.Fesser p.12.
b for **egressi** cf. ad 17.8.1, p.119.11-13*b;* ad 17.13.14, p.130.17; ad 17.1.4, p.105.15.

p. 133. 8-9 *a* **arripuimus negotiorum maximas moles.** For the verb cf. ad 17.1.10, p.106.11. Note the alliteration.
b for **moles** cf. ad 17.4.6, p.109.24-25*b;* 17.4.13 (p.111.2): used of an obeliscus; 17.7.13 (p.118.20): said of earth masses; ad 17.13.3, p.128.20; 15.8.2, p.58.9; etc. The pluralis is **poeticus.** For **negotium** cf. ad 17.1.3, p.105.5*b*.

struendo ... ponti. For the **gerundivum = part.fut.pass.** cf. ad 16.12.22, p.94.26*b*.

a **textis conpagibus ponti.** For **textis** cf. ad 14.2.10 (= I p.73): **contextis (c)ratibus** and Fesser p.12 (with lit.); ad 16.1.1, p.71.1*e:* **ordine contexto**; ad 17.1.2, p.104.7-9*c:* **ponte conpacto**; ad 17.1.2, p.105.4: **pontibus constratis**; ad 17.12.4, p.125.4: **ponte contexto**; ad 17.10.1, p.121.14: **contextoque navali ponte**; 14.10.6, p.29.3-4: **pontem suspendere navium compage**; 16.8.10, p.83.1: eamque (sc.fossam) **ponte solubili superstravit**.
b **conpagibus.** Cf. ad 16.12.44, p.98.20; ad 16.10.14, p.86.25; Verg.Aen. 1.122:
   Vicit hiems: laxis **laterum compagibus** omnes
   Accipiunt inimicum imbrem rimisque fatiscunt.
The subst. does not occur in Veget.r.m.Opt.Milev., though is does occur in Arn.adv.nat. and Claud.

telorum officeret multitudo. For the **personificatio** cf. ad 17.2.1, p.107.13. For the meaning of the verb cf. Krebs Antib.2 p.206 sq.; Heum.-Seckel p.388. **Officere c. gerundivo** seems a rarely occurring construction to me.

quo opera levi perfecto. Cf. **levi negotio** ad 16.12.22, p.94.26*a*. **Quo** refers back to the sentence: **primum ... multitudo.** For the **neutrum of the relativum** cf. ad 17.4.14, p.111.7-8 (pluralis); ad 17.5.15, p.115.20 (**nullo**).

hostilibus. Cf. ad 14.5.3 (= I p.85); ad 17.13.12, p.130.6*b*; ad 17.13.27, p.132.24-25.

calcatis. Cf. ad 17.10.1, p.121.14.

obstinatis ad mortem animis. Cf. ad 17.11.3, p.124.3; ad 17.13.14, p.130.16 (**obstinate**); ad 17.9.1, p.120.14*a* (**obstinatio**); ad 16.12.48, p.99.9-10*b* (**obstinatio**).

absque nostrorum dispendio. For **absque** cf. ad 14.3.4 (= I p.81). For **dispendium** cf. ad 16.12.41, p.98.9*a*. Cf.17.1.14: Hoc memorabili bello ... **dispendiis** rei Romanae peracto **levissimis**.

dispĕndio străvimus: Claus.II. Cf. ad 17.13.12, p.130.6*c;* ad 17.12.9, p. 126.2; ad 16.12.63, p.102.4 (**constrata**); ad 17.1.2, p.105.4 (**constratis**).

p. 133. 12 **parique petulantia.** Alliteration! Cf.26.7.11: et electi quidam stoliditate praecipites ad capessendum Illyricum missi sunt nullo praeter **petulantiam** adiumento confisi. **Petulantia** and **petulans** do not occur in Veget.r.m. Arn.adv.nat.Opt.Milev. In Claud. only **petulans** is found.
Cf.74 (Epigr.24) Deprec. ad Aleth.Quaest.7 sq.:
   Nulla meos traxit **petulans audacia** sensus
   Liberior iusto nec mihi lingua fuit.
   Versiculos, fateor, non cauta voce notavi.

p. 133. 12 For the adv. **petulanter** cf. ad 16.12.64, p.102.7-8.

p. 133. 12-13 *a* **agmina nobilium legionum.** Genit.identitatis. Cf. ad 15.10.4 (= IV p.55); ad 17.13.9, p.129.18*a*.
b The adj. means here: glorious, noble; the despot is flattering his soldiers. For at this time **the legiones** are no longer so glorious (for the various meanings of **nobilis** cf. ad 17.12.18, p.127.18-19c). For **agmina** cf. et. ad 17.13.6, p.129.7.
c Although **legio** still occurs as t.t. (cf.16.12.49, p.99.13: **Primanorum legionem**) and **legiones** is also used in a general sense (= army, troops, cf. 16.12.37, p.97.16: **gremio legionum protecti**; 17.10.7: rex cum **multiplices legiones** ... cerneret), other names are used more often by Amm.: **exercitus**, agmina, catervae, turmae, **miles (collect.)** numeri, cunei etc.

p. 133. 13 **Quados, Sarmatis.** Cf. ad 17.12.1, p.124.18.

p. 133. 13 **adiumenta.** Cf. ad 14.7.9 (= II p.27). Cf. et. 15.7.5; 18.2.13; 27.3.12. Cf. Veget.r.m.2.2 (= Lang p.36): Legio autem ... plena ... ex omni parte perfecta, **nullo extrinsecus indigens adiumento,** quantam libet hostium multitudinem superare consuevit.

p. 133. 13 *a* **adtrivimus:** we cut to pieces, destroyed totally. With this **military** meaning late Latin? Cf.Eutr.5.1: Romani consules ... victi sunt iuxta flumen Rhodanum et **ingenti internecióne attriti** etiam castra sua et magnam partem exercitus perdiderunt (**attriti** is wrongly put in brackets by some editors); Hist.Aug. (Treb.Poll.) Claud.7.6: Hos igitur Claudius ingenita illa virtute superavit, hos brevi tempore **adtrivit,** de his vix aliquos ad patrium solum redire permisit; Claud.10 (de nupt.Honor. et Mar.) 177 sq.:
   agnoscat famulum virgo Stilichonia (= Maria) pontum.

victrices nos saepe rates classemque paternam
veximus, **attritis** cum tenderet ultor **Archivis.**
b after **primum** (p.133.9) no **secundum** and **tertium** follow. From the context can be concluded that 2⁰ the **Sarmats** are defeated and 3⁰ the **Quads.** The accumulation of participium constructions obscures the meaning of the sentence.

aerumnŏsa dispĕndia. A repetition after 2 lines is quite remarkable. Claus.   p. 133. 14
II. For the adj.cf. ad 17.3.1, p.108.9. It has, at any rate, a solemn, old-fashioned sound.

inter discursus. Cf. ad 17.13.27, p.132.26. For the temporal **inter** cf. ad   p. 133. 14
17.4.1, p.109.4*a*.

a **repugnandi minaces anhelitus.** Cf.19.12.7: Perrexit (ut praeceptum   p. 133. 14
est) Paulus, funesti furoris et **anhelitus** plenus (note the ominous alliteration). Here the subst. means: the panting (breath-taking) exertion of the battle. Cf.Cic.off.1.36(131): Cavendum est autem, ne ... in festinationibus suscipiamus nimias celeritates; quae cum fiunt **anhelitus** moventur, vultus mutantur, ora torquentur; (And quite well comparable with our passage) Front.Strateg.2.1.7: Virginius cos. in Volscis, cum procurrere hostes effusos ex longinquo vidisset, quiescere suos ac defixa tenere pila iussit. Tunc **anhelantem** integris viribus exercitus sui adgressus **avertit.**
Anhelitus (and **anhelus, anhelare**) occur in Claud. and **anhelus** as varia lectio in Veget.r.m.3.11 (= Lang p.94), line 21. The **adj.** also in Arn.adv. nat. (Reiffersch.p.13.22). None of the 3 just-mentioned words in Opt. Milev. Cf. et. ad 16.5.14, p.77.16: **anhelare.**
b Not the **anhelitus** is threatening so much as the offering of resistance; so that, in my opinion, the 3 words are equal to: **minaciter repugnandi** anhelitus. For the **enallage** cf. Blomgren (op.cit.II) p.146 sq.

a **quid nostra valeat virtus experti.** Alliteration. For the conjunct.praes.   p. 133. 15
in the indirect question instead of the conj.imperf. (**repraesentatio**) cf. ad 14.7.9 Anm. (= II p.31).
(14.7.18 should be changed II p.31 into: **14.7.19).**
b Cf.14.10.14: qui sentit **expertus** nec fortitudinem in rebellis nec lenitatem in supplices animos deesse(?) (sc.Romanis).

aptatas. Also in 14.11.26; 16.10.8; 16.7.2; 31.2.6. (in 14.11.26 and 16.7.2   p. 133. 15
linked with **pinnas**). In 16.10.8 **aptata** in the claus.(I), while 2 lines previously **aptus** is used.

p. 133. 15-16 *a* **armorum abiecto munı̆mine.** Claus.II. Cf.15.10.1: Hanc Galliarum plagam ... **munimina** claudunt undique natura velut arte circumdata. But 19.7.3: ferrea **munimĕnta** membrŏrum: claus.I. Hagend.St.Amm. p.36: "Vox est poetarum fere propria, pro molestiore forma **munimentum** inde a Verg.Ovid.usurpata; in prosa oratione, quarto demum saeculo, si indicibus credimus, obvia". The word **munimentum** is used 41 times by Amm. (Hagend.ibid.). Cf.et. ad 16.12.58, p.101.6-7*d*.
b Cf. ad p.126.9*a*: **proiectis**; p.129.12: **proiecere** ... longius scuta.

p. 133. 16 *a* **pone tĕrga vinxĕrunt.** Seyf.: "und **lieszen sich die** zum Kämpfen bestimmten **Hände** auf dem Rücken **fesseln**;" Sabbah: "**ils lièrent** derrière leur dos **des mains** faites pour la lutte". The first translation comes up to our expectations, while the second one corresponds with the text. Rolfe, more or less like Seyf.: and **offered hands** that had been equipped for battle **to be bound** behind their backs". This also gives the solution to the problem, to my mind: they kept their hands behind their backs, **as if these were already bound,** in order to have them bound by the victors. Thus Amm. shortens the above-mentioned train of thought into these 3 words.
b For **terga** cf. ad 17.13.28, p.133.6*b*. For **pone** cf. ad 15.10.4 (= IV p.56).

p. 133. 16-17 *a* **restareque solam salutem contemplantes in precibus.** Cf.Liv.7.35.8: ergo **una est salus** erumpere hinc atque abire; Verg.Aen.2.354:
 una salus victis nullam sperare salutem;
Liv.30.9.8; Cic.Verr.1.2(4); Cic.Caecil.21(71).
b Contemplare Part.perf. **with passive meaning:** 16.8.6: statimque **legibus contem⟨platis⟩?**; 31.5.9: barbarique **hoc contemplato** globos inrupere nostrorum; 31.15.6: verum introire non auso, qui missus est, per Christianum quendam portatis **scriptis** et recitatis, utque decebat **contemplatis(?)** (cf. Blomgren p.172).

p. 133. 17 **adfusi sunt vestigiis.** For the verb cf. ad 16.4.5, p.75.10*a*. **vestigiis = pedibus:** well-known poetism. Cf.Verg.Aen.5.566; etc.

p. 133. 17 **Augusti clementis.** For **Augustus** cf. ad 17.3.4, p.108.17*b*. For **clemens** cf. ad 16.5.12, p.77.10-11 **(clementia);** ad 17.12.12, p.126.19 **(clementia).** These 2 words express Constantius' vanity and love of glory, for he was anything but **clemens.** Cf. Pauw (op.cit.) p.105 sq.
Cf.Cod.Iust.1.1.1: Cunctos populos, quos **clementiae nostrae** regit tem-

peramentum (a⁰ 380); ibid.2.44.3: Eos, qui veniam aetatis **principali clementia** (= imperial mercy) impetraverunt ... (a⁰ 529). The emperors, of course, love to ascribe this virtue to themselves, but many do this without justification.
Cf.et. ad 16.12.52, p.99.26 - p.100.1*e*.

a **cuius proelia saepe conpererant exitus habuisse felices.** For **felix** cf. ad 17.1.14, p.107.4-5*a*. For the **felicitas** of Iulianus cf. 25.4.14, p.369.10 sq. p. 133. 17-18
b **comperio** is suitable here. The verb means more than just: to be told, viz. to be told definitely, - accurately. Cf.et. ad 17.2.4, p.108.3-4*b*.
c For **exitus** cf. ad 16.12.13, p.93.3.

XIII, 29

a **his sequestratis.** Büchele: "Kaum waren **diese** beseitigt". Sabbah: p. 133. 18
"Ces peuples mis à part". Seyf.: "Kaum was **dies** erledigt". The last translation is the right one, in my view: lit. after these problems (neutr.) had been pushed aside. Cf.Cod.Theod.11.7.18: recens conditae **legis** (sc.11.7. 17) in hac parte **auctoritate sequestrata** (Gothofr.: id est, abrogata, antiquata). Late Latin. Cf. Souter p.375; Heum.-Seckel p.536; Veget.r.m. 2.20 (= Lang p.54): Illud vero ab antiquis divinitus institutum est, ut **ex donativo**, quod milites consecuntur, **dimidia pars sequestraretur apud signa** et ibidem ipsis militibus servaretur. (= to put aside, to lay down).
b Cf. **hisque secundo finitis eventu** § 30, p.133.20 sq., just after **this** passage per variationem.

Limigantes. Cf.17.13.1, p.128.11.   p. 133. 18

periculi declinatio. Cf.Cic.Cluent.53(148): neque haec tua recusatio con- p. 133. 19-20
fessio sit captae percuniae, sed laboris et **periculi non legitimi declinatio;** ibid.Tusc.4.6(13): Quoniamque, ut bona natura appetimus, sic **a malis** natura **declinamus**, quae **declinatio** cum ratione fiet, cautio appelletur. This meaning (= the avoiding of = the flight from) does not occur very often. For the verb **declinare** cf. ad 17.12.7, p.125.17; ad 17.13.14, p.130. 17; ad 16.12.57, p.101.1*a*.

suffugia petere latebrarum palustrium. Cf.17.13.18: ad **suffugia** locorum p. 133. 20
palustrium ⟨se⟩ contulerunt (cf.adnot.p.131.6*a*, *b*).
adegit. For the infinit.constr. cf.Hotm.-Leum.p.580, 167*B*.

XIII, 30

p. 133. 21 **eventu.** Cf. ad 17.12.9, p.125.22.

   a **lenitatis tempus ǎderat tempestīvae.** For the **hyperbaton** cf. ad 17.1.6, p.105.21*a*. For **lenitas** cf. ad 14.7.12 (= II p.39). Claus.III.

   b Cf.28.1.43: Et quamlibet **tempestivum est** ad ordinem redire coeptorum; 30.9.1: oppidorum et limitum **conditor tempestivus** (sc. Valentinianus); 16.11.4: Laeti barbari ad **tempestiva furta** sollertes; 16.12.12: ergo quoniam negotiis difficillimis quoque seape **dispositio tempestiva** prospexit.

p. 133. 22 *a* **ad loca migrare compulimus longe discreta.** Cf.17.12.19, p.127.22: ad Victohalos **discretos longius** confugerunt (c.annot. ad l.).

   b Cf.17.13.3: abnuere parati si iuberentur aliorsum **migrare.**

   c For the construction of the **verba** compellendi cf. ad 15.5.14 (= III p.91).

p. 133. 22 **in perniciem nostrorum.** Cf. ad 17.13.13, p.130.11*b*, *c;* ad 17.11.3, p.124.3.

p. 133. 22 **nostrorum.** Here Amm. is probably thinking first of all of the soldiers, the Roman army. He often uses **nostri** in this way, e.g.17.12.7, p.125.16; 16.12.55, p.100.19; 16.12.15, p.93.11; 16.12.19, p.94.13; 16.12.36, p.97.2; etc. Cf.et. ad 17.1.13, p.106.25*a*.

p. 133. 23 *a* **se commovere possent ulterius.** Cf.17.13.2: ut ad longinqua translati amitterent copiam nostra vexandi.

   b **se commovere.** With the special meaning of: to be enterprising, to be pugnacious, (e.g. in war). Cf.Nep.Agesil.17.6: namque illi, aucto numero eorum, qui expertes erant consilii, **commovere se** non sunt ausi (concerning a plan to defect) = they have not dared to move a muscle; Liv.2.54.6; Cic. ad fam.6.20.3 (Thoranio exsuli): Tu cura ut valeas et **te istinc ne temere commoveas;** ibid.9.5.2: Ita verecundiores fuimus quam qui **se domo non commoverunt,** saniores quam qui amissis opibus domum non reverterunt; ad Att.3.13.1: posteaquam extenuari spem nostram et evanescere vidi, mutavi consilium, **nec me Thessalonica commovi;** etc. **Ire** with its short forms is often replaced in the **sermo cotidianus** by other verbs, such as ambulo, vado, curro, se auferre, se dare, se ducere, se subducere etc. (Cf. **Lorenz** ad Plaut.Pseud.535; **Landgraf,** Bem. zum sermo cotidianus ... Bl.f.d.bayr.Gymn.1880,535). Cf.et. ad 17.12.21, p. 128.3*b*.

p. 133. 23 **pepěrcimus plǔrimis** = plerisque (as often). Claus.II.

Zizaim. Cf. ad 17.12.20, p.127.28.

praefecimus Liberis. Cf.17.12.20, p.127.28: Zizaim regem isdem **praefecit.**

Liberis. Cf. ad 17.12.17 sq., p.127.15 sq.; ad 17.12.12, p.126.19-20*b*, *c*.

a **dicatum nobis futŭrum et fĭdum.** Claus.I. Hyperbaton + alliteration.
Dicatus = devoted, obedient, sacred. With this meaning late Latin. Not in Claud.Veget.r.m.Arn.adv.nat.Opt.Milev.Cf.Cod.Iust.2.7.25.3: ut idem viri ... bina solidorum pro singulis milia nihilque amplius noverint dependenda viris magnificis comitibus **dicatissimorum** (= **devotissimorum**; cf. ad 16.8.3, p.81.10-11*b*) **domesticorum,** id est equitum, pro eo, qui inter equites meriturus(?) est. (For **comes** and **domestici** cf. ad 14.11.19 = II p.132; ad 14.5.1 = I p.125).
b Cf.17.12.20: conspicuae fortunae tum insignibus aptum ... **et fidelem.**

plus aestimantes. The most frequently occurring constructions with **aestimare** are: ablat. or **genit.pretii,** ex + ablat., or adverbia, with our meaning (though Georges quotes for a **double accusat.** Sall.Jug. 85.41; Mart.11.1.7; and for a **double nominat.** in the passivum Sen. de brev.vit. 8.2). Like here **plus (accusativus)** 17.13.11, p.130.1: **minus criminis** aestimabant (accus.). Cf.et. ad 17.12.17, p.127.17. Besides **aestimare** one finds: **existimare** e.g. 17.4.13, p.111.3: nihilque committere in religionem rĕcte **exĭstimans,** si (claus.II); 17.9.5, p.120.28 sq.: et nequi nos turbarum exĭstimet concitŏres (claus.III; though here not metri causa); 16.2.8, p.73.14: nihil prolatăndum exĭstimans (claus.II) (here, however, one can also form another colon); 16.10.11, p.86.7: ut **existimări** dabătur (claus.I); 16.11.13, p.90.21: rudis etiam tum ut **exĭstimabătur** (claus.I; though here not metri causa); 18.8.4: metu indubitatae mortis cǎutum **existimăntes** (claus.III); 19.10.2: ab omni spe tuendae salutis exclŭsus ut **aestimăbat** (claus.III; another colon is possible); 19.10.3: si itaque his (sc.filiis) abolitis nihil triste accidere pŏsse **existimătis** (claus.III); 20.2.2: ex opinione plĕraque aĕstimans (claus.II); 20.3.1: pavidae mentes hŏminum **aestimăbant** (claus.III); 20.4.8: gloriosum esse **existimans** iussa morte oppetere (not in the claus.); 20.4.9: id optimum făctu existimăvit (claus.III); 20.8.7: si quid novatum est nŭnc ut exĭstimas (claus.II); 17.13.23: dum licentem amentiam libertătem existimărent (cl.III); 24.1.15: alia virtutis suae horrea repperĭsse **existimăntes** (claus.III).

auferre. Cf. Sabbah A.M.II p.186. note 115: "**Adfer(r)e** donné par G et par V (and some other manuscripts) doit être préféré à **auferre** proposé par E et par les éditeurs: l'opposition n'est pas entre **donner** et **enlever** un roi aux barbares. Constance croit qu'en consacrant officiellement le roi choisi par les Sarmates ... il fait davantage qu'en imposant aux barbares un roi amené de l'exterieur ...".

Auferre is given by Cl.Seyf.Rolfe. The version **auferre** can quite well be defended, in my view: for **auferre regem** (sc. Zizaim) results in **adferre regem** (sc. peregrinum). But the version **adferre** gives a more satisfactory sentence. And in that case one should on principle maintain the version of the best manuscripts.

p. 133. 25 *a* **hoc decore augente sollemnitatem.** Cf.27.10.2: et quoniam casu Christiani ritus invenit celebrari **sollemnitatem**; 23.3.7: sacrorum **sollemnitate** prisco more completa (sc. Matri deorum); 25.8.16: Profecti inde Thilsaphata venimus, ubi Sebastianus atque Procopius ... ut poscebat **sollemnitas** (= official custom), occurrerunt (sc. nobis). Late Latin and judic.lit. Cf. Souter p.381; Heum.-Seckel p.545. The **subst.** does not occur in Claud.Veget.r.m.Arn.adv.nat.Opt.Milev. Apart from Arn., the 3 other authors have the **adj.** Opt.Milev.3.12 (= Ziwsa p.100.16) "replaces" **sollemnitas** by **solemnis consuetudo** (sc.sacrificii divini). Cf.et. Krebs Antib. 2 p.585.
b **decore** = mark of honour, homage.

p. 133. 25-26 *a* **quod ... acceptus** = quod rector isdem (cf. ad 15.5.19,20 = III p.103) tributus (a nobis) **antehac quoque electus est et acceptus (ab eis)** Elsewhere Zizais is called **rex** (17.12.20; 17.13.30, p.133.25); but **rector** has here a more general meaning: chief, head, leader. (for **rector** t.t. cf. ad 16.5.13, p.77.11-14*c;* ad 14.10.8 = II p.106; ad 16.12.22, p.94.26).
b **quod.** For the constructions cf. ad 17.5.8, p.114.21-24*a*.
c **elēctus est et accēptus.** Claus.III + **homoioteleuton** (cf. ad 15.10.4 = IV p.56).

XIII, 31

p. 133. 26-27 **quadruplex.** It would be too simple for Amm.'s reader (listener), if after **primo, deinde,** he would next have written: **tertio.** This thirdly is implied in § 32: ⟨si⟩ ... **servarint.** Fourthly is then expressed by **postremo.** Cf.et. ad 17.8.5, p.120.5-7.

p. 133, 27 **praemium.** Here the emperor uses the **general** term for military rewards. (cf.20.11.12: multis nostrorum idcirco cadentibus, quod decernentes sub imperatoris conspectu, **(spe)praemiorum,** ut possint facile qui essent agnosci, **nudantes galeis capita** ...). For the **milit. rewards** cf. Müller Mil. (op.cit.I) p.620 sq.

procinctus. Cf. ad 16.11.6, p.89.7. p. 133. 27

absolvit. Cf. ad 17.8.3, p.120.1*a;* ad 15.1.1 (= III p.5). Here, to complete, to finish (class.). Cf.et. ad 17.1.1, p.104.4*a*. p. 133. 27

nos quaesivimus et res publica. When Amm. renders **Constantius'** words correctly here, he certainly characterises with **nos,** which is placed in front and emphasized, the absolute monarch, who puts himself ahead of the **res publica.** p. 133. 27-28

primo ultione parta ... deinde quod ... sufficiet, For this variation in the constructions cf. ad 17.13.5, p.129.4-5. p. 133. 28 / p. 134. 1

ultione parta. The subst. is post-class., since Livius. The usual constructions are: ultionem ab aliquo(a)(re) petere, -exigere, -quaerere. Whether **ultionem parere de** occurs more often, is not known to me. The subst. does not occur in Claud.Veget.r.m.Arn.adv.nat.; it is found, however, in Opt. Milev. and legal writings. p. 133. 28

grassatoribus. Cf. ad 16.11.5, p.89.1 = robbers, bandits. Not in Claud. Veget.r.m.Opt.Milev. Arnob.adv.nat., though it occurs in legal writings. (cf.Heum.-Seckel p.231). p. 133. 28

noxiis. Here perhaps: guilty, deserving (of) punishment. Cf. **innocuus** (16.2.6, p.73.9*c*), **innoxius** (16.11.6, p.89.3). p. 133. 28

abunde sufficiet. For the use of the adv. cf. Krebs Antib.1 p.59 (with lit.). Amm. also uses **abundanter** (in the compar.).27.3.3: quo (sc. Symmacho) instante urbs sacratissima otio copiisque **abundantius solito fruebatur.** **Abunde** (with **sufficere**) is here used somewhat abundantly. The adv. does not occur in Claud.Veget.r.m.Opt.Milev.Arn.adv.nat. p. 134. 1

a **ex hostibus capti⟨s vi⟩vis.** Thus Cl.Seyf.V sufficient captivis. Sabbah: **sufficient ex hostibus captivis.** Novák Rolfe: quod vobis abunde **sufficient ex hostibus capta.** p. 134. 1
sufficiet b Btl.Cl.Seyf... This **captis vivis** will have been derived from

391

17.8.5: Chamavos ... partim acriter repugnantes, **vivosque captos,** conpegit in vincula. But this, to me, is no reason to correct V's version The subject of **sufficiet** is: **ex hŏstibus captīvis** = that which you gain (have gained) from the (proceeds of the sold) prisoners of war (enemies). The plural **sufficient** can be defended, in my opinion. There is no need to object against the claus. (Cf. Blomgren p.9 sq.).

b Captured enemies form, especially in these countries, the most important booty. They could be sold immediately to slave-dealers accompanying the troops and thus bring some money into the usually empty pockets of the soldiers. Thus the killing-off of barbarians is disadvantageous to the Roman soldiers, although it is often reported by Amm. and his contemporaries, and certainly not always with distaste.

p. 134. 1-2 **his ... dexteris.** The sober contents of these fine words are: you need not count on an extra reward. Thus I do not wholly agree with the explanation **contentus** by Sabbah A.M.II p.187. note 116.

p. 134. 1 **virtutem sc. vestram:** personificatio. Cf. ad 17.2.1, p.107.13.

p. 134. 2 **sudore.** Cf.14.2.14: tresque legiones **bellicis sudŏribus** indurătae (poet.plur. cf. ad 17.2.1, p.107.14-15b. Claus.III). Cf.et. ad 17.9.6, p.121.4-5. Fairly often in Amm.

p. 134. 2 **quaesivit et dexteris.** Cf.16.11.12: libentius enim bellatores **quaesito dexteris propriis** utebantur (and annot.ad 1., p.90.12).

XIII, 32

p. 134. 2-3 **nobis ... nostri:** plur.maiestatis. **Nobis,** as opposed to **vobis** (p.133.28). You have found your reward and obtained possessions in the **hostes captivi.** We have **amplae facultates** and **opum magni thesauri,** because our **labores** and **fortitudo** have seen to it that the **patrimonia omnium** (the patrimony of all "Romans") have remained intact. All this in the spirit of the **dominus,** who takes credit himself for what is achieved by others; and as it is repeatedly read in authors of this era. The last sentence of § 32 then means: A good emperor is satisfied with this, viz. that his subjects keep their prosperity (and do not lose it in unfavourable wars). This is also in agreement with the successful end of wars (and especially of this last one).

p. 134. 2-3 **amplae facultates ... opumque magni thesauri:** chiasm (cf. ad 16.8.2, p.81.1-4*b* 3). It is possible that **thesauri** is used metaphorically here. But **thesauri** may also be a t.t. here. (cf. ad 15.5.36 = III p.127). Cf.et.Heum.– Seckel p.585; Willems (op.cit.I) p.599 (with lit.). **Facultates** is a normal word in judic.lit.: state of fortune, **fortune. Opes** has a wider scope than **facultates,** at least here.

⟨si⟩ ... **servarint.** Si Btl.Haupt.Cl.Seyf.Rolfe. Sabbah does not insert p. 134. 3
si, explaining (II p.187, note 117): "V G donnant **servarint** ... on peut penser à un **subjonctif de supposition** (Ernout-Thomas, Syntaxe, p.237. § 255)." For this conjunct. cf.Hofm.-Leum.p.571, 160. It seems simpler to me to consider **integra ... servarint** as the 2nd member of an asyndeton, which then explains the 1st member. **Servarint** is fut.exact. (For the **asyndeton bimembre** cf. ad 17.12.9, p.125.25*b*).

patrimonia. The subst. has, besides the general meaning of private p. 134. 3
property, in the time of the dominate also the special meaning of: private property (capital) of the emperor. (cf. Willems p.603; Heum.-Seckel p. 410). The latter is part of the **aerarium privatum,** managed by the **v.illustris comes rerum privatarum,** (cf. ad 15.5.4 = III p.73). The choice of this subst. may not be accidental: the **patrimonium** of the emperor and of his subjects depends upon the same adversity and prosperity.

successibus prosperis. Cf. ad 17.5.8, p.114.22-24*c;* ad 17.13.24, p.132.7*a;* p. 134. 5
ad 16.4.5, p.75.10.

XIII, 33

a **hostilis vocabuli spolium**: lit. a booty, consisting of the name of the p. 134. 5-6
enemy (-ies). Genit.explicat.
b for **hostilis** cf. ad 17.13.12, p.130.6*b*. For **vocabulum** cf. ad 17.4.11, p.110.15-16*a;* p.132.15.

a **secundo Sarmătici cognoměntum.** Cf. ad 17.13.25, p.132.14-15. V p. 134. 6
secundi. Cl.Seyf.Sabbah Rolfe: **secundo,** a conjecture of Vales. It is the question whether V should be corrected. The 3 above words are an explanation of: **hostilis vocabuli spolium** and mean: the title of Sarmaticus for the second time. Vales. appeals to **secundo** p.132.14; but there it is next to **appellatus,** which is normal, whereas here it belongs with **Sarmaticus.** And besides, **secundo Sarmatici** is in the genit., dependent on **cognomentum.** In my view, **secundi** gives the same meaning as **secundo**

393

(the adject, is then used predicatively), while the 3 words are joined in a more normal way.

b **cognomentum.** Cf. ad 14.5.8 (= I p.88); ad 14.7.18 (= II p.46); ad 16.11.11, p.90.7. Claus.III.

p. 134. 6-7 **quod vos unum idemque sentientes.** Cf. ad 17.13.25, p.132.14. Cf.Cic.Catil. 4.7.(14): Causa est enim post urbem conditam haec inventa sola **in qua omnes sentirent unum atque idem**; ibid.2.9(19): quibus hoc praecipiendum videtur - **unum scilicet et idem quod reliquis omnibus** - ut desperent id, quod conantur, se consequi posse; ibid.4.9(19): habetis omnes ordines, omnes homines, universum populum Romanum, id quod in civili causa hodierno die primum videmus, **unum atque idem sentientem.**

p. 134. 7 **mihi ... mĕrito tribuĭstis.** Alliteration and claus.III.

ne sit adrogans dicere. Cf. ad 17.5.5, p.114.8-9*a*, *b*. Almost the same wording there.

p. 134. 8 **post hunc dicendi finem.** Instead of, for instance, an ablat.absol. For **post** temp. cf. ad 17.12.16, p.127.8*b*.

p. 134. 8 **contio.** Cf.24.4.24: ita nunc enituerunt hi qui fecere fortissime, **obsidionalibus coronis donati et pro contione laudati,** veterem more; 14.10.10: **advocato in contionem exercitu** imperator ... ad hunc disseruit modum; 21.13.9: cum in unum exercitus convenisset **omnes centurias et manipulos et cohortes in contionem vocavit** (follows a speech); 21.5.1: **classico ad contionem exercitu convocato** (followed by a speech).

A speech (address) in a soldiers' meeting is called 27.6.5: **oratio contionaria.** And the speaking in this meeting is called 23.5.16: **contionari.** As no laws are passed or officials elected in a soldiers' meeting, **contio** has become the standard term for this meeting. (cf. Willems, op.cit.I, p.157 sq.; **Gell.13.15.3;** Mommsen Abr., op.cit.I, p.299 sq.; Lange Röm.Alt.² II p.418 sq.; Madvig I, p.219). Not in Veget.r.m.

p. 134. 8 **alacrior solito.** Cf. ad 14.6.9 (= I p.93).

p. 134. 8-9 **aucta spe potiorum et lucris.** V **lucris;** similarly Sabbah Rolfe. **lucri** T B G Seyf. **potioris** R B G. It seems simpler to me to read: aucta spe **potioris et lucri.** For the placing of **et** cf.19.8.12, p.172.10-11; Blomgren p.97 sq. (with lit.); 31.12.11, p.587,24 sq.: **digestaque = digesta quae** (Blomgren p.100); etc.

vocibus festis. Cf.Tac.ann.12.69: ibi monente praefecto **festis vocibus** ex- ceptus inditur lecticae (sc.Nero). Ernesti: **faustis.** Thus here Her.**faustis.** But the version is correct. Cf.Claud.26.205 sq. (de bello Get.): p. 134. 9

  Mandemusne Noti flabris, quoscumque timores
  Pertulimus, **festae** doleant ne tristibus **aures?**
And more frequently in Claud. Once in Veget.r.m.: **festis diebus** (2.23). Not in Arn.adv.nat.Opt.Milev.

in laudes imperatoris adsurgens. Cf.Flor.3.1.10: Eodem tempore **in ultio-** **nem** non tam imperii Romani quam pudoris Metellus **assurgit** (= ultionem capessit, ultioni accingitur; cf.ibid.2.12.3: Macedones ... **consurgunt** = bellum capessunt; 2.17.3: Hispaniae nunquam animus fuit adversus nos universae **consurgere** = bellum capessere); Verg.Aen.10.94 sq.: p. 134. 9

  Tum decuit metuisse tuis; nunc sera **querelis**
  Haud iustis **assurgis,** et irrita iurgia iactas.
(= surgis ad querelas fundendas: Forbiger).
The verb occurs a few times in Claud., but not with the above-mentioned construction and meaning. Not in Veget.r.m.Opt.Milev.Arn.adv.nat. Cf.et.Vell.Pat.2.51.3: Tum Balbus Cornelius ... illis incrementis fecit viam, quibus ... **in triumphum et pontificatum assurgeret** fieretque ex privato consularis.

deumque - vinci. Cf.Cic. ad Q.fr.1.3.2: Sed **testor omnes deos, me hac una** **voce a morte esse revocatum,** quod omnes ... dicebant; Liv.4.53.5: **consulibus deos hominesque testantibus,** quidquid ab hostibus cladis ignominiaeque aut iam acceptum esset aut immineret, **culpam penes Maenium fore,** qui dilectum impediret; Veget.r.m.3.22 (= Lang p.112): Nam disciplinae bellicae et exemplorum periti **nusquam maius periculum imminere testantur;** Opt.Milev.1.21 (= Ziwsa p.23): deinde **esse distantiam** delictorum aut **remissio testatur** aut poena; ibid.3.2 (= Ziwsa p.70): (lacrimas) **quas testatur** nulla **posse** consolatione **siccari.** The verb fairly often in Opt.Milev. and Claud. Not in Arn.adv.nat. p. 134. 9-10

ex usu. Cf. ad 14.10.3 (= II p.100). Cf.et. ad 15.1.2 (= III p.8): **ex more.** p. 134. 10

a **tentoria repetit laeta.** For the **tents** cf. Grosse Mil. (op.cit.I) p.302 sq.; p.307 note 1; Müller Mil. (op.cit.I) p.615; Veget.r.m. **(tentoria):** 2.7; 3.2; 3.26; **(tabernacula):** 2.10; 3.8; **(papiliones):** 2.13; 1.23; 1.3; 3.8. p. 134. 10
b Cf.Liv.31.21.5: Galli, clamore suorum ex agris revocati, omissa

praeda, quae in manibus erat, **castra repetivere** (= sought them again). In **this** combination probably a t.t.mil. Cf.et.Curt.Ruf.9.8.16: ... Alexander ... rursus **amnem**, in quo classem exspectare se iusserat, **repetit**; ibid. 3.8.2: Hi magnopere suadebant (sc.Dario) ut retro abiret spatiososque **Mesopotamiae campos repeteret**; ibid.8.1.7: Alexander quoque, Sogdianis rursus subactis, **Maracanda repetit**; ibid.4.6.20: Et Betis, interfectum (sc.eum) ratus, **urbem** ovans victoria **repetit**; ibid.3.5.6: sibi **easdem terras**, quas victoria peragrassent, **repetendas**; etc.

p. 134. 11 *a* **et reductus imperator ad regiam.** Seyf.: "Der Kaiser liesz sich zum Palast geleiten". Correct translation: dynamic medium.

b **regiam.** In **Acimincum?** (cf. ad 17.13.4, p.128.26*a, c*). Probably a town, not too far from **Sirmium**. Though **Singidunum** is also possible. For **regia** cf. ad 16.8.11, p.83.4*b, c*.

p. 134. 11 **otioque bidui recreatus.** The part. is reflexive. For the combination of the first 2 words cf.Cic. ad fam.10.17.1: Antonius Id. Maiis ad Forum Iulii cum primis copiis venit. Ventidius **bidui spatio** abest ab eo; Ter.Andr. 440 sq.:

nihil hercle: aut, si adeo, **biduist** aut tridui
haec sollicitudo, nostin? deinde desinet.

And more often in this way. **Biduum** does not occur in Claud.Veget.r.m. Arn.adv.nat.Opt.Milev. Cf. et. ad 16.12.19, p.94.13.

p. 134. 11 **Sirmium.** Cf. ad 15.3.7 (= III p.45); ad 16.12.66, p.102.12*b*.

p. 134. 12 **pompa triumphali.** Cf.25.9.9: set ne ob recepta quidem quae direpta sunt, verum ob amplificata regna **triumphalis glorias** fuisse delatas; Ovid.Pont. 3.4.95:

Quid cessas currum **pompamque parare triumphis,**

Livia? iam nullas dant tibi bella moras; Suet. Caes.37: Pontico **triumpho** inter **pompae** fercula trium verborum praetulit titulum: veni, vidi vici ... ; Mart.8.78.2: **Indica pompa** (of the triumphal procession of Bacchus).

p. 134. 12 **regressus est:** variatio, instead of **repetivit.** The shortest route goes in a roundabout way, along the Danube road until **Singidunum**, and from there via Altina, Idiminium. Noviciana, **Bassianae**, Fossae to **Sirmium** on the **Savus**.

militares numeri. For **militaris** ad 17.13.25, p.132.14; ad 16.3.3, p.74.17. Cf.14.7.19: isdem diebus Apollinaris ... per **militares numeros** inmodice scrutabatur ... Cf.Müller Mil.p.574: "Jeden Truppenkörper (which is not entirely correct) ohne Unterschied der Waffengattung nennt Amm., allerdings dem Gebrauche seiner Zeit folgend, **numerus**. In einigen Fällen ist es zwar möglich, die mit diesem farblosen Worte bezeichneten Truppenkörper zu ermitteln, in andern aber unthunlich. Unter **numerus** sind zu verstehen eine **Legion** 29.3.7; **auxilia palatina** 25.10.9; 20.4.7; 24.4.23; eine **vexillatio** 25.1.7; **unbestimmt** bleiben 27.10.6; 31.11.2; 31.13.18". Grosse Mil. p.25: "In älterer Zeit hatte der Ausdruck **numerus** eine doppelte Bedeutung, eine allgemeine und eine spezielle. Einerseits bezeichnet er jeden Truppenkörper, der unter dem einheitlichen Kommando eines Offiziers stand, **anderseits eine Abteilung, die weder Legion noch Cohorte noch Ala war**. So wurde er zum Sondernamen für all die nationalen Truppenkörper des 2. und 3. Jahrhunderts, die nicht in das herkömmliche Schema passen wollten. Es ist eins von den vielen Zeichen des erstarkenden Nationalismus im röm. Staate des 3. Jahrhunderts dasz die **numeri** nun den **regulären** Truppen angegliedert werden .... Diese Entwicklung findet nun ihre scharfe Ausprägung in der Terminologie des 4. Jahrhunderts, indem jetzt der Ausdruck **numerus**, griechisch ἀριθμός, im 6. Jahrh. κατάλογος nur noch in **allgemeiner** Bedeutung gebraucht wird. Jeder beliebige Truppenkörper heisst so, mag er auch daneben seinen Sondernahmen führen, ob Legion oder Ala, Cohorte oder Auxilium .... **Von den numeri konsequent ausgeschlossen sind nur die scholae** (cf. ad 14. 7.9 = II p.27 sq.; ad 14.11.19 = II p.133 sq.; ad 15.5.12 = III p.88 sq.), die Abteilungen der Hoftruppen, die für den Dienst unmittelbar um die Person des Kaisers bestimmt waren" (the reason for this is organisational: for they are under the authority of the **magister officiorum**). And for a complete survey: Mommsen, Das röm. Militärwesen seit Diokletian (op.cit.I).

a **destinatas remeărunt ⟨ad⟩ sēdes. ad** is not found in V. **ad** included by E Cl. Seyf. Rolfe. Sabbah adheres to V's version, rightly so, in my view. There are no objections against the clausula ⏓ ⏑ ⏓ ⏑, even if it occurs less frequently (cf. Blomgren p.93 sq., with several examples). Nor against **the accusat. without praeposition** (cf. ad 17.9.2, p.120.17-18*b*. 2).

b **destinatas** = appointed (beforehand), intended(-), selected. Cf.21.13. 8: revocatis omnibus praeter eos quos consuetudo praesidio Mesopotamiae **destinarat**, reversus est Hierapolin. With this meaning also often in the judic.lit. As t.t. the verb also has the meaning: **to send off to** (said of civil servants) (cf.Heum.-Seckel p.141; Souter p.98). For the meaning: **obstinate** (and also for the **adv.** and **substant.** with the same meaning) cf. ad 17.2.2, p.107.21-22*b*. Cf.et. ad 16.12.37, p.97.9-11*e*.

c **sedes**: garrison-towns; as, in my view, other words, such as **castra, castella, munimenta,** etc. would have been used, if this meaning were not intended here. P.132.11, 17.13.24: in avitis **sedibus** the word means no more than just: dwelling-places. But 17.2.1, p.107.9-10: **Sedes hibernas** = **hiberna.** In 17.12.11, p.126.17 **sedes** = dwelling-places; similarly 17.13.23, p.132.3. However, for this last concept Amm. has many variations: **lares, domicilia, sua (sc.territoria), terrae,** etc. Cf. et. ad 17.10.10, p.123.12*a, b*.

XIV, 1

p. 134. 14 For **caput 14** cf. **Pighi** N.St.Amm.p.198 sq. (with the introductory words: Much ado about nothing).

p. 134. 14 *a* **Hisce isdem diebus.** In the month of May, 358 A.D. (cf. Pighi, N.St. Amm., op.cit.XVI, p.136). The combination **hic idem** also: 16.7.4; 16.11. 7; 20.9.8; 23.6.24; 23.6.25; 23.6.69; 24.5.2; 26.8.10; 27.3.2; 28.4.13; 28.4.26; 30.2.5; 23.3.3. Cf.et.16.5.9: suo **quaeque** loco **singula** demonstrabuntur; Hagend.abund. (op.cit.I) p.210; B.J. de Jonge, Apul.Met.II comm.p.60 (with lit.).

b **hisce.** An archaistic, solemn word. For this form cf.Hofm.-Leum.p.285 sq., 201*d;* Ernout-Meltzer[3] (1920) (op.cit.I) p.64 sq., 119,120.

p. 134. 14 **Prosper et Spectatus atque Eustathius.** For these 3 persons cf. ad 17.5.15, p.115,20-23.

p. 134. 15 **ut supra docuinus:** sc.: 17.5.15, p.115.20 sq. For this kind of expressions cf. ad 17.12.20, p.127.29; ad 17.13.1, p.128.11*a*.

p. 134. 15-16 *a* **Ctesiphonta reversum regem adiere.** The town is also mentioned 21.6. 12; 23.6.23; 24.2.7; 24.4.8, 13,31; 24.5.6; 24.6.12; 24.7.1; 24.8.6; 29.1.4. On the left bank of the **Tigris,** opposite **Seleucia** on the right bank. Winter residence of the **Arsacids.** Most prosperous period under the **Sassanids,** thus also under **Sapor.** (cf. ad 16.9.3, p.83.24). Cf. Woordenb.der Oudheid, 4, 1969, p.755 **(with lit.,** Veenhof); Pieper, Tab.6 (and p.27); Tcherikover, Hellenistic Civilization and the Jews, p.290.

b **adiere.** For the t.t. **aditus** and **adire** cf. ad 15.5.27 (= III p.112). For the abbreviated form cf. ad 16.12.19, p.94.11-12; ad 17.13.28. p.133.8.

perferentes: the standard verb for the conveying of messages and letters. Cf.17.5.15, p.116.1: imperatoris scripta **perferentes** et munera; Cf.Cic. ad.fam.2.6.1: cum has quam primum ad te **perferri litteras** magno opere vellemus; ibid. ad Q.fr.3.1.18: scripsique ad Caesarem neque Vibullium Caesaris **mandata** de mea mansione ad Pompeium **pertulisse** neque Oppium; ad Q.fr.1.1.1: tamen existimavi a me quoque tibi huius molestiae **nuntium perferri** oportere; ad fam.14.1.1: et **litteris** multorum et **sermone** omnium **perfertur** ad me; etc.

poscebantque rebus integris pacem. Cf.17.5.13: est enim absonum et insipiens ... ea prodere quae ... diu servavimus **inlibata;** 17.5.11: et suades **integro corpori** adimere membra quaedam; and the comm. ad 17.5.13, p.115.10 sq. Note the alliteration.

mandatŏrum ⟨**principis**⟩ **mĕmores.** Cf.21.7.4: mandatorum **principis** memor. The clausula can, in my opinion, not be an objection against the version of V (also followed by Seyf.Sabbah, while Cl. Rolfe insert **principis**). Cf. ad 17.13.33, p.134.12-13a. Neither is the addition necessary to make things clearer, because the **imperator** is mentioned immediately before this. (for **imperator** and **princeps** cf. ad 16.12.67, p.102.16).

a **nusquam ab utilitate Romanae rei maiestateque discedebant.** res Ro- **mana** also e.g.17.1.14 p.107.3-4: bello ... dispendiis **rei Romanae** peracto levissimis; p.109.18, 17.4.5: Octaviano **res** tenente **Romanas;** 17.5.14, p.115.18: in proeliis quibusdam raro **rem** titubasse **Romanam;** 19.1.4: verum caeleste numen ut **Romanae rei** totius aerumnas ... concluderet. Cf.et ad 16.11.7, p.89.10 (**Romaniae**).
b Cf.17.5.12: praefectus praetorio meus, opinatus adgredi negotium **publicae utilitati** conducens ... (comm. ad 1. p.115.6-7c, 2); ad 17.13.1, p.128.12a.
c **maiestate.** Cf. ad 17.5.12, p.115.9-10d.

a **amicitiae foedus sub hac lege firmari debere adseverantes.** Cf.17.5.10, p.114.29: Sospitati quidem tuae gratulor **ut futurus (si velis) amicus** ... 17.5.11, p.115.3: ut salus eius (sc.corporis) deinceps locetur in solido, **quod refutandum est potius quam ulla consensione firmandum** (and comm. ad 1.).
b Therefore, what is meant here is a **foedus amicitiae causa factum.** Cf. Willems p.346: "Le traité d'amitié est conclu à perpétuité, après une guerre, ou sans que l'état de guerre ait procédé, **et il assure des relations**

amicales entre Rome et un Etat qui conserve son entière indépendance. Un tel traité détermine le mode dont la sûreté et les intérêts des nationaux de chaque Etat seront protégés, quand ils seront de séjour sur le territoire de l'autre Etat (**recuperatio**)"; with the lit. quoted there.

c Cf.20.4.4: qui relictis laribus ... **sub hoc** venerant **pacto,** ne ducerentur. For this modal usage of **sub.** cf. Reinhardt p.62. Cf.et. ad 17.4.13, p.111. 6b.

d The contents of the **lex** (= condition) are expressed in the sentence **ne ... moveretur.**

e for **adseverare** cf. ad 17.11.4, p.124.9.

p. 134. 19-20 *a* **ne super turbando Armeniae vel Mesopotamiae statu quicquam moveretur.** For **super** cf. ad 16.12.70, p. 103,9-10*b*; ad 17.4.1, p.109.6*a*.

b **turbando** = ± mutando (cf.Flor.1.9.3: Tantumque libertatis novae gaudium incesserat (sc.cives Romanos) ut vix **mutati status** fidem caperent). With the literal meaning: to confuse, throw into commotion, etc., the verb occurs not only often in, for instance, Livius, but also in Veget. r.m. and Curt.Ruf. and Claud. For the subst. **turbamentum** cf.25.7.12; 26.7.8. Cf.et. ad 17.1.7, p.105.22-23*c*.

c **statu.** Cf. ad 16.12.12, p.92.24*a*.

d For **Armenia** and **Mesopotamia** cf. ad 17.5.6, p.114.12.

e Cf.17.5.6: **Armeniam** recuperare cum **Mesopotamia** debeo, avo meo composita fraude praereptam; 17.5.11: **Mesopotamiam** poscis ut tuam, perindeque **Armeniam** et suades integro corpori adimere membra quaedam. And for the **entire context** cf.comm. ad 1. p.113.25-26 sq.

XIV, 2

p. 134. 20 **diu igitur ibi morati**: viz. at **Ctesifon,** from the beginning of May 358 A.D. until ± May 25th of the same year. (cf. Pighi, N.St.Amm.p.136).

p. 134. 20-22 **cum ... regem ... obduriscentem ... cernerent.** For the **partic. construction** cf. ad 17.12.5, p.125.11. **Cernere c. acc.c.infin.** among others: 17.12.4, p.125.6; 24.2.15, p.336.20.

p. 134. 20 **obstinatissimum.** Cf. ad 17.13.28, p.133.11.

p. 134. 21 *a* **nisi harum regionum dominio sibi adiudicato** = nisi harum regionum dominium sibi adiudicatum esset. This sentence must be joined to **the following: obduriscentem ... pacem.**

b It is quite possible that Amm. is influenced here by the Greek, where εἰ μή occurs with a part.fut.e.g. in Plat.Crit.52 B (in the **nominat.**) and ἐὰν μή witn the **genit.abs.** e.g. Dem.c.Timocr.46. One should also compare the "free" use of **nisi** sometimes in the Digests (examples in Heum.-Seckel p.367); and of **tamquam with partic.** (ad 17.4.15, p.111.19-20*a*); of **licet with part.** (ad 17.12.11, p.126.13); **ut with part.** (ad 17.8.3, p.119. 27-p.120.1*a*).

dominio: complete property. Amm. here uses, as so often, a t.t.judic., which is typically Roman (cf. Sohm, Inst.[16], 1919, p.382). The verb **adiudicare** also belongs in the same sphere (= to award property by the **iudex** in a **iudicium legitimum** during a trial on the distribution of goods; cf. Sohm ibid. p.389 sq. = 63 III). Cf. et Willems (op.cit.I) p.71 sq. **(with lit.).**

p. 134. 21

obduriscentem ad. Cf.Cic.ad fam.2.16.1: nisi ... diuturna desperatione rerum **obduruisset** animus **ad** dolorem novum; Verr.5.13(34), without **ad**; Phil.2.42(108), without **ad**; ad Brut.ep.1.18: **obdurescunt** enim magis quotidie boni viri **ad** vocem tributi; ad Att.10.9.1: without **ad**; ad Att. 13.2.1: sed iam **ad ista obduruimus**; de fin.3.11(37): aut quis **contra studia** naturae tam vehementer **obduruit** ...? Tusc.3.28(67): ... **obduruisseque sese contra fortunam** arbitrantur. Where in the last 3 sentences (28(66), in fine) 3 forms of the verb **suscipere** have been used, I think a "hidden" quotation is not impossible. In any case the verb occurs fairly often in Cic. Not in Claud.Veget.r.m.Opt.Milev.Arn.adv.nat.

p. 134. 21

suscipiendam. Cf. ad 17.13.23, p.132.3*e*.

p. 134. 22

negotio ... infecto. Cf.Sall.Iug.104.1: Marius postquam **infecto** quo intenderat **negotio** Cirtam rediit (v.l. **confecto**) = **re infecta**. It should also be borne in mind that in vulgar Latin **negotium** = **res** (cf. Krebs Antib.2 p. 140, with lit.).

p. 134. 22

XIV, 3
post quod. For **post temp.** cf. ad 17.12.16, p.127.8*b*.

p. 134. 22

id ipsum ... impetraturi. This refers to 17.14.1: poscebantque ... moveretur.

p. 134. 23

a **condicionum robore pari.** These words may refer to the 2 envoys, mentioned in § 3, but also to the Persian emperor. The 2nd view is held

p. 134. 23

401

by Sabbah: "pour se heurter à des conditions aussi dures et **obtenir le même résultat**" (for this it is necessary to explain **id ipsum** as: **idem;** for this confusion of **ipse** and **idem** cf.Hofm.-Leum.p.479 sq., 80 e-f, with lit.); cf. Sabbah II p.187, note 120. I find this a forced translation. Seyf. is inaccurate: "um **denselben** Auftrag **unter den gleichen Bedingungen** durchzuführen", thereby neglecting **robore**. In my opinion the translation is as follows: with instructions to obtain **precisely this (see previous note) by (setting) the same strong conditions** (as did the previous envoys).

b For **robore** cf. ad 16.12.1, p.91.5; ad 16.12.24, p.95.3-4; ad 17.13.27, p.132.27*a*.

robur c.genit., of concreta as well as abstracta, occurs very often in the Latin of all periods. Our expression should be considered a poetism = condicionibis firmis.

c Cf. ad 17.12.11, p.126.12-13: cum **impetrandi** spe similia **petituros.**

p. 134. 23 **Lucillianus ... comes.** Cf. ad 14.11.14 (= II p.127). For **comes** cf. ad 14.5.1 (= I p.125); ad 14.7.9 (= II p.29); ad 14.7.9 (= II p.28); ad 14.11.19 (= II p.132); ad 15.5.4 (= III p.73); ad 17.10.5 p.122.8.

p. 134. 24 **Procopius tunc notarius.** Cf. ad 17.5.2, p.113.27-28*b*. Also mentioned: 18.6.17-18; 23.3.2; 23.3.5; 25.9.12; 26.6.1-9; 26.1.10 etc.; 26.9; 31.3.4. Cf.26.6.1: Insigni genere **Procopius** in **Cilicia** natus et educatus ea consideratione, qua propinquitate **Iulianum** postea **principem** (1) contingebat, a primo gradu eluxit et ut vita moribusque castigatior, licet occultus erat et taciturnus, **notarius** (2) diu perspicaciter **militans** (= to serve at the king's court) et **tribunus** (2) iamque **summatibus** (3) proximus post **Constanti obitum** (4) in rerum conversione velut imperatoris cognatus altius **anhelabat** (cf. ad 17.13.28, p.133.14) **adiunctus consortio comitum** (5) et apparebat eum, si umquam potuisset, fore quietis publicae turbatorem (for (1) cf. ad 16.12.67, p.102.16; for (2) cf. ad 14.5.6 = I p.128; Willems p.544 sq., p.555 (with lit.); for (3) cf. Souter p.400; Heum.-Seckel p.568 sq. = upper class, leading circles; for (4) = Nov. 361 A.D.; for (5) see previous note). With the words **et adparebat ... turbatorem** Amm. expresses an opinion which does not stroke with the following §§ of cap. 6. The impression one gets is rather that **Procopius** feared for his life (probably rightly) and, by way of emergency measure, later let himself be proclaimed emperor. Which, of course, need not exclude the fact that he did have ambitions in that direction; though not in the way as described in the last line of 6.1. Amm. is here the defendant of the establishment, of "legality"; as also appears from the history of **Silvanus** (cf. ad 15.5.2 =

III p.68). And further on in the mocking description of the usurpation of **Procopius** (26.6.15 sq.), which took place on September 28.365 in Constantinople. He is betrayed to **Valens** and put to death on May 27.366 (26.9.9). Together with **Lucillianus, Procopius** is held for a long time in **Ctesiphon.** From there he sends in 359 a secret measage to **Amida** (18.6. 17-18). In 363 he becomes commander of a body of troops, together with **Sebastianus** (23.3.5; 26.6.2). In 23.3.2 Amm. tells that **Julianus** appoints **Procopius** as his successor, without any witnesses, which fact is also alluded to in 26.6.2 (**obscurior fama**). In 25.9.12 we are informed that **Procopius** must see to it, that **Julianus'** mortal remains are brought to **Tarsus,** to be buried there, but: **confestim** corpore sepulto **discessit** nec inveniri potuit **studio quaesitus ingenti,** nisi quod multo postea apud Constantinopolim visus est **subito** purpuratus. Which can well be described as "going underground". For the homonyms, which are sometimes difficult to distinguish. cf. Seeck B.L.Z.G. (op.cit.I) p.247. Cf.et. Stein, Spätröm.Gesch. (op.cit.I) p.264, 270 sq. (with lit.); D.A.Pauw (op.cit.) p.171,177; **Brok** (op.cit.XVI) p.57, p.52 sq. (with lit.), p.238, p.251 sq.

postea. See previous note and 26.6.12 sq.   p. 134. 24

a   **nodo quodam violentae necessitatis adstrictus.** This more objective   p. 134. 24-25
judgment is probably more correct and fair than 26.6.1 (last sentence). Cf.et.26.6.12.
b   As is already indicated by **nodo, necessitas** is here not, as so often: difficult circumstances, precarious situation. (cf.26.9.9: consiliorum inops Procopius, ut in **arduis necessitatibus** solet cum **Fortuna** expostulabat luctuosa et gravi: the **necessitates** are the result of his **Fortuna**), but = ± **fatum, fortuna.** With **this** meaning also used 14.11.26: Eademque (sc. Adrastia) **necessitatis insolubili retinaculo** mortalitatis vinciens fastus tumentis in cassum etc. Cf.et. ad 17.9.6, p.121.4.
c   Cf.14.11.1: Ubi (at Milan) curarum abiectis ponderibus aliis, **tamquam nodum et obicem difficillimum** Caesarem convellere nisu valido cogitabat; Cod.Just.4.29.23: **Antiquae iurisdictionis** retia et **difficillimos nodos** resolventes et supervacuas distinctiones exsulare cupientes sancimus .... This metaphorical use of **nodus** occurs very frequently, among others in **Cic.** Cf.et.Opt.Milev.3.10 (= Ziwsa p.95): (Christus) qui **nodo pacis** iungit utrumque parietem; Claud.10.78 (de nupt.Hon.et. Mar.):

   Hic habitat **nullo constricta** Licentia **nodo;**
ibid.15.10 sq. (de bello Gild.):
   Iam domitus Gildon. **nullis** victoria **nodis**

    Haesit, non terrae spatio, non **obiice** ponti;
ibid.48 (Magnes) 36 sq.:
    Ille lacessitus longo spiraminis actu
    Arcanis trahitur gemma de coniuge **nodis;**
Iust.Phil.13.7: Ibi Battus dux eorum, **linguae nodis** solutis, loqui primum coepit; (and lit., with a different compositum of **stringere)** Tac.Germ.38.2: insigne gentis obliquare crinem **nodoque substringere** (Meyer: the tying up into a knot and putting up (of hair)); ad 17.3.1, p.108.7-8: **stringere.**

p. 134. 25 *a* **ad res consurrexerit novas.** Cf.28.3.4: Valentinus quidam ... **ad res perniciosas consurgebat et novas;** Suet.Jul.Caes.9.3: pactumque, ut simul foris ille, ipse Romae, **ad res novas consurgerent** (Fletcher, Rev. de philol. LXIII. 1937); ad 17.13.13, p.130.11*a*.

b **consurrexerit.** V Cl.Seyf. Sabbah. **Consurrexerat** Nov.Rolfe. **Consurrexit** HAG. It seems to me fundamentally more correct to maintain V's version. We then have here a futurum exactum, at which Sabbah II p.188 notes: "... un futur II **dans lequel la valeur du perfectum s'est affaiblie,** comme chez les comiques et dans la langue familière (Ernout-Thomas Synt. p.226, § 246)". Sabbah means, therefore, that the **fut.exact. here = fut.I.** But this does not explain the **futurum!** The explanation, in my view, is a psychological one. Paraphrase: Procopius ... who later **will rise** to incite a rebellion (as you, readers, **will read).** But although, with a little more difficulty, the fut.II **as such** can also be explained in this way. (cf. ad 17.13.32, p.134.3). Cf.et.Hofm.-Leum.p.563,155a: "... Zwischen Fut.II und I bestand ursprünglich ein Aktionsartenunterschied: **fecero, faxo** ist **perfektiv** "ich werde zur Ausführung bringen", **faciam** ist **imperfektiv** "ich werde mit der Ausführung beschäftigt sein". Noch bei Cic. scheint der Unterschied des durativen I und des perfektiven II Futurs gelegentlich zu spüren, vgl.z.B.Att.3.19.1: si ea (sc.salus) praecisa erit ... hanc miserrimam vitam vel **sustentabo** vel, quod melius est, **abiecero".** Hofm.-Leum. points out that in **Plaut.,** for instance, there are passages where there is no difference between fut.I and fut.II: the metrum is decisive.

Finally, it should be mentioned that in late Latin, in subordinate clauses, the fut.II, **in activum as well as in passivum,** is practically equal to the fut.I (cf.Hofm.-Leum.p.564, 155*b*, β, γ, with lit.); and that in late Latin **fut.** and **conjunct.** can be easily confused, because in vulgar Latin the **futurum** is beginning to disappear, to be replaced by circumscriptions. Cf. et Svennung Pall. (op.cit.II) p.464-469; Kalb, röm. Rechtssprache (1961 Neudr.) p.70, § 73.